ACSAC '99

Proceedings

15th Annual Computer Security Applications Conference (ACSAC '99)

December 6–10, 1999

Phoenix, Arizona

Sponsored by

Applied Computer Security Associates

In cooperation with

ACM Special Interest Group on Security, Audit, and Control

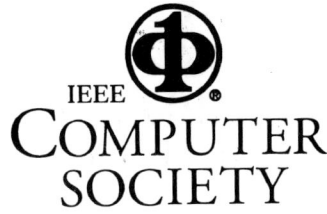

Los Alamitos, California

Washington • Brussels • Tokyo

Copyright © 1999 by The Institute of Electrical and Electronics Engineers, Inc.
All rights reserved

Copyright and Reprint Permissions: Abstracting is permitted with credit to the source. Libraries may photocopy beyond the limits of US copyright law, for private use of patrons, those articles in this volume that carry a code at the bottom of the first page, provided that the per-copy fee indicated in the code is paid through the Copyright Clearance Center, 222 Rosewood Drive, Danvers, MA 01923.

Other copying, reprint, or republication requests should be addressed to: IEEE Copyrights Manager, IEEE Service Center, 445 Hoes Lane, P.O. Box 133, Piscataway, NJ 08855-1331.

The papers in this book comprise the proceedings of the meeting mentioned on the cover and title page. They reflect the authors' opinions and, in the interests of timely dissemination, are published as presented and without change. Their inclusion in this publication does not necessarily constitute endorsement by the editors, the IEEE Computer Society, or the Institute of Electrical and Electronics Engineers, Inc.

IEEE Computer Society Order Number PR00346
ISBN 0-7695-0346-2
ISSN 1063-9527

Additional copies may be ordered from:

IEEE Computer Society	IEEE Service Center	IEEE Computer Society
Customer Service Center	445 Hoes Lane	Asia/Pacific Office
10662 Los Vaqueros Circle	P.O. Box 1331	Watanabe Bldg., 1-4-2
P.O. Box 3014	Piscataway, NJ 08855-1331	Minami-Aoyama
Los Alamitos, CA 90720-1314	Tel: + 1-732-981-1393	Minato-ku, Tokyo 107-0062
Tel: + 1-714-821-8380	Fax: + 1-732-981-9667	JAPAN
Fax: + 1-714-821-4641	mis.custserv@computer.org	Tel: + 81-3-3408-3118
E-mail: cs.books@computer.org		Fax: + 81-3-3408-3553
		tokyo.ofc@computer.org

Editorial production by Lorretta Palagi and Bob Werner

Cover art design and production by Joseph Daigle/Studio Productions

Printed in the United States of America by The Printing House

Table of Contents

15th Annual Computer Security Applications Conference—ACSAC '99

Message from the Conference Chair	xi
Conference Committee	xii
Program Committee	xiv
Tutorial Committee	xiv
Reviewers	xv
Speaker Biographies	xvi

WEDNESDAY MORNING, DECEMBER 8

Keynote Speech
Speaker: Lieutenant General Michael V. Hayden, United States Air Force

Distinguished Lecture
How to Cheat at the Lottery (or, Massively Parallel Requirements Engineering) xix
Speaker: Dr. Ross Anderson, University of Cambridge Computer Laboratory

WEDNESDAY 10:30 A.M., DECEMBER 8

Track A: Electronic Commerce
Chair: Ravi Sandhu, George Mason University

Modular Fair Exchange Protocols for Electronic Commerce 3
  H. Vogt, H. Pagnia, and F. C. Gärtner

Trustworthy Access Control with Untrustworthy Web Servers 12
  T. Wilkinson, D. Hearn, and S. Wiseman

A Language for Modelling Secure Business Transactions 22
  A. W. Röhm, G. Herrmann, and G. Pernul

Track B: System Engineering
Chair: Jan Filsinger, NAI Labs

Safe Areas of Computation for Secure Computing with Insecure Applications 35
  A. L. M. dos Santos and R. A. Kemmerer

Architecture and Concepts of the ARGuE Guard 45
  J. Epstein

Using Abuse Case Models for Security Requirements Analysis _____ 55
J. McDermott and C. Fox

WEDNESDAY 1:30 P.M., DECEMBER 8

Track A: Networks
Chair: Christoph Schuba, SUN Microsystems Laboratories, USA

A Parallel Packet Screen for High Speed Networks _____ 67
C. Benecke

An Asynchronous Distributed Access Control Architecture for IP over ATM Networks _____ 75
O. Paul, M. Laurent, and S. Gombault

Secure Communications in ATM Networks _____ 84
M. Laurent, A. Bouabdallah, C. Delahaye, H. Leitold, R. Posch, E. Areizaga, and J. M. Mateos

Track B: Panel Session—The Collection and Use of Meaningful Red Team Metrics
Chair: J. L. Connolly, MITRE Corporation

Panelists: Chris McBride, OASD (C3I)/IA
              Ed Schneider, IDA
              Mike Skroh, DARPA
              Greg Whitlow, USN

WEDNESDAY 3:30 P.M., DECEMBER 8

Track A: Security Analysis
Chair: John McDermott, James Madison University

Using Checkable Types in Automatic Protocol Analysis _____ 99
S. H. Brackin

SCR: A Practical Approach to Building a High Assurance COMSEC System _____ 109
J. Kirby, Jr., M. Archer, and C. Heitmeyer

Application-Level Isolation Using Data Inconsistency Detection _____ 119
A. Fayad, S. Jajodia, and C. D. McCollum

Track B: Workflow
Chair: LouAnna Notargiacomo, Trusted Computer Solutions

A Prototype Secure Workflow Server _____ 129
D. L. Long, J. Baker, and F. Fung

Napoleon: A Recipe for Workflow 134
   C. Payne, D. Thomsen, J. Bogle, and R. O'Brien

Tools to Support Secure Enterprise Computing 143
   M. H. Kang, B. J. Eppinger, and J. N. Froscher

THURSDAY 8:30 A.M., DECEMBER 9

Track A: Crypto
   Chair: Dan Gambel, Mitretek Systems

An Effective Defense Against First Party Attacks in Public-Key Algorithms 155
   S. M. Matyas, Jr., and A. Roginsky

Towards a Practical, Secure, and Very Large Scale Online Election 161
   J. Karro and J. Wang

Design of LAN-Lock, A System for Securing Wireless Networks 170
   R. E. Newman, M. V. Hoyt, T. Swanson, P. Broccard, M. Sanders, and J. Winner

Track B: Panel Session—Composition Problems of Component TOEs – Entrust, Oracle, and Windows NT/2000
   Chair: L. Ambuel, TRW

   Panelists: M. Donaldson, CESG
                 D. Harris, ORACLE
                 M. Lai, Microsoft
                 M. LaRoche, ENTRUST
                 J. Straw, Syntegra

THURSDAY 10:30 A.M., DECEMBER 9

Track A: Security Services
   Chair: Jody Heaney, MITRE Corporation

Toward a Taxonomy and Costing Method for Security Services 183
   C. Irvine and T. Levin

TrustedBox: A Kernel-Level Integrity Checker 189
   P. Iglio

Adding Availability to Log Services of Untrusted Machines 199
   A. Arona, D. Bruschi, and E. Rosti

Track B: Security Policy
Chair: Marshall Abrams, MITRE Corporation

Policy-Based Management: Bridging the Gap 209
  S. Hinrichs

Security Policy Coordination for Heterogeneous Information Systems 219
  J. Hale, P. Galiasso, M. Papa, and S. Shenoi

The ARBAC99 Model for Administration of Roles 229
  R. Sandhu and Q. Munawer

THURSDAY 1:00 P.M., DECEMBER 9

Track A: Public Key Infrastructures
Chair: Frank Sledge, TRW

A Distributed Certificate Management System (DCMS) Supporting Group-Based Access Controls 241
  R. Oppliger, A. Greulich, P. Trachsel

Fast Checking of Individual Certificate Revocation on Small Systems 249
  S. Russell

A Model of Certificate Revocation 256
  D. A. Cooper

Track B: Forum—Information Security Education for the Next Millennium: Building the Next Generation of Practitioners 265
Chair: Ron Ross, NIST

  Participants: Blaine Burnham, Georgia Institute of Technology
  Cynthia Irvine, Naval Postgraduate School
  Charles Reynolds, James Madison University
  Ravi Sandhu, George Mason University
  Rayford Vaughn, Mississippi State University

THURSDAY 3:00 P.M., DECEMBER 9

Track A: Public Key Infrastructures
Chair: Klaus Keus, GISA/BSI

Generic Support for PKIX Certificate Management in CDSA 269
  S. Erfani and S. Chandersekaran

Efficient Certificate Status Handling Within PKIs: An Application to Public Administration Services 276
  M. Prandini

Track B: Mobile Code
Chair: Dan Thomson, Secure Computing Corporation

User Authentication and Authorization in the Java Platform ___ 285
   C. Lai, L. Gong, L. Koved, A. Nadalin, and R. Schemers

Transactions in Java Card ___ 291
   M. Oestreicher

FRIDAY 8:30 A.M., DECEMBER 10

Track A: Panel Session—Legal and Technical Responses to Protecting the U. S. Critical Infrastructures ___ 299
Chair: Art Friedman, NSA

Panelists: Scott Charney, Department of Justice
             Ellie Padgett, NSA
             Mark Rasch, Global Integrity
             John Thomas, Averstar

Track B: Middleware
Chair: Vince Reed, MITRE Corporation

A Middleware Approach to Asynchronous and Backward Compatible Detection and Prevention of ARP Cache Poisoning ___ 303
   M. V. Tripunitara and P. Dutta

A Resource Access Decision Service for CORBA-Based Distributed Systems ___ 310
   K. Beznosov, Y. Deng, B. Blakley, C. Burt, and J. Barkley

Non-repudiation Evidence Generation for CORBA using XML ___ 320
   M. Wichert, D. Ingham, and S. Caughey

FRIDAY 10:30 A.M., DECEMBER 10

Track A: Security Architectures
Chair: Daniel P. Faigin, The Aerospace Corporation

Security Relevancy Analysis on the Registry of Windows NT 4.0 ___ 331
   W. Du, P. Garg, and A. P. Mathur

Security Architecture Development and Results for a Distributed Modeling and Simulation System ___ 341
   R. B. Neely

SecurSight: An Architecture for Secure Information Access ___ 349
   J. G. Brainard

Track B: Intrusion Detection
Chair: Jeremy Epstein, NAI Labs

SAM: Security Adaptation Manager 361
   H. Hinton, C. Cowan, L. Delcambre, and S. Bowers

An Application of Machine Learning to Network Intrusion Detection 371
   C. Sinclair, L. Pierce, and S. Matzner

A Process State-Transition Analysis and Its Application to Intrusion Detection 378
   N. Nuansri, S. Singh, and T. S. Dillon

Author Index 389

Message from the Conference Chair

As we bring 1999 to a close, we bring about closure of yet another decade. We can all reflect back to the beginning of the 1990's and see just how far we have come in understanding computer security. Information is a hot commodity. Protection of that information takes many forms. It affects so many industries: commerce, banking, medical, transportation, etc. It can touch many aspects of our daily lives.

Our knowledge base has grown tremendously in the last ten years bringing about stronger products and applications. It brings comfort one minute and fear the next. Information can get to the opposite side of the world with the click of a button; as long as everything surrounding it works as expected. So how do we continue to provide that information and yet maintain the protection of the information?

The next millennium will bring even more interesting challenges in the field of information security and my committee and I look forward to bringing you the practical solutions to match the challenges.

Dee Akers, The MITRE Corporation
Conference Chair

Conference Committee

Conference Chair
Dee Akers,
The MITRE Corporation

Panel/Forum Chair
Jody Heaney,
The MITRE Corporation

Media/Publications Chair
Dr. Frank Sledge,
TRW Corporation

Program Chair
Klaus Keus, German
Information Security Agency

Tutorial Chair
Daniel Faigin, The Aerospace Corporation

Special Events
Noelle Hardy, Arca Systems

Program Co-Chair
Jeremy Epstein, NAI Laboratories

Case Studies Chair
Steve Rome, National Security Agency

Publicity Chair
Vince Reed,
The MITRE Corporation

Publicity Co-Chair

Jay Kahn,
The MITRE Corporation

Web Advisor

Robert H'obbes' Zakon,
The MITRE Corporation

ACSA Chair

Dr. Marshall Abrams,
The MITRE Corporation

Registration Chair

Jim Litchko

Special Interest Liaison

Art Friedman,
National Security Agency

ACSA Treasurer

Ann Marmour-Squires,
TRW Corporation

Recording Secretary

Dan Gambel, Mitretek Systems

Photo not available
Guest Speakers Liaison

Steve LaFountain, National
Security Agency

Photo not available
Student Paper Chair

Dr. Matt Bishop, University of
California–Davis

Photo not available
Treasurer

Dr. Ron Gove, Science
Applications
International Corporation

Program Committee

Klaus Keus, German Information Security Agency, GERMANY, *Program Chair*
Jeremy Epstein, NAI Laboratories, USA, *Program Co-chair*
Jan Filsinger, NAI Laboratories, USA
Jody Heaney, The MITRE Corporation, USA
John McDermott, James Madison University, USA
LouAnna Notargiacomo, Trusted Computer Systems, USA
Steve Rome, National Security Administration, USA
Ron Ross, NIST, USA
Ravi Sandhu, George Mason University, USA
Dan Thomsen, Secure Computing Corporation, USA

Tutorial Committee

Daniel Faigin, The Aerospace Corporation, USA, Tutorial Chair
Tim Levin, Anteon, USA
Vincent LeVeque, SAIC, USA
Patricia Daggett, Data General Corporation, USA
Frank Belvin, The MITRE Corporation, USA
Jeremy Epstein, NAI Laboratories, USA
Lauren Uroff, XYPRO Technology Corporation, USA
Klaus Kleus, German Information Security Agency, GERMANY
Stuart Schaeffer, The Aerospace Corporation, USA
Cynthia Irvine, Naval Postgraduate Institute, USA

Reviewers

Marshall Abrams, The MITRE Corporation
Gene Bacic, Texar Software, Inc.
Dave Bailey, Arca Systems
David Bell, EDS
Jon Beskin, NAI Laboratories
Matt Bishop, University of California–Davis
Aaron Cohen, JOTA System Security Consultants Inc.
Edward J. Coyne, Science Applications Int. Corporation
Mary Denz, Air Force Research Laboratory
Pete Dinsmore, NAI Laboratories
Al Donaldson, ESCOM Corporation
Ken Elliott III, The Aerospace Corporation
Jeremy Epstein, NAI Laboratories
Gerd Enste, Debis IT-Security Services
Ellen Flahavin, NIST
Daniel Faigin, The Aerospace Corporation
Jan Filsinger, NAI Laboratories
Art Friedmann, National Security Agency
Dan Gambel, Mitretek Systems
Thomas Gast, German Information Security Agency
Virgil Gligor, University of Maryland
Ranwa Haddad, The Aerospace Corporation
Ramzi Haraty, Lebanese American University
Noelle Hardy, Arca Systems
Jody Heaney, The MITRE Corporation
Patrick Horster, University of Klagenfurt
Sushil Jajodia, George Mason University
George Jelen, G-J Consulting
Dale Johnson, NAI Laboratories
Mike Joyce, EDS
Klaus Keus, German Information Security Agency
Peter Kraaibeek, Consecure GmbH
Helmut Kurth, Industrie Anlagen Betriebsgesellschaft
Steve LaFountain, National Security Agency
Carl Landwehr, Mitretek Systems
Steven B. Lipner, Microsoft
Teresa Lunt, Xerox PARC
Leo Marcus, The Aerospace Corporation
John McDermott, James Madison University
Art Minado, National Security Agency
Mike Nash, Gamma Secure Systems Ltd
Patrick Nilson, SEMA Group
LouAnna Notargiacomo, Trusted Computer Systems
Rolf Oppliger, Bundesamt fuer Informatik (BFI)
Charles Payne, Secure Computing Corporation
Guenther Pernul, Universität GH ESSEN
Reinhard Posch, University of Technology, Graz
Ralph Puga, Network Associates
Steve Rome, National Security Agency
Ron Ross, NIST
Bernard Roussely, NATO NC3A
Ravi, S. Sandhu, George Mason University
Christina Serban, AT&T Laboratories
Qi Shi, Liverpool John Moores University
Christoph Schuba, Sun Microsystems Laboratories
Roland Schützig, Arthur Andersen AG
Gregg Tally, NAI Laboratories
Dan Thomsen, Secure Computing Corporation
Pat Toth, NIST
Gene Troy, NIST
Rayford Vaughn, University of Mississippi
Jean Viale, SCSSI
Paul Williams, Admiral Management Services Ltd.
Ed Wojciechowski, NSA/NCSC
Petra Wohlmacher, Universitaet Klagenfurt Institut fuer Informatik-Systemsicherheit

Speaker Biographies

Keynote Speaker: Lieutenant General Michael V. Hayden, United States Air Force

Lieutenant General Michael V. Hayden is Director, National Security Agency/Chief, Central Security Service (NSA/CSS), Fort George G. Meade, MD. The NSA/CSS is a combat support agency of the Department of Defense with military and civilian personnel stationed worldwide. He is the department's senior uniformed intelligence officer. The general entered active duty in 1969 after earning a bachelors degree in history in 1967 and a master's degree in modern American history in 1969, both from Duquesne University. He is a distinguished graduate of the University's Reserve Officer Training Corps program. General Hayden has served as commander of the Air Intelligence Agency and Director of the Joint Command and Control Warfare Center, both headquartered at Kelly Air Force Base. He also has served in senior staff positions in the Pentagon; Headquarters U.S. European Command, Stuggart, Germany; National Security Council, Washington, D.C., and the U.S. Embassy in the People's Republic of Bulgaria. Prior to his current assignment, General Hayden served as deputy chief of staff for United Nations Command and U.S. Forces Korea, Yongsan Army Garrison.

Distinguished Lecturer: Dr. Ross Anderson, University of Cambridge Computer Laboratory

Ross Anderson is a faculty member of the University of Cambridge Computer Laboratory, where he teaches and leads research in computer security, cryptology and software engineering. His most innovative recent work is on "Soft Tempest" — the use of software techniques to reduce the radio frequency information leakage from PC monitors and keyboards. This software is now fielded in a number of computer security products including PGP. He is a co- author of Serpent, a leading candidate in the current competition to find an Advanced Encryption Standard. He also has well known publications on the tamper resistance of smartcards, techniques for removing copyright marks from digital media, and the robustness of cryptographic protocols. Other papers document the failure modes of a number of real world systems including automatic teller machines, prepayment electricity meters, and goods vehicle tachographs. The unifying theme of his work is to provide robust control mechanisms for tomorrow's heterogeneous distributed systems.

Distinguished Lecture

How to Cheat at the Lottery (or, Massively Parallel Requirements Engineering)

Speaker

Dr. Ross Anderson, University of Cambridge Computer Laboratory

How to Cheat at the Lottery
(or, Massively Parallel Requirements Engineering)

Ross Anderson

University of Cambridge Computer Laboratory,
New Museums Site, Pembroke Street, Cambridge CB2 3QG, UK
Ross.Anderson@cl.cam.ac.uk

Abstract

Collaborative software projects such as Linux and Apache have shown that a large, complex system can be built and maintained by many developers working in a highly parallel, relatively unstructured way.

In this note, I report an experiment to see whether a high quality system specification can also be produced by a large number of people working in parallel with a minimum of communication.

1 Introduction

Experienced software engineers know that perhaps 30% of the cost of a software product goes into specifying it, 10% into coding, and the remaining 60% on maintenance. This has profound effects on computer science. For example, when designing new programming languages the motive nowadays is mostly not to make coding easier, but to cut the costs of maintenance. There has also been massive interest in open source software products such as Linux and Apache, whose maintenance is undertaken by thousands of programmers working worldwide in a voluntary and co-operative way.

Open source software is not entirely a recent invention; in the early days of computing most system software vendors published their source code. This openness started to recede in the early 1980s when pressure of litigation led IBM to adopt an 'object-code-only' policy for its mainframe software, despite bitter criticism from its user community. The pendulum now seems to be swinging back, with Linux and Apache gaining huge market share.

In his influential paper 'The Cathedral and the Bazaar' [1], Eric Raymond compares the hierarchical organisation of large software projects in industry ('the cathedral') with the more open, unstructured approach of cooperative developers ('the bazaar'). He makes a number of telling observations about the efficiency of the latter, such as that "Given enough eyeballs, all bugs are shallow". His more recent paper, 'The Magic Cauldron' [2], explores the economic incentives that for-profit publishers have found to publish their source code, and concludes that IBM's critics were right: where reliability is paramount, open source is best, as users will cooperate in finding and removing bugs.

There is a corollary to this argument, which I explore in this paper: the next priority after cutting the costs of maintenance should be cutting the costs of specification.

Specification is not only the second most expensive item in the system development life cycle, but is also where the most expensive things go wrong. The seminal study by Curtis, Krasner and Iscoe of large software project disasters found that failure to understand the requirements was mostly to blame [3]: a thin spread of application domain knowledge typically led to fluctuating and conflicting requirements which in turn caused a breakdown in communication. They suggested that the solution was to find an 'exceptional designer' with a deep understanding of the problem who would assume overall responsibility.

But there are many cases where an established expert is not available, such as when designing a new application from scratch or when building a competitor to a closed, proprietary system whose behaviour can only be observed at a distance.

There are also some particular domains in which specification is well known to be hard. Security is one example; the literature has many examples of systems which protected the wrong thing, or protected the right thing but using the wrong mechanisms. Most real life security failures result from the opportunistic exploitation of elementary design flaws rather than 'high-tech' attacks such as cryptanalysis [4]. The list of possible attacks on a typical system is long, and people doing initial security designs are very likely to overlook some of them. Even in a closed environment, the use of multiple independent experts is recommended [5].

Security conspicuously satisfies the five tests which Raymond suggested would identify the products most likely to benefit from an open source approach [2]. It is based on common engineering knowledge rather than proprietary techniques; it is sensitive to failure; it needs peer review for verification; it is business critical; and its economics include strong network effects. Its own traditional wisdom, going back at least to Auguste Kerkhoffs in 1883, is that cryptographic systems should be designed in such a way that they are not compromised if the opponent learns the technique being used. In other words, the security should reside in the choice of key rather than in obscure design features [6].

It therefore seemed worthwhile to see if a high quality security specification could be designed in a highly parallel way, by getting a lot of different people to contribute drafts in the hope that most of the possible attacks would be considered in at least one of them.

2 Experimental design

The opportunity to test this idea was provided by the fact that I teach courses in cryptography and computer security to second and third year undergraduates at Cambridge. By the third year, students should be able to analyse a protection problem systematically by listing the threats, devising a security policy and then recommending mechanisms that will enforce it. (The syllabus and lecture notes are available online at [7].)

By a security policy, we mean a high level specification which sets out the threats to which a system is assumed to be exposed and the assurance properties which are to be provided in response. Like most specifications, it is a means of communication between the users (who understand the environment) and the system engineers (who will have to implement the encryption, access control, logging or other mechanisms). So it must be clearly comprehensible to both communities; it should also be concise.

The students see, as textbook examples of security policy:

- the Bell-LaPadula model, which is commonly used by governments to protect classified information and which states that information can only flow up the classification hierarchy, and never down. Thus a civil servant cleared to 'Secret' can read files at 'Secret' or below, but not 'Top Secret', while a process running at 'Secret' can write at the same level or above, but never down to 'Unclassified';

- The Clark-Wilson model, which provides a reasonably formal description of the double-entry bookkeeping systems used by large organisations to detect fraud by insiders;

- The Chinese Wall model, which models conflicts of interest in professional practice. Thus an advertising account executive who has worked on one bank's strategy will be prevented from seeing the files on any other banking client for a fixed period of time afterwards;

- The British Medical Association model, which describes how flows of personal health information must be restricted so as to respect the established ethical norms for patient privacy. Only people involved directly in a patient's care should be allowed to access their medical records, unless the patient gives consent or the records are de-identified effectively.

The first three of these are documented in [8] and the fourth in [9]. Further examples of security policy models are always welcome, as they help teach the lesson that 'security' means radically different things in different applications. However, developing a security policy is usually hard work, involving extensive consultation with domain experts and successive refinement until a model emerges that is compact, concise and agreed by all parties.

Exceptions include designing a policy for a new application, and for a competitor to a closed system. In such cases, the best we can do may be to think long and hard, and hope that we will not miss anything important.

I therefore set the following exam question to my third year students:

> **You have been hired by a company which is bidding to take over the National Lottery when Camelot's franchise expires, and your responsibility is the security policy. State the security policy you would recommend and outline the mechanisms you would implement to enforce it.**

3 The UK National Lottery

For the benefit of overseas readers, I will now give a simplified description of our national lottery. (British readers can skip the next two paragraphs.)

The UK's national lottery is operated by a consortium of companies called Camelot which holds a seven year licence from the government. This licence is up for renewal, which makes the question topical; and presumably Camelot will refuse to share its experience with potential competitors. A large number of franchised retail outlets sell tickets. The customer marks six out of 49 numbers on a form which he hands with his money to the operator; she passes it through a machine that scans it and prints a ticket containing the choice of numbers plus some further coded information to authenticate it.

Twice a week there is a draw on TV at which a machine selects seven numbered balls from 49 in a drum. The customers who have predicted the first six share a jackpot of several million pounds; the odds should be (49 choose 6) or 13,983,816 to one against, meaning that with much of the population playing there are several winners in a typical draw. (Occasionally there are no winners and the jackpot is 'rolled over' to the next draw, giving a pot of many millions of pounds which whips the popular press to a frenzy.) There are also smaller cash prizes for people who guessed only some of the numbers. Half the takings go on prize money; the other half gets shared between Camelot, the taxman and various charitable good causes[1].

The model answer I had prepared had a primary threat model that attackers, possibly in cahoots with insiders, would try to place bets once the result of the draw is known, whether by altering bet records or forging tickets. The secondary threats were that bets would be placed that had not been paid for, and that attackers might operate bogus vending stations which would pay small claims but disappear if a client won a big prize.

The security policy that follows logically from this is that bets should be registered online with a server which is secured prior to the draw, both against tampering and against the extraction of sufficient information to forge a winning ticket; that there should be credit limits for genuine vendors; and that there should be ways of identifying bogus vendors. Once the security policy has been developed in enough detail, designing enforcement mechanisms should not be too hard for someone skilled in the art – though there are some subtleties, as we shall see below.

The exam was set on the first of June 1999 [10], and when the scripts were delivered that evening, I was eager to find out what the students might have come up with.

4 Results

Thirty four candidates answered the question, and five of their papers were good enough to be kept as model answers. All of these candidates had original ideas which are incorporated in this paper, as did a further seven candidates whose answers were less complete. As the exam marking is anonymous, the 'co-authors' of this specification are a subset of the candidates listed in the ackowledgements below. The question was a 'good' one in that it divided the students up about equally into first, second and third class ranges of marks. Almost all the original ideas came from the first class candidates.

The contributions came at a number of levels, including policy goal statements, discussions of particular attacks, and arguments about the merits of particular protection mechanisms.

4.1 Policy goal statements

On sorting out the high level policy statements from the more detailed contributions, the first thing to catch the eye was a conflict reminiscent of the old debate over who should pay when a 'phantom withdrawal' happens via an automatic teller machine – the customer or the bank [4].

One of the candidates assumed that the customer's rights must have precedence: *'All winning tickets must be redeemable! So failures must not allow unregistered tickets to be printed.'* Another candidate assumed the contrary, and thus the *'worst outcome should be that the jackpot gets paid to the wrong person, never twice.'* Ultimately, whether systems fail in the shop's favour or the customer's is a regulatory issue. However, there are consequences for security. In the context of cash machine disputes, it was noted that if the customer carries the risk of fraud while only the bank is in a position to improve the security measures, then the bank may get more and more careless until an epidemic of fraud takes place. We presumably want to avoid this kind of 'moral hazard' in a national lottery; perhaps the solution is for disputed sums to be added back to the prize fund, or distributed to the 'good causes'.

As well as protecting the system from fraud, the operator must also convince the gaming public of this.

---

[1] Appointing the members of the committees that dish out the money is a source of vast patronage for the Prime Minister and, according to cynics, is the real reason for the Lottery to exist.

This was expressed in various ways: *'take care how you justify your operations;' 'don't forget the indirect costs of security failure such as TV contract penalties, ticket refund, and publicity of failure leading to bogus claims;' 'at all costs ensure that there is enough backup to prevent unverifiable ticket problems.'* The operator can get some protection by signs such as *'no winnings due unless entry logged'* but this cover is never total.

Next, a number of candidates argued that it was foolish to place sole reliance on any single protection mechanism, or any single instance of a particular type of mechanisms. A typical statement was: *'Don't bet the farm on tamper-resistance'*. For example, if the main threat is someone forging a winning ticket after tapping the network which the central server uses to send ticket authenticator codes to vending machines, we might not just encrypt the line but also delay paying jackpots for several days to give all winners a chance to claim. (Simply encrypting the authentication codes would not be enough, if a technician who dismantled the encryption device at the server could get both the authentication keys and the encryption keys.) Translated into methodology, this suggests a security matrix approach which maps the threats to the protection mechanisms, and makes it easy for us to check that at least two independent mechanisms constrain every serious threat.

Various attempts were made to reuse existing security policies, and particularly Clark-Wilson. These were mostly by weak candidates and not very convincing. But three candidates did get some mileage; for example, one can model the lottery terminal as a device that turns an unconstrained data item (the customer selection) into a constrained data item (the valid lottery ticket) by registering it and printing an authentication code on it. Such concepts can be useful in designing separation-of-duty mechanisms for ticket redemption and general financial control, but do not seem to be enough to cover all the novel and interesting security problems which a lottery provides.

Some candidates wondered whether a new franchisee would want to extend the existing lottery's business model, such as by allowing people to buy tickets over the phone or the net. In that case, one should try to design the policy to be extensible to non-material sales channels. (Internet based lottery ticket sales have since been declared to be a good thing by the government [11].)

Finally, some attention needs to be paid to protecting genuine winners. The obvious issue is safeguarding the privacy of winners who refuse publicity; less obvious issues include the risk that winners might be traced, robbed and perhaps even murdered during the claim process. For example, the UK has some recent history of telephone technicians abusing their access to win airline tickets and other prizes offered during phone-in competitions; one might be concerned about the risk that a technician, in cahoots with organised crime, would divert the winners' hotline, intercept a jackpot claim, and dispatch a hit squad to collect the ticket. In practice, measures to control this risk are likely to involve the phone company as much as the lottery itself.

4.2 Discussions of particular attacks

This leads to a discussion of attacks. There were several views on how the threat model should be organised; one succinct statement was *'Any attack that can be done by an outsider can be done at least as well by an insider. So concentrate on insider attacks'*. This is something that almost everyone knows, but which many system designers disregard in practice. Other candidates pointed out that no system can defend itself against being owned by a corrupt organisation, and that senior insiders should be watched with particular care[2].

Moving now to the more technical analysis, a number of interesting attack scenarios were explored.

1. A number of candidates remarked that in the absence of enforceable limits on ticket sales per machine, an operator could issue large numbers of tickets without any intention of paying for them. In extremis, he might issue all 13,983,816 tickets required to win a jackpot. The obvious fix is to have a value counter to enforce a system of credit limits – but where? If the terminal cannot be completely tamperproof, we need an online solution. But this is not enough: three candidates warned about possible traffic insertion attacks at the server end, so having synchronised value counters at both the terminal and the server might be a good idea[3]. So would banking industry style batch controls and totals.

2. Three candidates discussed tricking genuine terminals into attaching to a fake server. The goal might be fraud (after the draw, forge tickets with authenticators calculated using the fake server

---

[2] One of the companies that originally made up the Camelot consortium had to leave after its chief executive was found by the High Court to have tried to bribe a competing consortium during the bidding for the original lottery franchise.

[3] but see section 4.3 below on the problems of redundancy

key) or denial of service (undermine the lottery's credibility by causing vendors to print tickets which cannot be redeemed if they win). The obvious fix is to have the terminals authenticate the server.

3. There was concern about the prospect of a winning ticket being claimed simultaneously at several shops. The general consensus was that an online operation with guaranteed commit-abort semantics and strong authentication of the terminal should be required to pay a winning ticket.

4. Candidates disagreed about the threat from refunds. If refunds are allowed, then someone might get a refund on a forged ticket and later present the original if it wins. (Historically, refund mechanisms have been a source of fraud with systems such as prepaid electricity meters [5]). The simplest solution is not to allow any refunds at all; and alternative is to allow them only in very restricted circumstances (only for data entry errors, only while the customer is still in the shop, only up to close of play, only while the terminal is online, and subject to collection and audit of all refunded tickets along with all locally paid winning tickets).

5. Although tamper resistance cannot be relied on completely, it can still be helpful. But should we protect the whole vending machine or just an embedded crypto module? If the latter, there is a risk that vendors will tamper with the rest of the system so that it reports only a proportion of their takings, in effect competing with the lottery by issuing the other tickets on their own account. So it is probably a good idea to make the whole vending machine tamper resistant, except for those components such as the receipt printer where user access is unavoidable.

6. It may be a good idea to allow small claims to be cashed anywhere in the system. This way, any bogus tickets should be spotted as quickly as possible. This will also help the operator detect any rogue merchants running completely bogus vending operations with unauthorised equipment.

7. This will not help, however, with another possible attack on the vending machine's tamper resistance. This is where a wiretap is used to reveal which machine sold a winning ticket (whether directly, or from published information about where a prizewinner lives); the attacker then burgles the shop, steals the machine and digs the authentication keys or logs out of it. So vending machines should not contain enough information to forge a ticket, except in the instant that a genuine ticket is being printed.

There are some secondary design concerns here. How will the machines validate the lower-value tickets that are paid out locally – only online? Or will some of the authenticator code be kept in the vending station? But in that case, how do we cope with the accidental or malicious destruction of the machine that sold a jackpot winning ticket, and how do we pay small winnings when the machine that sold the ticket is offline?

8. Close attention has to be paid to failure modes. If random errors and system failures can lead to individual gain then, as with some burglar alarm systems [12], deliberate attempts to cause failure can be expected. They may lead not just to occasional frauds but also to more widespread service denial.

9. Some attention has to be paid to whether the system should collect evidence with a view to resolving possible disputes with franchisees, and if so what form it should take. The naive approach is to ask for everything to carry a digital signature, but this is largely irrelevant to the kind of attack one expects from the experience of electricity token vending [5] – namely that a vendor sells a large number of tickets and then reports the machine stolen. The solution is likely to involve contractual obligations, insurance, and monitoring of vending machines by the central server.

10. There should be enough privacy protection to prevent punters learning the pattern of bets; even if the draw is random, other people's choice of numbers will not be, and this will skew the odds. The published history of jackpots gives some information on this (it is already extensively analysed) but one should not give out any more information, unless the operator decides to as a matter of policy. If it were believed that insiders had an advantage by knowing the popularity of each number, this could seriously erode confidence. (There is no realistic way to stop a clever vending agent rigging up some means of collecting local statistics, but at least the authentic national statistics should be protected.)

11. Some candidates suggested using the BBC's broadcast radio clock signal as an authentication

input to the vending terminals; but one candidate correctly pointed out that this signal could be jammed without much difficulty. This was a highly effective suggestion, in the sense that when it was mentioned to a colleague who had recently done an audit of a different online gaming system, his response was 'Oh s***!'

4.3 Reasoning about particular protection mechanisms

The third type of contribution from the candidates can be roughly classed as reasoning about particular mechanisms.

1. Five candidates discussed the kind of authenticator needed to validate the ticket. One suggested a digital signature; one reasoned that a MAC[4] would do; three pointed out that even a random number generated by the central server would be enough (though a MAC might be more convenient).

2. There was some discussion of how one should eliminate single points of vulnerability such as the encryption devices that would generate authenticators if this were done algorithmically. There was also some reasoning about separation of duty, such as how to prevent any single individual from being able to validate a jackpot win. One might, for example, have 'orange' and 'blue' encryption boxes (if encryption were used to generate authenticators) or databases (if the authenticators were randomly generated) and have the call centre send out an orange manager and a blue manager to visit the winner and check the claim.

3. There was also discussion of the nature of the Trusted Computing Base[5]. Is this all of the central server or just part of it? How much protection can you get by separating function across replicated hardware, such as multiple databases or crypto boxes at the centre, or by having part of the authenticator computed centrally and part by the vending machine? In the latter case, do you need to have all the vending machines online when claims are paid, or do you upload winning authenticators – in which case what did you gain by decentralising part of the codes before the draw? The efficacy of replication is well known to be bounded by common mode errors (particularly specification errors [13]). And in any case, how do you prevent yourself being laid open to service denial attacks? There are similar tradeoffs involving security and resilience when we consider whether to put the value counters at the server, in the terminals, or in both. Managing these tradeoffs may involve several iterations of a detailed design, with criticism from a number of bright people in parallel.

4. Some candidates discussed the level of reliance that could be placed on physical ticket security technologies, such as holograms; the general consensus was that the stock is bound to be stolen. Thus the primary protection should be digital not physical. However, having a printed serial number on the ticket costs little and may do some good if it is also an input to the MAC or other authentication process. This way, a crook has to do some physical forgery as well. Serial numbers might also provide a second level control against wiretap attacks, as one might transmit only the first few digits of the serial number to the server and arrange matters so that the remaining digits were a MAC computed with a key known only to the ticket printing company.

5. The candidates came up with quite a number of checklist items of the kind that designers often overlook – e.g. 'tickets must be associated with a particular draw'. This might seem obvious, but a protocol design which used a purchase date, ticket serial number and server-supplied random challenge as input to a MAC computation might appear plausible to a superficial inspection. The evaluator might not check to see whether a shopkeeper could manufacture tickets that could be used in more than one draw. Experienced designers appreciate the value of such checklists.

6. The user interface design also needs some care. We mentioned above that one should ask for telephone claims of big wins after the draw, then delay payment for a week or two in the hope that any duplicated winning ticket will become evident. This delay can be used for (and excused by) due diligence activities such as getting a sworn statement from each jackpot winner that the ticket is theirs, and that they are not cheating on a partner or a syndicate with an equity stake

---

[4]For the benefit of readers without a security background, a MAC – or message authentication code – is a cryptographic checksum computed on data using a secret key and which can only be verified by principals who also possess that secret key. By comparison, a digital signature can in principle be verified by anybody. See [8] for more detail

[5]the set of hardware, software and procedural components whose failure could lead to a compromise of the security policy

in the win – an activity which has given rise to most of the publicised disputes over the years.

7. As the company will want to convince outsiders that it is not cheating, it might veer towards involving third parties in many of the protection mechanisms. For example, in order to secure the database of bets before the draw, it would be natural to use a third party timestamping service rather than simply having a spare copy of a CD of the database; if a spare database were preferred, then one might leave it with a bank rather than at an in-house backup site.

8. How much audit effort is needed? Certainly, one should collect both winning and refunded tickets for examination. Key staff should be watched; a Jaguar in the car park should sound an alarm more quickly than it did in the Aldrich Ames case. There are many other details, such as:

   - what will be the controls on adding vending machines to network (and for that matter adding servers);
   - how long should logs be kept;
   - how to deal with refunded tickets;
   - how to deal with tickets that are registered but not printed (these will exist if you insist that unregistered tickets are never printed);
   - what system will be used to transfer takings from merchants to the operator (we don't want a fake server to be able to collect real money);
   - what audit requirements the taxman will impose;
   - what sort of 'intrusion detection' or statistical monitoring system will be incorporated to catch the bugs and/or attacks that we forgot about or which crept in during the implementation. E.g., we might have a weird bug which enables a shopkeeper to manufacture occasional medium-sized winners which he credits against his account. If this is significant, it should turn up in long term statistical analysis.

As we work through these details, it becomes clear that for most of the system, 'Trusted' means not just tamper resistant but subject to approved audit and batch control mechanisms.

4.4 How complete are the above lists?

At the time I set the exam question, I had never played the lottery. I did not perform this experiment until after marking the exam scripts; this helped ensure an even playing field for the candidates. In fact, by the time I got round to buying a ticket, I had already written the first draft of this article and circulated it to colleagues. My description of the ticket purchase process in that draft had been based on casual observation of people ahead of me in Post Office queues, and was wrong in an unimportant but noticeable detail: I had assumed that the authentication code was printed on the form filled by the customer whereas in fact it appears on the receipt (which I have therefore called 'the ticket' in this version of the paper). None of my colleagues noticed, and none of them has since admitted to having ever played. Indeed, only one of the candidates shows any sign of having done so. I had expected a negative correlation between education and lottery participation (many churches already denounce the lottery as a regressive tax on the poor, the weak and the less educated) but the strength of this correlation surprised me.

So the above security analysis was done essentially blind – that is, without looking at the existing system. Subsequent observation of the procedures actually implemented by Camelot suggests only two further issues.

1. Firstly, the Camelot rules allow small franchisees to pay wins of up to £500, while the agencies in main Post Offices can pay up to £10,000. This seems a better idea than our 4.2.6; it makes it a lot harder to run a bogus vending operation. Wins in the £500–£10,000 range are much commoner than jackpots, and main Post Offices are much harder to 'forge' than corner shops.

2. Secondly, the tickets are numbered as suggested in 4.3.4, but printed on continuous stock. The selected bet numbers and authentication codes are printed on the front, while pre-printed serial numbers appear on the back. This may have both advantages and disadvantages. If a standard retail receipt printer is used, it can produce a paper audit roll with a copy of all tickets printed. This may well be more convincing to a judge than any cryptographic protection for electronic logs. On the other hand, the audit roll might facilitate ticket forgery as in 4.2.7, and there may be synchronisation problems (the sample ticket I purchased has two successive serial numbers on

the back). When synchronising tickets with serial numbers, one will have to consider everything from ticket refunds to how operators will initialise a new roll of paper in the ticket printer, and what sort of mistakes they will make.

The final drafting of the threat model, security policy and detailed functional design is now left as an exercise to the reader.

5 Discussion and Conclusions

Linux and Apache prove that software maintenance can be done in parallel; the experiment reported in this paper shows that requirements engineering can too.

There has been collaborative specification development before, as with the 'set-discuss' mailing list used to gather feedback during the development of the SET protocol for electronic payments. However, such mechanisms tend to have been rather ad-hoc, and limited to debugging a specification that was substantially completed in advance by a single team. The contribution of this paper is twofold: to show that it is possible to parallelise right from the start of the exercise, and to illustrate how much value one can add in a remarkably short period of time. Our approach is a kind of structured brainstorming, and where a complete specification is required for a new kind of system to a very tight deadline, it looks unbeatable: it produced high quality input at every level from policy through threat analysis to technical design detail.

The bottleneck is the labour required to edit the contributions into shape. In the case of this paper, the time I spent marking scripts, then rereading them, thinking about them and drafting the paper was about five working days. A system specification would usually need less polishing than a paper aimed at publication, but the time saved would have been spent on other activities such as doing a formal matrix analysis of threats and protection mechanisms, and finalising the functional design.

Finally, there is an interesting parallel with testing. It is known that different testers find the same bugs at different rates – even if Alice and Bob are equally productive on average, a bug that Alice finds after half an hour will only be spotted by Bob after several days, and vice versa. This is because different people have different areas of focus in the testing space. The consequence is that it is often cheaper to do testing in parallel rather than series, as the average time spent finding each bug goes down [14]. The exercise reported in this paper strongly supports the notion that the same economics apply to requirements engineering too. Rather than paying a single consultant to think about a problem for twenty days, it will often be more efficient to pay fifteen consultants to think about it for a day each and then have an editor spend a week hammering their ideas into a single coherent document.

Acknowledgements

I am grateful to the security group at Cambridge, and in particular to Frank Stajano, for a number of discussions. I also thank JR Rao of IBM for the history of the 'object code only' effort, and Karen Spärck Jones who highlighted those parts of the first draft that assumed too much knowledge of computer security for a general engineering audience, and also persuaded me to buy a ticket.

Finally, the students who contributed many of the ideas described here were an anonymous subset of our third year undergraduates for 1998–9, who were:

PP Adams, MSD Ashdown, JJ Askew, T Balopoulos, KE Bebbington, AR Beresford, TJ Blake, NJ Boultbee, DL Bowman, SE Boxall, G Briggs, AJ Brunning, JR Bulpin, B Chalmers, IW Chaudhry, MH Choi, I Clark, MR Cobley, DP Crowhurst, AES Curran, SP Davey, AJB Evans, MJ Fairhurst, JK Fawcett, KA Fraser, PS Gardiner, ADOF Gregorio, RG Hague, JD Hall, P Hari Ram, DA Harris, WF Harris, T Honohan, MT Huckvale, T Huynh, NJ Jacob, APC Jones, SR King, AM Krakauer, RC Lamb, RJP Lancaster, CK Lee, PR Lee, TY Leung, JC Lim, MS Lloyd, TH Lynn, BR Mansell, DH Mansell, AD McDonald, NG McDonnell, CJ McNulty, RD Merrifield, JT Nevins, TM Oinn, C Pat Fong, AJ Pearce, SW Plummer, C Reed, DJ Scott, AA Serjantov, RW Sharp, DJ Sheridan, MA Slyman, AB Swaine, RJ Taylor, ME Thorpe, BT Waine, MR Watkins, MJ Wharton, E Young, HJ Young, WR Younger, W Zhu.

References

[1] The Cathedral and the Bazaar. Eric S. Raymond, http://www.tuxedo.org/~esr/writings/cathedral-bazaar/

[2] The Magic Cauldron. Eric S. Raymond, http://www.tuxedo.org/~esr/writings/magic-cauldron/

[3] A Field Study of the Software Design Process for Large Systems. Bill Curtis, Herb Krasner, Neil Iscoe, Comm ACM 31.11 (Nov 88) pp 1268-87

[4] Why Cryptosystems Fail. Ross Anderson, Comm ACM 37.11 (Nov 1994) pp 32-40, http://www.cl.cam.ac.uk/users/rja14/wcf.html

[5] On the Reliability of Electronic Payment Systems. Ross Anderson and S Johann Beduidenhoudt, IEEE Trans. Software Engineering 22.5 (May 1996) pp 294-301, http://www.cl.cam.ac.uk/ftp/users/rja14/meters.ps.gz

[6] La Cryptographie Militaire. Auguste Kerkhoffs, Journal des Sciences Militaires, 9th series, IX (Jan 1883) pp 5–38 and (Feb 1883) pp 161-191; http://www.cl.cam.ac.uk/~fapp2/kerckhoffs/

[7] Security. Ross Anderson, University of Cambridge Computer Laboratory, http://www.cl.cam.ac.uk/Teaching/1998/Security/

[8] Computer Security. Dieter Gollmann, John Wiley and Sons, 1999; ISBN 0-471-978442-2

[9] A Security Policy Model for Clinical Information Systems. Ross J Anderson, Proceedings of the 1996 IEEE Symposium on Security and Privacy, pp 30–43, Oakland, CA, 1996; conference paper is http://www.cl.cam.ac.uk/ftp/users/rja14/oakpolicy.ps.Z; full BMA version is http://www.cl.cam.ac.uk/users/rja14/policy11/policy11.html

[10] The 1999 papers are at http://www.cl.cam.ac.uk/tripos/y1999.html; see http://www.cl.cam.ac.uk/tripos/y1999PAPER7.pdf for paper 7 in which this question is number 6

[11] New Age lottery will be played on the net. Rupert Steiner, Sunday Times 25 July 1999 p 3.3

[12] Denial of Service: An Example. Roger M Needham, Comm ACM 37.11 (Nov 1994) pp 42–46

[13] Safeware. Nancy Leveson, Addison-Wesley (1994).

[14] Murphy's law, the fitness of evolving species, and the limits of software reliability. Ross J Anderson, Robert M Brady and Robin C Ball; Cambridge University Computer Laboratory Technical report no. 471, http://www.cl.cam.ac.uk/ftp/users/rja14/bab.ps.gz.

Track A

Electronic Commerce

Chair

Ravi Sandhu, George Mason University

Modular Fair Exchange Protocols for Electronic Commerce

Holger Vogt[*] Henning Pagnia Felix C. Gärtner[†]

Darmstadt University of Technology
Department of Computer Science
D-64283 Darmstadt, Germany
{holgervo|pagnia|felix}@informatik.tu-darmstadt.de

Abstract

Recently, research has focused on enabling fair exchange between payment and electronically shipped items. The reason for this is the growing importance of Electronic Commerce and the increasing number of applications in this area. Although a considerable number of fair exchange protocols exist, they usually have been defined for special scenarios and thus only work under particular assumptions. Furthermore, these protocols provide different degrees of fairness and cause different communication overhead.

The purpose of this paper is to present a unifying solution to the problem. We do this by defining a suite of protocol modules which allow to compose protocols where the achieved degree of fairness can be enhanced step by step. The advantage of the stepwise approach is that after each step one can decide if the provided degree of fairness is acceptable or if one is willing to spend more in order to reach a higher degree of fairness. We show the applicability of our approach by deriving a novel efficient fair exchange protocol.

1. Introduction

"Electronic commerce" via the Internet is currently one of the most rapidly increasing markets. In e-commerce, companies use the network for advertising as well as for supporting their business transactions, while most often the Internet is used for internal communication, marketing and support. There is also a steadily increasing number of providers which also sell their products electronically. One of the next major challenges in electronic commerce will probably be the establishment of pay-per-use applications for digital services, i.e. services which can be entirely rendered via an electronic network. Examples for such services are the delivery of video or audio data, the purchase of computer software, the transfer of digital money, the writing of a receipt, or querying a database, but also the provision of telephone lines or Internet access.

A common characteristic of electronic services is that they normally cannot be revoked, i.e., once the service has been granted then the service provider has no effective means to force the recipient to return it. This is particularly true if the two business partners reside in different countries with differing regional law regulations. Therefore, the exchange of two digital services should take place simultaneously in order to guarantee fairness for both involved parties. Unfortunately, real simultaneousness can in general not be achieved because digital services cannot be granted instantaneously. The reason for this is that any type of data always requires a certain amount of time to be transmitted. Hence, during the exchange either party might intentionally interrupt the transmission at any time or the network itself might fail, thereby interrupting communication. If at this time one party has already completed its service but the other party has not, then the exchange was unfair.

As already mentioned, services can be either the delivery of arbitrary (digital) items or the provision of a service, like the provision of a communication link. For the latter type of service *gradual exchange* protocols [14] can be used. The basic idea behind gradual exchange is to repeatedly grant small low-value portions of the services. Hence, interrupting the exchange can only lead to one party gaining a small advantage over the other. Thereby the amount of "unfairness" which a participating party may experience is minimized. A precondition for gradual exchange protocols is that the services in question must be divisible into parts of "near-to-equal" value. Obviously, the smaller these parts become the more communication overhead increases. Conversely, splitting the service into larger parts leads to a

---

[*]This author's work was supported by the Deutsche Forschungsgemeinschaft (DFG) as part of the PhD program (Graduiertenkolleg) "Enabling Technologies for Electronic Commerce" at Darmstadt University of Technology.

[†]This author's work was supported by the Deutsche Forschungsgemeinschaft (DFG) as part of the PhD program "Intelligente Systeme für die Informations- und Automatisierungstechnik" at Darmstadt University of Technology.

non-negligible loss in case the protocol is interrupted. In order to avoid this situation a different protocol for fairly exchanging the individual parts is required. For services or items which are not divisible in the sense described above, such a protocol must be used anyway.

The first protocols of this type (and also the simplest ones that have appeared in the literature) always involve the active participation of a trusted third party (also called "trustee") in every run. Such protocols have been presented by Bürk and Pfitzmann [5] and by Franklin and Reiter [6]. Requiring the active participation of a trusted third party in every exchange has some obvious drawbacks (such as the potential performance bottleneck or the need for permanent availability). These drawbacks can be partly circumvented by *optimistic* fair exchange protocols [2–4]. In optimistic exchange protocols both participating parties try to handle the exchange on their own and only call for the participation of a trusted third party if something went wrong during the exchange. If the protocol is known to ensure fairness both parties are aware that they cannot gain an advantage by acting maliciously. Therefore, the situation in which the assistance of the trustee is required is not likely to happen in practice.

Protocols which do not involve a trusted third party require special item properties in order to work correctly (for example the divisibility of money in Jakobsson's *ripping coins* [8]) or make it necessary to resolve a dispute externally. In the latter case it is important that sufficient evidence is gathered to make the participants concern provable. This can be done, for example, by using the notion of a publicly visible *blackboard* [11] or by using the existing Internet infrastructure [13].

The fair exchange protocols which have been presented in the literature are diverse and at first sight appear incomparable, even in the amount of fairness they offer. In this paper we present a unifying approach to describe fair exchange protocols. By analyzing the exchange process we show that many existing protocols are in fact a composition of different protocol modules with distinct functionality. By separating the concerns and identifying these modules we are able to construct a new and even more efficient protocol for fair exchange.

The remainder of the paper is structured as follows. We discuss different notions of fairness in Section 2. Subsequently, we present our modular approach to fair exchange protocols in Section 3. This is where we show how to compose given modules into a suite of protocols solving the fair exchange problem for different levels of fairness. We conclude our paper with a discussion of our approach and some future research directions in Section 4.

2. Fairness

An intuitive way to define fairness is the following: An exchange is both, *completed* and *fair* if both parties have received the desired item. If neither party receives nor loses anything valuable then the exchange is incomplete but still fair. All other outcomes are unfair since one party has gained an advantage over the other. A protocol is called fair if under all valid conditions the exchange always ends fair.

A straightforward way to guarantee fairness is to design a protocol such that after each protocol step fairness holds. (Otherwise, the party which has gained an advantage could immediately interrupt the protocol which now ends unfair.) One possibility to achieve this is to use an active third party which first collects both items and then — after checking their validity — performs the swap. Obvious disadvantages of this protocol exist:

1. The third party must be completely trusted, i.e., it must follow the protocol and particularly not collude with either party.

2. The third party cannot be implemented stateless since it must wait for the items of both parties before the exchange can commence. This implies a non-negligible memory overhead and the need for complex mechanisms for crash recovery.

3. A considerable amount of work is delegated to the third party, resulting in high computational load.

We will discuss methods alleviating these problems later in this section.

2.1. Validation of items

A problem which is inherent to all exchange protocols is how to check the items. In order to be able to do this it is important that a sufficiently detailed specification exists for both items. For some kind of items, for example digital money, the validation is rather simple. Another example is a widely used software package which can be checked by computing a cryptographic hash value and comparing it against a trusted reference value which is publicly available [6]. Problems with this solution however can occur if the software contains a serial number or an individual watermark for copyright protection. There are other items which are difficult to check: E.g., a common description of a software package usually contains a list of features which cannot be checked during a formal verification process. Promises like "high performance" are not accurate enough in order to be verified formally. What the customer expects from this will usually not meet reality. Therefore, for an accurate validation a complete and formal specification is required. Besides the fact that in some cases this is impossible to obtain, in most other cases it is very costly. Consequently, for the exchange we can at best guarantee that a delivered item meets a given specification. But we cannot guarantee that it meets the other party's expectations which might go beyond. So overall, we must assume that for the items a sufficiently accurate specification exists against which they can be verified (although this might be costly).

2.2. A hierarchy of fairness definitions

Several definitions of fairness have been proposed [1, 7, 16]. The most prominent definition is the one by Asokan [1] in which he distinguishes between strong and weak fairness. For weak fairness it is required that — in case of a failed exchange — either party can prove that it has behaved correctly, i.e., it has followed the prescribed exchange protocol. The proofs must then be shown to an arbiter outside of the system who has the power to establish fairness, usually by forcing both parties into cooperation. The problem with this is that in most countries it is still unclear how such a proof must look like in order to fulfill local law regulations. In any case, a lawsuit is expensive and its outcome might be rather uncertain. Therefore, it is desirable to resolve as many conflicts as possible within the exchange system itself. If the third party is sufficiently powerful it can automatically process the proofs and decide how to proceed. The advantage of this is that conflicts are now automatically processed within the exchange system, thus improving the degree of fairness.

In extension to the definitions of Asokan [1], we propose the following hierarchy of fairness guarantees:

F_6: Fairness can be guaranteed automatically by the system without further cooperation of the other party.

F_5: Fairness can be guaranteed automatically by the system with eventual cooperation of the other party.

F_4: Fairness can be achieved automatically by the system through providing a compensation for a suffered disadvantage.

F_3: Fairness can only be guaranteed outside the system without further cooperation of the other party.

F_2: Fairness can only be guaranteed outside the system with eventual cooperation of the other party.

F_1: Fairness can only be achieved outside the system by providing a compensation for a suffered disadvantage.

F_0: No fairness.

The fairness definitions F_4 to F_6 are supposed to be stronger than the others because conflicts can be resolved automatically without the need for a subsequent external dispute. Strong fairness by the definition of Asokan [1] corresponds to F_6. As Asokan does not make any assumptions about the willingness of the parties to cooperate, F_5 can also be regarded as strong fairness. Gärtner et al. [7] call F_5 *eventually strong fairness*. The difference between F_6 and F_5 lies in the additional assumption made about the participants, i.e., whether they can be eventually forced to cooperate. In practice, this can be achieved by using a trusted computing environment such as a smart card. The categories F_3 and F_2 match Asokan's weak fairness definition. The categories F_1 and F_4 describe a different fairness concept in which it is assumed that a non-delivered item can be substituted by a different one (e.g., a payment) which compensates the loss. Because this does not match the original intention of the exchange process we have ranked compensation as a method to achieve fairness which is weaker than the others.

2.3. Special item properties

Special properties of the exchanged items can help the third party to resolve conflicts. In this section, we describe two of these properties in more detail, namely "generatability" and "revocability" [1].

2.3.1. Generatability

A generatable item is an item which can be generated by the trustee in case the receiving party can prove that it has behaved correctly. There are different methods to make an item generatable, among them are the following:

1. A party forwards a copy of its item to the trustee who stores it for a possible subsequent dispute. The party is provided with a signed receipt which can be presented to any other party as a proof that the item is generatable by the trustee.

2. A party encrypts its item by a random key. This key is then deposited at the trustee who returns a receipt for it, which the party can from now on use as a proof for the generatability of the key. Note, that this receipt cannot be regarded as a proof for the generatability of the item, since it cannot be guaranteed that the encrypted item can successfully be decrypted.

3. A party encrypts its item by a random key and ensures that this key can be decrypted by the trustee. This can be done with the help of a public key cryptosystem: the party encrypts the random key with the trustee's public key and forwards this — as part of the exchange

protocol — to the other party. The latter cannot decrypt this random key and hence not the item, but the trustee could do so (provided that the correct item was correctly encrypted).

The burden which is placed on the trustee decreases from method 1 to method 3. While in method 1 the trustee must store the entire item he only needs to store the decryption key in method 2. Method 3 is the most efficient one in terms of storage space: the trustee can use a single key — namely the own private key — for decrypting any item which was made generatable.

2.3.2. Revocability

An item is called revocable if the trustee can revoke it in case it has sufficient evidence to do so. Revocable items are, for example, payments since payment systems usually support revocability. Other items which might be revocable are digital signatures or certificates which provide the right to use a service. It should be noted that items must not be revocable by a party itself. Otherwise, after a correctly terminated fair exchange, one of the parties could easily revoke the delivered item and thus gain an unfair advantage over the other party. Only the trustee should be allowed to revoke items.

3. Modular fair exchange protocols

In this section we show how different notions of fairness can be realized by combining appropriate program modules to an exchange protocol as shown in Figure 1. The advantage of this modular approach is that for different scenarios suitable solutions can be composed. These solutions may depend on the properties of the exchanged items, the power of a third party, the effort which is acceptable for the exchange, or on other properties like anonymity of the parties. We first describe the underlying system model. Then we present the required modules and discuss possible implementations.

3.1. System model

We consider a system to consist of a finite set of processing elements (also called nodes) which communicate through asynchronous message passing. The parties involved in a fair exchange (customers, vendors, trustees) are assumed to reside on distinct nodes which usually are geographically separated. Messages are sent through a communication subsystem which allows direct communication between any two nodes in the system regardless of the underlying physical topology. Message passing is point-to-point and reliable with FIFO delivery order. We place no timeliness restrictions on the relative processing speed of individual nodes so that we have the *asynchronous* model of distributed systems [15]. While trustees are assumed to follow the protocol correctly, customers and vendors can act maliciously by stopping to proceed further in a protocol or by sending corrupted messages. We assume however that such incorrect behavior can be detected either by a party which follows the protocol correctly or by a trustee.

3.2. Definition of fair exchange modules

In an exchange protocol at least two parties are involved: The customer C and the vendor V. Some actions also require the cooperation of a trusted third party or trustee T. The customer has an item i_C and the vendor possesses the item i_V. Although in most cases, the customer's item will be a payment, we use i_C as a more universal notion for it here.

3.2.1. Module M_1: Negotiate

In a first step the customer and the vendor negotiate about the exchange. They have to agree on a specification (i.e., a formal description of each other's item) which enables them to verify whether the item received during the exchange protocol is the one which was expected. When both parties know which items shall be exchanged, they also agree on which fair exchange protocol should be used and which modules are used in order to implement it. Additionally, they agree on the name of the trustee possibly involved if the protocol relies on one. If the protocol uses compensation as a method for re-establishing fairness (cf. fairness definitions F_1 and F_4) then the two parties must also agree on an appropriate compensation. After completion of "Negotiate" the exchange itself can be started.

3.2.2. Module M_2: Prepare to exchange

The vendor promises that he will deliver his item i_V after the customer has sent the item i_C. This is a verifiable commitment which can be used in an external dispute (e.g., a lawsuit) in case that the vendor has misbehaved. If the vendor refuses to give this commitment, the exchange protocol is aborted. In this case, fairness F_6 is achieved since nothing valuable has been exchanged yet.

3.2.3. Module M_3: Exchange

The customer sends i_C to the vendor, who checks this item against the specification. If it is the expected item, he sends i_V to the customer, who also checks the specification obtained in module M_1. The outcome of this action can be that

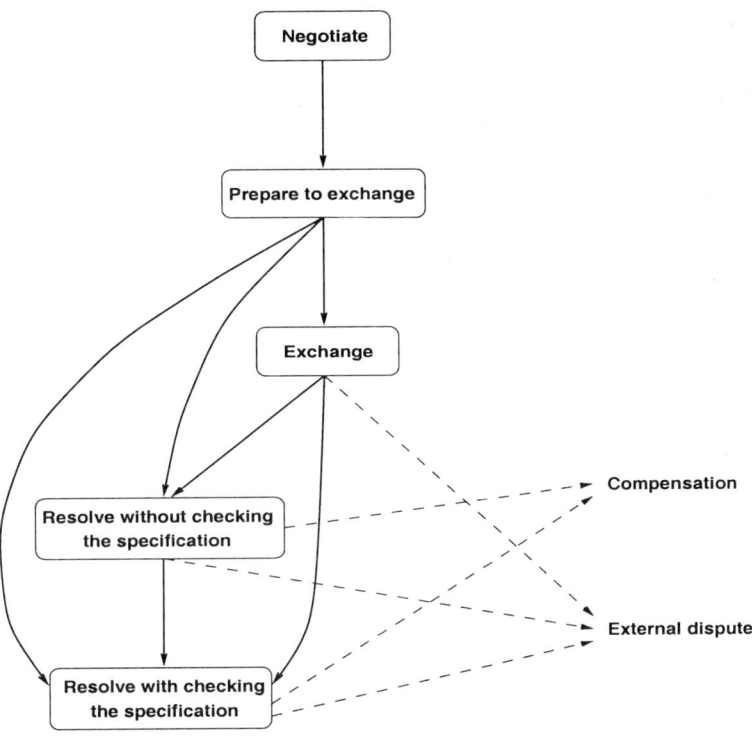

Figure 1. Composing fair exchange protocols by using the modular approach

1. both parties have the expected item,

2. none of them has an item, or

3. the vendor has i_C, while the customer has received nothing.

In the first two cases fairness F_6 is achieved, and the protocol can terminate at this point. In case 3, fairness must be re-established in one of the subsequent steps. One possible solution is to start an external dispute which however, guarantees only a lower degree of fairness (F_1, F_2, or F_3). Alternatively, the modules M_4 and M_5 can be used.

3.2.4. Module M_4: Resolve without checking the specification

If item i_V is generatable then the trustee tries to generate i_V for the customer. If the trustee succeeds, fairness F_6 is recovered. If not, either an external dispute has to be started or module M_5 must be invoked. Alternatively, compensation can be invoked if it was pre-arranged in module M_1. If the delivered item i_V does not match its specification (obtained during module M_1), module M_5 should be started. In most cases, we expect the trustee not to run into problems when trying to generate the item, because the vendor has already committed himself to deliver his item during module M_2 which can subsequently be used as a proof against him.

3.2.5. Module M_5: Resolve with checking the specification

The trustee checks the specification of the vendor's item i_V against the delivered or generated item. If this verification fails or if i_V is not available, the trustee has two possibilities: He can either use compensation (achieving fairness F_4) if pre-arranged or he can re-establish the state, in which neither the vendor nor the customer has the other's item (fairness F_6). If this cannot be done, fairness cannot be guaranteed within the system and an external dispute must be started.

3.2.6. Combining the modules

We can now set up fair exchange protocols by combining these modules. This approach is very flexible, because it provides several protocol variations: if after the execution of a module the fair exchange is completed, then subsequent steps using the other modules are not needed. It is also possible to use only a subset of the five modules by simply omitting one or more modules. However, the sequence of the modules must not be changed because this would result in incorrect protocols. Figure 1 gives an overview of the possible combinations. If a solution outside of the system is acceptable, the exchange protocol can also end with an external dispute.

3.3. Module implementations

In this section, we provide pseudo-code for possible implementations of the modules. The exchange is hereby considered to be the exchange between payment (which was i_C in the previous section) and the product that the customer wants to buy (which was i_V). In the following, we do not consider compensation as a method to gain fairness in order to ease presentation. It can however be easily incorporated into the implementations. We use the notation ⟨event⟩ : ⟨description⟩ to describe the individual steps of the implementation, where ⟨event⟩ can be the sending of a message from participant X to Y (designated by $X \to Y$) or some local computation of a participant (designated by its name). The ⟨description⟩ is a brief explanation of the type of message sent or the type of actions performed locally. We assume that secure cryptosystems are available and denote encryption and decryption functions using key x by e_x and d_x, respectively. We use the capital letters D_x and E_x whenever an asymmetric cryptosystem is applied for party x. A participant can also produce digital signatures. To ease reading, we will abbreviate signing a message m and obtaining a signature s by $s := sign(m)$. Finally, we also assume the availability of a strongly collision-free cryptographic hash function h. All these assumptions do not impose restrictions on the practicality of our approach, since sufficient means exist to realize these functions in practice [9].

3.3.1. First implementation of module M_1

A straightforward way to implement the negotiation module is the following:

Protocol I_{1a}

$C \to V$: $spec_{prod}$, T, set of possible protocols supported by C
$V \to C$: $spec_{pay}$, T, set of possible protocols supported by V

The customer and the vendor exchange the specification of the items which they want to receive and agree on a trustee T which can possibly be invoked. They also determine which exchange protocols are acceptable to both of them. Then the customer dynamically chooses one of these protocols with which he proceeds. For the following implementations it is assumed that for every message it is known to which protocol it belongs. This prevents various attacks that can be constructed by mixing steps from different protocols.

3.3.2. First implementation of module M_2

The "Prepare to exchange" module can be implemented like this:

Protocol I_{2a}

$C \to V$: order product
V : choose a random key R
encrypt product with R, i.e.
$EP := e_R(\text{product})$
compute hash $H := h(EP)$
encrypt R for the trustee, i.e.
$R_T := E_T(R)$
$Sig_V := sign(spec_{prod}, spec_{pay}, T, H, E_T(R))$
$V \to C$: Sig_V, EP, R_T
C : compute hash $H := h(EP)$
verify signature Sig_V

In this implementation the customer receives the product encrypted with a random key R, the key R encrypted with the trustee's public key, and a signature from the vendor to commit on this exchange. The main idea is that the further exchange process is reduced to the exchange of payment and R. Furthermore, the trustee will be able to compute R, after the vendor has sent the correct value R_T.

After execution of this module, it is still possible to abort the exchange if, for example, signature verification has revealed a bad signature.

3.3.3. First implementation of module M_3

The exchange can be implemented like this:

Protocol I_{3a}

$C \to V$: payment
V : check payment
$V \to C$: R
C : decrypt product, i.e.
$\text{product} := d_R(EP) = d_R(e_R(\text{product}))$
check product against $spec_{prod}$

This type of exchange is called an optimistic exchange [2], because no third party is required unless a conflict occurs. As most exchange processes can be assumed to run without failures, optimistic protocols can substantially reduce the load that is put on the third party. If a conflict occurs, the customer must decide which actions should be used in order to re-establish fairness.

3.3.4. First implementation of module M_4

Module M_4 is a solution for re-establishing fairness, if the previous modules failed to achieve fairness. It can be implemented like this:

Protocol I_{4a}

$$\begin{aligned}
C \to T \quad &: \quad \text{payment, spec}_{prod},\ \text{spec}_{pay},\ T,\ H,\ R_T,\\
&\quad\ Sig_V\\
T \quad &: \quad \text{verify signature}\\
&\quad\ \text{decode key: } R := D_T(R_T)\\
&\quad\ \text{check payment}\\
&\quad\ \text{deposit payment}\\
T \to C \quad &: \quad R\\
C \quad &: \quad \text{decrypt product, i.e.}\\
&\quad\ \text{product} := d_R(EP) = d_R(e_R(\text{product}))\\
&\quad\ \text{check product against spec}_{prod}
\end{aligned}$$

The trustee decrypts R, which he sends to the customer in exchange for the payment. The product is decrypted by the customer, so that he has to check it by himself. This implementation obviously relies on the vendor, who has to provide the correct values, so that the trustee can generate the correct key R. Since the vendor might have sent incorrect values, fairness cannot be completely guaranteed.

3.3.5. First implementation of module M_5

In this implementation the trustee checks the specification of the product. When he detects a failure, he must be able to revoke the payment, if it was already sent to the vendor. This guarantees fairness F_6 after the execution of this module.

Protocol I_{5a}

$$\begin{aligned}
C \to T \quad &: \quad \text{payment, spec}_{prod},\ \text{spec}_{pay},\ T,\ EP,\ R_T,\\
&\quad\ Sig_V\\
T \quad &: \quad \text{verify signature}\\
&\quad\ \text{check payment}\\
&\quad\ \text{decode key } R := D_T(R_T)\\
&\quad\ \text{decode product, i.e.}\\
&\quad\ \text{product} := d_R(EP) = d_R(e_R(\text{product}))\\
&\quad\ \text{check product versus spec}_{prod}:\\
&\quad\ \text{if "product OK" then}\\
&\quad\quad\ \text{deposit payment}\\
&\quad\quad\ T \to C \ : \ \text{product}\\
&\quad\ \text{elseif "product not OK and payment was}\\
&\quad\quad\ \text{already sent to the vendor" then}\\
&\quad\quad\ \text{revoke payment}
\end{aligned}$$

3.3.6. Second implementation of module M_5

One of the last steps of implementation I_{5a} is that the trustee sends the product to the customer. The following alternative implementation can be used in order to minimize the amount of transferred data:

Protocol I_{5b}

$$\begin{aligned}
C \to T \quad &: \quad \text{payment, spec}_{prod},\ \text{spec}_{pay},\ T,\ EP,\ R_T,\\
&\quad\ Sig_V\\
T \quad &: \quad \text{verify signature}\\
&\quad\ \text{check payment}\\
&\quad\ \text{decode key } R := D_T(R_T)\\
&\quad\ \text{decode product, i.e.}\\
&\quad\ \text{product} := d_R(EP) = d_R(e_R(\text{product}))\\
&\quad\ \text{check product versus spec}_{prod}:\\
&\quad\ \text{if "product OK" then}\\
&\quad\quad\ \text{deposit payment}\\
&\quad\quad\ T \to C \ : \ R\\
&\quad\quad\ C \quad\ : \ \text{decrypt product, i.e.}\\
&\quad\quad\quad\ \text{product} := d_R(EP))\\
&\quad\ \text{elseif "product not OK and payment was}\\
&\quad\quad\ \text{already sent to the vendor" then}\\
&\quad\quad\ \text{revoke payment}
\end{aligned}$$

This solution works better than I_{5a} if, for example, the customer has only a slow modem connection to the trustee. In this case I_{5b} should be used for minimizing the transmission time.

3.3.7. Second implementation of module M_2

The implementations above are particularly designed for optimistic fair exchange protocols. For an exchange involving an active trustee, the modules M_2 and M_3 can be implemented in the following manner.

Protocol I_{2b}

$$\begin{aligned}
C \to T \quad &: \quad \text{payment, spec}_{prod},\ \text{spec}_{pay}\\
V \to T \quad &: \quad \text{product, spec}_{prod},\ \text{spec}_{pay}
\end{aligned}$$

3.3.8. Second implementation of module M_3

Because the trustee possesses both, payment and product, he can check in advance if these items match their specification. If the checks fail, the exchange will abort without losing fairness.

Protocol I_{3b}

$$\begin{aligned}
T \quad &: \quad \text{check payment, check product versus}\\
&\quad\ \text{spec}_{prod}\\
T \to C \quad &: \quad \text{payment}\\
T \to V \quad &: \quad \text{product}
\end{aligned}$$

3.4. Composing protocols

The module implementations described in the previous section can be combined in different ways according to the rules displayed in Figure 1. The most important compositions are listed below:

P_1: $\langle I_{1a}, I_{2b}, I_{3b}\rangle$
This is the basic active exchange protocol for fairness F_6 which is used in several protocols (e.g. [5], [6]).

P_2: $\langle I_{1a}, I_{2a}, I_{3a}, \text{external dispute}\rangle$
This is a protocol for a weaker fairness (F_2/F_3). A detailed discussion of this class of protocols can be found in [1].

P_3: $\langle I_{1a}, I_{2a}, I_{3a}, I_{4a}, \text{external dispute}\rangle$
This is another weak fairness (F_2/F_3) protocol for the scenario of non-revocable payments.

P_4: $\langle I_{1a}, I_{2a}, I_{3a}, I_{5a}\rangle$
This is an optimistic protocol which ensures fairness F_6 inside the system. See [12] for a complete description.

P_5: $\langle I_{1a}, I_{2a}, I_{3a}, I_{5b}\rangle$
This describes a variation of P_4 with a fewer amount of transferred data in the case of conflict.

P_6: $\langle I_{1a}, I_{2a}, I_{3a}, I_{4a}, I_{5a} \text{ or } I_{5b}\rangle$
This is a very efficient optimistic fair exchange protocol providing fairness F_6, which will be elaborated on at the end of this section.

P_7: $\langle I_{1a}, I_{2a}, I_{4a}, \text{external dispute}\rangle$
This is an alternative implementation for the active protocol P_1. The NetBill payment protocol [16] uses a similar idea to ensure fairness.

P_8: $\langle I_{1a}, I_{2a}, I_{5a} \text{ or } I_{5b}\rangle$
This protocol is also a variation of the active protocol P_1.

The protocols P_1, P_2, P_4, and P_7 correspond to the existing protocols cited in the short protocol descriptions given above. The other protocols are so far unpublished.

P_3 is a novel variation of a weak fairness protocol which first makes an attempt to re-establish fairness automatically inside the system. Only if this fails an external dispute is started.

As already stated above, P_5 is a variation of P_4. The only difference between the two protocols is that at the end of Module M_5 the trustee does not send the product to the customer but the key R. The customer then decrypts the product himself.

In protocol P_8 after the exchange was prepared by the customer and the vendor, the trustee is used to finally perform the swap of product and payment. It should be noted that although P_8 invokes I_{5a} it is not necessary to use a payment system with revocability. The reason for this is that the payment was never sent to the vendor during the previous steps and therefore it does not need to be revoked. Different to this, the protocols P_4, P_5, and P_6 require the payment to be revocable.

Protocol P_6 is an interesting novel protocol which is now described in more detail.

Discussion of protocol P_6. After the negotiation phase in I_{1a} some preconditions for P_6 must be checked: In module M_5 the trustee should be able to revoke the payment. This is necessary for the (rather improbable) case that the vendor has received the payment during I_{3a} but the trustee is not able to generate the product in I_{4a}, due to a misbehaving vendor in I_{2a}. Without revocability the customer can either initiate an external dispute (this is equal to protocol P_2 or P_3) or he must rely on an active trustee (this ends up in protocol P_1 or P_7). The advantage of revocable payment is that with its help fairness can be guaranteed inside the system and that the trustee is not actively involved in any fault-free exchange. This is true for protocol P_6 which tries to involve the trustee as seldom as possible. This effectively reduces communication traffic caused at the trustee, since we can assume that most exchanges are executed without experiencing any failure. Thus, in the normal case the protocol terminates immediately after performing the exchange in I_{3a}.

The implementation I_{4a} attempts to re-establish fairness in the case of a failure. As in most cases the trustee will be able to compute the key R, so that the customer can decrypt the product. A lot of failures can be solved by invoking I_{4a}. Furthermore the implementation of I_{4a} is very efficient because only a minimal set of values has to be transferred to and from the trustee.

It should not be necessary to call I_{5a} or I_{5b} very often, so that even expensive computations during these modules (e.g. for checking the product) might be tolerable.

It should be noted that an additional property of this protocol is that it allows the customer to remain anonymous when buying a product from the vendor. In this case however, both the payment-system and the communication connection between the two parties must support anonymity.

4. Conclusions

Fair exchange is a problem of substantial practical significance in electronic commerce. Products, payments and services must be exchanged fairly to ensure the continuing growth of the electronic marketplace. In order to increase the trust that participating parties place in exchange services it is important to state precisely the guarantees of different protocols with respect to fairness and efficiency. When this has been done, customers and vendors can select a certain protocol that suits the application or situation needs best. For example, if products of considerable value (like a new CAD-program) are exchanged, both parties will probably favor a protocol which guarantees a strong fairness F_4–F_6 even if this comes at a higher cost (because they might have to pay a trustee). On the other hand, both parties might be willing to agree on a weakly fair F_1–F_3 protocol if they simply exchange the latest football results.

The fair exchange protocols which have been presented in literature are diverse and at first sight incomparable even in the degree of fairness they offer. We have analyzed the exchange process and we have tried to show that a lot of these protocols are in fact a composition of several modules with distinct functionality. By separating the concerns and identifying these modules we were able to construct a set of new and even more efficient protocols for fair exchange.

Moreover, by using our compositional approach it is now possible to construct exchange protocols for a given level of fairness and given item properties almost dynamically. In practical settings this enables the vision that a customer can choose an item from an on-line catalogue, select the desired level of fairness and have the rest of the exchange be executed automatically; it is no longer necessary for the user to select a specific protocol which is clearly a step towards more user friendliness.

The compositionality of our protocols also lends itself to modular verification of the protocols in the direction of the well-known software engineering paradigm of stepwise refinement. For this, it is however necessary to formalize the module specifications much more rigorously. We expect that this will reveal some potential for methodological improvements of our approach since the distinction between module specification and implementation has not been sharp enough. This is obvious from the fact that some combinations of modules (e.g., $\langle I_{1a}, I_{2b}, I_{3a} \rangle$) are not possible. A clearer differentiation between both concepts will lead the way to a more rigorous verification. This and the implementation of the given suite of protocols within our experimental testbed will be the focus of our continuing work.

References

[1] N. Asokan. *Fairness in electronic commerce*. PhD thesis, University of Waterloo, May 1998.

[2] N. Asokan, M. Schunter, and M. Waidner. Optimistic protocols for fair exchange. In T. Matsumoto, editor, *4th ACM Conference on Computer and Communications Security*, pages 8–17, Zurich, Switzerland, Apr. 1997. ACM Press.

[3] N. Asokan, V. Shoup, and M. Waidner. Asynchronous protocols for optimistic fair exchange. In *Proceedings of the IEEE Symposium on Research in Security and Privacy*, pages 86–99, May 1998.

[4] N. Asokan, V. Shoup, and M. Waidner. Optimistic fair exchange of digital signatures. In K. Nyberg, editor, *EUROCRYPT '98*, Lecture Notes in Computer Science, pages 591–606. Springer-Verlag, 1998. A longer version is available as Technical Report RZ 2973 (#93019), IBM Research, November 1997 at http://www.zurich.ibm.com/Technology/Security/publications/1997/ASW97b.ps.gz.

[5] H. Bürk and A. Pfitzmann. Value exchange systems enabling security and unobservability. *Computers & Security*, 9(8):715–721, 1990.

[6] M. K. Franklin and M. K. Reiter. Fair exchange with a semi-trusted third party. In T. Matsumoto, editor, *4th ACM Conference on Computer and Communications Security*, pages 1–5,7, Zurich, Switzerland, Apr. 1997. ACM Press.

[7] F. C. Gärtner, H. Pagnia, and H. Vogt. Approaching a formal definition of fairness in electronic commerce. In *Proceedings of the International Workshop on Electronic Commerce (WELCOM'99)*, Lausanne, Switzerland, Oct. 1999.

[8] M. Jakobsson. Ripping coins for fair exchange. In L. C. Guillou and J.-J. Quisquater, editors, *Advances in Cryptology—EUROCRYPT '95*, volume 921 of *Lecture Notes in Computer Science*, pages 220–230. Springer-Verlag, 21–25 May 1995.

[9] A. J. Menezes, P. C. V. Oorschot, and S. A. Vanstone. *Handbook of Applied Cryptography*. CRC Press, 1997.

[10] S. Mullender, editor. *Distributed Systems*. Addison-Wesley, second edition, 1993.

[11] H. Pagnia and R. Jansen. Towards multiple-payment schemes for digital money. In R. Hirschfeld, editor, *Financial Cryptography: First International Conference, FC '97*, volume 1318 of *Lecture Notes in Computer Science*, pages 203–215, Anguilla, British West Indies, 24–28 Feb. 1997. Springer-Verlag.

[12] H. Pagnia and H. Vogt. Exchanging goods and payment in electronic business transactions. In *Proceedings of the Third European Research Seminar on Advances in Distributed Systems (ERSADS)*, Madeira Island, Portugal, Apr. 1999.

[13] J. Riordan and B. Schneier. A certified e-mail protocol with no trusted third party. In *Proceedings of the 13th Annual Computer Security Applications Conference*, Dec. 1998.

[14] T. W. Sandholm and V. R. Lesser. Equilibrium analysis of the possibilities of unenforced exchange in multiagent systems. In C. S. Mellish, editor, *Proceedings of the Fourteenth International Joint Conference on Artificial Intelligence*, pages 694–703, San Mateo, Aug. 20–25 1995. Morgan Kaufmann.

[15] F. B. Schneider. What good are models and what models are good? In Mullender [10], chapter 2, pages 17–26.

[16] J. D. Tygar. Atomicity in electronic commerce. In *Proceedings of the 15th Annual ACM Symposium on Principles of Distributed Computing (PODC'96)*, pages 8–26, New York, May 1996. ACM.

Trustworthy Access Control with Untrustworthy Web Servers

Tim Wilkinson, Dave Hearn and Simon Wiseman
Defence Evaluation and Research Agency
Malvern, England

{t.wilkinson,d.hearn,s.wiseman}@eris.dera.gov.uk

Abstract

If sensitive information is to be included in a shared web, access controls will be required. However, the complex software needed to provide a web service is prone to failure. To provide access control without relying on such software, encryption can be used. Bob is a prototype system that supports complex access control expressions through the transparent use of encryption.

1. Introduction

The business benefit of an Intranet web is that information is available to those that need it in a timely fashion. However, most large organisations have some information that is considered sensitive and is not needed by all users. For example, Human Resources data might need sharing amongst members of the HR department, while other people are prevented from accessing it.

Existing solutions to this problem, for example [1], rely on complex web server software working correctly and being configured correctly, which means there is considerable risk that the controls will fail. In many commercial organisations, as long as the information remains on the company Intranet, the risks involved will be worth taking, given the relatively limited damage that would be caused if the controls fail. However, an organisation which handles particularly sensitive data, such as health care records or defence intelligence information, may find the risk unacceptable.

With increased use being made of electronic commerce to make trading more efficient, the boundaries of an Intranet are fast being eroded. Increasingly, an organisation will host some proprietary information belonging to its trading partners on its Intranet and these partners may need some access to the Intranet in order to conduct business. Typically, the partners will be in competition with each other and the host organisation would need to ensure that the information belonging to one partner is not revealed to another (either accidentally or deliberately). Should an access control failure occur, damage to the host organisation's reputation might lead to lost business and even claims for damages. In these circumstances, a commercial organisation may find the risk of complex access control software failing hard to justify to the shareholders or potential customers.

One way of controlling access to information in a web without relying on the web server software is to use separate servers for information of different sensitivities. Unfortunately this solution does not scale when many combinations of information sensitivity and user trustworthiness are required.

The only way a single untrusted web server can be used to handle information of different sensitivities is to remove responsibility for access control and separation from the server software. This can be achieved by encrypting documents, in a key not available to the server, before they are given to the server. This removes access control responsibilities from complex web server software and becomes a matter of distributing data decryption keys appropriately. Unfortunately, the general problem of key distribution is by no means a simple task, but some options are described in section 3.

This paper describes a prototype system called Bob that uses an encryption based approach to provide trustworthy access control in a web based on untrustworthy web servers. Bob was initially developed by the Defence Evaluation and Research Agency (DERA) for the UK Ministry of Defence. The concept, however, is a generic one and additional work has shown how Bob can be used to protect Electronic Patient Records in a medical environment.

In the next section the basic access control scheme is described, then the problem of key distribution is discussed. The question of how the release of information into the web is controlled is then tackled as well as possible ways of reconciling the conflicting requirements of data discovery and confidentiality. Finally, techniques for handling dynamically created content are considered.

2. Access Control

2.1 Access Control Expressions

The access control scheme can be described in terms of groups, each containing a number of users. These groups will usually represent a particular business function, project or trading partner. Each file accessed through the web server is labelled with an Access Control Expression (ACE), which indicates those users who are permitted to observe the file.

An ACE is a formula defined in terms of groups combined with operators "&" and "|", which are 'and' and 'or' respectively. Files with an ACE of the form "X & Y" can be observed by any user who is in group X and group Y, while files with ACEs of the form "X | Y" can be observed by any user who is either in group X or group Y.

Complex ACE formulae can be used, and some examples are shown below:

ACE	required groups
X & Y & Z	X Y Z
X & (Y | Z)	X Y or X Z
(W | X) & (Y | Z)	W Y or W Z or X Y or X Z

Suppose an organisation had a number of departments that handle sensitive information, including Engineering (ENG) and Finance (FIN). In addition, the organisation handles sensitive information belonging to its customers, who include ACME and DERA. A group would be created for each department and for each customer, and staff would be placed in these groups according to the departments for which they work and the customers that they serve.

Now sensitive engineering data about work for ACME would be labelled "ENG & ACME". An engineer who was not working on the ACME project would not be in the ACME group and so would be unable to see this data. Similarly, sensitive financial data about work for ACME would be labelled "FIN & ACME".

However, if the organisation were working on a joint project for ACME and DERA, the engineering details might be labelled "ENG & (ACME | DERA)", in which case any engineer working on an ACME (or DERA) project will be able to see details of the joint project as well. Alternatively, the data might be labelled "ENG & ACME & DERA", in which case only engineers who work on both ACME and DERA projects would be able to see the data.

2.2 Access Mediation

The ACE applied to a file accessed through the web server is not in itself used to mediate access. Instead, when the file is released into the server its ACE is used to determine the way the file's data is encrypted. The scheme uses a mixture of symmetric and asymmetric cryptography as follows.

When a file is released, a new symmetric key is generated and this is used to encrypt the file. This key is called the file's data key. The resulting encrypted data is prepended with a header before being released to the web server. The header contains the information that allows legitimate recipients to decrypt the encrypted data.

An asymmetric key pair is generated for each group in the access control scheme. This key pair is used to distribute a file's data key to those who are permitted to observe the file. One key of the pair is a key encrypting key and the other is a key decrypting key. The encrypting key is used to release information to the group, and the decrypting key is used by members of the group to observe data released to them.

In the simple case where the ACE is just a single group, the file's data key is encrypted using the group's encryption key. The result is placed in the header along with the file's ACE, as shown in figure 1. The way in which the data key is encrypted in general is explained in Annex A.

ACE
original MIME type
data key encrypted in group encryption keys
file's data encrypted in data key

Figure 1: Format of protected file

To observe a file, the ACE in the header is examined to determine how the encrypted data key should be recovered. In the simple case, where the label is just a single group, the group's decryption key is used to recover the file's data key from the header. Once the data key is obtained, the file's data can be decrypted. If the group's decryption key is not available, because the user is not a member of the group that is permitted to observe the file's data, there is no way the file's data can be accessed.

When HTTP is used to retrieve a file from a web server, the reply includes information about the type of the file. This information is included in the HTTP Content-Type reply header field, whose format is a MIME type. Standard web servers use so-called 'mailcap' files to determine, on the basis of file extension, which MIME type is to be associated with each file they deliver. In Bob, all encrypted files are given an extension of ".bob" and a MIME type of "application/x-bob" is associated with this.

When Bob format data is decrypted, in a manner that is described later, the type of the result is changed to the original type taken from the header. This means the browser knows how to handle the data in the normal way.

2.3 Protecting the Group Keys

Most applications of public key cryptography assume that a user's application software can be trusted to protect keys from disclosure and to use them only in accordance with the user's wishes. Here, however, the assumption is that complex web server software cannot be trusted, and so the same level of distrust must be levelled at the workstation applications. Thus a group's decryption key must not be made available to a user's ordinary application software, as this could pass the key to other users who are not part of the group.

The solution is shown in Figure 2. An HTTP decryption proxy is installed on the user's workstation and access controls provided by the workstation's operating system are set so that the proxy has access to a file containing the user's group decryption keys, but the user's application software is denied any access to this file. The access controls are also used to protect the proxy's binary image and configuration data from modification. The need for operating system access controls to protect the use of cryptographic mechanisms is discussed fully in [2].

The job of the decryption proxy is to transparently decrypt any encrypted data retrieved from a web server and to restore the original MIME type of the data. The proxy is trusted to keep the group decryption keys and all document keys private, regardless of what data it handles (for example, it defends against buffer overrun problems).

The user's web-enabled applications, including their browser, would be configured with the local decryption proxy as their web proxy, while the decryption proxy would be configured to chain-on to the network's real web proxy if one is required.

A group's decryption key is protected so that an application cannot pass it on to users who are not in the group, as this would give the recipient access to all files released to the group. Similarly, a file's data key is protected, otherwise this would give the recipient access to the particular file. However, once a file has been decrypted and given to an application, the cryptography does not stop the application passing the decrypted data to another user. This is part of the general problem of controlling the release of data while using untrustworthy application software, which is discussed in section 4.

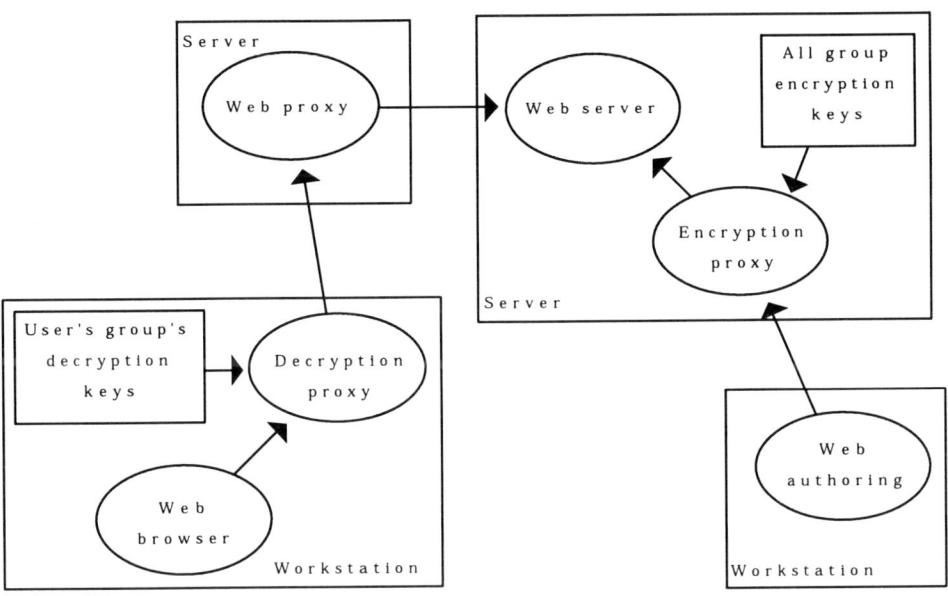

Figure 2: Overall architecture

Protecting a file's data key from disclosure also affords extra protection to the group decryption key. A user in possession of a document key, and the same key encrypted with a group encryption key, has the potential to mount a brute force attack to obtain the group decryption key. With a single document key, the user has only a small amount of information on which to base their attack, but if they can find several documents released to the same group, the brute force effort required will decrease.

Application software used by authors to create web content must be prevented from modifying group encryption keys. This is because the application, which must be considered untrustworthy, could gain access to all data subsequently released by replacing the group encryption key with one for which it knows the corresponding group decryption key. Since there is no need for anyone to know the encryption key, it seems prudent to keep it private as well as to prevent its modification.

Note that, having protected both the encrypting and decrypting keys from disclosure and modification, it would be possible to use symmetric cryptography for the group keys. The advantage of asymmetric cryptography, however, is that it gives extra protection in the event that proxies are compromised. For example, should a server's group encryption keys be divulged, no data is compromised if asymmetric cryptography is used.

Web content is typically created on a workstation and uploaded into the web server using FTP or HTTP. The process of releasing web content can be controlled by placing a proxy, for the appropriate protocol, between the web authoring application and the web server. This encryption proxy needs access to the all the group encryption keys, so it can encrypt a released file in accordance with its ACE. The encryption proxy is trusted to allow the group encryption keys to be modified only under strictly controlled circumstances, discussed in the next section. In addition, the proxy keeps the encryption keys private, though this is less important.

Figure 2 shows the placement of the encryption proxy in the current Bob implementation. As an alternative, the proxy could be placed on the user's workstation, which has the advantage of protecting the data's from eavesdropping as it passes from workstation to server. The disadvantage, however, is that the encryption keys need to be more widely distributed.

In order to know how the file's data should be encrypted, the encryption proxy needs to know the file's ACE. The way this is conveyed from the web authoring software running on the user's workstation to the proxy is discussed in section 4.

If encryption is to be used for access control, the problem of key revocation and replacement must be addressed. Key replacement will be needed occasionally to defray the risk of key compromise, and may also be performed on demand when keys are known to have been compromised. Keys might be compromised because proxies fail to hold the keys securely, the Public Key Infrastructure (PKI) might fail to deliver them securely, or a brute force attack might be successful.

A group key can be replaced by creating a new group identity and associated key pair. All users in the affected group can then be put in the new group, and the new decrypting key distributed accordingly. Then, all files with ACEs that mention the affected group are found and their ACEs are updated to replace the affected group with the new group. In addition, the data key is recovered and re-encrypted in accordance with the new ACE. Once all files have been processed, the original group is redundant and users can be removed from it. Performed in this way, group key replacement need not be completed as an atomic action and may even be carried out as a background task, depending upon urgency.

An individual document key can be changed easily. It is simply a matter of recovering the original file data key, using the decrypting key of some group which can access it, decrypting the data, and replaying the normal process associated with publishing.

3. Key Distribution

3.1 Public Key Infrastructure

The decrypting group keys of the groups to which a user belongs, need to be distributed privately to the decryption proxy on the user's workstation. One way of achieving this is to make use of public key technology. Each proxy would be identifiable by a distinguished name and associated public key, most likely wrapped together into an identity certificate. The proxy would hold the complementary private key in private local storage. An administrator wishing to place a consumer group decryption key into a proxy would obtain the identity certificate corresponding to the proxy. After verifying the certificate, the public key contained within it can be used to encrypt a group key for forwarding to the proxy. Only a holder of the proxies' private key can unwrap the group key.

At this point the message containing the hidden group key can be presented to the user of the system by, for example, electronic messaging. Once the message has been inserted into the proxy, the proxy can unwrap the message to reveal the group key and place it in private storage. Additional fields could be associated with the key, such as a time after which the key is invalid.

There is still an issue of how the proxy's private key is made available to the proxy initially. In organisations that prefer central key generation, the private key could be physically or electronically delivered to the proxy in a secure manner, and then imported through a trusted import function. Alternatively, the proxy could generate its own private key at installation time, and export the corresponding public key for signature by a certification authority.

3.2 Key distribution with NT security

While the ultimate solution is to distribute keys through a public key infrastructure, as discussed above, a lighter-weight alternative is possible using the security mechanisms of a networked operating system. These mechanisms only work in well-managed closed networks, so the technique will not always be applicable, but where the operating system's environmental assumptions hold it is perfectly adequate.

A key distribution scheme for Bob has been implemented using the security functionality provided by Windows NT. The relevant features are Services and Named Pipes.

A Named Pipe is a communications pipe mechanism whose use is subject to NT security in much the same way as files. A server process on one machine can create a named pipe and set its access control list so that only processes running under certain user accounts can connect to it. When a client process does connect to the pipe, the server process can establish the identity of the client account.

A Service is a process that is started when a machine boots and generally runs under a special system account, rather than one associated with a particular user. Ordinary users may subsequently log-in to the machine and the service continues to run.

More details about these features and a description of how they can be used to build systems for handling sensitive information is given in [3].

Figure 3 shows the general arrangement of processes and services used to distribute group keys. A simple database of group decryption keys is stored on a key server host. The decryption proxy on each workstation is installed as a service and this runs under a special system account. These proxies obtain the user's group keys from a process, the Key Server, using a Named Pipe. The Key Server could reside on the web server host, though it would be better to install it on a more tightly controlled machine.

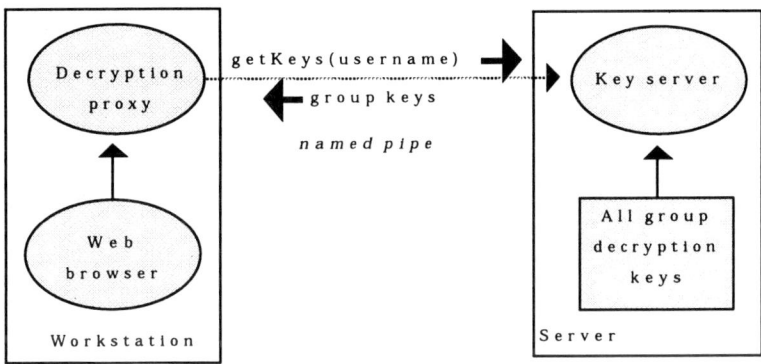

Figure 3: Distributing keys using NT security

The decryption proxy runs as soon as the workstation boots. Whenever it detects that a user has logged-on to the workstation, the proxy connects to the key server's Named Pipe and sends the account name of the user who has just logged on. The key server obtains a list of groups to which the user belongs and then returns a list of decryption keys for these groups to the decryption proxy.

Once the decryption proxy receives the list of group keys for the user, it can transparently decrypt any encrypted data returned from the web server. However, the proxy must ensure that any incoming connections are not from a remote workstation, in case a user in a different group is logged-on there.

The access control lists on the key server's Named Pipe are set so that only the service account used by the decryption proxies can access it. A user's application processes therefore cannot obtain any decryption keys from the web server.

4. Controlling Release

On a well-managed web site, files are not changed in an ad-hoc way. Subsets of web pages and links are updated or otherwise modified, and then uploaded to the server in a publishing operation. It is within this publishing function that access control requirements can be stated and release can be sanctioned.

The first step in publishing is for an author to create one or more documents for publication. Each document needs to have an ACE associated with it. The way this is done depends upon the application used and the environment in which it runs. A simple version might use Microsoft Word to create the documents, in which case the ACEs can be held as document properties. If the workstation provides support for labelled documents, the ACEs could be derived from the security labels of the documents. The Bob demonstration does this, using NT workstations augmented with Deep Purple [4] to provide the labelled documents.

Once the documents have been assembled, they must be released to the web server. Since the assumption is that application software is not sufficiently trustworthy to protect documents from disclosure, the release process must be controlled. In Bob, release is handled by a trustworthy service running on the user's NT workstation. Ordinary applications can request this service to release files to the web server. To defend against an application making inappropriate requests to release some data, the user is asked to confirm each request.

The release service obtains the user's sanction using a trusted path interface, to avoid the sanction being spoofed by an application. A trusted path interface is supported directly by Deep Purple, which uses NT's standard access controls on Desktops to implement it. As part of the release sanction, the user is asked to confirm the ACE for the product to be released. This prevents the application from changing the ACE after the user has set it and before the file is released.

The release service may also check the content of the files to be released to ensure that no data is hidden from the casual reader. This is important as an application may attempt to leak data by hiding it in files that are to be released. While checking for hidden text, the service may also generate a summary of the file's content. This can be presented to the user when they are asked to confirm the release, so that an application that attempts to change the data being released may be discovered.

For example, suppose an author prepares a web "page" comprising some HTML text and two images in GIF format. The release service can check that the application has not hidden sensitive data in comment tags in the HTML, and if any is found the user can be warned not to release the data. In the trusted path dialogue, which asks the user to confirm the release request, the "page" would be summarised, so the user can see the number of paragraphs of text and the number of images being released. If this summary is not as expected, the user has a chance of rejecting the confirmation request.

The release sanction can be obtained separately for each "page", or a single sanction for all the "pages" to be released as one "product" can be obtained. Whilst the former is in principle more secure it could also be seen as an inconvenience. It is common for users to take more care over a single operation than one they need repeat many times. Hence better overall security might be obtained by adopting a more relaxed approach in which one update involving several "pages" is sanctioned as a whole.

Assuming the user confirms the intention to release the data, the release service proceeds to upload the files to the encryption proxy on the server. It is important to prevent applications directly uploading data to the server's encryption proxy, as this would provide them with a way of leaking data. This protection can be achieved by using cryptographic techniques, but in a closed NT based environment named pipes can be used.

5. Searching and Dynamic Content

The usual approach to information discovery is to allow web sites to be indexed by a search engine, and to allow users browsing the site to search the indexes. The Bob approach is to protect sensitive data from complex web servers that are hard to trust. Search engines are also complex software, and at present there seems to be no reason to trust them more than a web server.

Hence it is not appropriate to provide search engines with sensitive data in plain text, and yet it is pointless to provide them with the data in an encrypted form because they then cannot index it. Thus a balance needs to be struck between confidentiality of information and the ability to locate information.

Data that all users are permitted to view need not be encrypted. A search engine can then be used to index this unencrypted data and allow it to be searched, without the complex software being trusted. If, as part of the process of preparing sensitive documents for the server, the author creates an abstract which is visible to all, the abstract can be made available via the search engine and would provide a means for information discovery. The abstract can include a link to the encrypted document, so that it is readily available to any user that is a member of the intended audience.

Another issue is dynamic content, where web pages are generated on demand based on the data in a database. For example, when a user browses a dynamic page, a CGI script may access a database and create some HTML that is returned to the user.

With Bob, the script passes the appropriate request to the database, but the sensitive results are returned as encrypted Bob files. These are embedded indirectly into the generated web page by using HTML <OBJECT> tags. Each <OBJECT> tag is a link to an encrypted result, but the data referred to is displayed in place in the web page, rather than being shown as a hyperlink. Thus if the user's groups are such that they can access all the results, the page is completely filled in, while if they are not some fields will display an error message.

The Bob encryption process could be included in the database engine, by exploiting the Object Relational features of Oracle 8 or Informix IUS [5], or a separate trusted server process could be interposed between the scripts and the database. Alternatively, the sensitive data could be encrypted before it is placed in the database. This has the advantage that the database engine need not be trusted to handle the sensitive data properly, but the disadvantage is that the data cannot be searched or manipulated (e.g. projection) within the database.

Independently of when the data is encrypted, its release into the database must be sanctioned, as the producer is not involved when the data is served out to a requestor. Techniques for doing this using object-relational database engines are discussed in [5].

6. Performance

The use of encryption as an access control mechanism adds an overhead to the release of documents into the web server and to their retrieval by a browser.

Consider first the simple case, where an ACE contains just one group. The release of a document requires that a data key is generated, the file is encrypted in the data key and the data key is encrypted in the group key. To retrieve a document, the data key must be decrypted using the group key and the file must be decrypted using the data key. Overall, the impact on performance is negligible and no noticeable delay is introduced.

In the general case, however, the overhead can be much higher. When a document is released, the data key must be encrypted using a group key many times. The number of encrypts using some group key is the number of elements in the ACE. This could be noticeable in terms of performance and latency, but any decrease would be negligible compared to the overhead of checking whether the document is suitable for release.

The overhead can sometimes be reduced as some ACEs can be re-written to have fewer terms while retaining the same meaning in terms of access control. For example, the ACE (A&B)|(A&C) can be re-written as A&(B|C), and this requires one less encrypt.

Generally, retrieving a document with a complex ACE is faster than releasing it. This is because there are many different collections of group keys that permit the data key to be recovered, and it is possible to choose the smallest such collection, to which the user belongs, by consulting the file's label. For example, suppose the ACE is (A&B)|(C&D&E)|(F&G) and the user is in groups C through G. By consulting the label in the file's header, it is possible to determine that only two decrypts are required, using the keys of groups F and G, whereas seven encrypts would have been needed to release the file.

Although there is a performance overhead introduced by the decryption of the file's data key, this can be performed in parallel with the transmission of the file's encrypted data. Thus this introduces no delay when retrieving a file with a long ACE.

7. Similar products

Although the use of encryption to protect access to resources is not a new idea, the technique employed in Bob has three significant features.

First, the encryption and decryption is not visible to the end-users. Contrast this with the Formlock[1] product from General Network Services, Here, when a user attempts to retrieve an encrypted document they are presented with a dialog box asking them what action should be taken.

Second, Bob's access control scheme supports complex access control expressions. Various cryptographic envelope schemes, for example IBM's Crytolopes[2] and DigiBox from InterTrust[3], also use encryption to control the distribution of data, but in contrast to Bob these control access simply by controlling the distribution of decryption keys to individuals.

Third, the encryption in Bob is used in a way that removes the need to trust complex, and hence untrustworthy, software. In common with other cryptographic access control solutions, Bob does not need to trust the web server, but unlike some other solutions it also does not need to place trust in the client's browser and associated plug-ins. Instead, Bob's implementation minimises the need to trust software hosted on the workstation, limiting it to just that which handles keys.

8. Conclusions

Web server and browser software is complex and its security features are prone to failure or misconfiguration, and hence cannot be trusted to handle sensitive information appropriately. Bob avoids this problem by ensuring that the web server only handles encrypted data and that release of data from the browser is carefully controlled. With Bob access control in the web is reliant upon:
- operating system access controls in the workstations and servers;
- the correct operation of the special encryption and decryption proxies;
- ensuring released data is labelled with an appropriate access control expression;
- the generation and distribution of the group encryption and decryption keys.

Using encryption to protect information does not solve all the problems, because it is necessary to defend the cryptographic elements from misuse by the untrustworthy servers and applications [2]. The basic protection mechanisms needed in the workstations and servers are found in Windows NT and Unix, but initial key distribution remains a difficult problem to solve in general. Key distribution in a closed NT environment is, however, straightforward.

The Bob solution does not remove the need for trusted software, but it reduces the scale considerably. Rather than trusting web servers and browsers, including all their plug-ins, only the encryption and decryption proxies and the release server need to be trusted. These are quite easy to trust as they are small and simple.

---

[1] http://www.gns.ca/
[2] http://www.software.ibm.com/security/cryptolope/
[3] http://www.intertrust.com/

Controlling the release of data into the server is not a trivial problem, because to be effective the controls must be closely integrated with web authoring application software. Such software is relatively immature, but progress in standardising distributed web authoring and versioning extensions to HTTP[1] should simplify the design of the release service and make it more widely applicable.

Finally, the addition of access controls into a web conflicts with the natural intention of a web to be freely accessible. This creates considerable tension, as evinced by the problems associated with search engines. This aspect of the problem is worthy of more research.

9. References

[1] "Role Based Access Control for the World Wide Web", J.Barkley *et al*, Procs. 20th National Information Systems Security Conference, Baltimore, October 1997.

[2] "The Inevitability of Failure: The Flawed Assumption of Security in Modern Computing Environments", P.Loscocco *et al*, Procs. 21st National Information Systems Security Conference, Crystal City, October 1998.

[3] "Adding Security Labelling to Windows NT", S.Wiseman, Information Security Technical Report, Vol 3, Num 3, Elsevier 1998.

[4] "Private Desktops and Shared Store", B.Pomeroy and S.Wiseman, Procs. 14th Annual Computer Security Applications Conference, Scottsdale, December 1998.

[5] "Securing an Object Relational Database", S.Lewis and S.Wiseman, Procs. 13th Annual Computer Security Applications Conference, San Diego, December 1997.

---

[1] http://www.ics.uci.edu/pub/ietf/webdav/

Annex A: Encrypting File Keys

A file's header contains the file's ACE and the file's data key encrypted in a way determined by the file's ACE. The function for encrypting the data key of a file D whose ACE is A is denoted H(D,A), and is defined as follows:

$\wedge$ is the concatenate operator

$H(D, G) = e_G(D)$
$H(D, x | y) = H(D,x) \wedge H(D,y)$
$H(D, G \& x) = e_G(H(D,x))$
$H(D, (x|y) \& z) = H(D, (x \& z) | (y \& z))$

where
 D is the file data key
 G is a simple ACE of one group
 x, y and z are arbitrary ACEs
 $e_G(\alpha)$ is the result of encrypting α in the
  encrypting key associated with group G

To observe a file, it must be decrypted using its data key. This can be recovered from the file's header if certain group decrypting keys are known. The ACE determines which combinations of group decrypting keys permit the data key to be recovered.

The function that is used to recover a data key from the encrypted data E and ACE A in the header is denoted R(E,A). This either retrieves the decryption key or returns an error. It is defined as follows:

$R(E, G)$ = If user in G then $d_G(E)$ else fail
$R(Ex \wedge Ey, x | y)$ = either $R(Ex, x)$
  or $R(Ey, y)$
  or fail if both fail
$R(E, G \& x) = R(d_G(E),x)$

where
 E, Ex and Ey are encrypted key data from the
  header
 G is a simple ACE of one group
 x and y are arbitrary ACEs
 $d_G(\alpha)$ is the result of decrypting α in the
  decrypting key associated with group G

A Language for Modelling Secure Business Transactions

Alexander W. Röhm, Gaby Herrmann, Günther Pernul
Department of Information Systems
University of Essen, Germany

{roehm | herrmann | pernul}@wi-inf.uni-essen.de

Abstract

Among other areas electronic commerce includes the fields of electronic markets and workflow management. Workflow management systems are usually used to specify and manage inter- and intra-organisational business processes. Although workflow management techniques are capable to specify and conduct at least parts of market transactions, these techniques are not or very rarely used for this purpose yet. In both fields users demand security and integrity to protect for example their privacy, their property rights or digital payments. To satisfy these security demands a variety of existing security services, mechanisms, protocols, and organisational measures are existent and may be used. At one hand side, to encourage using these techniques it is necessary to have a tool which enables a firm's executive to formulate market transactions security demands at a high abstraction level. On the other hand executing market transactions needs a more formal, machine readable description of the transaction and its security requirements. In this paper we present a methodology to specify secure protocols, which are usable to automatically conduct business processes as well as market transactions.

1 Introduction

By using the Internet for commercial purpose the significance of electronic commerce increases due to Internet's openness, which offers new opportunities and therefore changes our way of doing business. Electronic commerce is "... the sharing of business information, maintaining business relationships, and conducting business transactions by means of telecommunications networks" [14]. Electronic commerce reduces transaction costs due to the use of information technology (IT) and electronic markets in the Internet are therefore supposed to produce lower prices and bigger margins than traditional markets [8]. Why do many executives and consumers still hesitate to conduct their business activities in the Web? Our hypothesis is that users want to have integrated tools guaranteeing security and fair trade. The tools must be embedded in a legal system which protects from fraud and larceny. Executives who are responsible for trouble free and optimal execution of electronic business transactions want secure and fair trade and they therefore need possibilities to analyse and specify their security needs by using appropriate techniques.

In recent years a boom in the research field of electronic commerce is taking place. Mainly through the rapid adoption of the Internet by the users today nobody doubts the fact that electronic commerce is a strategic sector. This trend also inspired the research fields of IT-security, workflow management, business (re)engineering and others. The outcome of this research is that we have solutions in many areas like cryptographic mechanisms, secure payment protocols, workflow management systems and new promising business models. Up to now the integrated view of abstract specification and enabling technologies are rarely addressed. The relation between these areas is displayed in figure 1.

Some work about security for workflows, business processes, and market transactions has already been done. But most of them focus on authorisation mainly, for example Thomas and Sandhu [13], Bertino et al. [1], and Bußler [2]. For an appropriate integrated view on secure business transactions we need a broader view on security [7]. For example, non-repudiation of a message containing a document or originality of a payment token may be demanded for business transactions.

There are also a lot of single solutions for electronic commerce that allow fair exchange, secure payment, signing of digital contracts, and so on. But if you consider yourself to be in the position to realise a business model for the production, offering and selling of a digital product in the Internet your best choice would be hiring a software expert with a security expertise.

comes visible by focusing on virtual enterprises which execute distributed business processes over open communication networks. By using the same underlying technologies the same security requirements may be taken into account. In this paper we use the concept of business transaction to describe both market transactions and business processes.

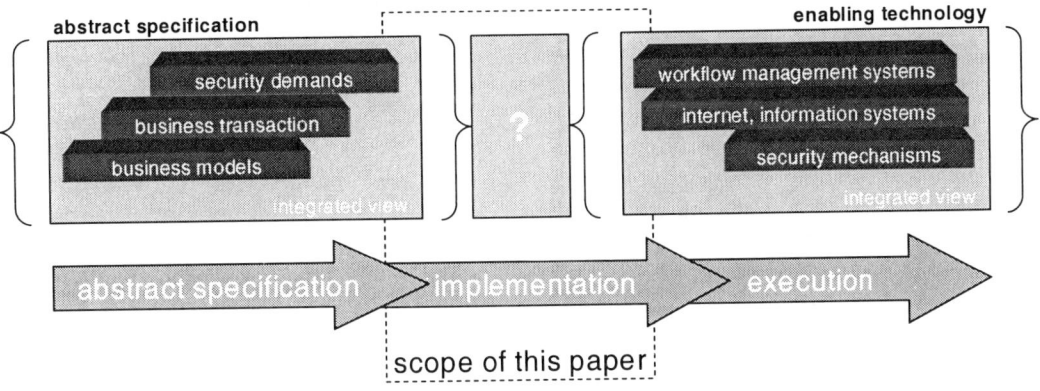

Figure 1: Scope of modelling secure business transactions

Taking into account that business models change relatively often the integration gap between the left and the right side of figure 1 shows its importance.

In this paper we present a language to specify secure business transactions which is integrated in a model, that describes the whole way of an electronic business transaction: from its abstract specification by an executive its implementation in machine readable form and finally to its execution. We see our work as a first step to close the gap in figure 1.

The structure of this paper is as follows: We first describe the integrated model in which ALMO$T is embedded in chapter 2. Chapter 3 contains the outline of the specification language ALMO$T (A Language for Modelling $ecure Business Transactions). ALMO$T can be used to specify protocols that realise security and integrity requirements of business transactions. The goal is to meet the users security needs. Chapter 4 gives an overview how the execution of business transactions is done with ALMO$T followed by the conclusion in chapter 5. In two appendixes we include the definition of ALMO$T with a BNF grammar and a real world example of a business transaction realised in ALMO$T.

2 Secure Electronic Business Transactions

Modelling methods for business processes are used to specify processes in firms. Anyway, they may be used to specify market transactions, too. Focusing on security requirements of electronic business processes and market transactions an alignment may be recognised. This be-

2.1 Electronic Business Transactions

Market transactions and business processes are interrelated. While business processes describe the activities inside the firm, market transactions describe the coordination of the (potential) business partners. More precisely, a business process is a general activity (or set of inter-related activities) with the intention to support an organisation to reach its (business) targets. Commonly, in each business process a relationship to business process partners exists. The interactions with business partners takes place on markets by market transactions. A market transaction is the process of a barter, where either tangible or intangible goods are exchanged between the different parties involved. Therefore, a market transaction is usually defined as a set of interactions between market participants in different roles having the goal to make and fulfil a contract concerning the exchange of goods.

Business transactions have immanent security requirements like confidentiality and legal binding of information, privacy, non-repudiation of having participated in a communication and so on. One of the most important security requirement for trade is to provide the integrity of traded goods, which means to conserve the value of traded goods by protecting their specific property rights. Integrity of a good may differ depending on the type of the good. As an example free tradable rights on electronic markets like emission permits (see example in appendix B) are valuable as original, only. To guarantee integrity of an emission permit the requirement originality has to be maintained. Looking on emission permits additionally anonymity may be important for economic reasons [9].

We introduce this idea of digital goods' integrity by extending the traditional view of integrity of a message because we see the importance for secure electronic commerce. Integrity of goods depend on the circumstances of the application. In contrast the integrity of a message results from the conditions of the communication.

Another important security demand is fairness, which also is not possible to ensure on basis of messages and communications. Fairness means that either all of the business partners got everything they expected, or none got anything and none lost anything at the end of a transaction. It is obvious, that realisation of the integrity of the good is part of the realisation of fairness. Especially, this is true when coin-based electronic payments are viewed as a type of digital good. When a business partner has sent a coin it immediately lost its value for him.

Security requirements result from different circumstances from internal of the enterprise or from the environment the enterprise is acting in (e.g. laws or ethical requirements). Each security requirement may occur at different security levels, because different transactions may have different risks. Therefore, different security mechanisms with different strength are needed.

2.2 Model and Realisation

To solve the security problems mentioned in the previous subsection an infrastructure which realises the security services and mechanisms is needed. To make these realisations usable for the person who specifies the secure business transactions, a way to combine existing solutions with new ones must be provided. In this section we first describe a model that shows the whole way from the specification at a high level of abstraction to the realisation of secure business transactions. Then we describe the basic properties of the security infrastructure in which a specified secure business transaction can be conducted, followed by some remarks on security service's characteristics.

2.1.1 Specification Model

To support realisation of secure electronic business transactions we have developed a three-layered architecture (for more information see [10]). At the upper layer graphical concepts to specify security requirements of business transactions are offered. To fulfil a specified security requirement the corresponding business process must include functionality which guarantees it. Usually such functionality is neither included in business process models nor in workflow management software and thus modifications or extensions are necessary. Such modifications are supported by a repository of use-cases located at the highest layer of the architecture. A business process is described by different perspectives (cf. [3]) which produces an integrated, consistent, and complete view of it. Use-cases offer modifications of different perspectives of the business process model to realise the demanded security requirements.

The representations of business processes have relationships to an infrastructure for electronic markets. That's why to realise a business process an enterprise may act on an electronic market, e.g. to offer its products or to use some services offered by other market participants (e.g. notary service). An electronic market is represented as a three-dimensional polygon which is structured in three layers correspond to the phases of a market transaction (information phase, negotiation phase, execution phase1); the edges represent different participants of the market. Besides the economic parties supplier, demander and intermediaries also parties, who realise trusted services2 and information services are needed to build a secure electronic marketplace. Trusted services are important for contracting and for digital goods which often need authenticated time, originality, and similar properties. For future electronic markets we also expect a lot of new tasks for trusted third parties. Information services provide technical information about the market infrastructure and the network. Examples are certificate directories or a special host which processes inquiries like: "What is the network address of a trusted third party issuing secure time stamps?". Business transactions are specified to describe the processes that are executed locally at each party and the protocols which are steering the co-operation between the parties.

The middle layer of the proposed architecture offers a repository of already modelled solutions of basic security elements and of activities linked with security requirements. Basic security elements are abstract descriptions of security mechanisms which enclose all information for their realisation. For example, verify digital signature R of alleged signatory S. An example of an activity linked with security requirements is the activity "deliver a licence anonymously under consideration of its originality".

These solutions are created by security experts located in the involved enterprises or employees of a third party of the market (enterprise) offering solutions of security problems. The ALMO$T language is the main

---

1 Sometimes instead of the execution phase two phases are define: the settlement and the adjustment phase.
2 Parties which realise trusted services are usually called trusted third parties.

means to bridge the gap between basic security elements and activities lined with security requirements respectively and soft- and hardware modules used for their realisation. It is located at the middle layer. For example, to realise basic security element "verify digital signature of signatory" the software building blocks "request certificate of signatory" and "proof digital signature using MD5 and RSA" are needed. Specifications on the middle layer should be built as kind to execute automatically.

At the lowest layer of the architecture a repository with hard- and software building blocks is included. They are combinable to realise security services.

Protocols specified with ALMO$T, as each other kind of protocol too, may be used in a business transaction only if all participants of that business transaction accept it and act according this protocol. If no agreement about a procedure to realise a certain degree of required security is reached, at least one participant of the business transaction must modify its security requirements or the business transaction may not be executed with these participants.

2.1.2 Characteristics of Security Services

In many cases the local usage of security services and mechanisms is not sufficient, and an infrastructure to offer additional services is necessary. In this subsection we discuss characteristics of such services.

In the example of an application of the digital signature the trusted service public-key-certification and the less trusted service public-key-directory are necessary. Theses services are offered by third parties, which can be part of the global environment, the local environment (e.g. the enterprise), or in the private environment of a particular participant. For example, a directory may offer its services globally to all participants or only to participants inside a corresponding enterprise in an address book, which contains public keys of communication partners and which is stored in the enterprise's local environment. Moreover, a participant of a business process may realise his/her private directory.

Using third parties of different environments may lead to different results. For example, usage of a third party from the local environment to obtain a certificate of a public key may lead to an obsolete public key because the corresponding certificate is declared invalid in the global environment but the local directory was not updated.

In most business processes third parties are involved, especially in secure business processes. Services of third parties may be used online which means the service is produced at the moment the service is needed, which includes a communication between the business participant and the party offering the service during usage of the service. In some cases the demanded service is produced in advance and the result is stored e.g. in the local environment of the business participant. For example, to register the originality of a document the third party must be involved in the business process online. But to obtain a certified public key an online service is not always necessary. If the corresponding certificate is stored locally the service may be produced offline. For security requirements the distinction between offline and online is relevant, because the use of online services may result in less availability and higher risk of vulnerability.

To sum it up, services may be established in different environments (private, local, and global) and the produced services may be integrated into business transactions either in advance (offline) or simultaneously (online).

3 ALMO$T

In this section we explain the overall design of ALMO$T. What we present is an approach which uses object-oriented ideas and notations for two reasons. First, because this results in a paradigm, which is easy to understand and straightforward to use and second, the realisation of the infrastructure is almost completely written in the object-oriented language Java. The syntax of ALMO$T-statements are given in appendix A.

3.1 Special Objects, Classes and their Interfaces

Because certain objects and classes occur in almost any business process, we include them as predefined classes and objects such as `doc`, `kCrypto` and `net`. For example, `doc` is the base class for documents, `kCrypto` the base class for key-based cryptography. The underlying communication network is a special object called `net`. If a special net should be used for communication (e.g. Internet) it can be derived from the class net as an additional object.

All classes are part of the same class hierarchy that is shown in figure 2. The root of this hierarchy is the abstract base class `object`. All other objects in ALMO$T are extensions of this class. The interface of `object` includes the method for assignments `set` and methods for comparisons, which are denoted by the corresponding mathematical relation combined with a question mark (e.g. =?, ≤?).

Similar to the class `object` there are predefined interfaces for the classes `boolean`, `doc`, `net`, `kCrypto`. Objects for key-based cryptography offer the methods `encrypt`, `decrypt`, and `verify`. These methods need the parameters doc (representing the data to process) and the key to use (e.g. `RSA.encrypt(key,data)`, where `RSA` is an extension of `kCrypto`). The methods `send` and `receive` of a network object `net` refer to the sent/received documents. They are used in combination with the communication net on which the data should be sent or received. Assigning a new value to an object the method `set` is used (e.g. `rating.set(clear accept)`). A document is an object which consists of a set of attributes. To access an object that is an attribute of a document, the `get_attr` method of the class `doc` is applicable. `doc.get_attr(tip)` delivers the value of the attribute `tip` of the object `doc`. Predefined classes are summarised with their interface in table 1.

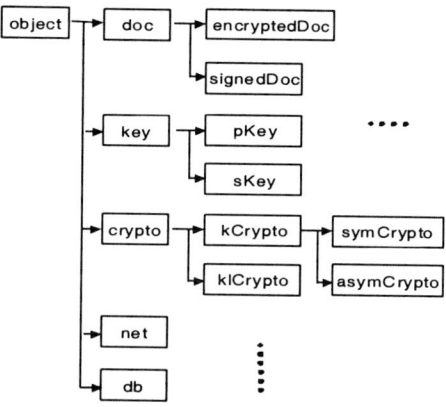

Figure 2: Class hierarchy of ALMO$T

object	abstract base class f. objects
`create(object)`	standard constructor
`<rel>?(object)`	compares two objects according to `<relation>`∈ {=,≠ ...}
`set(object)`	assigns a value to the object
boolean	objects of boolean type
`<op>(boolean)`	`<op>`∈ boolean operators
doc	base class for all documents
`attach(doc)`	attach doc to the document
`detach(doc)`	detach doc from the document
`get_attr(id)`	selector for attributes
`set_attr(id, object)`	equivalent to `get_attr(id)set(object)`
kCrypto	base class for key-dependent cryptography
`encrypt(key,doc)`	encrypt doc by using key
`decrypt(key,doc)`	decrypt doc by using key
`verify(key,doc)`	verify doc by using key
net	communication network
`send(doc,id)`	send doc to id
`receive(doc,id)`	receive doc from id
db	database object
`remove(object)`	removes object from database
`add(object)`	adds object to database
`get(object)`	get object from database

Table 1: Classes and their interface

3.2 Multiparty Business Transactions and Environments

In general more than one party may be involved in a business transaction. Therefore, ALMO$T allows to specify business transactions for single parties involved as well as together for all parties part of the business transaction from in- and outside a company. A specification of a business transaction is an object and the actions performed are its methods. To specify a multiparty business transaction for n different parties a table with n rows allows parallel specification of the business transaction for all participants. Because different parties are specified in one view an environment structure must be part of ALMO$T. This has an important impact on security due to the fact that the public services as well as the private-key must have its own definite place in the environment. For that reason a cascading environment structure has been chosen. Listed from the inner environment level to the outmost the different environments are:

- the *temporal* environment of the method,
- the *private* environment of the party,
- the *local* environment, to which a set of parties have access, and
- the *global* environment.

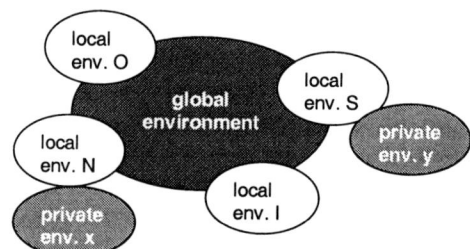

Figure 3: Environments

Used objects may be located at different levels. For example, an object may be located global to each business party or local to a single business party. Assume two objects with the same identifier `directory` are located at two different environment levels, e.g. global and local environment. Using one of these objects may lead to a different result in comparison to the use of the other one. Therefore, the priority of the environments is given by the following search order for identifiers: At first the temporal environment is searched for an identifier and if found the other levels are not been searched anymore. Otherwise the same procedure goes on until the outmost environment level (the global environment) is reached.

It is possible to define explicitly the environment in which an object is used. If a search strategy is explicitly given in a statement, as in the example `env.local(pKeyring(Boss))`, the standard search strategy (temporal → private → local → global) is not applied to the identifiers. For example: `env.global(db.get(Boss))` looks for our boss in the database of the global environment.

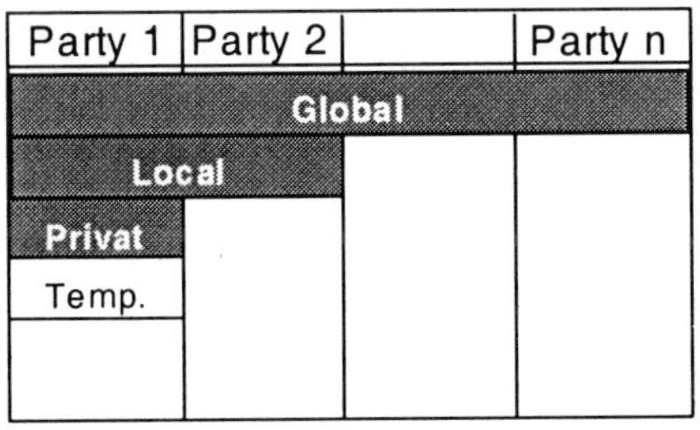

Figure 4: Multiparty business transactions

Figure 4 illustrates the relationship between different environments. The global environment is relevant for each participant of a business transaction. The whole infrastructure together with its objects that realise trusted or non-trusted services is located in the global environment. Each local environment is relevant for one enterprise and each private environment represents the objects internal to a party. Private environments must not overlap any other environment. Here are the most sensible objects located (such as secret keys or original objects like digital coins).

3.3 Constructs

In business processes it must be possible to change the control flow depending on certain conditions. For example, in signing a contract different roles are used depending on contract's value. That is why the if_else-construct is introduced. Additionally, a construct to model iteration loops is needed, which is realised in ALMO$T by the while_do-construct. The set of production rules (see appendix A) must be extended by the following rules:

```
if_else   → if <statement> <sequence> if_end |
            if <statement> <sequence> else
                          <sequence> if_end
while_do  → while <statement> do <sequence>
                          while_end
```

The extended production-rule of statement must is

```
statement → if_else | while_do
```

3.4 Conventions

For a better understanding of grammar expressions we introduce some naming conventions. As shown above third parties may be trusted or not. Because this distinction is important for the selection of third parties, this characteristic should be denoted. We use the prefix "t_" to denote the feature trusted and we use no prefix to denote non-trusted third parties. The prefix "t_" may be used to express the characteristic "trust" of other objects, too. The identifiers of all objects representing a database start with "db_". Table 2 summarises these conventions.

`t_<object>`	<object> must be trusted
`db_<object>`	db_<object> is a database

Table 2: Summary of naming conventions

In business transactions there are objects which may be used in many cases. Such commonly used objects in secure business transactions are for example the public-key pairs of participants. For these cases identifiers are reserved and predefined in ALMO$T. For example, `pKey` represents the public key and `sKey` the secret key of the party executing an activity located in the private environment. `pKeyring` represents a collection of public keys.

`pKey, sKey`	public key respectively secret key belonging to the party conducting the business transaction
`pKeyring`	list of previously obtained public keys of business partners
`env`	environment selection object
`global(object)`	<object> from global environment
`local(object)`	<object> from local environment
`private(object)`	<object> from private environment

Table 3: Summary of predefined objects

To denote a special environment to search for an object we use the object `env` which has the selectors `private`, `local`, and `global` for the respective environment level. Table 3 summarises some predefined objects.

3.5 Using ALMO$T

Although our model bridges the technical part of the gap described in the introduction (figure 1), it is not yet an integrated approach. More than in other areas in IT-security the aspect of "proper use" is a very sensible and vital one. On the other hand there is the demand of efficiency from the business point of view. Therefore, we have to discuss some issues of the way how ALMO$T is intended to be used.

Because the task of achieving a generic, flexible, efficient electronic commerce solution that also reaches some degree of security is a very complex task, we are aware that the ideas we describe are only a first step towards the goal.

Up to now we identified four properties that will promote security and efficiency:

- having a visual concept
- having different levels of abstraction
- having a reuse concept and
- transparency

Therefore, we are realising a graphical editor providing this properties. With this editor it is possible to edit ALMO$T specifications at different levels of abstraction. These different levels of abstraction are also represented in the class hierarchy in figure 2. For example the user may abstract from the security mechanism. Instead of using the object `RSA` it is possible to use the abstract class `asymCrypto`. The person who specifies a business transaction in this abstract way does not specify the concrete security mechanisms. This may be done later, supported by the editor. This might be useful to react on changes on the security policy of the company or discovered weaknesses of security mechanisms. Additionally, these abstract specifications serve as design pattern for further specifications. For example, looking at the first statement of T2 of activity negotiations in appendix B:

```
net.send(RSA.encrypt(pKeyring.get(D),draft.
modified()),D)
```

If the used cryptographic method should not be fixed at specification time, but the usage of any asymmetric cryptographic method that is to be selected, the statement may specified as follows:

```
net.send(asymCrypto.encrypt(pKeyring.get(D)
,draft.modified()),D)
```

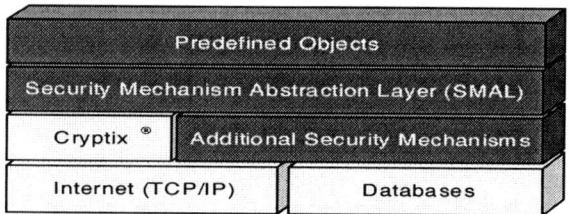

Figure 5: Realisation of objects

A class browser component of the editor will support reusing by allowing to store and browse security mechanisms, protocols and even already specified business transactions by their security properties. When selecting a solution the user simply drag-n-drop a graphical symbol that identifies the solution he/she intends to use.

4 Execution

In appendix B we give an impression of our formalism by specifying the example of the purchase of a digital good (a digitally represented emission permit). The specified example uses the following basic elements: encryption, decryption, and verification of the object `RSA`, the `add`, `remove` and `get` methods of a database, and the `send` and `receive` methods of the networks.

For executing this specification we have implemented a software library shown in figure 5, which contains basic elements, especially security mechanisms (lowest layer of the proposed architecture, subsection 2.2.1). The modules are implemented in JAVA by using the Cryptix 1.0 library [12] which provides basic public-key crypto-

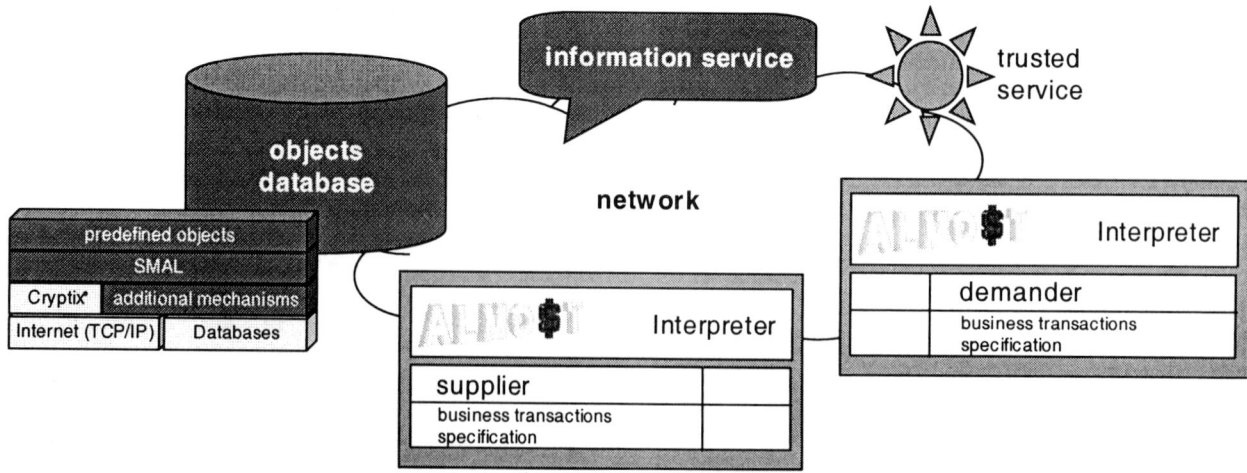

Figure 6: Execution of business transactions in an electronic commerce infrastructure

graphic mechanisms (e.g. RSA) and a collection of cryptographic mechanisms such as DES, IDEA, Blowfish, MD5, MD4, and SHA. All further cryptographic mechanisms in the SMAL are implemented by our own. In the first prototype we will use PGP 2.6.3i message and file formats for compatibility reasons [15]. For the certificate directory we use an Oracle 7.2 database with a jdbc Java interface and CORBA compatible object request broker3. The certification authority which currently is under development will provide X.509v3 [6] certificates and support the ISO certification infrastructure [5].

The realised objects are loaded from the different libraries during the time, when the specified business transaction is started in the ALMO$T-Interpreter. Each object or at least its interface (in the case the object is realised externally) is stored in a database and can be accessed according to the environment layer where it is defined. For example, to get public key of the supplier S in the version of global environment `env.global(pKeyring.get(S))`, communication with a component offering a directory service is necessary (example for an information service in figure 6). Other external objects are for example certification authorities, who are offering trusted services.

5 Conclusion

In this paper we introduced the specification language ALMO$T for specification of secure business transactions, which is usable for the specification of business processes in workflow management as well as for electronic markets transactions. The way to do that is to combine services provided in private, local and global environments that are represented as objects of which methods can be called from within a business transaction. Together with the specification model the whole way from abstract business transaction specification to the realisation and execution in an infrastructure was considered. An example was given in Appendix B.

In our future work we will address the usability issues by research in the way how an abstract security policy may be achieved with concrete mechanisms and protocols as we sketched in section 3.5. Additionally, the tasks of employees in an enterprise may be typed. An approach to define the authorisations and duties of such a type is the role-concept [11]. We consider to include the role-concept in ALMO$T.

6 References

[1] Bertino, E.; Ferrari, E.; Atluri, V.: A Flexible Model Supporting the Specification and Enforcement to Role-based Authorisations in Workflow Management Systems. Proceedings of Second ACM Workshop on Role-based Access Control, 1997.

[2] Bußler, Ch.: Access Control in Workflow Management Systems. Proceedings of IT Security'94, Oldenbourg-Verlag, 1995, pp. 165-179.

[3] Curtis, B.; Kellner, M.; Over, J.: Process Modeling. Communication of the ACM, vol.35, no.9, 1992, pp. 75-90.

[4] I-Kinetics Inc.: http://www.i-kinetics.com/ (last accessed 9/1997)

[5] International Organisation for Standardization (ISO): Information processing systems - Guidelines for the Use and Management of Trusted Third Parties - Part 2: Technical Aspects. International Standard ISO/IEC Working Draft 14516-2, Genf, 1995.

[6] International Telecommunication Union: Information Technology - Open Systems Inter-connection - The Directory: Authentication Framework. ITU-T Recommendation X.509, 1993.

[7] Karlapalem, K.; Hung, P.: Security Enforcement in Activity Management Systems. NATO ASI on Advances in Workflow Management Systems and Interoperability, Istanbul, 1997, pp. 166-194.

[8] Malone, T; Yates, J; Benjamin, R: Electronic Markets and Electronic Hierarchies. In, Communications of the ACM, vol.30, no.6, 1987, pp. 484-497.

[9] Röhm, A. W., Gerhard, M.: A Secure electronic market for Anonymous Transferable Emission Permits. In: Proceedings of Thirty-First Hawaii International Conference on System Sciences HICSS-31, 1998.

[10] Röhm, A.W.; Pernul, G; Herrmann, G.: Modelling Secure and Fair Electronic Commerce. Proceedings of the IEEE Annual Computer Security Application Conference ACSAC, 1998, pp. 155-164.

[11] Sandhu, R.S.; Coyne, E.J.: Role-Based Access Control Models. IEEE Computer, February 1996, pp. 38-47.

[12] Systemics Ltd: http://www.systemics.com/software/cryptix-java/ (last accessed 9/1997)

[13] Thomas, R.; Sandhu, R.S.: Task-based Authorization: A Research Project in Next-generation Active Security Models for Workflows. Proceedings of NSF Workshop on Workflow and Process Automation in Information Systems: State-of-the-art and Future Directions, Sheth, A. (ed.), Athens Georgia, 1996.

[14] Zwass, V.: Electronic Commerce: Structures and Issues. International Journal of Electronic Commerce, vol.1, no.1, Fall, 1996, pp. 3-23. http://www.cba.bgsu.edu/ijec/

[15] Zimmerman, P.: PGP User's Guide, Volume I: Essential Topics. October 1994.

---

3 product of i-kenetics [4]

Appendix A: Syntax of ALMO$T-Statements

Our language is based on the grammar G = (VN,VT,P,S) explained in the following. Non-terminals are VN = {bt, sequence, statement, identifier, object, method, arguments, digit, letters, integer, real, boolean}, where "bt" represents a business transaction. "statement" represents an activity. "object" represents an object, "method" represents a method of the object, and "arguments" are the objects passed to a method, when it is called. Additionally the boolean values true and false and also the integer and real constants are objects (7) and can be deduced to terminal symbols by the rules (1), (2), (3), and (4).

The set VT of terminals includes the identifiers of objects used in business transactions, produced by the rules (6), (1), and (5). It includes especially the object ε that represents an empty statement. The start-symbol S is defined by S = bt. The set P consists of the following production rules (where A°B means the concatenation AB of A and B):

(1) digit   → 0|1 ... |9
(2) boolean   → true|false
(3) integer   → digit | integer°digit
(4) real   → integer, integer
(5) letters   → a|b|c...|z|A|B...Z|-|_| digit
(6) identifier → letter | identifier°letter
(7) object   → identifier | integer | real | boolean
(8) method   → identifier
(9) arguments → arguments, arguments | object | object.method(arguments) | ε
(10) statement → object.method(arguments) | object
(11) sequence   → ε | sequence statement
(12) bt   → sequence

Appendix B: Example Specification

To explain our methodology we use as example the business process of purchasing an anonymous emission permit on an electronic market. To simplify our example, we leave out the role of the broker. An emission permit is a licence, which allows its owner to emit a certain amount of toxins into an ecological area. The model of emission permits is a successful tool for environmental policy. Its weakness are the high transaction cost, that can be reduced when digital emission permits are used in the way described in detail in [RöGe98]. This market transaction serves as a real world example, which we will realise in ALMO$T.

The information phase begins with the demander asking for offers (step 1). Afterwards he/she receives offers from potential suppliers (step 2). The negotiation phase consists of two activities: "negotiation" and "completion-of-contract". In the negotiation activity the demander creates the first draft contract and then the two business partners exchange draft contracts until they agree and conclude. Step 3 represents the exchange of draft contracts from demander to supplier and step 4 represents the exchange vice versa. Activity "completion-of-contract" is responsible for legal binding of the contract. To realise legal binding of contract first the demander sends the signed contract to the supplier (step 5) then the supplier asks an information service for the public key of the demander (step 6) and verifies demander's digital signature. If the signature is valid, the supplier signs the contract, too and sends it back to the demander (step 7). The demander checks supplier's signature by using its public key received from an information service (step 8). The execution phase begins with step 9 where the demander generates a session key and sends it encrypted with the public key of the issuer (trusted third party) to the supplier. The supplier sends his/her original permit together with the encrypted session key to the issuer (step 10). The issuer generates a new original and encrypts it with the session key. Then he/she sends it to the supplier (step 11), who gives it to the demander (step 12), who pays electronically (step 13).

In figure 7 the secure delivery of the original, anonymous document representing the emission permit is modelled.

Explanations to the notation:
- The first row includes the roles involved in the corresponding activity.
- In the given example: supplier (S), demander (D), and issuer of emission permits (I).
- The second row (named as G) represents the global environment.
- The row named "L" represents the local environment of the firm the role at the top of the corresponding column belongs to.
- Row "P" represents the private environment of the roles given at the head of each column.
- Row "T" represents the temporal environment of the roles given at the head of each column.
- T1, T2 name task1 and task2.
- (Ti,Y) represents the actions of Y in task Ti (Y∈{S,D,I})

The ALMO$T specification of activities "negotiation" and "completion-of-contract" representing the negotiation phase of the example are not included in this paper, but may be found on the web (www.wi-inf.uni-essen.de/~ifs/publikationen/)

The activity "delivery" guarantees the anonymity of the demander in the execution phase and the originality of the permission permit traded. To guarantee the originality of the permit, the demander generates a session key K for confidential communication with the issuer and send K encrypted with the public key of the issuer (RSA.encrypt(pKeyring.get(I),K)),S)) via the supplier to the issuer (T1 and (T2,S)). Additionally to the session K the supplier sends the permission permit (O) to the issuer (T2,S).

The issuer checks the originality of the permission permit[4], creates an new version number for the permission permit and sends it encrypted with the session key K via supplier to the demander (T3,I). The demander checks the encryption of the permission permit and stores it[5].

Activity delivery			
	D	S	I
G	net, RSA, IDEA, V		
L	db_disk		
P	pKeyring, sKey	pKeyring, O, sKey	db_originals, pKeyring, sKey
T	K, m, O	m	K, m

T1	K.set(V.random(128))
	net.send(RSA.sign(sKey,
	   RSA.encrypt(
	     pKeyring.get(I),K)),S)
		net.receive(m,D)
		while
		RSA.verify(pKeyring.get(D),m).=?
		                                  (false)
		do net.receive(m,D)
		while_end	

T2		m.attach(RSA.encrypt(
		   pKeyring.get(I),O))
		net.send(RSA.sign(sKey,m),I)
			net.receive(m,S)
			while
			RSA.verify(pKeyring.get(S),m).=?
			                                    (false)
			do net.receive(m,S)
			while_end
			RSA.decrypt(sKey,m)
			O.set(detach(m))

T3	IDEA.decrypt(K,net.receive(O,S)
	)
	While
	RSA.verify(
	   pKeyring.get(I),O).=?(false)
	do IDEA.decrypt(
	   K,net.receive(O,S))
	do_end
	db_disk.add(O)
		net.receive(m,I)
		net.send(m,D)
			If O.=?(db_original.get(O))
			db_original.remove(O)
			db_original.add(
			   O.set_attr(ver,V.random(128)))
			K.set(RSA.decrypt(
			   sKey,detach(m)))
			net.send(RSA.sign(
			   sKey,IDEA.encrypt(K,O),S)
			if_end

Figure 7: Execution phase of the purchase of an emission permit

---

[4] The case that the permission permit is not original is not specified in the example.
[5] The case the verification fails is not specified in the example.

Track B

System Engineering

Chair

Jan Filsinger, NAI Labs

Safe Areas of Computation for Secure Computing with Insecure Applications

André L. M. dos Santos and Richard A. Kemmerer
Reliable Software Group
Computer Science Department
University of California
Santa Barbara, CA 93106 USA
{andre, kemm}@cs.ucsb.edu

Abstract

Currently the computer systems and software used by the average user offer virtually no security. Because of this many attacks, both simulated and real, have been described by the security community and have appeared in the popular press. This paper presents an approach to increase the level of security provided to users when interacting with otherwise unsafe applications and computing systems. The general approach, called Safe Areas of Computation (SAC), uses trusted devices, such as smart cards, to provide an area of secure processing and storage.

This paper describes preliminary results of using the Safe Areas of Computation approach to protect specific browsing applications. The intent is for protected browsers to be used to interact with institutions that have requirements for high security, such as financial institutions that enable users to perform sensitive operations for electronic commerce or online banking.

1 Introduction

The Safe Area of Computation (SAC) approach uses a collection of trusted devices that enforces the protection of users from the insecurity of specific applications. Each of these devices is called a Safe Area of Computation. The goal of such devices is to provide islands of security that interact with an ocean of insecurity.

The main goal of the SAC approach is to provide security for client-server applications. The approach can be used to protect stand-alone applications too. However, due to space limitations this paper only describes its use for protecting client-server applications. In a client-server configuration Safe Areas of Computation provide:

a) *Strong authentication.* A client SAC exchanges cryptographic messages with a server SAC in order to perform mutual authentication. At the end of the exchange the client SAC and the server SAC will have agreed on a secret key.

b) *Secure channels.* Both the client and the server SAC will use the secret key that was agreed on in the authentication step to encrypt and decrypt messages that are exchanged, thus providing a secure channel.

c) *Access control.* Every client SAC has an access control list that specifies for each application being secured, the types of data that the user can access. In addition, if the type is hierarchical, the access list entry also specifies the clearance level of the user for that type. In order to access data the user's access control list must contain an entry of the type specified by the data's security label and the user's clearance level must dominate the security label of the data.

An important goal of SAC is to provide strong security even for users that are not concerned with security. The price paid for this security is that the SAC approach requires the user to deal with a hardware token, which is the client SAC. Although this requires an initial adaptation to its use, the benefits of the additional security provided outweigh the initial discomfort. The only requirement for a user is to insert the client SAC in a reader before performing a secure transaction, in the same way that ATM cards are currently used for interactions with bank ATM machines.

The SAC approach provides access control in a generic way. The approach uses generic hierarchical security labels and access control lists without predefining what the labels and clearance levels are. This enables contextual interpretation and implementation of more than one security policy concurrently. A bank can, for example, use security labels to specify what banking transactions a user can perform, while a digital library can use labels to specify what type of documents a user can access and if the documents have clearance levels what level is required. Although this paper uses documents to demonstrate the use of security labels, many different access policies can be modeled in the same way.

The SAC approach can be better understood with an example. Therefore, the next section gives a high level example of how the SAC approach can be used to protect data distribution over the Internet. Section 3 describes the details of the data structures used in the SAC approach and the overall architecture of the system. A prototype implementation of the SAC approach is described in section 4. Finally, conclusions and future work are presented in the last section.

2 Overview of the Use of SAC for Secure Internet Transactions

Currently, many Internet transactions are claimed to be secure because they use Secure Socket Layer (SSL) to establish an encrypted link between the client and the server. Although the SSL protocol is likely to be secure, it is generally misused. The result is that the transactions are not secure. Some of the problems are:

a) *Users don't check certificates.* The usage of SSL does not guarantee that a user is interacting with the site that he/she wants to interact with. It only guarantees that the site implements SSL. A user needs to check the site certificate in order to verify the name under which the site is certified. This is usually neglected even by users that are aware of the existence of certificates, and it is unknown to the rest. Another problem is that some sites do not get a certificate using the same name by which they may be known to the user.

b) *Anybody can have a certificate.* Anybody can apply for a certificate and receive one.

c) *User credentials are stored in an unsafe place.* Most of the sites that use SSL do not require a user to have a credential to authenticate his/herself to the site. However, even when a site requires a credential and the browser supports the use of credentials, this alone does not guarantee that the user identified is the one interacting with the site. For example, credentials that are stored in an unsafe place, such as the user's computer, can be stolen. These credentials can then be used later by an attacker.

d) *The loss of a credential may not be noticed by the user.* Credentials that are stored in unsafe areas can be compromised without the user ever noticing. In contrast, if a token is used for safe transactions, the stealing or loss of a user's token is easily noticed by the user.

Commercial products that use smart cards to store certificates in order to prevent attacks against these certificates already exist. These products represent a move in the right direction and provide some protection against attacks to a user's credentials. They, however, use the smart card primarily for certificate storage, while still making most of the decisions in an unsafe area.

The goal of the SAC approach is to protect specific servers. Thus, it does not use the general approach of certificates. Figure 1 shows a high level view of the SAC approach to protecting Internet transactions. Each client has a client SAC, which holds its access control list and other security relevant information, and each server has a server SAC. There are two different types of server sites: central authority sites and service provider sites. Initially there is a single central authority site with which the client SAC can communicate. A central authority site is the only site that can add access to other sites to a client SAC. However, once a service provider site has been added to a client site, Internet transactions are performed between the service provider site and the user without intervention from a central authority. A service provider can also modify the portion of the client SAC's access control list that refers to that particular service provider, and it can remove all of the user's access to the site. It cannot, however, modify the user's access list for any other site.

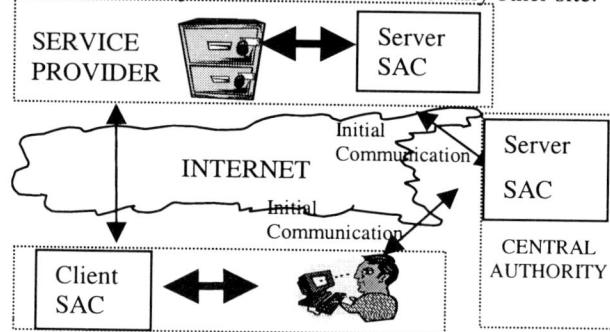

Figure 1: SAC approach for Internet Transactions

The use of the SAC approach for Internet transactions has many desirable features. The protocol used by the SAC approach provides strong authentication and prevents spoofing attacks against a user in a user-friendly manner. A private identification number (PIN) is used to authenticate a user to the SAC. This number can be any easy to remember number. To protect the data in the SAC, in case the SAC is lost or stolen, the client SAC has a lock out procedure that locks itself after a specified number of wrong attempts. Because of this, any dictionary attack against the client SAC has a high probability of being unsuccessful. In addition, because the SAC is tamper resistant, the data cannot be copied for repeating the attack. After entering the PIN, a user does not need to perform any additional authentication. The PIN is the only secret information that a user has, and it is only useful in the presence of the correct client SAC. In addition, any spoofing attack will not be successful since the protocol does not reveal any secret in the clear and the user can at most be tricked into revealing his/her PIN. A critical element of the SAC protocol is that the SAC exchanges a secret key in the authentication step. Thus, an attacker who tries to perform a man-in-the-middle attack, during authentication, will be unsuccessful, because either the user exchanges the secret key with the attacker, which does not authenticate the user to the server, or with the server, which does not reveal the secret key to the attacker. The use of the server public key by the user and the user's public key by the server for encryption guarantees that only the end parties can decrypt and retrieve the secret key.

Another desirable feature of the SAC approach is that the use of access lists and security levels enables the personalization of a user's services without overloading the server. Personalized data that is security related is safely stored in the client SAC. This data is used by the SAC to determine if the user can access the data requested, and only pre-authorized access is transmitted. Thus, any access that would not be authorized will not even be transmitted to the server, which reduces the load on the server. Although only pre-authorized requests are transmitted to the server, there is a back up check at the server to prevent any malicious requests.

A user can only be impersonated if his/her PIN is compromised and his/her SAC is lost or stolen. If this is the case, the user can easily notice the loss and the particular SAC can be disabled the first time that it is used. Furthermore, in the event that the SAC is not disabled, it can only be used to the extent of the user's clearance. For example, in the case where a bank is the service provider, a user can choose not to have access that allows money transfers over the Internet, which the SAC will enforce. Then if this client SAC is compromised it will still only have limited access, such as the ability to check the user's balance.

The client SAC must be a device that is either integrated into a computing base or that is easy to carry and can interact with a computing base. Smart cards are plastic cards that resemble magnetic strip cards, which most users are already familiar with and that most users associate with secure operations. Smart cards are an appropriate choice for the client SAC requirements. Current production versions of smart cards can have a cryptographic co-processor, 16 Kbytes of EEPROM, 2 Kbytes of RAM and 32 Kbytes of ROM. This is sufficient to implement a SAC client, although it still places some restrictions on the number of service providers that can be accessed by one card. In addition, smart cards and their readers are dropping in price, their memory size is increasing, and computer operating systems already support smart card readers.

3 Details of the SAC Approach

In a client-server configuration a client SAC interacts with a server SAC through an insecure medium. In this configuration, the user is not protected when interacting with either a client or server SAC alone. For example, in order to safely browse the web a user must interact with a server through a client site, both of which have safe areas of computation. If either the client or server site does not have the SAC, that particular interaction will not be protected.

The SAC, however, does not need to enforce the security policy of the computing system as a whole. The purpose of the SAC is to enforce a security policy tailored to the interactions of specific applications that a user needs to accomplish securely. The use of generic trusted areas that implement security critical functions to protect particular applications makes this approach different from approaches that use specific hardware for integrity checks of the computing system [9].

A security perimeter is defined as the imaginary boundary of a trusted computing base (TCB) within which all security-related functions are executed [8]. The trusted devices that compose a SAC define the SAC's security perimeter. The SAC can be as simple as a standalone smart card or secure coprocessor or it can be a collection of trusted processors, keyboards, displays, interfaces, etc.. The idea is to increase the number of safe operations that can be performed by adding trusted devices. As each new trusted device is added the security perimeter is extended.

3.1 SAC Data Structures

In the SAC approach data is organized in multi-level security containers. The container model used is a variation of the container model described in [5], which was proposed for military multi-level security documents, where each container is an abstraction for a set of data that has some attribute in common.

The SAC approach guarantees that only data to which a user has clearance is released outside the SAC. However, it is a function of the application software to present these containers and a description of the data inside the containers to the user for browsing and possible selection, after the SAC has approved access to them. To achieve this the SAC approach represents information by metadata, which has three fields: description, security level, and pointer. The metadata can be related to containers or to data. For containers the pointer field in the metadata information is a pointer to the container header, and for data this field is a pointer to actual data. The security level field represents the level a user must be cleared to in order to receive the data or header pointed to. A user who does not have the necessary clearance will not even know about the existence of the data or header to which the pointer points. The description field is used by the software that the SAC is protecting. It contains all information necessary to the software to interpret the metadata and to present it to the user for browsing and selection (e.g., MIME type information).

A header is a set of zero or more metadata entries. The possibility of a header having zero entries enables a pointer to a container header to have any security level without releasing additional covert information about the existence of classified data. In particular, this enables an unclassified pointer to a classified container header. This fact is used by the SAC approach to enable users to start their sessions with unclassified pointers to (possibly empty) container headers. An analysis of these pointers does not reveal the existence or the number of containers with classified data since the pointers can, and some will, point to empty container headers.

Consider a user making a query to request images of Santa Barbara, California. An example return value from the query could be the information shown in Table1. In practice there would be many entries, each with metadata that satisfies the query parameters. Since the security level of the example container "Satellite images of Santa Barbara from July 14th, 1998" is unclassified, any user would be able to request the container header. If a user requests the container header, the information in Table 2 will be sent in a secure way to the client SAC. This information represents the metadata that can be used to request further data or containers. Using containers inside other containers, any level of indirection, with possibly different clearance requirements, can be supported using this approach.

The user is shown representations of only the metadata from Table 2 to which he/she has clearance. For instance, if the user does not have secret clearance, the "Satellite Image 4 (infra-red)" metadata will not be shown. That is, the decrypted metadata about "Satellite Image 4 (infrared)" will never leave the client SAC. Based on the information shown the user may then choose and request further metadata of interest.

DESCRIPTION	SECURITY LEVEL	POINTER
Container: "Satellite images of Santa Barbara. 07/14/ 98"	Unclassified	ContainerServer ::DB0::satellite: :SB071498
:	:	:

Table 1: Pointer to a container with satellite images

DESCRIPTION	SECURITY LEVEL	POINTER
Visible Container: "Container of classified Satellite Images"	Confidential	ConfidentialSer ver::DB0::sat::S Bvis071498
Infra-Red Image: "Satellite Image 3" (infra-red)	Unclassified	Mainserver::DB 1::sat::SBir0714 98
"Satellite Image 4" (infra-red)	Secret	SecretServer::D B0::sat::SBir07 1498

Table 2: Header of the container in Table 1

3.2 The Client-Server SAC Architecture

When used in a client-server configuration, the SAC architecture is as shown in Figure 2. The following subsections describe the client SAC and server SAC in more detail.

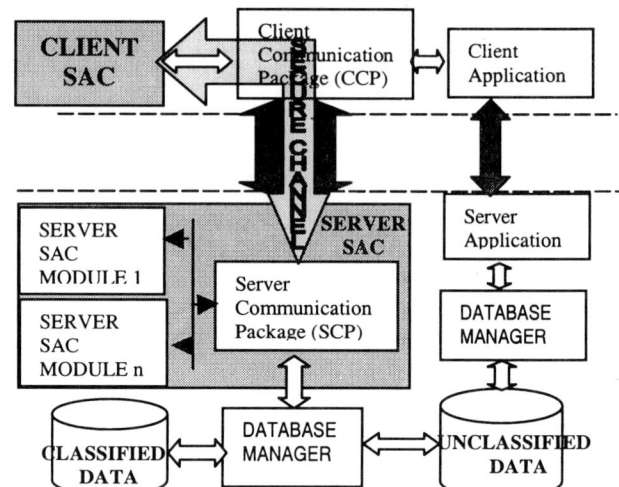

Figure 2: SAC in client-server configuration

3.2.1 The Client SAC

The client SAC and Client Communication Package (CCP) together are used to provide security without interpreting or presenting the data to users for browsing and selection. After the client SAC receives encrypted metadata from the server SAC, it decrypts it and uses the security level fields to check if a specific user has the appropriate clearances to receive the metadata. If the user is allowed to access the data, then the client SAC hands the decrypted metadata to the particular application via the CCP. The application then presents this metadata to the user to browse and query. The application software primarily uses the description field of the metadata to accomplish this, but in some cases may additionally use the other fields.

The CCP is not inside the security perimeter and is not considered a safe area. Because of this it does not deal with clear text data until the data has been authorized for access. The application software interacts directly with the CCP using generic functions, it does not interact with the client SAC. The generic functions provided deal with user and server authentication, requests for headers, and requests for data. Each of these is discussed in the next subsections.

The initial queries of the server application do not involve the SAC's; that is, the initial query of the server is made directly from the client application to the server application over an unprotected communication channel. The metadata returned by this query is a set of unclassified descriptions of the data or container in addition to their pointers. The disadvantage of this approach is that a user may be returned a pointer to a container that has no data. This, however, is not believed to be critical since the user will immediately find that he/she is following a link that will result in no data after requesting the container header with no data. The advantage of this approach is that if a user wishes to browse only unclassified data, then the SAC components will not be involved and some may not even be present.

3.2.2 User and Server Authentication

In order to start a session with a secure server the user must be authenticated to the client SAC and the client SAC and server SAC must mutually authenticate themselves. If this is not done or if the authentication fails, then any additional requests from the application software to the CCP will be denied.

The application software interacts with the user to request a pin code. After this pin code has been entered, the application software calls a CCP function "boolean AskSACAuthentication(char *pin)". This function takes as input a 4 digit pin code, represented as an array of characters. The choice of a 4 digit pin code is used due to an embedded functionality in most smart cards, which uses a 4 digit pin code to authenticate a user to the card. The card does not allow any transaction with it without the correct pin code. Although four is a small number of digits, which could suggest a brute force attack, the card only allows three wrong pin codes to be presented in a sequence. If a fourth wrong pin code is presented, the card will lock itself and will not work anymore. In order to unlock a card and return it to service, a special sequence of commands must be invoked on the locked card along with the use of a secret master key.

After the user has been authenticated to the client SAC the client SAC uses the Feige-Fiat-Shamir identification scheme [3] to identify itself to the server SAC. It then uses the Diffie-Hellman key-exchange algorithm [2] to agree on a session key. To prevent a man-in-the-middle attack, the client SAC and the server SAC use digital signatures based on the RSA algorithm [7] to sign the key-exchange. All information exchanged by the SACs will then be protected against eavesdropping by DES [6] using the session key. This provides a virtual secure channel between the client SAC and the server SAC.

3.2.3 Request for Headers

From the client SAC perspective, the starting point of any transaction request is an unclassified metadata. This metadata is the result of a query run without the use of any SAC component. If the metadata pointer points to a container, then a header describing this container can be requested. The headers are all encrypted and are assumed to be small, so they can be efficiently decrypted inside the security perimeter of the client SAC.

In order to request a header, the application software calls the function "int RequestHeader(DataPtr req, DataPtr **ans)". This function uses the struct DataPtr, which is defined as:

typedef struct _DataPtr{
    char description[100];
    char pointer[50];
    unsigned char securityLevel;
} DataPtr;

When requesting a header, the security level field of DataPtr is filled in by untrusted software (including CCP), which resides outside the client SAC. For this reason, the SAC approach does not rely solely on this information to grant or deny access to data. Thus, the SAC approach guarantees that even if a user provides a wrong or malicious security level to the client SAC, the server will not be misled into sending data that the user is not allowed to access. To assure this the server SAC will perform a backup check between the claimed security label and the security label that is linked to the header, which is stored in the server database.

When the function returns, the application software will receive an array of DataPtr in the ans argument. The number of elements in this array is specified by the integer returned by the function. The elements returned are only those elements of the container to which this user has access.

3.2.4 Request for Data

A request for data can be made if the user has a DataPtr structure that points to data. The request usually happens after a header is received and the available data is shown to the user. The user chooses the data of interest and the application software will make a request on behalf of the user. It is the function of the application software to arrange the data to be shown to the user and to handle his/her selections.

When the application software wants data, it calls the function "boolean RequestData(DataPtr req, char filename[8])". The requested data is specified in the argument req, in the same way that requests for headers are specified. The function returns true if the data has been received by the client computer, and the filename argument contains a pointer to the file that has the requested data in clear text. Currently it is the responsibility of the application software to sanitize the file after using it.

3.3 The Server SAC

The individual Server SAC modules and Server Communication Package (SCP) are sensitive software that must be protected. The protection of these modules is centralized in the server that uses the SAC approach for security. The administrator of the server must ensure the protection of this server, which is usually easier than ensuring the protection of the distributed clients. In addition, it is expected that the system administrator of this server is more security aware than the individual clients. For these reasons, the tamper resistant area where these modules run may be implemented using existing hardware on the server, such as implementing it in kernel space.

The Server SAC has a database, which contains client SAC public keys to identify and interact with each user. Every time a user initiates an authentication with the server the SCP spawns a new server SAC module with properly initiated parameters, including the user ID, the user's public key, and the server private key. The SCP also checks if the specific user needs to have any of his/her accesses updated, such as for adding a new service provider. To accomplish this, the SCP uses a database of access control list (ACL) modifications. The modification, if there is any, is requested by the server SAC through the secure channel, immediately after the channel is established.

The Safe Area of Computation in the server is composed of the dynamic set of server SAC modules, the databases that store keys and ACL modifications, and the Server Communication Package. This area, which must be well protected, is shown in Figure 3

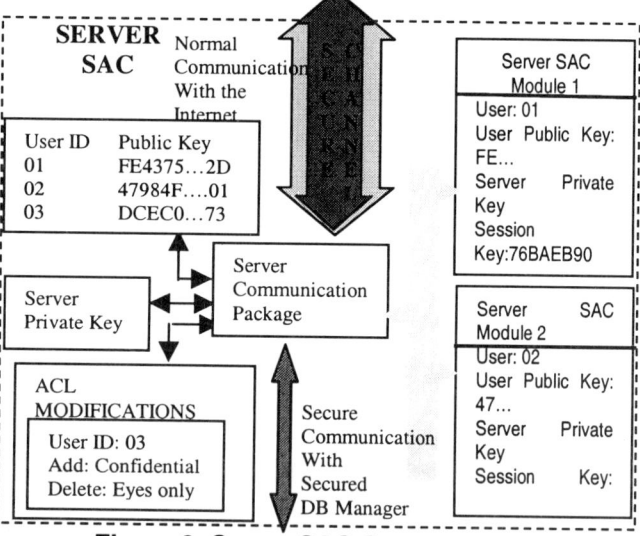

Figure 3: Server SAC Components.

The following subsections explain the communication of the server with the Internet and with the secured database and discuss the security of the server.

3.3.1 Server SAC Communication with the Internet

Communication with the Internet is handled by the Server Communication Package (SCP). Every time a client SAC issues a request to the server through the Client Communication Package, the SCP sends the request to a specific server SAC module. After this server SAC module processes the request it sends an answer to the SCP, which sends it back through the secure connection used by the client to issue the request.

Every communication out to the Internet and from the Internet is encrypted when the secure channel is used. Every pair of server SAC module/client SAC have specific cryptographic keys to encrypt and decrypt their transactions. This means that although only one secure channel is shown in Figure 3, there will be one distinct secure channel for each client. Thus, any adversary in the Internet cannot maliciously eavesdrop on a transaction that is conducted through the secure channel. In addition, since the keys are unique, malicious impersonation is not possible.

3.3.2 Server SAC Communication with the Secured Database Manager

The Server Communication Package also manages communication with a secured database manager, which handles all accesses to classified data. Since the database manager sends sensitive unencrypted data in answer to requests, the line of communication between the SCP and the secured database manager must be secure.

The request that is sent to the secured database manager is the data pointer sent from the client SAC and decrypted by the server SAC. Neither the server SAC nor the SCP interprets the pointer. As a result, the SAC approach can accommodate any database format without the need for any change, assuming the pointers are consistent with the secured database manager format. The requirement is that the database manager exports a function call, so that the SCP can send the pointer and receive back the security level of this data in addition to the data requested.

3.3.3 Security of the Server

A proper implementation of the server is an implementation where the modules shown in Figure 3 are kept in a safe area. In addition, this implementation trusts the data received from the secure communication with the secured database. This is a blind trust and nothing is done to guarantee the integrity of the data.

There is a possibility of denial of service attacks due to the fact that in every transaction with a client the server first needs to identify which user is requesting the transaction. This verification is accomplished by appending the user ID encrypted with the server's public key to the transaction. A malicious attacker cannot benefit from this since he/she will not be able to complete an authentication nor be able to get the session key used by a legitimate user interacting with the server. The attacker can, however, flood the server with transactions from possibly existing user IDs. This will require the server to process all these requests and may force legitimate users to restart sessions because of time-outs.

4 A Prototype SAC for Internet Transactions

As a proof of concept, the SAC approach was implemented for secure Internet transactions. It uses the configuration shown in Figure 4 to protect the transactions. The data used in this implementation is generic MIME data. The intent was to explore the ability of a browser to directly handle many types of MIME data securely. The transactions use the Netscape Navigator browser, and Plug in technology is used to communicate with the Client Communication Package (CCP).

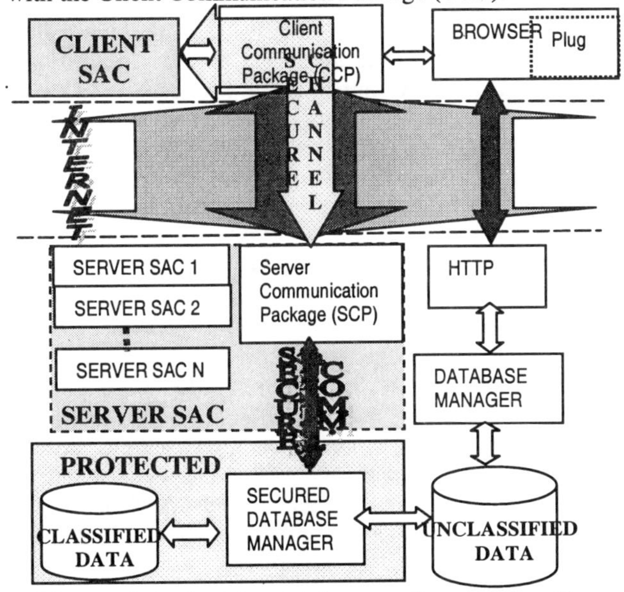

Figure 4: Safe Internet transactions using the SAC approach

When a client visits a secure server, the first (main) page in the secure server loads the Plug in, which loads the CCP and the client SAC. The client SAC is presently implemented by a program in the user's computer, but is currently being implemented using smart cards. The Plug in pops up a window requesting the pin code from the user. After the user enters this information, it calls the authentication function.

If the user is authenticated, one of the frames in the main page allows the user to request a search from the secure server. The answer to this search is a set of unclassified pointers to collections.

The following subsections detail the components in Figure 4 and describe the steps of a simple transaction.

4.1 Components of the Internet Prototype

In this section each of the components is described.

4.1.1 Plug In

The current version of the implementation assumes a user interacting with the secure server using the Netscape Navigator browser. The Plug in technology was chosen to implement the active interaction between the browser and the Client Communication Package (CCP). The same design may be used with ActiveX controls for interactions using the Microsoft Internet Explorer browser and Java applets with special capabilities.

By implementing this program as a Plug in, all the visual interfaces are provided to the user. The user interacts with the server using these visual interfaces, and the Plug in program interacts with the CCP when it needs classified data.

4.1.2 Client Communication Package

While the Plug in has a specific design developed to satisfy a particular application and server, the Client Communication Package (CCP) is designed to be generic and to support the functionality of the SAC approach. The CCP does not require a safe area and never deals with sensitive plain text data that has not been first approved for release by the Client SAC.

The CCP implements all functionality that can run in the unprotected area. This includes manipulation of sensitive data that has been cleared by the Client SAC. In addition, it implements the Internet communication line, which is used to exchange encrypted data between the client SAC and the server SAC and in which the virtual secure channel is established.

4.1.3 Client SAC

The Client SAC is assumed to have limited memory and low processing power because it will eventually be housed in a smart card. The code that provides security, as well the cryptographic keys, are stored inside its security perimeter.

Because the client SAC has low processing power, it would take a long time to decrypt large files. Therefore, file decryption is performed by the CCP, outside of the client SAC. The server SAC encrypts each file with a unique one-time key and sends the encrypted result to the CCP using a standard Internet connection. The key is then sent through the secure channel to the client SAC. The client SAC can then hand the CCP this key to decrypt sensitive data file. Thus, the client SAC always controls the decryption of sensitive data. This sensitive data is either used directly by the CCP, such as metadata in the clear, or is a key that can be used by the CCP to decrypt other sensitive data. The sensitive data or key will only leave the security perimeter if the access control list (ACL) inside the client SAC certifies that this user is cleared to access the data.

4.1.4 HTTP Server
The SAC approach does not make any assumption about the http server. That is, the generic nature of the approach does not require any particular http server. Although not currently implemented, the http server could transmit and receive encrypted sensitive data that is sent from the CCP to the SCP or vice-versa without compromising the security of the data. This would be accomplished by adding a communication channel between the http server and the SCP using a technology that extends the http server, e.g. CGI and servlets.

4.1.5 Secured Database Manager
The secured database manager handles sensitive data and should be kept in a protected area satisfying only requests from trusted sources. No sensitive data will be leaked if the SCP runs in a safe area and its communication with the secured database manager is secure.

4.1.6 Server Communication Package
The Server Communication Package (SCP), unlike the Client Communication Package, needs to run in a protected area in the server. The reason for this is that it interacts directly with the secured database manager to request sensitive data.

The function of the SCP is to interact with different clients and to dynamically allocate a specific Server SAC for each client. Each server SAC establishes a separate secure channel with the corresponding client SAC. A spawned server SAC uses the SCP as an auxiliary module to communicate with its respective client SAC in a secure way. In addition, the SCP is used to communicate and request data from the secured database manager.

4.1.7 Server SAC Module
One Server SAC module is spawned for each user that is successfully authenticated to the server. The Server SAC module has the necessary keys to interact with a particular client SAC.

The server SAC modules are kept inside the server SAC, while interacting with the corresponding client. When the client SAC ends a session with the server, the corresponding server SAC module is deleted. However, a session between a client and a server SAC module often has transactions that cannot be anticipated. Therefore, it may be desirable to keep that specific server SAC module around. Time-outs are used in the current implementation to solve this problem and to determine if a session has finished. This can cause some users to restart a session after a time-out.

4.1.8 Database Manager
In order to lower the workload when dealing with unclassified data, the server may run a second database manager that does not require a protected area. The system is responsible for assuring that this database manager can only access non-sensitive data. Using this approach the http server can request non-sensitive data directly from the unclassified database manager. This unclassified data can be used later to fetch classified data through the Safe Areas of Computation.

4.2 Example Session
The following sections describe in detail each step of a session. They discuss what tests and functions are executed in order to provide security.

4.2.1 Authentication
The Plug in interacts with the user, with the browser, and with the Client Communication Package providing the particular functionality needed by a specific application. The Plug in, Client Communication Package, and Client SAC, are implemented as programs that run in the user's computer and that must be installed before any transaction can be accomplished. The Client SAC, which is a very sensitive set of modules, is currently being migrated to a smart card.

When accessing the protected server, the user displays a page that resides in this server. This page will load the Plug in, which starts the client SAC and the Client Communication Package programs. A window pops up requesting the user to enter a pin code in order to authenticate the user to the client SAC.

After the user enters a pin code and clicks the OK button the process of authentication starts. If the user enters the correct pin code, he/she will be authenticated to the client SAC. The client SAC will then authenticate itself to the server SAC, using an Internet connection opened by the CCP. The result of the successful authentication process is a session key that provides a secure channel over the standard Internet connection.

4.2.2 Request for Container Pointers
After the authentication and secure channel establishment takes place, the user can request containers by making queries. The browser issues a query, through an insecure Internet connection to the http server. The http server queries the database manager, which will run the query on the unclassified data and return unclassified information that points to container headers. This information is composed of text information to be displayed to the user, an internal pointer to be used when requesting the container, and the security level of each container, as was shown in Table 1.

The list of available containers is returned to the user's browser through the Internet connection. Since this information is unclassified it is displayed to the user as a list without restriction.

4.2.3 Request for Container
The user selects a container from the list. When the user clicks a "Get Container" button, requesting the container,

the Plug in sends this request to the Client Communication Package (CCP), which forwards the request to the client SAC, specifying the pointer to the container header and its security level. If the user has the clearance necessary to request the container header, as specified by the security level of the container and the access control list, then the client SAC uses the secure channel to request the container header. Since the data used in the request is sent through the secure channel, neither the CCP nor the Internet can tamper with the request.

The request includes the security level of the container to which the clearance was checked and a header with the user ID. The security level will be used to prevent software outside the client SAC from maliciously faking a request. The user ID is used in order to identify which spawned server SAC module has established a secure channel with the particular user.

4.2.4 Server Processing of Container Requests

The appropriated server SAC module, from the possibly many spawned by the Server Communication Package (SCP), receives a request for a container from the client SAC that is associated with it. The server SAC uses the SCP to request the container specified by the pointer sent by the client SAC. The SCP requests the container from the Secured Database Manager using this pointer.

The Secured Database Manager fetches the requested data (a container header) and returns it to the SCP, together with the security level associated with this data. The SCP returns the container with this security level to the appropriated server SAC module. The result is tested against the security level sent by the client SAC when requesting the specific container. If both security levels are not the same the operation fails and an error is sent to the client SAC. This is the second time that the security level of the requested data is checked and will catch malicious requests, where the security level has been changed before it is sent to the client SAC. In the case where the security levels agree, the server SAC will send the container and the security level received from the SCP back to the client SAC through the secure channel.

4.2.5 Requests for Data

The client SAC receives the container header through the secure channel and processes it. Before processing any of the data inside the header the client SAC uses the access control list and the security level of the header received from the server SAC, to check if the user has access to this header. This is the third time that the clearance is checked and should never fail. A failure at this point is unexpected and should be logged for further studies.

The client SAC checks the user clearance for each data or container embedded in the container, as represented in the container header. It sends the client communication package only the information for the data and containers to which the user has clearance. The CCP will send this information to the Plug in, which shows it to the user for browsing and selection.

After browsing the information about the metadata inside the container, the user can select one of interest by clicking the "Get Data" button. The client SAC makes the request in the same way that it requests container headers.

4.2.6 Server Processing of Data Requests

The process of directing a request for data to the correct server SAC module is the same as the process of directing a request for a container. The correct server SAC module again uses the Server Communication Package (SCP) to request the data from the secured database manager. When the server SAC receives the potentially large data back, it generates a one-time key to encrypt this data. The server SAC will only continue operations, as in the request for a container header, if the security level of the data reported by the secured database manager agrees with the security level reported by the client SAC when requesting the data.

The server SAC encrypts the data using DES and the generated one-time key, and sends it to the SCP, which sends it to the Client Communication Package (CCP) via the standard Internet connection between them (outside the secure channel). Additionally, the server SAC uses the secure channel to send the key used for the encryption and the security level of the data to the client SAC. The client SAC will release the key to the CCP only if the user is cleared to access this data. This is the third check of clearance, analogous to the procedure used when requesting container headers.

4.2.7 Results of Requesting Data

The Client Communication Package receives the encrypted data from the Server Communication Package and the key for the decryption of this data from the client SAC. It uses this key to decrypt the data and to write it to a local file, which is returned to the Plug in. The Plug in shows the data to the user as appropriate to the particular application.

The Plug in must interpret the data in a way appropriate for the application. The SAC approach only delivers the data to the Plug in without interpreting it. A specific application can use the description field to specify possible formats. In the prototype, the description field includes the MIME type of the data, which is easily interpreted by the browser.

4.2.8 Access Control List Updates

The steps above describe a simple session. Additionally, the current implementation supports dynamic modification of the client SAC access control list (ACL). For this the server SAC may send a request to the client SAC to update its ACL when the client SAC authenticates itself. The request is sent through the secure channel just after it is established. This request is a list of accesses to add and delete. It is not possible to tamper with this data since it uses the established secure channel, which uses a different session key each time.

5 Conclusions and Future Work

The technologies currently used for interactions between users and sites on the World Wide Web have many security weaknesses. This paper presented the SAC approach, which uses trusted devices to improve the security of user interactions with a site. An advantage of the SAC approach is that standard applications only need to be modified to use the generic functions provided by the SAC Client Communication Package to get secure access to sensitive data. The prototype Internet SAC showed how this could be easily implemented using Plug in technology. This initial implementation was tested exchanging MIME data, particularly images and html pages. Images were classified with different security levels to demonstrate the container model.

The use of safe areas of computation for protecting user transactions is intended to make these transactions more secure. An advanced test bed for the current system is being implemented to protect Internet transactions of a user with the Alexandria digital library [4]. For this test bed two smart card operating systems are currently being used: CardOS M3 from Siemens and MultOS from MAOSCO. A test bed for protecting a financial institution is also planned.

The SAC approach uses access control lists implemented on the client SAC. Employing a user-specific, or device-specific access control list enables the personalization of the accesses and restrictions a user will have (e.g. only allowing the checking of a bank account balance and not allowing withdrawals). This personalization has the advantage of providing access to only the services that a user signs up for, which limits the possibility of impersonation of the user to only these services.

Another advantage of storing the access control lists on the client SAC is that when the server receives a request for a service, the client SAC has already authorized this request at the client host. The result is that the server does not need to again verify that the specific client has the necessary access rights for the requested service. However, if this redundant verification is desirable, it could be done for a small set of critical services. The security provided would be in addition to that already provided by the client SAC alone.

The implementation of the protected browser demonstrated that much of the burden of providing a user-friendly interface is placed on the application specific non-secure software. It is not a function of the SAC components. In addition, the SAC approach does not impose additional requirements that would make the application software less user-friendly.

The grouping of users and/or data providers is one way to lower the memory requirements for the client SAC. This means, however, that private keys will be shared inside a group, which represents a security weakness. The grouping used and the feasibility of grouping is an area for further investigation.

It is possible to charge for information using electronic commerce techniques and electronic cash. There are already some standards for these transactions. The best way to do this and the best technology available is another area to be investigated.

Currently, traffic analysis prevention is not considered to be a requirement; however, in future implementations it may be required. Thus, the interactions between the user's computer and the secure server for the first search will need to be protected. This could be accomplished using the protection of SSL. However, even the use of SSL will not prevent a man-in-the-middle attack whose goal is traffic analysis [1]. Because of this, functions for protecting queries will need to be implemented by the SAC for use if traffic analysis protection is desirable.

6 Acknowledgements

This research was partially supported by PulsePoint Communications and the University of California through a Micro Grant. It was also partially supported by Siemens AG and Mondex International.

References

1. F. De Paoli, A.L. dos Santos, and R. A. Kemmerer, "Web Browsers and Security", Mobile Agents and Security, LNCS 1419, pp. 235-256, Springer-Verlag, 1998.
2. W. Diffie and M. E. Hellman, "New directions in cryptography", IEEE Transactions on Information Theory, v. IT-22, n. 6, Nov. 1976.
3. U. Feige, A. Fiat, and A. Shamir, "Zero knowledge proofs of identity", Proceedings of the 19th annual ACM symposium on the theory of computing, 1987.
4. J. Frew, et. al., "The Alexandria Digital Library Architecture", Proc. of the Second European Conference on Research and Advance Technology for Digital Libraries, September 1998.
5. C. E. Landwehr, C. L. Heitmeyer, and J. McLean, "A Security Model for Military Message Systems," ACM Trans. on Computer Systems Vol. 9, No. 3 (Aug. 1984), pp. 198-222.
6. NBS FIPS PUB 46, "Data Encryption Standard", National Bureau of Standards, U.S. Department of Commerce, 1977.
7. R. L. Rivest, A. Shamir, and L. M. Adleman,"A method for obtaining digital signatures and public-key cryptosystems", Communications of the ACM, v. 21, n.2, Feb 1978.
8. D. Russel and G. T. Gangemi Sr., "Computer Security Basics", O'Reilly & Associates, Inc., July 1991.
9. B. S. Yee. "Using Secure Coprocessors". PhD dissertation, Carnegie Mellon University, 1994.

Architecture and Concepts of the ARGuE Guard

Jeremy Epstein
jepstein@nai.com
NAI Labs
McLean Virginia

Abstract

ARGuE (Advanced Research Guard for Experimentation) is a prototype guard being developed as a basis for experimentation. ARGuE is based on Network Associates' Gauntlet firewall. By integrating capabilities developed under several government programs, we were able to create a system which is easier to extend than other guards, provides significant new features (such as integration with an intrusion detection system), and yet has a reasonable degree of assurance.

1. Introduction

Standalone system high networks are a thing of the past. Historically, networks of different classifications were usually not connected. When connection was imperative, a person in the middle was required to review all data flowing between the networks (a slow and error-prone process). Today, even users of highly classified networks need instantaneous access to resources on the Internet. For example, planning a military operation requires access to public "open source" news and weather information (e.g., CNN). Additionally, organizations need to allow limited subsets of users on the outside to access resources inside the classified networks, especially in coalition environments.

Connecting such networks together historically required a guard, a special purpose device designed to prevent information flowing from the inside (the more highly classified side) to the outside (the less highly classified side). Guards differ from firewalls in their primary intent: a firewall is mostly concerned with keeping unauthorized users out, while a guard has the additional goal of preventing information on the inside from being sent to the outside.

Existing guards suffer from several key problems:
- They were either built on special purpose operating systems to maximize their resistance to attack (which made them both expensive to obtain and manage), or they were built on weak COTS operating systems (which made them vulnerable to attack). Examples of the former class include the C2 Guard [Fiorino], which is built on the XTS-300 B3-rated operating system [XTS-300]. Examples of the latter class include the ISSE guard [ISSE], which is built on an ordinary Solaris operating system.[1]
- The guards were also built for particular applications, and were generally hard to extend to other uses. For example, a DISA-sponsored study [SGS] found approximately 50 different guards built by the US Department of Defense. None of these guards have the capability to deal with modern middleware protocols such as IIOP (used by CORBA).
- In many cases, guards require a human to "certify" each piece of data (e.g., E-mail message) to be released from the inside to the outside, which is difficult to do accurately. In general, the certification occurs inside the enclave, using trusted software which puts a digital signature on the data to be released. The signature is then verified by the guard before release. This technique relies on the correct operation of the user's approval software (i.e., the correct functioning of the user's workstation). For example, Secure Computing's Standard Mail Guard [Smith] requires that the user invoke a Fortezza card to perform signing of each message to be released, without any assurance that the Fortezza card is signing what the user intended. The SMG can verify that the signature was applied correctly, but cannot determine whether the signed data is in fact appropriate for release, or even if it is what the user intended to release. Even aside from assurance issues, this scheme is inappropriate for connections involving lower level protocols (e.g., IIOP), since users cannot realistically approve each object invocation.
- As special purpose devices, guards lack integration with other security devices, such as working with intrusion detection systems. They require a separate set of management capabilities, and cannot be managed along with the rest of the network.

Our goal in designing ARGuE was to use a modern firewall as a base, thus providing a strong platform that has already withstood concerted attack. We then

---

[1] Earlier versions of the ISSE were built on the Harris Nighthawk, a B1 UNIX system.

extended the firewall in ways to provide modular functionality that provides a reasonable degree of assurance. Our goal was not to build an accredited (or even accreditable) guard; as such we have not developed any of the formal documentation required to field a product. Rather, our goal was to explore how we could use existing commercial and research technologies to provide a prototype of a next generation guard.

The remainder of this paper is organized as follows: Section 2 describes the ARGuE capabilities and architecture. Section 3 describes the current status of our work, limitations, and our future research directions. Section 4 concludes the paper.

2. ARGuE Capabilities

This section describes the Gauntlet capabilities, how we extended it to create the prototype guard (ARGuE), and the ARGuE architecture.

As described above, our goal was to build a guard with reasonable assurance, yet based on COTS products for low cost, flexibility, etc. Our method of achieving assurance was to build on a strong firewall platform, adding multi-part proxies (described below) that reduce the risks inherent in all firewall proxies, and strengthen the foundation by using operating system level wrappers to constrain the behavior of the proxy. Collectively, we believe this layered defense approach results in a guard that provides both functionality and assurance.

2.1 Gauntlet Capabilities

By building ARGuE (Advanced Research Guard for Experimentation) on the Gauntlet firewall, we gained several key capabilities.

First, Gauntlet has a strong pedigree, having been installed in thousands of sites. Although it has never been evaluated for use in Multi-Level Secure (MLS) environments, its ability to withstand attack is understood.

Second, as a COTS software product Gauntlet is a low-cost solution, running on COTS hardware architectures such as Intel PCs, Sun SPARC, and Hewlett-Packard PA-RISC.

Third, existing Gauntlet facilities provide many of the necessary features for a guard, including Virtual Private Networks, and the ability to block based on IP addresses.

Fourth, Gauntlet is readily extensible by including a Proxy Development Toolkit (PDK). The availability of existing protocol proxies allows incremental development of the guard. Initially, the guard can use existing proxies (with the limited filtering capabilities they provide), replacing them as more sophisticated filtering proxies become available.

Fifth, Gauntlet includes sophisticated management capabilities, including integration with Network Associates' Cybercop intrusion detection products.

2.2 ARGuE Extensions to Gauntlet

ARGuE extends the Gauntlet product in several ways: by adding "safer" multi-part proxies for critical protocols;

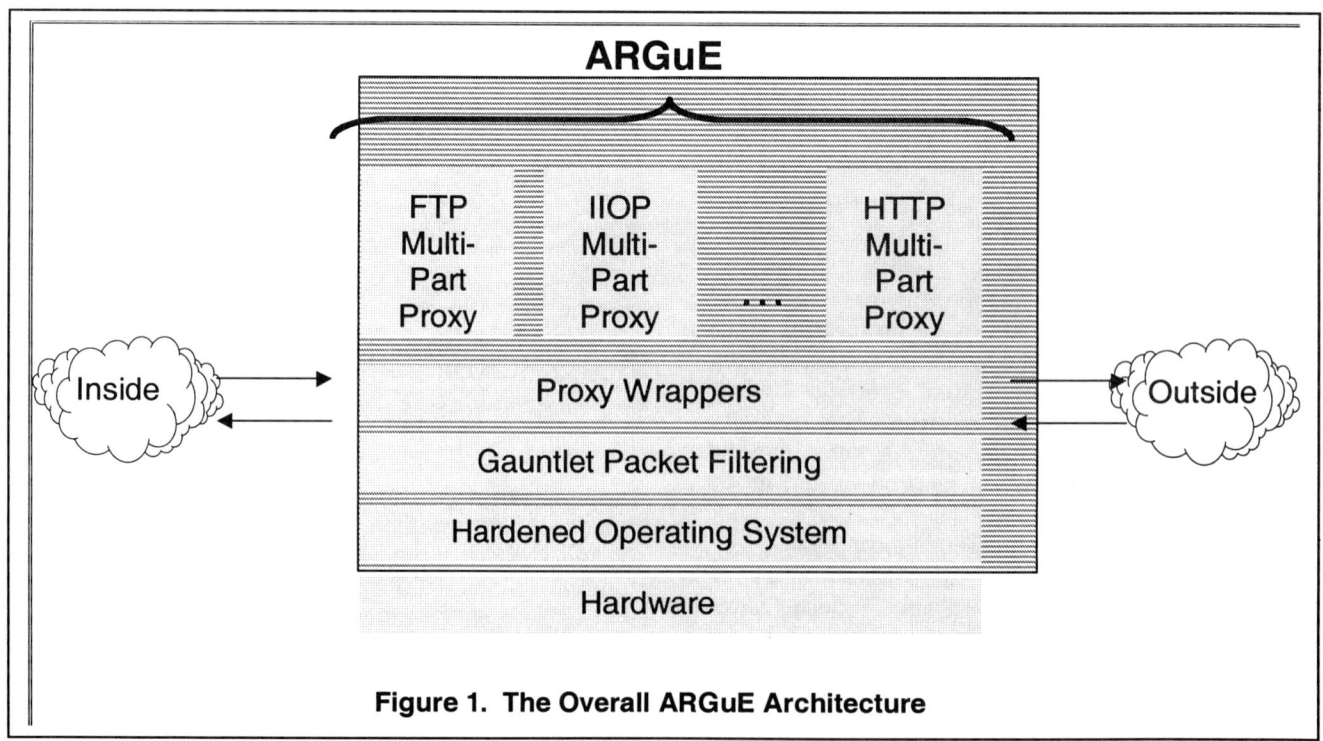

Figure 1. The Overall ARGuE Architecture

by providing "data sealing" capabilities; by integrating wrappers technology for constraining incorrect proxy behavior; and by providing data and application-specific intrusion detection information.

Figure 1 shows that an ARGuE system is made up of a Gauntlet with one or more multi-part proxies, where each proxy is constrained using wrapper technologies.

2.2.1 The Multi-Part Proxy Architecture

Proxies in most firewalls (including Gauntlet) are trusted software that communicate between the "inside" and "outside" networks. Figure 2 shows a traditional proxy, which provides communications between one inside and two outside networks. In general, such proxies allow unlimited communication from inside to outside, and limited communication from outside to inside. Any flaw in the proxy (including subversion), can cause the proxy to provide direct communication from the outside to the inside.

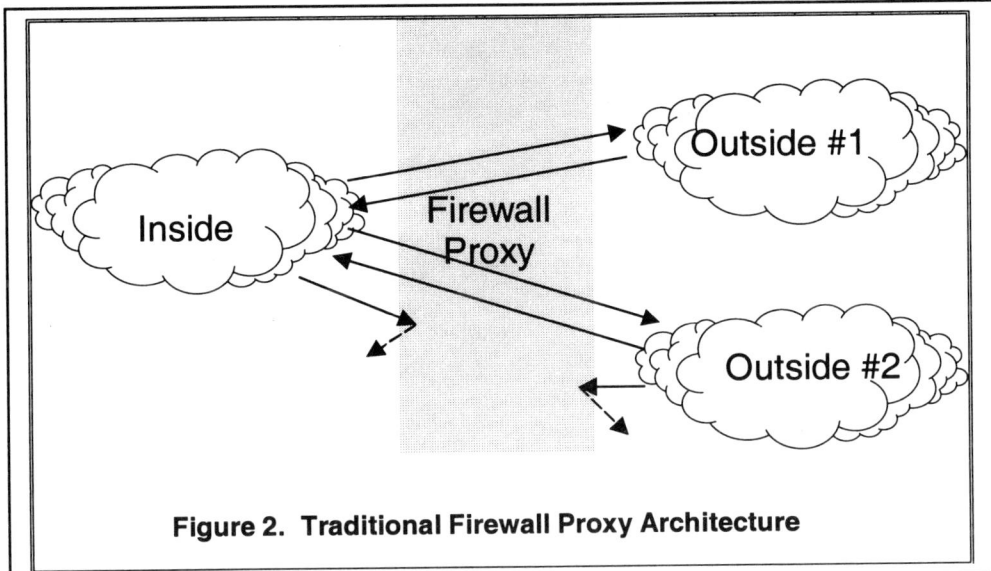

Figure 2. Traditional Firewall Proxy Architecture

By contrast, the ARGuE multi-part proxy, shown in Figure 3, divides the work of the proxy into several programs: one that communicates with (each) outside network, one that communicates with (each) inside network, and one in the middle that provides for filtering between each combination of inside and outside networks.

The inside listener/sender performs two functions: it listens for protocol operations (e.g., IIOP requests or replies) coming from the inside network and translates (externalizes) them into files, and it listens for the results of the content-based filter and translates the externalized files into protocol operations (e.g., IIOP requests or replies). Each outside listener/sender performs the analogous function for its attached outside network. The content-based filters review the file created by the inside or outside listener/sender, performing any necessary content-based decision-making depending on the direction of the transfer, and forwards the request to the opposite side. The content-based filter can also modify the file, thus performing sanitation (e.g., excising dirty words or "fuzzing" data values).

The use of files as the transfer mechanism is to reduce the binding between the different parts of the system. However, there is no fundamental architectural reason why the connection needs to be using a file. For example, a different implementation might use UNIX shared memory segments as the communication method, using appropriate permissions on the memory to control which

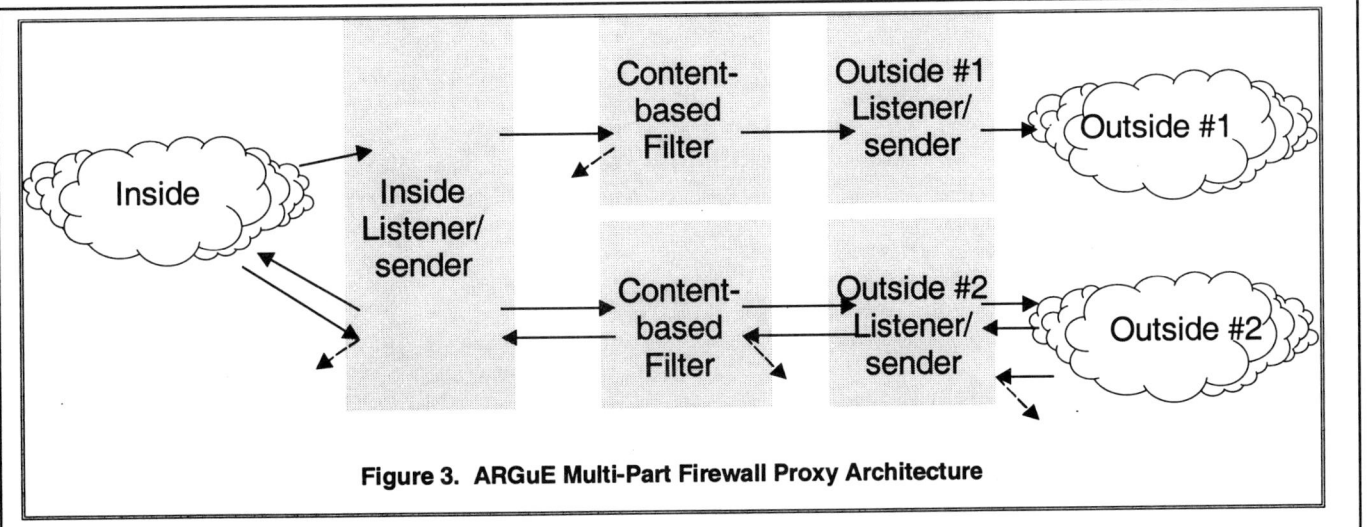

Figure 3. ARGuE Multi-Part Firewall Proxy Architecture

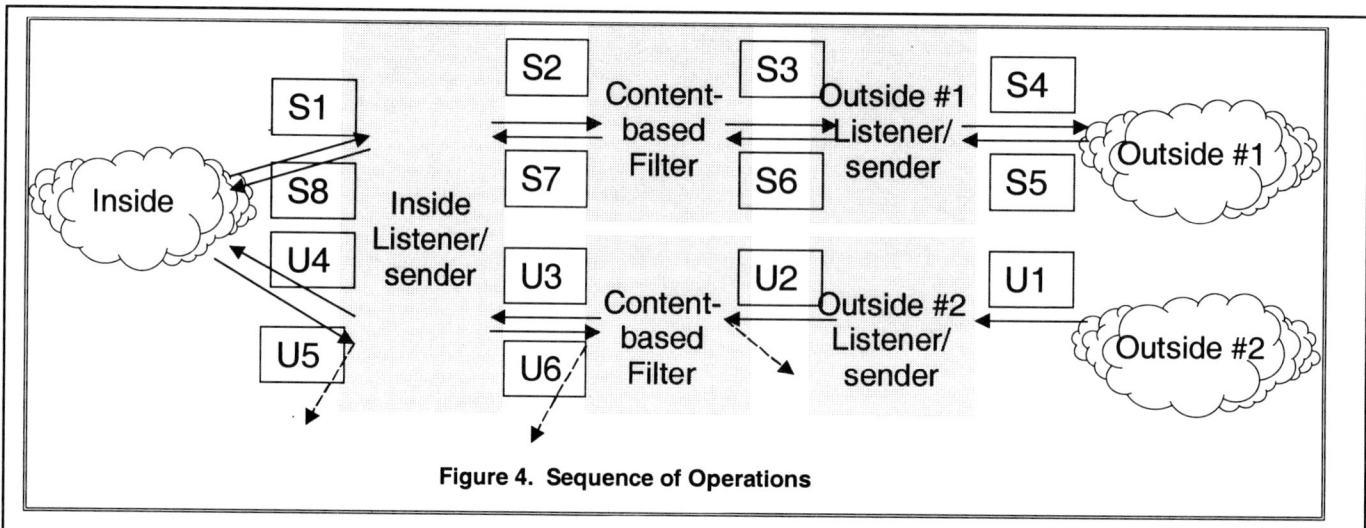

Figure 4. Sequence of Operations

processes can read and write. Using shared memory would probably be faster than the existing file-based mechanism.

Figure 4 shows the sequences for a typical successful or unsuccessful protocol operation.

Consider the sequence of operations shown in the upper portion of Figure 4. The operation starts on the inside, where the client application sends a request (S1) to the inside listener/sender. Access controls may be performed at this step before the request is externalized into a file and transferred (S2) to the content-based filter. The filter makes a decision based on the contents of the request, and forwards the file (S3) to the outside listener/sender. The file is converted from the file format back into the original protocol format, and sent to the server on the outside network. When the server responds (S5), the outside listener/sender may perform access controls, and then converts the response to a file, continuing back through the content-based filter (S6) to the inside listener/sender (S7), where it is converted back into a protocol stream and sent to the originating client.

The lower portion of Figure 4 shows an unsuccessful operation, beginning on the outside (although an unsuccessful operation could begin either on the inside or outside). In this case, the request is sent to the outside listener/sender (U1), which may perform access controls before converting the request to a file (U2) and sending it to the content-based filter. After reviewing the contents of the request, the filter may reject the request (the dotted line), or it may forward the request on to the inside listener/sender (U3), which converts the file back to a protocol request, and sends it to the inside server (U4). The server's response (U5) is sent to the inside listener/sender which may perform access control and reject the response (shown as the dotted line), or accept it and forward it (U6) to the content-based filter, which may also reject the request (the dotted line).

One complicating factor in the unsuccessful case is that if the response is rejected (at any of the locations shown in Figure 4), the client is left waiting for a response. Depending on the application architecture, it may be necessary to generate a synthetic response to the client indicating that the request or response has failed. In some cases it may be sufficient to reject it without

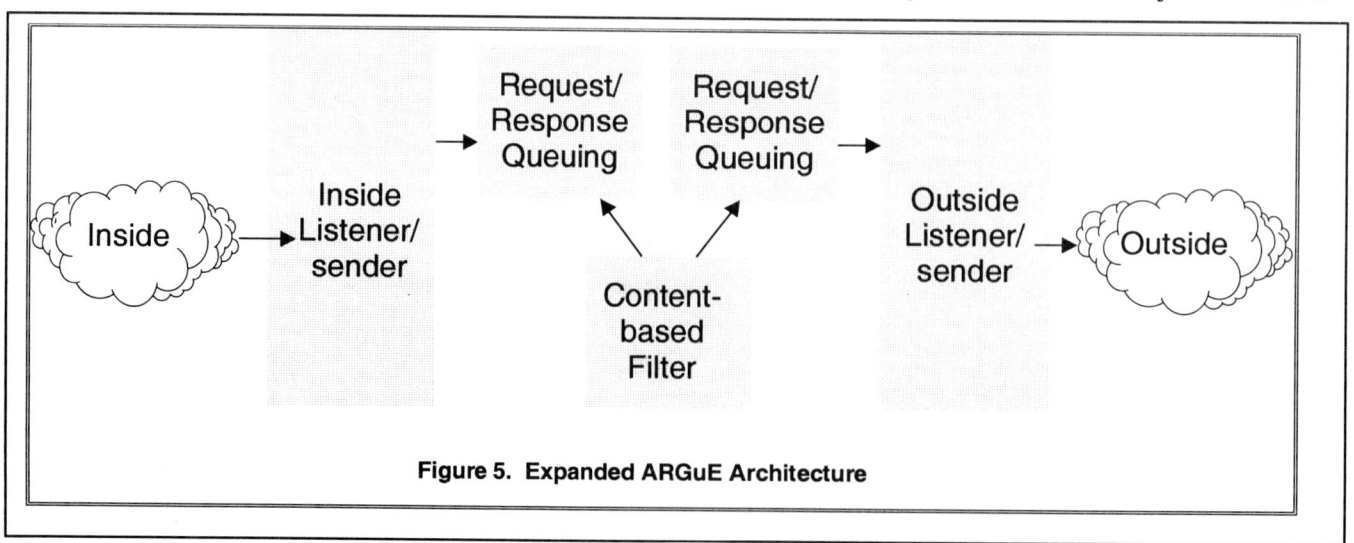

Figure 5. Expanded ARGuE Architecture

indicating whether it was the request or the response that was unsuccessful; in other cases it may be necessary to indicate what the cause of the failure was. In any case, some information leakage will occur as a result of the synthetic response, so careful definition of the generic response is necessary.

Figure 5 shows an expanded version of the architecture, adding the queuing and dequeuing components which are not shown in Figure 3. Each queuing component has an input and an output directory for each transfer direction. Only filters copy files from the input directories to the output directories.

The concept of a multi-part proxy was inspired by the C2Guard [Fiorino], which uses a similar sequence (shown in Figure 6) to split up the operation. The C2Guard consists of three computers: a Sun Solaris system that queues files from the inside and passes them over a serial line to the Wang XTS-300; the XTS-300 running the content-based filters; and a second Sun Solaris system that accepts the files over a serial line from the XTS-300 and transfers them to the outside. (The process is equivalent for files being transferred from the outside to the inside.) The queuing and dequeuing computers are required to be dedicated to that purpose; they accept (and send) files using NFS and FTP. In environments where protocols such as IIOP are required, another pair of computers (shown as the protocol/file translators) are required to translate from the native protocol to file format and back. The key difference is that ARGuE requires a single computer to provide all of the capabilities (protocol handling, queuing, and filtering) as opposed to three or five computers as in the case of the C2Guard.

2.2.2 Writing Content-based Filters

Each multi-part ARGuE proxy consists of the five parts enumerated above:
1. the inside listener/sender,
2. the inside request/response queuing,
3. the content-based filter,
4. outside request/response queuing, and
5. outside listener/sender.

Of these five parts, the first two and last two are generic for a given protocol. That is, all installations of ARGuE which use IIOP as the transfer mechanism will use identical software. The content-based filter, however, is highly application specific.

There are two parts to content-based filtering: figuring out what is to be filtered (i.e., the organizational security policy), and translating those rules into filtering code. Of these, the first is clearly more difficult, because organizations frequently do not know what makes data sensitive, especially at the protocol level where the higher level semantics are stripped away. It is further complicated with classified data (i.e., when connecting classified to unclassified networks) in that few individuals are willing to take the risk of identifying information as unclassified. It is far simpler to claim that all data is classified, thus leading to the traditional unconnected system-high systems. Determining what is to be filtered is a primarily social exercise, not a technical one, and as such is not further explored in this paper.

The ARGuE design allows for use of any executable program as a filter. Thus, the filter could be written in a low level language like C, in a scripting language such as Perl, or in an interpreted language such as Java. Since the filtering is done directly on the boundary controller

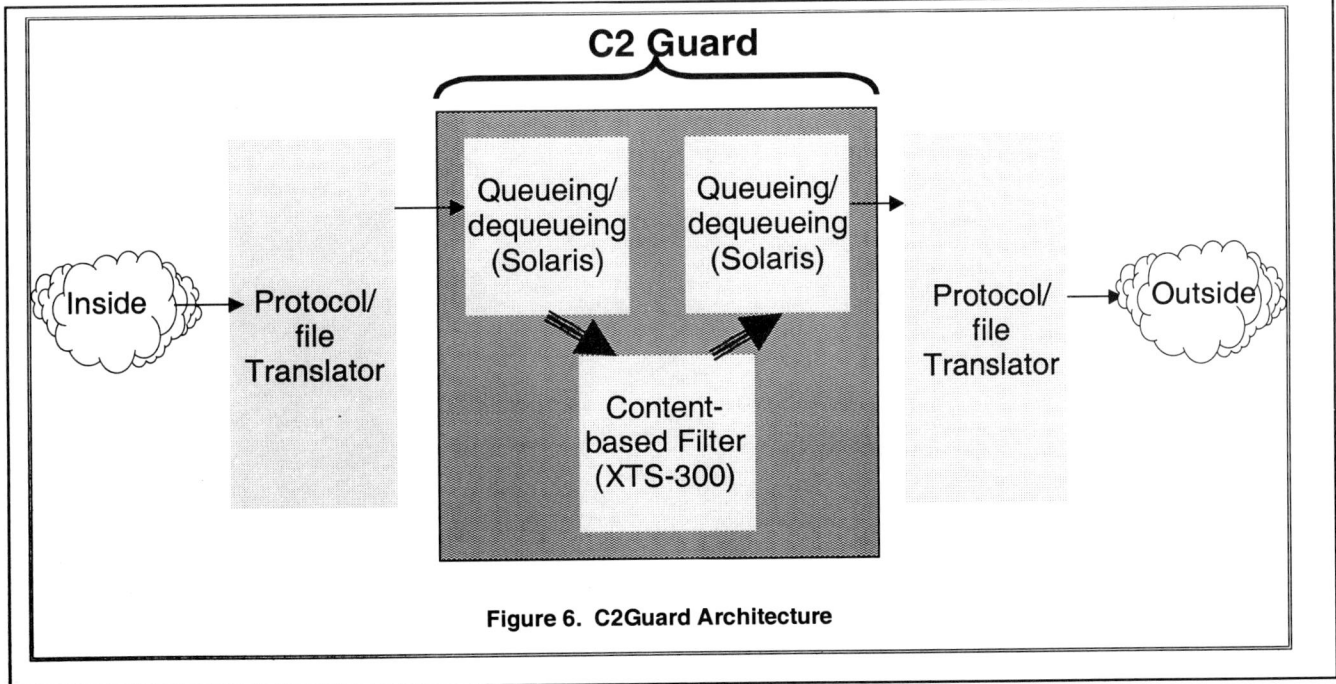

Figure 6. C2Guard Architecture

machine, any vulnerabilities in the filter may make it vulnerable to outside attacks. While we could use our Wrappers technology to limit the capabilities of the Perl or Java interpreters, there seemed to be little to be gained by that choice, and much to lose if there are other types of vulnerabilities in Java that we are not currently aware of. For these reasons, we rejected use of Perl or Java, primarily because of the complexity they introduce.

Instead, we decided to use Felt [Guttman], a language developed specifically for filter development. Felt provides constructs for parsing input files into fields and filtering based on content values. It can also be extended by writing C code, which can be embedded in the filter definition.

While it is non-procedural (with the exception of C extensions), Felt is still a programming language, and as such, requires significant expertise to write filters. Since filters are application specific, the effort involved in development is a significant cost in fielding a guard, as opposed to the generic parts of the system which can be amortized over multiple instances. As an area for further research, we are investigating whether a graphical user interface (GUI) could be used to present templates to a non-programmer who is knowledgeable about the security constraints, and have that person fill in the content limitations. The result of the GUI would be a Felt program, which could then be reviewed along with the GUI inputs to verify that it meets the organizational security requirements.

2.2.3 Data Sealing in ARGuE

In some cases, data comes into a system from the outside, is stored, and is then exported back either to its origin or to some other outside organization. In these cases, filtering can be avoided if the data can be recognized as having previously been imported, using the theory that if something came in then it must be acceptable to send out again.

In ARGuE, we implemented this concept by allowing filters to place digital signatures on data items as they transit from the outside to the inside. An inside-to-outside filter can then verify the digital signature as part of the filtering process, most likely in preference to performing content-based filtering.

The most difficult part of data sealing is determining what to do with the seal data (i.e., the data that makes up the seal itself). Our goal was to add seals to CORBA (IIOP) traffic, preferably without changing either the client or server application. We considered three approaches:

1. Figure 7 shows the initial approach where the seal would be embedded in the Interoperable Object Reference (IOR). This method was not feasible because it interfered with the operation of the CORBA application.
2. Figure 8 shows the second approach where the seal is calculated and embedded in a field designated as part of the application definition. This method worked acceptably, although it required that both the client and server applications be aware of the seal to reserve space for the seal storage. Additionally, it required that the server application store the seal with the data and retrieve it whenever retrieval is required. Thus, it was operable, but it did not meet our goals.
3. Figure 9 shows the third approach where the seal is calculated in the guard and stored there. Neither the client nor the server need be aware of the seal

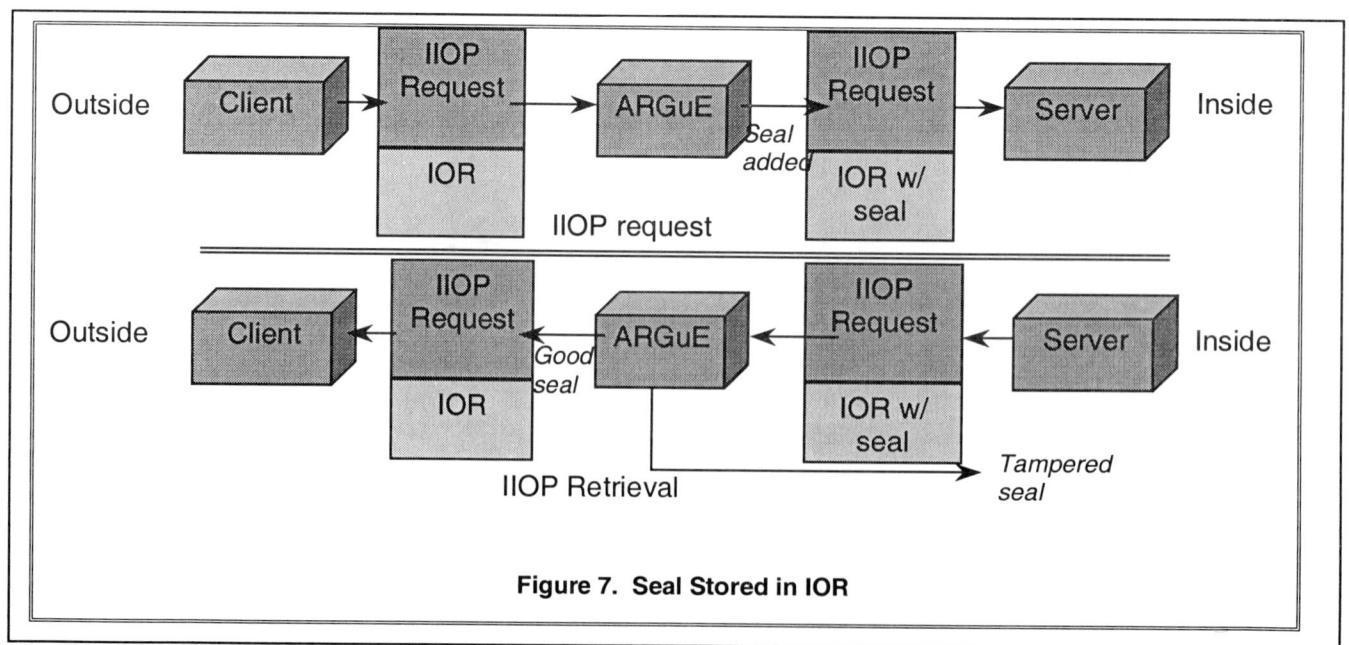

Figure 7. Seal Stored in IOR

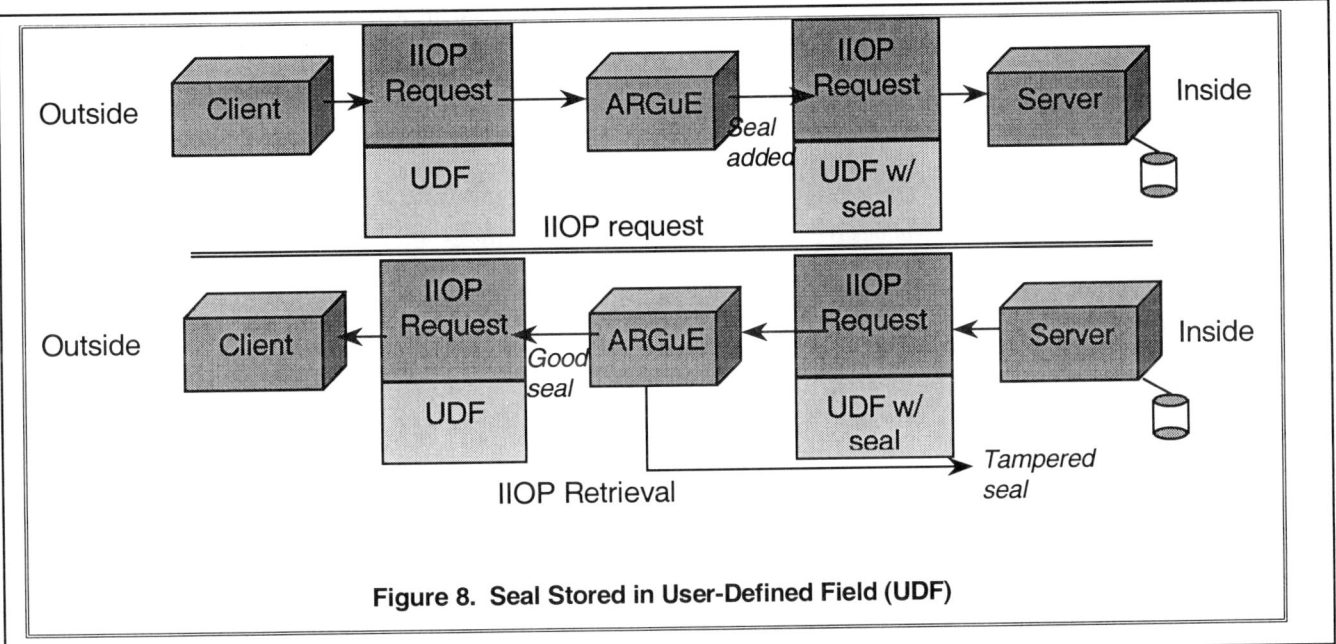

Figure 8. Seal Stored in User-Defined Field (UDF)

calculation, as it is kept exclusively within the guard. However, there are several problems with this approach. The guard must have a mechanism to determine whether a particular piece of data being presented for release has a corresponding seal in the database. The simplest method is for the guard to recalculate the seal, and then search its database for a previous instance of the seal value. Presuming that the digital signature algorithm is sufficiently strong that collisions are acceptably unlikely, this method will allow release of previously signed data, but will not allow release of unsigned data. A concern is that the guard cannot know when it is safe to discard any of the seals it has kept in its database, since it does not receive any notifications that the server has discarded data (the server being unaware of the presence of the database in the guard).

While any of these methods can be implemented, ARGuE currently uses the second and third of these methods (with the second being preferred).

One of the more difficult aspects of data sealing is determining what can realistically be sealed, and still have the seal be meaningful. For instance, if a seal were applied to a one byte value, then there would be too few realistic seals to be meaningful. There is no "magic" correct size for sealed data, but it is a consideration in

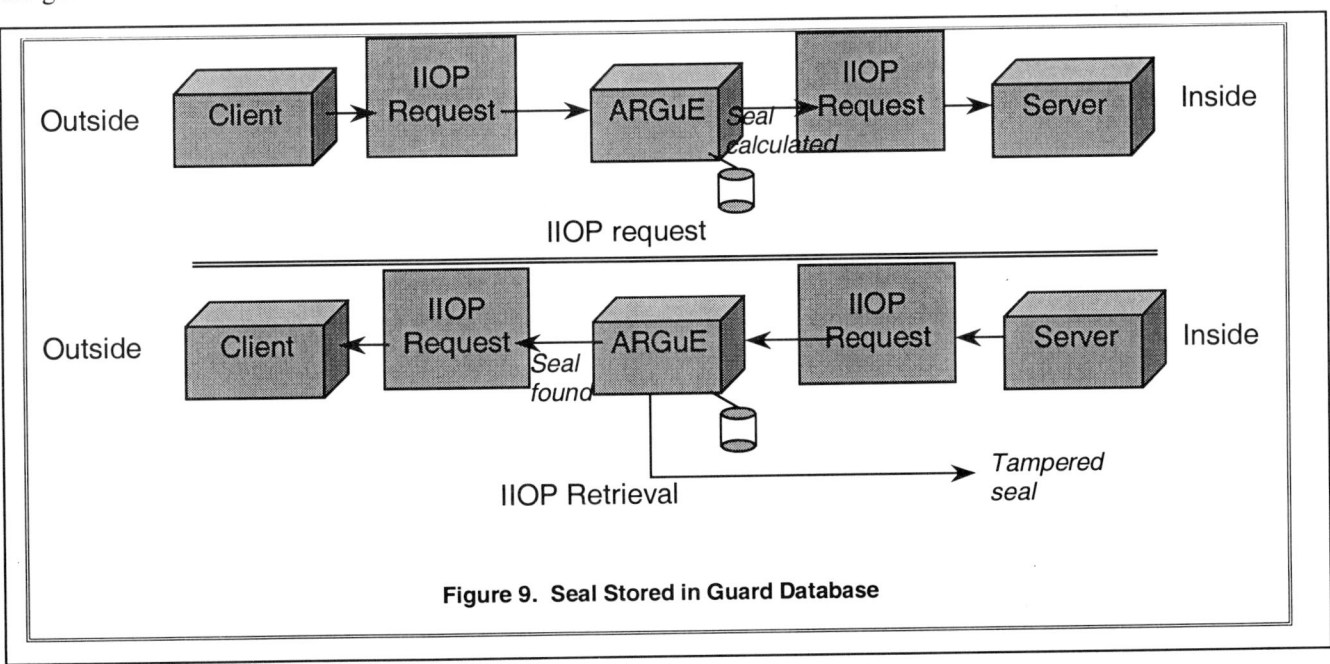

Figure 9. Seal Stored in Guard Database

developing the application-specific filtering software that adds and verifies seals.

2.2.4 Wrappers to Constrain Proxies

One of the concerns associated with having all of the guard processes on a single platform is that a flaw in any of the processes could lead to undesired results. For example, a flaw in the content-based filter or in any of the listener/sender processes could allow traffic to flow directly from the inside to the outside, bypassing the content-based filtering.

At first blush it might seem that existing operating system controls could be used to constrain behavior of the proxy. However, our base is the UNIX version of Gauntlet, and UNIX, like most operating systems, does not provide a thorough access control system. For example, while it is possible to control access to individual files within the Gauntlet (which ARGuE uses through use of unique UIDs and GIDs to represent each part of the multi-part proxy), there is no means to control which TCP/IP ports may be accessed by an application, other than the restriction that unprivileged processes cannot bind to ports below 1024. Our goal was to provide finer grained controls on the operation of the proxy parts.

Our means of controlling the proxies is to develop wrappers, using the Wrapper Definition Language (WDL) [Fraser]. There are three wrappers associated with each ARGuE multi-part proxy:

- A wrapper for the listener/sender programs, parameterized to allow it to bind to specified TCP/IP ports on the appropriate network interface (i.e., so the inside listener/sender can access the inside network, and the outside listener/sender can access the outside network, but not vice versa), and to allow it to access files in its corresponding directories, but not the directories belonging to the opposite side. This wrapper will vary depending on the protocol being processed by the proxy, especially insofar as the port numbers that can be bound.
- A wrapper for the queuing/dequeuing programs, parameterized to allow it to access the correct directories only, but not allowing them to access any TCP/IP ports.
- A wrapper for the filtering program, allowing it to operate on the queuing directories, but not allowing it to access any TCP/IP ports.

The wrappers are designed to allow the corresponding program to do little as possible, to minimize the risk of erroneous or malicious code. For example, the wrapper for the listener/sender program allows the following:

- Fork a child process
- Use semaphores used for synchronizing the different parts of ARGuE
- Make open() calls on files in specified directories (with limitations on what directories can be opened for reading and what directories can be opened for writing)
- Make read() and write() calls to access already opened files
- Make unlink() calls to remove files from specified directories
- Exit

2.2.5 Integration with Intrusion Detection

The final part of ARGuE is integration with intrusion detection technology. The Intruder Detection and Isolation Protocol (IDIP) [IDIP] can be used both to identify potential attacks, and to cause real-time changes in configurations to respond to those attacks.

IDIP integration is currently limited to notification of potential attacks. The listener/sender processes can detect incorrectly formatted protocols (by comparing the data received to the expected protocol), and can send appropriate notifications. The filter is capable of generating application specific alerts, depending on values received. For example, if data representing the amount of a bank deposit is being passed through ARGuE, an intrusion detection system might be configured as follows:

- For deposits less than $1000, no alert is ever generated.
- For deposits less than $10,000 made during banking hours, no alert is generated, but if outside of normal hours then a low level alert is generated.
- For deposits less than $100,000, an alert is generated, but the transaction is allowed to go through.
- For deposits less than $1,000,000, an alert is generated and the transaction is blocked, but other transactions are permitted.
- For deposits greater than $1,000,000, an alert is generated, and future transactions are refused (perhaps because it indicates a significant security breach).

The most interesting alerts are application specific, and hence require knowledge and planning on the part of the filter developer.

One of the critical issues in interacting with an intrusion detection system is where to report problems. We decided to report problems detected by the inside listener/sender and by the filter to devices on the inside, and problems detected by the outside listener/sender (but not the filter), to devices on the outside. It is unclear whether outsiders should also be notified of potential attacks found by the filter. We believe that attacks on the filter are most likely to be attempts to release data which fails the filtering criteria, and is more likely to indicate an error in the program sending the data (or the filter itself) than a concerted effort by an inside user to leak information.

3. Current Status, Limitations, and Future Work

ARGuE has been demonstrated in several government testbeds to connect together networks of the same classification (but where we pretended that the data was of different classifications). Protocols transferred in these demonstrations included IIOP (CORBA) and FTP. In the latter case, the data was stored within the file being transferred using XML. Use of XML meant that the filter had to parse the XML to find the relevant data to be filtered; an additional step.

ARGuE has several significant limitations:
- It is not, and is not planned to be accredited. It is only a testbed.
- There are inherent delays introduced by the architecture. Since filtering is not possible until an entire operation is available for review, the listener/sender processes accumulate an entire request. If the protocol being processed is FTP, this means that the entire file is collected into the ARGuE device before filtering begins and subsequent transfer. Thus, the transfer time is at least twice what it would be if ARGuE were not reviewing the data. Use of shared memory instead of files (as described earlier) would reduce this latency somewhat, but the requirement for assembling the entire operation would remain. The doubling of transfer time is therefore fixed, while the interim processing may be speeded up.
- Addition of each new protocol requires different listener/sender pairs. While it may be possible to adapt these from existing firewall proxies, they have different requirements, and hence will always be less flexible than corresponding firewalls. Additionally, the wrappers will differ somewhat for each listener/sender pair, thus increasing development effort.
- Developing filters is still hard, especially for protocols where the level of detail available in each request is small, and hence difficult to determine whether a particular message should be allowed through. For organizations accustomed to "out of the box" firewalls, the software development effort is a significant issue (although no worse than other guards).
- Because the filters are dynamically invoked for each message, they are inherently stateless. This has been adequate for our current purposes, but may not be in the future.
- CORBA implementations do not have fixed TCP ports, as do other network services such as SMTP or HTTP. Most CORBA implementations provide a mechanism to specify a particular TCP port to be used. Since the proxies must listen on particular ports, this requires application effort. However, this is no worse than the effort required to use CORBA applications through a firewall.

Our future directions include an in depth look at the assurance granted by the multi-part proxies (as compared to the traditional single part proxy), and the value of wrappers on proxies. As noted above, we also plan to build a graphical user interface to make it easier for non-programmers to specify filtering rules, and to compare the quality of filtering rules generated by non-programmers with those developed by programmers. Additionally, we plan to integrate ARGuE with central network management capabilities, so the set of filtering rules can be dynamically changed under the control of an administrator (perhaps in response to an operational need to transfer data, or to restrict traffic when a leak is suspected).

4. Conclusion

ARGuE provides significant features normally found in guards. The concept of a implementing a multi-part proxy within a single computer is unique to ARGuE, and provides assurances not typically found in firewalls, especially when married with the wrapper technology. The data sealing capability, while certainly not new, provides a useful capability in environments where data is imported and subsequently exported.

5. Acknowledgements

We are indebted to Sami Saydjari at DARPA who encouraged this effort, to Don Faatz at MITRE who contributed many of the ideas toward this architecture, to Debi Robertson for her tireless efforts to help us gain access to the Felt compiler used for data filtering, and to all our colleagues at NAI Labs who provided the inspiration, technologies, and work environment that made the CORBA Guard possible. In particular, James Croall developed the first version of the ARGuE software, Brian Schechter made significant enhancements and developed the data sealing capabilities, Matt Woods wrote many of the initial filters, and Chris Marcellin wrote the proxy wrappers. Finally, we appreciate the many constructive suggestions from the referees.

6. References

[ISSE] "Imagery Support Server Environment (ISSE) Guard System Description", http://www.itd.sterling.com/rome/projects/products/isse/ISSE_SD.html

[Smith] Richard Smith, "Constructing a High Assurance Mail Guard," *Proceedings of the*

	17th National Computer Security Conference, Baltimore MD, October 1994.
[Fiorino]	Thomas Fiorino *et al*, "Lessons Learned During the Life Cycle of an MLS Guard Deployed at Multiple Sites", *Proceedings of the Eleventh Annual Computer Security Applications Conference*, New Orleans LA, December 1995.
[Fraser]	Timothy Fraser, Lee Badger, and Mark Feldman, "Hardening COTS Software with Generic Software Wrappers", *Proceedings of the 1999 IEEE Symposium on Security and Privacy*, Oakland CA, May 1999.
[Guttman]	Joshua Guttman, John Ramsdell, and Vipin Swarup, *Felt, a Security Filter Compiler*, Personal Communication, November 1998.
[IDIP]	"Dynamic, Cooperating Boundary Controllers Final Technical Report", Boeing report D658-10822-1, August 1998.
[SGS]	"Security Guard Study", Defense Information Systems Agency, August 1995.
[XTS-300]	Final Evaluation Report, Wang Government Services, Inc., XTS-300 (Report CSC-EPL-92/003.C), National Computer Security Center, 1992.

Using Abuse Case Models for Security Requirements Analysis

John McDermott and Chris Fox
Department of Computer Science
James Madison University
Harrisonburg, Virginia 222807
E-mail: {mcdermot, fox}@cs.jmu.edu

Abstract

The relationships between the work products of a security engineering process can be hard to understand, even for persons with a strong technical background but little knowledge of security engineering. Market forces are driving software practitioners who are not security specialists to develop software that requires security features. When these practitioners develop software solutions without appropriate security-specific processes and models, they sometimes fail to produce effective solutions.

We have adapted a proven object-oriented modeling technique, use cases, to capture and analyze security requirements in a simple way. We call the adaptation an abuse case *model. Its relationship to other security engineering work products is relatively simple, from a user perspective.*

1. Introduction

A valid security engineering process, as typified by the Common Criteria [1], is a complex activity involving many special work products: security objectives, security requirements, security policies, functional specifications, and security policy models. These work products are essential in a process that aims to create trustworthy information security products. But the work products and relationships between them can be hard to understand, even for persons with a strong technical background, but little knowledge of security engineering.

Security specialists use mathematical security models [6, 8] to understand security problems and find solutions for them. Use of these models is essential to the creation of trustworthy information security products. But these models are complex and subtle. They are not easily understood by persons who are not security specialists. They must be interpreted for the system to which they are applied. Security specialists can construct these interpretations, but the construction can be time consuming.

On the other hand, market forces are driving software practitioners who are not security specialists to develop software that requires security features. When these practitioners develop software solutions without appropriate security-specific processes and models [2], they sometimes fail to produce effective solutions [7].

While we do not have a solution to this problem, we have adapted a proven object-oriented modeling technique, *use cases*, to capture and analyze security requirements in a simple way. We call the adaptation an *abuse case* model. As we employ it, an abuse case model is considerably easier to understand than a mathematical security model. Its relationship to other security engineering work products is relatively simple, from a user perspective

2. Use Cases

Use cases are abstract episodes of interaction between a system and its environment. A use case characterizes a way of using a system, or a dialog that a system and its environment may share as they interact.

We define a *use case* as a specification of a type of complete interaction between a system and one or more *actors* (discussed below). A use case must be complete in the sense that it forms an entire and coherent transaction. For example, making a cash withdrawal at an ATM machine, placing a call on the telephone, or deleting a file from a file system, are examples of complete interactions with various sorts of systems that would qualify as use cases.

An abstraction of an external agent that interacts with the system is called an *actor*. Actors represent entities outside a system that interact with it in some way. Actors may be human or non-human. Actors may interact with a system by exchanging data with it, invoking one of the system's operations, or having one of the actor's operations invoked by the system. Actors are abstractions of actual individual users or systems typifying the roles played in system interactions. Some examples of actors are *Dispatcher*, *Clerk*, *Printer*, *Communications Channel*, and *Inventory System*.

A *scenario* is a description of a specific interaction between particular individuals. A use case abstracts scenarios that are instances of the same kind of interaction between a system and its actors. The following description is a scenario:

> Mary Smith places her bank card into an active ATM machine. The system prompts her for her PIN number, and she types 2384. The machine displays a transaction menu. Mary chooses a balance inquiry on her checking account. The system reports that she has $1329.67 in her account, and again displays the transaction menu. This time Mary chooses to end the interaction, and the system releases her card. Mary removes it and the system returns to its ready state.

A use case abstracts scenarios such as this to provide a general specification for similar interactions. The following illustrates an ATM balance inquiry transaction use case:

> A balance inquiry begins when a Customer inserts his or her bank card into an active ATM machine in its ready state. The system prompts for the Customer's PIN. The Customer types the PIN. If the PIN is incorrect, the system displays an error message and asks the Customer to try again. The Customer gets three tries. After the third failure, the system keeps the card, displays a message telling the Customer to see a teller, and after twenty seconds, returns to its active state. If the Customer enters a valid PIN, the system presents a transaction menu. The Customer chooses a balance inquiry on either checking or savings. The system displays the current balance and re-displays the transaction menu. This continues until the Customer chooses to terminate the interaction. The system releases the bank card. The Customer removes the card and the system returns to its ready state. If the bank card is not removed within 40 seconds, the system retrieves the bank card.

Notice that the use case describes the possible courses of events that may occur in various scenarios.

Use case models are documented using two notations: use case diagrams and use case descriptions. Use case diagrams are part of the Universal Modeling Language (UML), an industry standard collection of notations for analysis and design [5].

A use case diagram is a schematic representation of actors and a system's use cases. Each actor is represented by a stick figure; the actor's name appears near the figure. Use cases are represented by ovals with the name of the use case either below or within the oval. Finally, an association line connects the actors with the use cases in which they participate. These symbols are shown below, in Figure 1.

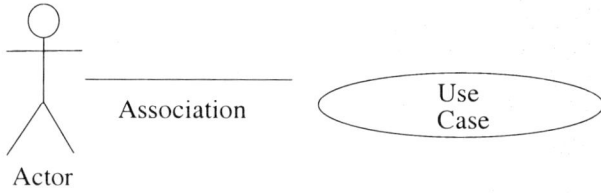

Figure 1. Use Case Diagram Symbols

Each use case should have an accompanying *use case description* that explains how the actors and the system interact. There is no standard notation or format for use case descriptions. Virtually any notation able to describe interactions between two or more entities may be used. Typically, use case descriptions are written in natural language. The simplest or most abstract use case description may be only a few sentences. More detailed use case descriptions are refined by adding details about the interaction and references to requirements for requirements traceability.

A special case of abstraction involves varying levels of detail about the interaction protocols between actors and the system. For example, an ATM balance inquiry use case description may simply state that the user identifies herself to the system, specifies a balance inquiry transaction on one of her accounts, is informed of the balance in response, and then the user terminates the interaction. This description abstracts protocol details. A use case description with more protocol detail might go into the specifics of ATM cards, PIN numbers, the ATM display and menus, and the button presses the user makes to accomplish the transaction.

Use cases that abstract the details of interaction protocols are called *essential use cases*; those that include protocol details are called *real* or *implementation use cases* [3].

3. A Use Case Model For An Internet-Based Information Security Lab

Here is a complete use case model that will show how actors, use cases, associations, diagrams, and use case descriptions fit together. This model is a simplified version of the one we are using to design and set up an Internet-based information security lab in our own department.

An Internet-based information security lab, or *lab*, is a collection of systems and software used for teaching information security. Laboratory exercises give students practical experience with security vulnerabilities, security testing, and defenses. The students are not physically in the laboratory, but access it through the Internet. The lab comprises four kinds of entities: *servers*, *sources*, *targets*, and *exercises*. The first three are specially configured host systems in the lab. Servers provide presence for the students in the lab; servers do not participate in the exercises. Sources and targets participate in the exercises, with at least one source and target for each exercise. The exercises are either exploits or defenses, from the student's point of view. Each exercise has two parts: *documentation* and *implementation*. The documentation is provided by the instructor and usually consists of files and code samples that explain the exercise. Students are allowed to access the documentation for an exercise and are expected to construct and demonstrate an implementation. The instructor also provides a model solution which is not given to the students until the exercise is completed. Before each exercise, the lab is configured by an administrator. After the exercise is complete, the administrator restores the lab to an appropriate configuration.

3.1 Use Case Diagram

The use case diagram for the lab is show below as Figure 2. There are three actors and eight use cases.

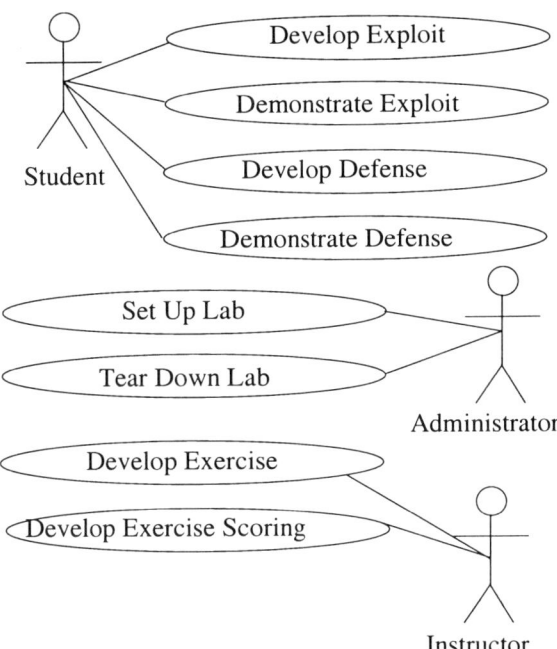

Figure 2. Use Case Diagram for an Internet-Based Information Security Laboratory

3.2 Use Case Descriptions

Here is a use case description from the model depicted in Figure 2. The first use case describes the interaction that takes place when a Student develops a security exploit as part of an assigned exercise. The second use case describes how a lab Administrator configures the hosts and networks of the lab for a particular exercise. Lab setup occurs for each exercise, because the exercise security configuration is quite frequently different from one that would be recommended for an operational system. Our descriptions are abstract and informal, as we would use for requirements elicitation. The actual lab will include several kinds of networks (Fast Ethernet, ATM, IPv4, IPv6) and hosts (Windows NT and Linux), and it is difficult to be specific in a small amount of space.

Develop Exploit

A Student first logs in to the lab server using a either a secure browser or command shell, from a remote location. The lab server authenticates the Student using a public key authentication algorithm and opens a session for the Student in her private workspace. The Student reads the description of the exercise, due dates, assigned hosts, list of references, and scoring rules from a text file provided by the lab server at her request. The Student studies the references that are outside the lab. The Student requests references that are stored in the lab, from the lab server. The lab server returns the references that are permitted by the current security policy of the lab server. The Student then logs on to the target host, via the lab server. The Student requests pertinent configuration information from the target host. The target host returns the configuration information permitted by its local security policy and the security policy of the lab server. The Student studies the configuration of the target host. The Student may request an editor from the lab server. The lab server will provide one if the Student is authorized according to the security policy. The Student then uses the editor to write a plan for the exploit, copies of configuration files, and programs needed to demonstrate the exploit. Alternatively, the Student may use editors and software tools on her local system outside the lab and then request to upload them onto the lab server via the secure shell. If this is permitted by the current security policy, then the lab server accepts the files and stores them in the Student's workspace. When the Student is satisfied that her exploit is ready she requests that the lab server install the necessary files on the source machine. If this is permitted by the security policy then lab server installs the necessary files on the source machine. The Student then tests her solution against the target and modifies the configuration files, procedures, and programs until the exploit succeeds or the Student gives up. The Student then saves her solution files on the server and logs out.

4. Abuse Cases

We define an *abuse case* as a specification of a type of complete interaction between a system and one or more actors, where the results of the interaction are harmful to the system, one of the actors, or one of the stakeholders in the system. We cannot define completeness just in terms of coherent transactions between actors and the system. Instead, we must define abuse in terms of interactions that result in actual harm. A complete abuse case defines an interaction between an actor and the system that results in harm to a resource associated with one of the actors, one of the stakeholders, or the system itself. For example, it may be possible to define an interaction that reveals a session key to an actor that should not see the session key. However, we would not call this interaction an abuse case, because no actor has used the compromised key to divulge the contents of a message or make an unauthorized change to stored data. If we extend the interaction to include the posting of the key on a public web site then we have an abuse case.

A further distinction we make is that an abuse case should describe the abuse of privilege used to complete the abuse case. Clearly, any abuse can be accomplished by gaining total control of the target machine through modification of the system software or firmware. In many cases it is not necessary to abuse this much privilege in the real system, so we need to include abuse of privilege that is less than maximal. To guard against simple abuses, an abuse case should describe interactions involving the minimal abuse of privilege necessary to accomplish the harm intended by the abusing actor. However, in the real system, an attacker may employ more than minimal effort. For this reason, we describe the range of privileges that might be used to accomplish the abuse, up to the maximum we intend to deal with.

Finally, we also include a short description of the specific harm that will occur as a result of the abuse. This description should be in terms from the user's domain.

We can describe abuse cases using the same strategy as for use cases: use case diagrams and use case descriptions. We do not use any special symbols for abuse cases in diagrams, that is, an abuse case diagram is drawn with the same symbols as a use case diagram. This allows us to create abuse case specifications in standard notation such as UML and to use design tools such as *Rational Rose* [4]. We distinguish the two by keeping them separate and labeling the diagrams. Abuse cases are not shown on a use case diagram and use cases are not shown on an abuse case diagram. Abuse cases can also range in levels of abstraction and we use both essential abuse cases and real abuse cases.

The actors in an abuse case model are the same kinds of external agents that participate in use cases. However, they should not be the same actors. If a human that is represented by an actor from a use case might also act maliciously in the corresponding role, then a new actor should be defined in the abuse case. For example, in our Internet-based information security laboratory, a malicious student might attempt to copy another student's solution. If we were to model this as an abuse case, we would define a new actor *Malicious Student* for the abuse case, rather than have the *Student* actor associated with the abuse case. If outsiders or unauthorized users are a threat, then new actors will have to be added to represent them. We do this to emphasize that a different role is active during abuse, even if the abusing actor also fulfills other roles. Some customers and users can be very sensitive about discussions of possible insider threats.

Actors in use cases are defined only briefly. In an abuse case, we give a more detailed description of the actor. Actor descriptions are very useful in abuse case modeling. Three characteristics of each actor are critical to understanding an abuse case: the actor's *resources*, *skills*, and *objectives*. The third characteristic may seem redundant if our abuse cases are at the same level of abstraction as essential use cases. However, the objectives of an actor are not really captured in the abstract abuse cases. Instead, we describe the actor's objectives as long-term goals that the actor potentially seeks over more than one abuse case. For example, the abuse case model of our information security laboratory includes two actors *Script Kiddie* and *Nazgul* [9]. The Script Kiddie's objective's include demonstration of skills by breaking in to a large number of systems while the Nazgul's objectives include industrial espionage, terrorism, and war. The resources available to an actor include other persons and organizations that might assist the actor, in addition to the tools and systems the actor may be using. Finally, resources include the amount of time an actor has to devote to the abuse case.

The description of an abuse case can also slightly differ from the approach taken with use case descriptions. We can describe abuse cases in exactly the same way that we describe use cases. However, we sometimes take a different approach. A use case description centers around a single abstract transaction or sequence of events, because a use case describes a desired interaction. On the other hand, because we are not sure where flaws will occur, an abuse case describes a family of undesirable interactions. The final "implementation" of an abuse case will be through the exploitation of requirements oversights, design flaws, and implementation flaws. Since we want to use the abuse case model to reduce the number of requirements oversights and design flaws, we may choose describe many abstract "transactions" that might take place to accomplish the same abuse. Each feature or component of the target system that might be exploited in an abuse case will be considered in the abuse case description. So each security relevant feature or component in the target system adds an abstract transaction to the family.

In our limited experience, we have used a tree, or sometimes a DAG structure to describe abuse cases in this way. We use a structure that could be a sub-tree of an attack tree, as used in penetration testing. The root of the sub-tree is the system we are modeling and the leaves are the resources or components of the system that are the targets of the abuse case. The interior nodes represent subsystems, applications, and individual classes within the applications. Each path from the root to a leaf shows which subsystems, applications, and classes might be misused in order to affect the leaf node in the desired way. Multiple paths through the tree indicate alternative means of accomplishing the abuse. In our experience, the interior nodes of the tree are entities that may be regarded as subjects, while the leaf nodes are objects.

To summarize,

Use Case	*Abuse Case*
• A complete transaction between one or more actors and a system.	• A family of complete transactions between one or more actors and a system, that results in harm.
• UML-based use case diagrams.	• UML-based use case diagrams.
• Typically described using natural language.	• Typically described using natural language. A tree/DAG diagram may also be used.
	• Potentially one family member for each kind of privilege abuse and for each component that might be exploited.
	• Includes a description of the range of security privileges that may be abused.
	• Includes a description of the harm that results from an abuse case.

In our experience, we develop the abuse case model one step behind the use case model. We use each component of the use case model to construct the corresponding component of the abuse case model:

1. *Identify the actors*. After the actors of the use case model have been identified, identify the actors of the abuse case model. If an actor in the use case model might attempt harmful use of the system, then add a corresponding malicious actor to the abuse case model. After the insider roles are represented, then actors

should be added for any intruders that might be a problem. Distinguish outsiders primarily on the basis of skills and resources. Requirements documents may give some help in identifying actors for abuse cases but a careful analysis of the system environment should also be done. It is important for the security specialist to discuss the potential actors with users and customers.

2. *Identify the abuse cases.* For each actor, determine their interactions with the system. Name each abuse case. At this point, it is helpful to draw an abuse case diagram.

4. *Define abuse cases.* As the interface to the system becomes more refined and the specific components are identified, the abuse case can be described. Since we use a tree structure to describe the possible points of abuse, we defer the definition until there is enough system structure to work with. The definitions can be refined as the description of the system is refined.

3. *Check granularity.* There may be too few abuse cases or there may be too many. Deciding how many are needed is largely a matter of experience and consideration of the specific target system. In our experience there are two ways we can wind up with too many abuse cases: 1) including possible but unlikely cases, or 2) modeling with too much detail. The latter problem results in several abuse cases that are distinguished only by details that are inappropriate for the purpose. For example, in most situations we would not need two abuse cases involving password theft that differed only in the kind of command shell used to accomplish the theft. We must be cautious when discarding an abuse case as unlikely. Some abuse cases may be too complex and others may be too abstract. A good abuse case model will have uniform granularity of detail in its cases, and not too many of them. Some abuse cases may need to be refined or abstracted to achieve uniform granularity.

4. *Check completeness and minimality.* Each abuse case description should be checked to see if it describes an interaction that results in harm to a user or stakeholder in the system. We should also check to see if a critical abuse case may have been omitted. An abuse case in the model may lack an abuse based on the minimal privilege needed to accomplish the harm. Requirements documents and the use case model should be reviewed, along with descriptions of anticipated security features. Users and customers should be consulted to be sure that no critical abuse has been overlooked.

5. An Abuse Case Model For An Internet-Based Information Security Lab

An example will help to make things clear. The following example shows how we would construct an abuse case model, at the essential use case level of abstraction, for our Internet-based information security lab. We present a simplified model that is based on the actual model we developed to construct a security model and policy for our Internet-based information security laboratory.

Figure 3 shows the abuse case diagram for the lab. Our model has three actors and eight abuse cases. The first thing to notice is that we have two abuse cases that are distinguished primarily by the capabilities of the actor that interacts with our lab: *Browse Exercise with Warez* and *Browse Exercise with Scalpel*. By "warez" we mean packages and tools that allow a user to mount attacks on a system from a GUI, without knowledge of the principles involved in carrying out the attack. By "scalpel" we mean a well-engineered attack designed specifically to penetrate our system. This kind of modeling can be helpful in identifying the level of security needed by users or customers.

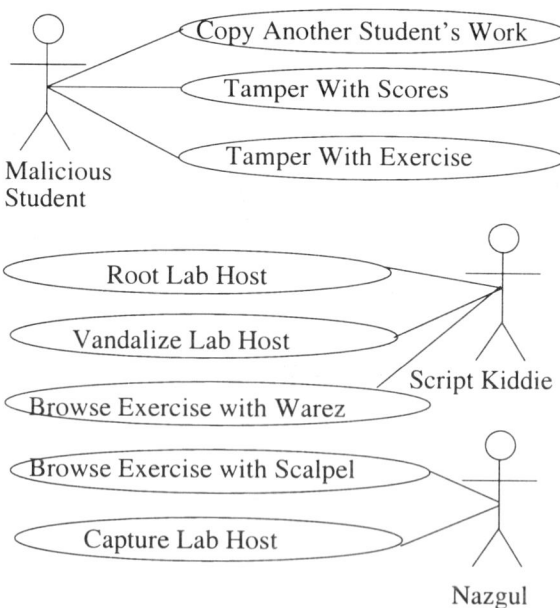

Figure 3. Abuse Case Diagram for an Internet-Based Information Security Laboratory

5.1 Actor Descriptions

Here are the actor descriptions for two of the actors in our abuse case model for the Internet-based information security lab. These two actors represent different classes of outsiders that, for whatever reason, we believe might attempt to abuse our system. The actual human who might assume the role of a Nazgul in attacking our system may also interact with it in the role of Script Kiddie, in order to probe for weaknesses. In this case, we are stating that such a person would apply no more resources, skills or time than any other attacker in the Script Kiddie role.

Script Kiddie

Resources

The Script Kiddie operates alone, although he or she may exchange some information with fellow Script Kiddies. The Script Kiddie has hardware, software, and Internet access that might be available to an individual through purchase with personal funds or by theft from an employer. Our model assumes that the Script Kiddie is willing to spend about 24 hours trying to defeat the security of a particular system.

Skills

Script Kiddies have limited technical skills. The majority of their activities are carried out using tools and techniques devised by other people.

Objectives

Script Kiddies may have a variety of criminal objectives including vandalism and theft. They also are interested in demonstrating their technical prowess.

Nazgul

Resources

Nazguls operate on behalf of groups that have budgets set aside to accomplish some form of harm. They may have technical assistance from an organization that is tasked with supporting them. They have hardware, software, tools, and Internet access provided by a business, a government, or a quasi-government. They have significant access to documentation of the systems they intend to abuse and may be able to test or simulate an intended exploit on a copy of the target system. We assume that Nazguls may spend up to 90 days in preparation and execution of an attempt to breach the security of the system.

Skills

Nazguls have superior technical skills. They can design operating systems, network protocols, computer hardware, and cryptographic algorithms. They apply software engineering technology, mathematics, computer engineering, and similar disciplines to their exploits.

Objectives

Nazguls are primarily interested in accomplishing the objective of the organization that supports them. They also seek to increase their own skills and knowledge, but not to demonstrate them to anyone. Organizations that support Nazguls do so to carry out espionage, warfare, terrorism or similar harmful activities.

5.2 An Abuse Case Description: Browse Server Exercise With Warez

Our abuse case description is intentionally very abstract, corresponding to an essential use case. We don't have the space to present a more detailed abuse case and we also want to show what an initial abuse case might look like. We would use this kind of abuse case description early in the requirements phase of a project. For example, we intend to incorporate both Windows NT and Linux based hosts in our lab and the abuse cases are meant to apply to either kind of host. However, in the requirements analysis, it is not significant whether the abuse occurs via Windows NT or Linux. Later, in design or testing, the specific features of NT or Linux would be significant.

Notice that our description does not include the logical case where the actor (Script Kiddie) fails to gain access to the exercise materials. Since this case involves no harm, we omit it.

We have included part of a tree diagram (Figure 4) depicting the various ways that the abuse case may be accomplished. The meaning of the tree diagram is intentionally vague, to avoid complexity that is of little benefit to users. We read the diagram like a decision tree, with each path from root to leaf defining an abstract abuse case transaction that could occur. For example, Figure 4 does not show all paths of the tree corresponding to the *Browse Server Exercises With Warez* abuse case, but it does depict the complete path for an abuse that exploits vulnerabilities in the file manager of a target host, to browse the documentation for an exercise.

Browse Server Exercises With Warez

Harm: The users of the lab will be legally, ethically, and morally responsible for increasing the abilities of the Script Kiddie. The users may also be responsible for allowing information about previously unknown exploits to be released.

Privilege Range: The Script Kiddie might carry out this abuse using privileges in the following range:

1. Installation of modified system utilities with root/administrator privileges on a source or target host
2. One-time control of a root/administrator account on a source or target host
3. One-time control of a root/administrator session on a source or target host
4. Installation of modified utilities with user privileges on a source or target host
5. One-time control of a single instructor session on a server host
6. One-time control of a single student session on a server host

Abusive Interaction: Using the TCP/IP protocol suite and a hypothetical attack tool called Warez 1, the Script Kiddie requests or attempts to initiate a session on some lab host. The initial session could be on a target host, a source host, or a server host. The lab host establishes the session with the Warez 1 tool. If the initial session has sufficient privilege, then the Script Kiddie will request either a file manager, a debugger, a programming editor, or a command shell to browse exercise documentation and example exercise implementations stored on a lab server. If the initial session has sufficient privileges or there is a flaw in the system software of the host, then the lab host permits browsing of the exercises on the server host. If the initial session does not have sufficient privileges to browse exercises stored on a server, then the Script Kiddie uses additional tools Warez 2 through Warez N to request an increase in privilege. The lab machine, source, target, or server, may or may not grant an increase in privilege. If the Script Kiddie cannot obtain an increase in privilege from the system software, then the Script Kiddie requests copies of the exercise materials directly, via the available file manager, debugger, editor, or command shell of the host. One or more of these applications permit (via a flaw) browsing of exercise documentation or exercise implementations stored on a lab server.

If any of the exercise materials could serve as additional warez to the Script Kiddie, then the Script Kiddie saves or downloads them.

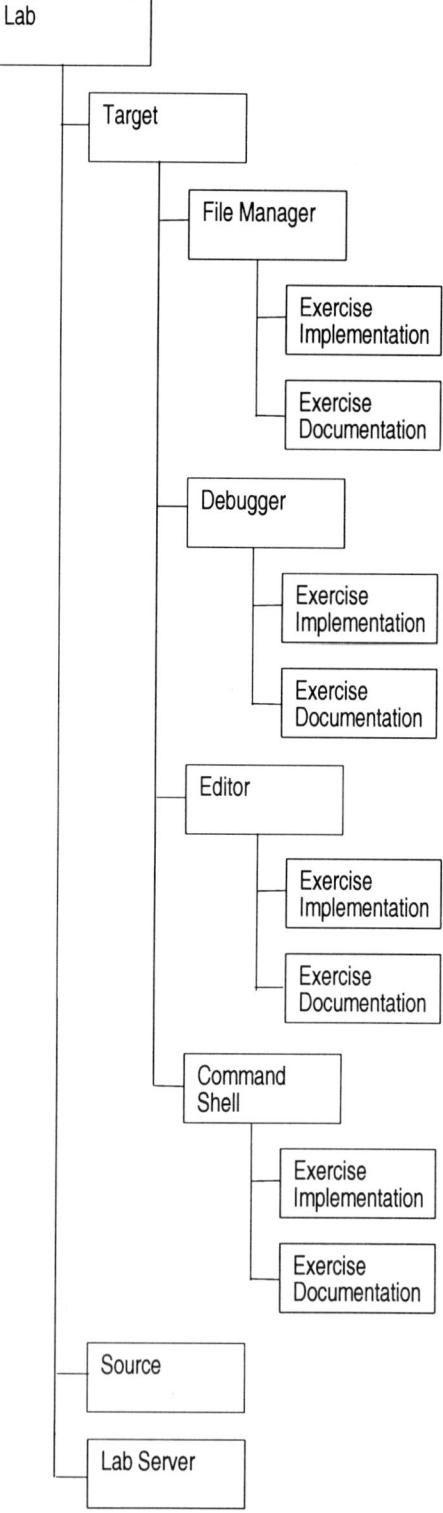

Figure 4. Tree Diagram for Abuse Case: Browse Server Exercise With Warez

The applicable abuse cases can been identified and defined in a level of detail like our example, with the help of the users and customers. Later, each abuse case can be refined and described more rigorously, as needed. One must be careful not to expend too much effort on rigorous descriptions of abuse cases early in the project. Changes in requirements or system architecture may overtake some of them and they will disappear.

6. Applications Of Abuse Case Modeling

Abuse case models can be helpful during the requirements, design, and testing phases of a security engineering process.

In a requirements phase, abuse case models can be used to increase both user and customer understanding of the security features of a proposed product. They can be made simple and abstract enough to be understood by users from a wide range of application domains. They can be used to show customers what will be prevented and what will not, in terms of their application domain. For this same reason, abuse case models are also useful for security requirements elicitation. Users can decide, in terms of their own application domain, which threats apply and which threats should be countered by product security features. Many fine security models have been developed that model various kinds of protection, in mathematically sound ways. Use of these models is essential for any product that aims at complete security. However, these models are subtle and very abstract. It can be difficult for users or customers to apply them in their own domain. Practitioners who use and translate these security models may expend a great deal of time transforming a policy to the user's domain, only to find that the policy is not what the users intended. Abuse cases may help security practitioners and users save time in arriving at a good understanding of security requirements.

During the design and testing phases of a security engineering process, we can apply abuse cases through a *refutation process*. As we analyze and design the system, we refute each use case to the appropriate level of assurance. This is one reason for describing the actors in greater detail in an abuse case. Our refutation may depend on the skills, resources, or objectives of the actor. For example, we may argue that 40-bit cryptographic keys are sufficient to refute an abuse case involving a Script Kiddie actor, because of their specified resource limitations, but not against a Nazgul. In other instances, our refutation may be based on the properties of a design feature. The strength of the refutation can be used to characterize the assurance we have. A refutation arrived at during an informal code walk through is not as strong as a refutation based on formal methods. Abuse cases can be ranked or weighted according to the assurance that should be applied to them. The assurance budget for a project can then be allocated by abuse case, according to the ranking.

During testing, we can design our security function tests to refute abuse cases. For example, we can apply the abuse case directly as a family of test cases. We form a test team that has the same skills and resources as the actors associated with the abuse case and let them exercise our system features. We can also combine testing with other refutation arguments. We may argue that neither an editor nor a debugger can browse exercises, if the current session lacks the necessary security permissions. We can then use testing to show that all exercises are configured with the security attributes needed to prevent browsing and that all passwords are sufficiently strong. We can also rank abuse cases in order to allocate testing resources.

Abuse cases can also be used to make design trade-offs. Since both use cases and abuse cases are readily understood by users and customers, they can be used to explain security-related design trade-offs. Customers will be better informed when choosing between modified functionality in a use case and the residual risk in an unrefuted abuse case.

7. Conclusions

By borrowing the concepts and notation of a proven modeling technique, we can model significant forms of abuse that we wish to prevent. An abuse case model is easily understood not only by users and customers, but also by the many developers who understand either use case models or UML. This is a significant benefit since many developers who work on the security features of software do not understand mathematical security models. Abuse cases are also more easily understood by other project engineering personnel who are not familiar with mathematical security models.

Abuse cases are much simpler than mathematical security models but they can be an effective tool for capturing security requirements. They are particularly useful in communicating with users and customers during requirements analysis and may be easier to understand when trade-offs must be made between security and functionality.

Abuse case models are not a substitute for mathematical security models. We intentionally make abuse case models ambiguous and incomplete and do not worry about their soundness. Abuse case models do not replace any other part of a sound security engineering process. The same qualities that make them powerful in security requirements analysis render them unfit as tools for high assurance. On the other hand, we have found them to be very useful as a complementary tool, when used during the requirements, design, and testing phases of a project.

References

1. COMMON CRITERIA IMPLEMENTATION BOARD, *Common Criteria for Information Technology Security Evaluation, version 2.0.* May 1998, Common Criteria Project Sponsoring Organisations.

2. CUSUMANO, M. and SELBY, R. How Microsoft builds software. *CACM*, 40, 6, June 1997, pp. 53-61.

3. LARMAN, C. *Applying UML and Patterns: An Introduction to Object-Oriented Analysis and Design*, Prentice-Hall, 1998.

4. RATIONAL CORPORATION, *Rational Rose*, http://www.rational.com.

5. RUMBAUGH, J., JACOBSON I., and BOOCH, G. *The Unified Modeling Language Reference Manual.* Addison Wesley, 1999.

6. SANDHU, R. and MUNAWER, Q. The RRA97 model for role-base administration of role hierarchies, *Proceedings of the 14th Annual Computer Security Applications Conference*, December 1998, Phoenix, Arizona, pp. 39-49.

7. SCHNEIER, B. and MUDGE. Cryptanalysis of Microsoft's Point-to-Point Tunneling Protocol (PPTP), *Proceedings of the 5th ACM Conference on Computer and Communications Security.* November 1998, San Francisco, California, pp. 132-141.

8. THOMSEN, D., O'BRIEN, D. and BOGLE, J. Role based access control framework for network enterprises, *Proceedings of the 14th Annual Computer Security Applications Conference.* December 1998, Phoenix, Arizona, pp. 50-58.

9. TOLKIEN, J. *Lord of the Rings.* Houghton Mifflin, 1974.

Track A

Networks

Chair

Christoph Schuba, SUN Microsystems Laboratories, USA

A Parallel Packet Screen for High Speed Networks

Carsten Benecke
DFN-FWL
Universität Hamburg
Vogt-Kölln-Str. 30
22527 Hamburg
benecke@fwl.dfn.de

Abstract

This paper demonstrates why security issues related to the continually increasing bandwidth of High Speed Networks (HSN) cannot be addressed with conventional firewall mechanisms. A single packet screen running on a fast computer is not capable of filtering all packets traversing a Fast/Gigabit Ethernet. This problem can be addressed by using parallel processing methods to implement a fast, scalable packet screen for Ethernets. The paper shows how hardware may be utilized to distribute the network load among such parallel packet screens. Empirical results using 'off–the–shelf' equipment indicate that this approach is usable.

1. Introduction

Firewalls are a widely employed mechanism for protecting networks from unauthorized access. They implement access control and audit functions at the interface between two or more networks with different security levels, thus enforcing a security policy.

Packet screens are simple building blocks for firewalls which allow packet based access control by checking the packet headers against filter rules. Access to hosts, networks, or services is usually controlled using a set of rules based on IP addresses, UDP/TCP ports, TCP flags, and network interfaces. Rules often include a component indicating which action is to be taken, should a packet be in contravention of the aforementioned rules. Based on this check, a packet may be either discarded, forwarded, or redirected [1].

The 'typical' topology of two networks connected via a packet screen is investigated in section 2. Performance measurements of typical activity show that a single workstation is not able to process the full traffic bandwidth in a high speed network (HSN), such as Fast Ethernet or ATM. The packet filter is therefore more than likely to represent a bottleneck to traffic in fast scaling networks with increasing bandwidth.

Section 3 presents parallel processing as a way to improve the overall throughput of a packet screen. Network equipment (e.g., hubs and switches) is used to distribute the load over the parallel devices. A simple algorithm allowing the packet filtering load to be shared among a number of parallel devices is introduced in section 4. Measurements of the prototype implementation show a significant increase in filtering performance. Some performance results are discussed in section 5. Moreover, the prototype can be adapted to full duplex Fast Ethernet networks (see section 6). Section 7 provides information regarding the reliability of the parallel packet screen.

Section 8 concludes with a discussion of open issues and ongoing improvements.

2. Firewall Topology

Figure 1 shows a simple setup of two IP networks separated by a single packet screen. All packets sent from one network to the other must pass through the packet screen. This applies the preconfigured filter rules when processing the packets. All filter rules are usually applied to the packets sequentially (in exactly the same order as they were configured). The load on the packet screen therefore not only depends on the number of packets arriving, but also on the number and order of the configured filter rules associated with each network interface.

In a high speed environment (Fast Ethernet, Gigabit Ethernet, or ATM) the single packet screen becomes a bottleneck for the communication between the individual separate networks [4]. Whereas, with typical packet sizes of 200–500 bytes, the throughput of the packet screen represents the limiting factor, for large packet sizes a single packet

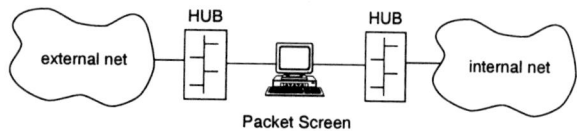

Figure 1. Packet Screen

screen may operate at wire speed. Applications often do not fully utilize the facilities available, 'preferring' to send smaller packets than the underlying transport mechanism can convey. Figure 2 shows the performance breakdown at the choke point of a single packet screen. The packet screen connects two 100 Mbit/s Fast Ethernet networks.

The number of packets sent and received is shown for a unidirectional UDP stream. The plots summarize the packet throughput of a direct connection through a single packet screen. The freely available tool `ip-filter`[1], modified to remove its caching mechanism to remember the action (drop or forward) associated with the previously filtered packet, provides the filter functionality. In disabling the caching, the worst case scenario is simulated: arbitrary network traffic where no two consecutive packets have equal attributes which would allow a cached decision to be of use.

The source and destination (Sun Ultra II workstations) are able to send and receive (`snd = rcv H2H`) a maximum of 34676 packets (message size of 16 byte) per second if there were no packet screens between them while the packet screen (a Sun Ultra I) limits the throughput to 12635 packets (`rcv, 0 FR`), i.e. 36%. This situation is exacerbated by increasing the number of filter rules to be applied to each packet. A humble ten filter rules (FR) reduce the throughput to 31% (`rcv, 10 FR`), a much more realistic hundred filter rules (`rcv, 100 FR`) reduces the total throughput to 3333 packets/s. This is less than 10% of the original capacity available to the source and destination hosts when communicating directly. In real environments, a caching mechanism (see above) will, to some degree, compensate for the reduced performance due to a large number of filter rules. It is therefore important to increase the filter system's underlying capacity to forward (i.e. process) packets in order to compensate for the bottlenecks described.

3. Parallel Packet Processing

The prementioned discussion shows there is a need for fast packet screens tailored to HSN. Employing faster processors for packet screening does not scale satisfactorily. Every 'single universal-processor' based approach will, eventually, become a bottleneck for a fast scaling high speed network. On the other hand it is doubtful if a special hard-

---

[1]available at `http://coombs.anu.edu.au/ipfilter/`

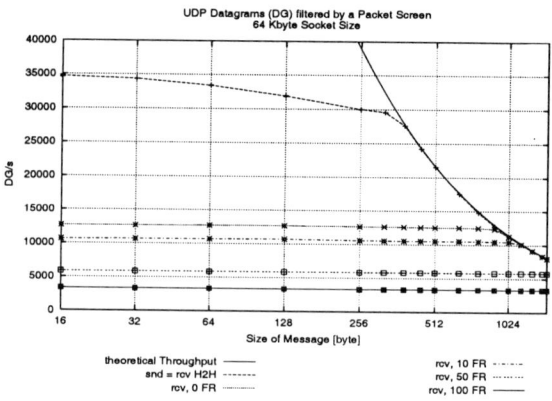

Figure 2. Performance of a Packet Screen

ware solution (e.g., a 'Packet Screen ASIC', [9]) is flexible enough to meet future security requirements[2]. This paper recommends a much more flexible and scalable approach to increasing the total filtered packet throughput: parallel processing. This section shows how 'off–the–shelf' components, such as the workstations used for the tests described, may successfully be employed in parallel packet processing (see section 3.1).

Two important problems are addressed. First, the packet stream must be distributed among the parallel packet screens. This process must be very efficient in order to avoid creating a new bottleneck. Second, the problem of how to distribute the load among the processors involved (workstations) constituting the parallel packet screen is to be solved. Section 3.3 discusses several alternatives of an algorithm which provides this functionality.

3.1. Packet Parallelism

There are many methods of distributing the load among a number of processors[3] [8]. Two basic approaches can be taken, in order to speed up processing. First, the protocol stack of the workstation can be parallelized [10] and, second, incoming packets can be processed simultaneously [5]. The latter approach is often called as *packet parallelism* and fits well to the construction of the parallel packet screens described herein:

- All packets can be processed independently because the sequence of arriving packets needs not be preserved, as IP may deliver them in any order. Furthermore, there is no need to store information pertaining

---

[2]The adaption to new security flaws is very expensive if special purpose hardware is employed. On the other hand, software filters are easy to upgrade.

[3]The term *processor* and *workstation* are used interchangeably. As single processor workstations are employed in the tests, parallel processing requires at least two processors/workstations.

to the packet's connection context unless 'dynamic filter rule' or 'context sensitive packet screen' technologies are required. In this case the inter-packet dependencies are likely to impose constraints on the process of packet distribution among the processors. Should dynamic filter rules be employed the processors may be required to exchange status information.

- Only small changes to the code of existing packet screen software are necessary. As all workstations make use of the same code[4], the only additional function needed is an algorithm to balance the packet load among the parallel workstations (see section 3.3).

- A very fine granularity of activity can be achieved, simply because each component in the parallel packet screen can process packets from any connection. Even the throughput of one single TCP-connection can be increased, since packets can be distributed among the processors.

3.2. Packet Distribution

The system shown in figure 1 can be extended to include more than one workstation for screening. An example utilizing three workstations which process arriving packets in parallel is shown in figure 3. The Ethernet hubs shown are required to propagate incoming packets to the workstations. Hubs (multi-port repeaters) usually forward all incoming packets from all interfaces (ports) to all other interfaces. This means that distribution (forwarding) of the incoming packets to the workstations is completely transparent. Since all packets are forwarded to every port on the hub, there is no need to explicitly address the packet screen components. This is a useful feature, as it means that the packet screen can, to a large extent, be hidden (if so desired). One advantage of this feature is that an 'invisible' packet screen is more difficult to attack.

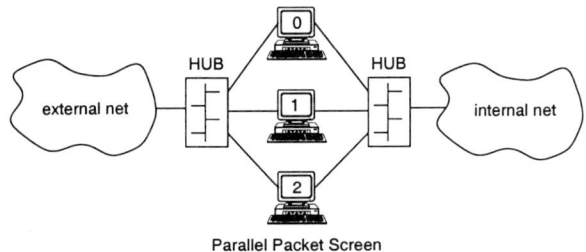

Figure 3. Parallel Packet Screen

---

[4]This is usually a kind of filter software which is compiled into the kernel or loaded at run time in the form of a 'loadable module'.

3.3. Distributed Packet Selection

The employment of hubs as shown allows the packets to be distributed to all attached packet screen components. In order to increase the packet throughput, the packet load should be shared by all processors. To this end, the packets to be processed are selected by each processor, all others are discarded.

The packet selection algorithm[5] must fulfill a number of requirements:

1. The algorithm should not be centralized. Should a single entity be responsible for selecting and forwarding the packets, it may become a bottleneck for total system throughput. A distributed algorithm can, on the other hand, increase total system reliability, as no single point exists which can lower system performance (or indeed bring it to a standstill).

2. The algorithm should be independent of the number of processors. It should allow the system to be scaled so that the number of processors may be increased in order to adapt the packet screen to faster networks or more complex screening operations.

3. The algorithm should be fast. The additional overhead due to packet selection should be minimized: the selection time (T_d) should be very short in comparison with the screening time (T_t):
$\bigvee$ packets : $T_d \ll T_t$

4. The algorithm should map each incoming packet to exactly one processor, each packet will therefore be processed only once. This behavior is required, firstly for efficiency, and, secondly, in order not to forward duplicate packets or to drop packets in the selection process.

5. The algorithm should evenly distribute the packets among the processors. All processors experience the same level of utilization.

Hash-Function for Packet Selection
A hash-function usually provides a fast scalable technique to map input symbols onto a chosen range of values. A very simple, fast hash function (requirement 3) can therefore be used to map the incoming IP packets onto their respective processors. In order to select a single processor for each packet (requirement 4), the hash function must map input symbols onto a range of processor identifications (see below).

The input symbols of the hash function must be present in the packets arriving for selection. Each packet screen can

---

[5]The selection algorithm is not responsible for filtering/screening.

thus apply the algorithm to the packets in order to match requirement (1). The packets contain a variety of information which can be used for the hash calculation:

IP address The major drawback of using the datagram source and/or destination address in the hash calculation is that all packets with the same address (either sender or recipient) are mapped onto the same workstation/processor. Should there be only one high bandwidth connection, the mapping would cause a system bottleneck. On the other hand, some 'stateful packet screens' could require all datagrams from a host be processed by a single processor in order for context sensitive screening to be possible. In this case, the parallelism could be increased by including port numbers in the hash calculation.

IP identification This value is required to be unique for each unique datagram and is usually incremented as each datagram is sent by the IP host. The value is a good choice for distributing the datagrams among parallel facilities: even the packets of a single connection can be processed in parallel.

IP header checksum All IP hosts calculate a checksum for the complete IP header information (for calculation the checksum field itself is assumed to be zero).

The major drawback of all the IP header values discussed above is that the values cannot be used for non-IP-packets (e.g., ARP packets or packets of other protocol suites). Therefore the following values may also be used:

Frame checksum If information about the underlying network layer (layer two) protocol is available, values contained within its structure can be used. Should the underlying network be, for example, Fast Ethernet, the frame checksum can be employed in the hash calculation. Indeed the use of the frame checksum is applicable to all protocol suites being of practical relevance. Moreover, similar units can be selected for other frame types (e.g. the 'Frame Check Sequence' of an FDDI frame).

Combinations It is also possible to use a combination of the values discussed above. Indeed, in some cases it may even be necessary to combine IP addresses with port numbers.

As the objective of the hash process is to obtain an even distribution of packet processing among the packet screen components, increasing the number of input symbols (hash calculation values) may produce a more even distribution.

Algorithm for Packet Selection
Packet selection may be summarized as follows:

1. All parallel processors (packet screen with n processors) are enumerated from $0, \cdots, n-1$ to identify the processors.

2. Hubs propagate the incoming packets to all processors.

3. All processors perform the hashing based on a predefined set of packet information[6] in order to map each incoming packet to a number within the range of $0, \cdots, n-1$.

4. The processor whose ID matches the mapping of the hash function is responsible for screening the packet.

5. All other processors (which IDs do not match the hash result) discard the packet.

4. Prototype Implementation

This section discusses a prototype implementation based on the public domain software `ip-filter`, which is available for most UNIX systems.

A first approach is to use the IP-packet checksum modulo number of processors to select which packet screen component should process the packet. Further research may be required to find more appropriate hash functions for packet selection.

For best performance, we have implemented the packet selection algorithm within the Fast Ethernet device driver. Of course it is also possible to implement the algorithm as part of the filter functions, but changing the device driver permits to discard non-selected packets as fast as possible (e.g., before sending them upstream to the ip-filter module).

Next to IP packets, there are two other packet types in the TCP/IP protocol suite[7] which are transported in Ethernet frames. These are 'Address Resolution Protocol' (ARP) and 'Reverse Address Resolution Protocol' (RARP) packets [6]. As the mainstream IP packet selection should not be disrupted, a value which starts at the same frame offset as the IP checksum in Ethernet frames, is used to distribute ARP and RARP packets. At this offset a frame contains the third and fourth bytes of the (R)ARP packet's Ethernet sender address.

5. Performance of the Parallel Packet Screen

This section discusses both the empirical as well as the analytical results for the packet throughput and the gainable

---

[6]The prototype uses the checksum of the IP-packet modulo the total number of processors as a hash function (see section 4).

[7]Only the TCP/IP protocol suite is discussed: other suites require additional / other checks.

speedup due to parallel processing. All plots (figures 2 and 4) show confidence intervals for a 99% confidence level.

5.1. Empirical Results

Figure 4 shows the performance of parallel packet screens with two to four processors. Sender, receiver, and packet screen are connected to a Fast Ethernet at 100 Mbit/s. The snd plot shows the unidirectional load of packets dispatched from the sender in datagrams/s. The rcv plots show the number of packets received at the destination after passing through a (parallel) packet screen with WS processors (workstations). A single packet screen is able to forward about 12700 packets/s, which still suffices to reach the maximum possible packet throughput of a Fast Ethernet for packet sizes larger than 896 bytes.

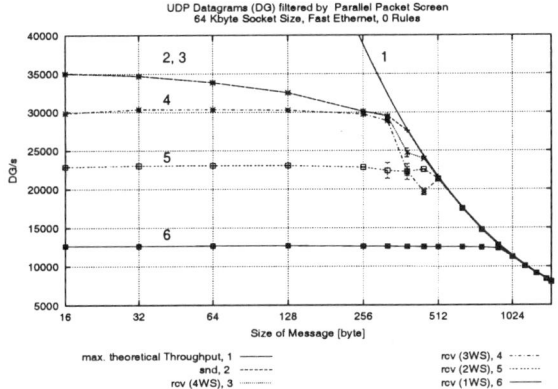

Figure 4. Performance of Parallel Packet Screen based on Fast Ethernet Hubs

A two WS packet screen is capable of processing about 22000 packets/s. As can be seen in figure 4, this throughput is sufficient to convey the full workload of a Fast Ethernet for packet sizes larger than 512 bytes. Three WS are able to forward about 30000 packets/s and four WS seem to be able to cope with the load offered for almost all packet sizes[8].

The small message sizes (16 to 256) almost have no influence on the throughput. The increase in packet throughput gained by parallel processing for small message sizes is listed in table 1. The value of 2.95 for a 4WS is calculated from figure 6 since at least two simultaneous senders were required to offer an adequate load.

---

[8]The snd plot and the rcv (4WS) plot overlap in almost all points. The lower throughput for messages with 384 bytes is reproducible but not yet analyzed.

Processors	Speedup
1	1
2	1.82
3	2.3989
4	2.9557 (see figure 6)

Table 1: Speedup of Parallel Packet Screen

On the one hand, the increase in processing capability is not linear, as all workstations must perform selection tasks on all arriving packets. This is the limiting factor for high parallel setups (see analysis below). On the other hand, the increase is adequate so that the load presented by fast 'state of the art' workstations can be coped with.

5.2. Analytical Results

In order to predict the gainable speedup due to parallel processing it is necessary to make some assumptions. First of all, it is assumed that the algorithm discussed in section 3.3 will result in an evenly distributed packet load among all n processors. This is true for the lab setup but may not be true in some special environments. Second, all the processors are of the same kind. Once again this is true for the lab setup but in real world environments different kinds of machines may be used for parallel processing. These two assumptions result in a balanced load among all processors, e.i., the observable utilization of all processors is the same.

Making these assumptions there is a probability of $P_I = 1/n$ that any of the n parallel processors (I) select an incoming packet, and a probability of $\overline{P_I} = 1 - 1/n$ that a processor will discard an arbitrary packet. This in turn implies that for every filtered packet (service time B_{fil}) an average of n selection operations (service time B_{sel}) is necessary.

Thus the maximum packet throughput of a *single processor* ($Pmax_I$) with respect to n parallel instances is:

$$Pmax_I(n) * n * B_{sel} + Pmax_I(n) * B_{fil} = U = 1$$
$$Pmax_I(n) = \frac{1}{nB_{sel} + B_{fil}} \quad (1)$$

U denotes the utilization of the processor. The overall packet throughput of *all n processors* is therefore:

$$Pmax_n(n) = Pmax_I(n) * n = \frac{n}{nB_{sel} + B_{fil}} \quad (2)$$

Finally the gainable speedup ($G(n)$) is denoted by

$$G(n) = \frac{Pmax_n(n)}{Pmax_I(1)} = \frac{n(B_{sel} + B_{fil})}{nB_{sel} + B_{fil}} \quad (3)$$

$$G(n) = \frac{B_{sel} + B_{fil}}{B_{sel} + (1/n)B_{fil}}$$

with an upper limit (theoretical max. speedup) of

$$\lim_{n \to \infty} G(n) = \frac{B_{sel} + B_{fil}}{B_{sel}} \quad (4)$$

Based on the empirical results from section 5.1 B_{sel} and B_{fil} are calculated for packets with 32 bytes[9] message size (user data) and a total number of zero filter rules[10]:

$$\begin{aligned} B_{sel} &\approx 9,29420E^{-6}\frac{s}{P} \\ B_{fil} &\approx 6,96224E^{-5}\frac{s}{P} \end{aligned} \quad (5)$$

By using these values in equation 3 the theoretical speedup with respect to n is calculated in table 2:

Processors	Speedup
*1	1
2	1,7893
3	2,4281
*4	2,9557
5	3,3988
6	3,7763

Table 2: Theoretical Speedup

The values for one and four processors (marked with a *) have been used to calibrate equation 3. Thus the calculated speedup matches the empirical value of table 1. The values for two and three processors can be used to verify the analytical results. Notice that the difference between empirical and calculated speedup is less than 2% for two and three processors.

So the calculated speedup is comparable to the empirical results (see table 1). Thus equation 3 can be used to predict the gainable speedup for more than four processors. E.g., it is possible to increase the throughput to 378% by using 6 instances which is sufficient to catch up with the theoretical throughput of a Fast Ethernet (100 Mbit/s) for packet sizes larger than 200 byte of user data as there is almost no dependence on the packet size.

Equation 4 provides a value of $\approx 8,49$ as the maximum speedup for this setup. On the other hand it is quite obvious

[9]This is an example. Other message sizes could have been used as well.
[10]packet forwarding only, no screening, unit of measurement is seconds/packet

that parallel processing works even better for setups with $B_{sel} \ll B_{fil}$, e.g. by increasing the number of filter rules.

As a rule of thumb: the more filter rules the better the speedup due to parallel processing.

6. Switched based Approach

The major drawback of the solution presented above, is that of the half duplex mode of the hubs employed. Hubs implement a shared segment and all connected workstations compete with each other for the available bandwidth. In conditions of heavy network load, this means that the number of collisions on the Ethernet will increase dramatically. Figure 5 shows the performance degradation originating from collisions in two networks where a sender in each network sends datagrams to a recipient in the other network via a four WS packet screen. The senders and recipients are all distinct machines and both datagram streams are sent simultaneously. The plots show the sums of individual throughputs for both senders and recipients. Even though the packet screen is able to filter about 37500 packets/s, many packets (medium to large sizes) are lost due to the massive collision rate at the hubs. For packet sizes of 256 to 576 there is a dramatic throughput decrease which is bigger than expected. Even though increasing the size of the packets eases the situation somewhat, the effect of collisions is still visible. The number of packets received never equals the number sent.

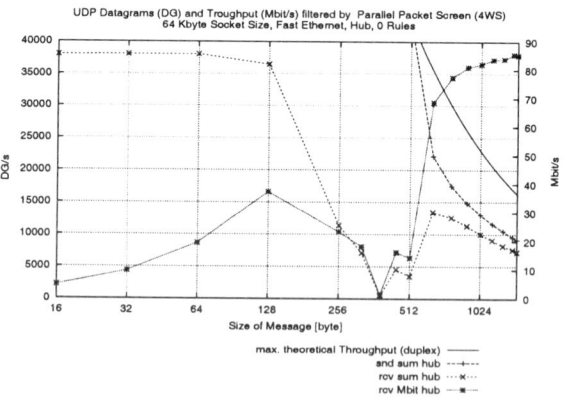

Figure 5. Bidirectional Packet Load and Effects of Collisions

In addition, most modern networks are moving from shared to switched media. If two fully switched fast Ethernet's are joined by a parallel packet screen based on hubs, the total bandwidth of 200 Mbit/s (full duplex) is reduced to at most 100 Mbit/s.

This section describes an extension to the parallel packet

screen approach allowing the use of switches to effect packet distribution. As switches support full duplex mode, the packet screen can also be driven at full duplex mode. Switches usually forward datagrams from one interface to exactly one other interface, a method is therefore needed which facilitates the forwarding of datagrams from one network to all workstations in the parallel packet screen.

The switch based approach suggested uses multicast addresses, whereby all workstations constituting the parallel packet screen are configured to receive packets for a special multicast address. Switch interfaces connected to one of the packet screen workstations are thus merged into a multicast group. The workstations are configured to reply to ARP queries for this multicast address. Furthermore, all workstations constituting the packet screen are configured with the same IP address.

A host from either network wanting to send datagrams to the other network looks up its configuration and receives the IP address of the packet screen which is the next hop address (router). The Ethernet address is received via an ARP query broadcast to any workstation attached to the switch. One of the packet screen workstations will select the packet as described above (section 3.3). Since the queried IP address is statically bound to the multicast Ethernet address, the packet screen will respond with this multicast address (see [6]). The host thus receives ('learns') the multicast address as the physical address of the next router.

Whenever the host sends datagrams containing the multicast address, the switch forwards the datagrams to all attached packet screen workstations, because they have been joined together to form a multicast group. This setup allows the use of the network (switches) to distribute the load while permitting it to be used in full duplex mode.

Figure 6 shows the performance of the switched based approach. The maximum packet throughput (about 37500 packets/s) stays the same since the filtering devices have not changed. Since no collisions occur the throughput stays almost constant until the number of packets received equals the number of packets sent (sizes ≥ 640 bytes). The maximum throughput is reached for 1472 byte messages at 189 Mbit/s.

The results demonstrate that the parallel packet screen approach is well suited to the switched network architecture.

7. Reliability

As shown it is possible to increase the packet throughput of a packet screen by parallel processing. On the other hand the failure probability also increases unless additional mechanisms are deployed. As a very simple failure model, it is assumed that a processor either works well or is subject to a "crash" failure [2], e.g., the workstation goes offline

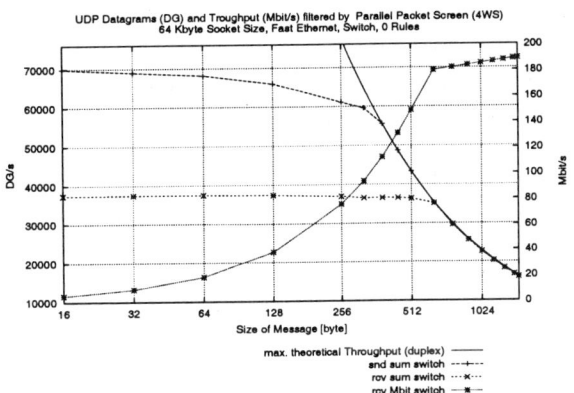

Figure 6. Bidirectional Packet Load, Switched based Approach

and is no longer able to process any packets.

This model is known as a "n of n system" where all of the n components (processors) must be alive. If one of the n processors fails, approximately every nth packet is discarded (see section 5.2). This results in a systematic packet loss.

Usually X_i indicates whether a component i of a system S is defect or intact:

$$X_i(t) = \begin{cases} 0, & \text{if component } i \text{ is intact at time } t \\ 1, & \text{if component } i \text{ is defect at time } t \end{cases} \quad (6)$$

If there is for example a probability of survival of 85% for a single processor packet screen after a certain time $t > t_0$, that is ($P(X(t) = 0) = 85\%$), then the probability of survival of a parallel packet screen that is composed of n equal components is [7]:

$$\begin{aligned} A_{nofn}(t) &= \prod_{i=1}^{n} P(X_i(t) = 0) \\ A_{nofn}(t) &= (P(X_i(t) = 0))^n \end{aligned} \quad (7)$$

If we deploy four processors the probability of survival after the same time t decreases from 85% to $0.85^4 \approx 52\%$!

As a rule of thumb: the more parallel processors the lower the survival probability. Thus the more parallel processors the shorter the time to repair.

After a crash a systematic packet loss occurs. As about every nth packet is lost the packet throughput after a crash (P_{crash}) decreases to:

$$P_{crash}(n) = Pmax_n(n) - \frac{Pmax_n(n)}{n} = Pmax_n(n)(1-\frac{1}{n}) \quad (8)$$

This behavior is undesirable although higher level protocols such as TCP may be able to overcome this problem. Ongoing work focuses on a more general approach.

By sending periodic "heart beat" signals the processors can monitor each other. If a crash is detected by any of the other processors, the remaining workstations can reconfigure themselves to the new number of available processors. After a short reconfiguration systematic packet losses are no longer visible. Each of the n parallel processors acts as a functional/active redundancy for all other processors. By using this algorithm it is possible to increase the availability of the parallel packet screen.

Moreover, the performance is also increased by the reconfiguration. After the reconfiguration the throughput is reduced from $Pmax_n(n)$ to $Pmax_n(n-1)$. This is still a better value than $Pcrash(n)$:

$$Pmax_n(n-1) > Pcrash(n) \quad (9)$$
$$\frac{(n-1)}{(n-1)B_{sel} + B_{fil}} > \frac{n}{nB_{sel} + B_{fil}} - \frac{1}{nB_{sel} + B_{fil}}$$
$$\frac{n-1}{(n-1)B_{sel} + B_{fil}} > \frac{n-1}{nB_{sel} + B_{fil}}, n \geq 2$$

Equation 9 shows that reconfiguration is also important to increase the throughput after the crash of a processor. This result is independent of the number of processors (n). After repairing and reintegrating the crashed processor into the parallel setup another reconfiguration can restore the maximum packet throughput to $Pmax_n(n)$.

8. Conclusion

This paper discusses the need for a scalable high speed packet screen capable of filtering packets in high speed networks. Parallel processing is used to increase the throughput of the packet screen. The use of hubs and switches to distribute the load over a number of parallel filtering devices allows highly scalable parallel packet filter devices to be constructed using 'off–the–shelf' components.

Performance measurements show a significant improvement in packet processing performance, which allows secure high speed networks to be built. This technique should be combined with mechanisms to speed up proxies on bastion hosts in order to build more sophisticated high speed firewalls [4]. Moreover, ongoing work shows that the underlying algorithm (see section 3.3) is also applicable to speed up network monitors and encryption/decryption boxes for virtual private networks.

While performance can be improved using the parallel processing architecture, the method set out above does have a drawback: an associated increased failure probability. Measurements show that a fail-stop breakdown of one device significantly reduces the throughput of TCP connections. This behavior is due to the loss of data packets and acknowledgments: the distributed selection of packets is not self stabilizing. Ongoing work is directed towards group management protocols [3] for status exchange and fault detection (see section 7) with the objective of increasing both performance and availability by parallel processing.

References

[1] D. B. Chapman and E. D. Zwicky. *Building Internet Firewalls*. O'Reilly, 1995.
[2] F. Cristian. Understanding fault-tolerant distributed systems. *Communications of the ACM*, 34(2):56–78, February 1991.
[3] F. Cristian. Reaching Agreement on Processor Group Membership in Synchronous Distributed Systems. Research Report RJ 5964 (59426), IBM Research Division, 1998.
[4] U. Ellermann and C. Benecke. Firewalls for ATM Networks. In *Proceedings: INFOSEC'COM*, Paris, June 4./5. 1998.
[5] M. Goldberg, G. Neufeld, and M. Ito. *A Parallel Approach to OSI Connection-Oriented Protocols*, pages 219–232. North-Holland, 1993.
[6] D. C. Plummer. An Ethernet Address Resolution Protocol. Request For Comments 826, Network Working Group, 1982.
[7] W. G. Schneeweiss. *Grundbegriffe für praktische Zuverlässigkeitsanalysen*. Datakontext-Verlag, Köln, 1981.
[8] C. Woodside and G. Franks. Alternative Software Architectures for Parallel Protocol Execution with Synchronous IPC. *IEEE/ACM Transactions on Networking*, 1(2):178–186, April 1993.
[9] J. Xu and M. Singhal. Design of A High-Performance ATM-Firewall. In *Proceedings: 5th ACM Conference on Computer and Communications Security*, San Francisco, California, November 4–5 1998.
[10] M. Zitterbart. *Funktionsbezogene Parallelität in transportorientierten Kommunikationsprotokollen*. Number 183 in Fortschritt-Berichte, VDI Reihe 10. VDI-Verlag, 1991.

An Asynchronous Distributed Access Control Architecture for IP over ATM Networks[*]

Olivier PAUL Maryline LAURENT Sylvain GOMBAULT

ENST de Bretagne, RSM Department
2 rue de la châtaigneraie - BP 78 35512 CESSON Cedex - France
Email : {Olivier.Paul|Maryline.Laurent|Sylvain.Gombault}@enst-bretagne.fr

Abstract

In this article, we describe a new architecture providing the access control service in both ATM and IP-over-ATM networks. This architecture is based on agents distributed in network equipment. It is well known that distribution makes the management process more difficult. This issue is raised and we provide an algorithm to distribute the access control policy on our agents. The comparison with other approaches shows that this architecture provides big improvements in ATM-level access control, scalability and QoS preservation.
Keywords: *Access Control, Management, Security, ATM, Agents, IP-over-ATM.*

1. Introduction

In the recent past, much attention has been paid developing security services for ATM networks. This resulted in the creation of many working groups within (and outside) the standardization bodies. One of them is the security Working Group of the ATM Forum created in 1995, which released its version 1.0 specifications in February 1999. Confidentiality, authentication, integrity and some kind of access-control have been considered. Access control as defined by the ISO in [1] is a security service used to protect resources against unauthorized use.

The ATM technology has been specified to transport various kinds of flows and allows users to specify the QoS (Quality of Service) applying to these flows. Communications are connection oriented and a signalling protocol is used to set up, control and release connections. In this article we show that the classical approach supplying the access control service (commonly called firewall) is unable to preserve the QoS. We then describe a new access control architecture for ATM and IP-over-ATM networks which does not alter the negotiated QoS.

The next section analyses current solutions providing the access control service in the ATM and IP over ATM networks. Section 3 describes the way to provide the access control service through an asynchronous distributed architecture. As a conclusion we make a comparison between our solution and other proposed approaches and we show that our architecture is a good alternative to current solutions.

2. Proposed solutions

Several solutions have been proposed in order to provide some kind of access-control in ATM and IP over ATM networks. This section is divided into three parts. In the first part we consider the adaptation of the Internet «classical» firewall architecture to ATM networks. In the second part we describe the solution proposed by the ATM Forum. In the third part we describe various solutions proposed to improve the «classical» firewall solution. As a conclusion we make a comparison between all these solutions.

2.1. Classical solution

The first solution [12] is to use a classical firewall located between the internal and public networks in order to provide access-control at the packet, circuit and application levels. As such the ATM network is considered as a level 2 layer offering point to point connections. As a result access-control at the ATM level is not possible and end to end QoS is no longer guaranteed.

At the IP and circuit levels, IP packets are reassembled from the ATM cells. Access-control is supplied using the information embedded in the TCP, UDP and IP headers. Packets are filtered by comparing the fields in the headers such as the source and destination addresses, the source and destination ports, the direction and the TCP flags with a pattern of prohibited and allowed packets. Prohibited packets are destroyed whereas allowed packets are forwarded from one interface to the other. When the same QoS is negotiated on both sides of the firewall, the end to end QoS may be modified in the following ways:

---

[*] This work is funded by DRET.

- Reassembly, routing, filtering and deassembly operations increase the Cell Transit Delay.
- Internal operations done over IP packets may increase the Cell Loss Ratio.
- The time spent to reassemble and disassemble the packets is proportional to the packet sizes, which are variable. As a result, the Cell Transit Delay Variation may be different from the CTDV value negotiated on each side of the firewall.
- Routing and filtering actions operate at the software level. Thus the load of the system may cause variations in the Sustainable and Minimum Cell Rate.

Application procedures are then filtered at the application level by proxy applications in accordance with the security policy. Like with the IP or circuit level filters, the QoS is affected, but much more strongly, since the traffic has to reach the application level. Moreover since the filtering operations are provided in a multitasking environment, desynchronization between the flows can occur.

This kind of solution is reported to have performance problems in a high speed network environment ([4], [6]). The latest tests ([7]) show that this access control solution is unsuccessful at the OC-3 (155 Mb/s) speed.

2.2. The access control service as considered by the ATM Forum

The access-control service as defined in the ATM Forum security specifications ([13]) is based on the access-control service provided in the A and B orange book classified systems. In this approach one sensitivity level per object and one authorization level per subject are defined. These levels include a hierarchical level (e.g. public, secret, top secret, etc.) and a set of domains modelling the domains associated with the information (e.g. management, research, education, etc.). A subject may access an object if the level of the subject is greater than the level of the object and one of the domains associated with the subject includes one of the domains associated with the object.

In the ATM Forum specifications, the sensitivity and authorization levels are coded according to the NIST [5] specification as a label, which is associated with the data being transmitted. This label may be sent embedded into the signalling, or as user data prior to any user data exchanges. The access-control is operated by the network equipment which verifies that the sensitivity level of the data complies with the authorization level assigned to the links and interfaces over which the data are transmitted.

The main advantage of this solution is its scalability since the access control decision is made at the connection setup and does not interfere with the user data. However it suffers from the following drawbacks:

- The network equipment is assumed to manage sensitivity and authorization levels. This is not provided in current network equipment.
- A connection should be set up for each sensitivity level.
- The access-control service as considered in traditional firewalls (i.e. access-control to hosts, services) is voluntarily left outside the scope of the specification.

2.3 Specific solutions

The above limitations have been identified and many proposals have been made in order to supply the «traditional» access-control service in ATM networks. These solutions may be classified into two classes: industrial and academic solutions.

Industrial solutions

The first industrial solution (Cisco, Fore) uses a classical ATM switch that is modified to filter ATM connection set up requests based on the source and destination addresses. The problem with this approach is that the access-control is not powerful since the parameters are very limited.

The second one (Storagetek) is also based on an ATM switch. However this switch has been modified to supply access-control at the IP level. Instead of reassembling cells for packet headers examination like in traditional firewalls, this approach is expected to find IP and TCP/UDP information directly in the first ATM cell being transmitted over the connection. This approach prevents delays being introduced during cell switching. Storagetek has also developed a specific memory called CAM (Content Addressable Memory) designed to speed up the research in the access-control policy. This approach is the first one taking into account the limitations introduced by the classical firewall approach. However some problems have not yet been solved:

- Access-control is limited to the network and transport levels. ATM and application levels are not considered.
- IP packets including options are not filtered since options may shift the UDP/TCP information in the second cell. This causes a serious security flaw.
- The device is not easy to manage especially when dynamic connections are required, since connection filters have to be configured manually.
- Performances of the device are not very scalable. An OC-12 (622 Mb/s) version of this product was announced in 1996 but has not been yet exhibited.

Academic solutions

Both academic solutions being proposed are based on the above Storagetek architecture, but they introduce some improvements to cope with Storagetek problems.

The first approach [3] uses an FPGA specialized circuit associated with a modified switch architecture. At the ATM level, the access control at connection establishment time is improved by providing filtering capabilities based on the source and destination addresses. This approach also allows ATM level PNNI (Private Network to Network Interface) routing information to be filtered. At the IP and circuit levels the access-control service is similar to the one provided by the Storagetek product.

- This solution is interesting since it is the most complete solution being currently implemented. However it suffers from many limitations:
- Special IP packets (e.g. packets with optional fields in the header) are not processed.
- Only a small part of the information supplied by the signalling (i.e. source and destination addresses) is used.
- Access-control at the application level is not considered.

The second approach [16] is the most complete architecture being currently proposed. This solution provides many improvements in comparison with the Storagetek architecture. The most interesting idea is the classification of the traffic. The traffic is classified into four classes depending on the ATM connection QoS descriptors and on the processing allowed to be done over it. Class A provides a basic ATM access-control. ATM connections are filtered according to the information provided by the signalling (i.e. source and destination addresses). Class B provides traffic monitoring. The analysis of the traffic is made on a copy of the flow. When a packet is prohibited, the reply to this packet is blocked. Class C is associated with packet filtering. IP and transport packet headers are reassembled from the ATM cells and analysed. During this analysis the last cell belonging to the packet called LCH (Last Cell Hostage) is kept in memory by the switch. The analysis should be at least faster than the time spent by the whole packet crossing the switch. When the packet is allowed, the LCH is released, but when the packet is prohibited the LCH is modified so that a CRC error occurs and the packet is rejected. For class D, the access control processing is similar to that of the firewall proxy.

This classification expects the switch to separate traffic with QoS requirements from traffic without QoS requirements. As such the traffic with QoS requirements is allowed to cross the switch without being delayed. Table 1 gives the filtering operations depending on the level implementing the access control and the traffic QoS requirements.

Table 1. Use of the access control classes

Level/Application	With QoS requirements	Without QoS requirements
Application	No Access control	Class D
Transport	Class B	Class C
ATM	Class A	Class A

This approach is very interesting since it introduces many improvements (traffic classification, LCH) over all the other proposals. However some problems remain:

- Few parameters are used to supply the access control service at the ATM level.
- Access control is not provided at the application level for applications requiring QoS.
- Traffic monitoring only applies to connection oriented communications, and UDP packets cannot be filtered using this technique.
- This architecture is complex so that it is likely that scalability is not offered
- No implementation has been exhibited.

The problems most often met are the lack of scalability and the impact on QoS introduced by the access control service. As a consequence, it appears of interest to develop a scalable architecture that could provide the access control service while maintaining the negotiated QoS.

3. An agent based access control architecture

3.1. Introduction

The goal of our architecture is to provide a scalable access-control service without altering the QoS negotiated for a connection. We selected a distributed architecture approach in order to have more scalability than in a centralized approach. As stated in [14] a distributed architecture induces many advantages. These advantages are as follows:

- Better fault tolerance. If a device providing the access control service fails, this device is the only one affected. Other devices are able to continue to communicate.
- Security level improvement. For an intruder to control the whole network, it is necessary to subvert all the access control devices one after the other.
- Protection against internal attacks. Internal attacks against internal devices can be avoided and detected since all the devices are protected.
- Realistic information about the flows. [11] shows that firewalls and intrusion detection tools systems rely

upon a mechanism of data collection which is fundamentally flawed. These systems watch all the traffic on the network, and scrutinize it for patterns of suspicious activity. However there is not enough information on the wire on which to base conclusions about what is actually happening on networked machines. Two classes of attacks (traffic insertion and evasion) which exploit this fundamental problem are exhibited thus showing that centralized traffic analysis systems cannot be fully trusted.
- A distributed architecture is not prone to these attacks since all the necessary information about the connections can be found on the end devices themselves.
- Performance improvement. For centralized devices to filter traffic, it is necessary to reassemble frames and packets in order to isolate flows that require filtering. Therefore, overhead is introduced by the controller. On the other hand, in a distributed architecture, the traffic is naturally reassembled. As a consequence, the access control processing introduces much less overhead than in the centralized approach.
- Scalability improvement. The access control processing can be distributed over several devices. As a result, very high rates can be supported, without needing a powerful centralized device.
- Efficiency improvement. As mentioned in section 1 many protocol stacks can be used above the ATM model. Providing access control mechanisms for all these protocols on a single device is not very efficient. In a distributed architecture, access control mechanisms and access control policy can be specific to the protocol stack being used. This results in less complex and thus more efficient equipment.

A distributed framework has also some disadvantages. It is more difficult to manage. Detecting attacks against several devices requires each device to cooperate with one another, which is not an easy task. The main disadvantage is that every device on the network has to be modified in order to supply the access control service. Another problem with a distributed architecture is the mean to exchange access control information.

In section 3.2 we show how a management agent can be modified in order to supply the access control service. Section 3.3 gives some indication to solve the problem of managing the distributed architecture. Finally section 3.4 describes a method to efficiently distribute the access control policy on our access control agents.

3.2. Access control enforcement

It is well known that communication devices keep information about ongoing communications in their protocol stack. Some of this information has been standardized for management purpose [15]. The access to these data is performed through a piece of software called management agent. We demonstrated in [9] that most of the relevant information from an access control point of view can be accessed through this kind of agent.

Our architecture is based on a modified management agent. This agent can be located on a terminal device or on an intermediate device as illustrated in figure 1.

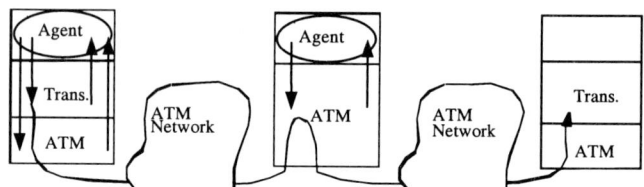

Figure 1. Access control enforcement points

The agent has to be modified in order to introduce the access control operations. It periodically polls objects located in the protocol stack describing communications. It then compares the values of these objects with the allowed values. The allowed values describe part of the access control policy to be applied in that agent. Thus the allowed values may vary from one agent to another. When prohibited values are detected, the agent interacts with the protocol stack in order to stop the prohibited action. A more detailed description of the agent architecture can be found in section 3.4. Our architecture has the following advantages:
- The information used to provide the access control service is examined asynchronously by the agent at the application level. Thus no impact on the QoS can be induced.
- The modifications of the system providing the access control service are small. Only our access control agent has to be added.

However, selecting the polling rate may not be easy. Indeed a too short interval of polling introduces unuseful overhead for the system whereas a too long interval of polling decreases the security level provided by the agent since some events will be missed by the agent thus introducing possible security flaws.

3.3. Access control management

As explained in section 3.1 a distributed architecture is quite difficult to manage. To solve this management problem, the three elements depicted in figure 2 are defined:
- The Access Control management application is responsible for configuring each agent with the relevant access control rules. It should also retrieve access control results from the agents and should analyse them to detect distributed attacks.
- The access control MIB is located on the access control agent device and is remotely managed by the

manager through the agent. This MIB includes both access control rules, and results from the access control process.
- The management protocol used to carry information between the access control manager and the access control agent has to supply integrity, authentication, access control and confidentiality services. The SNMPv2 [15] and SNMPv3 [2] protocols seem to be good candidates since they supply all these services.

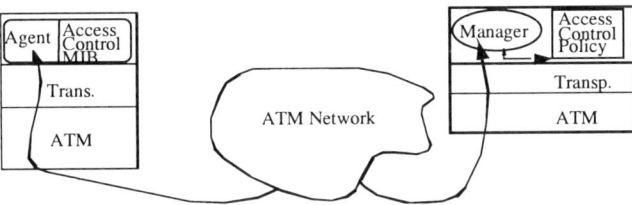

Figure 2. Access control management architecture

3.4. Access control policy distribution

One of the biggest problems in managing our access control architecture is to decide how to distribute the access control policy on our access control agents. The first step in solving this problem is to find a way to express the access control policy.

Expressing the access control policy

In order to express the access control policy we define an Access Control Policy Description Language (ACPDL). This language is based on the Policy Description Language [8] currently being defined by the Policy working group at the IETF. In our language an access control policy is described by a set of rules. Each rule is made up of: a set of conditions and one action which has to be executed if the conditions are met. The following BNF (Backus-Naur Formalism) expression describes the rule syntax.

```
Rule ::= IF <Conditions> THEN <Action>
```

All the conditions have the same generic structure (BNF notation):

```
Condition    ::=    <ACCESS    CONTROL
PARAMETER>    <RELATIONAL    OPERATOR>
<VALUE>
```

Depending on the level in the protocol stack, various access control parameters may be used:
- At the ATM level useful access control parameters have been described in [10], which include the traffic type, connection identifiers, addressing information, QoS descriptors and service identifiers.
- At the transport level most of the included parameters are commonly used to provide access control in firewalls (e.g. addressing information, ports, etc.).
- At the application level we define two generic parameters: the application user identifier and the application state.
- Timing parameters have also been included in order to specify when a rule should apply.

Actions also have a generic structure (BNF notation).

```
Action ::= <ACTION> <ACTION LEVEL>
```

The action can be to permit or to deny the communication. The level describes the layer (i.e. ATM, Transport, Application) where the action has to be executed.

Figure 3 provides an example of how a rule prohibiting connections between two ATM devices for the Video On Demand service can be expressed using the ACPDL. In this example both devices are identified by their ATM addresses and the video service is identified by the Broadband Higher Layer Identifier (BHLI).

```
IF (SRC_ADDRESS =
47.00730000000000000002402.08002074E4
57.00) AND (DST_ADDRESS =
47.00730000000000000002404.0800200D6A
D3.00) AND (BHLI_TYPE = 04) AND
(BHLI_ID = 00A03E00000002) THEN DENY
ATM_CONNECTION ;
```

Figure 3. Access control rule example

Distributing the access control rules

Before describing our distribution method, we have to describe our agents' internal structure in order to explain how access control rules are executed. As shown in figure 4 an agent is made up of two main parts. The first part is dedicated to access control management whereas the second part provides the access control service. The access control part also include two parts. The first one, called Access Controller is common to each agent. Its goal is to translate the access control rules retrieved from the Access Control MIB into Access Control commands. The access controller interacts with the second part called AC library through the Access Control Interface. The goal of the AC library is to hide the implementation of the access control objects to the access controller. The AC library translates commands received through the AC interface into real system commands and sends these commands to the real system through the system interface. This translation process is described in figure 4.

Since the AC interface is the same for each system, matching access control conditions and actions to access control objects is an easy task. Depending on the role of the network element on which it is located, each agent may provide a mapping between an Access Control Object and a System Object or not. Therefore describing which access control objects are implemented on equipment is important for the distribution process. One possible way to describe these objects could be to use the Management Information Bases (MIBs) defined by the standardization organisations since some of these MIBs include the most useful objects from an access control point of view ([9]). Since all of our access control conditions and actions cannot be mapped on existing management objects new MIBs have to be defined.

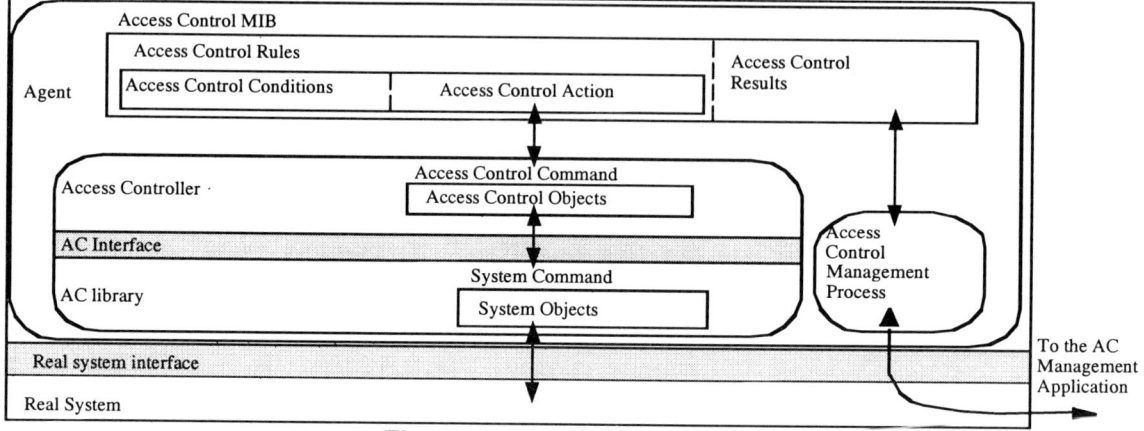

Figure 4. Agent's internal structure

The goal of the distribution algorithm is to efficiently assign access control rules to our access control agents. This distribution process must follow two laws:

- A rule must not be assigned to an agent where this rule cannot be executed. A rule cannot be executed when an access control object required by the rule cannot be mapped to a real system object by the AC library (1).
- A rule must not be assigned to an agent where this rule will never be executed. A rule will never be executed when:

- The rule is located on a terminal device and the rule does not apply to this device (2).
- The rule is located on an intermediate device D but does not apply to D and does not apply to a device interconnected by D (3).

To follow these laws the distribution process has to use a description of the network which has to be protected. Since we want to provide the access control service at the ATM, MAC, IP and application levels, the network is sliced into three layers (i.e. ATM, MAC, IP). Each slice is modelled by a tree describing interconnections between network devices at a single level.

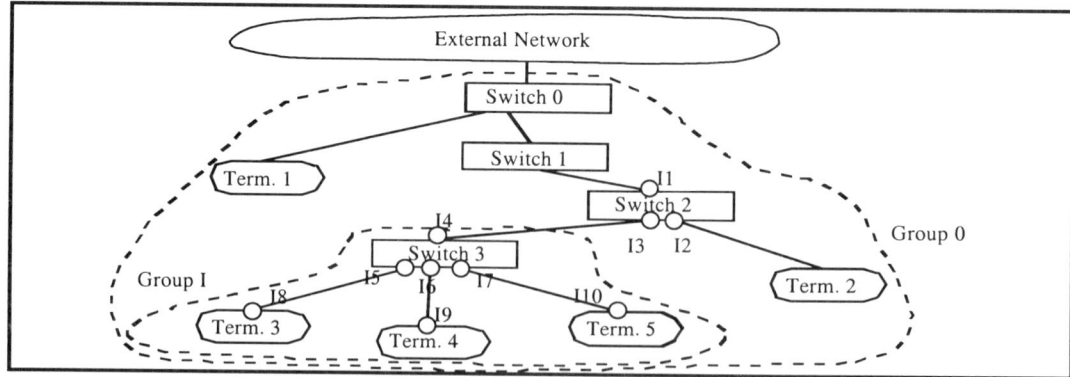

Figure 5. Network model at the ATM level

As shown in figure 5, two kinds of elements can be described. There are intermediate elements which interconnect other elements (i.e. switch devices in our example) and non intermediate elements which are called terminal elements (i.e. Term. devices).

Since a terminal element at the ATM level can behave like an intermediate element at a higher layer, a distinction has to be made for each layer. Figure 6 describes possible mappings between network elements at the ATM and IP levels. Possible mappings include a one to one mapping (i.e. one ATM element for one IP or MAC element) which is the most common case. The one to many (i.e. one ATM element for many MAC elements) case may happen in an emulated LAN environment when several LANs are configured over the same physical network. The one to zero mapping case happens when the device only provides ATM connectivity (e.g. ATM switches). Finally, the zero to many mapping case happens when the device is interconnected to the ATM network through a non ATM link.

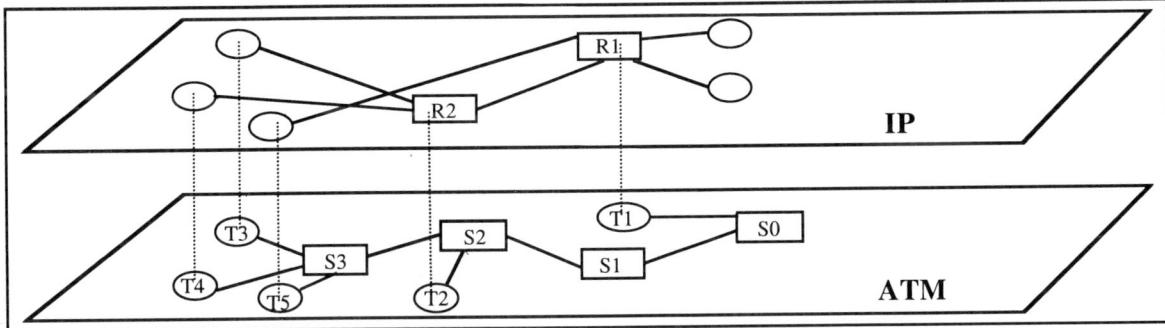

Figure 6. Interlayer relationships

In order to describe interactions between these elements we use three classes of objects:

The Interface class describes an interconnection point between two elements. Examples of interfaces are given in figure 5 where Switch 3 has three interfaces called I1, I2 and I3. Each Interface object is associated with the corresponding level (i.e. ATM, MAC, IP), type (i.e. Intermediate, Terminal) and address. Three functions (I.level, I.type, I.address) have been associated with the Interface class to manage this information.

The Group class describes the interconnections between interface objects. Each Group object is associated with its level (i.e. ATM, MAC, IP), list of connected interfaces and master interface (i.e. the interface to leave the group). Figure 5 describes two groups called Group 0 and Group I. In this example, Group I includes six pairs of interconnected interfaces and has I4 as master interface. Three functions (G.level, G.connects, G.master) have been associated with the Group class to manage this information.

The Device class describes the interfaces belonging to a same physical device. Each Device object is associated with a set of interfaces and the access control objects implemented by the access control agent located on the device. Figure 6 shows an example of relations described by the Device class. In this example, the device associated with T2 and R2 holds four interfaces (One at the ATM level and three at the IP level). Two functions (G.maps, I.stores) have been associated with the Device class to manage this information.

Figure 7 provides the distribution algorithm. The algorithm implements the three distribution laws ((1), (2), (3)) and uses the Access Control Policy modelled by a set of rules ({rule}) and the network description modelled by the three sets described above ({Group}, {Device}, {Interface}).

Four external functions are used:
- objects(r) provides the set of access control objects required by the access control rule r.
- interface(r) provides the set of interfaces to which the access control rule r applies.
- Associate(r,d) associates rule r with device d.
- Dissociate(r,d) dissociates rule r from device d.

```
For each i ∈ {Interface} do
 G = {g ∈ {Group}/i ∈ g.connects};
 D = {d ∈ {Device}/(i0,i1) ∈ d.maps,
  (i0=i|i1=i)};
 M = {m ∈ {Group}/m.master = i};
 N = {k ∈ {Interface}/k ∈ m.connects,
  m ∈ M};
 For each r ∈ {Rule} do
  For each d ∈ D do
   Associate(r,d);
   If ∃ o ∈ objects(r)/ o ∉ d.stores
   then
    Dissociate(r,d); /* case (1) */
   Else
    If i ∉ interface(r) then
     If i.type = «terminal» then
      Dissociate(r,d); /* case (2) */
     Else
      If ∃ j ∈ interface(r)/j ∉ N
      then
       Dissociate(r,d); /* case (3) */
```

Figure 7. Distribution algorithm

Optimisations

Providing more information about our security policy allows us to optimise our distribution process. Both optimisations in this section are based on the fact that the type of our access control policy is «What is not explicitly permitted is prohibited». With this kind of access control, a «Deny rule» always describes a subset of a «Permit rule». This type of access control policy is the most common but the opposite type (i.e. «What is not explicitly prohibited is allowed») would result in similar optimisations.

Our first optimisation applies to «Deny rules». The distribution of these rules must follow the following laws:
- If a «Deny rule» can be distributed over several cascading agents, the rule has to be distributed to the element closest to «terminal» devices (4).
- «Deny rules» don't have to be duplicated since a single «Deny rule» can block a communication (5).

These laws provide a better efficiency since it allows a smaller subset of rules to be attached to each access control agent.

Figure 8 provides the optimisation algorithm. This algorithm implements distribution laws (4) and (5). We define two additional external functions:
- action(r) provides the type of action specified by the access control rule r.
- associated(r,d) informs whether if access control rule r has been associated with device d by the basic distribution algorithm.

```
For each r ∈{Rule}/action(r) = «DENY»
 do
 For each d ∈{Device} do
  I = {i ∈ {Interface}/
   (i0,i1)∈ d.maps,(i0=i|i1=i)};
  G = {g ∈ {Group}/g.master ∈ I};
  M = {m ∈ {Interface}/m ∈ g.connects,
   g ∈ G};
  E = {e ∈ {Device}/(i0,i1) ∈ e.maps,
   e ≠ d, (i0 ∈ M| i1 ∈ M)};
  If associated(r,d) then
    If ∃ e ∈ E/associated(r,e) then
     Dissociate(r,d); /* case (4) */
For each r ∈ {Rule}/action(r) = «DENY»
 do
  D = { d ∈ {Device}/associated(r,d)};
  Let be d ∈ D;
  For each e ∈ D/e ≠ d
    Dissociate(e,d);   /* case (5) */
```
Figure 8. "Deny" based optimisations.

The second optimisation applies to «Permit» rules. These rules have to be duplicated between the source and the destination of each communication that has to be controlled. The basic distribution algorithm provides this property. However when the communication to be controlled takes place between two internal devices, our basic distribution algorithm distributes these rules between the root of our network tree to the first device interconnecting our two devices. These rules are useless and have to be removed. Moreover removing these rules also provides an address spoofing protection because communications coming from the outside with external addresses will be discarded since not explicitly permitted.
- Rules describing communications between two internal devices have only to be distributed on the smaller subset of agents interconnecting these devices (6).

Figure 9 provides the optimisation algorithm. This algorithm implements distribution law (6).

```
For each r ∈ {Rule}/action(r)=«PERMIT»
 do
 G = {g ∈ {Group}/interface(r) ⊂
  g.connects};
 Let be h ∈ G/∀ l ∈ G, h.connects ⊂
  l.connects;
 N = {n ∈ G/n ≠ h};
 M = {o ∈ {Interface}/o =n.master,
  n ∈ N};
 D = {d ∈ {Device}/∃(i0,i1) ∈ d.maps,
  (i0 ∈ M|i1 ∈ M)};
 For each d ∈ D do
  If associated(r,d) then
    Dissociate(r,d); /*case (6)*/
```
Figure 9. "Permit" based optimisation.

Once rules have been associated to devices, the management application is able to configure the relevant agents using the management protocol.

4. Conclusion

As a conclusion, table 2 compares all the competing approaches designed to provide access control on both ATM and IP over ATM networks. As we can see, our approach has the following advantages:
- Good access control at the ATM level.
- Very good scalability thanks to a distributed architecture.
- Good performance through an efficient distribution method.
- No impact on the QoS thanks to the asynchronous information retrieval process.
- Good manageability through a management and security integrated approach.

Table 2. Comparison of the different approaches

Property/Approach	Classical Firewall	ATM Forum	Filtering Switch	ATM Firewall	Dowd & al.	Xu & al.	Paul & al.
ATM level access control	No	No	Poor	No	Poor	Poor	**Good**
Transport level access control	**Good**	No	No	Average	Average	Average	Average
Application level access control	**Good**	No	No	No	No	Average	Poor
Label based access control	No	**Good**	No	No	No	No	No
Scalability	Poor	**Good**	**Good**	Average	Average	Average	**Good**
Level of modification	**Poor**	Large	**Poor**	**Poor**	**Poor**	**Poor**	Average
Impact on the QoS	Large	**No**	**No**	Poor	Poor	Poor	**No**
Level of security	**Good**	**Good**	Poor	Average	Average	**Good**	Average
Manageability	**Good**	Poor	**Good**	Poor	Poor	**Good**	**Good**
Implementation	**Yes**	No	**Yes**	**Yes**	**Yes**	No	No

This work could be usefully continued in two directions. The first direction is its implementation since this might give us interesting feedback on the real performance and security level provided by the architecture. The second direction is the extension of our architecture to other types of networks, our architecture being easily adaptable to other kinds of network that are based on a layer 2 switching and that consider QoS as an important constraint.

5. References

[1] ISO 7498-2:1989, Information processing systems -- Open Systems Interconnection -- Basic Reference Model -- Part 2: Security Architecture, ISO, 1989.

[2] Basking in Glory-SNMPv3, Dan Backman, Network Computing, August 1998.

[3] An FPGA-Based Coprocessor for ATM Firewalls, J. McHenry, P. Dowd, F. Pellegrino, T. Carrozzi, W. Cocks, in proceedings of IEEE FCCM'97, April 1997.

[4] Firewalls: Don't Get Burned, David Newman, Helen Holzbaur, and Kathleen Bishop, Data Communications, March 1997.

[5] Standard Security Label for Information Transfer, Federal Information Processing Standards Publication 188, National Institute of Standards and Technology, September 1994.

[6] ATM Net Management: Missing Pieces, Joe Abusamra, Data Communications, May 1998.

[7] Firewall Shootout Test Final Report, Keylabs, May 1998, Networld+Interop'98.

[8] Policy Framework Definition Language, draft-ietf-policy-framework-pfdl-00.txt, John Strassner, Stephen Schleimer, Internet Engineering Task Force, 17 November 1998.

[9] Où trouver les informations de contrôle d'accès dans le cas des réseaux ATM, O. Paul, M. Laurent, Technical report, ENST de Bretagne, August 1998.

[10] Manageable parameters to improve access control in ATM networks, O. Paul, M. Laurent, S. Gombault, 5th Workshop of the HP OpenView University Association HPOVUA'98, April 1998.

[11] Insertion, evasion, and denial of service: eluding network intrusion detection, T. Ptacek, T. Newsham, Technical report, Secure Network, January 1998.

[12] A network firewall, M. Ranum, Proc. World Conference on System Administration and security, 1992.

[13] ATM Security Specification Version 1.0, The ATM Forum Technical Committee. February 1999.

[14] On the modeling, design and implementation of firewall technology, Christoph Schuba, Ph.D. Thesis, Purdue University, December 1997.

[15] SNMP, SNMPv2 and CMIP, The pratical guide to network management Standards. William Stallings. Addison-Wesley. 1993.

[16] Design of a High-Performance ATM Firewall, J. Xu, M. Singhal, Technical report, The Ohio State University, 1997.

Secure Communications in ATM Networks

Maryline Laurent, IRISA
Ahmed Bouabdallah, Christophe Delahaye, ENST de Bretagne
Herbert Leitold, Reinhard Posch, IAIK
Enrique Areizaga, Fundacion Robotiker
Juàn Manuel Mateos, Inelcom Ingeniera

Abstract

The ATM Forum international consortium recently approved the first version of its security specifications aiming to protect communications over Asynchronous Transfer Mode (ATM) networks by offering data confidentiality, partners authentication, etc. This paper describes the architecture of one of the first ATM Forum compliant security prototypes being currently developed in the European project SCAN (Secure Communications in ATM Networks). Additionally to the security management functions specified by the ATM Forum to exchange encryption keys and negotiate security services, SCAN implements the possibility for end-users to modify the data flow encryption algorithm during a connection in progress, and the possibility to keep the encryption algorithm choice confidential. Moreover a flexible implementation is offered allowing future users to develop their own security protocols and their own ATM security monitoring applications.

1. Introduction

The Asynchronous Transfer Mode (ATM) technology success is due to its ability to support multimedia applications needs offering high bit rates and real time guarantees. Another ATM interesting feature is the early introduction of security services into ATM specifications, thus resulting in an efficient security solution to protect the ATM traffic against eavesdropping, traffic tampering, and masquerade. The introduction of the confidentiality, integrity, and authentication services into ATM appears helpful for the deployment of security sensitive multimedia applications such as the telemedecine applications where patient files are expected to be kept confidential, and modified only by authorized persons [1]. This paper describes the architecture and choices elected in project SCAN (Secure Communications in ATM Networks) to develop a prototype ensuring ATM traffic encryption at 155 Mbps, with inherent security management. This prototype is expected to be at least ATM Forum compliant, offering data encryption on a connection basis, and allowing security information to be exchanged through ATM signaling. The prototype is limited to point-to point communications environment, and additionally to the ATM Forum specifications, it implements the possibility to modify the data encryption algorithm during a connection in progress, and to improve the security level by maintaining security sensitive information secret.

This paper focuses mainly on security management aspects detailing the solutions chosen for updating session keys, and for negotiating the security services and mechanisms that will be used to protect subsequent exchanges. Attention is paid to describe the open interfaces of the prototype, which provide flexibility so that future users can develop their own security protocols fitting their own security needs, and national legislation.

More precisely, section 2 introduces ATM and the ATM security needs allowing readers to understand the remainder of the paper. Section 3 describes the security services and functions specified in current ATM Forum specifications. The following sections give a SCAN technical description, presenting the data encryption mechanism (section 4), the session key update (section 5), the security parameters negotiation (section 6), and the signaling protection (section 7). The security parameters monitored by users are presented in section 8 as SCAN security policy. The architecture of the SCAN prototype is provided in section 9, along with its open interfaces in section 10. Finally, section 11 gives some conclusions, and section 12 a list of useful acronyms.

2. Introduction to ATM security

The ATM technology is connection-oriented, that is, prior to any data exchange, it is necessary to set up connections (or virtual channels) over which data are later sent. To distinguish between connection monitoring operations and data exchange processing, the ATM protocol reference model is divided into planes. As depicted in figure 1, three planes are defined:

- The control plane to monitor signaling information that is, to set up, release, and control ATM connections
- The user plane to transfer data through data channels.
- The management plane to maintain the ATM network operational, propagating possible alarms and ATM traffic statistics.

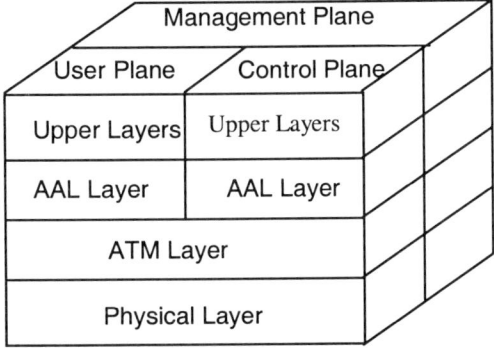

Figure 1   The ATM reference model

The management and control planes communicate over the ATM network through reserved virtual channels. However possibility is given to the management planes to exchange management information over the data channel being managed. As such, the management flow is the only one offering synchronization with the data flow.

Remote entities' control planes communicate thanks to signaling messages. Signaling messages contain a header specifying the message type, and many signaling IEs (Information Elements) informing of connection specific needs such as the quality of service, the upper application type, etc. Signaling messages include setup, connect, status, and release messages. The setup message is sent by the connection initiator, and propagates through the ATM network to the responder which should send back a connect message to complete the connection establishment. For a connection to be released, two processes are available. The soft one is to send a release message, waiting for a release complete message to release the resources allocated to the connection. The other approach is to send a release complete prior to deallocating the resources. Other signaling messages are defined, such as status informing of the control plane state associated to a specific connection, and restart to reinitialize a connection.

ATM is a cell-switching network. That is, any information sent over the network is in the form of 53-byte ATM cells including a header which specifies the ATM connection identifiers called VPI/VCI for Virtual Path/Circuit Identifiers. For the management planes to communicate, specific OAM (Operation And Maintenance) cells are defined. However for user planes and control planes to communicate, it is necessary to segment data frames, and signaling messages into ATM cells. As such, three layers modeling the processing to be done to obtain those ATM cells are defined in the ATM reference model: the physical layer mainly responsible for information transportation; the ATM layer mainly in charge of multiplexing and switching functions; the ATM Adaptation Layer (AAL) whose main function is to adapt services needs to ATM streams by performing segmentation into (/reassembly of) cells for instance.

The ATM model analyzis leads to the conclusion that the ATM traffic divides into three ATM flows types, data, management, and signaling flows. As such, three flows can be subject to attacks while in transit [2]. Data flows can be eavesdropped, and tampered, resulting in more or less severe losses. Signaling messages, and especially setup messages are vulnerable to eavesdropping, tampering, and masquerade. Eavesdropping setup messages informs the eavesdropper of the end-entities that need to communicate, and the type of application that will be used. Masquerades consist in constructing setup messages with a bogus source ATM address. The management flow is vulnerable to tampering attacks, since injecting alarms into the ATM network for instance may lead to improper connections releases.

It is clear that ATM flows require protection. However, since connections are expected to be of various sensitivity levels, it is necessary that first the security services used to protect data are negotiated. As a result, ATM security studies expect to introduce the following protections:

- Signaling protection by offering the authentication, integrity, and confidentiality services.
- Data protection, ensuring the confidentiality, integrity, and authentication of data.
- Security parameters negotiation. Three approaches may be considered whether security parameters are exchanged between security equipments through signaling messages, data channel, or OAM cells.

The OAM cells protection is not studied in current works, since OAM cells are not implemented in most of current ATM equipments, and since the OAM cells size is fixed thus precluding any authenticator or integrity check value to be introduced.

The next section describes the ATM Forum security specifications 1.0 emphasizing the required security services.

3. The ATM Forum specifications 1.0

Since 1995, the security working group of the ATM Forum has been working on ATM security aspects approving the first version of the ATM security specifications [3] [4] in February 1999. Those specifications aim to provide confidentiality of data, and integrity, and authentication of both data and signaling messages. Required services are as follows:

- Data confidentiality. Data are encrypted on a cell-by-cell basis encrypting only the 48-byte ATM cell payload. The encryption algorithms being considered include DES (Data Encryption Standard), TripleDES, and FEAL, and the operational modes offered are the ECB (Electronic CodeBook), CBC (Cipher Block Chaining), and the counter mode. Because of US legislation exportation restrictions, DES is expected to be used either with 40-bit or 56-bit effective keys.
- Data integrity, and authentication. AAL frames are protected by appending a cryptographic checksum to AAL frames. Possibility is given to provide replay/reordering protection by introducing a sequence number into AAL frames before calculating the cryptographic checksum.
- Security parameters negotiation.
  Two approaches are allowed, whether the security parameters are sent through signaling messages, or in-band through the data channel. The first one consists in appending a security IE (SIE) to setup, and connect messages. This SIE exchange allows the connection partners to negotiate the security services, and mechanisms, and to exchange the encryption keys to be used to protect their data transfer. For the encryption keys to remain confidential, and for the connection partners to be sure of their respective identity, existing two-way Security Message Exchange (SME) protocols are used.
  Protocols considered in the ATM Forum specifications refer to three levels of key: the session key used to encrypt data, the master key used to encrypt session keys when updating session keys during a connection, and the top-level key which is an asymetric key used to authenticate and initialize the first session key, and master key securely.
  An alternative to the signaling approach is to block the data traffic as soon as the connection is established, to realize the security negotiation through the data channel, and finally to unblock the data transfer. To avoid that the called partner considers incoming security information as data, the connection initiator indicates that the negotiation is done in-band thanks to a SIE within the set up message. The negotiation is done encapsulating the same SIEs than in the signaling approach, into simplified signaling messages. One advantage over the signaling approach is that the SIE length is not limited in the in-band approach, thus allowing long-length information such as keys certificates to be included into the SIE. For reliable SIE exchanges, additional in-band control messages are defined such as CONFIRM-AP to acknowledge the final SIE, and FAULT to indicate why the negotiation fails. The in-band approach is expected to use three-way SME protocols.
- Signaling protection. Any signaling messages may be authenticated and integrity protected by introducing a digital signature into an SIE. Especially, if an SME protocol is employed, protection is offered for setup and connect messages by calculating the signature over the SIE fields specified by the SME protocol. It is still offered for any other signaling messages (release, status, restart), and for setup and connect messages (if the SME protocol is not used) by introducing a signature calculated over part of the SIE.
- Session key update through OAM cells. For encrypted connections to be as secure as possible, session keys are expected to be updated from time to time. Because of their synchronization with the data flow, OAM cells were selected to carry session keys. Two steps are defined for session key updating. Firstly, a session key is sent encrypted under the master key through a specific OAM cell called SKE (Session Key Exchange) cell. Secondly, the session key is activated thanks to an SKC (Session Key Changeover) cell. During SKC cells transmission, the data traffic is blocked over the connection so that the data following the first SKC OAM cell received are decrypted under the new session key. Obviously if only one pair of SKE/SKC cells is sent, and one of them is lost during transfer, this results in subsequent data remaining undecryptable for the receiving end-station. To counteract that, the ATM Forum proposes to send a flow of similar SKE cells followed by a flow of similar SKC cells so that at least one SKE and one SKC cells are assumed to be received, thus resulting in a correct session key update. To preclude possible bursts from erasing all the transmitted OAM cells flows in the network, SKE and SKC cells are sent with a delay between each transmission.

In the security specifications of February 1999, it is envisaged that access control is offered by appending a security label to the setup and connect messages, which indicates the sensitivity level of the connection (public data, proprietary, company confidential, etc.). Security equipments (switches, end-stations) are expected to check this label against the label assigned to the links used to reach the destination. If no links have the sufficient level, the connection is aborted.

Project SCAN security aspects are close to the ATM Forum specifications, so that next sections describing SCAN security functions are closely related to the present section.

4. Data confidentiality

A hardware cryptographic unit called HADES (see section 9) is embedded into an ATM NIC card and is used to encrypt data traffic up to 155 Mbps with compliance with the ATM Forum. That is, it encrypts ATM cell payloads only. Available encryption algorithms are DES, and TripleDES with the ECB or CBC operational modes.

One problem to be solved when considering data cells encryption at 155 Mbps is the key agility problem presented for the first time in [5]. This problem arises when fast session keys change is required. This happens when each incoming cell needs to be encrypted with a session key different from the previous one. This means that in the worst case, a session key needs to be downloaded every 2.83 µs (($53*8$)/ ($149.76*10^6$)) [6]. SCAN solves this problem using fast access CAM (Content Access Memory) memory.

Since session keys as defined in the ATM Forum are unidirectional, each connection is provided with a pair of keys, one for encryption, and one for decryption. Session keys are downloaded from the NIC card drivers (the IE/OAM module described in section 9) using SCAN specific session key downloading cells (later referred to as AAL0 cells). AAL0 cells inform the HADES unit of the algorithm and mode of operation to be used over one VPI/VCI connection, and the session key(s) that should be employed for either encryption or decryption. AAL0 cells include two 64-bit session key fields, both of them being required when the TripleDES encryption algorithm is selected. AAL0 cells include also a 64-bit Initialization Vector useful for the CBC mode of operation.

AAL0 cells are locally identified by some specific connection identifiers M-VPI/M-VCI, and a specific payload type. These M-VPI, and M-VCI values are selected by the NIC card driver at the HADES unit initialization thanks to a configuration-VC cell which is identified itself by the means of the unused connection identifiers VPI/VCI=0/0. Upon reception of an AAL0 cell, the HADES unit downloads the new session key for encryption or decryption, and discards it, so that AAL0 cells remain local to the ATM end-station.

5. Session key update

Session keys used to encrypt data are updated during connections in progress with compliance with the ATM Forum specifications using the SKE/SKC cells (cf. section 3). In SCAN, session keys are updated either periodically, or depending on the amount of data cells being sent encrypted under the same session key over the connection. Session keys are unidirectional so that each party is responsible for updating its encryption key as frequently as it needs. As part of the security policy parameters, the session key update period expressed in seconds or in number of cells can be configured by each party from the user space using a specific interface (see sections 9 and 10).

Once the session key update completes, the HADES cryptographic unit should be informed of the new encryption or decryption key to be considered over one unidirectional connection. That is, after SKC cells transmission, and prior to unblocking the data traffic, it is necessary that the HADES unit is informed of the new encryption session key to be considered thanks to an AAL0 session key download cell. The remote party should download the same session key for decryption after the first corresponding SKC cell is received.

6. Security parameters negotiation

Like in the ATM Forum specifications 1.0, two approaches are considered in SCAN for negotiating the security parameters used to protect subsequent data transfers. These are the following:

- Negotiation through signaling messages. This approach being supported in the ATM Forum specifications 1.0 allows the future SCAN prototype to interoperate with other non-SCAN ATM security equipments at the condition that the SIE being constructed is ATM Forum compliant (see section 6.1). Like in the ATM Forum, only two-way SME protocols are supported in the signaling approach.
- Negotiation through OAM cells. This approach is SCAN specific, and consists in encapsulating security parameters into newly defined "negotiation OAM cells" dedicated to security. This approach is interesting if permanent connections are considered as no security parameters negotiation through setup signaling messages is allowed. Negotiation through OAM cells is also interesting when master keys (cf. section 3) need to be updated during a connection in progress, when the security officer modifies the security policy to be enforced over the connection, or when a great number of errored data cells are

received, thus implying that the previous session key update was errored.

Contrary to the ATM Forum in-band approach supporting only the three-way SME protocols, the SCAN OAM cell negotiation approach enables both the two and three-way SME protocols to be used. Another advantage is that the negotiation can occur at any time during the connection, and not only when establishing a connection. As such, end-stations are allowed to renegotiate security parameters as often as they need. Actually, in SCAN, possibility is given to initiate a new security parameters negotiation either periodically, or depending on the percentage of cells received with an errored-content, thus allowing possible improper session key updates to be detected.

Since the negotiation OAM cells aim is similar to what is done in the ATM Forum security specifications 1.0 at connection setup through the SIE, it was decided that the SIE is reused to realize a context negotiation by encapsulating the SIE within negotiation OAM cells. Since the SIE may be bigger than the 46-byte payload offered in OAM cells, SIE segmentation should take place before its encapsulation into negotiation OAM cells. As such the principle adopted by the ATM Forum for the session keys exchange which consists of sending the same session key updates OAM cells several times to be sure that at least one cell arrives at the destination does not apply for the negotiation OAM cells. The solution elected in SCAN to ensure that reliable SIE exchanges through negotiation OAM cells is to define a cell-loss recovery protocol based on sequence numbers and acknowledgement OAM cells. This protocol has been validated, and is described in section 6.2.

Since the OAM cell negotiation approach allows connection partners to initiate a new session key update or a new security context negotiation at any time during a connection, collisions between those mechanisms can occur, leading to improper session keys updates for instance. As such a collision manager is introduced, to decide which mechanism is to be stopped to allow the other one to complete. The general rule enforced is that a negotiation has precedence over a session key update, and when two negotiations are initiated simultaneously, the connection partner with the greater ATM address should stop the negotiation it initiated.

6.1 SCAN Security IE

One aim of SCAN is to be at least ATM Forum compliant. As such, to realize security parameters negotiation, SCAN constructs the SIE as specified in version 1.0 of the specifications [3], using the two and three-way RSA-based SME protocols. The ATM Forum SIE format is given in figure 2. Only fields meaningful for SCAN are present and are explained hereafter:

- The SIE identifier identifies the SIE from other signaling IEs.
- The 2-bit Coding Standard is used to distinguish between the ITU-T and the ATM Forum compliant SIE.
- The remaining SIE fields are divided into Security Association Sections (SAS). Each SAS includes the security information that is exchanged between two security agents, which may be either end-stations as considered in SCAN or intermediary equipments.
- The Version field identifies the ATM Forum specifications to which the SIE is compliant.
- The Scope, Target Security Entity ID, and Security Entity ID fields allow one security agent to identify itself as the SIE target security agents.
- The Relative ID field identifies the security association the SAS refers to.
- The following fields relative to the SME protocol are identified by the SME Format-SME Type fields. SME Type identifies whether the SME protocol is two or three-way exchange.
- The Security Services Specification Section includes the security parameters relative to the data protection (encryption algorithm, and mode of operation, etc.) and the SIE construction (SME protocol, signature algorithms, etc.).
- The Confidentiality Section includes the master key, and session keys, which are all encrypted by the means of the SME protocol.
- The Authentication Section contains a timestamp, a random number, and the digital signature calculated over the fields specified by the selected SME protocol.

Security IE Identifier		
Coding Standard		
Length		
Security Association Section ID		
SAS Length		
Version		
Scope		
Relative ID		
Target Security Entity ID		
SME Format-SME Type		
Security Entity ID		
Security Services Specification Section		
Confidentiality Section		
Authentication Section		

Figure 2 The SIE of the ATM Forum

Besides the security parameters, end-partners authentication, and secure keys transfer, SCAN provides end-partners with the possibility to ensure the confidentiality of security services and parameters being negotiated during a connection in progress or at connection setup. This possibility is interesting because an eavesdropper positioned at a point on the network can easily select sensitive connections to disrupt by filtering setup signaling messages or negotiation OAM cells according to the security services required. Indeed more security services are needed over a connection, more likely it is that the connection is sensitive. By encrypting some of those security parameters, this eavesdropping attack becomes less efficient. To do that, a new section called SCAN Confidentiality Section is introduced in the SIE replacing the ATM Forum Confidentiality Section. The distinction between the SCAN specific SIE and the ATM Forum compliant SIE is done thanks to the Coding Standard field.

The SCAN Confidentiality Section includes the ATM Forum Confidentiality Section and subpart of the Security Services Specification Section relative to data protection. The encryption is done over the content of the SCAN Confidentiality Section so that the keys and data protection parameters (data encryption algorithm, and mode of operation, session key update mechanism) remain confidential. The encryption algorithm used is the same as this employed for keys encryption, that is, it is specified in the Security Services Specification Section in cleartext.

6.2 The cell-loss recovery protocol

The purpose of this protocol is to ensure that a SIE being exchanged over the network encapsulated into negotiation OAM cells is received with no losses and correctly ordered. As such, when segmenting a SIE, each SIE segment is numbered with a sequence number and each negotiation OAM cell includes the sequence number associated to the SIE segment it carries. A group of negotiation OAM cells are acknowledged at the same time by a newly defined "acknowledgement OAM cell" which includes the sequence number of the next negotiation OAM cell expected.

The complexity of the protocol is due to possible losses occurring in the network, and the SIE processing time being undefined since dependent on the SME protocol security mechanisms used. The difficulty is that session keys should be updated at the end of the SIE exchanges, but should only take place after the last SIE is processed for the decryption session key to be decrypted and ready to be downloaded into the cryptographic unit. Because of it, and because of the specific role of the acknowledgement cell in the last SME flow, three kinds of acknowledgement cells are defined:

- Intermediate acknowledgement cells are used to acknowledge negotiation OAM cells which are not the last one in the last SME flow. For bandwidth optimization purpose, their transmission is done when a cell loss is detected, or when no negotiation OAM cells have been received for a long time while the SIE is not fully received yet.
- Final acknowledgement cells are sent to acknowledge the last negotiation OAM cell of the last SME flow.
- Other acknowledgement cells are sent to specify that a partner is ready for session key changeover processing.

Since no means is used to be sure that the latter two kinds of acknowledgement cells arrive to the destination, the same mechanism as this used for session keys downloading SKE/SKC cells transmission is employed (cf. section 5). That is, a number of similar acknowledgement OAM cells are sent with a delay between their transmission.

In order to preclude that both partners wait indefinitely for negotiation OAM cells or acknowledgement cells because of possible losses during transfer, two periods are introduced: IePeriod and AckPeriod. IePeriod (respectively AckPeriod) is the maximum delay between a full SIE transmission and the acknowledgement cell reception (resp. intermediate acknowledgement cell transmission and SIE reception). When IePeriod (resp. AckPeriod) elapsed, the SIE (resp. intermediate acknowledgement cells) is fully transmitted again. To avoid infinite SIE (resp. intermediate acknowledgement cells) transmissions, a maximum number of SIE transmissions MaxTryIe (resp. MaxTryAck for the maximum of intermediate acknowledgement cells retransmissions) is defined as part of the local security policy.

Once the negotiation is completed and the corresponding acknowledgement cells are sent, the new session keys exchanged by the SME protocol can be activated. One solution would be to block the data traffic over the connection during the negotiation duration so that the session keys can be downloaded into the cryptographic unit after the negotiation completion. The problem is that the negotiation duration is not known and that it is inappropriate to block the data traffic for a long time. As such, a better solution is to realize session key exchange in two steps, as being done when updating a new session key. That is, once the negotiation is completed, each connection partner activates its new session key using the SKC (Session Key Changeover) cells (see section 5).

7. Signaling protection

Like in the version 1.0 of the ATM Forum specifications, SCAN proposes that any signaling message (setup, connect, release, status, etc.) is protected proving the origin and integrity of the message. This protection is already ensured if the SME protocol is selected, but it remains limited to the setup and connect messages. As such, it is important to provide another method to ensure authentication and integrity of any signaling messages. This method is later referred to as "**authentication only**", and consists in introducing a digital signature into the SIE Authentication Section field (cf. figure 2). Contrary to the signature generated by the SME protocol, the signature generated for the authentication only is calculated over the entire Security Association Section. The available signature generation algorithm in SCAN is the RSA algorithm.

8. SCAN security policy

Users (e.g. the security officer) are allowed to define the security services and mechanisms to be used over connections from the user space (the Security Policy module mentioned in section 9). That is, each possible ATM destination is provided with a list of authorized encryption algorithms, and modes of operation, a list of authentication algorithms, a list of "in-band" SME protocols to be used for negotiation through OAM cells, and a list of out of band SME protocols to negotiate through ATM signaling, all of them being ordered according to preferences. For SCAN, six encryption algorithms/modes of operation, one authentication algorithm (RSA), four "in-band" SME protocols (two or three-way RSA-based SME protocols + security parameters confidentiality) and two out-of-band SME protocols (two-way RSA- based SME protocol + security parameters confidentiality) are implemented.

Moreover possibility is given to users to monitor security management parameters local to end-stations from the user space. Those parameters include the periodicity rules for new session key update and new security parameters negotiation expressed in seconds, number of cells encrypted under the same session key or percentage of errored-data cells received.

Other security management parameters are session key update oriented, such as the maximum number of SKC/SKE cells to be sent to be sure that at least one arrives at the destination, and the delay between two SKC/SKE cells transmissions. Also they include the cell-loss protocol parameters AckPeriod, IePeriod, MaxTryIe, and MaxTryAck defined in section 6.2.

9. SCAN architecture

Realizing the high-speed ATM cells encryption prototype requires developing an ATM NIC (Network Interface Card) card, the NIC monitoring drivers, and some security management software modules. A SCAN specific ATM NIC card development was necessary to plug a cryptographic unit realizing the High-speed ATM DES/TripleDES (HADES). This HADES unit intercepts the ATM cells flow between the AAL and ATM layers, at the ATM Forum standardized UTOPIA (Universal Test and Operations Physical Interface for ATM) interface for encryption.

The prototype is expected to be operational in the Windows NT 5.0 and Windows98 environments. Drivers are developed using Network Driver Interface Specification (NDIS) version 5. As depicted in figure 3, additionally to the NIC driver, the SCAN software includes three security management modules:

- The SP (Security Policy) module allows users (or the security officer) to inform the IE/OAM module of the security policy (cf. section 8) to be applied for a specific ATM destination.
- The IE/OAM module is responsible for most of the SCAN security management aspects, that is, session keys update, session keys download into the HADES unit, and the security parameters negotiation either through OAM cells or signaling.
- The KM (Key Management) module implements the RSA-based SME protocol, and the RSA authentication service, and therefore participates to the SIE construction together with the IE/OAM module.
- The NIC driver manages the NIC hardware resources, and the NDIS driver memory. It should deviate signaling messages so that all of them go through the IE/OAM module. Contrary to the IE/OAM module, it has access to the data traffic so it is required to inform the IE/OAM of the number of data cells being sent over a connection or the percentage of errored-content data cells received, to make it initiate new session keys updates or new negotiations.

What makes the SCAN prototype attractive with respect to other market ATM security products is its flexibility. Implementing the SP module in the user space allows future users to easily develop their own SP module, as part of an application for instance, with their own user interface to specify their security policy. The KM module being in the user space makes it possible to use SME protocols (respectively, authentication algorithms) other than the SCAN ones by merely replacing the KM module with another module. The latter aspect is interesting considering that some SME protocols (resp.

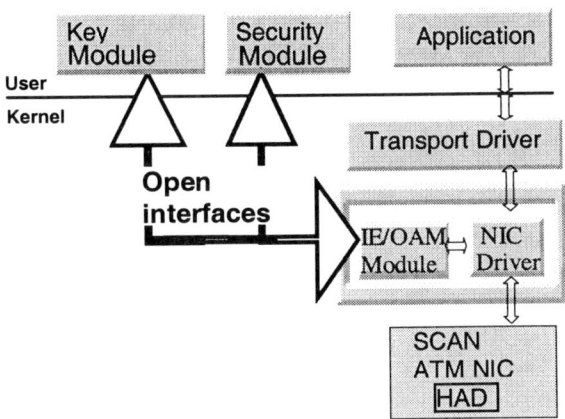

Figure 3 The software modules architecture

authentication algorithms) are prohibited in some countries and the communications protection level may strongly vary depending on people's security needs. Inherent interfaces between the KM and IE/OAM modules, and between the SP and IE/OAM modules are described in the next section.

10. Open interfaces

In SCAN, future users are allowed to develop their own SP and KM modules (see section 9), to integrate them in some applications, and to select more appropriate SME protocols and authentication algorithms than those proposed in SCAN. As such, two interfaces, one between the IE/OAM and SP modules and one between the IE/OAM and KM modules are specified and made publicly available in documents [7] and [8]. Messages exchanged at those interfaces along with their respective propagation direction, the parameters they contain, and their functions are specified in tables 1 and 2.

What clearly appears in table 1 is that the SP module can be used as a connections monitoring tool since it is informed of the security parameters being negotiated over a connection, and it is allowed to release any connections in progress.

For a better understanding of the KM/IEOAM interface, the following notions need first be explained:

- **Indexes**. Details of the SME protocols and authentication algorithms are only known by the KM module. The SME protocols and authentication algorithms being available in the KM module are referred to as indexes in the SP and IE/OAM modules and are listed in a configuration file along with their description in natural language. As such, when defining the security policy, the SP module consults the available protocols and algorithms along with their description in the configuration file. To preclude the SP (users) from selecting a three-way SME protocol for negotiation through signaling, and a protocol realizing some security parameters confidentiality while the ATM Forum compliance is required, 1-byte SME protocol indexes include in their first two bits the two/three-way exchange information, and the provision of the security parameters confidentiality.

- **Partial SIE construction**. The SIE is partly constructed in the IE/OAM and the KM. That is, the IE/OAM is responsible for all the data protection aspects (negotiation of the data confidentiality service, and session key update mechanisms) while the KM is responsible for the SME protocol and authentication service ones (algorithms selection, signature generation/verification). As such, the IE/OAM constructs a partial SIE, and sends it to the KM for completion. To do that, it is required that the KM informs the IE/OAM of the fields to be included, as mentioned in the first four messages of table 2.

Message type	Direction	Message content	Functions
Security Policy Consultation Request	IE/OAM -> SP	Local connection ID ATM partner address	Request for the security policy to be enforced with that ATM partner
Security Parameters	IE/OAM <- SP	Local connection ID Security parameters (SME index, local parameters, etc.)	Response to the previous request message, or Notification of the security policy modifications
Security Parameters Negotiation Result	IE/OAM -> SP	Local connection ID Security parameters (SME index, confidentiality algorithm)	Notification of the security parameters resulting from the negotiation
Release Connection	IE/OAM <-> SP	Local connection Ids	Release of one or more connection(s)

Table 1 : Messages at the SP/IEOAM interface

Message type	Direction	Message content	Functions
SME Protocol Features Consultation Request	IE/OAM -> KM	Local connection ID SME protocol index	Request the SME protocol features useful for the partial SIE construction
SME Protocol Features Consultation Response	IE/OAM <- KM	Local connection ID SME protocol index SME protocol features	Inform of the fields of the partial SIE when an SME protocol is selected depending on the flow number
Authentication Service Features Consultation Request	IE/OAM -> KM	Local connection ID	Request the authentication service features useful for the partial SIE construction
Authentication Service Features Consultation Response	IE/OAM <- KM	Local connection ID Authentication service index Authentication service features	Inform the fields of the partial SIE when the authentication service is selected
SIE for Security Negotiation	IE/OAM <-> KM	Local connection ID SME protocols list SIE	Includes the partial or full SIE used for negotiating the security parameters
SIE for Authentication Only	IE/OAM <-> KM	Local connection ID Authentication algorithms list SIE	Includes the partial or full SIE used only for authentication
Release Connection	IE/OAM <-> KM	Local connection IDs	Release of one or more connection(s)

Table 2 : Messages at the KM/IEOAM interface

Security services and mechanisms	Version 1.0 of the ATM Forum specifications	SCAN
Data confidentiality	ATM layer over the cell payload DES/TripleDES ECB/CBC/ Counter mode	ATM layer over the cell payload DES/TripleDES ECB/CBC
Data integrity	AAL layer	
Session key update	OAM cells MD5/SHA-1	OAM cells MD5
Security parameters negotiation	Through signaling or the data channel	Through signaling or OAM cells
Possible SME protocols	2-way protocol (signaling) 3-way protocol (data channel)	2-way protocol (signaling) 2/3-way protocol (OAM cells) 2/3-way RSA-based protocols (+MD5) SME protocols may include security parameters confidentiality
Signaling protection	Access control Authentication MD5/SHA-1/RIPEMD-160 +RSA/DSA/DESCBC/ DES40CBC/ Triple DES CBC/ FEAL CBC	Authentication MD5+RSA algorithm

Table 3 : Security service placements and security mechanisms offered in SCAN vs the ATM Forum

11. Conclusions

In this paper, we describe the technical choices elected in project SCAN to ensure the ATM traffic encryption at 155 Mbps providing ATM Forum compliance and offering a flexible implementation. This paper presents first the security services and mechanisms currently supported by the version 1.0 of the ATM Forum security specifications [3], and then it details the SCAN security functions being currently under development.

As depicted in table 3, SCAN implements the data encryption and session keys update as specified in the ATM Forum specifications, however it does not support the integrity service proposed by the ATM Forum. Like in the ATM Forum, SCAN proposes that the negotiation of security services used to protect subsequent data exchanges is done at connection setup by introducing a SIE (Security Information Element) dedicated to security into setup signaling messages. What differs from the ATM Forum specifications is the possibility to renegotiate the security services during a connection in progress by encapsulating the same SIE into SCAN specific "negotiation OAM cells". Because of the limited OAM cells payload size, SIEs are segmented prior to their encapsulation. To allow a reliable SIE transfer through OAM cells, a cell-loss recovery protocol has been defined, and validated.

In SCAN two kinds of SIE are implemented. One is ATM Forum compliant, allowing parties to authenticate to each other, to negotiate security parameters, and to exchange keys securely. The other one is SCAN specific. Additionally to the ATM Forum SIE functions, it ensures the confidentiality of part of the negotiated security parameters. Therefore SCAN improves the ATM connections security level since possible eavesdroppers can no longer deduce the data encryption algorithm used, and thus it makes it more difficult for them to break the encryption keys and to filter ATM connections.

Flexibility is targeted in SCAN implementation and is offered by exporting two security management software modules into the user space. One software module implements the security protocol related mechanisms, and the other one manages the security policy. The interfaces between those modules and the kernel space are publicly available, thus making it possible for future SCAN users to develop their own security protocols and their own security policy monitoring applications.

12. Acronyms

DES: Data Encryption Standard
CBC: Cipher Block Chaining
ECB: Electronic CodeBook
IE: Information Element
OAM: Operation And Maintenance
SIE: Security IE
SKC: Session Key Changeover
SKE: Session Key Exchange
SME: Security Message Exchange

13. Acknowledgements

Project SCAN (Secure Communications in ATM Networks) is funded by the European Commission, Directorate General XIII, ACTS Programme 3rd call, project number AC330.

14. References

[1] R.J. Anderson, "A security policy model for clinical information system", *IEEE Symposium on security and privacy*, pp. 30-43, 1996.
[2] M. Laurent, O. Paul, P. Rolin, «Securing Communications over ATM Networks: The Remote ATM Private Networks Inter connection Example», *Annales des télécommunications*, N°9-10, September-October 1998.
[3] ATM Forum, "ATM Security Specification Version 1.0", February 1999.
[4] T.D. Tarman, R.L. Hutchinson, L.G. Pierson, P.E. Sholander, E.L. Witzke, "Algorithm- Agile Encryption in ATM Networks", *IEEE computer*, Vol.31 N°9, pp. 57-64, September 1998.
[5] D. Stevenson, N. Hillery and G. Byrd, "Secure Communications in ATM Networks", *Communications of the ACM*, Vol.38, N°2, 1995.
[6] H. Leitold, R. Posch, E. Areizaga, A. Bouabdallah, M. Laurent, J.M. Mateos, O. Molino, "Security Services in ATM Networks", Interoperable Communication Networks ICON Journal, Baltzer Science Publishers, 1999.
[7] M. Laurent, "The Key Management Module Interface", ACTS deliverable D64, project SCAN, March 1999.
[8] M. Laurent, "The Security Policy Module Interface", ACTS deliverable D63, project SCAN, March 1999.

Track B: Panel Session

The Collection and Use of Meaningful Red Team Metrics

Chair

J. L. Connolly, MITRE Corporation

Track A

Security Analysis

Chair

John McDermott, James Madison University

Using Checkable Types in Automatic Protocol Analysis

Stephen H. Brackin *

Arca Systems / Exodus Communications
303 E. Yates St.
Ithaca, NY 14850

Abstract

The Automatic Authentication Protocol Analyzer, 2nd Version (AAPA2) is a fast, completely automatic tool for formally analyzing cryptographic protocols. It correctly identifies vulnerabilities or their absence in 43 of 51 protocols studied in the literature, and it finds errors in previously asserted authentication properties of two large commercial protocols. This paper describes the AAPA2 and its modeling of type, equality, and inequality tests performed by protocol participants. This description includes defining the AAPA2's Interface Specification Language, 2nd Version (ISL2), which expresses user assumptions about identifiably distinct plaintext types.

1. Introduction

Cryptographic protocols, called simply *protocols* for the remainder of this paper, are short sequences of message exchanges, usually involving encryption, intended to establish secure communication over insecure networks. Whether they actually do so, or can be subverted by an active wiretapper who blocks, replays, or modifies messages, is a notoriously difficult problem [1]. The basic issues are *authentication* (i.e., whether participants know whom they are communicating with), and *nondisclosure* (i.e., whether participants reveal information to anyone not meant to receive it).

Distortions on a protocol's execution by an active wiretapper, or *attacker*, who can potentially control all communication on the network are called *attacks*. Five of the many types of attacks that have been considered in the literature follow [13]:

- Freshness — the attacker replaces a message field with the same field from an earlier protocol run.

- Type — the attacker puts a message field of one type in place of a message field of another type.

- Binding — the attacker passes off one principal's public key as another principal's public key.

- Parallel Session — the attacker puts message fields from one protocol run into message fields in another protocol run, with two or more runs in progress simultaneously.

- Oracle — the attacker sends a message to a legitimate principal knowing that this principal's response will perform some computation useful to the attacker.

The Automatic Authentication Protocol Analyzer, 2nd Version (AAPA2) [9, 10] finds vulnerabilities to freshness, type, binding, parallel session, and some oracle attacks [8, 7]. The earlier Automatic Authentication Protocol Analyzer (AAPA) [3, 2, 5] finds vulnerabilities only to freshness attacks [6, 4].

For 51 of the 53 protocols in an on-line library, by Clark and Jacob, of protocols studied in the literature [13], the AAPA2 correctly identifies 13 as failed and 30 as not failed [8]. It misses vulnerabilities in 3 and raises false alarms in 5 others, though 2 of the false alarms obviously arise from its inability to model algebraic properties of operations used in these protocols [8]. Typos in [13] make it impossible to evaluate the AAPA2's performance on the remaining 2 protocols [8].

The AAPA, by contrast, correctly identifies only 6 of the Clark-Jacob protocols as failed and 33 as not failed [6, 8]. It misses vulnerabilities in 10 and raises false alarms in 2 others, though 1 of the false alarms obviously arises from the AAPA's inability to model algebraic properties of operations used in this protocol [6, 8]. (One of the AAPA "failure identifications" in [6] is actually a false alarm [8].)

The AAPA2 also finds authentication limitations [7] missed by the AAPA [4] in two large commercial protocols from CyberCash, Inc.

---

*This work was supported by the Advanced Research Projects Agency through Rome Laboratory contract F30602-97-C-0303.

All these AAPA2 and AAPA results are conditional on the assumption that the protocols are implemented in such a way that protocol participants perform the reasonable type, equality, and inequality tests, described in Section 2, that the AAPA2 assumes these participants perform.

The AAPA2 produces its results for the Clark-Jacob library, on a 128-meg Ultra 1, in an average of only 2.6 minutes per protocol [8]. The AAPA2 is 3 to 6 times slower than the AAPA, but this difference is almost entirely due to how the two are implemented. The AAPA2 is based on HOL98 [21], which uses Moscow ML, which is interpreted; the AAPA is based on HOL90 [20], which uses Standard ML of New Jersey, which is complied. The AAPA2 uses HOL98 capabilities to find multiple vulnerabilities in single protocols, something that the AAPA cannot do. Since the AAPA2 is still fast, this new functionality is far more important than the loss of speed.

Both the AAPA2 and AAPA produce their results by starting with specifications of protocols and their desired properties in a simple specification language. They both translate these specifications into Higher Order Logic (HOL), automatically construct proofs of the protocols' desired properties, and translate the proved and unproved results back into the simple specification language. They both examine only correct protocol executions, but they both ask whether the *possibility* of attacker interference makes it impossible for legitimate protocol participants to reach their desired authentication conclusions.

The AAPA2 and AAPA both construct their proofs using *authentication logics* derived from the Gong, Needham, Yahalom (GNY) logic [15], which itself is derived from the original Burrows, Abadi, and Needham (BAN)[12] authentication logic. These logics are collections of rules formalizing authentication inferences that an analyst could validly make on the basis of the information that a legitimate protocol participant has received. If the received information does not justify a desired conclusion, then this typically points to a protocol vulnerability that the analyst can easily exploit to construct an attack.

Authentication logics avoid the combinatorial explosion faced by tools that construct attacks on protocols [16, 19, 17], but they currently miss many failures because they over-simplify the problem. They currently make all their authentication deductions, for instance, by assuming that there have been no nondisclosure failures, even in response to attacks.

The AAPA2 represents a major step toward removing the over-simplifications that have limited the effectiveness of the authentication logics. While the AAPA2's BGNY2 authentication logic [9] still assumes that there have been no nondisclosure failures, it does *not* assume, as the AAPA's BGNY authentication logic [3] and all earlier authentication logics do, that protocol participants can always correctly identify and interpret the messages that they receive. Instead, the BGNY2 logic does the following:

- It assumes that legitimate protocol participants perform a computationally feasible set of type, equality, and inequality tests on the message fields that they receive, and it requires that these tests uniquely identify every field that is intended to convey an assertion.

- It requires that the assertion conveyed by every message field that is intended to convey an assertion be explicit in the field itself, not dependent on this field's context.

These additional message-identification and message-explicitness requirements are the main sources of the AAPA2's greater effectiveness compared to the AAPA.

This paper describes the BGNY2 logic's message-identification and message-explicitness requirements. Its description of the BGNY2 message-identification requirements includes giving the full definition of the AAPA2's Interface Specification Language, 2nd Version (ISL2), which allows the user to assume which plaintext types will be distinguished by the legitimate protocol participants' type tests.

The remainder of this paper is organized as follows. Section 2 describes the BGNY2 logic's message-identification requirements and how they incorporate information from ISL2 specifications. Section 3 defines ISL2 and how it expresses user assumptions about testably distinct plaintext types. Section 4 describes the BGNY2 logic's message-explicitness requirements, and how they signal potential ambiguity without raising too many false alarms. Section 5 gives an example, an ISL2 specification and AAPA2 analysis of the Wide-Mouthed Frog protocol. Finally, Section 6 gives suggestions for future work.

In the remainder of this paper, *field* denotes either a message field or a subfield of a message field, and *principal* denotes a legitimate protocol participant. The paper also describes inferences as being made by the principals themselves rather than by an analyst examining the data that these principals have received.

2. Message-Identification

This section describes the BGNY2 logic's message-identification requirements.

The identifications that principals can validly make on the basis of the tests that they perform depend on exactly what these tests are. Neither ISL2 nor BGNY2, though, model protocols in that detail. Instead, BGNY2 assumes that principals perform *all* the type and equality tests that they might reasonably be expected to perform, and some inequality tests.

The identifications that principals can validly make also depend on exactly what pieces of data are available to the attacker, since this determines which possible deceptions principals must avoid. Although it does cover a reasonably large subset of these possibilities, BGNY2 is currently inadequate on this score, which explains why the AAPA2 misses vulnerabilities to oracle attacks for 3 of the 51 Clark-Jacob protocols discussed in Section 1. Section 6 describes a feasible extension to BGNY2 that should correct this problem.

The following three subsections describe the type, equality, and inequality tests that BGNY2 assumes principals perform on all message fields that they receive that are intended to convey assertions. The fourth subsection describes what BGNY2 assumes is the set of all data items available to the attacker that might be used to convey an assertion. BGNY2 requires that the tests a principal performs on any message field intended to convey an assertion uniquely identify this message field among the members of this set.

2.1. Type Tests

As explained in Section 3, ISL2 allows the user to name different functions and pieces of plaintext, to define different types of plaintext, and to assign types to all function outputs and to all pieces of plaintext. BGNY2 assumes that the tests principals perform always distinguish objects of different types — BGNY2 takes this as the functional definition of "type".

If an ISL2 specification of a protocol identifies two pieces of plaintext as being of different types, then this means that user assumes that the software implementing this protocol will perform tests that always distinguish these two pieces of plaintext. These tests need not be explicit. For example, if trying to interpret a network address as a time stamp will cause the software implementing a protocol to produce a core dump, then the user can safely specify network addresses and time stamps as being of different types.

BGNY2 extends these ISL2 type assignments to type assignments for all fields exchanged in a protocol run by making the following assumptions:

- Encrypted and hashed fields are labeled with the names of the functions that produce them, so fields produced by different encryption and/or hash functions are always of different types.

- Tuples of different lengths are of different types.

- All plaintext fields are of different types from all encrypted and hashed fields.

- Algorithms sent as code are of a different type from all other forms of plaintext.

- Passwords, symmetric keys, and public or private keys are of types different from each other and from all user-specified types of plaintext.

These assumptions are realistic. In implemented protocols, encrypted or hased information is often labeled with the name and version number of the software used to produce it, so that the recipient can know which software to use for decrypting or recomputing this information. The attacker could falsify the labels on encrypted or hashed values, but not expect legitimate participants to willingly encrypt and send out information having a label other than the expected one. Software implementing a protocol will also malfunction if it does not check that the information it is operating on is of roughly the expected form.

In implementing these assumptions, BGNY2 defines a HOL concrete-recursive type :TypeName — essentially a parameterized, potentially infinite, enumerated type — whose elements name the types that principals assign to the fields that they receive and the fields that they expect to receive. The :TypeName constructors and their interpretations follow:

- CryptType: this constructor, parameterized by a function name, denotes the type of crypto-text produced by this function.

- FunType: the type of an algorithm sent as code.

- HashType: this constructor, parameterized by a function name, denotes the type of hash code produced by this function.

- PassType: the type of a password.

- PlainType: this constructor, parameterized by a user-defined plaintext type name, denotes this type of plaintext.

- PubKeyType: the type of a public or private key.

- SymKeyType: the type of a symmetric key.

- TnType: the type of the empty field.

- TxType: the type of non-existent fields.

- `TyType`: this constructor, parameterized by two `:TypeName` values, denotes the type of an ordered pair whose first element is of the first `:TypeName` type and whose second element is of the second `:TypeName` type.

BGNY2 assigns a `:TypeName` value to a field as a function of the field and a *function environment*, which the AAPA2 computes from a protocol's ISL2 specification. The function environment is a tuple of functions that express the assumptions the ISL2 specification makes about the algorithms, keys, and type tests used in the protocol. These functions tell the following:

- Which functions are encryption/decryption functions;
- Which functions are hash functions;
- Which functions are key-exchange functions;
- Which functions are tables of passwords;
- Which functions are tables of private keys;
- Which functions are tables of public keys;
- Which functions are tables of symmetric keys;
- Which functions preserve plaintext type; and
- Which user-defined type name is the type of each piece of plaintext.

2.2. Equality Tests

BGNY2, like the defaults for the Common Authentication Protocol Specification Language (CAPSL) [18], assumes that principals perform *all* the equality tests that they are capable of performing. If a principal holds a field and receives something that it expects to contain this field, possibly encrypted in a form that this principal can decrypt, then BGNY2 assumes that this principal will test that the field it receives contains the field that it holds.

If a principal holds a field, receives a field that it expects to contain the field that it holds, and finds that the field it receives indeed does contain the field that it holds, then this by itself proves nothing. If the field that the principal holds is something that this principal received as cleartext, for example, then the attacker might have replaced what this field should have been with what it is now in order to make the equality test that the principal just performed succeed when it should have failed! (Section 5 gives an example.) Only if the principal can be confident that the field it holds is playing the role that this field is supposed to play does the equality test give evidence that the message field this principal receives is what this message field is supposed to be.

BGNY2 addresses this problem using its `RightRole` construct, which asserts that a field is playing its intended role in the protocol run. A field is playing its intended role if it was placed in that role by a legitimate principal not influenced by an attack.

The BGNY2 rules formally defining `RightRole` [9] involve many HOL concepts extraneous to this paper. These concepts include inductively defined relations and the "deep embedding" of an authentication logic into HOL [3]. These rules' English interpretations, though, which follow, are straightforward:

- A principal can be confident that the fields it initially holds are playing their intended roles.
- If a principal can be confident that a field it receives is from another principal in the current protocol run and is of an expected form, then this principal can be confident that this field is playing its intended role.
- If a principal can be confident that a computed (e.g., encrypted) field is playing its intended role, and is capable of inverting the computation (e.g., decrypting), then this principal can be confident that the result of this inversion (e.g., the plaintext) is playing its intended role.
- If a principal can be confident that a hash code is playing its intended role and is capable of recomputing this hash code, then this principal can be confident that the field hashed is playing its intended role.
- A principal can be confident that a pair of elements is playing its intended role if and only if this principal can be confident that each element of this pair is playing its intended role.

BGNY2 interprets the results of a principal's equality tests by using the `RightRole` statements that this principal believes — i.e., the set of fields held by this principal that the principal can be confident are playing their intended roles. BGNY2 only allows a principal to infer the identify of a field from this principal's equality tests if the subset of these tests consisting of tests against values in the "playing their right roles" set uniquely identify the field.

2.3. Inequality Tests

BGNY2 assumes that principals perform a very limited amount of *inequality* testing. It assumes that if principals receive fields containing what they expect to be other principals' names, and they are capable of extracting these names, then they will object if these names are actually their own names. This is easy to implement, analogous to network software that detects and short-circuits messages sent from a site to itself.

2.4. Fields Available to the Attacker

In considering the possible fields that could be confused with an expected field, BGNY2 only considers fields sent during a correct protocol run. This excludes attacker-constructed fields and fields constructed by legitimate principals in response to oracle attacks. It is possible to model that level of attacker creativity, but doing so requires further complicating the logic — see Section 6.

BGNY2 does require, though, that fields be identifiably distinct from fields sent *later* in the protocol run. This models that the attacker can substitute fields from later points in earlier or parallel protocol runs if the tests that principals perform to determine freshness are inadequate, which they are in many protocols [8].

The AAPA2 gives a *warning* if it finds that a protocol has principals do something to check for freshness — e.g., check a timestamp — other than look for fields that they created earlier in the protocol run themselves. Since they can involve messages from different protocol runs, identification failures are particularly significant when they occur along with the AAPA2's warnings.

For practical purposes, BGNY2's model of the fields available to an attacker is also not so inaccurate as it might seem. The issue of message identification only arises for messages that are intended to convey assertions, and only messages whose sources can be reliably determined can reliably convey assertions. (BGNY2 restricts believing the assertion conveyed by a message to messages whose sources can be reliably determined.) Fields whose sources can be reliably determined always involve secrets assumed unavailable to the attacker, so the attacker can only obtain these fields from messages sent by legitimate principals. Feasible type tests also prevent what would otherwise be most oracle attacks, so the attacker can often only obtain fields that are sent during the normal execution of the protocol.

3. ISL2

This section gives the full definition of ISL2. It gives the BNF grammar for ISL2, with interspersed comments. These comments include notes on semantic restrictions imposed by the AAPA2, error messages produced by the AAPA2, and informal descriptions of the meanings of ISL2 constructs asserting properties of principals and fields.

A protocol specification has six parts: a name string that the AAPA2 uses to label its outputs; definitions naming the functions and pieces of plaintext used in the protocol; an optional abbreviations section that introduces substitutions for simplifying the remainder of the specification; the protocol's assumed initial conditions; the definition of a correct run of the protocol; and finally the authentication conditions a correct protocol run is expected to achieve.

```
<ProtSpec> ::=
  <Name> <Defs> [<Abbs>] <Init> <Prot> <Goals>
```

The name string begins and ends with the " character, but can contain any character besides the " character, denoted as in regular expressions by [^"]

```
<Name>   ::= 'NAME' ':' '"' <String> '"' ';'
<String> ::= [<String>] [[^"]]
```

The definitions section is a list of "declarations" or "relation specifications". A "declaration" asserts that a list of identifiers either names plaintext fields of a user-supplied type or names functions of a type determined by ISL2 keywords. A "relation specification" gives the inverse of an invertible function or an identity expressing the critical properties of a key-exchange function; it relates a function, function with key, or function applied to a list containing private and public keys to another function, function with key, or function applied to a list containing private and public keys.

The AAPA2 treats declaring two plaintext fields as being of different named types as assuming that the protocol is implemented in such a way that protocol principals never confuse one with the other. The AAPA2's current implementation requires that all principal names (or equivalently, network addresses) be assumed to be of a type different from all other plaintext types. The other plaintext fields can be assumed to be of any non-zero number of types. Plaintext type names can be arbitrary ISL2 identifiers.

The AAPA2 requires that every function be declared in such a way that the type of its outputs is well-defined. For encryption and hash functions, the AAPA2 assumes that their outputs are produced with headers that identify the algorithms used to produce them. A "type preserving" function — e.g., one that increments or decrements a nonce or timestamp — produces outputs of the same types as its inputs.

The AAPA2 also requires that all keys and passwords be given by functions. (Tables are a type of function.) This avoids the error, made with the AAPA, of having all specifications implicitly assume that a principal that holds a key always knows the role that this key will play in a correct protocol run. This correction allows a server, for instance, to hold a key that it shares with the principal who initiates a protocol run without having this server know *which* of the keys that it holds is the one that it shares with the initiator of the protocol run.

ISL2 identifiers are standard in that they can contain numeric characters or underscores if these characters are preceded by alphabetic characters, but nonstandard in two ways: they can begin with one of the special characters ~ or ^ meaning "not", so these characters can be used to construct intuitive names for the private key corresponding to a public key or the inverse of an invertible function; and they can contain the prime character '. In its output files, the AAPA2 translates both ~ and ^ to UN and translates ' to PR.

```
<Defs> ::= 'DEFINITIONS' ':' <DecOrRelList>
<DecOrRelList> ::=
 [<DecOrRelList>] <DecOrRel>
<DecOrRel> ::= <Dec> | <RelSpec>
<Dec> ::= <IdOrFun> ':' <IdList> ';'
<IdOrFun> ::=
 <Id> | (<Qualifier> 'FUNCTIONS')
<Id> ::= ['~' | '^'] <Chr> [<GenChrList>]
<Chr> ::= 'A'|...|'Z'|'a'|...|'z'
<GenChrList> ::=
 ( <Chr> | <Dgt> | '_' | ''' ) [<GenChrList>]
<Dgt> ::= '0'|...|'9'
<Qualifier> ::=
 'ENCRYPT' | ['KEYED'] 'HASH' |
 'KEYEXCHANGE' | 'PASSWORD' | 'PRIVKEY' |
 'PUBKEY' | 'SYMKEY' | 'TYPEPRESERVING'
<IdList> ::= [<IdList> ','] <Id>
```

If a relation specification says that one function is the inverse of another, both functions must be given with or both without keys; if both are given with keys, the ANYKEY value can be used as the key for both functions. For public-key encryption, the keys, and possibly the functions, will be different. For symmetric-key encryption, the keys (or ANYKEY values) will be the same, though the functions might be different. Representative examples in the various cases are

```
Minus1 HASINVERSE Plus1;
DES WITH ANYKEY HASINVERSE DES WITH ANYKEY;
RSA WITH Kp(A) HASINVERSE RSA WITH ~Kp(A);
```

If the relation specification says that one function value is equal to another, the same function must be given on both sides of the EQUALS, the function must have been declared as a key-exchange function, and this function must be given with lists of arguments whose first elements are private keys and whose second elements are public keys.

```
<RelSpec> ::=
 <Id> ['WITH' <GenKey>] <RelType> <Id>
 ['WITH' <GenKey>] ';'
<GenKey> ::=
 <Data> | ('(' <DataList> ')') | 'ANYKEY'
<RelType> ::= 'HASINVERSE' | 'EQUALS'
```

The optional abbreviations section simply defines identifiers as abbreviations for more complicated ISL2 expressions.

```
<Abbs> ::= 'ABBREVIATIONS' ':' <AbbList> ';'
<AbbList> ::= [<AbbList> ';'] <Abb>
<Abb> ::= <Id> '=' <DataList>
```

The initial-conditions section is syntactically an arbitrary list of ISL2 statements, though the proof attempt will fail with an error message if this list of statements includes other than Believes or Received statements.

```
<Init> ::=
 'INITIALCONDITIONS' ':' <StmtList> ';'
<StmtList> ::= [<StmtList> ';'] <Stmt>
```

Informal descriptions of the meanings of the various ISL2 statement constructors follow. These constructors' formal meanings are given via the function BGNY2 defined in the AAPA2's underlying HOL theory [9]. For brevity, these descriptions say "principal" rather than "principal named by a plaintext message field".

- **Believes**: The principal has adequate reason to believe the statement.

- **Conveyed**: The principal was the creator and source, during the current protocol run, of the field.

- **Fresh**: The field was created for the current protocol run.

- **Possesses**: The principal has received the field or is capable of computing this field from fields that it has received.

- **PrivateKey**: The key, for the algorithm, is one of the principal's private keys.

- **PublicKey**: The key, for the algorithm, is one of the principal's public keys.

- **Received**: The principal received the field before the current protocol run, or received this field as, or as part of, some message sent earlier in the current run.

- `RightRole`: The field is playing the role in the current protocol run that it plays in a correct run [9, 10]. `RightRole` often appears in the AAPA2's `.fail` and `.prvd` output files (see Section 5), but it is seldom useful in ISL2 specifications.

- `SharedSecret`: The field is unguessable, and if the pair of principals possess it, or come to possess it through secure means, then they are or will be the only ones, other than principals they both trust, who possess it.

- `Trustworthy`: If the principal was the source of a field with an associated statement, then this is adequate reason for believing this statement.

Statements are defined in terms of "statement sublists", which are lists of implicitly conjuncted statements separated by semicolons, and by lists of fields.

```
<Stmt> ::=
 (<Id> 'Believes' <Stmt>) |
 (<Id> 'Conveyed' <DataList>) |
 ('Fresh' <DataList>) |
 (<Id> 'Possesses' <DataList>) |
 ('PrivateKey' <Id> <Id> <Data>) |
 ('PublicKey' <Id> <Id> <Data>) |
 (<Id> 'Received' <DataList>) |
 ('RightRole' <DataList>) |
 ('SharedSecret' <Id> <Id> <DataList>) |
 ('Trustworthy' <Id>) |
 ('(' <StmtSubList> ')')
<StmtSubList> ::= [<StmtSubList> ';'] <Stmt>
<DataList> ::= [<DataList> ','] <Data>
```

A field is either an identifier — a piece of plaintext or an abbreviation — or an identifier previously declared as a function applied to a list of arguments, or an expression denoting signed or encrypted fields. The field `<x>h(k)` denotes `x` together with a message authentication code produced from `x` with key-dependent hash function `h` and key `k`. The field `[x](h,f)(k)` denotes `x` together with a signature that is the encryption, using function `f` and key `k`, of the hash of `x` produced using non-key-dependent function `h`. Finally, `{x}f(k)` denotes `x` encrypted with function `f` and key `k`.

Every hashed, encrypted, or signed field can optionally have an associated *extension*, which is a statement bound to the field that the protocol expects a principal to believe or else it would not send this field. For signed fields, the AAPA binds the extension to the message authentication code or encrypted hash code that serves as the signature part of the field. The field `t||(slist)` denotes field `t` with the implicitly conjuncted list of statements `slist` as an extension.

The ISL2 treatment of extensions comes from the GNY logic [15], but the AAPA2 restricts extensions to hashed or encrypted fields, since only hashed or encrypted fields are protected from being secretly modified in transit, only fields that cannot be secretly modified in transit can be confidently identified as coming from a particular principal, and only fields coming from a particular principal can be confidently believed to have the properties the protocol expects them to have.

```
<Data> ::=
 (<Id> [<Ext>]) |
 (<Id> '(' <DataList> ')' [<Ext>]) |
 ('<' <DataList> '>' <Id> '(' <DataList> ')'
  [<Ext>]) |
 ('[' <DataList> ']' '(' <Id> ',' <Id> ')'
  '(' <DataList> ')' [<Ext>]) |
 ('{' <DataList> '}' <Id> '(' <DataList> ')'
  [<Ext>])
<Ext> ::= '||' '(' <StmtSubList> ')'
```

Each message reception begins a new *stage* in a protocol run. The definition of a correct protocol run is a list of messages, separated by semicolons. Each message is given by a header giving the protocol stage, the sending principal, the receiving principal, and the field sent. The AAPA2 automatically adds the names of the sending principal and the intended receiving principal as the first two fields of every message sent.

```
<Prot> ::= 'PROTOCOL' ':' <MsgList> ';'
<MsgList> ::= [<MsgList> ';'] <Msg>
<Msg> ::= <Header> ':' <DataList>
<Header> ::= <Number> '.' <Id> '->' <Id>
<Number> ::= ('1'|...|'9') [<DgtList>]
<DgtList> ::= [<DgtList>] <Dgt>
```

Finally, the goals section gives the correct run's expected authentication properties, by protocol stage, as statements. A stage can have no associated statements, in which case it can be omitted, or it can have several associated statements, in which case these statements are given in a list with each statement terminated by a semicolon. While stages can be omitted, they must be given in increasing order.

```
<Goals> ::= GOALS ':' <GoalStmtList>
<GoalStmtList> ::=
 [<GoalStmtList>] <GoalStmt>
<GoalStmt> ::= <Number> '.' <StmtList> ';'
```

4. Explicitness Requirements

This section describes how BGNY2 protects against attacks that involve tricking the principals who receive message fields into interpreting these fields in ways that the principals sending these fields did not intend. Such attacks can involve modifying neighboring plaintext fields (e.g., "from" and "to" labels) or redirecting message fields to principals not intended to receive them. Binding attacks typically work in this way.

BGNY2 protects against such attacks by requiring that a principal only believe the statement bound to a message field if *every* piece of plaintext in this statement is explicitly contained in the message field itself. This prevents misinterpretations arising from attacker-induced distortions in the message field's context.

To avoid what would otherwise be a large number of extraneous explicitness failures, though, BGNY2 treats any field encrypted with a principal's private key as containing the name of this principal, and it treats any field encrypted with a symmetric key that is a secret shared by two principals as containing the names of these principals. Since being a private key or a shared secret depends on the current state of the protocol run, this introduces some dependence on context, but not any *new* dependence on context — i.e., any dependence on context not already present in the authentication logics' assumptions about shared secrets.

For the 51 Clark-Jacob protocols discussed in Section 1, BGNY2's explicitness requirements point up potential vulnerabilities in only 8 protocols, and for 6 of these protocols there are attacks that successfully exploit these vulnerabilities [8].

5. Example

This section gives an example of the very simple, but nevertheless failed, protocol, the Wide-Mouthed Frog protocol [13], and the AAPA2's analysis of it.

In this protocol, principals A and B communicate through a trusted server S, using symmetric-key encryption with keys that they each share with S, to exchange a newly created symmetric key for further communication. A begins the protocol by sending S a package, encrypted with a key Kas that A shares with S, containing a timestamp Ta, the name B of the principal that A wants to communicate with, and an unguessable, newly generated symmetric key Kab that S is to forward to B. S then sends B a package, encrypted with a key Kbs that B shares with S, containing S's timestamp Ts, the name A of the principal that wants to communicate with B, and the key Kab.

The protocol's ISL2 specification follows. In ISL2, a term of the form {x}f(k) denotes x encrypted with function f and key k, and the -> operator means "sends". Every message is implicitly labeled with the names of its sender and intended receiver — though the attacker can change these labels before the message is received. The || operator binds a statement to a field; the specification assumes that the principal sending this field will not send it unless this principal believes this statement. The statements in the INITIALCONDITIONS and GOALS sections, and bound to fields in the PROTOCOL section, are defined in Section 3, which also gives the full definition of ISL2.

NAME: "Wide-Mouthed Frog";
DEFINITIONS:
Name: A,B,S; Data: Ta,Ts;
ENCRYPT FUNCTIONS: E;
SYMKEY FUNCTIONS: Ka,Ks;
E WITH ANYKEY HASINVERSE E WITH ANYKEY;

ABBREVIATIONS:
Kab = Ka(B); Kas = Ks(A); Kbs = Ks(B);

INITIALCONDITIONS:
A Received E,Ka,B,S,Ta,Kas;
A Believes SharedSecret A B Kab;
B Received E,Kbs;
B Believes
 (Fresh Ts; SharedSecret B S Kbs;
  Trustworthy S);
S Received E,Ks,Ts;
S Believes
 (Fresh Ta; SharedSecret S A Kas;
  SharedSecret S B Kbs; Trustworthy A);

PROTOCOL:
1. A -> S: {Ta,B,Kab}E(Kas)
            ||(SharedSecret A B Kab);
2. S -> B: {Ts,A,Kab}E(Kbs)
            ||(SharedSecret A B Kab);

GOALS:
1. S Possesses Kab;
   S Believes SharedSecret A B Kab;
2. B Possesses Kab;
   B Believes SharedSecret A B Kab;

The following paragraphs give a brief introduction to AAPA2 operation; see [11] for more information. In constructing its proofs, the AAPA2 follows the algorithm described in [10]. On a stage by stage basis, it automatically constructs and proves, where possible, a collection of *default* goals that express the authentication properties of the protocol run that are likely to be of interest. The AAPA2 proves as many default goals as it can for a stage, then checks whether the proved default goals have the specified authentication goals for that stage as easy consequences.

If the AAPA2 is unable to prove all the specified authentication goals for a stage of the protocol, then it signals a *user-goal failure*. If the AAPA2 finds that a principal could otherwise infer the source of an encrypted or hashed field, but that this principal cannot distinguish this field from other fields that BGNY2 assumes are readily available to the attacker, then the AAPA2 signals an *identification failure*. If the AAPA2 finds that a principal could otherwise believe the statement bound to a field, but not every piece of plaintext in this statement is explicitly contained in the field itself, then the AAPA2 signals an *explicitness failure*.

The AAPA2 gives a *warning*, but does not call it a failure, if it finds that a protocol has principals do something to check for freshness — e.g., check a timestamp — other than look for fields that they created earlier in the protocol run themselves. It has these "second-class failures" as a convenience to users, since it would otherwise label most protocols as failed [8].

The AAPA2 completes each analysis by making *false* assumptions as necessary [10]. This enables it to find more than one problem in a specification in a single execution, and prevents earlier vulnerabilities from hiding later ones.

The AAPA2 produces terminal output describing its progress in analyzing the protocol, any failures that it encounters, and any false assumptions that it makes. After it finishes the protocol's last stage, it produces terminal output stating whether it raised warnings and/or found failures. If it finds one or more failures for an ISL2 specification in a file `foo.isl`, it produces a file `foo.fail` containing ISL2 descriptions of all its unproved default goals and a file `foo.prvd` containing ISL2 descriptions of any false axioms it assumed and all the theorems that it proved. It outputs axioms about sets in a pseudo-ISL2 that states equalities between sets of ISL2 statements or terms. If a "theorem" depends on one or more false axioms, the AAPA2 labels its output of that "theorem" with the names of these axioms.

The AAPA2 produces a formal analysis of the Wide-Mouthed Frog ISL2 specification, on a 128-meg Ultra 1, in 1 minute, 34 seconds. The AAPA2's terminal output, edited to take up less space, follows:

```
Beginning Wide-Mouthed Frog proofs
Warning!  Principal B believes term
  Ts
is fresh, but it does not create this term
Warning!  Principal S believes term
  Ta
is fresh, but it does not create this term
Proving default goals, stage 1
Identification failure, stage: 1!
Receiver's default tests do not distinguish:
  {Ta,B,Ka(B)}E(Ks(A))
from the following term(s) substitutable by
the attacker:
  {Ts,A,Ka(B)}E(Ks(B))
Making the false assumption
  AX1: {{Ta,B,Ka(B)}E(Ks(A)),
        {Ts,A,Ka(B)}E(Ks(B))} =
       {{Ta,B,Ka(B)}E(Ks(A))};
and continuing analysis of protocol
Proving user goals, stage 1
Proving default goals, stage 2
Proving user goals, stage 2
```

Warning(s) and failure(s): Wide-Mouthed Frog

Since the AAPA2's `.fail` and `.prvd` output files are typically useful only if it finds user-goal failures, and are indeed not useful for the Wide-Mouthed Frog example, this paper will omit giving them.

The AAPA2's analysis of the Wide-Mouthed Frog protocol shows this protocol's essential vulnerability: S cannot distinguish the field `{Ta,B,Kab}E(Kas)` from the field `{Ts,A,Kab}E(Kbs)`, so the attacker can mislabel a copy of a message field that S sends B for A and pass it off as a request *from* B to communicate *with* A, in the process updating the timestamp `Ta` to `Ts`. The attacker can repeat this process indefinitely, alternately pretending to be B and A, and keep A and B using the key `Kab` until the attacker has been able to determine this key.

6. Future Work

This section describes possible future work.

The AAPA2's major remaining limitation is that BGNY2 does not accurately model the set of data items available to the attacker. This is responsible for all 3 of the AAPA2's "misses" on the 51 Clark-Jacob protocols discussed in Section 1 [8]. Although it is provably impossible to *exactly* determine the set of data items available to an attacker in less than exponential time [14], it should be possible to incorporate a reasonable *superset* of this set into an extension of BGNY2 without significantly degrading the AAPA2's speed.

An extension of BGNY2 could define a superset of the data items available to an attacker as follows:

- Assume that the attacker has been able to induce an arbitrary number of previous and concurrent runs of the protocol.

- Assume that every output that could have been produced by a legitimate principal has been produced by this principal — i.e., assume that all possibilities covered by conditional tests have occurred.

Such a superset will be infinite, but the extended logic could still use unification techniques to prove that a fixed set of type, equality, and inequality tests performed by a principal will succeed in identifying a unique member of this set.

The extended logic could also incorporate use of this superset into all of its rules dealing with shared secrets, to require that everything treated as a shared secret is not even potentially made available to the attacker. By doing so, the extended logic would become the first authentication logic to address nondisclosure as well as authentication.

Finally, given the AAPA2's success with modeling type tests implicitly performed by protocol principals, the Common Authentication Protocol Specification Language (CAPSL) [18], a standard specification language being developed for all protocol designers and all protocol analysis tools, should incorporate such tests. CAPSL already allows user-defined types, but does not include operators that convert these types into functions testing whether particular fields are of particular user-defined types.

References

[1] R. Anderson and R. Needham. Programming satan's computer. In J. van Leeuwen, editor, *Computer Science Today*, number 1000 in Lecture Notes in Computer Science. Springer-Verlag, 1995.

[2] S. Brackin. Deciding cryptographic protocol adequacy with HOL: The implementation. In *Theorem Proving in Higher Order Logics*, number 1125 in Lecture Notes in Computer Science, pages 61–76, Turku, Finland, August 1996. Springer-Verlag.

[3] S. Brackin. A HOL extension of GNY for automatically analyzing cryptographic protocols. In *Proceedings of Computer Security Foundations Workshop IX*, County Kerry, Ireland, June 1996. IEEE.

[4] S. Brackin. Automatic formal analyses of two large commercial protocols. In *Proceedings of the 1997 DIMACS Workshop on Design and Formal Verification of Security Protocols*, Piscataway, NJ, September 1997.

[5] S. Brackin. An interface specification language for automatically analyzing cryptographic protocols. In *Internet Society Symposium on Network and Distributed System Security*, San Diego, CA, February 1997. IEEE.

[6] S. Brackin. Evaluating and improving protocol analysis by automatic proof. In *Proceedings of Computer Security Foundations Workshop XI*, Rockport, MA, June 1998. IEEE.

[7] S. Brackin. Automatically detecting authentication limitations in commercial security protocols. In *Proceedings of the 22nd National Conference on Information Systems Security*, Alexandria, VA, October 1999. IEEE.

[8] S. Brackin. Empirical Tests of the Automatic Authentication Protocol Analyzer, 2nd Version (AAPA2). Technical Report 99006, Arca Systems / Exodus Communications, Ithaca, NY, June 1999.

[9] S. Brackin. A highly effective logic for automatically analyzing cryptographic protocols. Technical Report 99023, Arca Systems / Exodus Communications, Ithaca, NY, May 1999.

[10] S. Brackin. Implementing effective automatic cryptographic protocol analysis. Technical Report 99032, Arca Systems / Exodus Communications, Ithaca, NY, June 1999.

[11] S. Brackin. User's Manual for the Automatic Authentication Protocol Analyzer, 2nd Version (AAPA2). Technical Report 98027, Arca Systems / Exodus Communications, Ithaca, NY, June 1999.

[12] M. Burrows, M. Abadi, and R. Needham. A logic of authentication. Technical Report 39, Digital Equipment Corporation, Systems Research Center, Palo Alto, CA, February 1990.

[13] J. Clark and J. Jacob. A survey of authentication protocol literature: Version 1.0. A continually updated library, available at www.cs.york.ac.uk/~jac/, of protocols analyzed in the literature.

[14] N. Durgin, P. Lincoln, J. Mitchell, and A. Scedrov. Undecidability of bounded security protocols. In *Workshop on Formal Methods and Security Protocols*, Trento, Italy, July 1999.

[15] L. Gong, R. Needham, and R. Yahalom. Reasoning about belief in cryptographic protocols. In *Proceedings of the Symposium on Security and Privacy*, pages 234–248, Oakland, CA, May 1990. IEEE.

[16] G. Lowe. Breaking and fixing the Needham-Schroeder public-key protocol using FDR. In *Proceedings of TACAS*, number 1055 in Lecture Notes in Computer Science, pages 147–166, New York, 1996. Springer-Verlag.

[17] C. Meadows. The NRL Protocol Analyzer: An overview. *Journal of Logic Programming*, 26(2):113–131, 1996.

[18] J. Millen. CAPSL web page. At www.csl.sri.com /~millen /capsl, 1998.

[19] J. Millen, S. Clark, and S. Freedman. The Interrogator: Protocol security analysis. *IEEE Trans. on Software Engineering*, SE-13(2):274–288, February 1987.

[20] K. Slind. HOL90.7. At research.att.com /dist /ml/hol90/hol90.7.tar.gz, 1994.

[21] K. Slind. HOL98. At www.cl.cam.ac.uk/Research /HVG/FTP, 1998.

SCR: A Practical Approach to Building a High Assurance COMSEC System[*]

James Kirby, Jr.   Myla Archer   Constance Heitmeyer

Code 5546, Naval Research Laboratory, Washington, DC 20375

{kirby, archer, heitmeyer}@itd.nrl.navy.mil

Abstract

To date, the tabular-based SCR (Software Cost Reduction) method has been applied mostly to the development of embedded control systems. This paper describes the successful application of the SCR method, including the SCR* toolset, to a different class of system, a COMSEC (Communications Security) device called CD that must correctly manage encrypted communications. The paper summarizes how the tools in SCR* were used to validate and to debug the SCR specification and to demonstrate that the specification satisfies a set of critical security properties. The development of the CD specification involved many tools in SCR*: a specification editor, a consistency checker, a simulator, the TAME interface to the theorem prover PVS, and various other analysis tools. Our experience provides evidence that use of the SCR* toolset to develop high-quality requirements specifications of moderately complex COMSEC systems is both practical and low-cost.

1 Introduction

COMSEC (Communications Security) devices, devices which manage encrypted communications, are vital to the correct operation of U.S. military systems. CD, the COMSEC device of interest in this paper, is designed to provide cryptographic processing for a U.S. Navy radio receiver. In addition to generating keystreams compatible with another cryptographic device and supporting multiple channels and multiple cryptographic algorithms, CD downloads associated algorithms and keys into working storage, assigns them to designated communication channels, maintains the association between an algorithm and its keys, and clears algorithms and keys from memory. CD, based on a technology called PEIP (Programmable, Embeddable INFOSEC Product) for implementing COMSEC devices in software as well as hardware, presents a new challenge in the development of COMSEC devices. While a solid base of experience exists for implementing trustworthy COMSEC devices in hardware, implementing COMSEC devices in software is rare.

During the last decade, numerous formal methods, many with automated support, have been proposed for developing high assurance software systems. Because studies (e.g., [6]) show that errors, such as security property violations, that are introduced early in system development are both the most common and the most expensive to fix, the goal of many formal methods is to discover and eliminate flaws during the early stages of system development. While mechanically supported formal methods hold great promise for identifying errors early, the exceptional user expertise and effort usually required to apply them present a major barrier to their use in the development of practical systems.

The SCR (Software Cost Reduction) method [15, 11] is a formal method which offers a user-friendly tabular notation for specifying system requirements, and a set of tools called SCR* for detecting, often automatically, flaws in the requirements specification. Although originally designed to specify the requirements of safety-critical control systems, SCR can also be used to specify the required behavior of other systems, such as COMSEC systems. To make SCR* useful to practitioners, the tools are designed to be as automatic as possible and to complement and support one another. Included among the tools in SCR* are an automated *consistency checker*, a *simulator*, and various verification tools.

To provide a high degree of assurance in the correctness of CD's specification, we have applied the SCR method, including the SCR* tools [12, 13, 11]. Our results suggest that applying the SCR method in the development of COMSEC devices of moderate size and complexity is practical, effective, and low-cost. In approximately one person-month, we were able to represent a significant subset of a prose requirements document for CD in the the SCR notation and to establish that the SCR specification satisfies a set of security properties. The product of this effort is a high-quality requirements specification in whose correctness we have a high degree of confidence. This requirements specification can guide both the development of the source code and the development of test sets for eval-

---

[*]This work is funded by ONR. For related work, see http://www.chacs.itd.nrl.navy.mil/SCR.

uating the conformance of the source code with the system requirements.

The paper is organized as follows. It first introduces the SCR method and the SCR* toolset in Section 2, and then describes in Section 3 how the tools were applied to CD. Section 4 discusses the results of applying SCR* to the CD specification. Finally, section 5 discusses related work, and Section 6 presents our conclusions.

2 The SCR Method and Tools

The SCR method is a formal method designed to specify and analyze the requirements of safety-critical control systems. Since its introduction in 1978, the SCR requirements method has been applied successfully to a wide range of critical systems, including avionics systems, space systems, telephone networks, and control systems for nuclear power plants. See, e.g., [15, 23, 8, 7, 22, 19].

An SCR requirements specification describes both the system environment, which is nondeterministic, and the required system behavior, which is usually deterministic [12, 14]. Quantities in the environment that the system monitors and controls are represented by *monitored* and *controlled* variables. SCR specifications also use two types of auxiliary variables: *mode classes* (whose values are called *modes*) and *terms*, both of which often capture historical information. In the SCR model, the system environment nondeterministically produces a sequence of input events, where an *input event* is a change in some monitored quantity. The system is represented as a state machine (i.e., automaton) whose current state is determined by the values of the state variables, where a state variable is either a monitored or controlled variable, a mode class, or a term. Executions of the system begin in some initial state, after which the system responds to each input event in turn by changing state and by producing zero or more output events, where an *output event* is a change in a controlled quantity. The system behavior is assumed to be *synchronous*: the system completely processes one input event before the next input event is processed.

An SCR specification defines the transitions of a system using of a set of tables. Each table describes the value of a given state variable in the new state. Each *dependent variable*, i.e., each controlled variable, term, and mode class, has a corresponding table. Two constructs used in the tables are conditions and events. A *condition* is a predicate on system states. An *event* occurs when the value of any variable changes. The notation "@T(c) WHEN d" denotes a *conditioned event* defined as

$$@T(c) \text{ WHEN } d \stackrel{\text{def}}{=} \neg c \wedge c' \wedge d,$$

where the unprimed conditions c and d are evaluated in the "old" state, and the primed condition c' is evaluated in the "new" state. Informally, this denotes the event "predicate c becomes true in the new state when predicate d holds in the old state". The table for a mode class is a *mode transition table*, which maps a source mode and an event to a destination mode. The table for any term or controlled variable is either an *event table*, which maps conditioned events to values of the variable in the next state, or a *condition table*, which maps conditions on the next state to values of the variable in the next state.

In addition to tables, an SCR specification contains dictionaries of *types*, *variable declarations*, *constant declarations*, *environmental assumptions*, and *specification assertions*. The specification assertion dictionary records required system properties, e.g., security properties. Our experience with practical systems is that most system properties can be represented as either state invariants or transition invariants, where a *state invariant* is a property that holds in every reachable state and a *transition invariant* is a property that holds in every reachable prestate/poststate pair (i.e., reachable transition).

The SCR* toolset [12, 13, 11] is a set of software tools developed by NRL to provide mechanized support for the SCR method. The tools include a *specification editor* for creating and modifying both an operational requirements specification (i.e., a state-machine representation of the required behavior) and a set of properties, such as safety and security properties; a *dependency graph browser* to display the dependencies among the variables in the specification; an automated *consistency checker* to expose missing cases, unwanted nondeterminism, and other application-independent errors [12]; a *simulator* to allow users to validate the specification; an interface to the *model checker* Spin [16] to detect violations of critical application properties; and an *invariant generator* [18] that computes state invariants from an SCR specification. To provide formal underpinnings for the tools and for the analysis techniques the tools implement, a formal model defines the semantics of SCR requirements specifications [14, 12].

Several additional tools have been recently integrated with SCR* by automatically translating the internal representation of an SCR specification into the input languages of the tools. These tools include *TAME* (Timed Automata Modeling Environment) [1, 2], an interface to the theorem prover PVS [25] for proving properties of automata models, a *validity checker* [4] which uses an integrated set of decision procedures to automatically check whether a given property is a state or transition invariant of an SCR specification, and a *test set generator* [9] that automatically generates test sets from an SCR specification.

3 Applying SCR* to CD

This section describes the translation of a subset of the prose specification provided by the CD developers into an SCR specification and the results of applying the SCR* tools to the SCR specification. The tools and analysis techniques that were applied include the consistency checker, simulator, invariant generator, Spin, TAME, and the validity checker. This section also describes our plan to use the SCR* testing tool to automatically construct test sets from the SCR specification of CD.

3.1 From Prose to SCR Requirements

To develop the SCR specification, we studied the CD Systems Requirement Document (SRD) provided by the CD project manager, focusing on the constraints it imposed on the required system behavior and representing those constraints using SCR constructs. The CD SRD, a traditional 2167A-style document, was sufficiently precise and complete about key and algorithm management, modes of operation, and security requirements relating to power, tampering, and zeroizing for us to capture the required behavior in the SCR specification of CD. We obtained security properties by examining the SCR specification and surmising the goals of the required behavior and by interpreting descriptions of functions in the CD SRD as security requirements. The CD project manager has reviewed the set of security properties that we formulated and confirmed that, except for one, they are reasonable security properties of CD. The exception, according to the project manager, was a property whose hypothesis (backup power is over voltage), would never be satisfied.

Our SCR specification describes the part of CD's behavior (as described in the SRD) that is consistent with the SCR model of black-box requirements. In SCR, the CD behavior is described in terms of inputs (the status of primary and backup power, data provided by the host, and positions of switches), outputs (indicator lights and status messages), and modes. In addition, our specification describes some memory management behavior that goes beyond SCR's usual modeling of black-box requirements. Usually, in SCR, memory is considered to be internal to the black box, and thus invisible from the outside, but we treat it as externally visible by defining controlled variables that represent the memory locations in which the CD software can store algorithms and keys. This memory management behavior models the rules in the CD SRD for loading algorithms and keys, associating them with channels, and clearing them from memory. There is (intentionally) not enough information in the CD SRD to specify the rules for cryptographic synchronization and generating keystreams. As a result, our SCR specification omits some required behavior that would be relevant and useful to reason about.

The CD SRD assumes that an unlimited number of algorithms and keys can be distributed among an unspecified number of storage locations and an unspecified number of channels. In the SCR specification, we assume that there are two key banks, each with two key storage locations; at most 1,000 different algorithms and 1,000 different keys; and two channels. The SCR CD specification has one more mode than described in the CD SRD: we add an Off mode so that the system is always in exactly one mode.

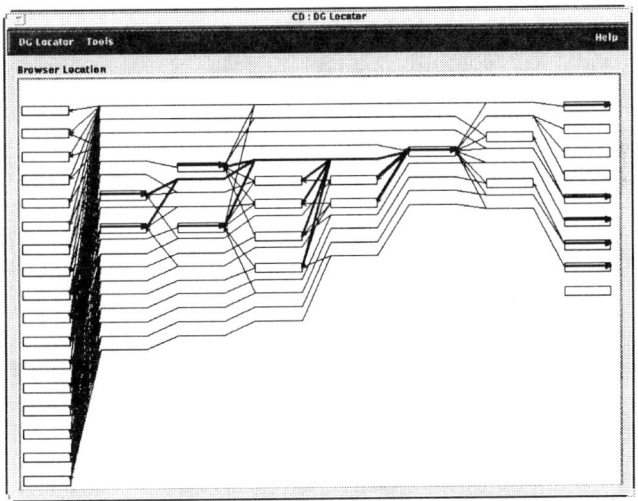

Figure 1. Full dependency graph for SCR CD.

Our SCR specification contains 39 variables—17 monitored variables, one mode class, two terms, and 19 controlled variables. Figure 1 shows the variable dependency graph for the complete SCR specification of CD. Variables are represented as boxes, and an arrow from one variable to a second variable indicates that the value of the first variable in the new state depends on the value of the second variable in either the current state or the new state. The heavy lines are backarrows; the number of backarrows reflects the complexity of the dependencies among the variables, which is also reflected in the complexities of the tables. Although this graph has cycles, the SCR* consistency checker was used to assure that there were no circular dependencies among the "new-state" variables (see Section 3.2).

Most of the effort spent in building the SCR specification of CD took place as a background activity over a nine-month period. The initial build of the specification required approximately one person-week. About one additional person-week was needed to refine and complete the specification, with frequent use of the consistency checker (see Section 3.2).

3.2 Applying the Consistency Checker

The consistency checker uses static analysis techniques to expose syntax and type errors, variable name discrepancies, unwanted nondeterminism (called *disjointness errors*), missing cases (called *coverage errors*), and circular definitions (i.e., cycles in the dependencies among new-state variables). The checks are fully automatic and thus require no user input or guidance. When an error is detected, the consistency checker facilitates error correction by providing detailed feedback. For some types of errors (e.g., disjointness and coverage errors), the checker, in addition to describing the error, will highlight where in the specification the error occurs, and display a transition or state that demonstrates the error.

The consistency checker may be used at any stage in the development of a specification. All checks, except those for missing cases and nondeterminism, execute in a few seconds and are typically invoked many times during an editing session. In developing the CD specification, we frequently used the less expensive consistency checks as "sanity" checks. Since applying the more expensive checks for missing cases and nondeterminism to the entire CD specification usually requires between five and nine minutes, we invoked these checks less frequently.

Error Message from Tool	SCR* Highlights	Diagnosis
"smOperation Mode Transition Table: Cycle Detection ERROR: Cycle #1: Table smOperation uses mode class smOperation in the Name field; Function is smOperation Mode Transition Table"	Name of mode class in mode transition table	Events in table for smOperation introduce a cycle in the new state variable dependencies

Figure 2. Consistency checker feedback.

Figure 2 gives an example of an error message generated by the consistency checker during our development of the SCR specification of CD. The first column gives the error message displayed by the tool. The second and third columns describe the part of the specification that is highlighted at user request and our diagnosis of the error. In this example, the error is a circular definition, i.e., a cycle among the new state dependencies. This cycle occurred on our first attempt to describe CD's mode transitions in cases where the prose requirements described entry into a mode as ultimately resulting in exit from that mode to some other mode.

3.3 Simulating the CD Specification

In contrast to other tools in SCR*, which are for verification, the simulator is a tool for *validation*. The purpose of verification is to prove that the specification satisfies selected system properties, such as state and transition invariants; the purpose of validation is to confirm that the specification captures the operational system behavior intended by the customer. The simulator permits application experts to validate the behavior defined by the specification before the system is built. They can do so by running scenarios through the simulator rather than by reading the detailed SCR specification.

A scenario is a sequence of input events, each of which assigns a new value to one of the monitored variables. For each input event in the sequence, the simulator updates the values of the dependent variables before processing the next input event. In addition to presenting the current state of the execution, the simulator can present a history of the execution and report when a scenario violates specified properties.

The simulator's standard generic interface presents the current state of an execution in terms of the current values of the state variables, i.e., the monitored variables, mode classes, terms, and controlled variables. A disadvantage of the generic interface is that it presents an abstract description of the system state that application experts find unnatural. To overcome this problem, the simulator supports the rapid construction of graphical front-ends customized for particular applications. Each application-specific front-end contains graphical representations of switches, indicator lights, dials, and other entities in the human-computer interface that, in contrast to the generic interface, clearly and directly communicate information about the system behavior to the user.

We found an application-specific front-end for CD useful in interacting with the CD project manager. After viewing a simulation of CD using the CD-specific front-end (built in less than a day), the CD project manager provided us with useful feedback on the SCR specification of the CD. Thus, evaluation of the CD specification through this front-end to the simulator allowed a very effective use of a very scarce commodity, the project manager's time.

3.4 Automatic Invariant Generation

The SCR* invariant generator is based on an algorithm for constructing state invariants from the functions defining the dependent variables. Consider a dependent variable v, defined by a mode transition table or an event table, which takes values in a finite set $\{a_1, a_2, \ldots, a_n\}$. The algorithm examines the conditions that can cause the value of variable v to change and generates for each a_i an invariant of the form

$$(v = a_i) \Rightarrow C_i,$$

where C_i is a predicate defined in terms of variables on which v depends. When v can take values in a very large (even infinite) set, the hypotheses $v = a_i$ are replaced by predicates defining a finite partition on the range of v; for example, when v has a numeric value, each predicate will define an interval. The appropriate intervals can often be computed automatically from the specification by identifying the values with which v is compared.

The automatic invariant generator currently provided in SCR* partially implements the algorithm for generating invariants from a mode transition table. The full algorithm, which we currently execute by hand, includes methods for generating invariants from event tables and condition tables and a strengthened method for mode transition tables; it will ultimately be implemented in SCR*. Figure 3 lists the nontrivial invariants that were generated automatically from the mode transition table for the CD mode class smOperation.

No.	Description	Generated Invariant
1	In Idle mode, the system is healthy and backup power is not overvoltage	smOperation = sIdle ⇒ mHealthyBackground AND mBackupPower ≠ overvoltage
2	In Standby mode, backup power is neither undervoltage nor unavailable	smOperation = sStandby ⇒ mBackupPower ≠ undervoltage AND mBackupPower ≠ unavailable
3	In Traffic Processing mode, the system is healthy and backup power is not overvoltage	smOperation = sTrafficProcessing ⇒ mHealthyBackground AND mBackupPower ≠ overvoltage
4	In Configuration mode, the system is healthy and backup power is not overvoltage	smOperation = sConfiguration ⇒ mHealthyBackground AND mBackupPower ≠ overvoltage

Figure 3. Nontrivial invariants generated automatically for the mode class smOperation.

Although the invariants generated from the specification are not the strongest possible invariants, they are often sufficient to establish interesting safety properties [18]. While applying the full invariant generation algorithm to CD did not provide results sufficient by themselves to establish the security properties we wished to verify, the generated invariants did play an extremely useful role: they provided every auxiliary lemma we needed to complete the proofs of all valid security properties that we investigated. Although there is no guarantee that this will always happen, that it did happen for CD suggests that applying invariant generation is a useful first step in verifying a set of properties, particularly since, once the full algorithm is implemented in SCR*, invariant generation will be fully automatic.

Three of the seven properties that we analyzed could not be proven automatically with either TAME or the SCR* validity checker (see Sections 3.6 and 3.7). To prove these properties, a total of five auxiliary invariants were needed. Of these five invariants, which are listed in Figure 4, invariants 1A, 2A, and 3A can be derived from invariants generated by the implemented algorithm. For example, invariant 1A is implied by invariant 4 in Figure 3, one of the invariants generated automatically from the mode transition table for smOperation. Invariant 4A follows immediately from additional invariants which were generated by hand using the strengthened algorithm for mode transition tables. The contrapositive of invariant 5A is generated by applying the algorithm by hand to the event table defining the integer-valued variable cKeyBank1Key1.

No.	Description	Auxiliary Invariant
1A	In Configuration mode, backup power is not overvoltage	smOperation = sConfiguration ⇒ mBackupPower ≠ overvoltage
2A	In Idle mode, backup power is not overvoltage	smOperation = sIdle ⇒ mBackupPower ≠ overvoltage
3A	In Traffic Processing mode, backup power is not overvoltage	smOperation = sTrafficProcessing ⇒ mBackupPower ≠ overvoltage
4A	If primary power is unavailable, then CD is in Standby, Alarm, or Off mode	mPrimaryPower = unavailable ⇒ (smOperation = sStandby or smOperation = sAlarm or smOperation = sOff)
5A	If CD is in Off mode, then key 1 in keybank 1 is 0	smOperation = sOff ⇒ cKeyBank1Key1 = 0

Figure 4. Auxiliary invariants needed for CD.

3.5 Model Checking Properties

When, as in SCR, a software specification describes a finite-state automaton, one can model check its properties. Model checking performs an exhaustive search of the state space of the automaton. If the number of state variables is large, and particularly if—as is common in software specifications—the individual variables take values in a large (even infinite) set, the state space can become so large that direct exhaustive search of the entire space is difficult or impossible. This problem, referred to as the *state explosion* problem, can often be alleviated by abstraction.

For SCR*, we have developed automatable abstraction methods that reduce the state space either by eliminating variables irrelevant to a property (*variable restriction*) or by reducing the range of variable values (*variable abstraction*) [5, 11]. When, as often happens, even abstraction does not allow the state space to be searched exhaustively, a partial search of the state space can often find states that *violate* a specified property. In addition to finding property violations, most model checkers produce counterexamples in the form of scenarios (i.e., execution sequences) that lead to the bad state. Below, we refer to counterexample scenarios simply as *counterexamples*.

Since model checking is largely automatic, using a model checker to check the validity of a property before trying to establish the property with a theorem prover is often a useful screening strategy. If Spin finds a violation, it produces a counterexample, thus saving the effort needed to generate a counterexample from a dead-end in a proof. In checking security properties for CD, we followed this strategy.

No.	Description	Property
1	If CD is tampered with, then key 1 in keybank 1 is zeroized	@T(mTamper) $\Rightarrow$ cKeyBank1Key1$'$ = 0
2	When the zeroize switch is activated, key 1 in keybank 1 is zeroized	@T(mZeroizeSwitch = on) $\Rightarrow$ cKeyBank1Key1$'$ = 0
3	No key can be stored in location 1 of keybank 1 before an algorithm has been loaded into the first location of algorithm storage segment 1	cKeyBank1Key1 $\neq$ 0 $\Rightarrow$ cAlgStoreSegment1 $\neq$ 0
4	If backup power has an undervoltage when primary power is unavailable, the CD enters either Alarm mode or Off mode	@T(mBackupPower = undervoltage) WHEN mPrimaryPower = unavailable $\Rightarrow$ smOperation$'$ = sAlarm OR smOperation$'$ = sOff
5	If backup power is overvoltage then the CD is in Initialization, Standby, Alarm, or Off mode	mBackupPower = overvoltage $\Rightarrow$ smOperation = sInitialization OR smOperation = sStandby OR smOperation = sAlarm OR smOperation = sOff
6	If primary power has an overvoltage then either the CD is in Initialization, Standby, Alarm, or Off mode, or the CD enters Initialization mode	@T(mPrimaryPower) = overvoltage $\Rightarrow$ smOperation = sStandby OR smOperation = sAlarm OR smOperation = sOff OR smOperation$'$ = sInitialization
7	If primary power has an undervoltage then either the CD is in Initialization, Standby, Alarm, or Off mode, or the CD enters Initialization mode	@T(mPrimaryPower) = undervoltage $\Rightarrow$ smOperation = sStandby OR smOperation = sAlarm OR smOperation = sOff OR smOperation$'$ = sInitialization

Figure 5. Sample true properties for SCR CD.

Figure 5 lists seven security properties that the SCR specification of CD satisfies. Before we tried to prove any CD security property with TAME (see Section 3.6), we first used the Spin model checker to search for violations of the property. For each property, we used SCR* to automatically extract an abstraction from the CD specification and the property, using the variable restriction method described in [5, 11] to remove all variables irrelevant to the validity of the property. Then, by hand, we applied the variable abstraction method described in [11]. By limiting the range of values that certain variables can assume, this method usually produces a smaller abstraction. In our CD study, the abstractions for different properties varied very little. A typical abstraction contained 28 variables, a reduction of 28% from the 39 variables in the complete SCR specification.

Using Spin, we discovered a few property violations. In each case, closer examination of the property showed that the formulation of the property was incorrect. As one would expect, model checking was unable to find any violations of the properties subsequently verified by theorem proving. Because the model checker ran out of memory before the analysis was complete, we were unable to search the complete state space of any of the abstract specifications and therefore to *verify* any of the properties listed in Figure 5. The importance of the theorem proving phase was demonstrated when we were able to use theorem proving both to prove that certain properties were invariants and to establish that one property for which Spin was unable to find a violation is not an invariant (see below).

3.6 Checking Properties with TAME

The tool TAME provides an interface to PVS for proving properties of automata models. TAME's goal is to reduce the human effort required in using PVS to specify these automata models and to prove state invariant properties for the models. TAME was originally designed to specify and reason about Lynch-Vaandrager (LV) timed automata [21] but has been adapted to I/O automata [20] and the automata model underlying SCR (see [2]). TAME provides more than twenty specialized strategies that implement proof steps mimicking the high-level proof steps typically used by humans in proving invariant properties. Experience has shown that for automata models whose state variables have simple types (such as numerical, boolean, or enumerated types), nearly all state invariants can be proved using the TAME steps exclusively.

We have integrated TAME into SCR* by developing an automatic SCR-to-TAME translator and special TAME strategies for the automatic analysis of properties of SCR automata [2]. For many SCR automata—in particular, those not involving timing constraints or other complexities such as tolerances for controlled quantities—a single TAME strategy can automatically prove many state invariants.

As stated in Section 2, most invariant properties of interest for an SCR automaton are either state invariants (one-state properties) or transition invariants (two-state properties). State invariants are typically proved by induction, with a base case for the initial states and an action case for each kind of input event. Although induction can be used in proving transition invariants, it is seldom appropriate, since the transitions possible from any given state seldom have any connection to the transitions possible from one of its successor states. Rather, transition invariants are normally proved by reasoning directly about the transition relation of the SCR automaton.

In TAME, the strategy SCR_INDUCT_PROOF performs the standard parts of an induction proof for a state invariant, and SCR_DIRECT_PROOF does the same for a transition invariant. A universal invariant proof strategy identifies the invariant as either a one-state or two-state property and then applies either SCR_INDUCT_PROOF or SCR_DIRECT_PROOF as appropriate.

Properties 1, 2, and 3 in Figure 5 took a few days to prove because the initial TAME representation of

CD combined with the initial versions of the strategies SCR_INDUCT_PROOF and SCR_DIRECT_PROOF led to unmanageably large data structures in the PVS prover. These problems led us to improve both our translation scheme and our proof strategies. After these improvements were made, we were able to prove properties 5, 6, and 7 in Figure 5 in less than an hour. The proof of property 4 took longer—about 2 days—because we needed to discover and to prove two layers of auxiliary invariants. This time would have been greatly reduced if the full invariant generation algorithm (see Section 3.4) had been automated.

When TAME's universal invariant strategy fails to complete the proof of an invariant, two possibilities exist: either the invariant is false, or additional invariants are needed in the proof. Associated with every proof "dead-end" is a problem transition. For one-state properties, this is the transition of the action case in the induction proof in which the dead-end appears. For two-state properties, this is the transition from the given state via some enabled automaton action to the successor state; the strategy SCR_DIRECT_PROOF produces only dead-ends in which the action is known, and hence for deterministic SCR specifications, the successor state (in terms of the given state) is known. TAME provides an analysis strategy to display the details of any problem transition. Once these details are understood, the user can determine whether the transition is reachable—in which case, the property is false—or whether it is unreachable, either because it would violate some transition invariant, or because one or the other of the states in the transition violates some state invariant.

Applying abstraction to a specification is less important in theorem proving than in model checking. Since a theorem prover can reason about abstract values, reducing the range of a variable using variable abstraction results in little or no improvement in the number of cases the theorem prover must consider. However, variable restriction can reduce both the number of cases and the complexity of reasoning about state transitions. Therefore, prior to analyzing a property with TAME, we applied variable restriction to the specification. Because the resulting abstractions for the individual properties were very similar, we used the same abstraction for all.

Applying the TAME strategies to the seven properties in Figure 5 resulted in the automatic proof of four of the properties. For two of the remaining properties, we proposed an auxiliary invariant, which was proved automatically and then applied to complete the proof. Property 1 in Figure 5 is an example of a property requiring a single auxiliary invariant, invariant 5A in Figure 4, in its proof. Examination of the event table for the variable cKeyBank1Key1, in Figure 6 shows why the auxiliary invariant is needed:[1] when CD is in mode sOff, the event @T(mTamper) does not change the value of cKeyBank1Key1. Invariant 5A, which states that cKeyBank1Key1 is 0 in mode sOff, clearly covers this case.

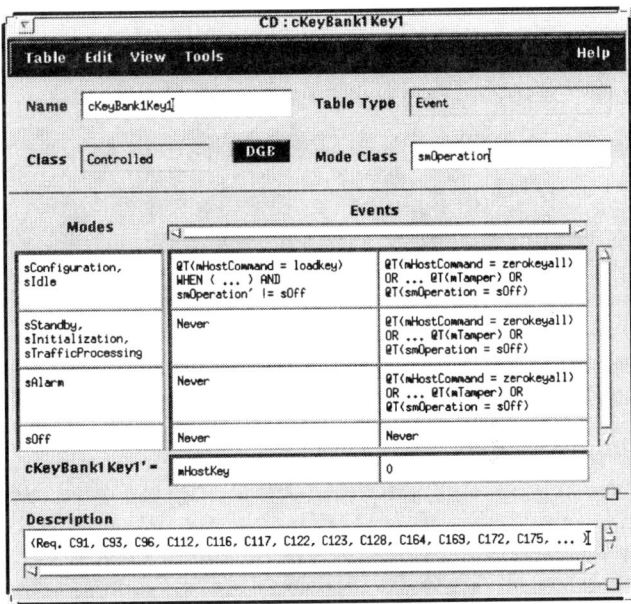

Figure 6. Event table for cKeyBank1Key1

In the case of the third remaining property, we suggested an auxiliary invariant that completed the proof. However, applying the automatic proof strategy to the auxiliary invariant resulted in several dead-ends, and we therefore proposed three additional auxiliary invariants. These three new invariants were then proved automatically using the universal invariant strategy. As noted in Section 3.4, each of the needed auxiliary invariants was subsumed or implied by invariants that either were, or could be, generated automatically. Thus, once the invariant generator is extended and communication between the invariant generator and TAME is possible, the class of invariants that can be proved automatically using TAME will be extended.

Figure 7 shows a proposed eighth property that does not hold in the CD specification. Although Spin

Description	Property
If CD is in Alarm mode, then key 1 in keybank 1 is 0	smOperation = sAlarm $\Rightarrow$ cKeyBank1Key1 = 0

Figure 7. A false property for SCR CD.

---

[1]Some of the conditions and events have been abbreviated using ellipsis.

was unable to produce a counterexample for this property, TAME's analysis of the property found 14 problem transitions. Some intelligent exploration using the SCR* simulator produced a scenario that leads to one of these transitions, thus demonstrating that the property does not hold in the SCR specification. Detailed examination of the feedback from TAME shows that no obvious invariants forbid the other problem transitions, so it is likely that they also correspond to counterexamples.

3.7 Applying the Validity Checker

The SCR* validity checker VC [4] checks the validity of first-order one-state or two-state properties directly by using an initial term-rewriting phase followed by application of a decision procedure that uses BDDs (binary decision diagrams) to evaluate propositional formulae and a constraint solver to reduce simple integer arithmetic formulae (Presburger formulae). The variable ordering used in the BDDs is particularly efficient for SCR specifications. VC can also perform an induction proof of a property by first applying a preprocessor to generate the appropriate base and induction cases and then applying the direct method to the generated cases. An automatic translation of SCR specifications into input for VC has been built.

VC has been applied to many of the same examples to which TAME has been applied, including the CD properties (after abstraction, as with TAME). The run time required by VC to analyze the CD properties was about half the time required by TAME. For the false property in Figure 7, VC produced a single problem transition, a special case of one of the 14 problem transitions reported by TAME. This is the same problem transition for which we used the simulator to find a counterexample. Thus, VC, like TAME, can be used in demonstrating that a property is invalid.

Unlike TAME, VC cannot be used to prove properties interactively. Therefore, the CD properties whose proofs required auxiliary invariants were checked after first including all necessary auxiliary invariants as assumptions, rather than by interactively invoking an analog of TAME's strategy for applying an invariant lemma. Mechanically checking the validity of complex properties (such as properties involving non-linear numerical constraints or numerical constraints over real numbers, or properties whose proofs require types of higher-order reasoning other than induction over reachable states) requires a general-purpose theorem prover, such as PVS through TAME. However, VC can provide an efficient first screening for invariance for any property of an automaton that involves only propositional logic, simple integer constraints, and universal quantification over states or state pairs.

3.8 Generating Test Sets

Applying the formal techniques described above produces very high-quality requirements specifications. Although such high-quality requirements specifications are valuable, the ultimate objective of the software development process is to produce high-quality *software*—software that satisfies its requirements. To weed out errors introduced by the implementation and to convince customers that the system performance is acceptable, the software needs to be tested. An enormous problem, however, is that software testing, especially of secure systems, is extremely costly and time-consuming. It has been estimated that current testing methods consume between 40% and 70% of the software development effort [3].

The high-quality specification produced by the SCR method can play a valuable role in software testing. We have developed an automated technique [9] that constructs a suite of *test sets* from an SCR requirements specification. Each test set is a sequence of system inputs in which each input is coupled with the required system outputs. To ensure that the test sets "cover" the set of all possible system behaviors, our technique organizes all possible system executions (i.e., traces) into equivalence classes and builds one or more test sets for each class. These test sets can then be used to automatically evaluate the implemented software. By reducing the human effort needed to build and to run the test sets, such an approach can reduce both the enormous cost and the significant time and human effort associated with current testing methods.

With our technique, a model checker's ability to produce counterexamples is used to construct the test sets. The requirements specification is used both to generate a valid sequence of inputs and as an *oracle* that determines the outputs the system is required to generate from a given system input. To obtain a valid sequence of inputs, the input sequence is constrained to satisfy the environmental assumptions in the SCR requirements specification.

We have built a prototype tool in Java that automatically translates an SCR specification into the language of either of two model checkers, executes the model checker to build the test sets, analyzes its outputs, and finally produces a file containing the generated test sets. Our prototype tool has been applied to a number of specifications, including a sizable component of a contractor-specified weapons system [11]. Given the tool's early success in constructing test sets efficiently, we expect that applying the tool to the CD specification should be equally successful. The CD project manager has expressed interest in using test sets generated by our tool to test the CD software.

4 Discussion

The Complexity of CD. Our SCR specification of CD reflects the application's significant complexity and moderate size. As noted in Section 3.1, the SCR specification has 39 variables, and the relationships among these variables is complex. In any state after the initial state, the monitored variable mHostCommand can take one of 17 values, and therefore, in any state of the CD, there are 16 possible input events involving changes in this variable. In addition, there are 17 other input variables. As a result, the mode transition table is large, involving 55 events to define 25 mode transitions, and many event tables in the specification are also large: the average number of events per table is 8, with the largest table containing 16 events.

Time and effort required. Despite the complexity of CD, the total time taken in this study to develop and analyze the SCR CD specification was only one person-month.[2] Formalizing the specification of CD in SCR, including the use of the analysis tools to perform sanity checks, took only two person-weeks, and even the most complex consistency checks ran in minutes. The graphical front-end for simulation of CD was constructed in one day. Improvements to formulation of the properties based on feedback from the model checker took only a few days. TAME and the validity checker underwent significant improvement during our analysis of the SCR specification of CD, and as a result, analyzing a property with these tools now takes at most a few minutes, and sometimes only a few seconds. The most labor-intensive part of the analysis of a property is analyzing proof dead-ends to determine their cause and their resolution. As noted above, we plan to fully implement the invariant generation algorithm. This extension of SCR* should reduce significantly the problem of discovering useful auxiliary invariants.

The practicality of SCR. For our SCR specification of CD, we analyzed eight security properties. For each property, we were able to definitively answer the question, "Does the operational specification satisfy this property?" When the answer was "No," we provided a counterexample illustrating the failure. Although the full set of security properties for CD (to which we do not have access) numbers in the hundreds, our success with the properties we considered and the relatively short time required support the proposition that SCR and the analysis techniques supported in SCR* provide a practical, low-cost approach to providing high assurance. Typical concerns expressed by practitioners regarding the practicality of formal methods are addressed in more detail in our discussion in [17] of the lessons we learned from our application of the SCR* tools to CD.

5 Related Work

RSML (Requirements State Machine Language) [10] is another requirements method in which, as in SCR, a system is specified as a state machine. RSML has been successfully applied to finding errors in the specification of a complex avionics system: the Traffic alert and Collision Avoidance System II (TCAS II). Like SCR specifications, RSML specifications include a set of tables and may be checked for consistency and for (a version of) completeness. SCR and RSML also have important differences. First, RSML has a Statecharts-style interface through which it explicitly supports specification features, such as hierarchical states and local variables, not explicitly supported in SCR (although similar effects can be obtained with SCR). Further, the AND/OR tables in RSML specify details of *transitions*, while SCR tables specify how *dependent state variables* are updated. Because a state machine has many more transitions than state variables, an RSML specification of a system contains many more tables than an SCR specification of the same system. Finally, automated support for the analysis of RSML specification properties beyond consistency and completeness is not yet extensive.

Reference [24] describes an earlier application of SCR to the development of another COMSEC device, the External COMSEC Adaptor (ECA). The development, from modeling the device through implementing and verifying its design, was done using the high-level SCR method, but not the SCR* toolset. The operational requirements were specified using SCR tables, and the critical requirements model—the desired properties—was specified using the CSP (Communicating Sequential Processes) language. In this effort, both formal and informal transitions between stages were used, with some automated support for the formal transitions from another mechanized theorem prover.

6 Conclusion

SCR offers a practical, low-cost approach to building a high assurance COMSEC device. Before implementation and design, the SCR* toolset can be used to build and analyze, often automatically, a mathematically precise requirements specification. Operational personnel can use the SCR* simulator to validate the behavior of the specified system. Further, model checking often can be used to identify security properties which the operational specification violates, and theorem proving can be used to verify the correct-

---

[2] Additional time was needed to make improvements in some of the SCR* techniques. These improvements were suggested by our experience with CD.

ness of security properties and suggest possible property violations. When analyses have established sufficient confidence in the requirements specification, the system can be built to satisfy that specification. A planned extension to SCR*, a tool to generate Java code from specifications, will help with this phase of development. Once the source code is available, test sets automatically generated from the operational requirements specification by the test set generator can be used to test the system implementation.

Acknowledgements

We thank Stan Chincheck and Tom Sasala for providing us with their prose specification of CD. We also thank Stan, Tom, and Bruce Labaw for many helpful discussions. Our colleague Ralph Jeffords executed by hand those parts of the invariant generation algorithm that are not yet mechanized. Our colleague Ramesh Bharadwaj and Steven Sims applied the SCR* validity checker to the CD properties, and Ramesh Bharadwaj discovered a counterexample corresponding to the problem transition found by this tool for the false property described above. Stuart Faulk, Ralph Jeffords, and Ramesh Bharadwaj gave us helpful comments on early versions of this paper.

References

[1] M. Archer and C. Heitmeyer. Mechanical verification of timed automata: A case study. In *Proc. 1996 IEEE Real-Time Technology and Applications Symp. (RTAS'96)*, pages 192–203. IEEE Computer Society Press, 1996.

[2] M. Archer, C. Heitmeyer, and S. Sims. TAME: A PVS interface to simplify proofs for automata models. In *Proc. User Interfaces for Theorem Provers 1998 (UITP '98)*, Eindhoven, Netherlands, July 1998.

[3] B. Beizer. *Software Testing Techniques*. Van Nostrand Reinhold, 1983.

[4] R. Bharadwaj and S. Sims. Salsa: Combining decision procedures for fully automatic verification. Draft.

[5] R. Bharadwaj and C. Heitmeyer. Model checking complete requirements specifications using abstraction. *Automated Software Engineering*, 6(1), January 1999.

[6] B. W. Boehm. *Software Engineering Economics*. Prentice-Hall, Englewood Cliffs, NJ, 1981.

[7] S. Easterbrook and J. Callahan. Formal methods for verification and validation of partial specifications: A case study. *Journal of Systems and Software*, 1997.

[8] S. R. Faulk, J. Brackett, P. Ward, and J. Kirby. The CoRE method for real-time requirements. *IEEE Software*, 9(5):22–33, September 1992.

[9] A. Gargantini and C. Heitmeyer. Automatic generation of tests from requirements specifications. In *Proc. ACM 7th Eur. Software Eng. Conf. and 7th ACM SIGSOFT Symp. on the Foundations of Software Eng. (ESEC/FSE99)*, Toulouse, FR, September 1999.

[10] M. P. E. Heimdahl and N. G. Leveson. Completeness and consistency in hierarchical state-based requirements. *IEEE Transactions on Software Engineering*, 22(6):363–377, June 1996.

[11] C. Heitmeyer, J. Kirby, B. Labaw, M. Archer, and R. Bharadwaj. Using abstraction and model checking to detect safety violations in requirements specifications. *IEEE Trans. on Softw. Eng.*, 24(11):927–948, November 1998.

[12] C. L. Heitmeyer, R. D. Jeffords, and B. G. Labaw. Automated consistency checking of requirements specifications. *ACM Transactions on Software Engineering and Methodology*, 5(3):231–261, April–June 1996.

[13] C. Heitmeyer, J. Kirby, and B. Labaw. Tools for formal specification, verification, and validation of requirements. In *Proc. 12th Annual Conf. on Computer Assurance (COMPASS '97)*, Gaithersburg, MD, June 1997.

[14] C. L. Heitmeyer, R. D. Jeffords, and B. G. Labaw. Tools for analyzing SCR-style requirements specifications: A formal foundation. 1999. Draft.

[15] K. Heninger, D. L. Parnas, J. E. Shore, and J. W. Kallander. Software requirements for the A-7E aircraft. Technical Report 3876, Naval Research Lab., Wash., DC, 1978.

[16] G. J. Holzmann. *Design and Validation of Computer Protocols*. Prentice-Hall, 1991.

[17] J. Kirby, M. Archer, and C. Heitmeyer. Applying formal methods to an information security device: An experience report. In *Proc. 4th IEEE International Symposium on High Assurance Systems Engineering (HASE '99)*. IEEE Computer Society Press, November 1999.

[18] R. Jeffords and C. Heitmeyer. Automatic generation of state invariants from requirements specifications. In *Proc. 6th International Symposium on the Foundations of Software Engineering (FSE-6)*, Orlando, FL, November 1998.

[19] R. R. Lutz and H.-Y. Shaw. Applying the SCR* requirements toolset to DS-1 fault protection. Technical Report JPL-D15198, Jet Propulsion Laboratory, Pasadena, CA, December 1997.

[20] N. Lynch and M. Tuttle. An introduction to Input/Output automata. *CWI-Quarterly*, 2(3):219–246, September 1989. Centrum voor Wiskunde en Informatica, Amsterdam, The Netherlands.

[21] N. Lynch and F. Vaandrager. Forward and backward simulations – Part II: Timing-based systems. *Information and Computation*, 128(1):1–25, July 1996.

[22] S. Miller. Specifying the mode logic of a flight guidance system in CoRE and SCR. In *Proc. 2nd Workshop on Formal Methods in Software Practice (FMSP'98)*, 1998.

[23] D. L. Parnas, G. J. K. Asmis, and J. Madey. Assessment of safety-critical software in nuclear power plants. *Nuclear Safety*, 32(2):189–198, April–June 1991.

[24] C. N. Payne, A. P. Moore, and D. M. Mihelcic. An experience modeling critical requirements. In *Proc. COMPASS '94*, pages 245–256, Gaithersburg, MD, June 1994. IEEE Press.

[25] N. Shankar, S. Owre, and J. Rushby. The PVS proof checker: A reference manual. Technical report, Computer Science Lab., SRI Intl., Menlo Park, CA, 1993.

Application-Level Isolation Using Data Inconsistency Detection

Amgad Fayad, Sushil Jajodia, and Catherine D. McCollum

The MITRE Corporation
1820 Dolley Madison Boulevard
McLean, Virginia 22102
{afayad, jajodia, mccollum}@mitre.org

Abstract

Recently, application-level isolation was introduced as an effective means of containing the damage that a suspicious user could inflict on data. In most cases, only a subset of the data items needs to be protected from damage due to the criticality level or integrity requirements of the data items. In such a case, complete isolation of a suspicious user can consume more resources than necessary. This paper proposes partitioning the data items into categories based on their criticality levels and integrity requirements; these categories determine the allowable data flows between trustworthy and suspicious users. An algorithm, that achieves good performance when the number of data items is small, is also provided to detect inconsistencies between suspicious versions of the data and the main version.

1 Introduction

Recently, increasing emphasis has been placed on supplementing protection of networks and information systems with intrusion detection [Lun93, MHL94, LM98], and numerous intrusion detection products have emerged commercially. When a suspicious thread of activity is discovered, the intrusion detection system or the system security officer must decide how to react and whether to allow continued access to the associated user, process, or host. Since the rate of detection (percentage of intrusions that are detected) is directly proportional to the rate of errors (percentage of reported intrusions that are not intrusions), if our goal is to achieve a high rate of detection, we must be prepared to tolerate a high rate of errors.

In [JLM98, LJM99], isolation at the application level was introduced as a means to achieve both a high rate of detection and a low rate of errors. The basic idea is to isolate a suspicious user S transparently into a separate environment that appears to S as the actual system. This approach allows S to be kept under surveillance without risking further harm to the system.

Jajodia, et al. [JLM98], investigated isolation at the database level, and considered the following attack scenario: Suppose a user S of the database comes under suspicion for some reason. To let S continue working and at the same time to isolate the database from any further damage from S, an on-the-fly "separate database version" is created to accommodate accesses by S. All transactions submitted by S are then directed to the separate database version, while transactions from other trustworthy users are applied to the main database version.

Advantages of using isolation at the database level follow: It permits finer grained monitoring of the suspicious user activities, the substitute host is not sacrificed, and the suspicious user S can interact with the system's resources. Therefore, if S proves to be innocent, S has not been subjected to denial of service and any valid results produced by S do not have to be discarded. The drawback of isolation at the database level is that in some cases merging data modified by a suspicious user, after he is found to be legitimate, can be time consuming [JLM98].

This paper's contribution to the database isolation scheme is in two areas. First, in most cases, only a subset of the data items needs to be protected from damage due to their criticality level or integrity requirements. In such a case, complete isolation of a suspicious user can consume more resources than necessary. Therefore, we divide, or categorize, data according to their criticality and integrity levels. Three categories are proposed: unconstrained, constrained but noncritical, and constrained and critical. These categories determine the allowable data flows between trustworthy and suspicious users.

Second, if a suspicious user is eventually identified as a legitimate user, an algorithm to detect mutual inconsistency is presented. The proposed algorithm has several advantages. First, the amount of work done by this algorithm is a factor of the number of data items accessed. By keeping the constrained but noncritical data items set small, better performance can be achieved. Second, this algorithm reports inconsistency in terms of data items instead of transactions. This process makes it easier for the database administrator to restore the integrity of inconsistent data items by executing appropriate compensating transactions [GMS87]. Third, this algorithm simplifies the case involving multiple suspicious users.

The remainder of the paper is organized as follows. Section 2 describes the categories of data items based on criticality and integrity requirements, and the resulting data flows between the trustworthy and suspicious users. Section 3 discusses the isolation architecture and provides an isolation protocol that preserves the data flows and an algorithm to implement the isolation. Section 4 describes the inconsistency detection algorithm. Section 5 shows examples of how the algorithm works. Section 6 shows the correctness of the algorithm. Section 7 reviews related work. Finally, Section 8 provides conclusions.

2 Categorizing Data and Resulting Data Flows

Traditionally, security technology views each access decision as Boolean: either the user request is granted or it is denied. When suspicious users are involved, the choice is not so straightforward. Certain portions of the database may be highly sensitive (e.g., data which, if revealed to competitors or adversaries, may compromise vital interests of the organization). Other portions of the database may have high integrity requirements and, therefore, any modifications by anyone not trustworthy should be disallowed.

In this paper, we place data items into three separate categories based on their criticality levels and integrity requirements. As shown in Figure 1, data items can be categorized based on their criticality and integrity ratings and suspicious users are allowed/disallowed R/W operations based on those ratings. For integrity reasons, we partition the data items as being either constrained or unconstrained. By definition, *constrained* data items are those to which the integrity constraints must be applied. A data item that is not constrained is said to be *unconstrained*. Based on security considerations, we partition the data items as being either critical or noncritical. We combine the two ratings to obtain the following three categories of data items:

- Unconstrained and noncritical data items – These data items have low criticality and integrity ratings.
- Constrained but noncritical data items – These data items have high integrity ratings; however, they have low criticality ratings.
- Critical data items – All data items that are highly sensitive are considered critical, regardless of their integrity ratings.

In the normal course of events when all users are believed to be trustworthy, each data item has only one version, that is, the main version; any updates by a user are seen by all other users of the database. Once a suspicious user is identified, the above categories determine the allowable data flows between trustworthy and suspicious users.

In general, data flows can be one of the following two types:

- *Disclosing* data flow, which permits data to flow from trustworthy users to suspicious users, or
- *Corrupting* data flow, which allows flow of data from suspicious users to trustworthy users

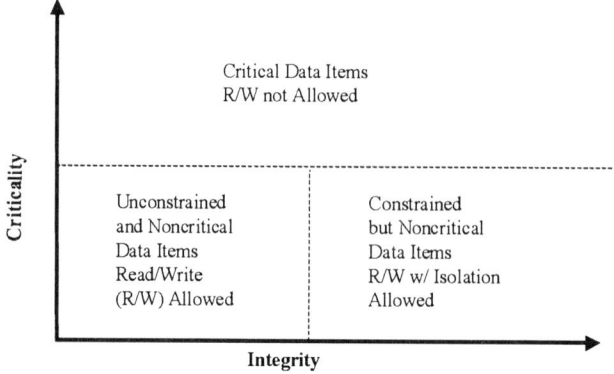

Figure 1. Categories of Data and Resulting Data Flows

A data flow can also be characterized according to its mode:
- *Full* data flow, in which all updates are shared by trustworthy and suspicious users
- *Blocked* data flow, in which updates from suspicious users are not given to trustworthy users but all updates from trustworthy users are given to suspicious users
- *Selective* data flow, in which some updates are shared by trustworthy and suspicious users

On unconstrained and noncritical data items, we allow full data flow that is both disclosing and corrupting. Therefore, there is no isolation on these items (i.e., all updates by trustworthy users are disclosed to suspicious users, and vice versa), and each unconstrained and noncritical data item has only one version.

On critical data items, we allow neither disclosing nor corrupting data flow. This means that suspicious users cannot read or write critical data items. We enforce a selective data flow policy on constrained but noncritical data items: We do not allow disclosing data flow; thus, suspicious users are not given any updates by trustworthy users to such items; suspicious users instead see the values of these items before the isolation was initiated. Trustworthy users, on the other hand, are given versions created by suspicious users; they have the option to select the version they would like to use.

3 Isolation Architecture and Algorithm

The architecture in this paper is similar to the architecture presented in [JLM98]. As shown in Figure 2, the *Intrusion Detector* identifies suspicious users and ultimately determines if a suspicious user is malicious or legitimate. The *Damage Recovery Manager* deals with handling data inconsistencies between the main database and the suspicious versions of the database.

When a user S is identified as being suspicious, S can read or write unconstrained data items and constrained but noncritical data items only. Whenever S modifies a constrained but noncritical data item d, the new value of d is labeled as suspicious (d_s). However, when S modifies an unconstrained and noncritical data item, no special labeling is performed; only the old value of d is replaced by the new value. Critical data items cannot be accessed by S; whenever S tries to access these data items, an error message is generated and given to S.

Only one version of unconstrained data items and critical data items is maintained. This is because changes to unconstrained data items by user S are automatically considered good, and user S is given neither read nor write access to data labeled critical. Only constrained but noncritical items may have multiple versions; exactly how these versions are created is explained in the isolation algorithm below.

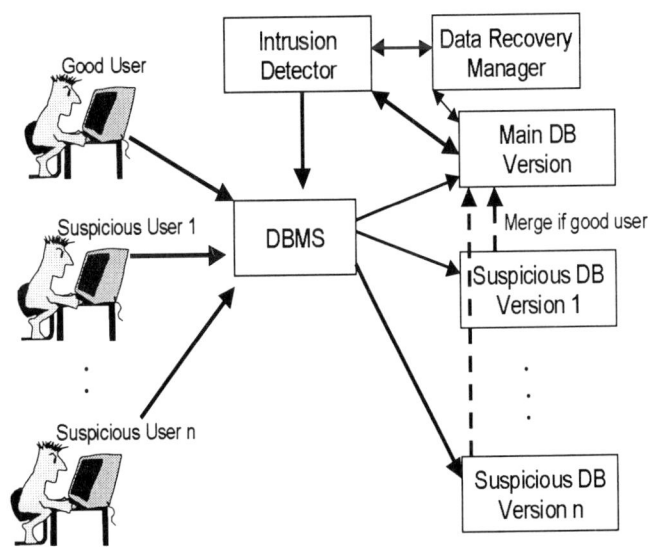

Figure 2. Isolation Architecture

The following list illustrates our isolation protocol, which is adapted from [JLM98].
- At the beginning of the main history, each constrained but noncritical data item x is associated with the same version number MAIN, denoted x[MAIN].
- When constrained but noncritical data item x is read or updated by a trustworthy transaction T, x[MAIN] is given to T, and after x[MAIN] is updated by T, if the version includes other version numbers, then a new version x[MAIN] associated with only one version number MAIN is generated which denotes the value that has been updated by T, and the old value with the same set of version numbers except that MAIN is excluded remains.
- When the first suspicious user S_1 is identified, We attach the specific version number INIT to each constrained but noncritical data item. As a result, a version of x may be associated with several version numbers, for example, x[MAIN][INIT] denotes the

value of x which should be the original value of x for each following suspicious database version, and it can be updated by a trustworthy transaction.

- Whenever there are no active suspicious histories in the database, the value of a specific signal variable RESETABLE is set to be TRUE if it has not been set yet.
- When a suspicious user S_i is identified (including the first one), a unique version number, for example, the time stamp t_i is attached to the INIT version of x. $x[INIT][t_i]$ denotes the value of x which has not been updated by S_i but can be updated by a suspicious transaction submitted by S_i.
- When x is read or updated by a suspicious transaction submitted by S_i, the version of x which includes the version number t_i will be given to S_i. If the version includes the version number INIT, then a new version $x[t_i]$ is generated which denotes the value that has been updated by S_i, and the old value with the same set of version numbers except that t_i is excluded remains.
- When a suspicious user S_i is going to be isolated, if the value RESETABLE is TRUE, then we first set the value RESETABLE to FALSE, and then attach both the INIT and the t_i version number to the current main database version, namely, data items associated with the MAIN version number and remove the old INIT database version.
- When a trustworthy user G_i attempts to read x, G_i is presented with the two copies of x, namely x[INIT] and $x[INIT][t_i]$. If G_i decides to use $x[INIT[t_i]]$, then a separate copy of x is no longer maintained. If G_i, on the other hand, decides to use the original value of x, then two copies of x are maintained.

The following terminology is used in the isolation algorithm. A data item d_i *precedes* data item d_j if d_i is written by a transaction which precedes a transaction that reads d_i and d_j or data item d_i is read by the same transaction which writes d_i and d_j. Data items d_i and d_j are *inconsistent* if d_i precedes d_j and vice versa. The *precedence-set* of a data item is the set of all data items which precede it. The *link set* of a data item d_i is the set of all data items that were written by the last transaction which wrote d_i. Throughout we assume that the write-set of each transaction is always contained in the read-set.

Procedure Isolation
begin
  for each Constrained & Noncritical (C&N)
  data item d **do begin**
    /* initialize the precedence/link-sets */
    link-set(d) = { };
    precedence-set(d) = { };
  end
  for each transaction T **do begin**
    if T is a trustworthy user transaction **then**
      apply the following to trustworthy
      user precedence/link-sets
    else
      apply the following to the corresponding
      suspicious user precedence/link-sets
  if accessed data item is critical and user is suspicious
    reject transaction
  if accessed data item is unconstrained & noncritical
    allow read/write w/o precedence/link-set updates
  if read-set(T) ∩ write-set(T) <> { } **begin**
    for all C&N d in write-set(T) **do begin**
      precedence-set(d) = precedence-set(d) ∪
          read-set(T);
    end
  end
  for all C&N d in read-set(T) **do begin**
    if link-set(d) ∩ read-set(T) <> { }**begin**
      for all C&N data items f in read-set(T)
      do begin
        precedence-set(f) = precedence-set(f) ∪
          link-set(d);
      end
    end
  end
  for all C&N d in write-set(T) **do begin**
    link-set(d) = write-set(T);
  end
end.

Figure 3. Isolation Algorithm

The algorithm maintains with each data item several pairs of sets, one pair corresponding to the trustworthy users and one pair corresponding to each suspicious user. Each pair consists of a precedence-set and a link-set. These sets are initialized to be empty. Whenever a transaction T is executed by a user, the corresponding pair is updated as follows: If the intersection of the read-set of T and the write-set of T is nonempty, then append the read-set of T to the precedence-set of each data item in the write-set of T. For each data item d in the read-set of T, if the intersection of the link-set of d with the read-set of T is nonempty, then append the link-set of d to the precedence-set of every data item in the read-set of T.

Copy the write-set of T to the link-set of each data item in the write-set of T.

In addition, the algorithm allows trustworthy users to select between suspicious values of data and the original value. If a trustworthy user G attempts to access a data item d which was modified by a suspicious user to the value d_s. G will be prompted to select between d and d_s. If G chooses d, then two versions of d will be maintained. Otherwise, one version of d will be maintained.

When a suspicious user accesses unconstrained and noncritical data items, the precedence/link-sets are not updated with these items. This is because only one version of unconstrained and noncritical data is maintained. If the suspicious user attempts to access critical data, the transaction will be rejected.

A more formal description of the isolation algorithm is given in Figure 3.

4 Data Inconsistency Detection Algorithm

When a decision is reached and the suspicious user S is found to be malicious, the corresponding suspicious database version is simply discarded. However, if S is found to be innocent, updates made by S must be merged with the main database version; any conflicting updates must be identified so that conflicts can be resolved.

Before we look for inconsistencies, we compute the transitive closure of each precedence set using Warshall's algorithm (e.g., see [Baa88]). Combine the trustworthy user precedence-sets with the suspicious user precedence-sets by computing the set unions.

Now we look for inconsistencies by performing the following: For each d_j and d_i, if dj is in precedence-set(d_i) AND d_i is in precedence-set(d_j), then we report that d_i and d_j are inconsistent. The system administrator must resolve all data items that cause inconsistencies (based on the algorithm).

A more formal description of the algorithm is given in Figure 4. Conceptually, this algorithm utilizes a precedence graph G consisting of data items as nodes, instead of a precedence graph that consists of transactions as nodes (as in [JLM98]). We construct a precedence graph G based on the computed precedence-sets. For data items d_j and d_i, we place a (directed) *precedence edge* from d_j to d_i if d_j precedes d_i. Cycles in the graph G indicate data inconsistency.

Note that in the event that multiple suspicious users are present, detection of inconsistency can be performed by computing the union of all the precedence-sets for each data item [Ram89].

Procedure Check Inconsistencies

begin
    apply *Warshall's algorithm* to compute
    transitive closure on precedence-sets;
for each data item d **do**
    full-precedence-set(d) =
        trustworthy-precedence-set(d) $\cup$
        suspicious-precedence-set(d);
end
for each data item d **do**
    for each f in precedence-set(d) **do**
        if d is in precedence-set(f) **then**
        /* *inconsistency detected!* */
        report d and f
    end
end.

Figure 4. Algorithm for Detecting Inconsistencies

5 Examples

In this section, we give two examples to illustrate how the algorithm works. For simplicity, we assume that all data items that are being accessed are constrained but noncritical.

Example 1. Consider the five transactions given below:
READSET(T_{s1}) = WRITESET(T_{s1}) = { d_1, d_2 }
READSET(T_{s2}) = { d_2, d_3 }, WRITESET(T_{s2}) = { d_3 }
READSET(T_{s3}) = { d_3, d_4, d_5 }, WRITESET(T_{s3}) = { d_4 }
READSET(T_{t1}) = WRITESET(T_{t1}) = { d_5 }
READSET(T_{t2}) = { d_1, d_5 }, WRITESET(T_{t2}) = { }

Here the subscripts s and t are used to denote the transactions executed by the suspicious and trustworthy users, respectively. Suppose the suspicious and trustworthy users execute transactions in the following order:

H = T_{s1} T_{t1} T_{s2} T_{s3} T_{t2}

Our algorithm will generate two sets of precedence sets, one involving the suspicious transactions and the other involving trustworthy transactions, as shown in Table 1. Since the precedence set $P(d_5)$ in the first column includes d_1 and $P(d_1)$ in the second column includes d_5, we conclude that both d_1 and d_5 are inconsistent.

Table 1. Precedence Sets for Example 1

Suspicious Precedence Sets	Trustworthy Precedence Sets
$P(d_1) = \{d_1, d_2\}$	$P(d_1) = \{d_5\}$
$P(d_2) = \{d_1, d_2\}$	$P(d_2) = \{\}$
$P(d_3) = \{d_1, d_2, d_3\}$	$P(d_3) = \{\}$
$P(d_4) = \{d_1, d_2, d_3, d_4, d_5\}$	$P(d_4) = \{\}$
$P(d_5) = \{d_1, d_2, d_3\}$	$P(d_5) = \{d_5\}$

Example 2. If we change the READSET(T_{s3}) to $\{d_3, d_4\}$, Table 2 shows the precedence sets for all the data items involved in the transactions. Unlike the previous example, no inconsistencies are indicated.

Table 2. Precedence Sets for Example 2

Suspicious Precedence Sets	Trustworthy Precedence Sets
$P(d_1) = \{d_1, d_2\}$	$P(d_1) = \{d_5\}$
$P(d_2) = \{d_1, d_2\}$	$P(d_2) = \{\}$
$P(d_3) = \{d_1, d_2, d_3\}$	$P(d_3) = \{\}$
$P(d_4) = \{d_1, d_2, d_3, d_4\}$	$P(d_4) = \{\}$
$P(d_5) = \{\}$	$P(d_5) = \{\}$

6 Correctness of the Data Inconsistency Detection Algorithm

Before we can give a proof of the correctness of the algorithm, we need to define the necessary terms.

Definition 1 [Ram89]. For data items d_i and d_j, we say that d_i *immediately precedes* d_j if one of the following items is true:
1) d_i is in the read-set and d_j is in the write-set of a transaction
2) The following conditions hold in a schedule S: there exist T_{lp}, T_{lq}, $p \leq q$, in S such that
a) T_{lp} updates d_i
b) T_{lq} reads d_j, and

a) There is a g in read-set(T_{lq}) intersection write-set(T_{lp}) and there is no $p<u<q$ such that g is in write-set(T_{lu}).

Definition 2 [Ram89]. The relation *precedes* is defined on the data items as the transitive closure of the relation *immediately precedes*.

Definition 3. For each data item d, we define the *precedence-set P(d)* as the set of all data items that *precede* d.

Definition 4. For each data item d, we define the *link-set(d)* as the set of data items in the write-set of the transaction that has most recently updated d and committed after isolation occurs.

The following theorem shows the correctness of the algorithm:

Theorem 1. After each transaction T, procedure *Isolation* updates the precedence-set of each data item correctly. That is, all data items, which immediately precede d, are in its precedence-set.

Proof. We provide a proof using induction on the number of transactions. If T is the first transaction, it is easy to see that the precedence-sets are up to date. Now we assume that after the kth transaction, the precedence-sets are up to date. We must show that after transaction k+1, the precedence-sets remain up to date. Now, let d_i be a data item. It easy to see from the definition that the algorithm adds all data items which immediately precede d_i which resulted from the k+1st transaction. Also, we claim that the link-sets are kept up to date. This follows from the definition of a link-set. QED

Given the correctness of the isolation algorithm and the correctness of Warshall's transitive closure algorithm, all data items, which precede data item d_i, are in its precedence-set. This ensures that the check inconsistencies algorithm detects all data items in need of correction.

7 Related Work

McDermott and Goldschlag [MG96a, MG96b] initiated this line of research with their work on data jamming. They identify several techniques to detect suspicious users.

Two papers directly relate to this work. Jajodia, et al. [JLM98], propose application-level isolation as a security mechanism to increase the security of information systems vulnerable to authorized malicious users. They develop an isolation scheme in the database context that isolates databases from any further damage caused by malicious users.

The current paper is different from [JLM98] in two respects. First, in this paper the database is partitioned into different categories, and these categories influence the data flows between suspicious and trustworthy users. Second, the way conflicts are identified during the merge of the suspicious versions and the main database version is very different. In [JLM98], the merge algorithm identifies all transactions that violate the serializability requirement. In contrast, the merge algorithm in this paper identifies all data items that may be inconsistent. We believe that it much easier for database administrators to take some compensating actions [GMS87] to restore the integrity of inconsistent data items than to try to identify the inconsistency by examining the cycles involving multiple transactions.

In [LJM99], Liu, et al., develop a probabilistic model to argue that intrusion confinement can be effectively used to resolve the conflicting design goals of an intrusion detection system by achieving both a high rate of detection and a low rate of errors. It is also shown that as a second level of protection in addition to access control intrusion confinement can dramatically enhance the security (especially integrity and availability) of a system in many situations. [LJM99] presents a concrete isolation scheme for file systems.

8 Conclusions

This paper expands the research on the concept of isolating suspicious users at the application level. First, we proposed categorizing data based on criticality and integrity requirements. Then we proposed an isolation scheme, which operates on only one of the categories proposed, namely constrained but noncritical data items. Finally we presented an algorithm which can efficiently detect inconsistencies in data items when suspicious users are present. Based on this paper, the following three conclusions apply: First, the complexity of the algorithm we presented is a factor of the number of data items accessed. Second, a small constrained but noncritical data set can help keep the overhead of this algorithm small. Finally, a potential disadvantage of this scheme is that resolving inconsistencies in data requires manual intervention.

Acknowledgement

This work was funded by Air Force Research Laboratory/Rome. We are grateful to Joe Giordano for his support.

References

[Baa88] S. Baase. "*Computer Algorithms.*" Addison-Wesley, Reading, MA, 1988.

[BHG87] P. Bernstein, V. Hadzilacos, and N. Goodman. "*Concurrency Control and Recovery in Database Systems.*" Addison-Wesley, Reading, MA, 1987.

[Dav84] Susan Davidson. "Optimism and Consistency in Partitioned Distributed Database Systems." *ACM transactions on database systems*, 9(3):456-481. September 1984.

[GMS87] Hector Garcia-Molina and Ken Salem. Sagas. *Proc. International Conf. on Management of Data*, pages 249-259, San Francisco, CA, 1987.

[JLM98] Sushil Jajodia, Peng Liu, and Catherine D. McCollum. "Application-Level Isolation To Cope with Malicious Database Users." In *Proc. 14th Annual Computer Security Applications Conference*, pages 73-82, Phoenix, AZ, December 1998.

[LJM99] Peng Liu, Sushil Jajodia and Catherine D. McCollum. "Intrusion Confinement by Isolation in Information Systems." In *Proc. XIII Annual IFIP WG 11.3 Working Conf. on Database Security*, Seattle, WA, July 1999.

[Lun93] Teresa Lunt. "A Survey on Intrusion Detection Techniques. "*Computers & Security*, 12(4):405-418, June 1993.

[LM98] Teresa Lunt and Catherine D. McCollum, "*Intrusion Detection and Response Research at DARPA,*" Technical Report, The MITRE Corporation, 1998.

[MG96a] J. McDermott, and D. Goldschlag. "storage jamming." In D.L. Spooner, S.A. Demurjian, and J.E. Dobson, editors, *Database Security IX: Status and Prospects*, pages 365-381. Chapman & Hall, London, 1996.

[MG96b] J. McDermott, and D. Goldschlag. "Towards a model of storage jamming." In *Proceedings of the IEEE Computer Security Foundations Workshop,* pages 176-185. Kenmare, Ireland, June 1996.

[MHL94] B. Mukherjee, L. T. Heberlein, and K. N. Levitt. "Network intrusion detection." *IEEE Network*, pages 26-41, June 1994.

[Ram89] K. V. S. Ramarao. "Detection of Mutual Inconsistency in Distributed Databases." *Journal of Parallel and Distributed Computing*, 6:498-514, 1989.

Track B

Workflow

Chair

LouAnna Notargiacomo, Trusted Computer Solutions

A Prototype Secure Workflow Server

Douglas L. Long, Julie Baker, and Francis Fung
Odyssey Research Associates
33 Thornwood Dr., Suite 500
Ithaca, NY
{dougl,julie,fung}@oracorp.com

Abstract

Workflow systems provide automated support that enables organizations to efficiently and reliably move important data through their routine business processes. For some organizations, the information processed by their workflow systems is highly valued and in need of protection from disclosure or corruption. Current workflow systems do not help organizations to adequately protect this important data. We describe a prototype secure workflow system that allows users to develop high-level workflow security policies and to automatically execute these policies within the workflow system. These workflow policies can use the workflow context to provide fine-grained, dynamic access control and other security services that enhance the organization's ability to control the information contained in its workflow system. In this paper, we will explain these security policy goals, our prototype policy editor, our prototype workflow server, and our underlying Java-based implementation.

1 Overview

Odyssey Research Associates is developing secure workflow technology that will help the enterprise to secure and protect its sensitive data as the data moves through the enterprise's day-to-day activities. ORA approaches workflow security from a policy-based perspective. In this approach, high-level security policy defines the protection requirements for all types of enterprise data and the workflow infrastructure uses this policy to automatically determine the security requirements for properly handling data as it moves through the workflow system. The chief benefit of this approach is that the workflow system can dynamically control access to data as it moves from one workflow activity to another, providing access control that is tightly coupled to the activities that are being performed. This tight coupling ensures that workflow users have access to the data they need, but only when they are performing activities that require this access.

The next three sections of this paper describe the three primary goals for our secure workflow system: dynamic access control, fine-grained data security, and active security. The following two sections describe our approach to secure workflow and the Java-based infrastructure that we have developed to implement it.

This work is funded under a Phase II SBIR, "Security Policy Modeling and Enforcement Tools for Clinical Workflows," sponsored by DARPA.

2 Dynamic Access Control

One of the primary motivations of our work is the need to provide dynamic access control for certain types of enterprise data. The need for an enterprise user to access a particular piece of enterprise data may change over time due to changes in duties, changes in assignments, or for other reasons. A valid reason for access today may not be valid tomorrow. Dynamic access control automatically reacts to these changes, allowing access control decisions to take into consideration factors other than the usual subject, object, and permissions typical of standard access control models. Dynamic access control adds new dimensions to access decisions, considering not just who and what, but why.

There is another reason for using dynamic access control. The greater the sensitivity of an item of information, the more tightly access to that item needs to be controlled. Dynamic access control provides a finer granularity for access control decisions that provides more precise control over who can access the data and why. Dynamic access control provides tighter control over who can access which data, which increases the security for sensitive data.

It is important to note that dynamic access control does not replace other access control models and mechanisms. It instead allows these methods to be used more effectively. Dynamic access control provides automatic policy-driven use of access control that allows the implementation of complex policies that cannot be effectively implemented manually.

ORA uses workflow as the basis for dynamic access control. Workflow defines processes and facilitates the assignment of the activities necessary to complete these processes. Each activity represents a distinct step in a process. The workflow system assigns specific activities to users based on the previously completed activities, the outcomes of those activities, the roles and responsibilities of the user, the process definition, and the state of the process instance. In other words, users perform work in the context of the workflow environment; this context provides much more information about why a user is performing a particular activity than is typically available. Since any data that a user needs to access to perform an activity is also accessed in the context of the workflow instance, this richer context is available for use in making access control decisions for this data. For example, users can be granted access to certain data while they are performing an activity that requires the access and denied access to the data when they are not performing a relevant activity. In this way, we can use the workflow context for making dynamic access control decisions.

Dynamic access control is not needed in every situation, but it is critical to providing adequate access control in some environments. Consider, for example, the clinical environment. A typical clinical environment may define roles, such as doctor, nurse, intern, clerk, etc., and use these roles for controlling access to medical records. While this scheme is sufficient to differentiate which users (roles) can read, write, and update which parts of a patient record, it does not provide the level of control over the patient record that is needed. For example, this scheme will allow any doctor to access any patient record at any time, regardless of whether or not the doctor is involved in the care of that patient. This inadequacy can lead to abuses: users can browse patient records to find personal information on celebrities, VIPs, friends, etc.; users can use this information in inappropriate ways; or users can even adversely affect the quality of patient care. The problem is that the need to access a patient's record is dynamic. Ideally, medical personnel should have no access to records of patients whom they are not treating, full access (appropriate to their role) to records of patients under their care, and limited access to records of patients whom they are no longer treating. Dynamic access control provides the necessary fine-grained access control and prevents the kinds of abuses cited above.

3 Fine-grained Data Security

Another primary motivation of our work is the need to provide fine-grained protection mechanisms for documents. Some parts of a document may be more sensitive than other parts and these parts may require stronger protection mechanisms than the less sensitive parts. On the other hand, the application of strong protection mechanisms to the entire document may unduly restrict access to the less sensitive parts of the document. Our solution to this problem is to provide for different levels of protection for different parts of a document. For example, some parts of the document may have access controls and other parts may be selectively encrypted. This solution enables organizations to balance the need for higher security with the need for access to data. Consider, once again, the clinical environment. An electronic patient record can be viewed as a single document that contains information with a range of sensitivities. Based on their role, different medical personnel require access to different parts of this document; some of these personnel require access to sensitive data, others do not. Our approach treats a patient record as a single integral document, but protects the different parts of the document according to the sensitivity of the data contained there.

For this project, we have developed a security policy editor that assigns security policy to the different parts of a document, based on the structure of the document. Any document (or as we shall see later, data source) that has sufficient structure can have policy assigned to its parts in this manner. The security policy editor uses XML Data Type Definitions (DTD) to describe the structure of a class of documents, allows the user to assign policy to the different elements in this structure, and outputs the resulting policy. This policy is used by the enforcement mechanism described in section 6 to control the security of all documents that are instances of this class. (Note that, for the current prototype, the structure of the documents that we work with is restricted to a particular hierarchical form; we have yet to consider arbitrary DTDs.)

4 Active Security

The final motivation of our work is the need to provide an active security environment that automatically implements the desired security policy with little or no intervention from end users. There are a number of reasons that end users cannot be completely depended on for policy implementation. End users are notorious for not wanting security to get in the way. End users are not always sufficiently educated about security and can often inadvertently bypass or disable security functionality without being aware they have done so. End users do not always remember to do the right thing. Finally, end users need assistance with complicated policies; policies that require users to take frequent manual actions are doomed to failure. Our approach to solving these problems is to build the policy into the workflow infrastructure. By making the workflow infrastructure responsible for security policy interpretation and implementation, we provide the end user with automated support that relieves the end user of much of the drudgery.

Consider the clinical environment once again. Medical end users require immediate access to medical records. This means that medical end users will not tolerate any delay in access to medical records due to security. For these reasons, security in clinical environments must be almost entirely transparent to the end user. In this environment, active security is essential to protecting patient privacy.

5 Secure Workflow

Odyssey Research Associates has developed a secure workflow system that protects enterprise data according to a workflow security policy. We have also developed a security policy editor that helps security administrators to define the workflow security policy. The secure workflow system consists of two types of servers: a workflow server and a data repository. As currently implemented, multiple data repositories may be used to support a single workflow server. The workflow server is responsible for all workflow-related functions: keeping track of process status, assigning activities, etc. Data repositories are responsible for the storage and retrieval of the data that workflow users require to perform assigned work activities. Workflow clients can only interact with the servers through protected interfaces. These protected interfaces are security aware in the sense that all actions performed using a protected interface must conform to the workflow security policy.

The design of the secure workflow server incorporates an off-the-shelf workflow engine that provides basic workflow services; we augment the basic workflow services by wrapping them with protected interfaces as described above. In order to use an off-the-shelf workflow engine effectively to build our secure workflow server, we require a standard object model for workflow services that we can use in conjunction with any off-the-shelf workflow engine. Fortunately, the Object Management Group (OMG) and the Workflow Management Coalition (WFMC) have joined forces to provide just such a standard model [5]. The OMG, supported by the WFMC, has adopted a workflow management facility. The OMG standard, originally known as the jFlow Workflow Management Facility, is co-authored by representatives of 20 companies and supported by 20 others, which altogether represent the workflow industry's major players. By adopting the jFlow standard, enhancing it with our policy enforcement mechanisms, and using a commercial workflow engine as a back-end server, we have been able to develop a secure workflow server with a significantly smaller investment of time and resources than would otherwise be possible.

The design of the data repository is also based on industry standards. We use XML DTDs to define the structure of the repository data. The interfaces that clients use to access repository data are based on the Document Object Model (DOM), which is an object model developed by the World Wide Web Consortium for representing XML documents and data [4]. As is the case with the workflow server, we have wrapped the DOM interfaces with protected interfaces that ensure that clients perform all data storage and retrieval actions in accordance with the workflow security policy. By using XML as the basis for the data repository, we can easily place any data that can be generated in an XML format into the data repository.

We also use XML DTDs to define the structure of the workflow data for the security policy editor. This allows us to tie the security policy to specific element types, which, in turn, allows a fine-grained specification of the security policy.

Figure 1 shows how all of these components fit together to provide a secure workflow system.

Note that policy creation, class generation, and placing of the initial set of repository data onto the data repository does not require access by workflow users and can therefore be done in a controlled environment. Once an administrator has initialized the repository through this administrative process, workflow users are able to access the data through the protected interfaces.

6 Active Security Infrastructure

To implement the protected interfaces we have developed a distributed, object-oriented, policy enforcement infrastructure. We also have developed tools that help implementers to build applications based on this infrastructure.

The distributed policy enforcement mechanism includes not only the component or components that store and adjudicate the security policy, but also those components that connect the security policy components with the rest of the system and ensure that the appropriate security policies are properly enforced. We take an object-oriented approach to the design of the security services and policy enforcement mechanisms. We provide the tools for developing a set of policy-aware objects that are capable of enforcing security policies developed using the security policy editor. We have developed an approach that makes it possible to add our policy enforcement mechanisms to existing sets of interfaces, with minimal impact on these interfaces. This

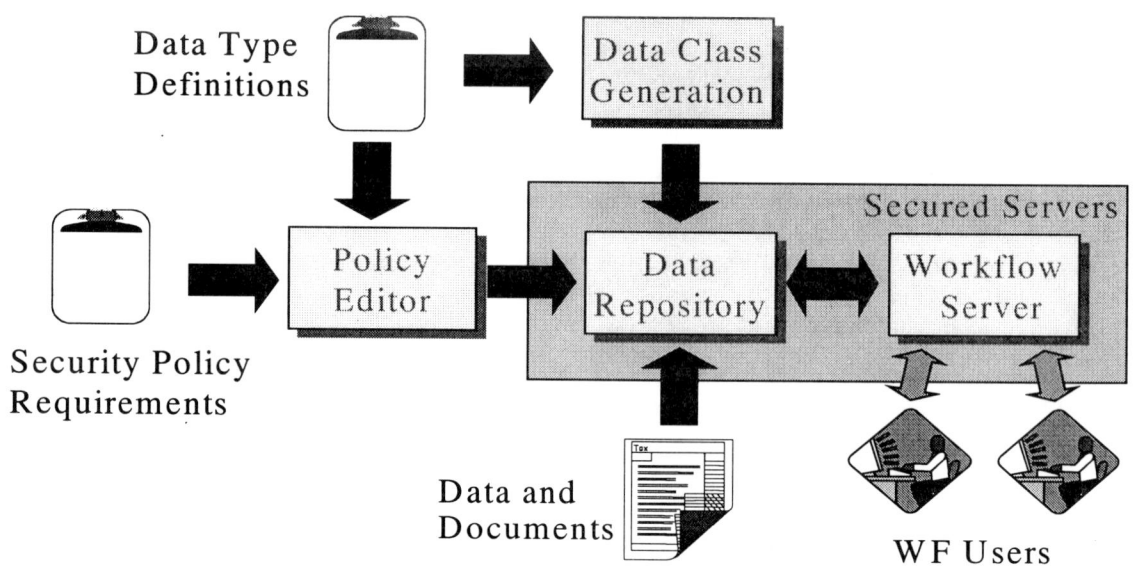

Figure 1. Secure Workflow and Data Repository

in turn allows us to take advantage of object models and standards that industry groups and other standards bodies are currently developing

The distributed policy enforcement mechanism includes not only the component or components that store and adjudicate the security policy, but also those components that connect the security policy components with the rest of the system and ensure that the appropriate security policies are properly enforced. We take an object-oriented approach to the design of the security services and policy enforcement mechanisms. We provide the tools for developing a set of policy-aware objects that are capable of enforcing security policies developed using the security policy editor. We have developed an approach that makes it possible to add our policy enforcement mechanisms to existing sets of interfaces, with minimal impact on these interfaces. This in turn allows us to take advantage of object models and standards that industry groups and other standards bodies are currently developing.

We considered several options, including Microsoft's COM, OMG's CORBA, and Java Remote Method Invocation (RMI) for implementing the secure workflow server. We ultimately decided to use Java RMI technology. We rejected COM because of the restrictions of COM technology to the Windows/Intel architecture. At the other extreme, we decided that we did not need the full power (and expense) of CORBA and its ability to integrate heterogeneous programming environments, languages, and legacy systems. The Java environment and Java RMI provide an elegant development environment (along with cross-platform portability) without the expense and overhead of a CORBA environment. However, we have purposely kept our object models and overall design very CORBA-like to maintain the potential for CORBA integration at some time in the future.

In our prototype workflow system, we protect objects by placing their implementations on secured servers and providing protected interfaces that provide and enforce secure access to server objects. Clients access server objects through proxy objects whose purpose is to enforce client-side security policy. A corresponding object on the server side implements the secure interface to the server object and enforces server-side security policy. Our security policy enforcement mechanism is layered on top of Java RMI in a way that transparently provides server objects with the security protection the policy requires. With our design, we can automatically generate all the code necessary for security policy enforcement directly from the specification of the Java interface to the server object implementation. The server object implementation does not require any modification in order to be secured. At runtime, the security policy is instantiated on the server and securely downloaded to the client proxy.

Part of our approach is to automatically generate all the code necessary for security policy enforcement directly from a Java interface's specification. From a Java interface definition, we generate a set of security-aware Java interfaces and classes. The generated interfaces and classes transform the original Java interface into a secure, remote interface capable of enforcing the security policy defined for the interface. Security policy enforcement is largely transparent to clients that use the transformed interface and to servers that provide implementations of the interfaces. We are using Spectangle, a tool developed by ORA as part of the CORBA/THETA project for the NSA [3], for the code generation. Spectangle provides a powerful, flexible code generation facility that is ideal for this project and allows us to automatically generate the security code for a Java interface in a cost-effective manner.

7 Conclusion

ORA has developed a prototype secure workflow server that automatically implements an enterprise security policy for workflow users and activities. We have developed a security policy editor that security administrators can use to develop appropriate workflow policies and we have developed a secure workflow server and secure data repository that enforce these policies for all interactions with workflow client software. In addition, we have implemented the servers using a distributed object-oriented policy enforcement infrastructure. This project has demonstrated how high-level security policies can be implemented in a workflow system, providing enhanced security services that protect sensitive data as it is moved through the system.

References

[1]. Roshan Thomas, "Security in Workflow Processes: Dynamic Security Models for Clinical Workflows," Odyssey Research Associates, December 4th, 1996.

[2] Douglas Long, Peter Samsel, "Security Policy Modeling and Enforcement Tools for Clinical Workflows, Semi-Annual Report," Odyssey Research Associates TM-98-0016, June 15, 1998.

[3] Maureen Stillman, Cheryl Barbasch and Matthew Stillerman, "Design of a CORBA-Compliant THETA," Odyssey Research Associates TM96-0026, March 1997.

[4] W3C, "Document Object Model (DOM) Level 1 Specification," World Wide Web Consortium October 1, 1998.

[5] OMG, "Joint Workflow Management Facility - Revised Submission," Object Management Group bom/98-06-07, July 4, 1998.

[6] Charles F. Goldfarb, Paul Prescod, The XML Handbook. 1998, Upper Saddle River, NJ: Prentice Hall PTR.

[7] Carla Marceau, "Specification-based code generation using literate programming tools," Odyssey Research Associates, December 5, 1996.

Napoleon: A Recipe for Workflow

C. Payne, D. Thomsen, J. Bogle and R. O'Brien
Secure Computing Corporation
2675 Long Lake Road
Roseville, MN 55113

Abstract

This paper argues that Napoleon, a flexible, role-based access control (RBAC) modeling environment, is also a practical solution for enforcing business process control, or workflow, policies. Napoleon provides two important benefits for workflow: simplified policy management and support for heterogeneous, distributed systems. We discuss our strategy for modeling workflow in Napoleon, and we present an architecture that incorporates Napoleon into a workflow management system.

1. Introduction

Last year at this conference we introduced Napoleon, a multi-layered, role-based access control (RBAC) modeling environment for distributed computing systems [10]. Napoleon's primary objective is to simplify policy management for the system administrators of distributed computing systems. It satisfies this objective by shifting the burden of policy management from the system administrator alone to all of the principals involved in the system's development, including application designers, system integrators and the like. Napoleon translates the resulting policy for each enforcement mechanism in the system. Napoleon is a practical solution for RBAC policy management.

This year we argue that Napoleon is also a practical solution for business process control, or workflow, policy management.[1] Napoleon addresses two challenges posed to workflow technology developers: simplify policy management [1] and support distributed computing systems [3]. Napoleon's layered model simplifies policy management by dividing the burden among all principals in the system's development, and Napoleon supports distributed computing systems by providing policy translators for the various enforcement mechanisms in the distributed system.

Modeling workflow in Napoleon is simple, because the underlying concepts of workflow are consistent with the Napoleon model. However, implementing workflow is more complicated. RBAC policies are primarily class-based, but workflow policies are very much instance-based. We discuss these issues and propose a solution that incorporates Napoleon into a workflow management system.

First we review the Napoleon model and software tool. Napoleon has evolved significantly since last year. In particular, the model is more general and more flexible.

2. Revisiting Napoleon

> Pastry is like mathematics. Everything is logical. If you know the basic building blocks, you can make anything.
>
> Jacques Torres
> Dessert Circus[11]

Napoleon is the common name for a family of desserts that are created by alternating layers of pastry with sweet, creamy filling and then finishing with a glaze of icing or a dusting of confectioners' sugar (see Figure 1 (a)).

Napoleon is also an acronym for the Network Application POLicy EnvirONment, a role-based access control (RBAC) modeling environment [10]. The environment consists of a policy model and a software tool for defining and managing the model. The software tool is implemented in Java with a model-view-controller architecture.

Like the dessert, the Napoleon policy model is multi-layered (see Figure 1 (b)). Each layer defines a set of roles that become policy building blocks for all higher layers. The bottom policy layer defines the most primitive access control policy. This policy layer is typically application-specific and is defined in terms of the access control mechanisms that manage the application's resources. The second through penultimate layers use the roles defined at lower layers to create even more abstract roles that simplify policy

---

[1] This investigation was performed under a Phase I SBIR from the National Institute of Standards and Technology (NIST) Contract No. 50-DKNB-8-90107. Phase II has been awarded and will begin in the fall of 1999.

only one key. Key chains can also contain other key chains, which supports role hierarchies. One of the innovations of Napoleon is that it associates constraints with each key chain. The constraints place additional restrictions on the use of the key chain. For example, a key chain may allow access to patient medical records, but constraints may prevent the holder of the key chain from accessing any records for which the holder is not the primary care physician. Figure 2 illustrates how keys and key chains are used to build semantic layers in the Napoleon model.

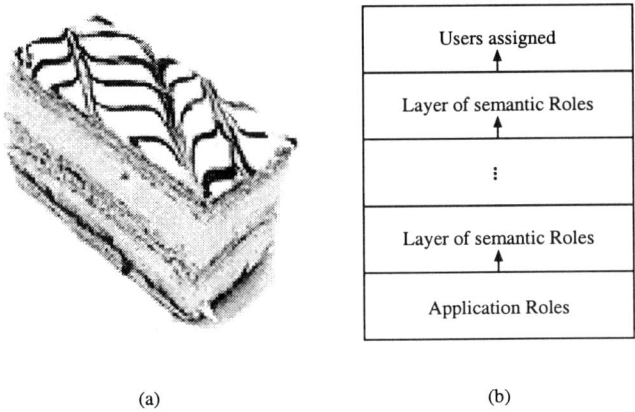

Figure 1. Two Napoleons

management. Roles defined in the top layer are assigned to users. Like the dessert, there can be an arbitrary number of layers, and new layers can be introduced as required.

Unlike the dessert however, each Napoleon policy layer is constructed by a different "chef." Application designers define the bottom layer because they understand best what their resources are and how access to these resources should be constrained. Several chefs may contribute to a single layer, e.g., there may be several applications represented in the bottom layer. System administrators define the top layer because they know who their users are. The chefs for intermediate layers vary with each model. An application suite designer may group the roles of participating applications into roles for the suite. A system integrator may create more abstract roles based on the suite roles. It is important to note that unlike the dessert, the layers in a Napoleon policy model may not be strictly one above the other. A particular layer may build on roles defined in any layer below it, not just the layer immediately below it. For example, the local system administrator is not restricted to roles defined in the penultimate layer. Roles assigned to users can be culled from any layer as needed.

The model described above, with its arbitrary number of layers, is a significant improvement over the original model [10]. The original model contained only two layers: one for the application designer and one for the system administrator. It did not consider the myriad of other principals that should define policy. The current model evolved from our attempts to include some of these principals and from our exploration of workflow support.

The current model continues the metaphor of a key to simplify policy management. A key corresponds to a role. Within each layer, keys are collected into key chains for easier handling. Keys cannot be exported directly to higher layers, but they can be incorporated into a key chain with

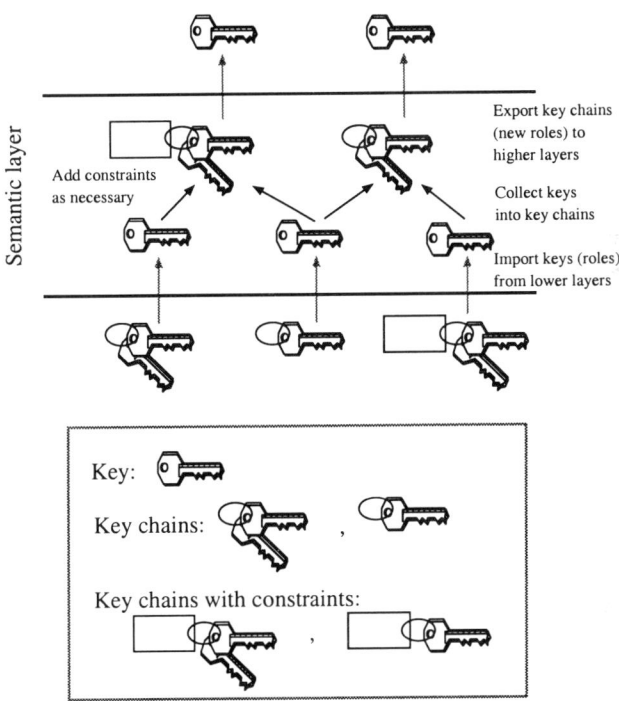

Figure 2. Building semantic layers with keys and key chains

Napoleon's software tool provides a graphic user interface (GUI), or viewer, for each layer of the model. While the middle layers of the model are identical structurally, they differ semantically depending on the chef, so a different viewer is possible in each case. The tool manages the export and import of keys between layers and directs the policy translators to convert the policy rules of the Napoleon model into the enforcement languages of the underlying policy enforcement mechanisms. The tool is very modular: new viewers and policy translators can be added easily.

2.1. Example

Consider a simple example of a hospital data system that is composed of two applications: a CORBA application used by the medical staff to record and share patient information and a COM billing application. The hospital purchases these applications from a third party integrator.

The system's RBAC policy is modeled in Napoleon as three layers, which are illustrated in Figure 3. In the bottom layer, the designers of the CORBA application and the COM application define their application policies independently. For CORBA and COM-based applications, the Napoleon software tool gathers automatically a list of supported operations, or methods, from the application's interface definition language (IDL) files. The application designer uses Napoleon's GUI to group these methods into convenient sets called handles and then to assign handles to keys. A key designates that the holder has permission to execute the associated methods. Since CORBA and COM are object-based, controlling access to an object's methods is sufficient for controlling access to the object itself.

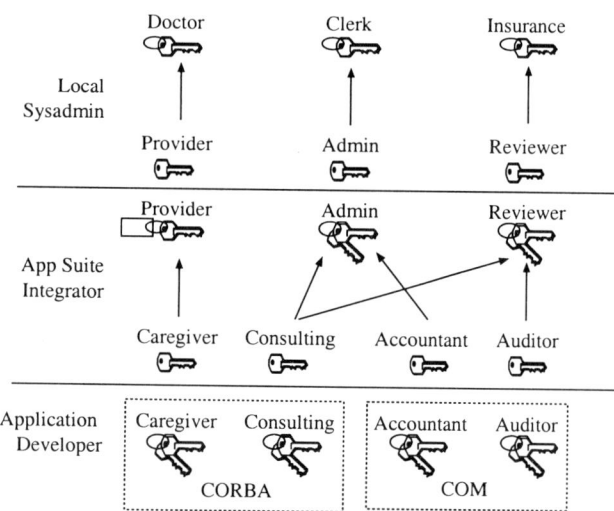

Figure 3. An example Napoleon model

To define the application security policy, the application designer uses the Napoleon GUI to collect keys into key chains and marks the key chains for export to higher model layers. By marking key chains for export, the application developer creates policy building blocks for other layers to build upon. It is similar to creating a software interface. Anything not explicitly included in the interface is not available for use outside the layer.

For our simple example, the CORBA-based, patient information application designer exports two key chains: a CAREGIVER key chain for creating and modifying patient records and a CONSULTING key chain for only viewing patient records. The COM-based billing application designer also exports two key chains: an ACCOUNTANT key chain for generating billing data and an AUDITOR key chain for only viewing billing data. These four key chains represent application-specific roles that are available as building blocks for higher layer policies.

In the middle layer, an application suite integrator imports the four key chains from the application layer. Once a key chain is exported, it is considered an atomic entity, so it is considered a key by all higher layers. The application suite integrator is charged with defining a policy that spans all applications in the suite. In this example, the application suite builds three key chains for export: the ADMIN key chain that contains the CONSULTING key and the ACCOUNTANT key, a PROVIDER key chain that contains the CAREGIVER key, and a REVIEWER key chain that contains the CONSULTING key and the AUDITOR key. The PROVIDER key chain includes constraints that the holder must be a primary care provider for the patient whose records are being accessed.

At the top layer, the three key chains exported from the middle layer (ADMIN, PROVIDER and REVIEWER) are available as simple keys. The four key chains exported from the bottom layer (CAREGIVER, CONSULTING, ACCOUNTANT and AUDITOR) are also available in the event that ADMIN, PROVIDER and REVIEWER are not sufficient, but they are not immediately visible.

While the hospital is tied to a regional information network, it employs a small staff that must wear many hats. The system administrator uses Napoleon to create three key chains to assign to users: the DOCTOR key chain contains only the PROVIDER key, the INSURANCE key chain contains only the REVIEWER key, and the CLERK key chain contains only the ADMIN key. The constraints applied to any keys contained in a key chain apply to the key chain also. For example, a user in the DOCTOR role can only modify patient records for which the user is the primary care physician.

Once the hospital's security policy is defined, the system administrator directs Napoleon to translate the policy for the CORBA and COM object managers. These object managers enforce the policy for their respective objects. In other words, as users attempt to access patient records or billing data, the object managers ensure that the users have the appropriate role and that stated constraints are satisfied.

We will return to this example later in the paper to consider workflow.

3. Workflow

A workflow is "the computerized facilitation or automation of a business process, in whole or part." [5] Workflow technology is a promising solution for protecting business assets, because it controls not only who has access to what but when that access occurs.

Figure 4 illustrates a simple workflow for processing employee expense reimbursements. We represent the workflow as a directed graph with one entry. Each node in the graph is a workflow activity, or *step*, and the edges determine the order in which steps must occur. Associated with each step are the object(s) that will be accessed (e.g., "check request"), the operation(s) that will be performed ("prepare") and the performer ("EMPLOYEE"). In this simple workflow, an employee must first prepare an check request form and have that form approved by a manager. Then a company accountant drafts the check, and finally the treasurer approves (signs) it. The most obvious constraint is that the steps must occur in order, but other constraints are possible. We may require that the approving manager be the manager for the employee. We may require also that no two functions be performed by the same individual, which is called separation of duties [9].

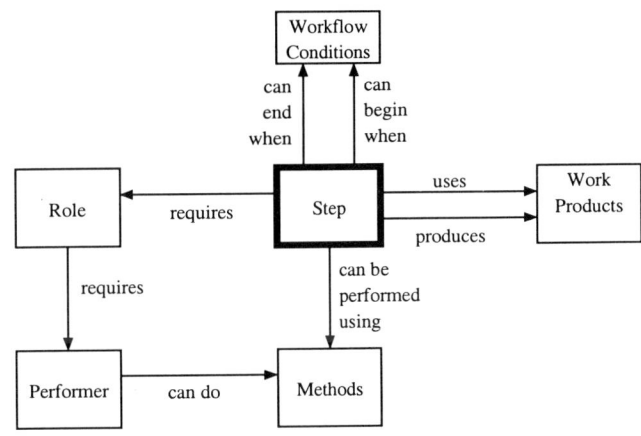

Figure 5. Fundamental concepts of workflow

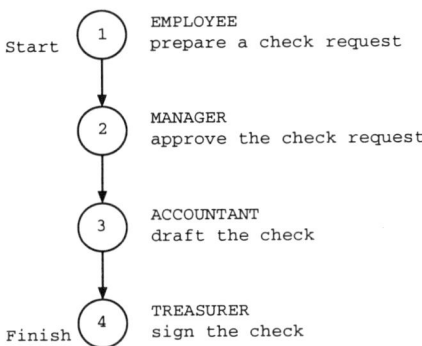

Figure 4. Simple workflow

Riddle [8] identifies the fundamental concepts of workflow and describes the relationships between them (see Figure 5).

- A *step* is a unit of work. It may require several resources to complete. Associated with the step are those resources and the role required to perform it.

- A *work product* is an artifact created or modified by steps. Steps use and produce work products.

- A *role* represents the accesses that are required to perform a step.

- A *workflow condition* is a predicate that must be satisfied during step performance. It is often expressed as entry and exit conditions on the step, that is, the step can begin when and can end when the conditions are true.

- A *performer* is a person or tool with the skills necessary to complete the step. A role may require special skills and therefore a specific performer.

- A *method* is an approach for carrying out a step. A step can be performed using one of several methods. The performer can do these methods.

Several of these concepts, such as roles, methods and performers, are also fundamental concepts for RBAC. Even *work products* is familiar; it is just a different name for the resources to be accessed. Only steps and workflow conditions are really new.

Riddle relates concepts a bit differently than the RBAC community, but the differences are superficial. Figure 6 illustrates Riddle's concepts using a role-based perspective, rather than the step-based view of Figure 5. From this perspective, we see that steps are like sub-roles. They define a group of accesses that are specific to a task. Workflow conditions determine when the sub-roles are active. A role, then, is a collection of steps and their associated workflow conditions.

Workflows are enforced by a workflow management system (WMS). The user interacts with the WMS to gain access to resources controlled by the workflow. Automated workflow technology has evolved significantly since it was introduced thirty years ago for office automation systems. Early workflow systems did not acknowledge the variety of ways that humans perform a task. So researchers focused on better modeling techniques, and today workflow research is more interdisciplinary: a combination of computer science and social science. The WMS must encompass non-computer activities such as meetings, handle unexpected contingencies, and allow new workflows to be constructed from existing workflows [3]. Workflow process models must be

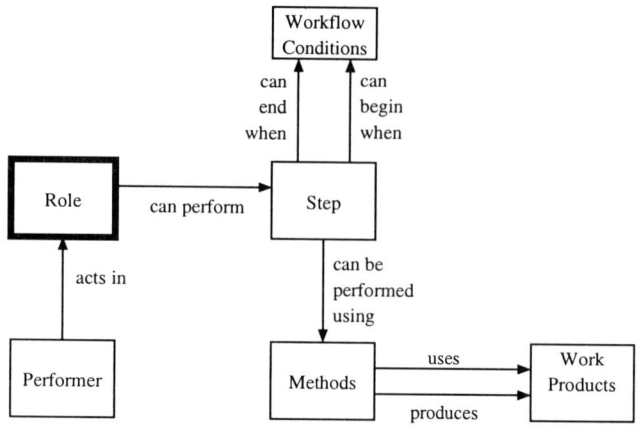

Figure 6. A role-based perspective of workflow

reconciled with the rich variety of activities and behaviors that comprise "real work" [1]. In short, workflow management is a complex activity, and we want to leverage existing technology as much as possible.

4. Napoleon and workflow

Abbott *et al* [1], Feinstein *et al* [4] and Bertino *et al* [2] note that workflow management can be simplified considerably by adopting an RBAC model. However, many role-based models fail to include the role authorization constraints that are required for workflow [2]. As Napoleon includes role constraints, it is a good candidate for workflow policy management.

Our design strategy for incorporating Napoleon into a WMS is to let each tool do what it does best. Napoleon is a policy management tool. While it may be tempting to extend Napoleon with workflow management features, the complexity of workflow management would overwhelm it. Instead, we let Napoleon serve as the policy management engine for a WMS. We use Napoleon to specify and enforce certain aspects of the workflow policy. The divisions of labor between Napoleon and the WMS are described below.

4.1. Specifying workflow in Napoleon

We begin by assuming that the workflow is defined in the WMS and imported into Napoleon. The workflow is imported as a collection of steps. Note that the workflow conditions associated with each step are not imported. We could model these conditions in Napoleon, but we will explain in Section 5 why we choose not to do so.

Our approach is to model workflow as a new layer in a Napoleon model. The new layer looks structurally like the other layers, that is, it has keys and key chains with associated constraints. The difference is in how we build and interpret it. We call the new layer the *workflow layer*, and we introduce a new "chef," the workflow administrator, to construct it.

The workflow administrator begins by assessing the keys that are available for the workflow. The workflow will require certain operations to be performed. If those operations are not represented in the available keys, the workflow administrator must create new keys. Once the necessary keys are imported, the workflow administrator collects the keys required for each step into a key chain that represents the step. The collection of key chains defined in this layer map one to one to the collection of steps in the workflow. The workflow administrator marks each step for export to the next layer, where they are assigned to the roles that will perform them. Several steps may be performed by the same role.

4.1.1. An example with workflow

To illustrate this process, let us return to the hospital scenario from Section 2.1. Suppose the system administrator, who also happens to be the workflow administrator, wants to specify the simple workflow illustrated in Figure 7. This workflow states that whenever a DOCTOR updates a patient's medical record with treatment information, the CLERK must prepare a bill for the treatment. The bill must then be reviewed by the INSURANCE representative, who may authorize partial payment. Finally, the CLERK bills the patient for the remaining balance. This workflow ensures that all bills are reviewed by the insurance representative before they are mailed to the patients, and it ensures that no insurance payment is authorized without a bill.

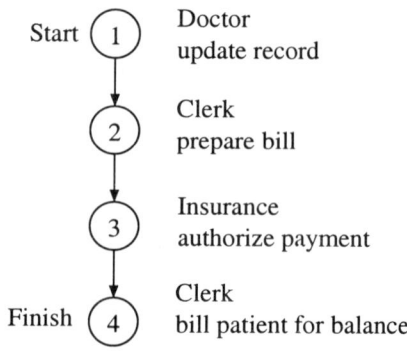

Figure 7. A simple workflow

Figure 8 illustrates how the new workflow layer is modeled in Napoleon. The bottom and second layers are constructed as before. Then the workflow administrator (who may be the system adminstrator) imports the keys (PROVIDER, ADMIN and REVIEWER) necessary to perform the workflow from the second layer. We assume these keys are sufficient, but the workflow administrator could revisit the lower layers and construct new keys if appropriate.

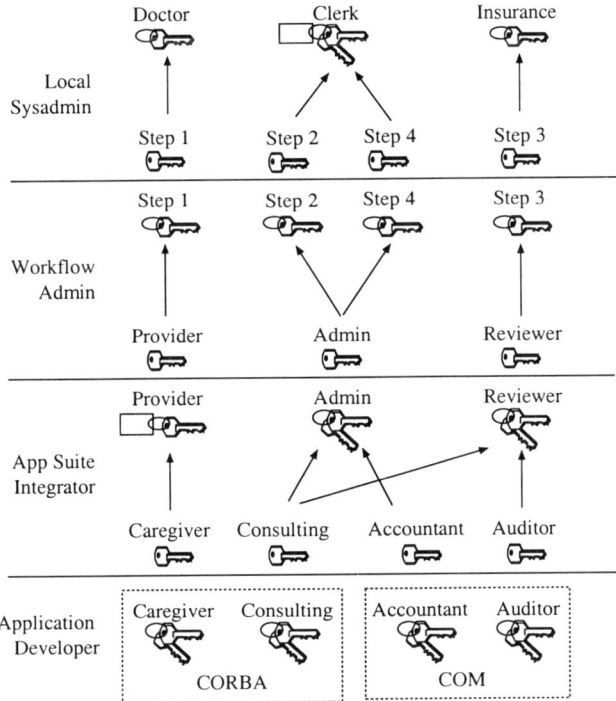

Figure 8. Modeling the workflow in Napoleon

These keys are collected according to the steps that require them. Step 1 requires only the PROVIDER key. Both step 2 and step 4 require the ADMIN key, so the ADMIN key appears on two separate key chains. If different operations are required between the two steps, we could introduce constraints on one or both of the key chains. Finally, step 3 requires only the REVIEWER key. The workflow administrator marks these four steps for export to the system administrator level, where they are assigned to the roles (DOCTOR, CLERK and INSURANCE) that will perform them. In the case of a role that can perform multiple steps (for example, CLERK), constraints are used to determine the appropriate step.

The main difference between a Napoleon model without workflow and a Napoleon model with workflow is that the latter divides roles into sub-roles by task. A Napoleon model simply describes sets of sets, so the division is natural. However, as we will discuss next, there are huge differences in how these models are enforced.

4.2. Enforcing workflow in Napoleon

Napoleon is designed to provide central policy management with distributed policy enforcement. Once the policy is defined, it is "pushed out" to the various enforcement mechanisms in the distributed system. If the policy changes, the new version is pushed out. Napoleon makes no access decisions itself.

Workflow management, on the other hand, requires some central policy enforcement. First, there can be many instances of a workflow active simultaneously. The accesses permitted a specific user may vary depending on the instance. Each access request must be bound to the appropriate instance, and that binding must occur in the WMS.

Second, for each workflow instance only one step (the *current step*) is active at any time. From an access control perspective, the permissions associated with the current step are granted only when the step begins and are revoked immediately after the step concludes. Each instance of a workflow may have a different current step at any point in time. The WMS must track the current step for each workflow instance in order to determine appropriate accesses.

Our initial investigation focused on ways to enforce workflow entirely within the local enforcement mechanisms. To satisfy workflow's central enforcement needs, we envisioned a *workflow object* would track the current step for each instance of a workflow. Napoleon would create the workflow object and bind it to the resources it controls. For each access request, the local enforcement mechanism would examine the corresponding workflow object and verify that the request is approved for the current step. If the request is approved, the local policy ("pushed out" as usual by Napoleon) would be enforced for that resource. The local enforcement mechanism would update the workflow object's indicator of *current step* as required.

There are several disadvantages with this approach. First, Napoleon must be modified considerably to create and distribute workflow objects. Second, each access request requires an additional permission check to the workflow object, which may be expensive. Third, we must trust the enforcement mechanisms to update the current step correctly. An enforcement mechanism could circumvent the workflow policy with malicious updates. Fourth, this approach would duplicate much of the workflow management processing already handled by the existing WMS. Clearly this approach is very invasive, so we refocused our efforts on a solution that leaves Napoleon and the local enforcement mechanisms relatively unchanged.

5. A Napoleon-based workflow management architecture

Olivier [7] notes that workflow policy enforcement can be partitioned into three layers, from lowest to highest: controlling access to resources, controlling access to steps and application-specific enforcement. A useful split occurs in the middle, or step, layer. Steps are a natural primitive for workflow designers. A WMS is specialized to create steps, determine their proper order and control execution of workflow instances according to that order. These operations are unique to workflow technology. However, access for a particular role to the resources associated with a particular step can be controlled by mechanisms that are commonly available in non-workflow domains.

Our solution exploits these partitions by assigning the step layer and the application-specific layer to the WMS and by assigning the resource layer to Napoleon. Workflows, their steps and workflow conditions are specified within the WMS. The steps are then exported to Napoleon, where resources and roles are bound to them. During workflow execution, the WMS manages workflow instances and directs Napoleon to grant and revoke access, as appropriate, to specific steps. Workflow conditions are enforced by the WMS because they determine when the access grantings and revocations should occur.

A high-level design of our solution is illustrated in Figure 9. This design illustrates two modes: policy specification mode and workflow execution mode. Operations for policy specification mode are noted in *italics*, while operations for workflow execution mode are noted in ordinary text. A classical workflow management system will isolate these modes into two modules: a *specification module*, which enables administrators to specify the workflow, and an *execution module*, which assists in coordinating and performing the procedures and activities [3]. Traditionally the specification module is used only in pre-execution; however, researchers are recognizing the need for the two modules to co-evolve to handle dynamic change and exception handling.

The best way to explain the architecture is with a simple scenario for creating and executing a workflow.

5.1. Start with the workflow class definition.

The workflow designer begins by specifying an access control policy that will apply to all instances of the workflow. The designer creates the workflow and its steps using the specification tools in the WMS. This information is then exported to Napoleon, where the binding of resources and roles to steps (as described in Section 4.1) occurs. Napoleon has already gathered a list of available object classes from the IDL files of its object managers. This list is also provided to the WMS for creating workflow instances (see Section 5.2 below).

When this process is complete, the designer has created an access control policy for a particular *class* of workflow. This policy names the roles required, it identifies the steps that each role may take and the class of resources that can be accessed at each step. However, the policy is incomplete. It does not have enough information to control a workflow instance. For example, it does not name individual objects. The objects that may be accessed will depend on the current step of a workflow instance. Therefore, Napoleon holds onto the policy for now; that is, it does not "push out" the policy for the enforcement engines.

5.2. Create a workflow instance.

At this point, Napoleon is loaded with a set of access control policies for workflow classes. A workflow instance gets created when some event occurs to trigger it. For example, a user requests a check reimbursement form, or a notification appears in a user's inbox. When such an event occurs, the WMS determines the appropriate workflow for the event and creates a new instance of that workflow. The workflow instance is stored locally at the WMS. The instance names the specific objects that may be accessed and the specific users that may access them.

When a workflow instance is created in the WMS, it must also be created in Napoleon. The WMS provides Napoleon with the necessary information to instantiate the appropriate workflow's class access control policy, which means providing constraints such as "if object is named foo.txt" that will be added to the instance copy in Napoleon. The instance policy names (via constraints) the specific objects that can be accessed. If all specific objects are not known when the instance is created, the WMS may provide additional constraints for that instance later.

In summary, the workflow instance definition in Napoleon looks like the class definition except that it also contains the constraints that name specific objects.

5.3. Execute the workflow instance.

The execution phase highlights the simplicity of this solution. The WMS controls the execution of the workflow instance. It determines the proper sequence of steps (e.g., what branches are executed), and it knows which steps are active. It decides when a step should start (become active) and when it is completed (and thus become inactive). The WMS does what it implies: it manages the workflow. However, it relies on Napoleon to manage the access control policy.

As the workflow executes, the WMS directs Napoleon to grant access to the active steps and revoke access to inactive

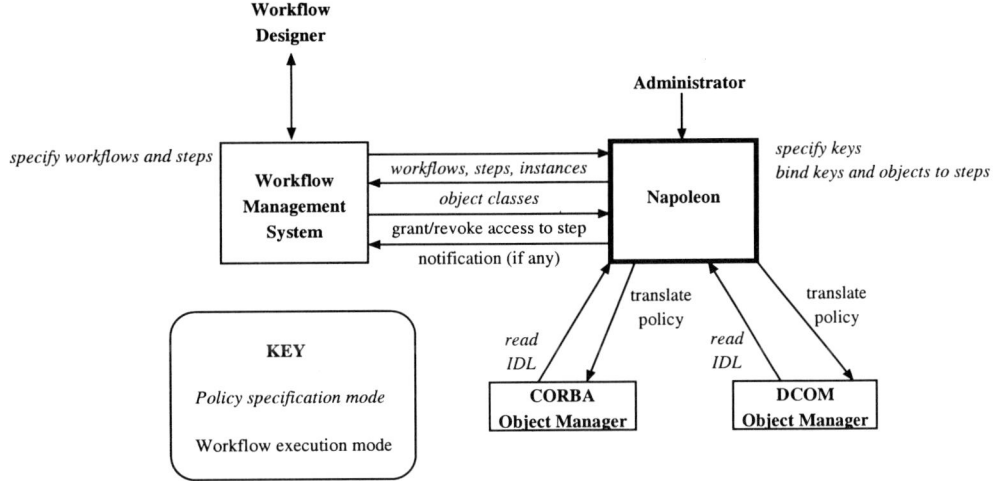

Figure 9. A Napoleon-based workflow management architecture

steps. No policy is translated for the object managers unless directed by the WMS. For example, suppose that step 1 of workflow instance P is active. Once step 1 is complete, the WMS will direct Napoleon as follows:

> Revoke access to step 1 in instance P, then grant access to step 2 in instance P.

Note that Napoleon runs in tandem with the WMS. With regard to policy translation, the only change in Napoleon's behavior is that it now "pushes out" the policy a step at a time rather than all at once.

6. Conclusions

We have described a workflow management architecture that incorporates Napoleon for workflow policy management. The architecture exploits the natural partitions in workflow policy management by assigning workflow-specific tasks to the WMS and workflow-generic tasks to Napoleon. This approach lets each tool do what it does best.

Napoleon offers many benefits to workflow management, including simplified policy management and support for heterogeneous, distributed computing systems. Napoleon's flexible model lets workflow be introduced at any layer.

The support for distributed systems lets a workflow's control extend beyond the local system or local network. A business's divisions may be far-flung across the Internet, so workflows may span several divisions or even several companies (supplier, distributor, etc.). Also, a workflow may need to control resources under the purview of legacy enforcement mechanisms as well as resources managed by newer standards like CORBA. In fact, the WMS does not have to know how the resources under its control are managed. Napoleon acts as a "universal adapter" between the WMS and the policy enforcement mechanisms.

7. Future work

An outstanding issue for Napoleon is how constraints should be implemented for CORBA and COM/DCOM objects. Neither system handles instance policies very well, although we have a sample approach for enforcing constraints in CORBA. The Object Management Group has looked at the issue [6], and we will look more closely at their findings and at related work by the Workflow Management Coalition (WfMC) [12]. We will examine the issue of constraints more fully in the next phase of this effort.

We will also consider other ways in which Napoleon may benefit workflow management, such as with support for hierarchical workflows.

Finally, we will identify a suitable WMS to prototype our architecture.

References

[1] K. Abbott and S. Sarin. Experiences with workflow management: Issues for the next generation. In *Computer Supported Cooperative Work (CSCW)*. ACM, 1994.

[2] E. Bertino, E. Ferrari, and V. Atluri. A flexible model supporting the specification and enforcement of role-based authorizations in workflow management systems. In *ACM Workshop on Role-Based Access Control*. ACM, 1997.

[3] C. Ellis and G. Nutt. Workflow: The process spectrum. In *Workshop on Workflow and Process Automation in Information Systems*. National Science Foundation, May 1996.

[4] H. Feinstein, R. Sandhu, C. Youman, and E. Coyne. Final report small business innovation research (sbir) role-based access control phase 1. Technical Report Department of Commerce Contract number 50-DKNA-4-00122, NIST, May 1995.

[5] D. Hollingsworth. Workflow reference model v. 1.1. Technical Report TC00-1003, Workflow Management Coalition, January 1995.

[6] Object Management Group. Workflow management facility. Technical report, Object Management Group, July 1998.

[7] M. Olivier, R. van de Riet, and E. Gudes. Specifying application-level security in workflow systems. In *9th International Workshop on Database and Expert Systems Architectures (DEXA '98)*. IEEE Computer Society, August 1998.

[8] W. Riddle. Fundamental process modeling concepts. In *Workshop on Workflow and Process Automation in Information Systems*. National Science Foundation, May 1996.

[9] R. Sandhu. Separation of duties in computerized information systems. In *Database Security IV: Status and Prospects*, pages 179–189. North Holland, 1991.

[10] D. Thomsen, D. O'Brien, and J. Bogle. Role based access control framework for network enterprises. In *14th Annual Computer Security Applications Conference*, December 1998.

[11] J. Torres. http://www.jacquestorres.com/ bookinformation / book1 / jtbook.htm.

[12] Workflow Management Coalition. Workflow security considerations — white paper. Technical Report WFMC-TC-1019, Workflow Management Coalition, February 1998.

Tools to Support Secure Enterprise Computing

Myong H. Kang, Brian J. Eppinger, and Judith N. Froscher
Information Technology Division
Naval Research Laboratory

Abstract

Secure enterprise programming is a difficult and tedious task. Programmers need tools that support different levels of abstraction and that track all the components that participate in distributed enterprises. Those components must cooperate in a distributed environment to achieve higher-level goals. A special case of secure enterprise computing is multilevel secure (MLS) computing. Components that may reside in different security domains have to cooperate to achieve higher-level missions.

To ease the programmer's burden, we are developing an MLS workflow management system (WFMS), called MLS METEOR. A programmer can specify a distributed programming logic through a GUI-based workflow design tool. Based on the programming logic, MLS METEOR will generate a distributed runtime system that handles communication among different hosts, even those that reside in different classification domains. The multilevel security enforcement of MLS METEOR does not depend on the WFMS itself but rather on the underlying MLS infrastructure and a few security critical components. This paper concentrates on the system organization of MLS METEOR and the rationale for this structure. We explain which portions of the system can be used in generic enterprise computing and which portions are specific to MLS computing.

1. Introduction

Globalization has replaced the separation that characterized the Cold War era. Unconventional coalitions among businesses and nations and among former adversaries are formed to advance common goals, then quickly dissolve as individual objectives change. Threats now lie in these essential connections among participating enterprises, which also enable profitable cooperation. To facilitate these alliances, businesses and the military rely on distributed information technology (IT) for most operations and must be able to respond quickly to new situations and threats in completely different environments. Hence, supporting IT resources must be flexible to allow for rapid reconfiguration.

The military has additional requirements that stem from the need to pull together coalitions in a short timeframe to achieve a common goal and to protect sensitive national security information. Each mission has different mission logic and deals with different computing resources that can belong to different classification domains. Therefore, distributed programs that support such missions have to deal with multilevel security (MLS) issues.

Another complication of distributed computing arises because the programs are very large. In general, distributed programs are much larger than conventional programs and often involve the integration of existing applications to achieve higher-level goals. Even though distributed object computing standards like CORBA and DCOM, have made a basic level of interoperability among distributed applications possible and have made distributed programming tenable, distributed programming is still a difficult and tedious task. Usually a team of programmers has to work on different parts of a program, which have to be assembled to provide the IT support for the mission. It is often difficult to have a global picture of the whole program and to monitor the progress of the work due to the magnitude of these programs and the wide distribution of resources.

The operational environment and dependence on cooperation among distributed IT resources mean that we need development and runtime tools that
- ease the programming burden of constructing large-scale, distributed systems and promotes reuse of existing components,
- provide a GUI-based distributed programming environment that offers different levels of abstraction so that not only the global picture of the program, but also more detailed views of a component, can be displayed for different users,

- allow easy (re)configuration of design to accommodate and promote integration with coalition partners,
- generate runtime code to handle the complexities of distributed communication (e.g., CORBA, DCOM, HTTP),
- can specify recovery strategies,
- reduce the design time and cost of MLS applications,
- generate secure runtime code to ensure the success of the mission since these systems operate in many different classification domains, and
- provide monitoring capabilities so that users at different classification domain can determine the status of work in progress at their level and the levels that they are allowed to monitor.

Even though there may be many ways to achieve these goals, we have started with the workflow paradigm, to which we can add new capabilities such as multilevel security, distributed scheduling, recovery, etc. In this paper, we view multilevel secure computing as a special case of secure enterprise computing. We may have to guard the connections among different security domains more strongly than the connections among business partners. However, the MLS programming principles is not much different from any other secure enterprise computing. In fact, we have designed the WFMS so that different security infrastructures can be used to facilitate cooperation among several enterprises.

This paper is organized as follows. In section 2, we briefly review our strategy to achieve the above goal for secure enterprise computing. We present the software structure for implementing such a system in section 3. We carefully organize the software so that only a small portion is specific to MLS computing. Section 4 concludes this paper and presents the status of the project and future work.

2. A Strategy for Secure Enterprise Computing

We presented a strategy to pursue the above goals in a separate paper [2]. In this section, we summarize the strategy for the sake of completeness.

The MLS workflow management system (WFMS) that we are building will provide equivalent functionality to a single-level WFMS and hooks into an MLS infrastructure for enforcing the MLS security policy. Tasks that may be single-level individually, but located in different classification domains, have to cooperate to achieve a higher-level MLS mission. Therefore, we need to provide an MLS distributed programming (design) tool that allows programmers to specify their distributed program logic (we sometimes call *mission logic* in this paper). This design tool allows MLS workflow designers to

- divide a design area into multiple domains,
- specify information flow, dependency, and the condition of the dependency among tasks that are in the same or different domains,
- specify dominance relationships among domains (e.g., Top Secret > Secret > Unclassified), and
- specify exception conditions and recovery strategies for exceptions.

On the other hand, the runtime engine needs to provide MLS services in a distributed and heterogeneous computing environment. The MLS runtime system must enforce the following information flow requirements:

- High users may have access to low data and low resources,
- High processes may have access to low data, and
- High data must not leak to low systems or users.

An MLS WFMS should obey this MLS policy. Atluri *et. al.* have investigated MLS workflow in general [1]. The development of high-assurance software, necessary to provide separation between unclassified and TS/SCI information, such as MLS workflow systems, has proven to be both technically challenging and expensive. Today's fast paced advances in technology and the need to use COTS products make the traditional MLS approach untenable. Therefore, we have chosen the approach for building MLS workflow by integrating multiple single-level workflows with an MLS distributed architecture. This is in line with modern distributed computing paradigms that support autonomy and heterogeneity.

To implement an MLS WFMS using the architectural method, the following technical approach has been established:

- Implement the necessary design tool for supporting MLS workflow. Even though this tool allows workflow designers to specify information and control flow among tasks in different domains, the operational environment of the tool will be system-high (i.e., the workflow design tool neither accesses sensitive data in multiple domains nor passes it around). Hence, we can implement this tool without too much concern for multilevel security issues (e.g., information leakage across classification domain boundary). This tool will be run on a single-level system.
- Choose a strategy for dividing an MLS workflow that was designed using the design tool into multiple single-level workflows.

- Choose an MLS distributed architecture where multiple single-level workflows can be executed.
- Choose a single-level WFMS to execute single-level workflow in each classification domain.
- Extend the workflow interoperability model to accommodate cooperation among workflows at different classification domains.
- Extend the single-level workflow enactment service (i.e., runtime engine) to accommodate communication among tasks in different classification domains.

In the following section, we describe the internal structure of the MLS WFMS that we are building using the above strategy.

3. System Organization

There are many ways to satisfy the requirements that were described in section 1. We believe that an MLS WFMS is a good way to meet those requirements. In general, a WFMS consists of two main components: a design tool and runtime tools. Our requirements contain an unusual requirement, which is MLS. However, the rest of requirements are generic enough for use by corporate environments. We believe the MLS requirement and the way we solve this MLS problem actually helps us to look into workflow interoperability from a fresh perspective [2].

We have developed generic platform independent distributed programming tools based on an object-oriented paradigm; hence, Java was chosen as our development language. We also want our design tool to be not only independent of the runtime engine, but also independent of the underling MLS infrastructure. Based on these requirements, we have developed the system organization as shown in figure 1.

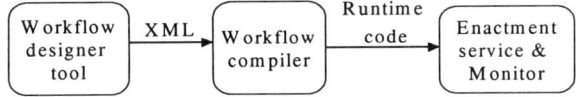

Figure 1: Internal structure of MLS METEOR

A workflow designer specifies mission logic through the workflow design tool (i.e., various workflow editors). The workflow design tool saves the design in XML (eXtensible Markup Language) [5]. When a workflow design is completed, the workflow compiler reads the XML representation of the design and performs the necessary design analysis and validation. Finally it generates runtime code for enactment services. Even though there are many workflow runtime engines, there are very few distributed runtime engines. We believe that OrbWork, an implementation of METEOR WFMS from University of Georgia and a distributed workflow runtime engine, is a good starting point. To satisfy MLS and other requirements, OrbWork has been extended. In the following subsections, we will explain each component in detail.

3.1. Workflow Design Tool

The workflow design tool is a generic distributed programming tool that can express programming logic through GUI-based editors. We have developed the workflow design tool based on the MLS distributed computing model.

3.1.1. MLS distributed computing model

MLS distributed programming adds another dimension of complexity to single-level distributed programming, which itself is not a trivial task. Therefore, we need a new programming model for MLS distributed computing that

- eases the burden of MLS distributed programming, especially in the context of large system integration,
- promotes the re-use of existing components,
- facilitates the specification of security requirements (e.g., roles),
- enables secure cooperation among autonomous systems at different classification levels, and
- provides a global picture of the whole mission and a proper view of a mission to users at different levels of abstraction,

In the MLS METEOR model, a *task* represents an abstraction of an activity. A task can be regarded as a unit of work that is performed by a variety of processing entities, depending on the nature of the task. A task can be performed by (*realized by*) a human, a computerized activity that executes a computer program, a database transaction, or possibly a network of interconnected tasks. Hence, a task provides one level of abstraction (view) and its realization provides a lower level of abstraction (view). Since the realization of a task may contain many tasks at different levels of abstraction, a task is a recursive reference in the METEOR model. In other words, one task from a particular user's point of view may be a network of many tasks from another user's perspective.

There are two types of tasks in the model:
- *Foreign task:* A task whose realization (i.e., strategy for implementation) is unknown to the workflow designer. It represents a task that is a part of cooperating independent system. It is required for a designer to declare a foreign task explicitly to provide a hint to the runtime code generator. A foreign task should have a minimal information set

- (e.g., where to send the request, how to receive output).
- *Native task:* A task for which the realization is known or the realization will be provided before runtime code generation (i.e., all other tasks except the foreign tasks).

For example, foreign tasks can be used to define communication and synchronization with a task in other classification domains. If an MLS workflow is created at the highest classification domain, then the complete MLS workflow with realizations of all its tasks can be specified. However, if the workflow designer creates an MLS workflow that requires input from (or output to) higher classification domains, then he may know only the interfaces to the tasks at the higher levels but not the detailed workflow process at higher levels.

A native task can be either a simple task or a network task. A simple task is a task that cannot be broken down further from a workflow designer's point of view. A *network task* represents the core of the workflow activity specification. Since a network task is one of the realizations of a task, it is always associated with a task called its *parent task*. A single network of tasks defines a relationship among workflow tasks, transferred data, exception handling, and other relevant information. It is a collection of either foreign or native tasks and transitions from one task to another. Figure 2 shows a simplified version of two levels of abstractions (views) where Task2 is the parent task of the projected workflow W_l, which contains tasks 4, 5, 6, and 7, and transition t_j represents a transition from Task1 to Task2. In Figure 2, Task1, Task2, and Task3 may belong to different classification domains. Hence, the MLS METEOR model can be thought of as follows: along the *xy*-surface, there are tasks in different domains and along the *z*-axis, there are different levels of abstraction.

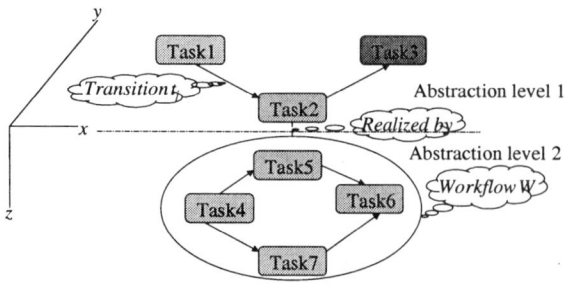

Figure 2: MLS METEOR Model

A task may play the role of a source task or a destination task (e.g., Task1 is the source task and Task2 is the destination task of the transition t_j in Figure 2) for a number of transitions. All of the transitions for which a task is the destination task are called the *input transitions* for that task (e.g., transition t_j is an input transition for Task2). Likewise, all the transitions for which a task is the source task are called its *output transitions* (e.g., transition t_j is an output transition of Task1). A transition may have an associated Boolean condition called its *guard*. A transition may be activated only if its guard is true. When there is a transition from task T_i to task T_j where T_i and T_j are in different classification domains, we call this an MLS *transition* from T_i to T_j.

An *external transition* is a special type of a transition in which the two participating tasks (source and destination) are not in the same workflow (i.e., transition to and from a foreign task). An external transition may lead to a start task of another workflow. Similarly, an implied transition leads from the final task and is used to notify the external entity that the network has terminated. Note that an MLS transition is turned into an external transition when an MLS design is divided into multiple single-level workflows for runtime.

External transitions are also used to specify synchronization points with some external events. Typically, external transitions may be used to specify communication and synchronization between two independent workflows. Here, an external transition leading into a task in the workflow is assumed to have an implied source task (outside the workflow). Similarly, an external transition leading out of a task in the workflow is considered to have an implied destination task (outside the workflow). External transition is a cornerstone of our strategy to support MLS workflow.

The classes (i.e., types of objects) that are associated with an input transition to a task are called the task's *input classes*, and those appearing on an output transition are called *output classes* of that task. If an output class is also not an input class then the class is *created* by the task. Specifically, an object instance of the specified class is created by the workflow runtime. An input class that is not an output class is *dropped (consumed)*. When input classes are unused by the task, they are transferred to the task's successor(s).

A group of input transitions is called an *AND-join* if all of the participating transitions must be activated for the task to be *enabled* for execution. An AND-join is called *enabled* if all of its transitions have been activated. All the input transitions of a task may be partitioned into a number of AND-joins. A group of input transitions is called an *OR-join* if the activation of one of the participating transitions enables the task.

A group of transitions is said to have a *common source* if they have the same source task and all lead either from:
- Its success state or
- Its fail state.

A group of common source transitions may form one of the following:
- *AND-split*: Each of the transitions in the group has the condition set to `true`. This means that all of the transitions in the group are activated once the task is completed.
- *OR-split* (selection): An ordered list of transitions where all but the last transition may have arbitrary conditions (i.e., the last transition on the list has the condition set to `true`). The first transition whose condition is satisfied will be activated.
- *Loop*: A special case of an OR-split, where the list is composed of exactly two transitions: continue and break. Continue implies branch taken and break implies branch not taken (i.e., fall through).

All tasks that we define in this paper are single-level tasks. What we mean by single-level is that the task receives input from one classification domain and produces output at the same classification domain. There are four special tasks: *begin, success, failure,* and *synchronization*. The synchronization tasks represent external transitions to and from other workflows. In general, workflow designers do not manipulate synchronization nodes directly. They are automatically generated by the system based on the specification of foreign tasks and input and output transitions to and from the foreign tasks.

An MLS *workflow* is a network of interconnected single-level (foreign or native) tasks from more than one classification domain. Note that we call a task single-level from one particular level of abstraction (view). Since a single-level task may be realized by an MLS workflow at a lower level of abstraction, it may have side-effects on different classification domains at lower abstraction levels. Hence, our distinction between single-level and multilevel is purely from the perspective of a specific abstraction level.

Let $CL(T_i)$ represent the classification domain of task T_i. The relationships between the classification domains form a lattice. An MLS workflow that is the realization of task T_i where $CL(T_i) = S_a$ must obey the following constraints:
- The *begin, success*, and *fail* nodes of the MLS workflow must be $CL(begin) = CL(success) = CL(failure) = S_a$.
- It may have tasks in other classification domains; however, if the $CL(T_j) = S_b$ where S_a does not dominate S_b, then T_j must be a foreign task. In other words, only tasks in S_c where $S_a \geq S_c$ may have realizations.

3.1.2. Design Editors

The workflow design tool should provide an easy way to capture the control and data flow among components. It should also provide an easy way to import existing designs or components to the current design environment. We provide various platform independent GUI-based editors to support the MLS distributed computing model. There are two starting points into a specific design process (see figure 3). They are the task and network editors, both of which will create an initial top level component (task). The arc and operator editors are mainly used in conjunction with the network and task editors to specify data and control flow. There are three additional editors that aid MLS workflow design: data, domain, and role editors. These three editors can be used independent of the specific workflow. For example, domain structure, especially in MLS, may be predefined based on physical separation. Also role hierarchy [6] may be predefined by organizations. This semi-independence enables a workflow designer either
- to use predefined data, and domain and role structures from a previous design or
- to define necessary data, domain and role structures during a workflow design.

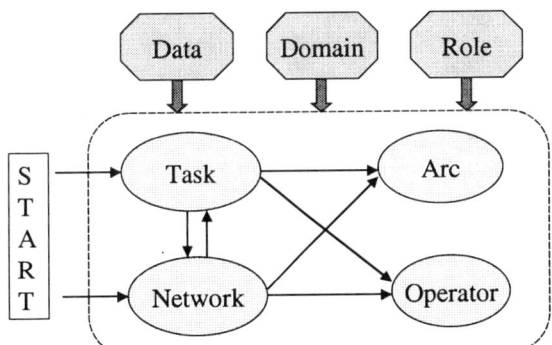

Figure 3: A typical design process and relationship among editors

The description of each editor follows.

Network Editor

A network editor, alternatively called a map editor, is a graphical programming tool that allows users to lay out the control flow of the intended mission logic. Hence, at the highest abstraction level, it provides a global picture of a mission. In this editor, the designer can
- divide the drawing area into many classification domains,
- drop tasks in the different domains, and

- draw arcs that represent control flow between tasks.

A designer can traverse the different abstraction levels to observe or specify different workflow logic with this editor. It also provides links to all other editors to refine a design. For example, if a designer wishes to specify operators (e.g., AND-split, loop) for a specific task, then he can do so by accessing the operator editor.

An ability to prescribe recovery routes and alternative tasks in case of failure is an important feature for an MLS WFMS. Our designer provides this capability through various editors. First, the network editor supports two types of arcs that represent transitions: one is success arc and the other is fail arc. Second, METEOR also supports system and user-defined exceptions that can be specified through the task editor. Using exceptions and fail arc, a workflow designer can specify a recovery strategy for predictable failures. Figure 4 shows a snapshot of the network editor.

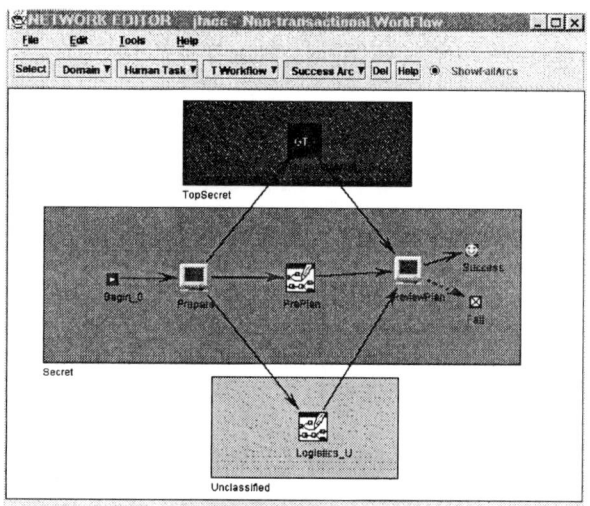

Figure 4: A snapshot of the network editor

Task Editor

The task editor provides the designer with a tool for describing the interface, operating environment, and implementation of the task. Since tasks can be connected together in the implementation of another task (i.e., network task), the task editor also provides information about connections to other tasks and their corresponding editors. In other words, the task editor provides a task-centric view of the workflow.

To describe the task interface, the designer provides a unique name for identifying the task, along with a textual description. The task's type specifies how the task is implemented. The two primary task types are network and simple, where simple tasks include: human, transactional and non-transactional. To complete the interface to a task the designer must specify the input data objects necessary to invoke the task along with the task's output data objects. The designer can specify multiple invocations, but during runtime all the data objects for one of the invocations must be available for a task to start. If the designer wishes to specify failure states for a task then special data objects, called exceptions, are used.

The designer must also describe the environment within which the task has been designed to operate. Of critical importance to an MLS design is what classification domain the task will be operating in. The designer can use compartments (e.g. data restrictions) to further restrict access to the task and its data. In addition the designer can specify what organization owns the task and what roles (which will map to a list of users at runtime) are allowed to perform the task. The designer can also specify the host where a task should be located and specify any system and operational constraints (e.g., allocated time to completion) for the task. During workflow design it is important that the designer considers constraints which have been specified in parent tasks.

The designer must also specify the task implementation (realization). The task's realization is highly dependant upon the type of the task. For a network task, the designer can use the network editor to describe the underlying workflow. For a simple human task, the workflow design tools will generate a generic html page based upon the inputs and outputs of the task. The designer can then specify an html editor and viewer that he can use to customize the HTML page for the desired result. When implementing a simple transactional task, the designer will be able to enter the database query commands that are necessary to carry out the commands. For a simple non-transactional task, the designer can enter the code necessary for invoking the task (e.g., executable code, CORBA invocation) or can enter a description of what needs to be done, and the runtime designer can actually implement the functionality. Both transactional and non-transactional tasks can be connected to existing legacy applications.

There are two other special tasks, which the task editor can edit. They are the abstract and the foreign tasks. A designer uses an abstract task to describe the interface and security of a task that some other designer will complete before runtime code generation. But a foreign task is used to describe the interface to a task that will be implemented by another designer and will be available only at runtime.

To achieve a task-centric view of the workflow, the task editor provides the necessary connectivity to look at the entire design. If the task is used within a workflow, the task editor provides the designer with a view of all the task's connections (arcs) whether input, output, or failure arcs. For each connection, the editor provides the designer with quick access to the associated arc, operator, and task editors. And the task editor provides the ability to view down to the implementation details.

Arc Editor

An arc in the network editor represents a transition from a source task to a destination task. In our implementation, arcs specify the data transferring from the source task to the destination task (i.e., input and output classes). The arc editor provides an easy way to map outputs from one task to inputs of another task in a given workflow. For example, one task has three outputs, type1, type1, and type2. Another task has three inputs type1, type1, and type2. Since there is an ambiguity of matching two type1 outputs to two type1 inputs, an arc editor provides a handy way for the designer to specify which output of a task corresponds to the input of another task.

Operator Editor

The new model uses operators to specify the input and output transitions for a task. Hence, a designer needs a capability to edit the structure of these operators. Due to the complexity of workflow design for most applications, it does not seem practical to attach complex operator structures to each task (i.e., three operator structures per task; input, success output, and failure output) in the network editor. So we provide a separate editor to organize the input transition operator and two output transition operators. The input operators are organized using a structure of AND-joins and OR-joins to combine transitions from other tasks. The two output transitions (one for success and one for fail) are organized using a structure of AND-splits, OR-splits, and a LOOP to distribute transitions to other tasks.

Domain Editor

The domain editor allows a designer to specify attributes of each domain (e.g., name, description). As mentioned in section 3.1.1, the dominance relationship among classification domains form a lattice. The domain editor allows the designer to specify the dominance relationship among classification domains. It also lets users change the GUI properties of classification domains (e.g., color). This editor provides a convenient place to specify receive and release policies between pairs of domains. This policy information can be used as a view into a complete list of policies that are described in a more comprehensive policy definition and enforcement tool.

Data Editor

Data for the workflow design tool is specified as an object interface. The data editor provides a graphical interface for a designer to specify new data and access already defined data. All data objects must extend an existing workflow data object, since the root workflow data object implements functionality required by the runtime of data object management. This is similar to the Java concept where the "Object" class is the root of the entire Java class hierarchy. The data editor allows the designer to specify the package, class name, what class the current class extends (single inheritance only), fields, and methods.

Workflow data is used for task invocations, outputs, and exceptions. In the case of exceptions, the data must extend an existing user exception or the root "UserException". Data is also used for the guards (conditional statements in operators). In a conditional statement, the designer will have access to all the fields and methods defined in the interface of the data object. The relationship among workflow data is shown in figure 5.

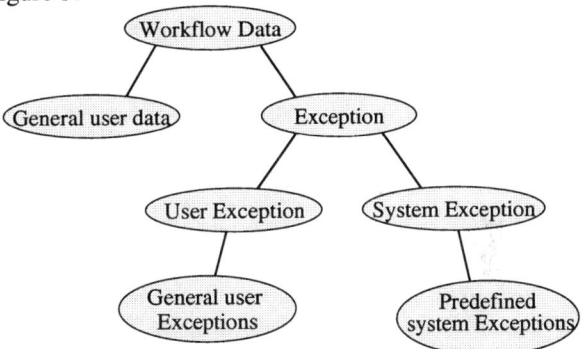

Figure 5: Data inheritance tree

Role editor

The role editor is similar to the classification domain editor in the sense that it allows a designer to define roles and the relationships among them (i.e., role hierarchies). In defining a role the designer can specify the name of the role, its description, and the privileges associated with the role. In general, role hierarchies reflect an organization's line of authority and responsibility. For example, if role A is higher than role B, then role A may have all the permissions that role B has and more. A designer can specify which role is more privileged than another in a given organization through this editor. The role editor will generate XML files on a per organization basis. These XML files can be used by an external application to assign users to roles and enforce permissions in the runtime system.

3.1.3. Coordination among Editors

Editors share common workflow related information and several of them might be displayed at the same time. If an object is modified after an editor displays information, then the editor needs to know about the changes so that it can refresh its display. We use a very simple scheme to ensure consistent display. There is an editor registry that maintains a list of active editors. When a user opens an editor, it registers itself to the registry. When a user closes an editor, it drops itself from the registry. When an editor modifies an internal workflow object, it notifies other active editors. It is each editor's responsibility either to update display if the editor uses the modified object or ignores the notification if the editor does not use the object.

The workflow design tool is not only a generic GUI-based, distributed programming tool, but also a good documentation tool that can capture the architecture of a complex distributed system design. Since the tool has to handle various inputs and outputs (e.g., mouse movement, context sensitive menu display), it becomes a fairly complex system. Since we do not want to make the design tool any more complex than is necessary, we created another module, the workflow compiler, to handle some functions that do not require much user interaction. In the next section we present the modules that bridge the gap between the workflow design tool and enactment services.

3.2. Workflow Compiler

There are two main reasons that we decided to separate the workflow compiler from the workflow design tool. First, even though the workflow design tool performs limited local design validation (e.g., task name conflict), it is logical to move global design analysis and code generation out of the workflow design tool for maintainability and extendibility reasons. Second, the workflow design tool is a generic distributed programming and documentation tool that can be used for many different purposes. Therefore, a different user community may have different analysis and validation requirements (e.g., vulnerability analysis). Also a different user community may prefer different enactment services. Hence we need to create a simplified (i.e., no GUI components) data structure that can be used by other people to write a new analyzer or runtime code generator.

Based on the above requirements, we structured the workflow compiler to perform three important tasks. They are:
- Analysis and validation of the design,
- Splitting an MLS workflow into multiple single-level workflows, and
- Generation of runtime code for enactment services.

The workflow compiler is organized in such a way that new analyzers or runtime code generators can be easily integrated. The internal structure of the workflow compiler is as shown in figure 6.

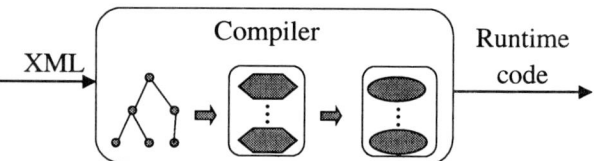

◆ : Global analysis and validation component

● : Runtime code generators

Figure 6: the structure of MLS METEOR compiler

The workflow compiler reads an XML representation of a design and converts it to an internal tree data structure. The analyzer and runtime code generator receive the internal data structure and perform their tasks. Runtime code generation largely depends on
- the specific runtime engine that will be used and
- the MLS infrastructure (see section 3.3.1) where the runtime engine is executed.

The process of splitting an MLS workflow design into multiple single-level workflows that we described in section 2 and also in [2] precedes runtime code generation. Initially, the extended version of OrbWork that is an implementation of METEOR is used as our target runtime engine. However, the structure of the MLS Meteor allows other runtime engines to be easily incorporated.

3.3. Runtime-system

An MLS workflow runtime management system accesses information in many classification domains. Therefore, the MLS requirement needs to be addressed by the runtime system. Our strategy for providing an MLS workflow management capability that can reduce MLS trust requirements is through composing multiple single-level WFMSs on a particular MLS infrastructure.

3.3.1. MLS Infrastructure

Composing an MLS workflow from multiple single-level workflows is the only practical way to construct a high-assurance MLS WFMS today. In this approach, the multilevel security of our MLS workflow does not depend on a single-level WFMS, but rather on the underlying MLS distributed architecture. The MLS distributed architecture will:
- Host multiple single-level workflows to be executed and

- Provide conduits for passing information among tasks in different classification domains.

A generic MLS distributed architecture is shown in Figure 7.

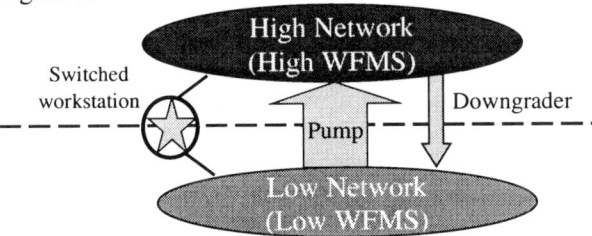

Figure 7: An MLS Distributed Architecture

In this architecture, switched workstations (e.g., "Starlight") enable a user to access resources in multiple classification domains and create information in domains that the user is authorized to access. One-way devices (e.g., a flow controller such as "A Network Pump") together with information release and receive policy servers provide a secure way to pass information from one classification domain to another. An information release policy server resides in a classification domain where the information is released, and an information receive policy server resides in a classification domain where the information is received as shown in Figure 8.

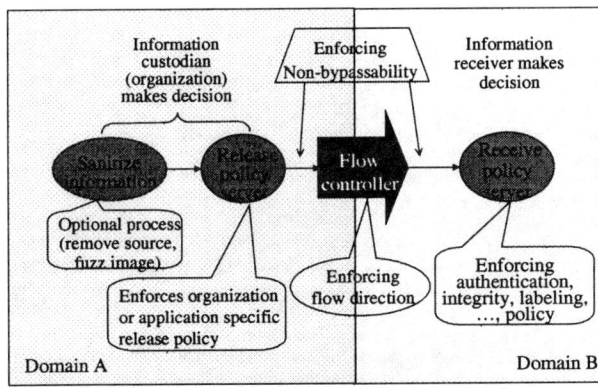

Figure 8: Information Release and Receive Policies in Conjunction with a Flow Controller

3.3.2. Single-level Enactment Services and Monitor

There can be many enactment services for a given workflow design. Currently we are using modified OrbWork [4] for our runtime engine. OrbWork is a single-level distributed workflow engine implemented in Java. It does not have a central scheduler for the whole workflow, rather there is a distributed scheduler per task that the workflow designer defined in the network editor. Each scheduler only knows its predecessors and successors.

Briefly, OrbWork works as follows. OrbWork schedulers are CORBA servers. Hence, they communicate with each other through CORBA's IIOP. OrbWork schedulers are also HTTP servers. When a human operator has to interact with a scheduler (e.g., human task), he can do so through the HTTP protocol. Also when a human workflow manager needs to intervene for some reasons, he can do so through the HTTP protocol.

OrbWork has two other CORBA servers: data servers and workflow monitor servers. Data servers act as a repository for data that needs to be passed among schedulers. The workflow monitor server receives progress reports from schedulers. Simplified communication paths among different components in OrbWork are shown in figure 9.

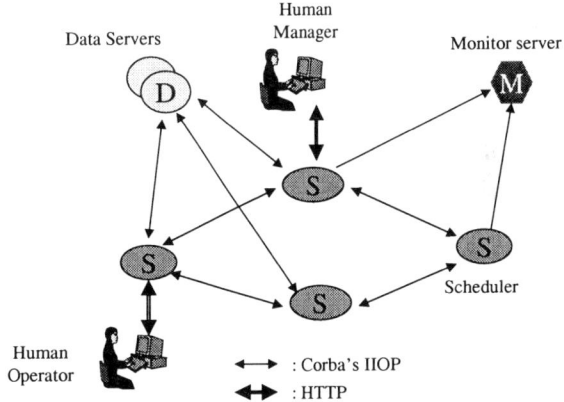

Figure 9: Communication among OrbWork components

3.3.3. MLS Enactment Services and MLS Monitor

As we presented in section 2 and in [2], our strategy for achieving MLS workflow is through the interoperability of single-level workflows that were generated from an MLS workflow design. For interoperability, the workflow runtime engine should be able to pass and receive the necessary information across domain boundaries. We extend OrbWork with the *synchronization node*. We can categorize synchronization nodes into release and receive synchronization nodes following our MLS infrastructure shown in figure 8. The responsibilities of synchronization nodes are as follows:

- To act as proxies for a task in another domain,
- To serve as exit and entry points to pass necessary information from one domain to another domain, and
- To ensure only proper information is passed to another domain (i.e., make sure release and receive policies are enforced).

For example, if there is an MLS transition from task A to task B as in figure 10, the release synchronization node acts as a proxy for task B and the receive synchronization node acts as a proxy for task A. Also release synchronization nodes serve as an exit point of the release domain and the receive synchronization node serves as an entry point for the receive domain. Therefore, release and receive policies can be enforced there.

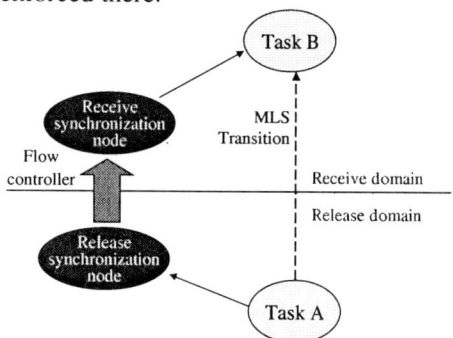

Figure 10: Break down of an MLS transition into multiple transitions

In our MLS workflow system, information exists as objects. Hence, there is the potentially that objects that contain variables and methods have to be passed across domain boundaries. Passing an object across classification domains can cause integrity and security violations. To mitigate risks associated with passing entire objects (i.e., state and definition of objects) across domain boundaries, currently, we only pass the necessary state information so that the objects can be reconstructed on the receiving domains. When a release synchronization node receives an object, it extracts the necessary information from the object and sends it through a flow controller. When a receive synchronization node receives, it instantiates the object in the receiving domain.

An MLS WFMS requires an MLS monitor. Workflow managers in a classification domain may need to know the progress of work in their classification domain and other domains that they are authorized to access. In other words, users of MLS workflow in different classification domains may have different views of the workflow they are running. Hence, an MLS WFMS should provide the capability to monitor activities in all domains the workflow manager is authorized to access. We are providing MLS monitoring capabilities that use similar techniques to those for data transfer from one domain to another. In other words, we place a monitoring proxy that receives monitoring information in a lower domain. This monitoring proxy corresponds to a release synchronization node and transfers the monitored information to a higher domain. In the higher domain, there is another monitoring proxy which corresponds to a receive synchronization node. This monitoring proxy relays the lower-level monitoring message to a higher-level monitor server. As in the case of data transfer, information must satisfy release and receive policy and must go though a boundary controller.

4. Conclusion

In this paper, we presented the system organization of MLS METEOR and the rationale behind the organization. MLS METEOR is an example of an MLS application that can run on the MLS infrastructure that was presented at this conference last year [3]. In this approach, multilevel security enforcement of MLS METEOR does not depend on the single-level WFMS but rather on the underlying MLS infrastructure and a few security critical components (i.e., synchronization nodes that enforce release and receive policy, and boundary controllers). Therefore, MLS METEOR allows a workflow designer to concentrate on the functionality of the system he is building.

Prototypes of all components (i.e., workflow design tool, workflow compiler, and extended OrbWork as an enactment service) have been implemented. We are in the process of integrating those components. Future work includes adding more advanced features and addressing other aspects of workflow (e.g., survivability).

References

1. V. Atluri, W-K. Huang and E. Bertino, "A Semantic Based Execution Model for Multilevel Secure Workflows," Journal of Computer Security, To appear.

2. M. H. Kang, J. N. Froscher, B. J. Eppinger, and I. S. Moskowitz, "A Strategy for an MLS Workflow Management System" To appear in 13th IFIP Conference on Database Security, Seattle, WA, 1999.

3. M. H. Kang, J. Froscher, and B. Eppinger, "Toward an Infrastructure for MLS Distributed Computing," 14th Annual Computer Security Applications Conference, Scottsdale, AZ, 1998.

4. K. Kochut, A. Sheth, and J. Miller, "ORBWork: A CORBA-Based Fully Distributed, Scalable and Dynamic Workflow Enactment Service for METEOR," UGA-CS-TR-98-006, Technical Report, Department of Computer Science, University of Georgia, 1998.

5. Extensible Markup Language (XML) 1.0," World-wide-Web Consortium, http://www.w3.org/TR/1998/REC-xml-19980210.html

6. R. Sandhu, E. Coyne, H. Feinstein and C. Youman, "Role-Based Access Control Models," IEEE Computer, Vol. 29, No. 2, 1996.

Track A

Crypto

Chair

Dan Gambel, Mitretek Systems

An Effective Defense Against First Party Attacks in Public-Key Algorithms

Stephen M. Matyas, Jr. and Allen Roginsky
IBM Corporation
Research Triangle Park, NC

Abstract

This paper describes a method for assuring that user-generated public and private key pairs are cryptographically strong. This assurance is achieved by limiting the number of attempts a user can make while generating the keys. Since it takes many billions of attempts to generate so-called "weak" keys, with any significant probability of success, our method precludes users from cheating.

The described method has a potential positive impact on several evolving cryptographic standards, where the strength of the keys used with public key cryptography are a matter of major concern. It has no negative impact on key generation performance. The method is simple and straightforward, and it can be easily performed with just a few computational steps.

1. Introduction

Two fundamentally different encryption techniques are known to cryptographers. They are the symmetric key algorithms and the public key methods. These techniques do not compete; instead, they complement each other.

Whenever a symmetric key cryptosystem is employed, two parties, usually named Alice and Bob, share a secret key which they use for both encryption and decryption. The best-known symmetric key algorithm is the Digital Encryption Standard (DES), described in [9]. It was approved by the American National Standards Institute (ANSI) 1981 as a standard of choice for the US financial industry. To use this algorithm, Alice and Bob must share a secret key K which of party uses for an encryption and another for the decryption of data. DES is a block cipher that operates on 64-bit-long blocks of data. It is called a symmetric-key algorithm because both parties user the same key. The key K has 56 bits of secret entropy.

Over the years, DES was meticulously studied by cryptanalysts all over the world. This analysis revealed no cryptographic weaknesses. However, with the recent advances in computer technology it became possible to attack DES by "brute force". This means that the entire space of all possible keys could be searched until the correct key was found. The most recent well-publicized brute-force attack against DES was mastered during the annual RSA Data Security Conference in January 1999. The secret key was discovered in 22 hours. This vulnerability is unacceptable for many real-life applications.

Various other symmetric key algorithms exist. We will mention the Triple DES method, where a block of data is first encrypted under one DES key, then decrypted using the second key and, last, encrypted with the third key. This procedure significantly increases the cryptographic strength of the algorithm, at the expense of the diminished performance.

In 2000 the National Institute for Standards and Technology (NIST) will select a new algorithm which will provide a long-term replacement for DES and Triple DES.

All symmetric key algorithms must rely on the existence of a complicated infrastructure that ensures that secret keys are distributed to pairs of users that need to know them. The integrity of these secret keys must also be guaranteed. In a network of n users there will therefore simultaneously exist n(n-1)/2 cryptographic keys. Every time a key changes, a complicated mechanism must be used to ensure that a replacement key is delivered to Alice and Bob. Even though some optimizations exist that allow a network to function with fewer keys, the problem of managing and distributing this large number of keys remains difficult to solve.

In 1976 W. Diffie and M. Hellman published a paper [11] where a solution to the key generation and distribution problem was presented. Much more importantly, this paper lays the groundwork for a creation of a new field: public key cryptography. The authors suggested that each user will be provided with two different keys, one known to the public and one kept private. They demonstrated that without the knowledge of each other's private keys, Alice and Bob could generate a key that could be used for DES or any other symmetric key algorithm. This key could not be discovered by anyone who did not know Alice's and Bob's private keys, even if a potential attacker intercepted the communications between Alice and Bob. Indeed, this communication did not have to be secret at all.

The reason that the Diffie-Hellman protocol worked was that a certain mathematical problem could not be solved without performing an extremely large number of calculations. This number is so large that finding the secret symmetric key that Alice and Bob generate is computationally impossible, if the underlying parameters (public keys) are chosen prudently. The difficult mathematical problem that makes it possible is that of solving a discrete logarithm problem in a particular finite group.

While this protocol also requires the existence of a trusted third party (TTP) that authenticates the users, the keys themselves can be generated independently by Alice and Bob. Furthermore, the mechanism of public key cryptography is ideally suited for other applications, such as digital signatures, and also for data encryption.

It turned out, that other mathematical problems can serve as underlying tools for public key cryptosystems. The RSA algorithm, named after its inventors Rivest, Shamir and Aldeman [1], utilizes the difficulty of factoring large integers into their prime factors. Yet another important example of the use of public key technology is that of an elliptic curve cryptosystem. It was first introduced by N. Koblitz in [2] and V. Miller in [3]. This system is also based on the computational difficulty of solving a discrete logarithm problem in a group but the group is different from that proposed in [11]. It is a group of points on an elliptic curve over a finite field.

To make these public key cryptosystems solid and operational, certain requirements must be imposed on public and private keys that Alice and Bob own. The sizes of the finite groups must be sufficiently large, the prime factors in the RSA algorithm must satisfy many specific constraints (for example, if p is an RSA prime, then both p-1 and p+1 must have large prime divisors – see [7]), the choice of an elliptic curve must be made very carefully, to avoid the so-called anomalous curves and to satisfy the so-called MOV condition [8].

If some of the conditions on public and private keys are not met, this might result in a weakening the security of the generated key or of that of a digital signature. A key that does not satisfy the conditions that a particular algorithm (Diffie-Hellman, RSA or Elliptic Curves) calls for is referred to as a "weak" key. The notion of weak keys is particularly important when the RSA method is employed.

Under normal circumstances, the probability of accidentally choosing a weak key is extremely low and the entire scenario may look to be too improbable to have occurred in real life. However, there is the possibility that a cheating party will deliberately try to generate a weak signing key, and then repudiate its signed messages by claiming that its signing key was "broken" by an attacker. This is called "the first party attack." The first party attack presents a significant problem to designers of public key cryptosystems. For this reason, the ANSI standard X9.31 [7] requires that the prime numbers p and q used in the generation of the public modulus satisfy certain additional properties, which ensure that the generated keys are not too weak for the purposes of the RSA digital signature algorithm.

The ANSI X9F1 committee was concerned that a first-party attacker would not follow the prescribed prime-generation procedure but would instead purposely construct bad primes. Therefore, the committee put a requirement in the X9.31 standard that the primes, p and q, must be generated from seed values (6 in number) and that the seed values must be saved in order to later prove that the prime numbers were generated in compliance with the prescribed procedure. The X9.31 protocol relies on the use of one-way functions to prevent an attacker from working backwards to determine the seed values that lead to the generation of a particular prime pair. Hence it forces an attacker to select seeds values and use a forward construction process. Although this is an improvement (i.e., it provides some defense against the first party attack), the protocol does not guarantee that an attacker cannot find "weak" primes. A cheating party (often referred under these circumstances as the "first party", because it is the party responsible for generating p and q and for signing messages with the generated signature key) can try many seeds until possibly it finds one that leads to the creation of "weak" primes. That is, it does not stop an attacker from performing an exhaustive attack using the "forward construction process." Such an exhaustive attack need not be performed in real time and, therefore, allows for billions of primes to be tested. Later the first party can say that this was the very first seed that it selected, and was just unlucky.

In this paper we show a way to eliminate the opportunities for the first party attacks described above. We believe that instead of introducing many complicated requirements that would ensure that no key selected by the first party attacker is weak, it is better to limit the possibilities of trying many candidate keys. Of course, a selected key could still be "weak," but this could occur only by pure chance. The ability to perpetrate a meaningful attack would have been removed.

Another point worthy of mentioning is that the seeds used in the generation of private keys should be distributed uniformly over the space of all possible seeds. The current standard (X9.31) satisfies this requirement, and it was therefore deemed essential that our solution method also guarantee a uniform distribution of seeds.

The rest of the paper is organized as follows.

In Section 2 we outline the general ideas and methodologies behind our algorithms. In the following three sections we will show how to use the existing mechanisms and the infrastructure of public key technology to create the keys with a guarantee they were not created by a first party attacker. In Section 3, the Diffie-Hellman ideas will be used, in Section 4 we will use the RSA method and in Section 5 – an Elliptic Curve Cryptosystem. Note that any protocol can be used to create keys for any other public key algorithm. Thus, the Diffie-Hellman method can help us generate the keys to be used with the elliptic curves, the elliptic curve protocol can, in turn, be used to generate the RSA keys, and so on.

In Section 6 we briefly talk about possible alternatives to the proposed algorithms. Section 7 addresses the security of the infrastructure needed to operate these protocols.

2. Solution Method

Here we describe a protocol between a user and a Trusted Third Party for generating a secret seed value. In this paper, the TTP will be a Certification Authority (CA) that participates in the generation of the seed. The CA is already used in cryptography and is a critical part of the public key infrastructure (see [5]). Hence involving the CA in the prevention of a first party attack does not introduce a new entity and thus does not significantly increase the overhead. We will assume, as it is usually done, that the CA is an honest partner in this protocol.

We describe three possible protocols that are almost equivalent, but rely on the strength of different public key algorithms, as follows: the discreet logarithm (DL) problem in a multiplicative group of a finite field, the RSA algorithm, and the elliptic curve algorithm. It is noteworthy that the choice of one or these three methods has nothing to do with the further use of the key that the method helps generate. Thus, an RSA algorithm can be used to generate a key later used in an elliptic curve cryptosystem, a DL approach can be used to create an RSA key, and so on. However, one should note that the elliptic curve logarithm problem is harder to solve for the given size of the of the security parameters, than either the problem of finding the RSA key or the discreet logarithm problem in a multiplicative group of a finite field.

The main idea behind our approach is to require that the user generates the public and private key pair from a secret seed value Xseed, where Xseed is computed from a portion of the seed selected by the user, denoted x, and a portion of the seed selected by a CA, denoted z, who cooperate using a prescribed key generation protocol. The CA also computes and returns a special value that the user can store for purposes of an audit, which enables the user to prove that the composite value Xseed was generated in accordance with the prescribed key generation protocol.

The prescribed key generation protocol is such that the user cannot create a seed unilaterally and if it tries many different times to generate an x (e.g., billions of times), hoping that the resulting seed value Xseed will lead to a weak key, the CA will undoubtedly catch the cheating party or at least detect that some party is attempting to cheat.

One significant advantage that each of the protocols presented below offers is that the random seeds that it creates are distributed uniformly over the space of all possible seeds. This means that the attacker will not be able to exploit any bias among the keys generated from these seeds. The requirement for uniformly distributed random seeds affects the design of the protocols somewhat. For example, by simply computing Xseed=x+z in Protocol 1, we would end up with a so-called "triangle" distribution of seeds.

To further increase the security and the independence of these protocols the CA may use a separate (secret, public) key pair for these protocols. This way even if the CA accidentally signs something related with its "main" public key, it will in no way impair the strength of our protocols. Similarly, our protocols have no adverse affect on the CA operations and on the security of the users' private keys.

We will now describe the three protocols in greater detail.

3. Generating Keys Relying on a "Conventional" Discrete Logarithm Problem

This algorithm is based, like the original Diffie-Hellman idea, on the difficulty of finding an integer y, given a large prime p, an integer g between 2 and p-1 and the value of $g^y \pmod{p}$. The input to this algorithm includes the following values: L - the length in bits of a seed to be generated; J - the bit length of the prime number that guarantees the security of this method. (The size of J must be such that it would be considered infeasible for an attacker to solve the corresponding discrete logarithm problem); p_0 - a publicly known prime number of the length at least J bits; g - a publicly known generator used to secure communications between the user and the Certification Authority. It also utilizes a cryptographic hash function H (see [10] and also [4]) and is depended on the CA's public and private key pair used for signing (PKca, SKca).

The output is a seed Xseed that can be used to generate keys for a public key algorithm..

The procedure to generate Xseed is as follows.

The user randomly generates an integer x between 1 and 2^L-1. The user then computes $y = g^x \pmod{p_0}$ and sends y to the CA. The Certification Authority generates uniformly randomly a (non-secret) integer z between 0 and 2^L-1, computes w=H(y* $g^z \pmod{p_0}$) and signs it with its private key SKca. This signed value is called Sigw. The CA next increments a counter to track the number of times this user asked for assistance establishing seeds. This can be done per user or for the entire CA. If the count is larger than some reasonable threshold for a particular user (or for the CA if the counters are not kept per user) then the Certification Authority might suspect that a user is attempting a first party attack and the CA will send a warning to a system administrator.

The CA now sends z and Sigw to the user. The user computes Xseed=x+z (mod 2^L). The values of Xseed are uniformly distributed over the set of integers between 0 and 2^L-1, since z is drawn uniformly randomly from the set of integers between 0 and 2^L-1.

The user the computes w=H($g^{x+z} \pmod{p_0}$) and verifies the signature on w (Sigw) using the public verification key of the Certification Authority, PKca. This ensures the user that an audit can be passed.

The user now saves Sigw and Xseed and proceeds to generate the public keys using Xseed as seed. If more than one seed is needed then a similar procedure can be used to generate each required seed.

If there is an audit, the user will have to prove that the proper procedure was followed. The user does the following:

Compute w1=H($g^{Xseed} \pmod{p_0}$) and compute w2=H($g^{Xseed'} \pmod{p_0}$) where Xseed' = Xseed + 2^L. Since 0<x+z< p_0, (the latter inequality holds since J>L+1), there is no "false" value Xs between 0 and 2^L-1 such that either $g^{Xs} \pmod{p_0}$ or $g^{Xs+2^L} \pmod{p_0}$ equals $g^{x+z} \pmod{p_0}$. Next the user validates w1 and w2 using Sigw and the public verification key of the CA, PKca. If either w1 or w2 is valid, then the user did everything according to the rule.

Note. Only one of the values w1, w2 is correct. The other one is not, so by making it valid for the purposes of the audit, we introduce a chance that a cheating user can pass the audit while using an incorrect seed. However, the probability of this happening is extremely low.

4. Generating Keys Using the RSA Method

The input to this procedure includes L - the length in bits of a seed to be generated; N - a publicly known composite number of the length L+1 bits ($N = p*q$, where p and q are large unknown primes. The secret parameters p and q are generated by the user and are certified by a trusted third party); e - an RSA public exponent and also H, PKca and SKca that are defined as in the previous section.

The output is a seed Xseed that can be used to generate keys for public key cryptography.

The procedure to generate Xseed is as follows.

First, the user randomly generates an integer x between 1 and N-1, such that it is mutually prime with N. Next the user computes $y = x^e$ (mod N) and sends it to the CA. The CA randomly generates a (non-secret) integer z between 1 and N-1, computes w=H(y* z^e (mod N)) and signs it with SKca. This signed value is Sigw. Note that if z takes all integer values between 1 and N-1, then, since x is mutually prime with N, $x*z$ (mod N) also takes all possible values between 1 and N-1. Each of these values will occur exactly once while z is changing between 1 and N-1, so the likelihood for $x*z$ (mod N) to take any given value is the same and is equal to 1/(N-1), hence resulting in a uniform distribution. Next the Certification Authority increases by 1 the count for the number of times the user asked for assistance establishing the seeds. The CA then sends z and Sigw to the user.

The user now computes Xseed= $x*z$ (mod N). If $Xseed \geq 2^L$ then the user must retry using a new x. Note also that since the probability of returning to Step 1 here is less than 0.5, one can expect to succeed in moving to the next step only after a small number of attempts. The user then computes w=H($(x*z)^e$ (mod N)) and verifies the signature on w (Sigw) using the public verification key of the CA, PKca. The user now saves Sigw and Xseed and proceeds to generate the public keys using Xseed as seed.

If there is an audit, the user will have to prove that the proper procedure was followed. The user will compute w=H($(Xseed)^e$ (mod N)) and then validate it using Sigw and the public verification key of the CA, PKca. If the signature is valid, the audit is passed successfully.

5. Generating Keys Using Elliptic Curves

The security of data exchange between the user and the CA is based here on the strength of the discrete logarithm problem for a group of points on an elliptic curve over a finite field. The reader can find a lot of information on this problem and on the use of the elliptic curve in cryptography in general in [6].

The following parameters must be provided as an input to this procedure: L - the length in bits of a seed to be generated; J - the bit length of the prime number n that guarantees the security of this method. (The size of J must be such that it would be considered infeasible for an attacker to solve the corresponding elliptic curve discrete logarithm problem. In any case, J>L+1; this assures that $x + z < n$); E - an elliptic curve over a finite field F_q.

This is a set of points that satisfy a certain algebraic relationship (see [6].) The number of points on this curve is nh, where n is a large prime (has at least J bits) and h is a small cofactor. G - a base point. It is a point of order n on E. The other input parameters H, PKca and SKca are defined like in previous two sections.

The output is a seed Xseed that can be used to generate keys for public key cryptography.

The procedure to generate Xseed is as follows.

The user randomly generates an integer x between 1 and 2^L-1. The user then computes a point Y=xG on the elliptic curve E and sends it to the Certification Authority. The CA randomly generates a (non-secret) integer z between 0 and 2^L-1. The CA then computes a point P=Y+zG on E. The coordinates of P are denoted x_P and y_P. The CA computes w=H(x_P) and signs it with SKca. As in the previous two algorithms, this signed value is called Sigw. The Certification Authority increases by 1 the count for the number of times the user asked for assistance establishing the seeds. The CA then sends z and Sigw to the user.

The user now computes $w = H(x_P)$, where x_P is the x-coordinate of the point $(x+z)G$ on E. The user then verifies the signature on w (Sigw) using the public verification key of the CA, PKca. The user now saves

Sigw and Xseed and proceeds to generate the public keys using Xseed as seed. This ensures that the user can pass an audit.

If an audit is performed, the user will compute w1 and w2, the hash values of the x-coordinates of the points (Xseed)G and (Xseed+2^L)G, correspondingly, on E, and then proceed as shown in Section 3.

6. Alternative Procedures

Each of the three protocols described above could be used in a slightly different manner. The certificate that the CA issues would contain either the value w or both w and Sigw. The advantage of this alternative algorithm is that the user does not have to store Sigw. A possible disadvantage is that it might require a slight change to the existing standard protocol between the user and the Certification Authority.

7. CA Security

One should notice that the proposed scheme requires the CA to sign many messages, in addition to its usual task of signing the certificates. This raises a question of whether it will be possible to learn more about the CA's private key or to use it as an oracle by making it sign various messages whose context the CA can not fully control.

We do not see it as a problem. The CA's private key is supposed to be absolutely secure so even if it signs many sets of data, no useful information should be derived from these signatures. In addition, it is possible to require the CA to have another (private, public) key pair to be used only to perform the operations outlined in this TR.

8. Conclusion

We presented an algorithm that assures that a seed used for the user-generated public and private key pair is strong. This assurance comes from the fact that a first party attack based on the multiple tries to find a weak key pair has been made impossible. The resulting seeds are distributed uniformly over the space of all possible keys. The principle innovation is to the Certification Authority limits the number of attempts the user can make in generating a public and private key pair. The security of the proposed method relies on the difficulty of solving one of the following problems: (1) the discrete logarithm problem in a multiplicative group of a finite field, (2) the integer factorization problem, or (3) the discrete logarithm problem in a group of points in an elliptic curve over a finite field. Regardless of what method was chosen to assure the security of our method, the generated keys can be used in any algorithm suitable for public key cryptography.

References

[1] Rivest, R.L., Shamir, A., and Adleman, L.M., "Cryptographic Communications System and Method," US Patent #4,405,829, 20 Sep., 1983.

[2] Koblitz, N., "Elliptic Curve Cryptosystems," Mathematics of Computation, 48 (1987), pp. 203-209.

[3] Miller, V., "Uses of Elliptic Curves in Cryptography," Advances in Cryptology - CRYPTO 85, Lecture Notes in Computer Science, 218 (1986), pp. 417-426, Springer-Verlag.

[4] Schneier, B., "Applied Cryptography," 2nd eddition, John Wiley & Sons Inc, 1996.

[5] Menezes, A.J., van Oorschot, P.C., and Vanstone, S.A., "Handbook of Applied Cryptography," CRC Press, 1997.

[6] Menezes, A.J., "Elliptic Curve Public Key Cryptosystems," Kluwer Academic Publishers, Fourth Printing, 1997.

[7] ANSI Standard X9.31-1998, Digital Signatures Using Reversible Public Key Cryptography For The Financial Services Industry (rDSA).

[8] ANSI Standard X9.62-1998, The Elliptic Curve Digital Signature Algorithm.

[9] National Bureau of Standards, NBS FIPS PUB 46, "Data Encryption Standard," National Bureau of Standards, U.S. Department of Commerce, Jan. 1977.

[10] ANSI Standard X9.30-1993, Part 2: "Public Key Cryptography Using Irreversible Algorithms for the Financial Services Industry: The Secure Hash Algorithm 1 (SHA-1)" (Revised). 1993.

[11] Diffie, W. and Hellman, M.E., "New Directions in Cryptography," IEEE Transactions on Information Theory, v. IT-22, n. 6, Nov 1976, pp. 644-654.

Towards a Practical, Secure, and Very Large Scale Online Election

Jared Karro and Jie Wang
Division of Computer Science
The University of North Carolina at Greensboro
Greensboro, NC 27402, USA
Email: {jqkarro, wang}@uncg.edu

Abstract

We propose in this paper a practical and secure electronic voting protocol for large-scale online elections. Our protocol satisfies a large set of important criteria that has never been put together in a single protocol before. Among all electronic voting schemes in the literature, Sensus, a security-conscious electronic voting protocol proposed by Cranor and Cytron [CC97], satisfies the most of what we desire. Sensus has been implemented and used in mock elections. However, Sensus suffers from several major drawbacks. For instance, we show that even if all voters follow the Sensus protocol honestly, some voters' votes may still be replaced with different votes without being detected. Our protocol overcomes these drawbacks.

1. Introduction

Democratic societies are founded on the principle of elections. However, it is not unusual that many eligible voters in a democratic society do not participate in elections. One of the common reasons for not participating is that voters find it inconvenient to go to the polls. In conventional elections, voters must go to a designated location near their residence. However, for various reasons voters are not always able to make it to these locations. They may be out of town on work or on vacation. Even if they are in town, their daily schedule may not permit them to get to the ballots.

With the rapid growth of the Internet, specifically the World Wide Web, voting online provides a reasonable alternative and in the future may replace conventional elections. Voting online would allow voters to participate in an election in any location that provides Internet access. Voters could cast their ballots while at work, at school, or in the comfort of their own home. Many public libraries have computers with Internet access that could also be used in elections. In some places, bookstores and coffee bars are also starting to provide Internet access. For those voters still without Internet access, voting districts would still have designated locations, only computers, instead of voting booths, would be used. There would be no need to limit voters to a district.

The idea of electronic election over computer networks has been studied intensively for over fifteen years. A variety of cryptographic voting protocols have been proposed to minimize election fraud and maximize voter privacy (for example, see [Be87, BT94, Ch88b, Co86, CF85, C+96, CGS, CC97, F+93, IV91, MV98, NS91, NS, N+91, Sal96, Sch96, SK94]). Most of the early-proposed protocols only deal with a few certain issues of elections, mostly for theoretical interests. As pointed out in [F+93] and [CC97], such protocols are impractical to implement for a large-scale geographically distributed voting district. For a survey of several such protocols we refer the reader to Section 3.2 in Cranor and Cytron's paper [CC97]. So far there has not been a single government election done over the Internet.

Fujioka, Okamoto, and Ohta [F+93] studied how to make online elections practical and proposed a voting protocol using cryptographic techniques of blind signatures and anonymous communication channels. Their protocol also uses central facilities to administrate elections and count votes. They justified that using central facilities is necessary for a voting scheme to be practical. Built on this work, Cranor and Cytron [CC97] recently designed and implemented a security-conscious polling protocol, called Sensus. However, Fujioka et al.'s protocol and the Sensus protocol suffer from several major drawbacks (we will describe these drawbacks in Section 3). Some of these drawbacks are due to the use of blind signatures in large scales and the unpractical assumption of using anonymous communication channels (note that CPU identification numbers have been embedded into the new Intel's Pentium III chips that can be broadcast over the Internet). These drawbacks hinder Sensus from being used in large-scale elections.

To design a voting protocol that is secure and usable in large-scale elections, it is necessary and important to identify a set of criteria to help achieve our goals. We will describe these criteria in Section 2. The rest of the paper is organized as follows. In Section 3, we will discuss several major drawbacks of the Fujioka-Okamaoto-Ohta voting protocol and the Sensus protocol. In Section 4, we will present a new design of an electronic voting protocol to overcome these drawbacks. Our protocol also uses central facilities, but it does not use blind signatures or anonymous communication channels. Moreover, our protocol can be used in elections where we wish to know who has voted and who has not. This property is desirable in Australian elections [MV98]. In Section 5, we discuss security measures and implementation issues of our protocol. In Section 6, we provide proofs that our protocol satisfies all the criteria defined in Section 2 and overcomes the drawbacks of the Sensus protocol. In Section 7, we outline a number of additional properties of our protocol.

2. System requirements

A good electronic voting system should not sacrifice voter privacy or introduce opportunities for fraud. For an electronic voting system to be useful and acceptable by voters, it must be at least as secure as conventional voting systems. We use the following set of nine criteria to ensure that an electronic voting system is secure and practical for large-scale elections.

- **Democracy.** Only eligible voters are permitted to vote, and they can do so only once.
- **Accuracy.** A voter's vote cannot be altered, duplicated, or removed without being detected. Invalid votes are not tabulated in the final tally.
- **Privacy.** Votes remain anonymous.
- **Verifiability.** Voters can be sure that their votes are tabulated correctly, but voters are not required to verify their votes in order to ensure election integrity.
- **Simplicity.** Voters can finish voting quickly, with minimal equipment or special skills.
- **Mobility.** Voters are not restricted to physical location from which they can cast their votes
- **Efficiency.** The election can be held in a timely manner (*i.e. all computations during the election are done in a reasonable amount of time and voters are not required to wait on other voters to complete the process*).
- **Scalability.** The size of the election will not drastically affect performance.
- **Responsibility.** Eligible voters who have not voted can be identified. (This is an optional requirement.)

Among these criteria, democracy, accuracy, privacy, verifiability, simplicity, and mobility are directly relevant to the voters, which are adapted from [CC97]. The criteria of efficiency, scalability, and responsibility are added to our system.

For the privacy criterion, we may further require that no voter can prove that he or she voted in a particular way to prevent vote buying and extortion. But as pointed out in [CC97], unless voters are required to cast their votes from inside a solitary voting booth, voters will be able to prove how they voted by allowing buyers to observe them while they are casting their votes. This requirement would comprise mobility, one of the major reasons to hold an online election.

The current US government elections do not satisfy the verifiability criterion. If an election booth has malfunctions, for example, then some voters' ballots may not be counted correctly and the voters are not able to detect it. In the past, elections have also been held in which ineligible voters, even the deceased, have been allowed to cast their ballot.

Conventional election systems also do not handle mobility easily. For those voters who will not be in their home districts during the election and wish to vote, they must file absentee ballots. But due to time constraints, this may not always be possible, as their absence may not be known until the last minute.

The criteria of simplicity, efficiency, and scalability imply that in such a voting system, voters cannot be required, or expected to communicate with other voters; and voters cannot be required to do all the computations of the election. This means that some central facilities must be employed by the system.

The responsibility criterion is not required in US elections, but it is required in Australian elections. By Australian laws, eligible voters are required to participate in government elections; they are subject to punishment if they do not participate without acceptable reasons [MV98].

3. Voting with blind signatures and anonymous communication channels

Many electronic voting protocols have been proposed during the past fifteen years as we mentioned in Section 1, but none of them seem to fit our set of requirements as nearly as Sensus. Many of these protocols, while of theoretical interest, are not practical to implement for a large number of geographically distributed voters [CC97]. Sensus, on the other hand, has actually been implemented and used in mock elections. Sensus is based on the voting protocol proposed in [F+93], which uses blind signatures and anonymous communication channels to administrate elections. In this section we will first outline these two protocols. We will then show that these two protocols suffer from several major drawbacks.

We begin with Fujioka et al.'s protocol [F+93], which consists of voters and three central facilities called *registrar*, *validator*, and *tallier*. Note that in [F+93], the validator is called the administrator and the tallier is called the counter. The registrar compiles a list of eligible voters, which could be performed before the actual election begins. (We note that the registrar facility is not mentioned explicitly in [F+93].) The protocol consists of seven phases outlined below, where the registration phase, not included in [F+93], is added here for completeness as in the Sensus protocol.

Registration phase. The registrar compiles a list of eligible voters prior to an election. Eligible voters generate public/private key pairs for signing ballots, and register to vote by sending the registrar their voter identifications and the public keys, which are placed in a registered voter list. (See [CC97] for a detailed implementation of this phase.) The registrar then sends the list to the validator.

Preparation phase. The voter V prepares a voted ballot b, encrypt it with a random string k he/she selects as in the bit-commitment scheme [Na90]. Assume that the committed ballot is x. The voter then blinds x into a new string e, signs e into a new string s, and sends (I, e, s) to the validator, where I is V's ID.

Authorization phase. Using the registered voter list, the validator verifies that the signature s belongs to a registered voter I who has not yet voted, signs the ballot e into a new string d, and returns d to the voter.

Voting phase. The voter V retrieves the blinding encryption layer, revealing an encrypted ballot y signed by the validator, and sends the pair (x, y) to the tallier via an anonymous communication channel as described in [Ch81, Ch88a, Pf84].

Collecting phase. The tallier checks the signature y, using the validator's public key, to make sure that x is from a legitimate voter, and places (x, y) on a list of valid ballots.

Opening phase. At the end of the election, the validator publishes the number of voters who were given the administrator's signature, and publishes a list of all triples (I, e, s) it has received; and the tallier publishes the list of valid ballots. The voter V then checks that the length of the list is equal to the number of voters, and that his/her vote (x, y) appears on the tallier's list, with index n. The voter then sends (n, k) to the tallier via an anonymous communication channel.

Counting phase. The tallier decrypts the corresponding committed ballot x using k and retrieves the ballot b, counts the votes, and announces the voting results.

The Sensus protocol, for a large part, is the same as Fujioka et al.'s protocol. It assumes that all communication between voter and election authorities occurs over an anonymous channel. What is different in Sensus is that it uses one more central facility called *pollster* and that the tallier does not wait till the end to process votes. The latter is done by modifying the opening and counting phases. In particular, after the collecting phase, the tallier signs the encrypted ballot x and returns it to the voters as a receipt. Upon receiving the receipt, the voter sends the tallier the ballot decryption key k, and the tallier uses the key to decrypt x to obtain b and add the vote to the tally. Sensus still relies on voters to perform verification as in the opening phase of Fujioka et al.'s protocol. The pollster acts as a voter's agent, performing all cryptographic and data transfer functions on a voter's behalf.

Next, we show that using blind signatures as in these two protocols would allow the tallier to cheat the election without been detected. We note that in the preparation phase, if several voters would choose the same random keys k and vote in the same manner, then their encrypted ballots x will be exactly the same, and so they will obtain the same y with the validator's signature. The tallier can then replace a few (not all) of these pairs (x, y) with some other legitimate pairs (x', y'). When each of the affected voters checks for its vote, he/she will see (x, y) in the published list and hence will not detect anything wrong. To make matters worse, the tallier may generate new votes to replace duplicated votes. Since voters would use the same pseudo-random number generator provided by the protocol to generate secret keys k, and since in a large-scale election many of the votes will be the same, it is likely that many of the pairs (x, y) will be the same. This would make the attack successful, which would violate the accuracy criterion. While it is theoretically possible to make all the random keys distinct, in practice this would not be easy to guarantee because keys are generated by individual voters.

Fujioka et al. [F+93] noted that the validator could submit votes for voters who decide to abstain. They then suggested that voters who abstain should submit a blank ballot to avoid this from happening. This is hardly a practical solution because if the voters decide to abstain, they probably would not take the time to submit blank ballots either. Likewise, the voters who abstain cannot be relied upon to make sure that no votes were cast for them. To solve this problem, it may be possible to have some sort of time expiration on the ballots. This however, may generate more problems.

Another drawback with the Sensus protocol and Fujioka et al.'s protocol is that they rely on anonymous communication channels to provide anonymity. But anonymity is hard to guarantee over the Internet. Although there are services that offer the ability to browse the Web anonymously, such as anonymizer.com, the only way to guarantee that all voters use these services is to force them to use certain sites. However, voters cannot know, with any certainty, that these sites do not collaborate with any of the central facilities involved. Cranon and Cytron [CC97] suggest that an anonymous channel could be secured through the use of a chain of World Wide Web facilities. The problem with this solution is that some organization must configure this to occur. It would be difficult to ensure the voters that none of the Web facilities in the chain are secretly collaborating with the authority. The task of anonymity on the Web may have been made even more complicated with the recent introduction of embedding CPU identification numbers into Intel's Pentium III chips. These numbers can be broadcast over the Internet, identifying the voter's Internet connection and the machine from which they are casting their votes. This would violate the privacy criterion.

Finally, in these two protocols, voters are relied upon to verify that their votes were counted. This is not practical, especially for voters who do not have convenient Internet access. These voters would have to revisit a polling place to verify their votes after the voting results are announced. Therefore, Sensus violates the simplicity and the verifiability criteria.

4. The proposed protocol

Our protocol does not use blind signatures or require anonymous communication channels. Instead, our protocol uses a secure form of communication (e.g. HTTPS in Netscape) for all transactions. Our protocol uses six central facilities. They are the *registrar*, the *authenticator*, the *distributor*, the *counter*, the *matcher*, and the *verifier*. The responsibilities of these facilities will be explained below when we detail our protocol. Our protocol consists of only four phases (procedures).

Registration phase.

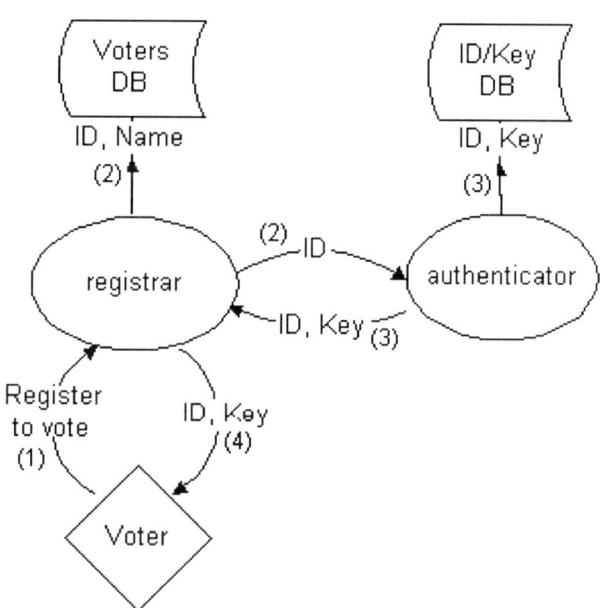

1. In order to vote, a voter must first register with the registrar to identify himself as an eligible voter.
2. Upon registering, the registrar assigns a unique identification number to the voter, places the voter's name and ID in the registered voter list, and sends the ID without the name to the authenticator.
3. The authenticator generates a unique pair of public/private keys for the ID it received, stores them in a list, and sends the pair of the public key s and the ID to the registrar.

4. The registrar then sends the pair back to the voter. (In so doing, the authenticator will not know whom the given key s belongs to without conspiring with the registrar.)

Remark. The key s may be valid for a long time for multiple elections, or could expire after a given time. If the key were to be kept for a long duration, it would probably be best to have the voter encrypt it with a password of his/her choice, so that no one else could use it. The original, unencrypted key would be destroyed and the encrypted key (still denoted by s) would be stored instead. This would also allow a voter's district to store the voter-encrypted keys to prevent the key from being lost or damaged, without worrying about someone getting access to the key. Voters just need to retrieve the key from their district, or floppy disk, before voting.

Pre-voting phase.

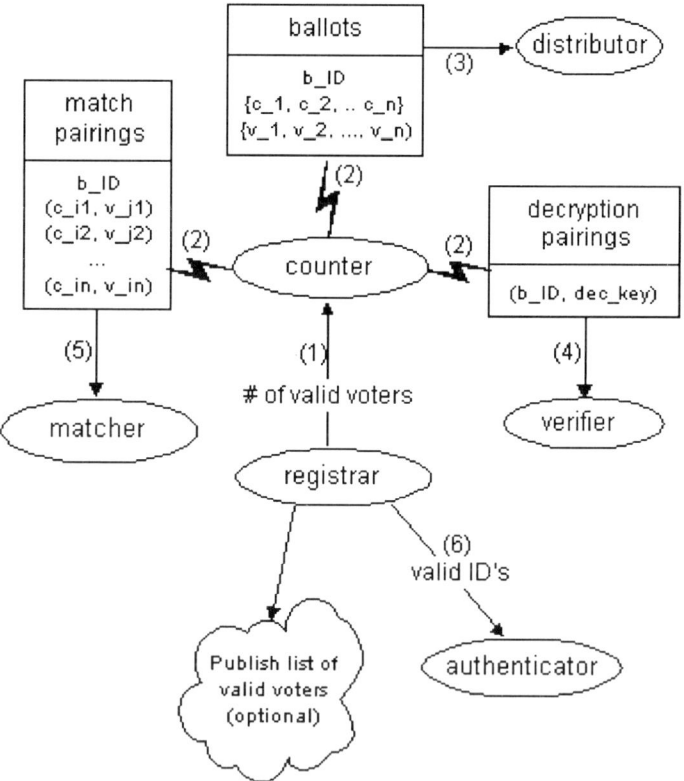

1. The registrar sends the number of eligible registered voters to the counter.
2. The counter generates a larger number of ballots than the number of registered voters. Each ballot consists of three things: each of the choices on the ballot, an encrypted version of each choice, and a ballot ID. The counter keeps record of the decryption key and the ballot ID for each ballot so that the counter can later decrypt the cast votes.
3. The counter sends the ballots to the distributor.

4. The counter sends a copy of the decryption table to the verifier.
5. The counter sends the match pairings (pairs of a ballots encrypted and decrypted choices) to the matcher.
6. The registrar sends the authenticator a list of ID's that are eligible for the given election. If desired, the registrar may publish the names of these voters.
7. If desired, the verifier can check the ballots and pairings to confirm that they were properly generated.

Voting phase.

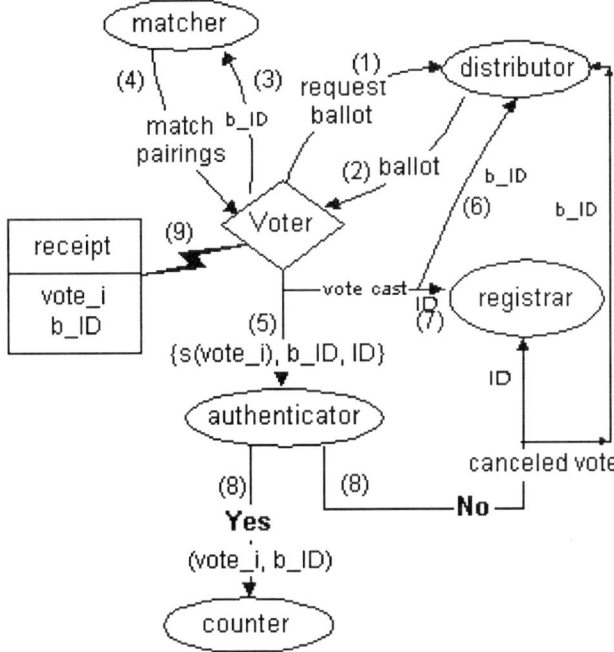

1. When the voter wishes to participate in the election, he/she contacts the distributor and asks for a ballot.
2. The distributor randomly selects a ballot and sends it to the voter.
3. The voter's web browser requests the matching pair for the received ballot from the matcher.
4. The matcher sends the voter the appropriate matching pair.
5. The voter then signs the encrypted version of the desired vote using his/her signature key s and sends them to the authenticator, along with the ballot's ID number, and the voter's own ID.
6. The voter's Web browser informs the distributor that the ballot with the given ballot ID has been cast. (In so doing, the distributor has a record of how many votes are actually cast, and by which ballots. This will prevent any facility from generating votes for unused ballots, solving a major problem in many of the previously discussed protocols.)
7. The voter's Web browser informs the registrar that the voter has cast a vote, but it is not required to tell the registrar which ballot ID it used.
8. The authenticator first checks the signature to authenticate the voter. The authenticator then verifies that the authenticated voter is permitted to vote in the given election. Once authenticated, the authenticator passes only the legitimate encrypted vote and the ballot's ID to the counter. If authentication fails, the authenticator will notify the voter that he/she is not allowed to vote. The authenticator would then notify the registrar and distributor with a cancellation.
9. The voter's browser generates a receipt when the authenticator confirms receiving the ballot packets.

Announcement phase.

The announcement phase requires no interaction between the different facilities. Each facility merely releases certain information to the public. To verify the integrity of the election, the verifier facility compares certain published lists. An individual voter could also compare some of these lists. The integrity of the election does not require a voter to do so, but allowing a voter to perform such checks increases the security as explained in Lemma 3 of Section 6.

- The counter decrypts the votes it has received and tallies the vote.
- The authenticator publishes list #1 containing the encrypted ballots and the ballot ID.
- The counter publishes list #2 containing its version of list #1. Both lists 1 and 2 should be identical.
- The authenticator publishes list #3 consisting of all voter IDs that cast ballots (in numerical order).
- The registrar looks at list #3 and confirms that only valid voters voted. (This list could also be published if desired.)
- The verifier confirms that lists 1 and 2 are identical. (To prevent cover-ups, it may be desirable to have lists 1 and 2 be sent to the verifier before they are published.)
- The verifier uses list 1 and the decryption table (from counter in the pre-voting phase) to confirm the results published by the counter.
- Voters can look at lists 1 and 2 to see their votes on both of these lists.
- The distributor looks at lists 1 and 2 to be ensured that only legitimate ballots appear. Any illegal ballots can than be removed and the results recalculated. The distributor could also release its list of ballot ID's, but this should be done after the authenticator and the counter released their encrypted ballot lists.
- The counter announces the election results, which can be verified by the verifier.

Remark. Revealing the source code, much in the same

way as with PGP, could allow laymen to check the validity and honesty of the facilities.

5. Security measures and implementation

To ensure that elections are held fairly, we must develop security measures to prevent individual modules of our voting protocol from conspiring with each other. We require that each of the facilities generate a pair of public and private keys of its own. These pairs should be replaced from time to time. To keep elections from being delayed, we recommend changing the keys between elections. We assume that not all of the facilities can be compromised at the same time. This is a reasonable assumption, for there is little one can do if all of the facilities are compromised simultaneously. In any conventional voting system, the overall security and integrity rely on humans. This means that the integrity of a traditional election is only as strong as that of the people running it. We will use a public-key encryption/decryption scheme where keys commune. To prevent facilities from communicating illegally, all facilities will monitor the facility-facility communication channel.

5.1. Data protection

Each facility is required to encrypt its database (list of data) on the fly, *e.g.*, one record at a time, using the public keys of all the facilities. By doing so, the only way to completely decode a piece of data would be to acquire the secret keys of all severs, which, by our assumption, is impossible. Because the database is encrypted piece by piece, the facility can easily extract the portion of the data from the database it needs to see and then sends it to the other facilities to decrypt it.

It is not necessary to encrypt election results, as they will be released at the end of the election. It would also be very easy to see any discrepancy in the results when all of the lists are released. It is necessary to encrypt the database of the distributor to protect the ballots that have not been given out.

5.2. Security of Communication Channels

We have two type of communication to deal with. The first type is between facilities, and the second type is between a voter and a facility.

Facility-facility communication. For this type of communication, we need to ensure that these communications cannot be intercepted or altered; we also need to ensure that facilities do not collaborate to compromise the integrity or anonymity of the election. We accomplish both of these goals using the following protocol. When facility A wants to transmit data to facility B, facility A sends the encrypted data to a randomly selected third facility C. Facility C then decrypts the data with its own secret key, verifies that the size and the structure of the data it received have not been altered, and sends the data to another randomly selected facility D. The process is continued until the data finally reaches facility B, and facility B will be able to read the data after it uses its private key to decrypt the data.

Since intermediate facilities cannot completely decrypt the data, they will not know what exactly is being sent. The protocol can ensure that the information being sent is of legitimate size and structure. The only way for an intermediate facility to cheat would be to rearrange the information so it matches this size and structure. This would cause some information, such as some of the ballots to be left off, but the other facilities would be able to notice this when tabulation occurs.

Since facilities could manipulate this process by breaking the illegal data into small parts and reporting sizes that make the data appear legitimate. The facilities should each keep a log of the status of the protocol. This way communication can only occur between two facilities at appropriate times and should be limited as to how many communications they are permitted.

To reduce the amount of traffic, as well as decryption computation, communication between facilities should be done in large blocks. For instance, the counter should send all of the ballots to the distributor, and the authenticator should send the counter encrypted ballots in a large number of blocks.

Voter-facility communication. Since we are dealing with the Internet, the most logical form of security for the interaction between the voter and the central facility would be to use HTTPS. HTTPS is already considered to be a secure form of communication for the Internet. It is considered to be a *de facto* standard, and as long as it is viewed as such, it would be reasonable to use HTTPS. If circumstances cause a new standard to arise, this new standard should be adopted for this type of communication.

The only alteration to the HTTPS protocol we will have to deal with is the fact that when the voter is being sent something it would be encrypted. Of course, the facility also would not be able to look up the requested information. Therefore, the facility encrypts the database and sends it to the other facilities to remove their encryption. The facility gets the information back, decrypts it with its secret key and then looks up the requested information.

6. Proof of anonymity and security

In this section provide proofs that our protocol satisfies all nine of the criteria defined in Section 2. Recall that we assume that not all facilities collaborate at the same time. We first prove the following lemma.

Lemma 1. If no facility knows all other facilities' secret keys, then any collaboration among facilities can be detected by a non-collaborating facility.

Proof. We note that each facility's data is stored in an encrypted form with all the other facilities' public keys. The collaborating facilities cannot bypass the other facilities, because without them the data cannot be decrypted. Hence, the only way for two facilities A and B to collaborate is to cheat: The sending facility A does not encrypt the data and sends the data directly to the receiving facility B. Such activities can be detected by a non-collaborating facility C by monitoring the data transactions in the follow ways.

Case 1. Facility A specifies that facility B is the destination facility and sends the data directly to B. Then the non-collaborating facility C can find out that A cheats because C must receive the data before B does.

Case 2. Facility A specifies that facility B is not the destination, but picks B to be the first facility to pass the data. Then the non-collaborating facility C can find out that A cheats after a few rounds of transactions because A is supposed to randomly pick a third facility to send the data and C should have a chance to receive it in a few rounds.

The similar proof can be applied for the case where more than two facilities collaborate. This completes the proof.

Based on Lemma 1, we assume that no facilities collaborate in the rest of the proofs presented below.

Lemma 2. The democracy criterion is satisfied.

Proof. We assume that no cheating occurs in the registration phase; otherwise, there is little we can do no matter what voting protocol is used.

We first show that only eligible voters are allowed to vote. If an ineligible voter tries to vote, the authenticator can notice this and will not allow the vote to be cast. If the authenticator cheats by allowing an ineligible voter to participate in the election, the registrar will notice this when it receives the list of ID's that voted. If the registrar allows an ineligible voter to vote, then either too many voters would be permitted to vote, or an eligible voter would be denied the right to vote by the authenticator. In the first case, since we know the exact number of eligible voters for the given election in the registration phase, the authenticator or the counter would notice that too many people were being allowed to participate. In the second case, the voter will be notified and so the voter can challenge the registrar or the authenticator. The voter could request the registrar to inform the authenticator that he/she is eligible, which may then result in the first case.

Next, we show that each eligible voter can only vote once. If a voter tries to vote twice, the authenticator would notice that the signature key s and ID had already been used. Depending upon the voting scenario, the new vote would either overwrite the old vote, or it would simply be ignored. If the authenticator tries to pass the new vote on anyway, it would have to place it in place of someone else's vote, because otherwise the lists posted at the end would not match in length. The registrar, however, has its own list of voters, and their ID's that actually voted. Eventually, there would be a conflict with these lists. This completes the proof.

Lemma 3. The accuracy criterion is satisfied.

Proof. Due to the fact that voters are given a receipt, and that they are allowed to view the published lists as described in the Announcement Phase, a voter's vote cannot be altered, duplicated, or removed without being detected. An attempt to alter or remove votes would be futile since the cheating party would not know which voters are going to check for their ballot. If a cheater changes a ballot and the voter whom cast the ballot examines the list, it would be evident that fraud had occurred. Appropriate measures could than be taken to remedy the error. In a large scale election, the cheater would be required to alter many ballots, increasing the likely hood of being caught.

There are three kinds of votes that are considered invalid, namely, votes made by ineligible voters, votes made by eligible voters but the votes are in incorrect formats, and votes generated by central facilities for unused ballots. For the first kind of invalid votes, as shown in the proof of Lemma 2, they will be detected before the final result is announced, and so they will not be counted. For the second kind of invalid votes, the counter will not be able to tally them since they are in wrong formats. For the third kind of invalid votes, since many lists are published at the end of the election, no facility can generate votes for unused ballots without being detected. This completes the proof.

Lemma 4. The privacy criterion is satisfied.

Proof. The only facility that can see the voters' names is the registrar. The registrar, however, can only see the encrypted ballot cast by a particular voter's ID. The registrar has no way to decrypt this vote without collaborating with the counter. We have shown in Lemma 1 that this cannot occur.

Lemma 5. The verifiability criterion is satisfied.

Proof. Voters can be sure that their votes were tabulated by verifying that their ID and encrypted key are in the lists posted by the authenticator and the counter. Moreover, the voters are not relied upon to verify their votes because this is the job of the verifier. Although we do not require voters to check their ballots, it can be assumed that some will. Therefore, since the verifier does not know who will check their ballots, the verifier cannot cheat without being detected.

Lemma 6. The simplicity criterion is satisfied.

Proof. The voter is required to do very little, except that he/she needs to register and vote. The facilities do the majority of the work, with the voter's computer doing very minor calculations, and voters can vote with minimal equipment and skill.

Lemma 7. The mobility criterion is satisfied.

Proof. This is straightforward since our protocol is to be used over the World Wide Web.

Lemma 8. The efficiency criterion is satisfied.

Proof. As we mentioned earlier that in our protocol, the facilities do the most of the computations. In particular, all the calculations, except the signatures, are done before the voting even occurs. This means that very little time is consumed in the actual voting process. The main delay in voting would be the actual network communication. If the voting population were divided into districts the network delay would be minimal. Keeping the facilities in a close physical proximity, connected via a high-speed network, would also minimize delays. We can run the facilities using powerful computers (or special-purpose computers) to increase efficiency.

Lemma 9. The scalability criterion is satisfied.

Proof. Since our protocol is to be run over the World Wide Web, it is easily scalable and divisible. If districts are desired or needed, our protocol will compensate for that by having each district running its own facilities. Large-scale elections would run smoother if they were partitioned, but it is not necessary to do so.

Lemma 10. The responsibility criterion can be satisfied.

Proof. As we mentioned before that the responsibility criterion is an optional requirement, which is not required in the US elections. But it is desirable in Australian elections. If this criterion is desired, the registrar can easily make it possible by publishing the names that have voted.

7. Additional Properties

In addition to the properties we proved in Section 6, we outline below some additional properties of our voting protocol.

- Our protocol can be easily modified to allow the facilities to hold multiple elections simultaneously. For instance, we can participate in a nationwide election at the same time we vote for local officials or ordinances. This could be achieved by adding an election ID to the ballots. The ID would tell the facilities what election the given ballot is for. Voters would request a set of ballots instead of a single ballot.
- Voters may be allowed to change their vote. This could be done in one of two ways. First, authenticator holds all votes till the end, to change a vote, the user just resubmits their vote. The authenticator throws out the old vote and keeps the new one. Second, when the authenticator sees that the voter has already cast his/her ballot for the given election, the authenticator asks the counter to remove the ballot from its list. The authenticator then sends the new vote to the counter. As an added benefit of this property, we can make vote selling more difficult, because the buyer now has to lock the seller until the end of the election to prevent the buyer from changing his/her vote.
- Our protocol can handle many types of elections (*e.g.,* several candidates, picking multiple candidates, write-in), with very limited modification.
- Interested parties could have their own facilities designed to check the integrity of the election.
- Using the distributor facility, we are allowing elections to occur on the Internet without worrying about hiding or masking IP addresses. The distributor facility also provides additional reliability on the integrity of the election.

Final remark. If the parties running the individual facilities would not collaborate (e.g., due to conflict interests) and they are in a secure environment, then some of the security measures such as encrypting data using public keys of all facilities could be removed.

Bibliography

[Be87] J. Benaloh. *Verifiable Secret-Ballot Elections.* PhD. Thesis, Yale University, 1987.

[BT94] J. Benaloh and D. Tuinstra. Receipt-free secret-ballot elections. In *Proceedings of the 26th ACM Symposium on Theory of Computing*, pages 544-553, ACM Press, 1994.

[Ch82] D. Chaum. Blind signatures for untraceable payments. In *Blind Signatures for Untraceable Payments*, D. Chaum, R. Rivest, and A. Sherman, eds., pages 199-203, Plenum Press, 1982.

[Ch81] D. Chaum. Untraceable electronic mail, return addresses, and digital pseudonyms. *Communication of the ACM*, 24(1981), pp. 84-88.

[Ch88a] D. Chaum. The dinning cryptographers problem: unconditional sender and recipient untraceability. *Journal of Cryptography*, 1(1988), pp. 65-75.

[Ch88b] D. Chaum. Elections with unconditionally secret ballots and disruption equivalent to breaking RSA. In *Proceedings of Advances in Cryptology (EUROCRYPT'88)*, vol. 330 of *Lecture Notes in Computer Science*, pages 177-182, Springer-Verlag, 1988.

[Co86] J.Cohen. Improving privacy in cryptographic elections. Yale University Tech. Rep. DCS/TR-454, 1986.

[CF85] J. Cohen and M. Fisher. A robust and verifiable cryptographically secure election scheme. In *Proceedings of the 26th IEEE Annual Symposium on Foundations of Computer Science*, pages 372-382, IEEE Computer Society Press, 1985.

[C+96] R. Cramer, M. Frankin, B. Schoenmakers, and M. Yung. Multi-authority secret ballot elections with linear work. In *Proceedings of Advances in Cryptology (EUROCRYPT'96)*, vol. 1070 of *Lecture Notes in*

Computer Science, pages 72-83, Springer-Verlag, 1996.

[CGS] R. Cramer, R. Gennaro, and B. Schoenmakers. A secure and optimally efficient multi-authority election scheme. Manuscript acquired from rosario@watson.ibm.com.

[Cr96] L. Cranor. Electronic voting: computerized polls may save money, protect privacy. *ACM Crossroads* (Electronic Journal), 1996.

[CC97] L. Cranor and R. Cytron. Sensus: A security-conscious electronic polling system for the Internet. In *Proceedings of the Hawaii International Conference on System Sciences*. Wailea, Hawaii, 1997.

[F+93] A. Fujioka, T. Okamoto. and K. Ohta. A practical secret voting scheme for large-scale elections. In *Proceedings of Advances in Cryptology (AUSCRYPT'92)*, vol. 718 of *Lecture Notes in Computer Science*, pages 244-251, Springer-Verlag, 1993.

[Iv91] K. Iversen. A cryptographic scheme for computerized general elections. In *Proceedings of Advances in Cryptography (CRYPTO'91)*, vol. 576 of *Lecture Notes in Computer Science*, pages 405-419, Springer-Verlag, 1991.

[MV98] Y. Mu and V. Varadharajan. Anonymous secure e-voting over a network. In *Proceedings of the 14th Annual Computer Security Application Conference*, pages 293-299, IEEE Computer Society. 1998.

[Na90] M. Naor. Bit commitment using pseudo-randomness. *In Proceedings of Advances in Cryptology (CRYPTO'90)*, vol. 435 of *Lecture Notes in Computer Science*, pages 218-229, Springer-Verlag, 1990.

[Ne93] P. Neumann. Security criteria for electronic voting. In *Proceedings of the 16th National Computer Security Conference*, pages 478-481, 1991.

[NS91] H. Nurmi and A. Salomaa. A cryptographic approach to the secret ballot. *Behavioral_Science*. 36(1991), pp. 34-40.

[NS] H. Nurmi and A. Salomaa. Secret ballot elections and public-key cryptosystems. Manuscript.

[N+91] H. Nurmi, A. Salomaa, and L. Santean. Secret ballot elections in computer networks. *Computers & Security,* 10(1991), pp. 553-560.

[Pf84] A. Pfitzmann. A switched/broadcase ISDN to decrease user obervability. In *Proceedings of the International Zurich Seminar on Digital Communication*, pages 183-190, IEEE Computer Society Press, 1984.

[SK94] K. Sako and J. Kilian. Secure voting using partially compatible homomorphisms. In *Proceedings of Advances in Cryptology (CRYPTO'94)*, vol. 839 of *Lecture Notes in Computer Science*, pages 411-424, Springer-Verlag. 1994.

[Sal96] A. Salomaa. *Public-Key Cryptography*. 2nd edition. Springer-Verlag, Berlin, 1996.

[Sch96] B. Schneier. *Applied Cryptology*, 2nd edition. John Wiley & Sons, New York, 1996.

Design of LAN-Lock, a System for Securing Wireless Networks

Richard E. Newman
Capt. Mark V. Hoyt
Tim Swanson
Computer & Information Science & Engineering
PO Box 6120
University of Florida
Gainesville, FL 32611-6120
352.392.1488/1220fax
nemo,mvh,tswanson@cise.ufl.edu

Phillipe Broccard
Mark Sanders

Joe Winner

Raytheon Systems Division
1501 72nd St. No. MS-50
St. Petersburg, FL 33710-4628
{prba,mwsa,jkwb}@eci-esyst.com

Abstract

Wireless LANs are becoming increasingly available, affordable and attractive due to their increasing speeds and decreasing costs, in addition to their ability to offer easy configuration and reconfiguration of nodes in a LAN. However, most commercial wireless LAN products have limited security over the link, and none that we are aware of use NSA-approved cryptographic methods. This paper describes a system developed jointly by a team at the University of Florida in its Integrated Process and Product Design (IPPD) course and a liaison engineer at Raytheon Systems Division that uses Fortezza cryptographic cards to provide authenticated, encrypted connections between hosts running MS Windows.

1. Introduction

Wireless LANs (WLANs) are attractive due to their ease of deployment and reconfiguration. In addition, they support roaming hosts, which allows users to carry their notebook or laptop computers with them as they go from location to location within a WLAN service area. With speeds increasing and costs decreasing, they should enjoy greater popularity as time goes on. Simply using hopping sequences or spreading codes in the spread spectrum techniques (Code Division Multiple Access, CDMA) employed by most such systems does not in itself prevent an eavesdropper from sniffing frames off the WLAN. As businesses are likely to use their WLANs to handle sensitive, proprietary or statutorily private data, it is crucial to protect the information sent over the WLAN. However, any solution must provide as much transparency as possible to the users, that is, it must have a low impact on performance and little or no impact on the applications that may be used.

These observations prompted Raytheon, Inc. to initiate a project with the IPPD program at the University of Florida to address these issues. The goal of the resulting project was to provide for limited communication security in a WLAN-LAN environment, with the following requirements:

1. it must run under Windows 95 or Windows NT (eventually both);

2. it must be compatible with the Raylink WLAN product;

3. it must use the Fortezza cryptographic PCMCIA card [1];

4. it must provide for communication with users on wired LAN hosts that do not have Fortezza cards;

5. it must be compatible with most if not all applications running on Windows;

6. it must be as transparent to the user as possible;

7. it must have a minimal impact on communication performance.

These requirements were intended to satisfy the largest base of potential users and to incorporate NSA-endorsed cryptographic systems.

As far as impact on performance is concerned, the system needs to be able to continue to support the applications commonly used, including some streaming video applications as the most demanding. Interactive video and audio place not only throughput demands on the system, but also delay requirements. Ideally, the additional security mechanisms should be able to match the throughput of the underlying network (about 2 Mbps), but a rate of 384 kpbs would suffice under most circumstances, as the 2 Mbps is shared by all the hosts in a WLAN group anyway.

The next section will discuss these requirements and their impact on system design in more detail.

1.1 Organization

The remainder of the paper is organized as follows. System architecture and the impact of requirements on it will be discussed in the next section. After that, a section will be devoted to each major component: Key Management, Layered Service Provider, and Proxy. We then report the performance results obtained so far, and conclude the paper.

2 LAN-Lock Architecture

This section describes the overall environment of the system and the architecture it uses.

2.1 Design Considerations

It was decided that the project should focus on protecting communications on the WLAN, and that sniffing on the wired LAN was a smaller threat (and one that was already tolerated); the wired LAN is assumed to be secure. Thus the system has to provide some means of allowing communications between wireless hosts (required to use encryption) and hosts on the wired LAN (most of which would be unable to access Fortezza functions, lacking in PCMCIA card readers). Figure 1 shows the environment in which the system is designed to work. This forces additional complexity into the system in that there must be an intermediary on the wired LAN that decrypts encrypted frames for the wired hosts lacking Fortezza capability, and encrypts frames from those hosts destined for the wireless hosts.

Wireless hosts should be required (insomuch as this is possible given the environment) to use cryptographic protection, so each wireless host runs a protocol that refuses communication if the packets are not appropriately encrypted from an authenticated host. Two wireless hosts not running this protocol may communicate directly without encryption or authentication, but this is impossible to prevent in any case as the user may always boot the host in whatever system configuration is desired. Communication with hosts on the wired LAN is only possible through Raylink Access Points (APs), which act as bridges between the wired LAN and the WLAN. In order to prevent inadvertent broadcast of unencrypted data over the WLAN, and to prevent wireless hosts from being able to communicate with

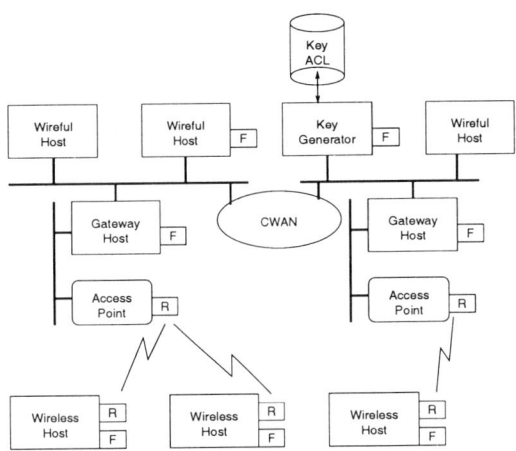

Figure 1. Physical architecture and operational environment for the LAN-Lock system

wired hosts without encrypting their messages, a gateway is placed between each AP and the rest of the wired LAN. The gateway enforces the requirement to encrypt messages over the WLAN, and so wireless hosts must obey the rules to gain access to the resources on the wired network.

A major consideration in the design is the layer at which the information is cryptographically protected. With sufficiently fast encryption, this may be performed at the link level, the network level, the transport level, the LSP level, or the application level [7, 8]. The choice was made to provide the protection at the LSP layer, for the reasons given below.

The link level is desirable from the standpoint of transparency and enforcement, but it presents problems in that the data would have to be intercepted and modified in the WLAN interface driver, since the interface card itself was not subject to modification. Modifying the driver would have been possible, but doing this creates the problems that only the cards for which modified drivers existed would be usable, and whenever the driver was updated, the new driver would have to be modified.

Neither the IP nor the TCP layer [8] in the protocol stack were viable, as we would first have had to obtain access to the protocol source code from Microsoft, an unlikely proposition. Further, not only would the same maintenance problems existed, but we would be limited to applications that used those specific protocols, or else had to modify UDP code, or IPX code, etc. in order to provide for wider availability.

Incorporating the protection in the application level had been done in several cases already, but requires modified applications. Those familiar with Kerberized applications know how restrictive this can be, as each new or modified application must be maintained, and every host using the application must have the modified version of it.

Below WinSock and above the transport layer in the protocol stack is the Layered Service Provide (LSP) region. The LSP mechanism was developed (mostly by Intel) to provide a way in which third party vendors could insert new capabilities into the protocol stack without altering applications or the networking kernel. Since the LSP sits above the transport layer, and is always called by WinSock, providing protection there allows compatibility with any application that uses WinSock on one hand, and any network protocols available from WinSock on the other. This also means that only one component of the system need be modified, and only the LSP code needs to be maintained. In short, implementation at the LSP level provided the transparency and interoperability desired, while keeping access and maintenance problems to a minimum.

Scalability is also an important factor. While each AP may only be able to handle around 60 hosts, the APs are connected to the enterprise's CWAN and so there may be hundreds of wireless hosts. While existing IEEE standards are used to handle roaming and so forth, the LAN-Lock system still needs to provide each wireless host with an appropriate set of keys and to be able to authenticate it. The keys must be distributed in a timely fashion to known, active hosts, and new hosts or hosts that are temporarily disconnected must be able to obtain appropriate keys on demand. These issues are dealt with in detail in the next subsection.

2.2 Key Management

In order to provide a uniform framework for key distribution and to manage key groups reflecting need-to-know categories, we chose to implement key generation and authorization as a centralized function. Given that it was likely for a single host to be connected to several other hosts at any given time, and there are a number of popular applications that require group communication, LAN-Lock uses a single key per category rather than generating a key on a per-session basis. In part, this is because the Fortezza card can only hold nine keys at a time in its key registers, so a host or a server that has more than nine connections would have to have multiple Fortezza cards (or do some relatively slow keys swapping) to manage keys otherwise.

Further, to provide for greater security the system only permits use of a given key for a limited amount of time (one hour by default). This places a requirement to be able to generate and distribute keys for up to a minimum of 500 hosts every hour, including up to four different keys per host. These four keys represent one general key and up to three group keys allowed by the system. Since the environment is not synchronous, the hosts and gateway must tolerate overlapping use of old and new keys, whence the requirement to have only four keys (each key requires a pair of Fortezza key registers: one to hold the current key and one to hold a key whose use is permitted for incoming messages).

A single key generator tracks the locations where keys need to be sent and which hosts should be given which group keys. This authorization information is kept in a separate configuration file on the generator maintained by a special program that insures integrity by only allowing the site security officer (SSO) to alter and sign it. The key generator verifies that the key access control list has the proper signature on it before using it.

The Fortezza card is used to wrap session keys (message encryption keys or MEKs) for distribution using the public key of the recipient [5, 6]. This allows the generator to create distributions without concern over whether the recipient currently wants a key or not, so much of the timing can be handled in this central location. Since only a host with an activated Fortezza card possessing the corresponding private key can unwrap the MEK, authentication is implicit. The key generator only needs to track which hosts are active and which public key to use for each host.

In actuality, the key generator (KG) does not send wrapped keys directly to the hosts, but rather to the key distribution servers (KDSs), one of which is associated with each gateway (though they need not be in general, it is convenient to have the key distribution servers associated with the gateways so that wireless hosts that do not have current keys can contact the distribution server at the gateway rather than having to go through the gateway). Preparing a key for distribution takes some time, as the recipient's certificate must be loaded into the card in order to wrap the key, so by using hierarchical distribution, the bulk of the load of wrapping keys can be passed on to the key distribution servers rather than remaining with the key generator. This does mean that the key distribution servers must also know for which hosts they need to prepare keys, and which keys to prepare, so the KG sends the (signed) key ACL to the KDSs.

The Fortezza card must be initialized, so a separate application with GUI allows the user to enter the personality and PIN to activate the card. It also tracks statistics on the bytes encrypted and decrypted, and allows the user to select which key to use for outgoing messages.

2.3 Layered Service Provider

Intel developed the Layered Service Provider (LSP) in cooperation with Microsoft to permit third party developers to insert protocol and processing layers between Winsock and the network protocol stack (above the transport layer). This allows processing transparent to the application and independent of the network protocols used, as long as the application uses Winsock.

Within LAN-Lock, the LSP module's primary task is to encrypt outgoing packets and decrypt incoming packets. To do this, it must know which keys to use and it must have those keys, so it is also required to add and delete headers, and handle keys.

Key handling consists of initially requesting keys from a KDS, which then identifies and authenticates the user and notes that the user's host is active and in its service area. The LSP must receive wrapped keys, unwrap them, and store them in the appropriate registers for later use. If a message arrives with a key that the host does not have, the LSP must request the key from the KDS. Normally, once the host is known to the KDS, the KDS will send the host key updates on a periodic basis, so it should be rare that an initialized host would not have a needed key.

2.4 Proxy

Since communications is desired between hosts without Fortezza capability on the (supposedly secure) wired LAN and wireless hosts that must use Fortezza encryption, some node on the wired LAN must provide for the cryption (taken to be encryption or decryption, whichever is appropriate [4]) between the two types of hosts. In order to prevent unencrypted traffic from inadvertently being sent over the WLAN, this node, the proxy, sits between the AP and the wired LAN and acts as a bridge. The cryption (and headers) are inserted above the transport layer, so any reliable transport service must notice the insertion/deletion of bytes from the connection as headers, MICs, and padding needed for encryption are added, or when same are deleted. Therefore, the proxy cannot simply act as a processing relay along a single connection, but must perform a relay between two connections: one between the proxy and the wireless host, the other between the proxy and the wireful host.

2.5 Summary

LAN-Lock then provides the transparent communication security desired using three main components: key management, LSP, and proxy. Auxiliary user interface programs provide for access to configuration information, such as key group access, Fortezza card initialization and certificate information. Each of these components will be discussed in detail in the following sections.

3 Key Management

A significant part of this project was design of an adequate facility to manage keys. Since the Fortezza cards use X.509 certificates (type I or type III depending on which version of the card you have), we assume the existence of the public key hierarchy needed to provide for identification, authentication, and secure session key distribution [2, 3]. Certificates are extracted from the cards and may be sent without increasing vulnerability through the network. Fortezza certificate management library routines support certificate verification, and checking against revocation lists.

3.1 Key Lifetimes

Since connections can last for hours or days easily, we believe it necessary to limit the duration use of any session key. Rather than make the key use duration depend on the amount of use it has seen (in the number of bytes or packets that have been encrypted using the key, for example), which would have required some clever and likely expensive monitoring of many distributed users, LAN-Lock uses a simple wall clock mechanism. Each key is intended to be used for one hour as the default, though this can be changed.

The operating environment is asynchronous, so it would be expensive and unnecessary to require all the hosts to change the key used at the same time (using barrier synchronization, for example). Instead, LAN-Lock has the hosts chose independently when to start using a new key, and accept on incoming messages both keys that they have not yet started to use as well as keys that they no longer use, as long as the incoming key is not too far out of the local window of use. To this end, the keys are labeled with the intended time interval of usage at the time they are distributed.

In order to accept a key that the host is not currently using, the host must have a copy of that key available, and for performance reasons, it must be in one of the nine Fortezza key registers. To minimize the number of registers used per key group (see below), only two registers per key group are used. In essence, each host has a current key and one other key they will accept. The other key may be the previous key or it may be the next key, and this will change as keys are distributed. The current key changes on the hour, so for at least 15 minutes after the hour a host will have the current key and the old key (see Figure 2). At some point after that and before 15 minutes prior to the next hour, a new key should arrive for the host to store in the register that held the old key. At that point, the host has the current key and the next key key. As long as no two hosts disagree about the time by more than 30 minutes, and as long as the distribution mechanism can deliver copies of the new key to all hosts within the half-hour period allotted, no host should receive a message that it cannot decrypt, assuming it has rights to the key group used for that message.

Note that the decision to change use from the current key to the new key (which should already have been delivered) is a local decision, whereas the keys are distributed according to the distribution system and its timing.

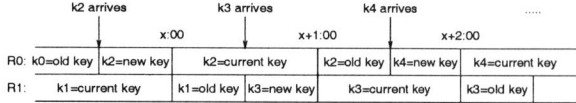

Figure 2. LAN-Lock management of session keys in Fortezza registers

In fact, the key management system on each host maintains the state of each register, and when a new key arrives to replace an old one, the system first marks that register as unused, then replaces the key then marks it as holding the next key to use for that key group. In this way, race conditions are avoided.

3.2 Key Groups

As mentioned above, it was desired that the users and data be partitioned into a small number of categories for isolation reasons, but it was not needed that these categories form the basis for a lattice security model. Since the Fortezza card has only nine usable key registers, and each key group requires two registers, this leaves the system with at most four key groups per host (or really, four per Fortezza card, but since most hosts have but one Fortezza card active at a time anyway, it amounts to the same thing). Since the gateway needs to be able to translate for all of its client hosts, it is limited to four groups per Fortezza card as well, so in effect the whole system is practically limited to four key groups at a time. The gateway could be extended to use more than one Fortezza card, but this is not currently the case.

Key group access rights are based on X.509 certificates. That is, the key Access Control List is indexed by certificate ID, as this is what is in effect authenticated. This key ACL is maintained by the SSO and is signed using the SSO's signature key, so the KG and KDCs can verify that it has not been altered by an unauthorized entity.

3.3 Key Generator

The Key Generator (KG) is required to generate new keys for each key group and start their distribution to the appropriate hosts. The KG maintains a clock that indicates when the new keys should be sent, and starts distribution at 15 after the hour. Note that the tokens can be generated before that, but they should not be sent until the KG can be confident that no hosts are still using the old key (otherwise, a host that has received the new key and replaced the old one cannot decrypt a message from a host still using the old key). At this point, the KG may send wrapped keys directly to host or to intermediate distribution points.

Each key destined for a particular host must be wrapped in a token specific to that host (or rather, specific to the certificate being used by that host). It is not necessary for the recipient to request the key, or for it to authenticate itself to the KG, since only the intended recipient should be able to unwrap the transmitted key using its private key. Key generation is relatively fast, but wrapping the keys takes longer, especially since the destination's public key has to be loaded in order to wrap the session key. For larger systems, a distribution hierarchy is needed to allow for scalability.

3.4 Scaling

In a CWAN with several hundred to thousands of users, it would be difficult or impossible for a single KG to wrap the keys for each host each hour. LAN-Lock uses a key distribution hierarchy that has Key Distribution Servers (KDSs) receive wrapped keys from the KG along with the (signed) key ACL, unwrap the keys and then for each key, wrap it for each authorized active recipient in its service area. This permits significant parallel processing by the KDSs and the KG, and increases the maximum number of hosts that the system can support for a given processing power and session key lifetime..

The KDSs also responsible for responding to requests from newly activated hosts and from hosts that have missed a key update message. Any request of this nature leads the KDS to verify that the requester is authorized to access the requested keys, then wrap them and send them if they are. The responses to asynchronous key requests have the same format as key update packets, naming the key group and the usage window for the key.

Later, in the section on performance, this paper will give key generation and wrapping speeds observed that indicate that the system design is adequate for timely key distribution.

4 Layered Service Provider

The main work of the system is done by the code in the Layered Service Provider (LSP). As explained above, this allows for great flexibility and transparency while remaining maintainable. Though the two sections below describe what the LSP does at the two different types of nodes that communicate over the WLAN, in fact the LSP code is the same on both type - a bit just changes the behavior of the code from one type to the other.

4.1 Wireless User Host

Most nodes are user hosts: wireless laptops required to use Fortezza encryption. On these, the main task of the

LSP is to crypt messages: encrypt outgoing messages using the current key of the selected group, and decrypt incoming messages using the key specified in the header. The key group is specified using a separate program with user interface; the default group is the general group. The LSP also rejects messages that are not encrypted to help prevent accidental or malicious transmission of unencrypted traffic over the WLAN.

When a host is initialized, it has to request new keys. Likewise, when a host receives a message for which it does not have the key (and the key is used within fifteen minutes of its intended use period), the host must request an appropriate key. To make this transparent to the applications, this is handled by the LSP layer. The LSP sends a request to the Gateway and awaits its reply before completing processing of the incoming message. It is possible that an incoming message may use a key that is too far out of its intended use period, in which case the LSP replies to that host with a rejection message, and the originator's LSP must update its current key before resending the message.

New key sets arrive asynchronously, and the LSP must recognize key update messages, verify that they are sent from an authorized source, and check that the key labels are appropriate (that they are indeed new keys and not a replay of some old key update message). If that is the case, then it stores the new keys in the appropriate registers by first invalidating the old key, then loading the new key, then updating the key database to indicate that the register holds the new key.

A timer set to expire on the hour informs the host's LSP when the current key should be changed. The LSP then changes the key status in its database, checking that the new key as been stored in the appropriate register. If not, keys are requested from the KDS. Changing the current key is only a matter of changing the register number used in the calls to the Fortezza driver.

Finally, the wireless host's LSP is responsible for determining when a connection is being made to a wireful host or a message is destined for a wireful host, and redirecting the packets to the proxy. It has to include information on the true destination of the packet when it does this so the proxy will be able to set up the appropriate relay, or it must change the destination port to one already set up by the proxy to handle that connection.

4.2 Gateway

The Gateway's main duty is to act as an enforcement mechanism to disallow messages from the wired LAN to be sent over the WLAN without encryption. The Gateway currently comprises three components: a KDS to receive keys from the KG and distribute them within its service area, the LSP that crypts messages passing through it, and a proxy that exists at the application level. It is not necessary that the Gateway hold the KDS, but it is done that way currently for convenience. The other two components are necessarily in the Gateway.

The KDS portion accepts wrapped keys from the KG, unwraps them, then rewraps them for distribution to the hosts in its service area. It also fields requests for missed key updates and initialization of the key database for newly activated hosts. While doing these tasks, it maintains a list of hosts currently in its service area so that it can send them key updates automatically.

The LSP code that handles message cryption is the same for the Gateway as for any other Fortezza-enabled host, except that the Gateway should never lack a valid key. However, it does have the additional duty to recognize LAN-Lock header information inserted at the LSP level that is used for key management and for setting up proxy relays.

A standard proxy such as Socks does not work in this environment. As the hosts are mobile, it is not appropriate to constrain a host always to contact the same proxy host for access across the LAN-WLAN boundary. Further, a wireful hosts may need to contact wireless hosts in more than one service area, so again a fixed proxy location does not work.

As mentioned above, each wireless host's LSP contacts the Gateway when a connection is to be established with a wireful host. The request is sent to a standard port, and contains information on the true destination IP address and port. The proxy must then set up a connection to that endpoint and establish an endpoint for the wireless host that is associated with that relay. This information is returned to the wireless host's LSP and logged in a table used to redirect messages to the proxy. The relay itself is simple - messages are simply collected from one connection and sent out on the other; no filtering is done. However, there are two little bits of complexity.

First, each relay must be multithreaded since traffic is asynchronous (no assumptions can be made about which endpoint will send the next message). Second, it is desired that the relay allow messages sent between wireless hosts and wireful hosts that have Fortezza capability remain encrypted end-to-end. This means that the relay needs to have access to information on which wireful hosts are currently Fortezza-enabled at the LSP level, so that incoming messages will remain encrypted over the wired LAN. Outgoing messages are not a problem as these are always encrypted anyway.

4.3 Wireful Hosts

It was originally our hope that the wireful hosts would need not be modified in any way if they did not have a Fortezza capability. However, if a wireful host is to be able to communicate with a wireless host, it must go through the proxy. This means that even the wireful hosts must have a modified LSP so that it can redirect communications intended for a wireless host to the proxy instead. Of course, wireful hosts that have Fortezza capability use the same LSP and auxiliary programs as the wireless hosts.

5 Performance Results

It is important that the system permit use of as many applications as possible in as transparent a way as possible. In terms of performance, this boils down to two main requirements: the keys must be distributed in a timely manner, and the unseen work by the LSP must not significantly impact delay or throughput. Limited success has been had on both counts.

5.1 Key Distribution

Using the hierarchical key distribution infrastructure described above, the design goal of 500 users can be met. Assuming 10 KDSs with the maximum of 61 hosts per AP, and assuming every host is given access to all four key groups, this amounts to 244 generations of transmission encryption keys (TEKs) used to wrap the message encryption keys (MEKs) at each KDS. The KG must perform 40 TEK generations and MEK wraps to distribute the keys to the KDSs, so in the worst case (longest path) from first starting to generate the wrapped keys to the last KDS sending the last key to the last host, at total of 288 TEK generations must be done. In addition to that, there is the matter of clock skew, which we take to be no worse than five seconds a day or 2.5 minutes per month. This gives a maximum relative skew of 5 minutes, so for distribution of all the keys within half an hour minus maximum relative clock skew, 25 minutes are available for the 288 TEK generation and MEK wrapping operations, or a bit over 5 seconds per such operation (taking the network propagation delays to be negligible). This is well within the measured time observed for the hosts and Fortezza cards we used, which were fractions of a second.

5.2 Encryption/Decryption

A bigger hit is taken in cryption operations at the LSP. Due to the constraints on the way that Winsock, the LSP and the Fortezza card need to handle memory, each message had to be copied twice in the LSP to process it. This causes significant delay in the current version, on the order of 0.5 to 1 second. We are currently investigating ways to decrease this delay.

In addition, there is the actual throughput of the system. For most messages, the message header size does not contribute significantly to the traffic volume, so the main source of decreased throughput is in the LSP processing and the Fortezza processing. Most of the LSP processing cost is in the copying mentioned above, and should be reduced with program optimizations and faster CPUs. However, the Fortezza cards have their own processing speed limitations, and these vary according to card manufacturer and version. Between the LSP and the Fortezza cards, we observed a throughput of about 500 Kbps. This is barely adequate for some interactive, high-bandwidth applications.

6 Conclusions

The LAN-Lock system design can achieve most of its goals as it is. It is transparent to applications and places a fairly low burden on the user to initialize the Fortezza card and to specify which key group to use. However, applications that bypass the LSP will not be processed by the LAN-Lock system, so these, such as network neighborhood, should be disabled on hosts if all message traffic is to be encrypted. System performance is adequate, but delays are longer than desirable for interactive applications, and throughput must be increased for some of the more bandwidth intensive applications.

7 Acknowledgements

Dr. Al Nauda of Raytheon was of great help establishing this project with the IPPD program and supporting our efforts. Chris Francis at Raytheon provided excellent technical help with Fortezza programming. We would like to thank the NSA and Blaine Burnham in particular for assisting us in obtaining Fortezza cards to use in our development and experiments. This work also builds upon an earlier project named SWARM, whose team blazed the way in development for LAN-Lock. SWARM development team members included Thomas Coscenza, Steve Farago, Blake Bouldin and Keith Nolan. Other LAN-Lock team members not involved with the development described here include Jian Huang and Roger Lie. The IPPD Program at the University of Florida is directed by Dr. Heinz Fridrich, without whose initiative IPPD and this project would never come into existence. There are several others who have helped in large and small ways with this project, and to whom we are grateful; please forgive us if we do not mention you here.

References

[1] J. Epstein and T. Williams. Using fortezza for transparent file encryption. *Twelfth Annual Computer Security and Applications Conference*, pages 140–147, Dec 9-13 1996.

[2] ISO. *Final Text of DIS 7498-2, Information Processing Systems - OSI Reference Model - Part 2: Security Architecture.* ISO/IEC, 1988.

[3] ITU-T. *X.509, The Directory - Authentication Framework.* CCITT, ITU-T, 1988.

[4] P. F. S. Reed, M. G. and D. M. Goldschlag. Proxies for anonymous routing. *Twelfth Annual Computer Security and Applications Conference*, pages 95–104, Dec 9-13 1996.

[5] A. S. Rivest, R. and L. Adleman. A method for obtaining digital signatures and public key cryptosystems. *Communications of the ACM*, 2:120–126, 1978.

[6] B. Schneier. *Applied Cryptography, 2nd Edition.* Wiley and Sons, 1996.

[7] W. Stallings. *Data and Computer Communications (5th Ed.).* Prentice-Hall, 1997.

[8] W. Stevens. *TCP/IP Illustrated, Vol. I.* Addison-Wesley, 1994.

Track B: Panel Session

Composition Problems of Component TOEs – Entrust, Oracle, and Windows NT/2000

Chair

L. Ambuel, TRW

Track A

Security Services

Chair

Jody Heaney, MITRE Corporation

Toward a Taxonomy and Costing Method for Security Services

Cynthia Irvine
Naval Postgraduate School
Monterey, CA

Tim Levin
Anteon Corporation
Monterey, CA

Abstract

A wide range of security services may be available to applications in a heterogeneous computer network environment. Resource Management Systems (RMSs) responsible for assigning computing and network resources to tasks need to know the resource-utilization costs associated with the various network security services. In order to understand the range of security services an RMS needs to manage, a preliminary security service taxonomy is defined. The taxonomy is used as a framework for defining the costs associated with network security services.

1 Introduction

Several efforts are underway to develop middleware *resource management systems* (RMSs) that will logically combine a wide range of network resources to construct a "virtual" computational system [2] [5] [10]. Geographically distributed, heterogeneous resources are expected to be used to support applications with a wide range of computation needs. Large parallelized computations found in fields such as astrophysics [11], aerodynamics, meteorology, etc. will require allocation of perhaps hundreds of individual processes. Multimedia applications, such as voice and video will impose requirements for low jitter, minimal packet losses, and isochronal data rates. Adaptive applications will need to adjust to changing conditions. The RMS in such an environment is responsible for: efficiently scheduling multiple simultaneous tasks onto specific network resources; supporting user requirements for performance and security (viz, QoS); and providing support for tasks to adapt to changing resource availability.

Users or applications submit tasks to the RMS, which schedules the tasks for execution. As part of the process of estimating efficient task schedules, the RMS must balance resource-usage costs against user benefits. Specifically, there might not exist sufficient resources to maximize the benefits to all users. Thus the RMS must quantify the costs associated with the entire range of network services. These costs include bandwidth, task execution speed, latency, storage, etc. Costing of security services in this context has received little attention. The challenge is to associate costs with the entire range of network security services.

The purpose of this paper is to present a preliminary taxonomy of security services, and to show how this taxonomy can be used as the foundation of a system for supplying security-costing information to an RMS. Section 2 presents our preliminary taxonomy. Section 3 is a sketch for how the structure of the taxonomy might be used to define quality of security service requests to an RMS. Section 4 examines how the cost of using various elements of the taxonomy might be presented to an RMS; and Section 5 is a discussion and conclusion.

2 Taxonomy of security services

Users and applications on the network are presented with various security *services* (e.g., authenticity, confidentiality, integrity, non-repudiation, etc.). A security service may be used to implement one or more security policies (organizational and automated [16]), and is, in turn, implemented by one or more security mechanisms (and of course, a given security mechanism may be used to implement different security services, e.g., "OS access controls," in Table 1). Some mechanisms provide fixed services, and some are variant.[1] Additionally, the RMS may make choices for the user regarding variant security mechanisms, as part of its schedule formulation or adaptive re-scheduling (see Section 4).

Each security mechanism is associated with a service area, which indicates the general topographical component of the network in which the security or protection is effective. The taxonomy identifies three service areas: end system (e.g., a client or server system), intermediate node (e.g., routers, switches), and network connection (i.e., the "wire" connecting various systems and nodes). Security

---

1. Variant mechanisms offer the user various "degrees," or strengths, of security (viz., over and above some minimum requirement). See [9] for details.

mechanisms associated with end systems and intermediate nodes protect resources (e.g., data and programs) that are associated with a node or system; for network connections, we are concerned with mechanisms for protecting information that is physically in transit.

Table 1 provides our preliminary taxonomy. It lists security services, example mechanisms and associated service areas. The service areas are designated: "IM" for Intermediate Node, "NC" for network connection, and "ES" for End System. The Total Subnet (TS) service area identifies mechanisms that cannot be assigned exclusively to either of IN, NC, or ES.

2.1 Rationale for the taxonomy

In constructing a taxonomy one wishes it to be both useful and complete. Since a taxonomy is simply an organizational artifice, it must have reason to exist, which is its usefulness. Additionally, the taxonomy fails if it does not account for all of the elements of the classes that it attempts to organize.

We have found this taxonomy to be a useful tool for characterizing the security services and requirements that a RMS might encounter in the network context. As such, it is useful for organizing a quality of security service request (see Section 3) and for presenting costs to a Resource Management System (See Section 4).

As for completeness, we assert preliminarily that the top level is complete. Our taxonomy includes the traditional security categories found in the literature, e.g., Pfleeger [12] (confidentiality, integrity, availability), Ford [4] (authentication, access control, confidentiality, integrity, non-repudiation), and Stallings [15](confidentiality, integrity, availability, authentication, nonrepudiation, access control). (Note that in the latter two examples we find "access control" to be redundant with availability, confidentiality and integrity). Empirically, all of the example mechanisms that we have examined so far have been accounted for in our top level list of security services.

The second level (viz., end system, intermediate node, and network connection) is a simple enough partitioning of the generic network topology that we claim it to be complete through inspection. The list of mechanisms in Table 1 is not intended to be exhaustive, but provides a framework for illustrating the taxonomy.

3 Quality of security service requests

The security service taxonomy can be useful in understanding how security is involved in a Quality of Service request. Security in the Quality of Service context has traditionally implied the general notions of one or more of the following: confidentiality, authenticity, access control, and integrity [3] [13]. However, there is no reason why a Quality of Security Service request could not include all of the elements from "Security Service" and "Service Area" in Table 1. In other words, we envision a security vector in a fully-functional Quality of Service request to include levels of service for the range of security services and mechanisms that we have identified, where "level of service" can indicate degrees of security with respect to assurance, mechanistic strength, administrative diligence, etc. Thus, a generic QoS request would look something like the following in a BNF-style notation:

QoS Request ::= task_specifier, security_vector, performance_vector, other_factors

And a security vector would appear as follows:

security_vector ::= security_component [, security_component]*

security_component ::= security_service, service_area, level

security_service ::= <services from Table 1>

service_area ::= [ES | IN | NC]

level ::= <mechanism-dependent security-level indicator>

A component may be included in the security vector for each variant security mechanism, i.e., for each mechanism in the network environment that provides to the user a choice of security "level." For example, a partial security vector might look like this:

data confidentiality, NC, crypto-high (e.g., 128-bit keys),

authenticity, NC, medium (e.g., public-key signature),

nonrepudiation, ES, high-assurance (e.g., Common Criteria rating EAL7 [1])

Here, for the sake of exposition, the "level" of each security component is somewhat arbitrarily assigned. Establishment of nomenclature and metrics for these levels is the subject of ongoing investigations [7] [18]. Translation mechanisms [6] may be utilized in presenting a high-level Quality of Security Service interface to the user, while managing parameters (such as a suitable translation of "level") to the underlying detailed security mechanisms.

4 Costing of security services

To motivate the need for security costing information, a specific RMS scheduling mechanism is described. We will

Table 1: Preliminary security service taxonomy

SECURITY SERVICE	SERVICE AREA	EXAMPLE SECURITY MECHANISMS
Data Confidentiality	IN	OS access controls, Cryptographic credentials
	NC	40-bit DES, 128-bit Blowfish
	ES	OS access controls, Cryptographic credentials
Traffic Flow Confidentiality	IN	Active network nodes monitor traffic and inject dummy packets in response to certain triggering conditions.
	NC	Communications use a Virtual Private Network with encapsulated packets
	ES	Traffic padding up to a defined maximum is provided. Beyond that maximum, traffic flow confidentiality cannot be guaranteed.
Data Integrity	IN	OS access controls, Cryptographic credentials
	NC	Cryptographic chaining, integrity sequence numbers, and digital signatures
	ES	OS access controls, Cryptographic credentials
Authenticity	IN	Active network supports internode authentication based on digital signatures
	NC	Data origin authentication, i.e., IP address, digital signatures
	ES	OS identification and authentication mechanism; use of Digital Signature Standard; use of trusted certificate authority
Non-Repudiation	IN	Active network nodes report transactions to secure logging facility
	ES	Digital notary and non-repudiation services
Guarantee of Service, Availability	IN	Active network nodes reserve bandwidth for network administrative traffic. Priority-based scheduling for application traffic
	NC	Bandwidth reservation protocol
	ES	Time-slicing scheduler, FIFO scheduler with preemptive interrupts
Audit and Intrusion Detection	IN	Auditing of network control functions
	TS	Rule-based and profile-based network intrusion detection, intrusion correlation engine to identify intrusions across a group of subnets
Boundary Control	TS	firewall, proxy server, guard

show how this work requires detailed security costing information.

Resource management systems are responsible for efficiently scheduling multiple tasks onto computing and network resources in a distributed, heterogeneous computing environment. RMSs support Quality of Service by scheduling to meet user requirements for performance and security, and by providing support for tasks to adapt to changing network resource availability.

An RMS schedules tasks for execution in the network in response to requests from users or applications. The task may be submitted with a QoS "specification," which articulates the user's desired quality of service, including security services. An RMS currently under investigation, the Management System for Heterogeneous Networks [5], has as its primary goal determination of the best scheduling

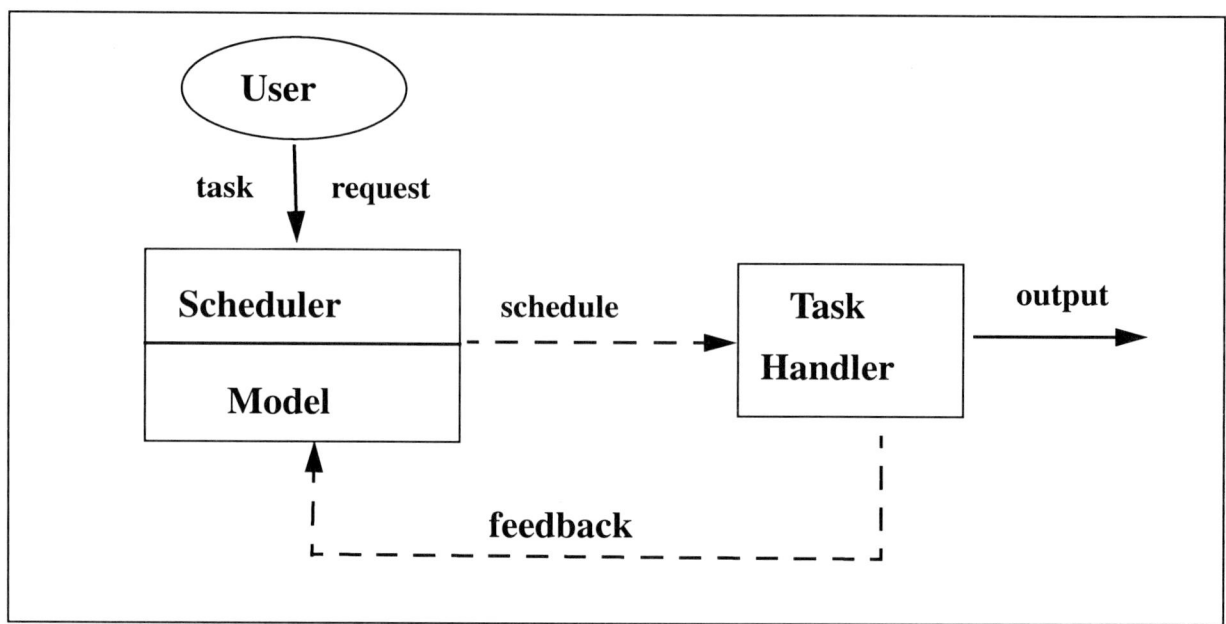

FIGURE 1. Resource Scheduler. The task handler is responsible for realizing the scheduler's execution plan and provides feedback to the scheduler so that it can dynamically adapt the schedule to evolving resource conditions.

support for many diverse applications, each with its own quality of service requirements, in a distributed, heterogeneous environment. MSHN preserves compatibility with existing security policies, applications and operating systems through its middle-ware role. This is in contrast to network operating systems, which *strictly* control the access to and utilization of resources, and usually require modifications to the OS, application, or security policy.

The MSHN RMS constructs task schedules based on a network infrastructure model. This model includes the resource and security requirements of current and waiting tasks, and the security and availability of network, computing and storage resources. The resulting schedules are provided to task handlers that run the tasks and provide feedback to the scheduler. If the model is inaccurate (e.g., security or resource availability changes), the RMS adjusts its model and potentially reschedules the tasks (see Figure 1).

RMS schedule construction consists of several logical phases, or steps:

1. In the reduction phase, the scheduler finds the *realizable* resource assignments for the task by discarding the possible assignments that will not work according to the model. In addition to resource availability matching (e.g., required service type vs. resource type), security plays a key role. Both the task and the resources are characterized by security requirements: those of the task must be met by a subset of the resources; those of the resources constrain the task. The task's security characteristics are compared to the minimum security requirements of the various resources and infrastructure components to determine where the task can run. Additionally, the task's minimum and maximum security requirements (e.g., reflecting the user's QoS security specification) are compared to the services available from the resources and infrastructure. The result is a set of resource-assignment "solutions," where each solution identifies various resources sufficient to run the task.

2. The resource usage costs, including costs for accessing security services, are derived for the various solutions.

3. In the optimization phase, an "optimum" solution is heuristically selected. The criteria for selection is to (attempt to) minimize costs and to maximize the QoS benefit to the users ([8] [9] [17]). More specifically, using realizable resources from the reduction phase, the scheduler attempts to create a schedule to meet QoS requirements for all of its tasks. In order to support as many tasks as possible, the scheduler must meet the typical task scheduling constraints while minimizing resource usage costs.

After step 3, some RMSs may make various network resource reservations. Finally, the task is submitted for execution.

If a particular security mechanism is "fixed" (i.e.,

Table 2: Security cost examples

Security Service	Service Area	Mechanism	Cost Measure
Data Confidentiality	NC	link layer 40-bit DES	Processor clocks per byte [14]
Message Non-Repudiation	ES	remote non-repudiation service	$2n$ bytes per message network bandwidth, plus c clocks per byte
Intrusion Detection	TS	experimental ID system	n Mbytes per second of overall bandwidth, plus m instructions per second, plus b bytes per second storage

always applied) then the overhead for the mechanism is part of the normal cost of running the task and the normal costing mechanism used by the RMS will suffice. For variant security mechanisms, however, the security overhead will vary, depending on the user's QoS request. For example, some task invocations will utilize little, if any, of the variant mechanism; other invocations may utilize the mechanism at an increased level; and, the scheduler may adapt security support (while maintaining any minimum system security policy requirements) in order to schedule the tasks most efficiently. The RMS must calculate how much the use of the security mechanism will increase the cost of the task, according to the specific security "level" requested. For this reason, the RMS must have access to detailed information about the resource cost (as well as the task's requested QoS) for each variant security mechanism. Near-optimal solution selection depends on the accurate estimation of per-task, per-resource, cost of security.

With respect to implementation, the RMS's costing information may be table-driven or algorithm-based, and the cost measurement scale may vary for each mechanism and resource (see Section 4.1, below).

4.1 Costing example

The security overhead for several security mechanisms is shown in Table 2.

The data confidentiality mechanism is a 40-bit DES encryption mechanism implemented in the link layer. For message non-repudiation, a commercial non-repudiation service mechanism is used. The cost of using this mechanism is a per-message exchange of n bytes with the remote non-repudiation server, and c clocks per message-byte to create the crypto-checksum for the message. The intrusion detection mechanism is shown to use a fixed overhead of the network bandwidth (e.g., for sampling and probing) along with constant processor and storage overhead

Costing information is provided to the scheduler, which will use these data and its current system model to select services, including those for security, that maximize the benefit for the collection of tasks it is serving [8].

5 Discussion and conclusion

A taxonomic framework has been presented for describing security services in terms of broad service categories, network "service areas," and security mechanisms. It has been shown that this taxonomy can be used for different purposes, including the specification of user Quality of Service requests, and the specification of security costs related to network tasks. With respect to Quality of Security Service, we have envisioned that users would be able to specify levels or ranges of desired security service, and as with other QoS parameters, could use these specifications to be able to trade off levels of task performance against requested levels of security.

Continued effort is required to determine the best units for the cost measures. For example, all measures could be unitless and normalized within a common framework. This approach would require a careful description of the semantics of the units with respect to each security service. Alternatively, units can be retained and the components combined into a "vector" to be used by the RMS scheduler.

Additionally, further work is required to expand the enumeration of specific security mechanisms with respect to the described taxonomy.

Acknowledgments

The authors wish to gratefully acknowledge partial support for this research from the DARPA/ITO program.

References

[1] Evaluation Criteria for IT Security, ISO/IEC CD 15408, Part 3: Security Assurance Requirements, November 1997. (commonly known as the *Common Criteria*)

[2] Foster, I., and Kesselman, C., Globus: A Metacomputing Infrastructure Toolkit. *International Journal of Supercomputer Applications*, 11(2):115-128, 1997.

[3] Foster, I, Kesselman, C., Tsudik, G., and Tuecke, S., A

Security Architecture for Computational Grids, *Proceedings of the Fifth Conference on Computer and Communications Security*, San Francisco, CA, 1998, pp. 83--92.

[4] Ford, W., Computer Communications Security, Englewood Cliffs, NJ: PTR Prentice Hall, 1994, page 22.

[5] Hensgen, D., Kidd, T., St. John, D., Schnaidt, M.C., Siegel, H. J., Braun, T. Maheswaran, M., Ali, S., Kim, J-K., Irvine, C. E., Levin, T., Freund, R., Kussow, M., Godfrey, M., Duman, A., Carff, P., Kidd, S., Prasanna, V. Bhat, P., and Alhusaini, A., "An Overview of the Management System for Heterogeneous Networks (MSHN)," *Proceedings of the 8th Workshop on Heterogeneous Computing Systems (HCW '99)*, San Juan, Puerto Rico, Apr. 1999, pp 184-198.

[6] Irvine, C., and Levin, T., A Note on Mapping User-Oriented Security Policies to Complex Mechanisms and Services, Naval Postgraduate School Technical Report, NPS-CS-99-008, June 1999.

[7] Juneman, R. R., Novel Certificate Extension Attributes--Novel Security Attributes: Tutorial and Detailed Design. Version 0.998, Novell, Inc. 122 East 1700 St., Provo, UT, August 1997.

[8] Kim, Jong-Kook, Hensgen, D., Kidd, T., Siegel, H.J., St.John, D., Irvine, C., Levin, T., Porter, N.W., Prasanna, V., and Freund, R., A QoS Performance Measure Framework for Distributed Heterogeneous Networks, to appear in *Proceedings of the 8th Euromicro Workshop on Parallel and Distributed Processing*, Rhodos, Greece, January 2000.

[9] Levin, T., and Irvine C., Quality of Security Service in a Resource Management System Benefit Function, NPS Technical Report, Forthcoming

[10] Litzkow, M. Livney, M., and Murtka, M. Condor: *A Hunter of Idle Workstations. In Proceedings of the 8th International Conference on Distributed Computing Systems*, San Jose, CA, June 1998, pp 104-111.

[11] Ostriker, J., and Norman. M. L., *Cosmology of the Early Universe Viewed Through the New Infrastructure.* C.A.C.M. 40(11):85-94.

[12] Pfleeger, C., Security in Computing, Prentice Hall PTR, Upper Saddle River, NJ, 1997, page 4.

[13] Sabata, B. Chatterjee, S., Davis, M., Sydir, J., and Lawrence, T., "Taxonomy for QoS Specifications," *Proceedings of the IEEE Computer Society 3rd International Workshop on Object-oriented Real-time Dependable Systems (WORDS '97)*, Newport Beach, CA, Feb 1997.

[14] Schneier, B., Kelsey, J., Whiting, D., Wagner, D., Hall, C., Twofish: A 128-Bit Block Cipher, Counterpane Systems, http://www.counterpane.com/twofish-paper.html, June, 1998.

[15] Stallings, W., Network and Internetwork Security, Prentice Hall, Englewood Cliffs, NJ, 1995, page 5.

[16] Stern, D. F., On the Buzzword "Security Policy", *Proceedings of 1991 IEEE Symposium on Security and Privacy*, Oakland, Ca., May 1991, pp. 219-230.

[17] Vendatasubramanian, N. and Nahrstedt, K., "An Integrated Metric for Video QoS." *ACM International Multimedia Conference*, Seattle, Wa., Nov. 1997.

[18] Wang, C., and Wulf, W.A., Towards a Framework for Security Measurement, *Proceedings of the Twentieth National Information Systems Security Conference*, Baltimore, MD, October 1997, pp. 522-533.

TrustedBox: a Kernel-Level Integrity Checker

Pietro Iglio
Fondazione Ugo Bordoni
Rome, Italy
e-mail: iglio@fub.it

Abstract

There is a large number of situations in which computer security is unpopular. In fact, common users do not like too much restricted security policies. Usability is often preferred to security. Many users want to be free to use their computers to run untrusted applications. Moreover, it is not possible to require that every computer user is a security expert. As a consequence, it is very easy for hackers to gain access to a computer system, and to perform a number of unauthorized operations.

In this paper we focus on the problem of system integrity. There are some applications in which system integrity is at least as important as privacy and service availability. For this purpose, we have designed and implemented TrustedBox, a kernel-level integrity checker that can be used to enforce a very restricted security policy and that allows users to use the same system to perform untrusted operations.

1 Introduction

Nowadays an increasing amount of critical tasks are carried out using computer systems. For this reason, computer security is, and will be, a primary goal in many modern commercial and governmental organizations. A lot of work has been done in recent years to protect systems against different kinds of attacks.

In spite of the progress in the field of computer security, there are some real life situations in which users are not protected enough when they carry out critical operations.

The main reason is that, in general, common users are not computer security experts. In most situations, they are not even computer experts. Such a lack of expertise is really helpful for hackers, because common users can hardly realize that the system has been compromised.

Moreover, a restricted security policy is often impractical because it would limit too much the usability of the system. In many organizations there is the need of using the same personal computer to edit documents, to surf the Web, to exchange e-mail, to run multimedia applications, and to perform critical tasks.

For example, it is a common practice to use the same personal computer to run untrusted applications (such as applications downloaded from the network) and to buy products through sites offering e-commerce services. This common practice can be very dangerous, for several hacker's toolkits are widely available through the Internet. By using these toolkits, hackers could break into systems and replace critical operating system components to gain remote control of the system and to leave hidden backdoors for future access.

NetBus [NTB] and BackOrifice [BKO] are just two examples of software tools that can be used by hackers to have the complete control of the victim's personal computer. Such programs can infect any computer running Windows™ 95 and Windows™ NT by installing themselves as hidden system components. On many hacker Web sites it is explained how to use any executable program as a *trojan horse* to infect a Windows system using NetBus or BackOrifice. Some software tools are even publicly available to simplify this task. Once the system has been infected, hackers can remotely read all keystrokes, read and upload files, etc. on the infected machine.

Similarly, tools such as Rootkit [VEN] can be used to attack UNIX™ systems and to install modified versions of critical system components in such a way that it is very hard to detect their presence.

Companies pushing on e-commerce services advertise the absolute security of all communications with their servers because they are using strong encryption. Nevertheless, they never say that encryption is useless if the client has been compromised. Therefore, most users do not even know that their system could be remotely controlled by a hacker that, bypassing all cryptographic protections, could read all keystrokes, including passwords, credit card number, and so on.

In this work we focus on system integrity. There is a number of situations in which compromising critical system components, application or data can cause serious damages. For example, there are some countries in which the digital signature legislation states that digital signatures can be used to sign legal statements, such as contracts or commercial agreements. In these countries, a compromised system running a modified version of the digital signature software run by a manager could lead to loss of money or other kinds of troubles. Similarly, a compromised Web server serving hacked pages could seriously damage the public image of a company.

In Section 2, we discuss the problem of protecting a user against a compromised system. First, we go through some typical approaches to the problem. Then, we explain why those approaches are still unsatisfactory to ensure a high-level of protection against experienced intruders. In Section 3, we present our solution. Details about the implementation are provided in Section 4. In Section 5 and Section 6, respectively, we show some examples of applications and we discuss some limitations of our solution. In Section 7, we compare our work with other existing solutions. Finally, we summarize our future plans and finish with our conclusions.

2 Is What You See What You Think It Is?

In the past years computer systems have constantly grown in complexity. About fifteen years ago personal computers were equipped with a very simple hardware and a primitive, single-task operating system that could run in a few kilobytes of memory. The number of users performing critical tasks by means of such systems was very low.

A modern personal computer is likely to have tens of applications installed, several gigabytes of hard disk storage, and hundreds of system components spread across the file system. Most operating systems are able to run more applications at the same time, and are based on an open architecture to be easily extended. Similarly, even the simplest application can have a very complex structure and be made of several components spread out in the system.

As a consequence, it is very hard to detect what is really going on when the system is running. From a user's point of view, the computing environments look simpler to use because of the progress of graphical user interfaces. The drawback is that a modern system is much more complex than those in use fifteen years ago. Of course, as complexity increases security is harder to enforce.

Even if a system is very carefully configured and a good security policy is somehow enforced, a single mistake made by an inexperienced user or, worse, by the system administrator could compromise the security of the whole system, or some parts of it. A single access to the system by an untrusted entity is sufficient to hide fraudulent code in the meanders of the system.

The basic problem is that, while much effort has been made to protect the system by unauthorized users, not too much care has been taken for the converse. Almost all modern operating systems provide authentication and access control mechanisms. However, to the best of our knowledge, there is no widely used operating system that provides a built-in mechanism for the user to authenticate the operating system itself, its critical components, and all running applications.

Common users, for example, are used to "authenticate" applications through their user interface. Nobody, of course, looks at the binary code of an application to check that the application itself is doing exactly what it has to do. How can users be sure that they are not performing critical operations on a compromised system?

Many solutions have been proposed to address this problem. A number of currently available tools, generally referred to as *audit tools*, fall into the following categories:

- **integrity checkers**: programs that compute a cryptographic signature for each critical system component or application, and compare the signature against a previously created database.
- **anti-virus programs**: programs that try to identify and block infecting programs by inspecting the content of files coming from an external source (e.g., a diskette or the network). They try to match the content of files with strings of bits from a database of known viruses.
- **static audit tools**: programs that check for system misconfiguration.

Note that some tools fall in more than one category. For example, some anti-virus programs include integrity checking capabilities.

We claim that none of the above approaches provides a satisfactory solution to the problem of protecting systems used to perform highly critical tasks.

A suitable configured integrity checking tool should always be used in a situation in which we want to be sure that a system configuration does not change over the time. Such tools can be used for monitoring the executable programs of the operating system, configuration files, and applications. The problem is that most of them do not perform continuous monitoring, but they have to be periodically run by the administrator. They can be useful to discover that a file has been modified, but they cannot prevent using modified files.

The limit of anti-virus programs is that they can successfully recognize only known computer viruses, or some known behavioral patterns (e.g., attempts to

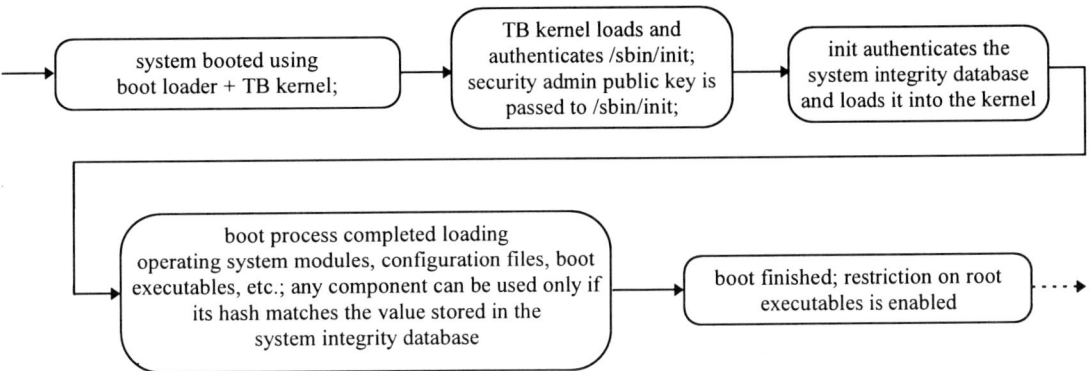

Figure 1: TrustedBox kernel boot process

replace the boot sector). They are not guaranteed to work against new and still-not-classified viruses. Most of anti-virus programs, for example, can detect BackOrifice and NetBus, but they would probably fail to detect variants of those spy programs.

Similarly, static audit tools provide a valuable help to discover some known attacks, but they can do nothing if the attack has not been classified yet. Another problem is that many of them do not perform continuous monitoring, but they need to be run by the system administrator. Finally, we must say that such tools do not generally check whether an application has been compromised.

In addition to the above problems, most audit tools suffer from an inherent limitation: they rely on the underlying operating system. An experienced hacker could replace or intercept critical system calls to deceive an auditing tool. For example, it could be possible to change the *open* system call in such a way that when the auditing tool requests a compromised file, the system call returns the original version of the file. Even better, the compromised operating system could intercept all user requests for the execution of the audit tool and run a fake version of the audit tool itself.

It is possible to compromise the operating system in a number of ways. Once an intruder or a trojan horse has gained *superuser* privileges, there is nothing to do, even using active audit tools. Everything that runs before the audit tool is executed could attack the audit tool itself. For example, the system administrator has generally enough power to kill any process, and to replace any executable program. Thus, if we assume that no encrypted file system is used on the victim's computer, then an intruder that gains physical access to the system could install the hard drive or another system, and modify any audit tool by using a raw disk editing tool.

3 The TrustedBox Approach

The solution we describe is suitable for a large number of situations in which users do not need to perform unsafe and critical operations at the same time. Such situations are fairly common: some users use their personal computer most of the day to write documents and, occasionally, they have to issue digital signatures; a company Web server running is performing a critical task (i.e. serving "official" Web pages approved by the company itself), and sometimes the Web master has to update pages and perform administrative tasks.

Under these circumstances, the TrustedBox approach has the following advantages:

- users can be effectively protected against highly motivated individuals that could somehow replace any file in the file system;
- users can use the same system, at different times, both for unsafe operations and highly critical tasks;
- the role of the security administrator is separated from the role of the system administrator; the system administrator does not even need to be a trusted entity;
- it is possible to enforce a restricted security policy for critical tasks;
- there is no need to modify existing applications to be aware of new security mechanisms;
- there is no need to keep a system used for critical tasks in a secure location with restricted access;
- it is inexpensive and practical;

We distinguish two security policies, a *relaxed policy* and a *restricted policy*, corresponding to two system states, the *untrusted state* and the *trusted state*.

When in untrusted state, the security policy could be relaxed in favor of usability. Users could have permission to download and run unsafe applications from the network, to enable dangerous network services, to allow system access to other users, and so on. In real life, it is very common that users have such requirements for their activity.

It is obvious, however, that a system running in untrusted state can be easily compromised. For this reason, users are required to switch to the trusted state when they have to perform critical tasks. To enter in trusted mode the user has to shutdown the system and boot with a *TrustedBox kernel* (TB kernel). This is necessary because any part of the system could have been modified, including the operating system itself.

A TB kernel is based on a regular kernel that has be modified to enforce the restricted policy. Our prototype is based on a UNIX kernel, but most concepts apply to other operating systems as well.

The TrustedBox kernel has been previously stored on bootable media (e.g. a diskette) that must be kept from the user in a safe place. The TB kernel contains a minimal kernel required to boot the system and access the file system. Note that the integrity of the whole system relies on the integrity of the boot media.

Once the kernel has been loaded, it verifies the integrity of the /sbin/init executable. Under the UNIX operating system, /sbin/init is the first program that is run at boot-time by the kernel, and it is responsible to complete the boot process. The integrity of /sbin/init is verified comparing its message-digest with the corresponding message-digest stored on the boot media.

When /sbin/init is launched, the TB kernel passes the public key of the security administrator as a command line option:

/sbin/init -pk *public-key*

Note that the public key is stored on the boot media, therefore it comes from a trusted source. The modified version of init uses the public-key to authenticate the *system integrity database*, a database containing the message-digest of all critical files, including executables, kernel modules, configuration files, etc.

Next, init loads the system integrity database into the kernel and continues a normal boot process. Kernel modules can be loaded, services started, and so on. However, since we are starting a trusted system that is stored on an untrusted file system (except the boot kernel), every single component is authenticated using the message-digest from the system integrity database. If the message-digest for a file does not match the value stored in the system database, the kernel refuses to open the file.

The diagram in figure 1 summarizes the trusted boot process. In the rest of this section we describe the restrict security policy that can be enforced using the TB kernel, plus some other details.

3.1 Security Policy in Trusted Mode

The TB kernel distinguishes between *trusted files* (i.e. files listed in the system integrity database) and *untrusted files* (the remaining files). In addition to the standard security mechanisms of the underlying operating system, the TB kernel imposes a number of restrictions concerning program execution and file system access. In particular, an application can be executed if and only if:

- the user is authorized to run the application, according to the standard security mechanisms of the underlying operating system;
- the application is listed in the system integrity database;
- the application message-digest matches the message-digest stored in the system integrity database;

Furthermore, an application can be executed with *superuser* privileges if and only if it meets the above requirements and is marked with the *super* option in the system integrity database. This restriction has been added because applications running with *superuser* privileges are so powerful that can bypass many security mechanisms, especially on UNIX systems. The security administrator can limit to the minimum the set of *superuser* applications that can be executed in trusted mode setting the *super* option only for the applications required to perform the critical tasks. It is possible, for example, to not permit the execution of any shell with root permission. Note that this is a strong restriction to the common operating system policy, where the *superuser* can execute every application.

Since some applications may need to run with root privileges during the boot process (e.g. /bin/sh can be needed to start some daemons), the restriction on the execution of *superuser* applications must be explicitly enabled using a new system call, *tbox_set_state*. Such system call is used to raise the TB state from *booting*, that is the initial state, to *running*, that is the normal state in which the user works.

A correctly configured system should raise the execution state to *running* once the boot process has been completed to enable the restriction on executables that run with root permission.

Note that the system call has been implemented in such a manner that, once the state has been raised to *running*, it cannot be changed for the rest of the session.

As far as non-executable files are concerned, the policy is slightly different. The TB kernel authorizes a regular process to open a file with *read* permission if and only if:

- the file does not appear in the system integrity database (i.e. it is an *untrusted file*);

or

- the file appears in the system integrity database and its message-digest matches the digest in the configuration file;

Permission to open untrusted files is granted so that it is possible to run a large number of applications that work on newly generated files or access to files modified during the trusted session. For example, a linker needs to access files created by a compiler. Since such files have been created during the current trusted session, they are not stored in the system integrity database (that must exist at boot time). Note that, unlike regular files, executable files can be only executed if they exist at boot time.

The authorization to open untrusted files can lead to security problems in some circumstances. For example, if our application needs a *perl* interpreter to run, once we must authorize the execution of the *perl* interpreter in trusted mode. In this way, it would be possible to execute any *perl* script, because the execution of a script, from a kernel point of view, corresponds to an "open" operation (and not to an "execution" operation). However, we want to have a strict control on the set of programs that can be executed (regardless of the fact that they are binary programs or scripts). To address this issue, an entry in the system integrity database for an executable program can be marked with a special flag, *open_only_trusted*, and the following rule holds:

- the TB kernel authorizes a process marked with a *open_only_trusted* flag to open a file for reading if and only if the file appears in the system integrity database and its message-digest matches the digest in the configuration file;

The last constraint allows the security administrator to safely authorize the execution of interpreters, because it enormously reduces the risk that users run *trojan horses* hidden inside untrusted scripts.

It is easy to understand that the TB kernel strongly relies on the integrity of any executable, library, configuration files etc. that is used when the system is in trusted state. For this reason, the TB kernel rule imposes this additional restriction:

- it is not possible to change any file, executable or not, that appears in the system integrity database;

As far as directories are concerned, it is possible to sign the content of a directory, i.e. to sign the listing of a directory at a given time. A directory listed in the system integrity database is said to be a *trusted directory*. Here are the limitations imposed by the TB kernel for trusted directories:

- it is not possible to change the content of a trusted directory (e.g. adding or removing files from that directory);
- it is not possible to open for listing a trusted directory whose signature does not match the value stored in the system integrity database;
- a trusted directory can only contain trusted files and other trusted directories;

The signature of a directory is useful to avoid any change to the boot process. Under many UNIX systems, in fact, the boot process is carried out running all programs belonging to some special directories (e.g. /etc/rc.d). The security administrator can "sign" a particular boot process signing these directories and all contained executables.

Finally, for any operation not mentioned here, the normal access control policy of the operating system is applied.

4 Implementation Details

As a proof of concept, we have developed an experimental prototype of the TB kernel based on a modified version of the Linux kernel. The prototype is not meant to be a complete and highly-secure implementation, but it is useful to evaluate the usability of a system running in trusted state. At the time of writing, the prototype does not implement integrity checking for directories and other minor details.

A substantial work has been done on the Linux kernel to change the semantics of some system calls (*open* and *execve*) and to add new system calls. The changes to the Linux kernel can be summarized as follows:

- an implementation of the SHA algorithm has been added at kernel level;

```
fb0347750f82b8bff5684f11fc586ebddd919878   /sbin/init
b1b67ad426bc408d68cb817aece75effde1533b3   /etc/syslog.conf
3dd6a70d8bec298033808cf9647c664043a7e91e   /etc/rc.d/
71c31f59ae2896a3ff6ca6e7092eece0f2db2bf3   /bin/ping super
ec636b4c89a82b5c239e3bcaf8ccce6c4d19e042   /mnt/nfs/data always
a09d4e2eef5b4014d8987fee1696749556e04e8c   /usr/bin/perl super, open_only_trusted
```

Figure 2: Example of system integrity database entries

- a new boot-time parameter has been added; the new parameter is used to pass the message-digest of the system integrity database to the kernel;
- the *open* and the *execve* system calls have been modified to implement the policy described in the previous section;
- a system call, *add_sid_entry*, has been added; this system call is used by the *trusted_init* program to load the system integrity database into the TB kernel;
- a new system call, *tbox_set_state*, has been added to enable the restriction on root executables;

Furthermore, we have obtained the *trusted-init* program modifying the normal *init* program to accept an extra parameter (the security administrator public key), authenticate the system integrity database and to load it into the kernel. In particular:

- the TB kernel runs *trusted-init* passing the public key stored on the trusted boot media;
- *trusted-init* passes the public key to a cryptographic module that verifies the signature of the system integrity database. The cryptographic module is statically linked, to avoid trusting external libraries or programs;
- *trusted-init* repeatedly invokes the *add_sid_entry* system call to pass each entry to the TB kernel;
- after that the last entry has been passed to the TB kernel, *trusted-init* calls *add_sid_entry* passing a special parameter that stops the kernel from accepting further entries. In this way, it is not possible for other programs to add new entries that are not stored in the system integrity database;
- *trusted-init* completes the normal boot process;
- after the boot process has been completed, the following invocation:

```
tbox_set_state(TBOX_STATE_RUNNING);
```

enables the restriction to run as root only executables that have been marked with the *super* flag.

The signature of the system integrity database is verified using a publicly available implementation of the RSA algorithm [RSA] using a MD5 hash algorithm. Of course, any other algorithm can be used with minimal changes, according to the security requirements of a particular application.

The boot diskette is prepared copying on it the TB kernel and the Linux Loader (LILO). Since the security administrator public key is too long to be passed as a kernel parameter, it has been hard-coded into the TB kernel. Currently, this requires that the kernel is partially re-compiled when the public key is changed. Changing the public key, however, should not happen frequently. However, we have planned the development of maintenance tools to simplify the process of storing the public key on the boot media.

The system integrity database is stored into a text file, /etc/sysintdb. A system integrity database entry has the following format:

```
hash filepath [super][always][open_only_trusted]
```

The `hash` value is an ASCII representation of the message-digest for `filepath`. The optional `super` keyword means that the file can be executed with root privileges. This keyword is meaningless if the file has no execute permission. The `always` keyword can be optionally specified to force integrity verification every time the file is open. This keyword is related to an optimization that is explained in the subsection "Performance Improvements". Finally, the `open_only_trusted` keyword is used to specify that the executable file can access only files listed in the system integrity database.

Some sample entries are shown in figure 2. The cryptographic signature of the system integrity database is stored into the /etc/sysintdb.sig file.

4.1 Performance Improvements

Invoking a message-digest calculation for each *open* and *execve* system call invocation introduces a performance overhead, since these system calls are used very frequently. In order to greatly reduce this overhead, we have adopted the following optimization: each file to be authenticated is authenticated only the first time it is accessed. Then the file is marked, for the rest of the trusted session, as *authenticated*. No other checks will be performed after that the file is marked as *authenticated* until the next system shutdown.

Note that, since it is not possible to open for changes a file listed in the system integrity database, the authenticated file will not change its contents for the whole session. However, it is possible to disable this optimization for some files specifying the `always` keyword in the system integrity database. In such case, the file will be checked at each access.

Further performance improvements could be gained using a faster implementation of the SHA algorithm, or a faster message-digest algorithm. Performance, however, was a secondary issue respect to security for the kinds of applications we had in mind during the design of TrustedBox.

5 Examples of Applications

As explained in the previous sections, TrustedBox provides a valuable help to run applications in a trusted environment without using dedicated machines with a very restricted and controlled access. Once the system has been correctly configured, it can be used even by inexpert users without too many restrictions. Their only responsibility is to perform highly critical tasks in trusted mode and to keep the boot media in a secure place.

An example of application in which TrustedBox can be really helpful to solve a lot of security and administrative issues is the generation of digital signatures. We can imagine the following scenario: a number of users in the same organization use digital signatures to sign critical documents, such as financial transactions or contracts. The same users, however, use their personal computers for other tasks, such as word-processing, e-mail exchange and Internet surfing.

The scenario described is very common, as digital signature is becoming very popular in many modern organizations. A security administrator is responsible to set up, on a isolated machine (disconnected from the network and running in single-user mode), a safe environment with the minimum set of applications required for the trusted mode. The safe environment can include, for example, a document viewer (such as a HTML browser), a smart-card driver and a software to digitally sign documents.

After that all the software has been carefully verified, the security administrator can use the appropriate maintenance tools to create the system integrity database and the boot diskettes that will be distributed to all employees.

The system administrator can than install the trusted configuration, along with the system integrity database, and all network connected machines that need to run the trusted environment. As previously pointed out, the security administrator and the system administrator can be two different entities, and the system administrator could even be untrusted. Once users have got their boot media, in fact, the integrity of the subsystem used for critical operations will be automatically checked.

There is no way the system administrator can install a modified configuration (assuming that the safe configuration has been correctly chosen, of course).

Users can now perform their regular tasks booting in untrusted mode: for example, they can edit documents and download documents to be signed from the network. Periodically, e.g. twice a day, they boot in trusted mode, view the documents with the authenticated viewer, and sign them using a smart-card.

Note that in a similar scenario the responsibility of the system administrator is greatly reduced. He must not keep under constant monitoring a large number of critical workstations and, on the other hand, users don't have to trust the system administrator when they sign critical documents. As far as users preserve the integrity of the boot media, there is no need to prevent physical access to their workstations when they are not running in trusted mode.

Another situation in which TrustedBox can be worth using is for running specialized servers, i.e. servers running a restricted number of applications. Examples are critical Web servers or firewalls. Running a system like a Web server in trusted mode could greatly limit the potential damage by an intruder that gains unauthorized access to the system. In the past months, for example, a number of Web sites have been hacked. A typical attack consists of a replacement of some Web pages with a modified version of the same pages. This kind of attack can seriously damage the credibility of a large organization.

If a TB kernel is used to run the Web server and the Web pages are added to the system integrity database, it would be virtually impossible to bypass the kernel-level imposed restrictions to modify trusted files.

Likewise, it would be really hard to modify the configuration of a firewall that runs on the top of a TB kernel. A security company could install and configure firewalls whose configuration cannot be modified even by the customer. In this way, it should be possible to avoid a potential dispute about a firewall misconfiguration, since the firewall could only run with the provided configuration.

6 Limitations of TrustedBox

Despite the valuable help of TrustedBox in the protection of system integrity, it has some inherent limitations.

From a security point of view, one of the most fundamental limitations is that TrustedBox does not authenticate the hardware and the firmware. In particular the software that is executed when the system starts up and that is responsible for starting the boot process (called BIOS on Intel-based machines), cannot be authenticated, as it is loaded before the kernel.

If the hardware or the firmware is compromised, in fact, the user cannot be sure that the kernel that is loaded upon start up is the trusted kernel that is stored on the boot diskette. Latest personal computers have a software upgradable BIOS, and several computer viruses do significant damage overwriting the system BIOS. Thus, a possible attack to the TrustedBox system could be done replacing the system BIOS with a modified version that, for example, performs a different bootstrap process. Since the authentication starts only after that the kernel has been loaded, there is no authentication of the underlying layers.

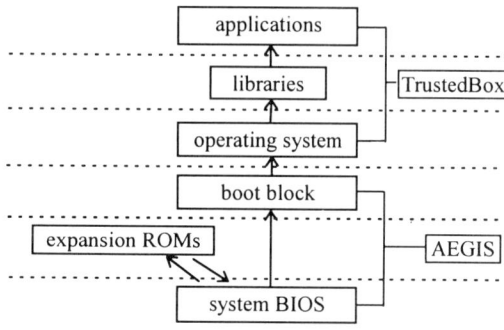

Figure 3: TrustedBox and the AEGIS architecture

This problem is discussed and addressed in [ARB], that proposes a secure bootstrap architecture. The secure bootstrap process, called AEGIS, ensures the integrity of the bootstrap code computing a cryptographic hash for the system BIOS, any other firmware (eg. graphic card and disk controllers) and the boot sector. The hash values are compared with a signature associated with each component and stored on a read-only memory. AEGIS relies on a trusted system ROM, containing the verification code and the cryptographic certificates. A basic assumption, of course, is that no unauthorized user can access the system motherboard and replace the ROM.

Since AEGIS addresses the problem of validating any layer that is not checked by TrustedBox, it is possible to say that using both of them on the same system would be a great security enhancement. In this scenario, AEGIS would be responsible for ensuring the integrity of the firmware bootstrap process, and TrustedBox would ensure the integrity of the operating system during the rest of the boot process and when the system is running, as shown in figure 3.

Another security problem with TrustedBox is that it can be subject to denial-of-service attacks. If an intruder changes or removes any signed executable file, for example, the system will not execute that file in trusted mode. However, this is a minor problem if compared to the damage of running a compromised executable during critical tasks. The system administrator should keep a backup copy of any signed file to quickly recover a compromised system. Alternatively, it could be possible to use same solution discussed for the AEGIS architecture in [ARB2]. This solution is based on a trusted repository, that can either be an expansion ROM board that contains verified copies of the required software, or it can be a network host. In the case of TrustedBox, the network host solution could be used, using a protocol with strong authentication to ensure the integrity of transferred data.

Another possible attack to a TrustedBox system could be performed modifying the warm-reboot procedure of the operating system in untrusted state. In fact, a compromised operating system could "pretend" that is doing a warm-reboot and that it is loading the TB kernel. As a consequence, the user could erroneously believe that the system is in trusted state and could perform critical tasks while the compromised system is running. For this reason, we strongly recommend that the trusted mode boot should be only performed after a complete system power-off. Unfortunately, we do not know any way to impose that users enter in trusted mode after a cold-boot.

Finally, there is a potential security problem due to the need to allow users booting from an external media. In many situations users are not permitted to boot a system from a diskette, as they could boot with an operating system that allows to access the file system bypassing all security checks. Since we cannot impose this restriction, one possible solution is to use TrustedBox in combination with a cryptographic file system, such as [CFS], or using a special boot device, as explained in the Section "Future Works". Another possible solution is the usage of a modified system BIOS that authenticates the boot media, so that it is not possible to bootstrap with a different operating system.

From a practical point of view, a major problem is the need to reboot the system to enter in trusted mode.

This could be a serious problem if the activity requires a frequent switch between critical tasks and non-critical tasks. This is an inherent limitation of our approach, that does not fit very well in such situations.

It could be possible to set up a configuration file to run as many applications as possible in trusted mode, but there are some tasks that cannot be performed with such a restricted security policy. One example is software development: it is not possible to compile and run applications in trusted mode, because any binary generated during the trusted session cannot appear in the configuration file and, thus, cannot be executed. A trusted session, however, could be used to compile secure applications or set up safe scripts without running them.

7 Existing Solutions

Many available security tools try to address the problem of system integrity. One of the most popular in the UNIX world is probably Tripwire [KIM]. Tripwire helps the system administrator to detect file tampering by comparing the cryptographic signature of each protected file against a signature stored in a database. Several signature algorithms can be chosen, including MD5 [MD5], MD4 [MD4] and SHA [SHA]. To prevent the database from being altered, the authors suggest to store it on some tamper-proof media. Similar tools are ATP [ATP], that employs a dual signature (32-bit CRC and MD5) to verify files, and Binaudit [BSP].

COPS is an intrusion detection tool that checks a UNIX host for well known vulnerabilities in the system set up. It focuses on things like inappropriate permissions set on files and directories, missing or inadequate password security, potentially dangerous *setuid* programs and similar problems. After its release, COPS has been extended to include an integrity checker, the *crc_check* program, based on a simple CRC checksum of the files being monitored.

As previously pointed out, a main disadvantage of such tools is that they rely on the integrity of the operating system and other critical programs. Even if such tools are stored on a read-only media, it is very simple, for example, to modify the source code of any public domain shell to trap any invocation of /usr/bin/cops or /usr/bin/tripwire and execute a tampered version of such tools. Another disadvantage is that traditional tools have to be run periodically and they cannot guarantee a constant integrity of the system. Therefore, such tools are a valuable help to detect tampering after it happens, rather than preventing it. As explained in the previous sections, the TrustedBox approach provides a constant monitoring of the system during the execution in trusted mode.

Domain and Type Enforcement (DTE) [WAL] is an access control technology that aims to minimize the damage root programs can cause if subverted. An operating system providing DTE can be configured to enforce a restricted security policy to confine root programs in domains from which they can access only a subset of system objects (files, devices, etc.). Some implementations of DTE are available, for example as extensions of a UNIX kernel. A drawback of the DTE approach is that, to be effective, some system applications should be modified to fully take advantage of DTE mechanisms.

Since DTE does not address the problem of system integrity, its approach is complementary to the TrustedBox approach. An implementation of DTE in a TB kernel could be useful to better define a restricted security policy required to carry out critical tasks.

An example of security application that is based on two different kernels is Sidewinder™ [THO]. Sidewinder™ is an Internet firewall based on a modified version of BDS-OS UNIX that includes DTE. It uses an operational kernel, with DTE enabled, and an administrative kernel, in which security policy checks are bypassed. System maintenance tasks are performed under the administrative kernel, that can be started by a user that is "physically" connected to the system and only after shutting down the operational kernel.

The difference between the Sidewinder and the TrustedBox approach is that the Sidewinder system administrator has to be trusted. This because any software modified or installed by the system administrator working in administrative mode will be executed in operational mode. Using TrustedBox, instead, nobody but the security administrator can alter the configuration that will be used in trusted mode. Only the security administrator can authorize changes to the system issuing a digital signature for the system integrity database. The Sidewinder approach can be good for a firewall, that is normally not accessed by untrusted users, whereas our approach is suitable for systems that are normally used to run untrusted applications.

8 Future Works

We are actively working on our prototype of the TrustedBox kernel to fully implement all discussed issues. Furthermore, we aim to provide administrative tools to simplify the task of the security administrator, to update the system integrity database, to create the trusted boot diskette and to set up an appropriate security policy.

An interesting future direction would be the integration of the TrustedBox approach with other kernel-level solutions to improve UNIX security, such as DTE and capabilities [MOR]. Also, we are planning the integration of TrustedBox with the AEGIS architecture, discussed in section 6.

Finally, we are investigating the possibility to use special boot devices, such as PCMCIA cards, to both authenticate the user that performs the system boot and to reduce the risk that the boot media is tampered. The firmware should authenticate the PCMCIA card, load the TB kernel from the PCMCIA card and start a regular boot process. The PCMCIA card would also be safer than a traditional diskette to store the trusted boot media, but with the drawback of additional hardware costs.

9 Conclusions

We have designed and implemented a secure operating environment that can run on the top of an untrusted file system to perform highly critical tasks in a safe manner.

Thanks to its mechanisms to define a restricted security policy, a well configured system running in trusted mode is much harder to attack compared to a conventional system, especially for intruders that aim at modifying the system configuration or replacing system components. On the other hand, the only user responsibility is to start the system with a trusted boot media.

If the security administrator and the system administrator are distinct entities, furthermore, users do not have to trust the system administrator, as normally happens.

The ability to boot in untrusted mode or in trusted mode, so that the same system can be used both for unsafe and secure operations, makes TrustedBox a very interesting and inexpensive solution for a large number of application fields.

Digital signature systems and secure servers are just two cases in which TrustedBox could be adopted, but it would be very easy to think about a number of similar situations.

References

[WAL] Walker K. M. et al., "Confining Root Programs with Domain Type Enforcement (DTE)", in Proceedings of Sixth USENIX Security Symposium, San Jose (California), 1996.

[KIM] Kim G. H., Spafford E. H., "The Design and Implementation of Tripwire: a File System Integrity Checker", in Proceedings of 2nd ACM Conference on Computer and Communications Security, 1994.

[BDG] Badger L. et al, "A Domain and Type Enforcement UNIX Prototype", USENIX Computing Systems, Vol 9, No. 1, 1996.

[THO] Thomsen D. J., "Sidewinter: Combining Type Enforcement and UNIX", Proc. 11th Computer Security Application Conference, Orlando (FL), 1995.

[VEN] Venema W., "Root Kit", Presentation at SURFnet CERT-NL SGC-SEC/SSC Workshop, May 1995.

[FAR] Farmer D., "The COPS Security Checker System", Proceedings of the Summer 1990 USENIX Conference, Anaheim, CA, p. 165.

[ATP] D. Vincenzetti, M. Cotrozzi, "ATP anti tampering program", proceedings of the Security IV Conference, Berkeley, CA, 1993. USENIX Association.

[BSP] M. Bishop, "Auditing files on a network of machines", Security Workshop, USENIX, 1988.

[ARB] Arbaugh W. A., Farber D. J., Smith J. M., "A Secure and Reliable Bootstrap Architecture", in Proceedings of IEEE Symposium on Security and Privacy, Oakland (California), 1997.

[ARB2] Arbaugh W. A., Farber D. J., Smith J. M., "Automated Recovery in a Secure Bootstrap Process", Internet Society Symposium on Network and Distributed System Security (SNDSS) in San Diego, March 11-13,1998.

[SHA] National Institute for Standards and Technology, "Secure Hash Standard", Federal Information Processing Standards Publication 180, Government Printing Office, Washington, D.C., 1993.

[MD4] Rivest R. L., "The MD4 message digest algorithm", Advances in Cryptology – Crypto '90, 1991.

[MD5] Rivest R. L., "RFC 1321: The MD5 message-digest algorithm", technical report, Internet Activities Board, April 1992.

[RSA] R. L. Rivest, A. Shamir and L. Adelman, "A method for obtaining digital signatures and public-key cryptosystem", Commun. Of ACM, Vol. 21, No. 2, pp. 120-126, Feb. 1978.

[CFS] M. Blaze. "A Cryptographic File System for UNIX", proc. 1st ACM Conference on Computer and Communications Security, Fairfax, VA, November 1993.

[MOR] A. G. Morgan, "Linux-Privs",
http://www.kernel.org/pub/linux/libs/security/linux-privs/doc/linux-privs.html/linux-privs.html

[NTB] NetBus: a remote administration and spy tool,
http://www.netbus.org

[BKO] Back Orifice Windows Remote Administration Tool,
http://www.cultdeadcow.com/tools/bo.html

Adding Availability to Log Services of Untrusted Machines

A. Arona, D. Bruschi, E. Rosti
Dipartimento di Scienze dell'Informazione
Università degli Studi di Milano
Via Comelico 39/41, 20135 Milano – Italy
{*arona, bruschi, rosti*}@*dsi.unimi.it*

Abstract

Uncorrupted log files are the critical system component for computer forensics in case of intrusion and for real time system monitoring and auditing. Protection from tampering with information can be achieved using cryptographic functions that provide authenticity, integrity, and confidentiality. However, they cannot provide the prerequisite for any further information processing, i.e., information availability. In this case, fault tolerant strategies can be of great help improving information availability in case of accidental or deliberate deletion.

In this paper we propose a system that increases log files availability in case of software deletion by reliably and efficiently distributing the logs on multiple independent machines. The proposed scheme is more efficient than simple replication, both from the storage space and the network bandwidth points of view. The proposed system has been implemented and its impact on performance has been measured. Since it operates as a postprocessor after log generation, the proposed system can be easily integrated with logging systems that provide various cryptographic functions for forensic purposes.

1. Introduction

One of the most common and serious consequences of computer system compromise is data deletion, in particular log files deletion in order to cancel the intruder's traces. Adopting all the countermeasures to increase information availability against users' malicious behavior is one of the basic tasks of any security system. Protection from tampering with information can be achieved using cryptographic functions that provide authenticity, integrity, and confidentiality. However, they cannot provide the prerequisite for any further information processing, i.e., *information availability*. Since information availability is the necessary precondition to any further processing aimed at preserving higher level properties such as integrity, authenticity, or confidentiality, many efforts have been put forth on improving data availability. The most popular solution, i.e., any type of RAID system [2], however, is of no help for the case we consider in this paper. RAID systems operate at file system level and are completely transparent at user level. Therefore, executing an "`rm -r /`" command would simply delete *all* files and the related redundant information that would allow to reconstruct lost data in case of single disk failures.

In this paper we address the problem of preserving information availability even after files are deleted using commands such as "`rm -r /`" in Unix system. The solution we propose is an efficient answer to the problem of recovering data after a successful and disastrous intrusion. From this point of view, the approach proposed in this paper increases availability in case of *software* and *hardware* malfunctioning, as opposed to the RAID approach, which is only intended to overcome *hardware* malfunctioning. Note that the proposed solution cannot prevent an intruder from turning off the logging facilities, but can limit the chances that the intruder removes the logs of the activities performed in order to gain access to the system.

Any reasonable proposal in the direction of increasing data hw/sw availability requires the use of a set of independent computers, hence of file systems, different from the one whose data must be preserved. Replicating the data on an independent machine, that is a machine that does not share any hardware or software component with the one where the data originally resides, is the simplest way of increasing availability. Note that replication on independent machines differs from RAID1 systems, i.e., RAID systems that mirror all the information on a duplicate set of disks, as both sets of disks in the latter provide a single logical file system, while the former involves logically and physically distinct systems. Replication on independent machines is expensive in terms of disk space and network bandwidth usage. With n hosts, where the value n depends upon the importance of the stored information, the storage and bandwidth requirements are n-fold the original one. Thus, the higher the level of availability required in the presence of (possibly) untrusted hosts, the higher the number of machines, which implies larger amounts of disk space and network bandwidth. An alternative solution to increase data availability, which at the same time guarantees also confidentiality, is using Shamir's Secret Sharing strategy [7]. However, Shamir's algorithm is no better than simple replication as for the disk space occupation and bandwidth requirement, since it leads to an n-fold increase in storage space and network bandwidth requirement.

The solution to the problem of increasing data availability we propose in this paper is both disk space and network bandwidth efficient, as it is based on the Information Dispersal Algorithm [5]. The Information Dispersal Algorithm allows to distribute a file F in n pieces, each of size $|F|/m$, to multiple hosts such that it can be reconstructed using any $m < n$ such pieces, with $n/m \sim 1$. Because of the dimensions of each piece, the overhead introduced in this case, both at network and storage level, is $|F|n/m$. In this paper we apply the Information Dispersal Algorithm to log files, as they are the critical component of computer forensics and post mortem analysis after computer intrusions as well as "live" activities such as auditing and monitoring. Their availability depends upon hardware reliability and system security. Log files deletion may be caused by a system crash or a successful system compromise. While using WORM devices or printers is a viable solution against the latter [3], it is of no use against hardware faults to which such devices are as vulnerable as any other writable storage device. It is well known that the level of hardware reliability can be improved but can never reach 100%. Security on untrusted machines is usually low and log files hardly ever survive intrusions. On the other hand, trusted machines are equally subject to hardware faults, which may cause the loss of the log files so that the actions preceding the fault cannot be analyzed. Guaranteeing log files survival to either software or hardware malicious events, that is guaranteeing log files availability, is the critical property any secure logging service implicitly relies upon. Once availability is guaranteed, integrity, authenticity, and confidentiality can be added to the service in order to make sure the information it provides is reliable/trustworthy.

We realized a filter that increases data availability, based on an optimized version of the Information Dispersal Algorithm, as it is more efficient with respect to encoding time, storage space, and network bandwidth usage than the original one presented in [5]. When n hosts are used, the number m of hosts, $1 \leq m \leq n$, that are sufficient to reconstruct the original information can be set depending upon the critical nature of the log files. However, unlike the Secret Sharing scheme, $m-1$ pieces may yield some information about the original one, although heuristics can be adopted that minimize the probability of such an event. The filter can be applied to any log generating process, whose output can be piped as input to the filter, or by applying it to the log files after they are being written, as in the case of web servers, ftp servers, routers, or system processes. A prototype has been implemented that operates with the system general purpose logging facility `syslogd`. Percentage space reductions with respect to simple replication in the range of 38% to 71% have been measured depending upon the message types and degrees of availability, i.e., minimum number of pieces necessary to reconstruct the original information.

Once service availability is guaranteed, the logging service can be enhanced in order to add integrity, authenticity, and secrecy. Cryptographic functions, such as encryption, digital signature, and (keyed) digest, can be easily added to the system proposed in this paper, together with an adequate key management system, either as a part of the application or as an autonomous system, e.g., a Certification Authority.

This paper is organized as follows. Section 2 briefly recalls the Information Dispersal Algorithm in the optimized version we developed. Section 3 presents the proposed filter and Section 4 illustrates its implementation. Extensions for forensic use are investigated in Section 5. Section 6 summarizes our contribution and concludes the paper.

2. The Information Dispersal Algorithm

In this section we illustrate the mathematical aspects of the Information Dispersal Algorithm, with particular emphasis on the optimized version we propose. Readers that are more interested in system details can skip this section, as it does not aid system understanding.

The Information Dispersal Algorithm (IDA) proposed by Rabin [5] distributes, after a suitable encoding, a piece of information I of length $|I|$ into n parts, any m of which are sufficient in order to reconstruct the original information I. Thus, even if $k = n - m$ systems are compromised and the pieces stored there are deleted, the original information can still be reconstructed correctly and completely. IDA is space efficient as the overall space occupation is $|I|n/m$, which is close to $|I|$ if n and m are chosen so that $n/m \sim 1$.

In this work we designed and implemented a more efficient version than the original one, which we call accelerated IDA (aIDA). In aIDA the encoding scheme is based on a Galois Field over 2^8 instead of the finite field Z_{257} used in [5]. Such a choice impacts on the protocol execution performance as summations and bit-wise XOR on bytes replace multiplications and summations on half words, respectively, which are used in the original description. Furthermore, it also impacts on the storage space required by the encoding scheme. While the original scheme based on Z_{257} encodes each byte in a two byte string, our scheme maps bytes to bytes, thus halving the size of the dispersed information produced by the original implementations. The implemented version is described in what follows.

Let I be a sequence of characters $b_1 \ldots b_N$, $N = |I|$, where each character is represented as an integer over a range $[0, B]$ and $B = 255$ if the usual 8-bit byte character representation is used. Each character b_i can then be represented as an element g_j of the Galois Field over 2^8, $GF(2^8)$. Note that, because an 8-bit representation is used, the proposed system can be used also with logging systems whose output has any binary format. Choose n vectors $a_i = (a_{i1}, \ldots, a_{im}) \in GF(2^8)^m$ for $1 \leq i \leq n$ such that every subset of m different vectors are linearly independent [5]. I can be divided in $\frac{N}{m}$ sequences, each of length m,

$$I = S_1, S_2, \ldots, S_{N/m}$$

where

$$S_i = g_{1+(i-1)m} \ldots g_{m+(i-1)m}, \quad i = 1, \ldots, \frac{N}{m}$$

and $g_j \in GF(2^8)$. I can then be encoded as the sequence $I_1, I_2, \ldots, I_n$ with $I_i = c_{i1} c_{i2} \ldots c_{iN/m}$ and

$$c_{ik} = (a_{i1} + g_{1+(k-1)m}) \oplus \cdots \oplus (a_{im} + g_{km}) \quad (1)$$

where $+$ and $\oplus$ are the summation over bytes and bit-wise XOR operations, respectively. Note that since $|I_i| = |I|/m$, the sum of the lengths $|I_i|$ is $|I|n/m \sim |I|$ if m is selected such that $n/m \sim 1$.

We now show how, with any m pieces out of the entire sequence of n, it is possible to reconstruct the complete information I. For ease of notation, let $I_1 \ldots I_m$ be the sequence of available uncorrupted pieces and let $\mathbf{A} = [a_{ij}], 1 \leq i, j \leq m$, be the $m \times m$ square matrix whose i-th row is the vector a_i defined before. Compute the inverse matrix $\mathbf{A}^{-1}$ and indicate the i-th row of $\mathbf{A}^{-1}$ with $\alpha_i = (\alpha_{i1} \ldots \alpha_{im})$. Then in general, for $1 \leq k \leq N/m$,

$$b_j = h^{-1}[(\alpha_{i1} + c_{1k}) \oplus \cdots \oplus (\alpha_{im} + c_{mk})], \ 1 \leq j \leq N \quad (2)$$

where $i = j \bmod m, k = \lceil j/m \rceil$ and h^{-1} is the function that maps each element in $GF(2^8)$ to the corresponding byte, which can be efficiently implemented with a table lookup using the argument as index. I is encoded and split using Eq. 1 and reconstructed using Eq. 2 after inverting matrix $\mathbf{A}$ once and for all. Each equation requires $2m$ operations for each character, thus reconstructing I requires $N 2m$ operations.

Table 1 shows a sample of performance measurements of aIDA against IDA with $n = 5$ and $m = 2$ and $m = 4$ for various input strings. For each input size, the piece size and the encoding times of the input string are given. Measurements were collected on the SGI Origin 2000 used for the experiments described in Section 4. The values reported are the average over ten runs, in order to account for possible measurement instabilities. However, negligible standard deviations were observed, so they are not reported. As the tables show, the advantage of using aIDA becomes greater as the input size increases or as the redundancy level increases.

Table 1. Encoding times in $m$secs (a) and piece size in bytes (b) using IDA and aIDA for various input sizes with $n = 5$ and $m = 2$ and $m = 4$.

	INPUT SIZE	$m = 2, n = 5$		$m = 4, n = 5$	
		IDA	aIDA	IDA	aIDA
(a)	70	0.226	0.176	0.216	0.172
	140	0.365	0.298	0.326	0.275
	210	0.498	0.419	0.444	0.384
	280	0.633	0.541	0.563	0.492
	INPUT SIZE	$m = 2, n = 5$		$m = 4, n = 5$	
		IDA	aIDA	IDA	aIDA
(b)	70	70	35	36	18
	140	140	70	70	35
	210	210	105	106	53
	280	280	140	140	70

3. The Log Availability Filter

In this section we describe the software fault-tolerant system we designed in order to increase log files availability at low storage and network bandwidth cost. Our system is a module that transparently operates on the system generating the log information and processes it before it is sent to the independent storing systems. Since the processing phase is decoupled from log generation, the module can be combined with any log generating routine. Because a set of independent machines is used to store the processed information, using such a filter protects both against hardware failures of the individual storing machines and against illegitimate software misuse thereof, such as deletion commands executed with superuser privileges by a malicious user. Appropriate security measures are assumed to be in place on the machine generating the log files. If such measures were to be broken, i.e., the logging machine were to be compromised, nothing could prevent the intruder to turn off the Filter or the logging facility itself.

The Log Availability Filter is based on the distribution of the log file on a set of possibly untrusted machines using aIDA. By splitting the log file on different machines using aIDA, both transmission and disk writing times decrease. Increasing the number of devices the log file is written to reduces the probability of hardware faults that will make the log files unavailable, i.e., the probability that all the device will break down, both at network and host level. Since the storing machines are independent servers, the probability of a hardware fault that will crash all of them decreases with the product of the individual fault probabilities. Furthermore, when a set of independent machines different from the one that generates the logs is used for storing the log file, a number thereof, from which the log file can be reconstructed, is reasonably expected to survive an intrusion. To improve security, the storing machines can be connected to the one generating the log entries on a serial line, so that they are usually not visible to the Internet.

The system architecture comprises a server, whose activities must be logged, that generates the log file and a set of satellite independent machines that individually store a piece of the log file. The Log Availability Filter transparently operates between the two, as illustrated in Fig. 1.

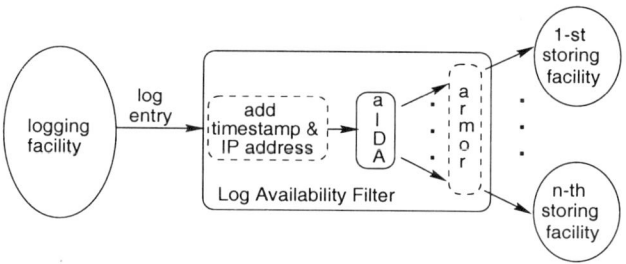

Figure 1. A schematic view of the Log Availability Filter architecture. Dashed lines indicate optional Filter phases.

The Filter operates in three steps, as log entries are generated. First, each log entry is time-stamped with the current local time and IP address of the host that generated it. The addition of such information is instrumental to ordered log reconstruction, as different logging machines may send their files to the same set of storing machines. However, the time-stamp and IP address might be eliminated if the logging service provides either of them or both already. In the second step the time-stamped entry is processed with aIDA producing a set of pieces, each one to be sent to a different machine. Each such piece is identified by a sequence number that is used for log reconstruction. Note that availability is achieved at log entry level, as log entries are processed individually as they are generated, thus improving the granularity of fault-tolerance. In the third step each piece is armored using only printing ASCII characters, e.g., with the Unix command `uuencode` [4] or the standard encapsulation format MIME [1], as a protection against corruption as the piece travels through intersystem gateways and character interpretation at the receiving host. Such a phase is optional and can be skipped when it is guaranteed that neither packet corruption nor early character interpretation may occur. Finally, the storing machines receive the pieces addressed to each of them and store them on disks.

With each entry being divided into as many pieces as there are storing machines, for any given number n of storing machines the number of pieces m that are needed in order to reconstruct the original entry is a configuration parameter of the Filter. The trade-off existing between the level of availability required and the level of confidentiality offered as a by-product by the Filter translates into conflicting requirements on the parameters of the encoding scheme. High availability implies small m, i.e., a small number of servers is sufficient to reconstruct the file. In this case, a large number of servers must be compromised in order to completely delete the log file but access to a small number of servers allows an intruder to gain access to the log file. On the other hand, with a large m, a large number of servers is needed to reconstruct the file and to be able to read it. In this case, a large number of servers must be compromised in order to have access to the file but it is enough to compromise few hosts to make file reconstruction impossible. Thus, large m implies higher confidentiality and lower availability. Note that, although aIDA does not offer encryption protection, the encoding scheme used can be adapted such that fewer than m pieces yield almost no information about the original content. Therefore, confidentiality is higher than with simple replication. Furthermore, a large m contributes to the space and transmission time efficiency of the protocol, while a small m increases the size of the individual pieces distributed on the machines, thus reducing the space efficiency of the protocol. The value $m = n/2 + 1$ strikes a balance between the two issues. If the log entries are encrypted, the level of availability can be increased, thus reducing m, without exposing the log file to confidentiality violations. Table 2 summarizes the properties of the encoding scheme as a function of m.

Table 2. Properties of the aIDA encoding scheme with respect to the number of pieces m for a system with n, $n > m$, storing machines.

m	availab.	secrecy	storage sp.	bandwidth
small	high	low	high	high
large	low	high	low	low

4. Experimentation

In this section we present the results of an implementation of the Log Availability Filter in conjunction with the general purpose logging facility `syslogd` available in Unix systems. A porting to NT environments is also planned, where the Filter must be adapted to interact with the `event logging service`, which collects system, applications, and security logs.

We focus here on the log file generated by the system routine `syslogd` and illustrate how our Filter can be integrated with such a routine. However, the Filter is general enough to be integrated with other logging routines either at system or at application level. Interface adjustments may be necessary in order to read log entries with non-textual format or that cannot be directly sent to the Filter instead or before they are written to disk. Possible improvements to our Filter are also discussed.

4.1. System Platform

The experimental platform comprises one log generating host and five storing hosts, as depicted in Fig. 2. The logging machine is an SGI Origin 2000 with four MIPS R10000 processors equipped with 1GB main memory, 32KB on chip data cache and 32 KB on chip instruction cache, 4 MB level 2 data/instruction cache. The five storing machines are SGI O2 workstations connected on a 100 Mbps Ethernet LAN.

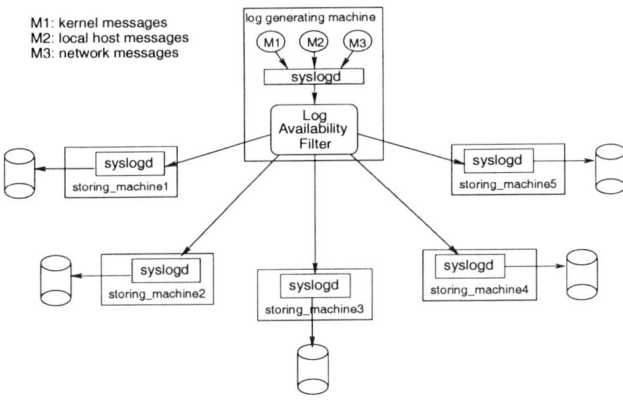

Figure 2. Experimental setting for the Log Availability Filter with 5 storing machines.

The `syslogd` command is a general purpose logging facility widely available on Unix systems [3]. Programs that need to have information logged can generate a syslog message. Syslogd reads the received message and logs it as a single-line character string into a set of files or devices (such as printers) or other hosts as described by the configuration file `/etc/syslog.conf`. Log messages can be received from one of three standard sources, indicated as M1, M2, and M3 in Fig. 2: a special device (`/dev/klog`) for messages generated by the kernel, a Unix domain socket for messages generated by processes running on the local host, and the UDP port 514 for messages generated over the (local area) network by other machines. Five actions may be specified in the configuration file: log to a file or device, send a message to a user, send a message to all users, pipe a message to a program, and send the message to the syslog of another host.

Our system is configured as the program to which the selected entry types are piped, according to the configuration file specification. In the more general case, when piping is not possible like with the `event logging service` in NT environments, the Filter can be adjusted so as to read log records from the log files used by the application, as they are written. The Filter takes care of sending the generated pieces for each entry to the destination hosts, where the local syslogd will receive them and store them on disk. Because the syslogd on the receiving host reads a character at a time and aIDA uses an 8-bit code, the third step, i.e., the armoring phase, is necessary in our case to prevent character interpretation ahead of time.

4.2. Experimental Results

Results for experiments with 5 storing machines are presented in this section. For our case study, we have considered three types of syslog entries, namely those generated by `rlogind` for a remote login connection attempt, `named` for a DNS query, and `sendmail` for an e-mail message transmission or reception. Entry length varies depending upon the host names that appear in it and whether their symbolic or numerical name is resolved locally. The `rlogin` entry we considered is 51 bytes long, the `named` entry is 158 bytes long and the `sendmail` entry is 205 bytes long.

We first analyze the bandwidth requirements in terms of message size. The time-stamp and host IP address add 19 bytes to each entry, thus the Filter actually operates on 70, 177, and 224 bytes long entries, respectively. Each of the n packets generated by aIDA for an entry is then piggybacked with the packet sequence number and the Filter process ID, for a total of eight additional bytes. Because of the way syslogd works, the Filter is executed every time an entry is generated on the logging host, thus each entry can be uniquely associated with the process ID of the Filter execution that processed it. This information, together with the packet sequence number, is necessary to correctly reconstruct the original entry at the storing host, as syslogd uses the UDP protocol, which does not guarantee order packet delivery. Armoring each packet expands its size by a further 35%. The original entry length, the time-stamped entry length, and the size of the packets actually sent over the network with and without armoring are reported in Table 3 for each entry type. Note that, for the same input string length, packet sizes differ from those reported in Table 1 because of the eight bytes added to each packet that specify the packet sequence number and the Filter process ID.

Table 3. Overall log entry size and individual packet size in bytes for various availability degrees for the `syslog` entry type considered when 5 storing machines are used. The size of the armored packets is given in parenthesis.

SIZE	rlogind	named	sendmail
ORIGINAL	51	158	205
W/T_ST & IP	70	177	224
$m=2, n=5$	43 (61)	97 (133)	120 (161)
$m=3, n=5$	32 (45)	67 (93)	83 (113)
$m=4, n=5$	26 (37)	53 (73)	64 (89)

Table 4 compares the total amount of bandwidth required by our system for various availability degrees and by simple replication using 5 hosts in both cases. In case of replication, we present results for time-stamped entries, in order to compare the two systems on homogeneous data sets. As the table shows, the proposed Filter is always more efficient than replication, even if armoring is used. The advantage of using our scheme with respect to replication is greater when armoring is not necessary, as in this case the percentage space reduction of our system ranges from 38% to 71%. However, when armoring is needed, the percentage space reduction of our system is still worth its cost since it ranges from 13% to 60%. In both cases, the minimum gain is for the high availability case (i.e., $m=2, n=5$) for short entries (i.e., `rlogind`) and the maximum gain is for the low availability case (i.e., $m=4, n=5$) for long entries (i.e., `sendmail` and `named`).

Table 4. Total bandwidth requirements in bytes for replication on 5 hosts and for three availability degrees using the Log Availability Filter, for plain and armored packets, with time-stamped entries in all cases. The percentage storage reduction is given in parenthesis.

STRATEGY	rlogind	named	sendmail
5 REPL.	350	885	1120
$m=2, n=5$, PL.	215 (38%)	485 (45%)	600 (46%)
$m=2, n=5$, AR.	305 (13%)	665 (24%)	805 (28%)
$m=3, n=5$, PL.	160 (54%)	335 (62%)	415 (63%)
$m=3, n=5$, AR.	225 (35%)	465 (47%)	565 (49%)
$m=4, n=5$, PL.	130 (62%)	265 (70%)	320 (71%)
$m=4, n=5$, AR.	185 (47%)	365 (58%)	445 (60%)

We now consider the execution time overhead introduced by the Filter. Since some phases of the Filter are optional, we have separately measured the times of each of them, so as to be able to correctly identify the system bottleneck, when the Filter is in place. The times (in $m$seconds) to add the time-stamp and IP address, to process the entry with aIDA, to armor all pieces, and finally to distribute the various pieces over the network for the various entry types and availability degrees are reported in Table 5. In order to account for possible measurement instabilities, each value is the average over ten runs. However, negligible standard deviations were observed, so they are not reported.

As the table shows, the time to add the time-stamp and IP address is basically constant, as expected since it does not depend on the input size. Armoring the packets introduces a very limited overhead, as the coding is a simple sequence of bitwise operations. The relatively large execution times of the aIDA phase[1] is however one order of magnitude smaller than the time to send out the packets. In fact, packet distribution is the system bottleneck and it is greater than the sum of the other components. Comparable, if not larger, times would be spent in case of replication, and in case of remote storing of log files, as suggested as a good security practice. Therefore, we conclude that the cost of adding availability to logging services in terms of processing overhead is not an issue.

Table 5. Execution times in $m$seconds of the phases of the Log Availability Filter for various degrees of availability.

AVAIL. DEG.	PHASE	rlogind	named	sendmail
all cases	ADD T_ST & IP	0.16	0.17	0.17
$m=2, n=5$	aIDA	0.2	0.40	0.49
	ARMOR	0.018	0.030	0.037
	SEND	2.3	2.3	2.3
$m=3, n=5$	aIDA	0.2	0.39	0.47
	ARMOR	0.02	0.031	0.037
	SEND	2.4	2.3	2.3
$m=4, n=5$	aIDA	0.2	0.40	0.46
	ARMOR	0.021	0.033	0.039
	SEND	2.1	2.0	2.0

4.3. Observations

We analyze here the proposed implementation and consider possible improvements to our system. We concentrate on the transmission aspects and on the logging mechanism.

Because `syslogd` uses the UDP protocol when transmitting the log to a machine other than the one that gen-

---

[1] The execution times of aIDA are generally larger than those reported in Table 1 because we account to aIDA the time for the allocation of some data structures, which are used in subsequent phases and which are not considered in the IDA vs aIDA comparison.

erated it, it is subject to packet loss. The use of our Filter provides tolerance also against UDP packet loss. The degree of availability, which protects from log file deletion in case of compromise of up to a certain number of machines, applies to packet loss as well. However, UDP packet loss may combine maliciously with system compromise so that an entry may not be recoverable although fewer than $n - m$ systems have been compromised. When the set of compromised hosts is disjoint or partially disjoint from the set of hosts that have not received their portion of log entry because of UDP packet loss, so that the union of the two sets contains more than $n - m$ machines, log file reconstruction becomes impossible because fewer than m machines have reliable data. Using a reliable transport protocol, namely TCP, would guarantee the system against packet loss, thus solving the problem of the combined effect of machine compromise and packet loss. The packet size would also decrease, as the packet sequence number and Filter process ID would not be necessary. In this case, syslogd could not be used directly on the storing machine as the packets recipient, since it listens on UPD port 514 by definition. Ad hoc clients should be developed and installed on the storing hosts that would receive the packets and pass them along to the local syslogd. The price of using a reliable transport protocol is paid with a performance degradation, as TCP is slower than UDP. However, in a local area network, where packet loss and retransmission are not frequent, performance degradation is expected to be limited.

As Table 5 shows, transmission is the Filter bottleneck. In order to optimize such a phase, we considered the possibility of using the UDP based multicast service. With multicast communication, a single message is sent to a registered group of hosts participating in the multicast instead of as many messages as there are hosts in the group. In this case too, a receiving client on the storing machines would be needed, as syslogd is not multicast enabled. Because of the nature of the communications in the Filter, where each recipient is sent a different message, multicast is not the correct solution from a logical point of view. However, it turns out to be a good solution from an implementation point of view, since the time to send all packets reduces to 0.55 $msec$ on the average, about one fourth of the unicast case, regardless of the availability degree, entry type, and number of recipients, i.e., participating hosts. Although the overall bandwidth requirement does not change with respect to the unicast communication case, when using multicast all messages are sent from a single socket, which explains why the send time is roughly constant in this case. Thus, if multicast were used, all of the storing machines would see the entire traffic for each log entry and would have to discard the packets destined to other machines. If they kept them all instead of dropping them, a further level of fault-tolerance would be introduced as a by-product that would reduce the chances of malicious combinations of UDP packet loss and packet deletion due to machine compromise.

The measures reported in the previous section are relative to the Filter execution time but do not take into account the time to launch its execution. The way syslogd works requires that, in case log entries are piped to a program, such a program be executed every time an entry occurs. A more efficient implementation that optimizes system overhead for program startup every time it must be executed would consider running the program (our Filter in this case) as a daemon. Such an alternative would require to modify the standard syslogd.

5. Logging as Evidence

A possible use of log files is to supply evidence in legal proceedings in case of computer security incidents. Legal acceptability of tracks as evidence depends upon admissibility, i.e., the conformity to the jurisdiction's legal rules, and weight, i.e., the degree of understanding and convincement for the court and judge(s). Admissibility strictly depends upon the country's body of laws regarding electronic documents and their generation and storage. Availability is the necessary prerequisite for legal evidence, although it is not sufficient. Authentication and integrity, which are usually among the requirements for legally valid electronic documents, are also necessary, to guarantee the origin of the logs and their non-modification [8]. Authentication of the log generating machine and integrity checksums to detect possible alterations of the logs, contribute to increase the legal weight of log files. Confidentiality may be required for privacy reasons, e.g., when the owner of the logging system is not the owner of the information being stored as in case of outsourced systems, but it does not add weight to the evidence.

The Filter we have presented guarantees log availability by distributing each log entry on a set of possibly untrusted hosts so as to hamper log file destruction. The logs processed with our Filter have no value as evidence in court, as much as the standard ones. However, they can be given legal weight if authentication of the logging machine and integrity checks of the log entry are added in the Filter processing, according to the jurisdiction's legal rules. Regardless of the specific solution adopted, a trusted machine is needed if log entry authentication is required. Different strategies can be devised in order to obtain a secure, in terms of confidentiality, integrity, and availability, log service. Two are the scenarios we can envision.

We believe that the most elegant and complete solution combines our Filter with the logging system such described in [6]. Schneier's system guarantees that in case of intrusion, an attacker will not be able to read nor alter or delete undetectably log entries made before the intrusion.

A trusted host that interacts with the logging machine is necessary for key management, which is limited to the initial sharing of a secret key with the logging machine from which the chain of keys used for authentication, MAC computation, and encryption is constructed, and the exchange of the first session key of the chain. Note that the sophisticated system proposed by Schneier guarantees the log confidentiality and allows to grant log access on a role-based security scheme, which is not a requirement for legal evidence.

The other scenario consists of a network of servers implementing the IPSEC communication protocol where our Filter is simply deployed as a log postprocessor. In this environment, log authentication and integrity can be achieved at network level since cryptographic functions can be computed using the session key established between the two hosts during the authentication phase. The deployment of our Filter in such an environment would complete the requirements for log legal evidence with availability, as authentication and integrity are provided by the environment itself. The role of the trusted host of Schneier's solution is played by the CA that manages the host public keys. Encryption, although not necessary for legal purposes, could be added either at application level or at network level.

6. Conclusions

The first step towards providing auditing capabilities that can be exercised after system compromise is preventing log file destruction, i.e., adding availability to log services. Mechanisms that can help detect file alteration and prevent unauthorized file reading complete the requirements for effective intrusion detection and auditing systems.

In this paper we have presented a software fault-tolerant system that adds availability to any system logging facility. The proposed system is based on an original implementation of the Information Dispersal Algorithm, which provides an efficient encoding scheme that significantly reduces storage space and network bandwidth requirements with respect to the simple replication strategy. A prototype was developed and the impact of its deployment in a real environment was measured. A variety of long entry types and degrees of availability have been considered and possible optimizations have been discussed. The application of the proposed system to the design of a legally valid logging system has been outlined and possible scenarios have been illustrated.

References

[1] N. Borenstein and N. Freed. Mime (multipurpose internet mail extensions): Mechanisms for specifying and describing the format of internet message bodies. *Internet RFC 1341*, June 1992.

[2] P. Chen, E. Lee, G. Gibson, and D. Patterson. Raid: High-performance, reliable secondary storage. *ACM Computing Survey*, 26(2):145, February 1994.

[3] S. Garfinkel and E. Spafford. *Practical Unix and Internet Security*. O'Reilly & Associates, 1996.

[4] G. Glass. *Unix for Programmers and Users: A Complete Guide*. Prentice Hall Int., 1993.

[5] M. Rabin. Efficient dispersal of information for security, load balancing, and fault-tolerance. *Journal of the ACM*, 36(2):335–348, February 1989.

[6] B. Schneier and J. Kelsey. Secure audit logs to support computer forensics. *ACM Transactions on Information and System Security*, 2(2), May 1999.

[7] A. Shamir. How to share a secret. *Communication of the ACM*, 22(11):612–613, November 1979.

[8] P. Sommer. Intrusion detection systems as evidence. *Recent Advances in Intrusion Detection, RAID 98*, September 1998.

Track B

Security Policy

Chair

Marshall Abrams, MITRE Corporation

Policy-Based Management: Bridging the Gap

Susan Hinrichs
Cisco Systems
shinrich@cisco.com

Abstract

In a policy-based system, policy goals are described with respect to network entities (e.g., networks and users) instead of enforcement points (e.g., firewalls and routers). This global view has several advantages: usability, global rules are closer to the goals of the human administrator; scalability, the policy system ensures that the enforcement points are configured appropriately, whether there are 1 or 100 enforcement points; and security, the policy system ensures that the policy is enforced consistently. This paper describes techniques for accurately translating from global policy rules to actual per-device configurations, and it describes how these techniques were used in the implementation of Cisco Secure Policy Manager.

1 Introduction

Policy has been frequently presented as a solution to management problems, but the definitions of policy vary widely. For the purposes of this paper, policy is a global goal statement or constraint. An example of a policy statement is "Engineering should have access to the department web server." This policy statement does not identify the implementation details of which machines belong to engineering and which port the web server is listening on. A policy statement should closely match the goals of the policy decision-maker to reduce the chance of entry error.

For a set of policy statements to be useful, it must be enforced by a set of appropriately configured devices, e.g., firewalls, encrypting-routers, or traffic-shapers. Device configuration is inherently myopic and literal. For example, a firewall does not know which machines are engineering machines. An enforcing firewall needs a rule like "permit TCP traffic on port 80 from 192.168.56.0/24 to 128.45.67.34/32".

There is a conceptual gap between the policy statement and the enforcing configuration that must be bridged to make policy useful in the real world. If there is only one enforcing device involved, the translation is relatively straightforward, but in a larger environment there may be 10's or 100's of enforcing devices that must be coordinated to implement the policy. At this point, the problem of manually doing this translation becomes far more daunting and error prone.

In many ways, this problem is analogous to the problem of compiling a program for a distributed machine[1]. The policy is the program, and the enforcing devices are the nodes in the distributed machine. We can use the same techniques from distributed compilation to perform the translation from policy to a set of consistent device configurations.

This paper describes how we used these compilation techniques in policy-based management during our construction of the Cisco Secure Policy Manager[1][2]. First, we describe the basic components of a policy specification. In Section 3, we describe the steps that a policy compiler performs to translate the global policy to device specific configuration. In Section 4, we provide a concrete example of policy expression and compilation by describing how these features were implemented in the Cisco Secure Policy Manager. We describe evolving policy standards and related policy work in Section 5, and we end with our conclusions in Section 6.

2 Policy expression

A policy statement is a guarded action; when the condition is matched the action constraint is enforced[3]. The policy condition can test against a number of properties. Most commonly, the condition tests against a property of the packet header, e.g., the source IP address or the destination port.

A policy condition can also test against global conditions, e.g., time of day, detected attack, or network

---

[1] Version 1.0 of this product was called the Cisco Security Manager. Version 2.0 and beyond is named Cisco Secure Policy Manager. For simplicity, this paper refers to all versions as Cisco Security Policy Manager.

load. To make such an external condition useful, the policy-based management system must have access to agents that monitor the state of the world. For example, intrusion detection systems sniff the local network to detect attack signatures and can be used to feed back information about the state of the network into the policy-based management system[4,5].

Finally, a policy condition can test against extended state associated with the network flow, e.g., a user associated with the source IP address. This kind of association also requires some additional infrastructure to be useful. An Authentication, Authorization, and Accounting (AAA) server and a Network Access Server (NAS) can use Radius extensions[6] to change configurations based on an authenticated user.

Policy actions are constraints or requirements associated with the network flows that match the guarding condition. Some policy actions include filtering actions, e.g., permit/deny, block java; cryptographic requirements, e.g., use an encrypting IPSEC tunnel; or quality of service requirements, e.g., give best effort service.

While we have described the policy statements as a set of simple guarded actions, the conditions and actions can be combined into an arbitrarily nested set of conditional statements. Figure 1 shows an example policy describing the constraints on HTTP traffic.

```
If Service is HTTP
   If Destination is S
      If Source is H
         Service level is premium
         Permit
      Else If Source is N1 or N4
         If Source is N4
            Use encrypting tunnel
         Permit
```

Figure 1: Example policy that specifies constraints on HTTP traffic.

Conditional nesting in the policy may aid administrators by allowing them to group features that should be considered together. An arbitrarily nested policy can be flattened into a canonical list form. If the conditional parameters are orthonormal, we can also build optimal search structures to traverse the policy conditions and find the appropriate set of actions[7]. Therefore, deciding whether to nest or to simply require a list of guarded actions is a usability issue not a performance issue.

However, order of the policy rules or policy trees is important. If the user specifies an order of evaluation, the policy-based tool must use this ordering to resolve potential conflicts.

While guarded actions can describe quite complex situations, the policy specification language described above is not Turing complete. There are no looping mechanisms or state assignments. This policy is merely a data flow specification. Without loops, we are guaranteed that evaluating the policy will complete in a fixed amount of time. This guarantee of fixed-time policy evaluation is a must for real-time packet filtering.

2.1 Policy targets

Guarded actions can be used to describe constraints against almost any domain. The action examples above reference the security and quality of service (QOS) domains. In addition, policy has also been proposed for putting constraints on routing. While policy can describe constraints on all these service domains, the operational constraints on these domains differ and these differences can influence the tradeoffs made in implementing a policy-based management system.

The security domain (filtering and cryptography) is the least forgiving of error. If you have a hiccup in the enforcement of your security policy, you may permanently lose connectivity or lose trust by allowing intruders access.

Routing policy has the biggest scaling problem. Huge numbers of routers must be coordinated to consistently enforce the policy goals. For this reason, routing policy tends to be more dynamic and tolerant of changes in the routes.

Depending on your administrative model, QOS policy enforcement falls somewhere between the security domain and the routing domain. An edge-oriented QOS administrative model will be on the same scale as firewall enforcement. A more detailed administrative model will impact more enforcing devices and have more of a scaling concern.

This paper concentrates on the security domain, though the techniques we describe should extend to QOS policy enforcement depending on the QOS administrative model.

3 Policy compilation

Once the administrator specifies policy goals, the enforcing devices must be configured to consistently enforce these policy goals. Traditionally, the administrator or some other technically knowledgeable person has been responsible for creating the device configurations. However, with information about the network topology, this kind of mapping from global intent to local mechanism is well suited to translation automation.

In this section we describe the kind of topology information needed to make this transformation. We also describe the compilation algorithm and various conflict detections and resolutions that can be performed during the translation. We close this section with an example policy translation.

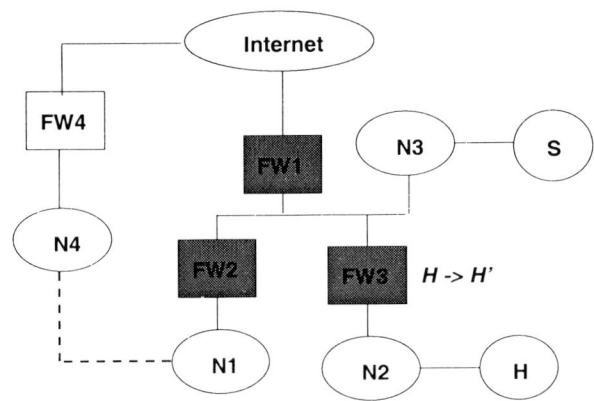

Figure 2: An example topology showing several enforcing firewalls separating networks.

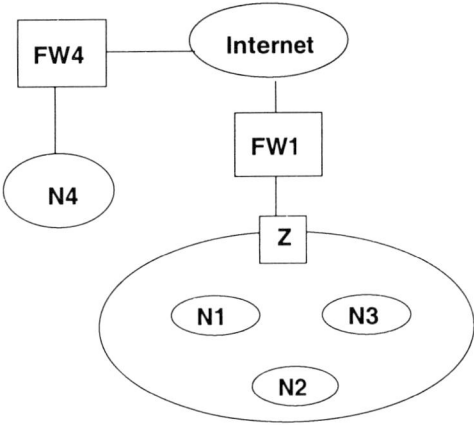

Figure 3: The example topology from Figure 2 with the topology under FW1 collapsed into a single cloud.

3.1 Topology information

The policy compiler must have accurate information about the network topology to perform an accurate mapping from global policy to local configuration. The policy compiler must know the relationships between networks, so it can model the paths where traffic can flow. It must also know the location of all enforcement points under its control.

Figure 2 shows an example topology. If the policy compiler is missing information about a possible path between networks N1 and N4 (as shown by the dashed line), there is the potential for a backdoor because the configuration for the nearby enforcing devices will not enforce the policy between N1 and N4 along that path.

Entering complete topology information by hand is tedious and error prone. Ideally, this topology information can be imported from an already existing database or discovered automatically. Also, in many cases, the complete topology is unnecessary. When implementing a security policy, you only care about the details of the topology near the enforcing devices (firewalls and routers).

The administrator can define a *cloud* to collapse the topology information about a larger set of networks into one virtual gateway that has many networks associated with it. The concept of a network cloud has been used by network designers for years to ignore irrelevant details when discussing a network architecture. The idea is that a subsection of the network can be replaced by a virtual gateway if the details of the network subsection are not relevant to the discussion at hand. Figure 3 shows an example of a network subsection replaced by a network cloud. In this case, we only care that traffic from firewall FW1 must send to default gateway address Z when sending traffic to networks N1, N2, or N3.

3.1.1 Domain of constant policy

The *domain of constant policy* is a concept defined in the Orange Book[8], and this concept appears under one name or another in almost all security management systems, e.g., zones in Lucent Managed firewalls, sites in Centri firewalls. When mapping a policy to a real network, the system must first identify enforcing devices and determine the sets of networks enclosed by the enforcing devices. Each completely enclosed set of networks is a domain of constant policy. By consistently configuring the devices on the perimeter of the domain, a single policy can be consistently enforced against the domain.

The domain of constant policy also defines a lower bound on enforcing granularity. The policy system cannot enforce any constraints on traffic that does not cross the border of a domain of constant policy.

In the topology shown in Figure 2, the gray firewalls enclose a domain of constant policy that includes N3. If firewall FW3 were not there, filtering rules between N2 and N3 could not be enforced.

If an edge of the domain is not protected, there is an unconstrained back door that a knowledgeable opponent could take advantage of. For example, if firewall FW4 were not present and the dashed connection between N1 and N4 were present, we could not reliably enforce any filtering rules about traffic between N1 and the Internet. A rogue program could route along the unprotected dashed link.

While the idea of domains of constant policy has originated in the security world, the same idea is needed in the quality of service arena. Nichols, Jacobson, and Zhang describe a similar idea of policy domains in [9] to automatically negotiate bandwidth requirements between administrative domains. If the borders are not clearly identified and enforced, rogue traffic could enter and leave the network through an unregulated path.

3.2 Pruning and renaming

Pruning is one of the first steps of compiling a logically shared-memory program to a distributed-memory machine[1]. For each node in the distributed system, the compiler prunes out sections of the program that are irrelevant to that node. In a distributed system with little regularity, you get N pruned programs for N computing nodes. In a distributed system with more topological regularity or a distributed program with more data symmetry, many of the pruned programs are likely to be the same.

Pruning is also the first step in compiling a policy down to the enforcing configurations. The policy compiler steps through each enforcing device and removes all rules that are not relevant to that enforcing device. The policy compiler steps through the global policy rules for each enforcing device. At each source and destination test, the compiler checks whether any path from the source to the destination passes through the target enforcing device. If there is no path through the target device, the test case is pruned out of the rules for the target enforcing device.

As the policy compiler prunes, it also performs address translation rewriting. The topology in Figure 2 shows an address translation rule on firewall FW3. As traffic from host H flows through firewall FW3, its address is changed. The configuration on firewall FW1 must be aware of this address change and enforce rules against the translated address H' rather than the internal address H. The compiler computes the translated addresses at the same time it calculates reachability with respect to the target enforcing device. The algorithm in Figure 4 summarizes the per-device rule calculation.

```
For each policy rule Ri
  devices = CalcPathNodes(Ri.src, Ri.dst)
  For each enforcing device Dj in devices
    Rd = Ri
    Rd.src = SrcAddrWRTDevice(Dj, Ri.src)
    Rd.dst = DstAddrWRTDevice(Dj, Ri.dst)
    Dj.Rules.Append(Rd)
```

Figure 4: The per-device rule generation algorithm.

For a system with R global rules and an average number of D devices on some path for each rule, this pruning calculation will take $O(RD)$ steps. In the worst case the graph is completely connected; D will be the number of enforcing devices in the topology graph.

When calculating the per-device configurations, the policy compiler can also optimize the search structure. Most enforcing devices only take a list of policy rules as input, but if a device can understand nested conditionals, the policy compiler can use d-dimensional trees to optimize the runtime packet search structure[7]. With an ideal d-dimensional tree, the device's runtime rule search should only take $O(d + \log R)$ steps where d is the number of conditional elements, i.e., the degree of the search space, and R is the number of rules.

3.3 Consistency checking

The policy compiler can also perform a large number of consistency checks and conflict detection steps.

Is the enforcement point capable of the request? It may be acceptable to have a device incapable of enforcing a request along the path as long as there is another capable device along the path. If it is an expensive check, the user may only want the check performed once even if multiple devices on the path are capable. However, it may be a good idea to leave in multiple security relevant checks particularly if the traffic is moving in and out of controlled networks. A knowledgeable opponent could use spoofing to insert bogus traffic after the only checkpoint on the path.

Does this enforcement point have sufficient resources to carry out the request? On many routers, the fixed set of security associations (SAs) places a strong limit on the number of IPSec tunnels that can be terminated at that router. Memory also places a limit on the number of filtering rules that can be implemented on a given firewall.

Are there conflicts between rules of the same action type? The policy compiler may get two filtering rules that conflict, e.g.,
src=192.168.1.1 dst=10.10.10.10 protocol=IP reject
src=192.168.1.1 dst=10.10.10.10 protocol=IP accept.

If both of these rules come from the same administrative tool, we can rely on the administrator to express an ordering. However, if the rules come from multiple administrative tools, it is not clear which rule takes priority. An external authority must be able to express some sort of priority for each rule set to resolve such conflicts.

Are there conflicts between rules of different action types? Actions that apply to filtering and tunneling may conflict. If the tunnel rules are applied before the filtering rules, the packet header information is no longer available to make filtering decisions. In this case, making a global decision to apply filtering rules before tunneling rules resolves any conflicts between tunneling and filtering.

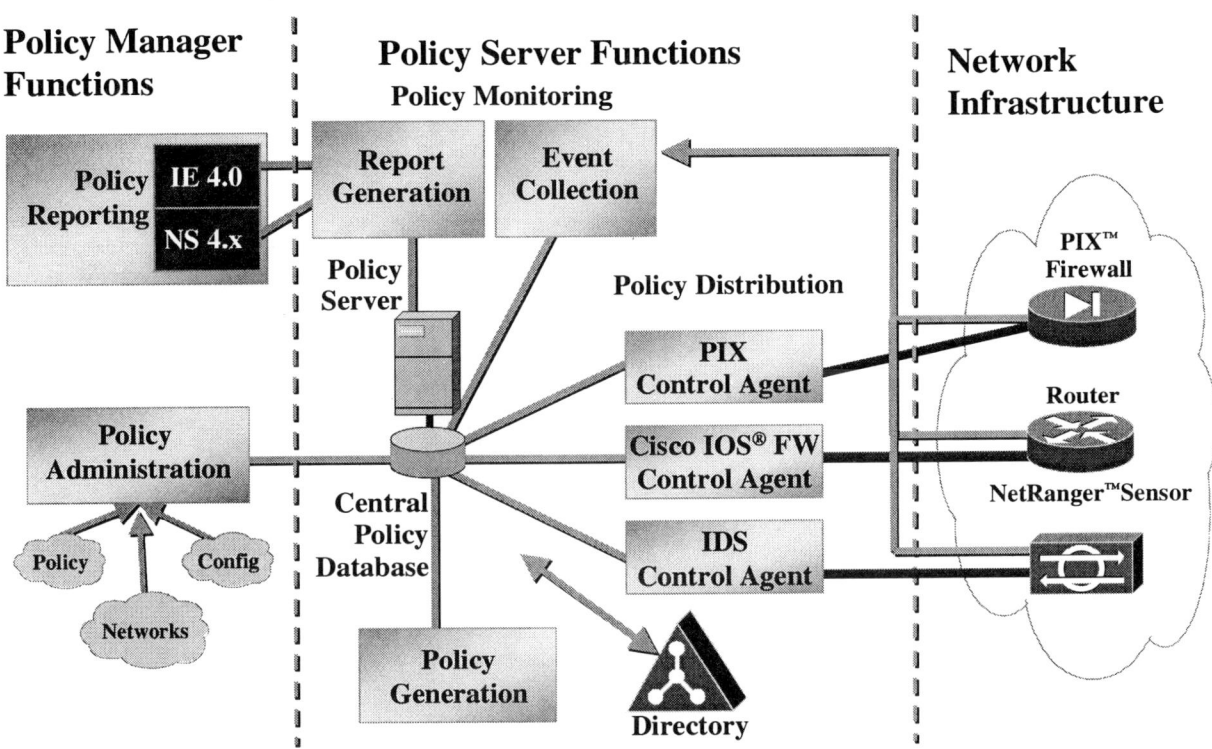

Figure 5: Architectural overview of the Cisco Secure Policy Manager.

Ideally, the policy compiler should be able to detect all conflicts during the initial compilation phase. It is easier and less error prone to centrally orchestrate policy implementation. However, in the real world, the policy compiler must be able to allow for the case where it does not have complete information about the enforcing devices. For example, it may generate a configuration for a device, but the device does not have sufficient memory to load all rules in the configuration.

3.4 Example compilation

Three permit rules arise from the example policy in Figure 1.
1. Svc = HTTP, Src = H, Dst = S, ServiceLevel = premium
2. Svc = HTTP, Src = N1, Dst = S
3. Svc = HTTP, Src = N4, Dst = S, Tunnel = Encrypting

Consider the example topology in Figure 2 without the dashed line connection. Since the topology is a tree, there is exactly one path that each flow can traverse. For rule 1, traffic from H to S traverses enforcing device FW3. In addition to filtering traffic, this device must also be able to enforce the quality of service constraint.

For rule 2, traffic from N1 to S traverses firewall FW2. This rule only specifies a traffic filtering constraint, so a standard firewall should be able to correctly enforce the rule.

For rule 3, traffic from N4 to S traverses enforcing devices FW4 and FW1. In addition to traffic filtering, the rule specifies that the traffic must pass through an encrypting tunnel; therefore, FW1 and FW4 must be capable of being configured as tunnel endpoints.

4 Cisco Secure Policy Manager infrastructure

The previous section described the general theory and issues of mapping global policy to specific device configurations. In this section, we describe how this theory has been implemented in the Cisco Secure Policy Manager architecture.

Over the past three years, our group has worked on a system for mapping user-specified policy to per-device configuration. Our work started with the Centri Firewall[10] and continues with the Cisco Secure Policy Manager[2]. Centri 4.0 controlled a single enforcing device, and it combined the policy expression and topology into a single tree. In Centri 5.0, we had to separate the policy and topology trees to enable policy expression as it applied to multiple enforcing devices. In the Cisco Secure Policy Manager, we expanded the set of target devices beyond the Centri NT-based firewall kernel.

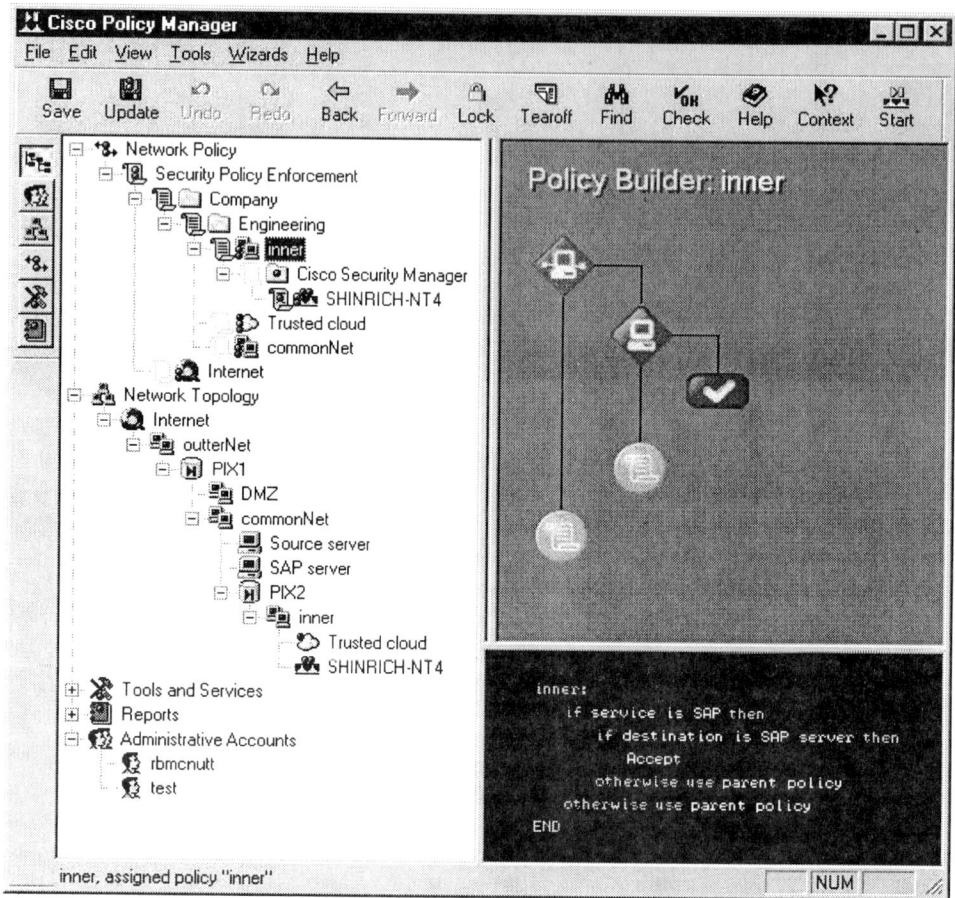

Figure 6: Screen shot of the Cisco Security Manager user interface showing the network topology tree and the policy enforcement tree.

Figure 5 shows an overview of the elements of the Cisco Secure Policy Manager architecture. Version 1.0 compiles policy down to enforcing devices that are PIX Firewalls. Version 2.0 also controls the IPSec features of the PIX Firewall and the firewall feature set and IPSec features of IOS routers. Future versions will also control the NetRanger intrusion detection sensors and other end-to-end network services. The elements of Cisco Secure Policy Manager currently communicate through a proprietary persistent object store

4.1 Administrative interface

The administrator enters policy through a graphical user interface (shown as policy administration in Figure 5). The user interface presents several trees of which two are the most important: the topology tree and the policy enforcement tree. We use these two trees to separate information about the physical relationships from information about logical relationships.

In the topology tree, the administrator specifies the topology, identifies the enforcement points and defines the relations between networks. The topology tree enables the administrator to collapse network details into a network cloud. The current topology editor is restricted to a tree. The topology editor provides a "short-cut" mechanism to express non-tree topologies. A short-cut is much like a soft link in the Unix file system or short-cuts under Windows. With a short-cut, the user can make further references to the same object in multiple places in the topology.

Figure 6 shows a screen shot of the topology tree in the left pane. This example shows a topology with two nested PIX Firewalls. The outer PIX Firewall (PIX1) has a third interface to connect it to a DMZ network in addition to an external interface to the "outterNet" network and an internal interface to the "commonNet". network. Most of the topology behind the inner PIX Firewall (PIX2) is collapsed into "Trusted cloud."

In the policy enforcement tree, the administrator defines policies using a nested-if specification. These policies are associated with network entity sources. The policy conditions can include information about traffic destination, network protocol, and time-of-day. The policy actions include permit/deny the traffic flow and requirements that the traffic must flow through a particular tunnel. Figure 6 also shows a screen shot of the policy enforcement tree. The policy attached to the inner network is displayed in the right-pane. This policy enables SAP traffic from the inner network to the company SAP server.

The source-based enforcement tree provides structure that enables the administrator to define policy inheritance. The source network objects can be placed in a hierarchy of folders in the enforcement tree. Policies can be attached to the folders or the network objects. The policy evaluation follows a best match algorithm. If we are looking for a policy for a particular host, we first find the object in the enforcement tree that most closely matches, e.g., host, network. Once this is found in the tree, the attached policy is applied. If there is no attached policy, we walk up the parents in the tree until we find a policy. If no policy is found, the default policy to deny all traffic is applied.

When a starting policy is found, it is evaluated with respect to the incoming traffic. If the evaluation ends on a "Use parent policy" node, the evaluation continues on the policy associated with the parent node in the enforcement tree. With this policy inheritance, the administrator can easily describe general policy cases, and then add exceptions for particular machines or users. Figure 7 summarizes this policy inheritance evaluation algorithm.

Policy inheritance makes it easy to make exceptions to a basic policy. In the policy shown in Figure 6, the inner network inherits from the policy attached to the engineering machine policy folder. The policy attached to this folder allows FTP to the departmental source control servers. This policy also inherits from its parent policy attached to the company network folder. This policy allows HTTP traffic to the Internet.

When all elements in the policy enforcement tree are based on an IP address, e.g., network hosts and IP ranges, the meaning of best match is straightforward. However, when authenticated users are allowed as sources of traffic, the meaning of best match is less clear. Suppose Joe has authenticated on the mail server and there is a policy that applies to both entities, which policy takes precedence? In Centri Firewall, user-based policies always took precedence,

and in most cases this was what the administrator expects, but in some cases (particularly for server machines) the administrator does not want user-based policies overriding the server's policy. This is an issue that we have not addressed in version 1.0 of Cisco Secure Policy Manager, but it will be an issue when we re-introduce user-based policies in a future version.

```
N = best match node in enforcement tree
    for p
while N ≠ ∅
  if N.policy ≠ ∅
    retval = N.policy.Eval(p)
    if retval = accept ∨
       retval = reject
      return retval
    else if retval = Use parent policy
      N = N.parent
  else
    N = N.parent
return reject
```

Figure 7 Summary of the policy enforcement tree evaluation semantics with respect to a particular packet.

After the administrator commits the policy changes, the user interface program stores the proposed policy as a set of global policy objects. These global policy objects are written in the persistent object store.

4.2 Policy compilation

The policy compiler is shown as the "Policy Generation" block in Figure 5. The policy compiler is notified when new policy objects are present in the database. The policy compiler takes the topology information and the global policy objects and generates a per-device policy list in a canonical form as described in Section 3.2. This compiled policy rule list is linked with the enforcing device and stored in the policy database.

The policy evaluation algorithm defined in Figure 7 describes the semantics of the policy enforcement tree evaluation, but it does not describe how the policy must actually be interpreted at run time. The policy compilation phase maps the policy enforcement tree to device-specific configurations. The policy compiler is free to perform semantic preserving transformations in the evaluation tree. In particular, the policy compiler flattens out the inheritance hierarchy and then re-optimizes the common policy rules.

4.3 Policy distribution

A device-specific control agent program is associated with each controlled enforcement point as shown in the "Policy Distribution" block in Figure 5. Multiple control agent programs may be running on different machines in the system to distribute the compilation load and keep the policy control closer to the controlled devices. The control agents perform two main functions: configuration creation and configuration deployment.

4.3.1 Configuration creation

The relevant control agents are notified when new policy rules lists have been generated. The control agent reads the new policy rule list out of the object store and translates the generic policy rule into the syntax of the enforced device. In many cases the translation is a simple syntax transformation from the canonical form to the particular device syntax. In some cases, the transformation is more substantial. For example, the PIX Firewall outbound commands are evaluated based on best match semantics, but the canonical rule set that the policy server generates assumes first match semantics.

For Cisco Secure Policy Manager, the control agents store the per-device configuration into a buffer of commands. When the per-device commands are approved, the control agent telnets in and downloads the commands just as if a human was entering the commands[2]. This is a clunky interface for a program. Seemingly innocuous changes in return messages between device versions can mess up the download program. We chose this mechanism for the first download mechanism because it required no change in the target devices. Future versions will use new download mechanisms better suited for program-controlled download, e.g., Common Open Policy Service (COPS), Lightweight Directory Access Protocol (LDAP).

The system can be run in a mode where the administrator gets a chance to review and approve the translation before it is downloaded to the enforcing device. Until the policy compilation technology matures and gains administrator trust, we expect most administrators to run in this manual approval mode. This is analogous to how programmers would double check compiler output in the early days of compiler technology.

4.3.2 Configuration deployment

Deployment of the approved configurations is a tricky problem that is also encountered in traditional network management. An unwise update order may block a nearer device before its configuration has been updated. For example, consider the topology in Figure 2. Assume machine H hosts the control agent for firewalls FW3 and FW1. If we change the configuration for firewall FW3 before we change the configuration for firewall FW1, we may get into a situation where firewall FW1 is unreachable.

Cisco Secure Policy Manager ensures that basic policy traffic is never prohibited. In addition to making sure that the policy-based traffic is always permitted, the Cisco Secure Policy Manger must ensure that the address translation does not make servers inaccessible[3]. This avoids the problem of being permanently cut off from the control agent.

However, even if the new policy allows the policy download traffic, updating a firewall configuration will likely kill off any existing connections (including the download of the current generation of configurations to another enforcement device).

A complete solution is a two-phase commit. The control agent downloads the new configurations, which the devices store in a separate memory bank. After the control agent detects that all devices under its control have successfully received the new configuration it would give the signal to swap configurations. Unfortunately, most network devices do not have memory to store the next configuration, so this solution cannot be implemented with today's network hardware.

Network management tools generally leave it to the user to specify the download order. The user understands the topology and can determine which devices are farthest away. Cisco Secure Policy Manager has topology information, so it can derive a good download order to help the user.

5 Policy standards and related work

Much standardization work has started in the area of policy-based management. Much of this work has been motivated by quality of service requirements rather than security. However, for such a general problem both policy targets should be able to use

---

[2] PIX Firewall uses an encrypted secure telnet. IOS can use IPSec to protect the telnet session.

[3] Consider the topology in Figure 2 with address translation rules. Assume the new configuration includes the address translation rule for machine H on firewall FW3. If we download the new configuration for firewall FW3 first, traffic from H will appear to come from H' on firewall FW1, but the original configuration on firewall FW1 only allows configuration traffic from address H. In this case, we must change the configuration on firewall FW1 before changing the configuration on firewall FW3, or we risk permanently breaking connectivity to firewall FW1.

similar techniques. Cisco Secure Policy Manager uses few of these standards because they were not available during development, but we anticipate using the standards as they evolve.

The IETF organized a policy working group to develop policy standards that would apply across multiple target domains. This group is trying to standardize on policy schemas that can be implemented in LDAP directories. With such a standard, policy rules from multiple tools and/or multiple administrative domains can be integrated and made available to standards compliant devices.

To date, this working group has published a draft on core policy schema[3]. The core schema defines the basic guarded agent structure defined in Section 2. All other domain-specific policy schemas should inherit from the core schema.

The COPS protocol has been defined in the RSVP Admission Policy (RAP) working group as a standard protocol for moving policy to the devices. This protocol was developed for the QOS domain, but it is general enough to be used for other target domains. First generation policy-based management tools such as Cisco Secure Policy Manager have relied on telnet and the current command line interfaces. COPS provides a more compact, standard protocol for automating policy changes.

COPS is almost to RFC-status[11] and is implemented in IOS. COPS is a general protocol that can be used in multiple ways. RSVP can use COPS to query policy information from a policy server[12]. COPS can also be used to provision policy information to the device itself for DiffServ[13].

Within the last couple years, the first generation global policy technology has come to light. In [14], Guttman describes a language for describing global filtering policies and algorithms for verifying the policy and generating local filtering rules. Our work differs in the input policy language. Guttman's language assumes that all input police rules are disjoint so policy rule order is unimportant. In our input language, policy rules may conflict so input rule order is important.

More recently Bartal, Mayer, Nissam, and Wool have described their work on the Firmato firewall tool kit[15]. Their work is a similar attempt to derive per-device configurations from a global policy. This work concentrates on firewall filtering. The policy description and inheritance scheme is different from the one described in this paper. The Firmato paper describes a conservative approach to pruning that places all possible enforcing configuration rules on every enforcing device.

6 Conclusions

Policy-based management holds much promise for delivering consistent, correct, and understandable network systems. The benefits of policy-based management will grow as network systems become more complex and offer more services (e.g., security and quality of service).

If the policy system has sufficient information about the network topology, the network administrator can rely on the compiler to take care of the details of generating consistent device configurations. This kind of automated resource management is similar to what existing compilers do, and we can use many algorithms and methods from the compiler world.

We are currently seeing the first generation policy-based management systems. While these first generation systems are useful, there are many areas for improvement in the next few years, e.g. improved download methods, better device support, improved mapping transformations. Policy-based management is proving to be an exciting area promising many rewards to the network administrator.

7 Acknowledgements

Many people at Global Internet and Cisco Systems have contributed over the years to the evolution of the global policy model and compilation algorithms implemented in the current Cisco Secure Policy Manager. These team members include Partha Bhattacharya, Alan M. Carroll, Nick Centanni, Shawn Dempsay, Doug Drew, Brad Frank, Xeuhong Gan, Jimmy Han, Yi Jin, Dima Lebedenko, Imin Lee, Da Li, William Li, Gary Lin, Erica Liu, Blaine McNutt, Tim Petty, Russell Rice, Chis Roulliard, Ken Rowe, Hari Shankar, Liman Wei, Rick Wells, Scott Wiegel, and Bosko Zivaljevic. Thanks also to Robin Lee for doing last minute editing.

8 References

1. D. Callahan and K. Kennedy. *Compiling Programs for Distributed-memory Multiprocessors*. Rice COMP TR88-74, Rice University, August, 1988.
2. Cisco Systems, San Jose, CA. *Cisco Security Manager Tutorial*, DOC-786905, 1999. Available at http://www.cisco.com/warp/public/cc/cisco/mkt/secruity/csm.
3. J. Strassner, E. Ellesson, and B. Moore. "Policy Framework Core Information Model". Internet Draft, May 17, 1999. Available at http://search.ietf.org/internet-drafts/draft-ietf-policy-core-schema-03.txt.

4. Cisco Systems, San Jose, CA. *NetRanger Overview*, DOC-787019. 1999. Available at http://www.cisco.com/netranger.
5. T. F. Lunt. "A survey of intrusion detection techniques". *Computers and Security* 12(1993):405-418.
6. C. Rigney, A. Rubens, W. Simpson, and S. Willens. "Remote Authentication Dial In User Service (RADIUS)". Request for Comments 2138, Internet Engineering Task Force, April 1997.
7. K. Mehlhorn. *Multi-dimensional Searching and Computational Geometry*. New York:Springer-Verlag, 1984.
8. *Trusted Computer System Evaluation Criteria*, DoD 5200.28-STD, December 1985.
9. K. Nichols, V. Jacobson, and L. Zhang. "A Two-bit Differentiated Services Architecture for the Internet", November 1997. Available at http://diffserv.lcs.mit.edu/Drafts/draft-nichols-diff-svc-arch-00.pdf.
10. Cisco Systems, San Jose, CA. *Securing Your Network with Cisco Centri Firewall*, DOC-CENTRIFW-SYN, 1997. Available at http://www.cisco.com/centri.
11. J. Boyle, et.al. "The COPS Protocol". Internet Draft, February 24, 1999. Available at http://search.ietf.org/internet-drafts/draft-ietf-rap-cops-06.txt.
12. J. Boyle, R. et. al. "COPS usage for RSVP". Internet Draft, February 26, 1999. Available at http://search.ietf.org/internet-drafts/draft-ietf-rap-cops-rsvp-04.txt.
13. F. Reichmeyer, et.al. "COPS Usage for Policy Provisioning". Internet Draft, February 1999. Available at http://search.ietf.org/internet-drafts/draft-sgai-cops-provisioning-00.txt.
14. J. D. Guttman. 1997. "Filtering Postures: Local Enforcement for Global Policies". *In IEEE Symposium on Security and Privacy*. pp. 120-9.
15. Y. Bartal, A. Mayer, K. Nissim, and A. Wool. 1999. "Firmato: A Novel Firewall Management Toolkit". In *IEEE Symposium on Security and Privacy*. pp. 17-31.

Security Policy Coordination for Heterogeneous Information Systems

John Hale * Pablo Galiasso Mauricio Papa Sujeet Shenoi [†]
Department of Computer Science, University of Tulsa, Tulsa, OK 74104

Abstract

Coordinating security policies in information enclaves is challenging due to their heterogeneity and autonomy. Administrators must reconcile the semantic diversity of data and security models before negotiating secure interoperation. This paper proposes an architecture that uses mediators and a primitive ticket-based authorization model to manage disparate policies in information enclaves. The formal foundation of the architecture facilitates static and dynamic analysis of global consistency and policy enforcement.

1. Introduction

Security managers have an arsenal of tools at their disposal for protecting information systems. However, they are not well-equipped to coordinate security policies between interconnected enterprises. Security in open heterogeneous environments is too often a patchwork of conflicting policies implemented in an *ad hoc* manner. Nevertheless, security managers of mission-critical information enclaves must guarantee the coherence of their policies within global, often hostile, environments.

Consider the information enclave shown in Figure 1. In this example, a toxin specialist is rendering medical advice to a M.A.S.H. unit treating a patient exposed to an unknown toxin. The specialist must integrate information from a variety of sources. Specifically, the specialist needs to know patient symptoms, toxins local to the region, and patient allergies.

Each site contains a piece of the puzzle. The M.A.S.H. unit maintains data regarding status and location of patients: $R_1(Patient, Symptom, Region)$. Military headquarters (HQ) maintains an object-oriented database of toxins detected in regions of battle, expressed as $R_2(Toxin, Region)$. The Poison Control Center (POISON CTL) maintains a list of poisons associated with symptoms

---
*To whom correspondence should be addressed (email: johnhale@utulsa.edu).

[†]Research supported by MPO Contracts MDA904-96-1-0114, MDA904-96-1-0115 and MDA904-98-C-A900.

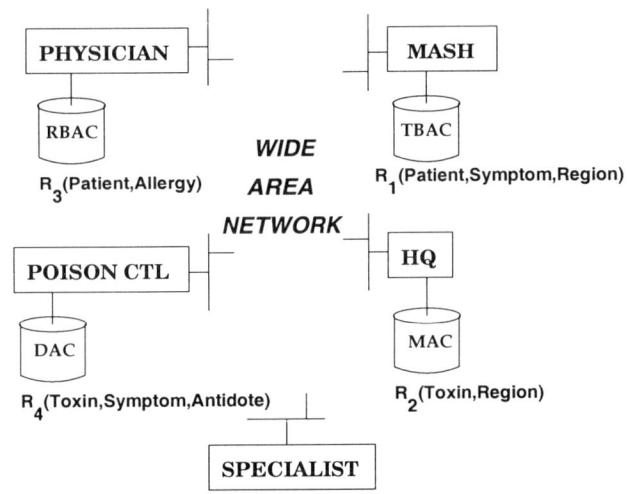

Figure 1. Heterogeneous information system.

and antidotes: $R_3(Toxin, Symptom, Antidote)$. Finally, the patient's physician maintains a database of patient allergies: $R_4(Patient, Allergy)$. The specialist must integrate this information to suggest a treatment for the patient at the M.A.S.H. unit.

Each site manages its own security policy. The M.A.S.H. unit employs Task-Based Access Control (TBAC) to permit fine-grained control in the execution of mission-critical tasks. HQ uses Mandatory Access Control (MAC) to provide access based on clearances. POISON CTL engages Discretionary Access Control (DAC) while the physician's database provides role-based access control (RBAC). The prevailing security policies may change at any time. E.g., an officer at HQ may decide to declassify "expired" data, or the administrator of the physician's database may elect to adjust the permissions of a given role.

Treating the specialist as a regular user in each system has disadvantages. Assuming that the relevant HQ data is classified <SECRET,COMBAT>, access to it implies clearing the specialist at this level. Subsequently, the specialist would have access to other sensitive data, circumventing the prevailing security policy. Implementing a flexible authorization model that delivers least privilege in the face of policy model heterogeneity remains an inherent challenge for information enclaves.

This paper describes a primitive authorization model as a common foundation embedded within a mediator architecture to facilitate policy coordination between enterprises. The next section presents a ticket-based access control scheme and uses it to model a variety of security policies. Section 3 proposes an architecture for integrating security policy mediators within an information enclave. It also considers the potential for security analysis supported by formal authorization semantics accompanying the ticket-based access control scheme. The final sections compare this approach with related work in the field and make some concluding remarks.

2. Modeling Security Policies

Our scheme employs a flexible ticket-based access control scheme to permit the implementation of a variety of authorization models for distributed objects [9]. A design priority is to provide developers of heterogeneous information systems with opportunities for secure interoperability by offering common access control mechanisms that underlie their authorization models. The model can be used for ubiquitous access control or in more practical, lightweight authorization service implementations.

2.1. Tickets

Tickets are tokens linked with permissions held by subjects. Ticket distribution and revocation are thorny issues in authorization models [8]. A naive distribution policy would prohibit all but the ticket "owner" from distributing tickets. Another policy might permit ticket holders to distribute tickets. This is more flexible, but requires constraining the circumstances under which holders pass tickets.

Revocation is more complicated for tickets with multiple privileges. Revocation must be partial, selective and transitive [8]. Partial revocation is the ability to remove a subset of privileges bestowed by a ticket. Selective revocation is the specification of a subset of ticket holders for revocation. Transitive revocation stipulates that revocation propagates through all principals receiving privileges. Clearly, a trade-off exists between the flexibility of a ticket-based authorization model and the effectiveness of its revocation scheme.

Our model incorporates mechanisms for adding and removing tickets from access control lists (ACLs). However, it does not have built-in facilities to ensure that the critical properties of revocation and distribution are respected. System developers build the necessary constraints when creating authorization schemes to enforce specific policies.

ACCESS TYPES
```
priv ::= ALL
       | priv'
priv' ::= KEY
        | LOCK
        | G . priv'
        | R . priv'
```

ACCESS CONTROL PREDICATES
```
EVAL:  cmd -> state -> state -> bool
TRANS: state -> state -> bool
```

ACCESS CONTROL COMMANDS
```
cmd ::= ADD priv token object object
      | REMOVE priv token object object
      | cmd ; cmd
```

Figure 2. Access control definitions.

2.2. Authorization Model

An authorization model resolves (s, o, a) tuples as true or false for subjects (s), objects (o) and access types (a). This information defines the global authorization state. Our ticket-based scheme defines an authorization state by a function $State : Object \rightarrow Privilege \rightarrow Token \rightarrow Bool$. Note that $< Object, Privilege, Token >$ denotes an authorization statement, where $Token$ identifies a label in a ticket that serves as a representative for a subject. The state $< o, p, t >$ means that object o associates privilege p with token t.

Privileges are either keys held by subjects or locks held by objects. E.g., if $Bill$ is a subject and $Door$ is an object, then $< Bill, \text{KEY}, sesame >$ implies that $Bill$ can use $sesame$ as a key in its access requests. On the other hand, $< Door, \text{LOCK}, sesame >$ means that $Door$ has a lock that can be opened by a subject holding $sesame$ as a key. Thus, the two tuples together imply that $Bill$ can access $Door$.

The recursive definitions in Figure 2 specify a general model of *grant* and *revoke* privileges, with higher order access types such as G.LOCK and G.R.KEY. G.LOCK (grant lock) permits adding a LOCK privilege to an object. G.R.KEY (grant revoke key) permits adding a R.KEY to an object. Note that every type other than KEY behaves as a lock. In general, a higher order privilege can always be decomposed into the form $< X.priv >$ where X identifies the permitted action (grant or revoke) and $priv$ identifies the privilege type.

The ALL privilege confers all privileges to a subject. A subject holding a key matching a lock held by an object with access type ALL has complete access to that component. The authorization state of an object can be modified by adding or removing ticket-privilege associations maintained in its access control list.

The command set in Figure 2 provides for dynamic and explicit authorization state modification. Commands can be embedded in messages as authorization requests. Subjects can add or remove ticket-privilege associations in objects for the tokens they hold as keys.

Rule 1: $\forall p : priv, o : obj, t : token, s : state;$
$$s \, o \, \text{ALL} \, t \Rightarrow s \, o \, p \, t$$

Rule 2: $\forall s_1, s_2. \exists c : comm;$
$$\text{EVAL} \, c \, s_1 \, s_2 \Rightarrow \text{TRANS} \, s_1 \, s_2$$

Rule 3: $\forall p, s_1, s_2, o_1, o_2, t;$
$$s_1 \, o_1 \, \text{KEY} \, t \wedge s_1 \, o_2 \, \text{G}.p \, t \Rightarrow$$
$$(s_2 \, o_2 \, p \, t \wedge (\forall o', p', t'. \, o' \neq o_2 \vee p' \neq p$$
$$\vee t' \neq t \Rightarrow s_1 \, o' \, p' \, t' = s_2 \, o' \, p' \, t')$$
$$\Rightarrow \text{EVAL} \, (\text{ADD} \, p \, t \, o_2 \, o_1) \, s_1 \, s_2)$$

Rule 4: $\forall p, s_1, s_2, o_1, o_2, t;$
$$s_1 \, o_1 \, \text{KEY} \, t \wedge s_1 \, o_2 \, \text{R}.p \, t \Rightarrow$$
$$\neg(s_2 \, o_2 \, p \, t \wedge (\forall o', p', t'. \, o' \neq o_2 \vee p' \neq p$$
$$\vee t' \neq t \Rightarrow s_1 \, o' \, p' \, t' = s_2 \, o' \, p' \, t')$$
$$\Rightarrow \text{EVAL} \, (\text{REMOVE} \, p \, t \, o_2 \, o_1) \, s_1 \, s_2)$$

Rule 5: $\text{EVAL} \, (c_1) \, s_1 \, s_2 \wedge \text{EVAL} \, (c_2) \, s_2 \, s_3$
$$\Rightarrow \text{EVAL} \, (c_1; c_2) \, s_1 \, s_3$$

Figure 3. Authorization semantics.

Figure 3 shows rules specifying the authorization model semantics. Rule 1 expresses the semantics for the ALL access type. Rule 2 formalizes the relationship between the predicates EVAL and TRANS used to specify the authorization state transition semantics. The predicate EVAL returns true when a command will take one state to another; TRANS returns true if a transition between states is possible.

Rule 3 defines the semantics of the ADD command. A subject must have *grant* privilege over an access type in an object to add a token of that type to the object. It also stipulates that subjects can only add tokens held by them as keys. For example, authorization tuples $< o, \text{G.R.LOCK}, a >$, $< s, \text{KEY}, a >$ and $< s, \text{KEY}, b >$ allow the command ADD R.LOCK b o s.

Rule 4 provides the semantics of the REMOVE command. It specifies when it is legal for a subject to remove authorization tuples. Using the previous example, an additional authorization tuple $< o, \text{R.R.LOCK}, b >$ would let s remove R.LOCK permissions from o. Once again, s must hold the token as a key. Rule 5 introduces command sequences to the system, formalizing the transitive nature of commands on authorization states.

2.3. Specification Language

The authorization scheme employs an object-based specification language to model protection schemes for a variety of information systems. The specification of DAC, RBAC, TBAC and MAC policies for relational and object-oriented databases is simplified by the language whose abstract syntax is given in Figure 4.

```
obj -> OBJECT ID(template)
        : METADATA mdinit
        : ACL := { aclinit }
        { (meth | subobj)* }

meth -> METHOD ID(return) ID(name) prms
prms -> (ID(type) ID(name)
           (, ID(type) ID(name))* )
        | ( )

subobj-> SUBOBJ ID(name) : ID(template)

mdinit -> := ID(template)

aclinit -> acle ( , acle)*
acle -> [ ID(name) , priv , ID(token) ]

priv -> ALL | priv2
priv2 -> KEY | LOCK | GRANT . priv2
         | REVOKE . priv2
------------------------------------
OBJECT R3(Patient,Allergy)
        : METADATA = empty
        : ACL := {[read,lock,Pat],
                  [read,lock,Phys],
                  [write,lock,Phys]}
        { METHOD Tuple read()
          METHOD Void write(Tuple t))}
```

Figure 4. Specification language and example.

The language employs a simple object model to facilitate the expression of abstract structural descriptions of information systems. The model forms a hierarchical system of objects that can be used to represent information protection units and system boundaries. For instance, an object can represent a table or tuple in a relational database, or it can represent a host or subnet on an enterprise network. The metadata facility in the model can be used to capture class and interface behavior in object-oriented databases. Methods, generalized for object-oriented systems, can be specialized to `read` and `write` as accessors for relational data.

Figure 4 also shows a low-level specification for the $R_3(Patient, Allergy)$ table in Figure 1. The specification names the protected object, describes initial metadata and access control configurations, and identifies the set of legal actions on the object. Note that the first element in each ACL triple refers to an action on the table. The second element confers a privilege to principals possessing tokens matching those held as the third element.

2.4. Mappings

Sophisticated authorization policies can be mapped into the primitive access control framework. This subsection illustrates the mapping process for DAC, RBAC, TBAC and MAC schemes in by expanding the example in Figure 1.

Discretionary access control (DAC) bases authorizations on subject identity. DAC is mapped to the ticket-based authorization model by associating tokens with subject identities.

Figure 5 illustrates enterprise structure and permission in the poison control center (POISON CTL in Figure 1). In it, `Al`, `Sue`, `Jim` and `Cy` are registered as physicians, while `Jan`, `Jim` and `Cy` have administrative privileges. Registered physicians have access to poison control data. For instance, `Al` (because he is registered as a physician) can issue a query on $R(Toxin, Symptom, Antidote)$. Queries from `Al` carry a ticket with the key that identifies him. $R(Toxin, Symptom, Antidote)$ must have a lock matching `Al`'s key.

This example also demonstrates a concept of ownership. `Cy` owns $R(Toxin, Symptom, Antidote)$; its ACL indicates that `Cy` can grant subject access (via `G.LOCK`) to the table. Thus, physicians must register with `Cy` for access to the toxin data. Moreover, `Cy` can write and grant write permission to the table.

Figure 5 shows a high-level specification expressing DAC configurations. The specification maps to the underlying authorization model and associates each protection unit (table) with a list of possible actions. Actions are associated with a set of subjects permitted to execute them.

The ability of a subject to assume multiple roles makes role-based access control (RBAC) an attractive scheme in many enterprises. Roles may be defined by groups of transactions and/or method invocations in the ticket-based access control scheme. Subjects typically assume a role at login, endowing method groups with "role" tickets. Corresponding locks must be distributed to the appropriate resources.

In the example enterprise, `Joe` plays the roles of accountant and patient. As an accountant, `Joe` can bill patients; as a patient `Joe` can look at his medical record (part of which lies in $R_4(Patient, Allergy)$). These actions are modeled in the object system by methods, `bill()` and `look()`, respectively. Invocations of `bill()`, associated with the accountant role, are endowed with an `Acct` key. Invocations of `look()`, associated with the patient role, are given a `Pat` key.

Figure 6 presents the enterprise with its RBAC authorization scheme. It also shows a high-level specification that maps RBAC configurations to the primitive authorization model. As with the DAC example, each protection unit (table) is associated with a list of permissible actions. Note that each action is associated with a role set.

Task-Based Access Control (TBAC) is motivated by the need for temporary trust while executing transactions. It regards individual transactions as trust units. Individual methods, procedures and functions are the natural manifestations of transactions in computer systems.

Figure 7 illustrates the M.A.S.H. enterprise employing a task-based access control model. Medics may only execute particular functions to complete specific tasks. For example, `Jane` can perform an examination – a process that accesses medical records, but only for the purpose of diagnosis. Furthermore, `Jane` can only access the stockroom database $R(Med, Qty)$ when treating patients.

A specification of the TBAC scheme adopted by the M.A.S.H. enterprise is shown in Figure 7. It associates abstract tasks with methods. However, trust in TBAC can be more fleeting than in RBAC; the same task that was authorized at one point in time might be unauthorized at another. To help implement such policies, the ticket-based authorization model facilitates temporary trust with dynamic distribution and revocation of keys and locks.

Mandatory Access Control (MAC) requires subjects and objects to be tagged with security clearance or classification levels defined by pairs of labels: a security level and a category, e.g., (`Top_Secret, Medical`). MAC models respect the Simple Property (no read up) and the *-Property (no write down/declassification).

The ticket-based access control scheme implements MAC by mapping tickets to MAC classification labels. Classes, instances and principals carry keys and locks associated with MLS classifications. Classification domains (comprising rank/compartment pairs) form a partial order. The ordering on levels is satisfied by embedding (within each message) all the tickets for all the levels dominated by a subject. The Simple and *-Properties are preserved by enforcing the use of accessor methods for all read and write operations.

The object-oriented database at headquarters that enforces a MAC policy is shown in Figure 8. Note that `Region` and `Toxin` are Secret classes (the compartment concept is omitted to simplify the presentation); `Sector_12` and `Sarin` are respective instances of these classes. Both classes and instances are regarded as objects in the underlying model and utilize a common protection mechanism

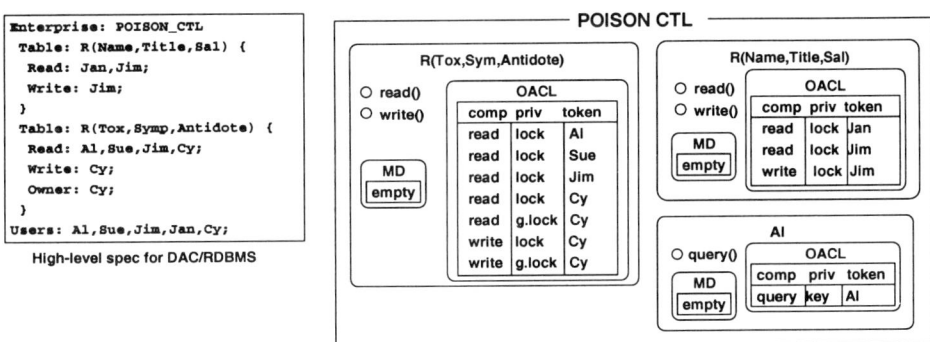

Figure 5. Poison Control – DAC.

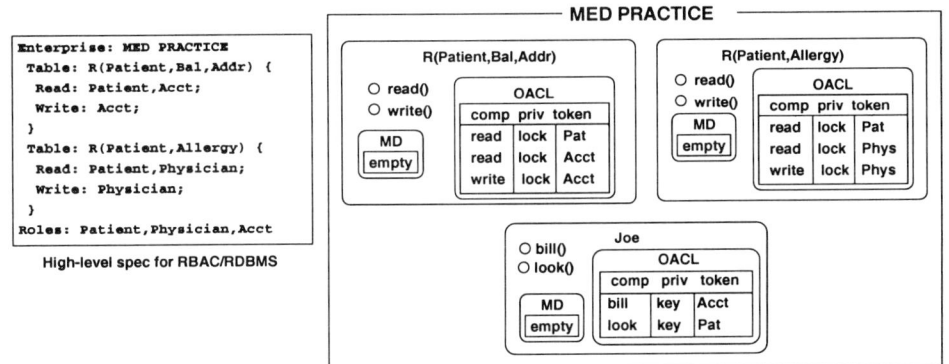

Figure 6. Healthcare example – RBAC.

(ACLs). The principal difference between classes and instances is that the metadata of an instance is empty since it cannot be used to create instance objects.

The protection scheme associates keys and locks with tokens mapping to classifications, e.g., S and TS. Other tokens, such as gter and atox, are used to enable private communication between method proxies in instances and method bodies in classes. Figure 8 also shows part of a high-level specification for the enterprise that expresses class, instance, method and slot protection policies.

3. Mediation Infrastructure

This section describes a middleware architecture for security policy mediation in federated information enclaves. It begins by assessing existing technology for software interoperability.

3.1. Interoperability

Achieving interoperability of heterogeneous distributed databases and applications presents many challenges. Identifying a suitable connectivity solution for an information enclave requires handling heterogeneity issues in operating systems and development platforms, and structural disparities in databases. Moreover, interoperation entails deriving a consistent global information schema and access policy from federated database systems. Our infrastructure employs JDBC, CORBA, and mediators –technologies that have surfaced to address issues in database connectivity and application integration.

JDBC attempts to accommodate database heterogeneity by delivering a common API that provides access to different relational databases [10]. JDBC drivers exist for most commercial relational database systems, including Oracle, Sybase and Informix. A standard data access interface, JDBC consists of a set of Java classes and interfaces for executing SQL statements. Applications using JDBC are written in Java, and are therefore platform independent themselves. The principal benefit of JBDC is that one does not have to write multiple applications to achieve heterogeneous database access and cross-platform application deployment. However, JDBC does not directly support security policy coordination between heterogeneous distributed databases.

The Common Object Request Broker Architecture (CORBA) is a general purpose architecture for application integration in distributed computing environments [15]. It supports interoperability via the Interface Definition Language (IDL) that allows language-neutral object interface specifications. CORBA's Object Request Broker (ORB) is a

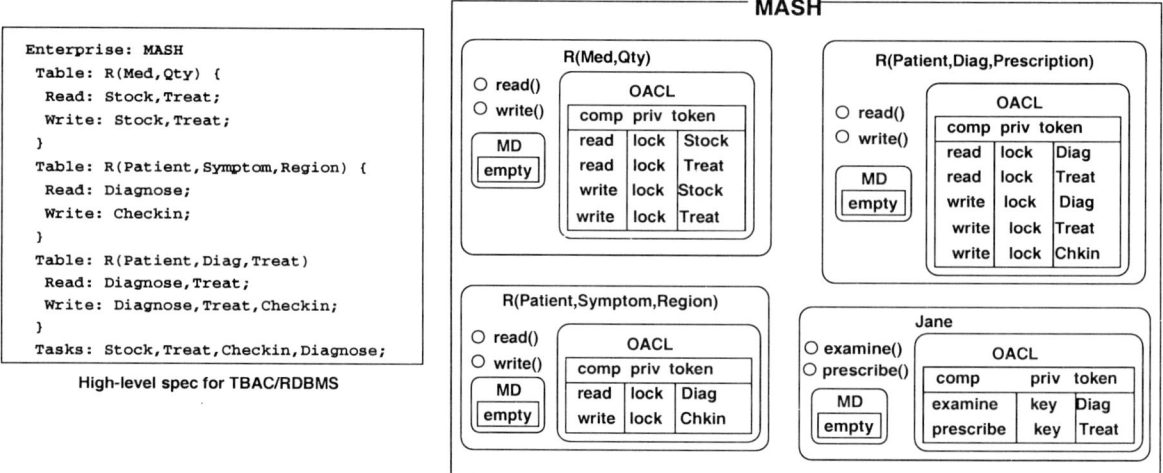

Figure 7. M.A.S.H. – TBAC.

transparent infrastructure that facilitates distributed communication across heterogeneous systems. CORBA includes a set of standard services for (among other things) naming, trading, transactions, persistence and security.

The CORBA Security Service (CORBASEC), based on the Distributed Computing Environment's (DCE's) security architecture, provides access control, authentication and nonrepudiation for distributed object systems [16]. CORBASEC adopts a flexible engagement model that permits security mechanisms to operate transparently or to be called directly by clients and servers. Authenticated principals are given credentials containing their security attributes that indicate the rights they own. CORBASEC promotes a number of secure interoperability schemes, differentiated by various security attribute/credential delegation options.

While CORBA facilitates application-level integration, it does not address higher-level issues. It offers a middleware solution for remote method invocation of heterogeneous distributed objects, but stops short of providing an infrastructure for policy mediation. In particular, CORBA (and CORBASEC) does not have mechanisms for reconciling disparate security policies and models in heterogeneous databases.

Mediators [22] facilitate a three-tiered architecture for enterprise computing. The bottom tier houses information resources and the top tier comprises high-level applications; the middle tier contains mediators that marshal feedback between them. Mediators can serve many purposes, including generating consistent global views from heterogeneous information resources, optimizing performance, analyzing and summarizing information, and authorizing access to information resources.

Security mediators provide managed gateways (sometimes implying human interaction) for database queries and responses. Security mediators can accept query requests from applications, pre-process requests, deliver queries to databases, receive and process results, and record activity in logfiles.

Mediators can also be used to reconcile security policy disparities in federated information enclaves. This approach employs CORBA and JDBC as foundations for integrating applications and heterogeneous distributed databases in open environments. Application subjects hold a partially implicit and potentially heterogeneous collection of rights to various information resources. Mediators in our architecture would determine these rights according to the prevailing "global" authorization policy synthesized from local policies.

3.2. Software Architecture

Security policy coordination of federated information enclaves is achieved within a special architecture that integrates CORBA, JDBC and mediators. JDBC provides a standard API for accessing heterogeneous databases, while CORBA enables cross-platform application-level integration. These technologies can be used in concert to provide a common interface for security policy mediators. Figures 9 and 10 illustrate the software architecture for security policy coordination in heterogeneous information systems.

Each enterprise manages its own policy mediator, which rests on CORBA and JDBC layers. Each mediator contains a current model of its database and prevailing security policy (Figure 10). This is held as a mapping to the primitive authorization model described in Section 2. As seen in Figure 9, mediators are also deployed at principals' sites. These mediators are responsible for fragmenting queries and disseminating them along with appropriate credentials to mediated information systems.

Mediators contain separate coordination policies for

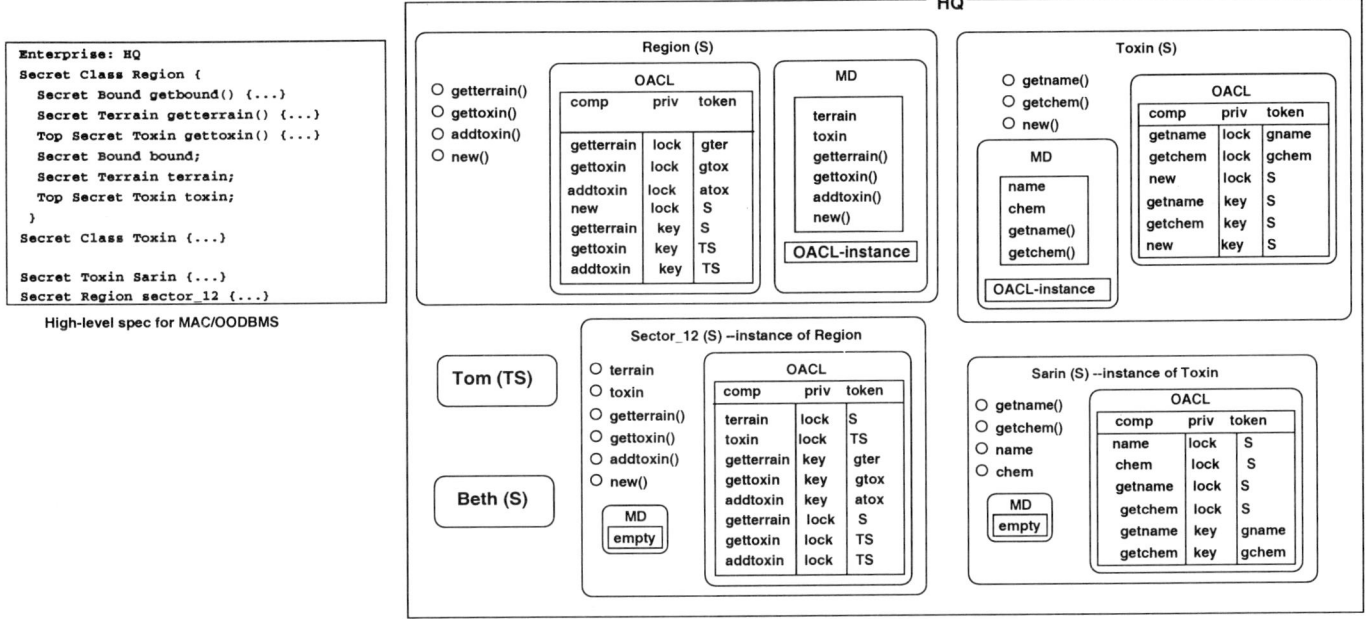

Figure 8. Headquarters – MAC.

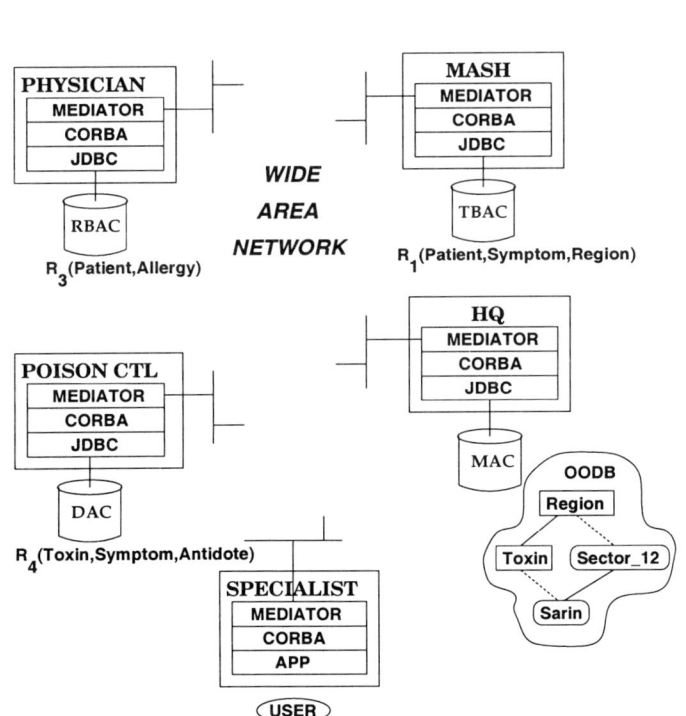

Figure 9. Software architecture.

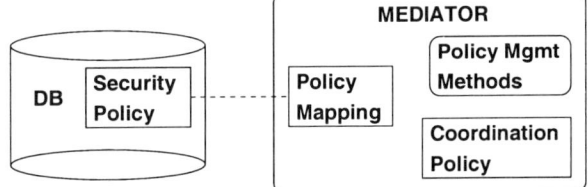

Figure 10. Policy mediator.

managing access by foreign principals. Foreign principals send credentials (called tickets in our authorization model) along with access requests. Mediators intercept access requests along with foreign principal credentials to enforce their specific coordination policies. Coordinating policies can take many forms, including:

- Mapping foreign principals to local principals
- Assigning local proxies to act as trusted delegates of foreign principals
- Requesting vouchers from trusted sources for foreign principals
- Mandating joint authorization with local principals

In the example in Figure 1, the specialist accesses heterogeneous databases, sending her credentials – say, a token pair $(Specialist, Jill)$ – to each intervening mediator. (We assume the credentials offered by the principal's mediator are authentic.) The coordination policy for the enterprise may dictate mapping a *Specialist* token from the foreign principal into a *Physician* role. The poison control center may not have a *Jill* registered and so the mediator might register her upon obtaining a voucher from a trusted source. The coordination policy at the M.A.S.H. unit could mandate the creation of a local proxy with limited authority to execute specific tasks for the foreign principal. Finally, joint authorization of the specialist and a local principal with suitable clearance could be mandatory at headquarters for accessing sensitive records.

The security policy mediation architecture extends the security perimeter of an enterprise by permitting controlled access to databases by foreign principals. The benefit of this architecture is increased functionality without the sacrifice of control. The challenge is to understand the resulting policy for the larger system.

3.3. Security Analysis

Guaranteeing the enforcement and consistency of global security policies is difficult for information enclaves. The use of a primitive authorization model as a common substrate for heterogeneous policies provides an opportunity for their formal analysis. Our architecture maps disparate security policy models to a common framework to permit the verification of global consistency and ensure enforcement.

Policy consistency is of primary concern in federated systems where security management is a decentralized process with no common authority. Enterprises may compose conflicting global policies from internally consistent ones. Adding an enterprise (and its security policy) to a federated system of enterprises can introduce conflicts in the global policy. Similarly, global policy consistency can be jeopardized when policies are adjusted. For example, a new or adjusted enterprise policy might allow principals to foil joint-authority requirements by enabling them to pose as dual identities (i.e. by allowing one principal to present two unique sets of credentials).

New or modified policies can be "statically checked" for global consistency when a policy compiler maps the high-level policy specification into the ticket-based access control model. The formalisms in the underlying model (see Figure 3) coupled with denotational semantics for policy specification languages can make such compile-time checks possible. This enables security managers to understand the broader implications of establishing new policies or adjusting existing ones.

Policy enforcement occurs dynamically, i.e., at run-time. Principal mediators bundle credentials with query fragments to distribute to remote information systems. Mediators at the information systems apply their coordination policy to incoming requests based on the bundled credentials. The combination of compile-time and run-time security policy analysis and management facilitates global policy consistency and enforcement.

4. Comparison with Other Work

A comparison with related work falls across several lines: authorization models, forms and levels of heterogeneity, and the overall approach.

Authorization models differ in protection granularity for objects and the basis of privilege for subjects. The growing popularity of RBAC [18] and TBAC [21] demonstrates the need for distinct models in different settings. The advent of semantically-diverse object-oriented databases has led to the development of even more models [2,4,12,17,20]. The integration of such variegated information systems mandates the coordination of equally diverse security policies.

There are many difficulties in coordinating security policies in federated systems, where enterprises must collaborate and yet maintain some autonomy [7]. Managing heterogeneity at the policy level is particularly challenging. De Capitini di Vimercati and Samarati [7] have proposed an authorization model that addresses these problems for tightly coupled federations. Their solution guarantees authorization autonomy by supporting decentralized access control between local sites but relying on a central authority for managing federated schema and objects. Our approach differs in that it focuses on loosely coupled federations where no central authority for federation management is possible.

The Argos system unifies heterogeneous access control models in an open distributed environment [13] by permitting the configuration of various identity-based authorization policies. Identity-based authorization models are prevalent, but our ticket-based access control scheme can be used to model radically different policy models. Argos also introduced the notion of domains for subject behavior and object protection rights. Domains generate classes of protection rights and behavior, materializing basic access types (e.g., read and write) from complex object systems. Argos remains one of the largest efforts to achieve a general multi-policy authorization service model and implementation for object-oriented databases.

Flexible schemes that support multipolicy access control are becoming increasingly relevant [1,3]. The architecture described in [3] employs flexible mechanisms and mediators [22] for tunable access control policies. Candan *et al.* [5] used the Heterogeneous Reasoning and Mediator System (HERMES) as a foundation for the secure mediation of databases. Their work promotes a principle of cautious cooperation to enforce local and global security policies while providing widely integrated services. Dawson *et al.* [6] describe a mediator architecture for reconciling heterogeneous data and MLS lattices in federated databases. However, our approach is unique in that policy heterogeneity is addressed at the model level, i.e., the integration of RBAC, MAC, and DAC policies.

The metapolicy concept –a policy about policies– was introduced in [11]. Metapolicies were applied to policy negotiation with the design of a formal "multipolicy machine" in [1]. Kuhnhauser and von Kopp Ostrowski [14] have engaged metapolicies to construct a formal framework that supports multiple access control policies for loosely coupled federations. The focus of their effort is to provide support for application-specific policy development, coexistence and re-use in open environments. Metapolicies in this framework are realized through the construction of cooperation and conflict matrices – policies themselves are the objects in these matrices. The implementation [14] uses "custodians," similar to the mediators used in this work.

5. Conclusions

Security managers struggle with policy coordination between enterprises in information enclaves implementing disparate data and security models. Mediators can be used in conjunction with other integration technologies to achieve a standard architecture for security policy coordination designs and analyses. The primitive authorization model embraced by the security policy mediation architecture presented in this paper provides a common foundation for policy coordination and facilitates static and dynamic analyses of security.

References

[1] D. Bell. Modeling the multipolicy machine. *Proceedings of the New Security Paradigms Workshop*, 2–9, 1994.

[2] E. Bertino, S. Jajodia and P. Samarati. Access control in object-oriented database systems: Some approaches and issues, in *Advanced Database Concepts and Research Issues (LNCS 759)* (eds. N. Adam and B. Bhargava), Springer-Verlag, Amsterdam, 17–44, 1993.

[3] E. Bertino, S. Jajodia and P. Samarati. Supporting multiple access control policies in database systems. *Proceedings of the IEEE Symposium on Research in Security and Privacy*, 94–109, 1996.

[4] H. H. Bruggemann. Rights in an object-oriented environment. *Database Security, V: Status and Prospects* (eds. C. Landwehr and S. Jajodia), Elsevier, Amsterdam, 99–115, 1992.

[5] K. S. Candan, S. Jajodia and V. S. Subrahmanian, Secure mediated databases. *Proceedings 12th International Conference on Data Engineering*, 28–37, 1996.

[6] S. Dawson, S. Qian and P. Samarati, Secure interoperation of heterogeneous systems: A mediator-based approach. *Proceedings of the 14th IFIP TC-11 International Conference on Information Security*, 1998.

[7] S. De Capitani di Vimercati and P. Samarati. Authorization specification and enforcement in federated database systems. *Journal of Computer Security*, **5(2)**, 155–188, 1997.

[8] V. Gilgor, J. Huskamp, S. Welke, C. Linn, and W. Mayfield. Traditional capability-based systems: An analysis of their ability to meet the trusted computer security evaluation criteria, Institute for Defense Analyses, IDA Paper P-1935, 1987.

[9] J. Hale, J. Threet, and S. Shenoi. A framework for high assurance security of distributed objects. *Database Security, X: Status and Prospects* (eds. P. Samarati and R. Sandhu), Chapman and Hall, London, 99–115, 1997.

[10] G. Hamilton, R. Cattell and M. Fisher. *JDBC Database Access With Java: A Tutorial and Annotated Reference*. Addison-Wesley, New York, 1997.

[11] H. H. Hosmer. The multipolicy paradigm for trusted systems. *Proceedings of the New Security Paradigms Workshop*, 19–32, 1993.

[12] S. Jajodia and B. Kogan. Integrating an object-oriented data model with multilevel security. *Proceedings of the IEEE Symposium on Research in Security and Privacy*, 76–85, 1990.

[13] D. Jonscher and K. R. Dittrich. Argos – A configurable access control system for interoperable environments, in *Database Security, IX: Status and Prospects* (eds. D. Spooner *et al.*), Chapman and Hall, London, 43–60, 1995.

[14] W. E. Kuhnhauser and M. von Kopp Ostrowski. A framework to support multiple security policies. *Proceedings of the 7th Annual Canadian Computer Security Symposium*, 1995.

[15] T. J. Mowbray and R. Zahavi. *The Essential CORBA: Systems Integration Using Distributed Objects*. John Wiley, New York, 1995.

[16] W. Rosenberry, D. Kenney and G. Fisher. *Understanding DCE*. O'Reilly and Associates, Inc., Sebastopal, California, 1993.

[17] A. Rosenthal, J. Williams, W. Herndon and B. Thuraisingham. A fine grained access control model for object-oriented DBMSs, in *Database Security, VIII: Status and Prospects* (eds. J. Biskup *et al.*), Elsevier, Amsterdam, 319–334, 1994.

[18] R. Sandhu. Access control: The neglected frontier. *Proceedings of the First Australian Conference on Information Security and Privacy*, 1996.

[19] R. Sandhu, E. Coyne, H. Feinstein and C. Youman. Role-based access control models. *IEEE Computer*, **29(2)**, 38–47, 1996.

[20] R. K. Thomas and R. Sandhu. Discretionary access control in object-oriented databases: Issues and research directions. *Proceedings of the Sixteenth National Computer Security Conference*, 63–74, 1993.

[21] R. K. Thomas and R. Sandhu. Task-based authorization controls (TBAC): A family of models for active and enterprise-oriented authorization Management, in *Database Security, XI: Status and Prospects* (eds. T.Y. Lin and S. Qian), Chapman and Hall, London, 166–181, 1997.

[22] G. Wiederhold. Mediators in the architecture of future information systems: A new approach. *IEEE Computer*, **25(3)**, 38–49, 1992.

The ARBAC99 Model for Administration of Roles

Ravi Sandhu and Qamar Munawer

Laboratory for Information Security Technology (LIST)
George Mason University, ISE Department MS 4A4, Fairfax, VA 22030
sandhu@gmu.edu, www.list.gmu.edu

Abstract

Role-Based Access Control (RBAC) is a flexible and policy-neutral access control technology. For large systems—with hundreds of roles, thousands of users and millions of permissions—managing roles, users, permissions and their interrelationships is a formidable task that cannot realistically be centralized in a small team of security administrators. An appealing possibility is to use RBAC itself to facilitate decentralized administration of RBAC. The ARBAC97 (administrative RBAC '97) model was recently introduced for this purpose. ARBAC97 has three sub-models called URA97 (for user-role administration), PRA97 (for permission-role administration) and RRA97 (for role-role administration).

In this paper we define enhancements to ARBAC97 to give us the new ARBAC99 model. Specifically the URA and PRA sub-models of ARBAC99 introduce significant new features relative to their counterparts in ARBAC97 (while RRA is left unchanged). ARBAC99 incorporates the concept of mobile and immobile users and permissions for the first time in this arena. This paper gives a formal definition of ARBAC99, motivates these enhancements and analyzes several subtle issues that arise in this context.

1 Introduction

Role-based access control (RBAC) is a promising access control technology for the modern computing environment (for recent literature, see [BFA99, GGF98, FBK99, NO99, SCFY96, San98, SBM99, ZSS99]). In RBAC permissions are associated with roles, and users are assigned to appropriate roles thereby acquiring the roles' permissions. This greatly simplifies management. Roles are created for various job functions in an organization and users are assigned roles based on responsibilities and qualifications. Users can be easily reassigned from one role to another. Roles can be granted new permissions as new applications come on line, and permissions can be revoked from roles as needed. Role-role relationships can be established to lay out broad policy objectives.

RBAC is policy neutral and flexible. The policy enforced is a consequence of the detailed configuration of various RBAC components. RBAC allows a wide range of policies to be implemented. Administration of RBAC must be carefully controlled to ensure the policy does not drift away from its original objectives. In large systems the number of roles can be in the hundreds or thousands, users can be in the tens or hundreds of thousands and permissions in the millions. Managing these roles and users, and their interrelationships is a formidable task that cannot realistically be centralized in a small team of security administrators. Decentralizing the details of RBAC administration without loosing central control over broad policy is a challenging goal for system designers and architects. There is tension here between the desire for scalability through decentralization and maintenance of tight control.

Since the main advantage of RBAC is to facilitate administration, it is natural to ask how RBAC itself can be used to manage RBAC. The use of RBAC for managing RBAC will be an important factor in its long-term success. There are many components to RBAC. RBAC administration is therefore multi-faceted. In particular we can separate the issues of assigning users to roles, assigning permissions to roles, and assigning roles to roles to define a role hierarchy. These activities are all required to bring users and permissions together. However, in many cases, they are best done by different administrators or administrative roles. Assigning permissions to roles is typically the province of application administrators. Thus a banking application can be implemented so credit and debit operations are assigned to a teller role, whereas approval of a loan is assigned to a managerial role. Assignment of actual individuals to the teller and managerial roles is a personnel management function. Assigning roles to roles has aspects of user-role and permission-role administration. More generally, role-role relationships establish broad policy.

An administrative model called ARBAC97 (administrative RBAC '97) was recently introduced by Sandhu et al [SBM99]. ARBAC97 has three components: URA97 is concerned with user-role administration, PRA97 is concerned with permission-role administration and is a dual of URA97, and RRA97 deals with role-role administration.

In this paper we introduce and formalize a significant enhancement to ARBAC97 to give us the new ARBAC99 model. Changes are specifically made to the URA97 and PRA97 models, while RRA97 remains unchanged. In other words, URA99 and PRA99 are respectively different from URA97 and PRA97 while RRA99 is identical to RRA97. The important difference between ARBAC99 and ARBAC97 is the concept of mobile and immobile users and permissions. We explain and motivate this distinction informally in the next section. Following this intuitive explanation we discuss the URA97 model and its enhancement to URA99. PRA99 is a dual of URA99 and is defined in this paper in this manner rather than being evolved from PRA97. We assume the reader is generally familiar with RBAC concepts. Our underlying RBAC model is the so-called RBAC96 model [SCFY96].

2 Mobility and Immobility

We now informally motivate the intuition behind URA97 and the notion of mobility and immobility of users introduced in URA99. Consider the role hierarchy of figure 1(a) and the administrative role hierarchy of figure 1(b). We will use these hierarchies in our examples throughout this paper. Figure 1(a) shows the regular roles that exist in an engineering department. In these diagrams senior roles shown towards the top inherit permissions from junior roles shown towards the bottom. Equivalently junior roles inherit members from senior roles. Thus permissions assigned to E1 are also available to members of PL1 but not vice versa. Alternately, members of PL1 are also members of E1 but not vice versa.

Figure 1(a) has a junior-most role E to which all employees in the organization belong. Within the engineering department there is a junior-most role ED and senior-most role DIR.[1] In between there are roles for two projects within the department, project 1 on the left and project 2 on the right. Each project has a senior-most project lead role (PL1 and PL2) and a junior-most engineer role (E1 and E2). In between each project has two incomparable roles, production engineer (PE1 and PE2) and quality engineer (QE1 and QE2). The role hierarchy can, of course, be extended to dozens or hundreds of projects within the engineering department. Moreover, each project could have a different structure for its roles. The example can also be extended to multiple departments each with different structure and policies.

Figure 1(b) shows the administrative role hierarchy which co-exists with figure 1(a). The senior-most administrative role is the senior security officer (SSO). The administrative roles junior to SSO consist of two project security officer roles (PSO1 and PSO2) and a department security officer (DSO) role with the relationships illustrated in the figure.[2]

There are two issues that need to be addressed in decentralized administration of user-role membership. Firstly we need to control the roles that an administrative role has authority over. We would like to say, for example, that the PSO1 administrative role controls membership in project 1 roles, i.e., E1, PE1, QE1 and PL1. Secondly, it is also important to control which users are eligible for membership in these roles.

URA97 addresses these two issues respectively by means of a *role range* and a *prerequisite role* (or more generally a *prerequisite condition*). A role range is specified by a junior and senior role. The range includes all roles between these two endpoints. The [and] brackets indicate that respectively the junior and senior end point is included in the range, whereas the (and) brackets indicate the end point is excluded. Thus [E1,PL1] consists of E1, PE1, QE1 and PL1, while [E1,PL1) omits PL1.[3] The prerequisite role specifies which users can be assigned by PSO1 to roles in the authorized range. For example, if a prerequisite role of ED is specified for PSO1 and role range [E1,PL1] then only those users who are already members of ED are eligible to be assigned to a role in [E1,PL1] by the PSO1 role. This simple idea is

---

[1]It is not necessary to have a junior-most role or senior-most role in every role hierarchy, so this is just an artifact of our example.

[2]In addition we assume there is a chief security officer who is authorized to make any change in the system, and as such is outside the purview of these administrative models.

[3]The reader may recognize this as standard mathematical notation for open and closed intervals.

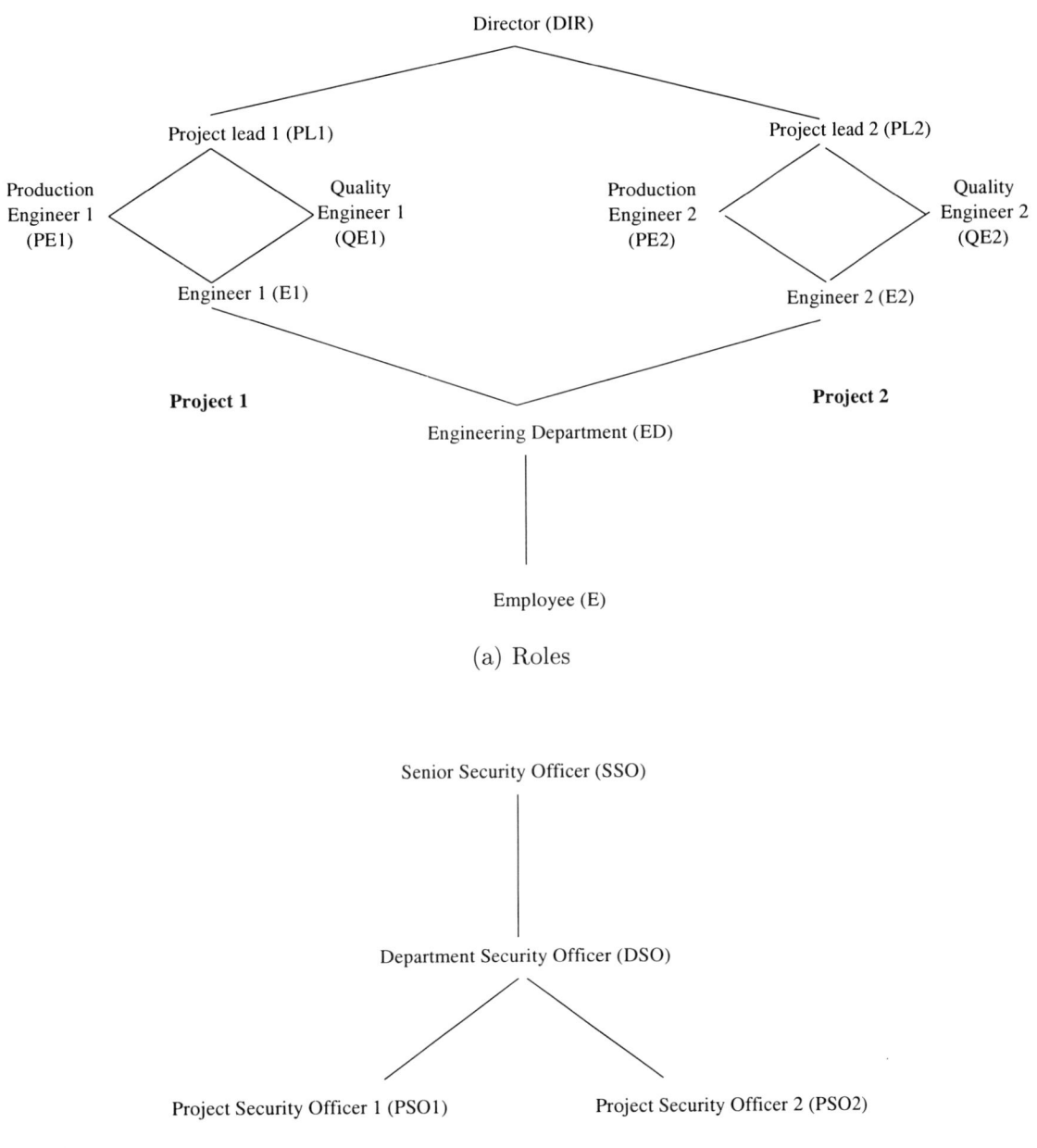

Figure 1: Example Role and Administrative Role Hierarchies

surprisingly powerful as demonstrated in [SBM99].

In URA97 there are two consequences of assigning a user to a role. Firstly the user is authorized to use the permissions of that role and its juniors. Secondly, the user also becomes eligible for assignment to other roles by appropriate administrative roles. These two aspects of role membership are tightly and inextricably coupled in URA97. The main innovation in URA99 is to decouple these two aspects.

URA99 distinguishes two kinds of membership in a role. Immobile membership grants the user the authority to use the permissions of a role but does not make that user eligible for further role assignments. Thus immobile members of a role only get the first aspect of role membership identified above. Mobile membership on the other hand covers both aspects.

This distinction between mobile and immobile users can be very useful in practice. For example, a user under training can be assigned to the ED role and thus participate in the engineering department while preventing junior administrators from assigning this user to projects. After completion of training the user's membership in ED can be upgraded to be mobile. Another example is a visitor who can be granted immobile membership in a junior role as an observer but cannot get assigned to more senior roles. Yet another example is a consultant who might be assigned to the E2 role as an immobile member. The consultant can participate in project 2 and use the general resources of the engineering department due to inherited membership in ED. At the same time the immobility of the consultant prevents junior administrators from assigning the consultant to project 1 roles.

There is a dual notion of mobility for permissions introduced in PRA99. PRA97 allows us to give PSO1 the authority to take a permission assigned to PL1 and grant it to roles in the range [E1,PL1]. The idea is that each project can delegate permissions of the project lead role to more junior project roles as the project security officers deem appropriate. While this may be acceptable for most permissions of the project lead role it is likely that some permissions are not suitable for such delegation. These permissions can be assigned to PL1 as immobile while the others can be assigned as mobile.

It is possible that this distinction between mobile and immobile users and permissions can be simulated in some way in ARBAC97 without directly incorporating it in the extended model ARBAC99. This would be an interesting theoretical exercise which is beyond the scope of this paper. Our objective in this paper is to understand the semantics of mobility and immobility and its interaction with the role hierarchy. As we will see there are a number of subtle issues that arise in formalizing this intuition.

3 The URA97 Model

In this section we briefly review the formal definition of the URA97 model. Our discussion is necessarily brief and the reader is referred to [SB97, SBM99] for detailed motivation and rationale for the design of URA97. URA97 was introduced by Sandhu and Bhamidipati [SB97] and was later incorporated in ARBAC97 [SBM99]. A number of implementations of URA97 on various platforms have also been reported in the literature [SA98a, SA98b, SP98, SB99].

URA97 has two components, one dealing with assignment of users to roles (the grant model) and the other with revocation of user membership (the revoke model).

3.1 URA97 Grant Model

The notion of a prerequisite condition is a key part of URA97.

Definition 1 Let R be the set of regular roles, U the set of users and $UA \subseteq U \times R$ the user-role assignment relation. A **prerequisite condition** is a boolean expression using the usual $\wedge$ and $\vee$ operators on terms of the form x and $\overline{x}$ where $x \in R$. For a given set of roles R let CR denotes all possible prerequisite conditions that can be formed using the roles in R.

Definition 2 A prerequisite condition is evaluated for a user u by interpreting x to be true if $(\exists x' \geq x)(u, x') \in UA$ and $\overline{x}$ to be true if $(\forall x' \geq x)(u, x') \notin UA$ where $\geq$ is the senior relation in the role hierarchy.

User-role assignment is controlled in URA97 by the *can-assign* relation as follows.

Definition 3 User-role assignments are authorized by the relation, *can-assign* $\subseteq AR \times CR \times 2^R$ where AR is the set of administrative roles and subsets of the roles R are identified using the range notation discussed in section 2. (URA97 requires that $AR \cap R = \emptyset$.)

The meaning of *can-assign*$(x, y, \{a, b, c\})$ is that a member of the administrative role x (or a member of an administrative role senior to x) can assign a

Admin. Role	Prereq. Condition	Role Range
PSO1	ED	[E1, PL1)
PSO2	ED	[E2, PL2)
DSO	ED ∧ $\overline{PL2}$	[PL1, PL1]
DSO	ED ∧ $\overline{PL1}$	[PL2, PL2]
SSO	ED	(ED, DIR]
SSO	E	[ED, ED]

Table 1: Example of *can-assign* in URA97

Admin. Role	Role Range
PSO1	[E1, PL1)
PSO2	[E2, PL2)
DSO	(ED, DIR)
SSO	[ED, DIR]

Table 2: Example of *can-revoke* in URA97

user whose current membership, or non-membership, in regular roles satisfies the prerequisite condition y to be a member of regular roles a, b or c.

An example of *can-assign* is given in table 1. PSO1 can assign membership in E1, PE1 or QE1 to members of ED. Similarly, for PSO2 with respect to E2, PE2 and QE2. DSO can assign users in ED to PL1 provided the user is not already a member of PL2. Similarly for PL2 with respect to PL1. SSO can assign members of E to ED and members of ED to any role in the engineering department.

3.2 URA97 Revoke Model

In classical discretionary access control the source (direct or indirect) of a permission and the identity of the revoker is typically taken into account in interpreting the revoke operation. URA97 takes a role-based approach to revocation so authority to revoke is independent of who actually assigned a user to a role, as follows.

Definition 4 The URA97 model authorizes user-role revocation by means of the relation *can-revoke* $\subseteq AR \times 2^R$.

The meaning of *can-revoke*(x, Y) is that a member of the administrative role x (or a member of an administrative role that is senior to x) can revoke membership of a user from any regular role $y \in Y$. Y is specified using the range notation. We say Y defines the *range of revocation*.

An example of *can-revoke* is given in table 2. The role ranges in tables 1 and 2 are closely related. This is likely to be the common case but URA97 does not require that *can-assign* and *can-revoke* have correlated role ranges.

To understand the semantics of revocation we introduce the following distinction.

Definition 5 Let us say a user u is an *explicit member* of role x if $(u, x) \in UA$, and that u is an *implicit member* of role x if for some $x' > x$, $(u, x') \in UA$.

For example, an explicit member of DIR in the engineering department role hierarchy is an implicit member of all other roles. It is possible for a user to simultaneously be an explicit and implicit member of a role.

Revocation in URA97 has impact only on explicit membership and is said to be weak. Thus a user may be revoked explicitly from E1 but continue to be an implicit member due to explicit membership in, say, PL1. Strong revocation requires revocation of both explicit and implicit memberships. So a user who is strongly revoked from E1 will be weakly revoked from E1 and all roles senior to E1. Strong revocation therefore has a cascading effect upwards in the role hierarchy. Of course, each of the weak revokes required for this purpose must be authorized. Strong revocation can be defined to have an all-or-nothing semantics (so no revocation takes place if even one of the required weak revokes fails) or a best-effort semantics (so all required weak revokes within the authorized revocation range take effect, while those outside the authorized range fail). In the formal URA97 model strong revocation is defined to be a series of weak revocations (although in an implementation direct support for strong revocation would be more efficient).

4 The URA99 Model

URA99 builds upon the URA97 model by introducing the following concept, motivated earlier in section 2. A user's membership in a role can be mobile or immobile. *Mobile membership* of user u in role x means that u can use permissions of role x and members of administrative roles can use this membership to put user u into other roles. *Immobile membership* of user u in role x means that u can use permissions of role x but members of administrative roles cannot use this membership to put user u into other roles.

To formalize this distinction we consider each role x as consisting of two sub-roles Mx and IMx. Membership in Mx is mobile whereas membership in IMx is immobile. For compatibility with URA97 we define the set of roles R to consist of the mobile and immobile sub-roles as follows.

Definition 6 For a given set of roles $R1$ we define the roles for URA99 to be $R = \{Mx, IMx \mid x \in R1\}$.

With this definition the user-assignment relation of URA97, $UA \subseteq U \times R$ essentially remains unchanged in URA99. Assignment of a user to Mx signifies that the user is a mobile member of x. Similarly, assignment of a user to IMx signifies that the user is an immobile member of x.

Combining mobile and immobile membership with the previously defined notion of explicit and implicit membership gives us four distinct kinds of role membership in URA99, as follows.

Definition 7 There are four kinds of user-role membership in URA99 for any given role x.

- *Explicit Mobile Member EMx*
  $u \in EMx \equiv (u, Mx) \in UA$

- *Explicit Immobile Member $EIMx$*
  $u \in EIMx \equiv (u, IMx) \in UA$

- *Implicit Mobile Member $ImMx$*
  $u \in ImMx \equiv (\exists x' > x)(u, Mx') \in UA$

- *Implicit Immobile Member $ImIMx$*
  $u \in ImIMx \equiv (\exists x' > x)(u, IMx') \in UA$

It is possible for a user to have all four kinds of membership in a role at the same time. However, we will define the semantics of URA99 so that there is strict precedence amongst these four kinds of membership as follows.

$$EMx > EIMx > ImMx > ImIMx$$

So even though a user can have multiple kinds of membership in a role, at any time only one of those is actually in effect.

To explain the inheritance of mobile and immobile memberships of a role we first consider the hierarchy of two roles shown in figure 2(a) where role $x1$ is senior to role $x2$. User Alice who is an explicit mobile member of role $x1$ (Alice $\in EMx1$) is an implicit mobile

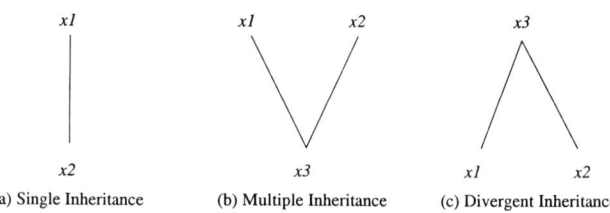

(a) Single Inheritance (b) Multiple Inheritance (c) Divergent Inheritance

Figure 2: Inheritance of mobility and immobility

member of $x2$ (Alice $\in ImMx2$). Similar inheritance applies to immobile memberships as well. Therefore, if Bob is an explicit immobile member of role $x1$ (Bob $\in EIMx1$) he is also an implicit immobile member of role $x2$ (Bob $\in ImIMx2$).

Next, consider the role hierarchy of figure 2(b). Let Bob be an explicit mobile member of role $x1$ and explicit immobile member of role $x2$. Now Bob is an implicit mobile member of $x3$ (because of his explicit mobile membership in $x1$) and is an implicit immobile member of role $x3$ (because of his explicit immobile membership in $x2$). According to the precedence rule mobile membership is stronger than immobile membership. This means that Bob will effectively have implicit mobile membership in role $x3$.

Finally consider the role hierarchy of figure 2(c). Say that Bob is an explicit mobile member of role $x3$. Therefore Bob is an implicit mobile member of roles $x1$ and $x2$ in the hierarchy. Let us also suppose that Bob is an explicit immobile member of $x2$. Then according to our precedence rule Bob will be immobile in $x2$ whereas mobile in $x1$. Bob's explicit immobile membership overrules implicit mobile membership.

The meaning of a prerequisite condition in URA97 is quite straightforward, because the notion of role membership is simple. In URA99 we need to interpret a prerequisite condition in terms of mobile-immobile and explicit-implicit memberships. URA99 prerequisite conditions are defined in terms of x and $\overline{x}$ as in URA97 (rather than in terms of Mx, IMx, $\overline{Mx}$ and $\overline{IMx}$). Membership and non-membership in a role is then interpreted as follows.

Definition 8 In the URA99 grant model a prerequisite condition is evaluated for a user u by interpreting x to be true if

$$u \in EMx \vee (u \in ImMx \wedge u \notin EIMx)$$

and $\overline{x}$ to be true if

Admin. Role	Prereq. Role	Role Range
PSO1	ED	[E1, PL1)
PSO2	ED	[E2, PL2)
DSO	ED ∧ $\overline{PL2}$	[PL1, PL1]
DSO	ED ∧ $\overline{PL1}$	[PL2, PL2]
SSO	ED	(ED, DIR]
SSO	E	[ED, ED]

Table 3: Example of *can-assign-M*

Admin. Role	Prereq. Role	Role Range
PSO1	ED	[E1, PL1)
PSO2	ED	[E2, PL2)
DSO	ED ∧ $\overline{PL2}$	[PL1, PL1]
DSO	ED ∧ $\overline{PL1}$	[PL2, PL2]
SSO	ED	(ED, DIR]
SSO	E	[ED, ED]
DSO	E	[ED, ED]

Table 4: Example of *can-assign-IM*

$u \notin EMx \wedge u \notin EIMx \wedge u \notin ImMx \wedge u \notin ImIMx$

In other words x denotes mobile membership (explicit or implicit) and $\overline{x}$ denotes absence of any kind of membership. Note that it is not possible for x and $\overline{x}$ to be simultaneously true. They can however be simultaneously false (when $u \in EIMx$ and $u \notin EMx$).

The *can-assign* relation of URA97 is replaced by two relations as follows.

Definition 9 User-role assignments as mobile members are authorized by the relation, *can-assign-M* $\subseteq AR \times CR \times 2^R$ and user-role assignments as immobile members are authorized by the relation, *can-assign-IM* $\subseteq AR \times CR \times 2^R$.

The meaning of *can-assign-M(x, y, Z)* is that a member of administrative role x (or a member of administrative role senior to x) can assign a user whose current membership, or non-membership, in regular roles satisfies the prerequisite y to a regular role $z \in Z$ as a mobile member. Whereas the meaning of *can-assign-IM(x, y, Z)* is that a member of administrative role x (or a member of administrative role senior to x) can assign a user whose current membership, or non-membership, in regular roles satisfies the prerequisite y to a regular $z \in Z$ as an immobile member.

Examples of *can-assign-M* and *can-assign-IM* are respectively shown in tables 3 and 4. Table 3 is identical to table 1. Of course, the prerequisite condition is now interpreted differently as discussed above. The top six rows of table 4 are identical to table 3. This means that mobile or immobile membership is granted at discretion of the individual administrators. URA99 requires that authorization for granting mobile or immobile membership be explicitly specified in this manner. There is no implication in general that authority to grant mobile membership implies authority to grant immobile membership (although this may be a common case). The last row of table 4 authorizes DSO to enroll any employee as an immobile member of ED. DSO does not have the power to enroll employees as mobile members of ED. That power is confined to SSO. In this example DSO can enroll an employee as a immobile member of ED and later the SSO can upgrade the membership to be mobile.

4.1 URA99 Revoke Model

The URA99 revoke model fixes a lack of symmetry between the grant and revoke models of URA97 which is quite independent of the issue of mobility. It also deals with revocation of mobile and immobile membership.

In URA97 the relation *can-assign* involves the prerequisite conditions but *can-revoke* does not. To see the utility of prerequisite conditions in this context consider that PSO1 controls user role assignments in project 1 roles. If Bob is a member of E1 then PSO1 can assign Bob to any role of project 1, namely E1, PE1, and QE1. These assignments are governed by the relation *can-assign*. Suppose PSO1 does not want Bob to be a member of any role outside project 1 because his membership in other roles may affect his performance in project 1. If Bob is assigned to a role that falls outside project 1 roles then PSO1 should have authority to revoke him from that role. URA97 does not provide this conditional authority to revoke a role. Prerequisite conditions in *can-revoke* are one means to provide this facility.

Following the approach of the grant model in URA99 we introduce two relations to authorize revocation of mobile and immobile membership as follows.

Definition 10 The URA99 model authorizes revocation of mobile membership by the relation *can-revoke-M* $\subseteq AR \times CR \times 2^R$ and revocation of immobile membership by the relation *can-revoke-IM* $\subseteq AR \times CR \times 2^R$.

Admin. Role	Prereq. Role	Role Range
PSO1	E	[E1, PL1)
PSO2	E	[E2, PL2)
DSO	E	(ED, DIR)
SSO	E	[ED, DIR]
PSO1	E1	[E2, PL2)
PSO2	E2	[E1, PL1)

Table 5: Example of *can-revoke-M*

Admin. Role	Prereq. Role	Role Range
PSO1	E	[E1, PL1)
PSO2	E	[E2, PL2)
DSO	E	(ED, DIR)
SSO	E	[ED, DIR]
PSO1	E1	[E2, PL2)
PSO2	E2	[E1, PL1)
DSO	E	[ED, ED]

Table 6: Example of *can-revoke-IM*

The meaning of *can-revoke-M(x, y, {a, b, c})* is that a member of administrative role x (or a member of a administrative role senior to x) can revoke mobile membership of a user from role a, b or c subject to the prerequisite condition y. Similarly for *can-revoke-IM* with respect to immobile membership.

An example of these relations is given in tables 5 and 6. The first four rows of tables 5 are essentially the same as table 2. The prerequisite condition E will evaluate to true for all employees so is redundant. It can equivalently be replaced by any predicate that is always true. The last two rows allow PSO1 to revoke project 1 users from project 2 roles and vice versa. Th top six rows of table 6 are identical to table 5, so in this example authority to revoke mobile membership also implies authority to revoke immobile membership. The last row of table 6 authorizes DSO to remove immobile users from ED (which DSO has the power to assign as per table 4).

The evaluation of a prerequisite condition for the revoke model of URA99 is different from the grant model. For the revoke model we do not distinguish mobile and immobile membership. Thus we have the following interpretation.

Definition 11 In the URA99 revoke model a prerequisite condition is evaluated for a user u by interpreting x to be true if

$$u \in EMx \lor u \in EIMx \lor u \in ImMx \lor u \in ImIMx$$

and $\bar{x}$ to be true if

$$u \notin EMx \land u \notin EIMx \land u \notin ImMx \land u \notin ImIMx$$

Note that unlike in the grant model x and $\bar{x}$ cannot be false at the same time. As in URA97 they are logical complements of each other.

4.2 URA97 as a Special Case of URA99

If all membership is restricted to being mobile than URA99 is identical to URA97. This can be achieved by setting *can-assign-IM* and *can-revoke-IM* to be empty. In this manner there is a simple relationship between URA97 and URA99.

5 The PRA99 Model

The PRA99 model deals with assignment and revocation of permissions to and from the roles. Like users, permissions can also be assigned to roles as mobile and immobile. Just as PRA97 relates to URA97, we have PRA99 as an exact dual of URA99. For sake of completeness we give a complete definition of PRA99 here. The main difference between PRA99 and URA99 is that in PRA99 implicit membership of a permission in a role is inherited upwards in the hierarchy. We give the definitions below without further commentary since they are so closely related to URA99 definitions.

Definition 12 The roles in PRA99 are the same as in URA99, that is, $R = \{Mx, IMx \mid x \in R1\}$. The permission role assignment relation is $PA \subseteq U \times R$.

Definition 13 There are four kinds of permission-role membership in PRA99 for any given role x.

- *Explicit Mobile Member EMx*
  $p \in EMx \equiv (p, Mx) \in PA$

- *Explicit Immobile Member $EIMx$*
  $p \in EIMx \equiv (p, IMx) \in PA$

- *Implicit Mobile Member $ImMx$*
  $p \in ImMx \equiv (\exists x' < x)(p, Mx') \in PA$

- *Implicit Immobile Member $ImIMx$*
  $p \in ImIMx \equiv (\exists x' < x)(p, IMx') \in PA$

Definition 14 Permission-role assignments as mobile members are authorized by the relation, *can-assignp-M* $\subseteq AR \times CR \times 2^R$ and permission-role assignments as immobile members are authorized by the relation, *can-assignp-IM* $\subseteq AR \times CR \times 2^R$.

Definition 15 The PRA99 model authorizes revocation of mobile membership by the relation *can-revokep-M* $\subseteq AR \times CR \times 2^R$ and revocation of immobile membership by the relation *can-revokep-IM* $\subseteq AR \times CR \times 2^R$.

Definition 16 In the PRA99 grant model a prerequisite condition is evaluated for a permission p by interpreting x to be true if

$$p \in EMx \vee (p \in ImMx \wedge p \notin EIMx)$$

and $\overline{x}$ to be true if

$$p \notin EMx \wedge p \notin EIMx \wedge p \notin ImMx \wedge p \notin ImIMx$$

Definition 17 In the PRA99 revoke model a prerequisite condition is evaluated for a permission p by interpreting x to be true if

$$p \in EMx \vee p \in EIMx \vee p \in ImMx \vee p \in ImIMx$$

and $\overline{x}$ to be true if

$$p \notin EMx \wedge p \notin EIMx \wedge p \notin ImMx \wedge p \notin ImIMx$$

6 Discussion and Conclusion

We have described the new ARBAC99 model for role-based administration of role-based access control. ARBAC99 is the first model that incorporates the notion of mobile and immobile users and permissions in administrative RBAC. It has three components: URA99 (user-role administration '99), PRA99 (permission-role administration '99) and RRA99 (role-role administration '99). It is an extension of ARBAC97 obtained by adding the concept of mobile users and permissions in the URA and PRA models. The RRA model is unchanged.

The basic intuition of ARBAC97 is not altered in this paper, that is, the decentralization of administration of user-role assignments, permission-role assignments and role-role hierarchies by means of administrative roles, prerequisite conditions and role ranges. Administrative roles are given autonomy within their administrative ranges as constrained by prerequisite conditions.

References

[BFA99] Elisa Bertino, Elena Ferrari, and Vijay Atluri. Specification and enforcement of authorization constraints in workflow management systems. *ACM Transactions on Information and System Security*, 2(1), February 1999.

[FBK99] David F. Ferraiolo, John F. Barkley, and D. Richard Kuhn. A role based access control model and reference implementation within a corporate intranet. *ACM Transactions on Information and System Security*, 2(1), February 1999.

[GGF98] Virgil D. Gligor, Serban I. Gavrila, and David Ferraiolo. On the formal definition of separation-of-duty policies and their composition. In *Proceedings of IEEE Symposium on Research in Security and Privacy*, pages 172–183, Oakland, CA, May 1998.

[NO99] Matunda Nyanchama and Sylvia Osborn. The role graph model and conflict of interest. *ACM Transactions on Information and System Security*, 2(1), February 1999.

[SA98a] Ravi Sandhu and Gail-Joon Ahn. Decentralized group hierachies in unix: An experiment and lessons learned. In *Proceedings of 21st NIST-NCSC National Information Systems Security Conference*, Arlington, VA, October 5-8 1998.

[SA98b] Ravi Sandhu and Gail-Joon Ahn. Group hierarchies with decentralized user assignment in Windows NT. In *Proc. International Association of Science and Technology for Development (IASTED) Conference on Software Engineering*, Las Vegas, Nevada, October 1998.

[San98] Ravi Sandhu. Role-based access control. In Zelkowitz, editor, *Advances in Computers, Volume: 46*. Academic Press, 1998.

[SB97] Ravi Sandhu and Venkata Bhamidipati. The URA97 model for role-based administration of user-role assignment. In T. Y. Lin and Xiaolei Qian, editors, *Database Security XI: Status and Prospects*. North-Holland, 1997.

[SB99] Ravi S. Sandhu and Venkata Bhamidipati. Role-based administration of user-role assignment: The URA97 model and its Oracle implementation. *The Journal Of Computer Security*, 1999. in press.

[SBM99] Ravi Sandhu, Venkata Bhamidipati, and Qamar Munawer. The ARBAC97 model for role-based administration of roles. *ACM Transactions on Information and System Security*, 2(1), February 1999.

[SCFY96] Ravi S. Sandhu, Edward J. Coyne, Hal L. Feinstein, and Charles E. Youman. Role-based access control models. *IEEE Computer*, 29(2):38–47, February 1996.

[SP98] Ravi Sandhu and Joon Park. Decentralized user-role assignment for web-based intranets. In *Proceedings of 3rd ACM Workshop on Role-Based Access Control*, pages 1–12, Fairfax, VA, October 22-23 1998. ACM.

[ZSS99] M. Zurko, R. Simon, and T. Sanfilippo. A user-centered modular authorization service built on an rbac foundation. In *Proceedings of IEEE Symposium on Research in Security and Privacy*, pages 57–71, Oakland, CA, May 1999.

Track A

Public Key Infrastructures

Chair

Frank Sledge, TRW

A Distributed Certificate Management System (DCMS) Supporting Group-based Access Controls

Rolf Oppliger   Andreas Greulich   Peter Trachsel
Swiss Federal Strategy Unit for Information Technology FSUIT
Monbijoustrasse 74, CH-3003 Berne, Switzerland
{rolf.oppliger,andreas.greulich,peter.trachsel}@isb.admin.ch

Abstract

Mainly for scalability reasons, many cryptographic security protocols make use of public key cryptography and require the existence of a corresponding public key infrastructure (PKI). A PKI, in turn, consists of one or several certification authorities (CAs) that issue and revoke certificates for users and other CAs. Contrary to its conceptual simplicity, the establishment and operational maintenance of a CA or PKI has turned out to be difficult in practice. As a viable alternative, this paper proposes an architecture for a distributed certificate management system (DCMS) that can also be used to provide support for group-based access controls. The architecture has been prototyped and is being used by the Swiss Federal Strategy Unit for Information Technology (FSUIT) to protect access to intranet resources.

1 Introduction

Network security is a hot topic today. Access control services are usually provided through the use of firewalls, whereas communication security services are usually provided through the use of cryptographic security protocols that work at the Internet, transport, and/or application layer of the TCP/IP communications protocol suite [1,2]. Mainly for scalability reasons, many of the cryptographic security protocols make use of public key cryptography and require the existence of a corresponding public key infrastructure (PKI). A PKI, in turn, consists of one or several certification authorities (CAs) that issue and revoke certificates for users or other CAs. The CAs may be organized in many ways, including, for example, a hierarchy or a decentralized web of trust (making heavy use of cross-certificates).

Since the term "certificate" was first used by Loren M. Kohnfelder to refer to a digitally signed record holding a name and a public key [3], it has been assumed that the only purpose of a certificate is to bind a public key to a globally unique name. In fact, this assumption has led to the design of several PKIs on top of existing naming schemes and directory services, such as provided by the ITU-T recommendations of the X.500 series. However, the singular use of the term "certificate" has recently been challenged with the use and proliferation of attribute certificates within the Internet community [4,5]. Unfortunately, standardization is far away from coming up with a commonly agreed and widely deployed format for attribute certificates, and the use of attribute certificates on a large scale and across applications is still not possible today (this will probably change when attribute certificates become widely deployed on the Internet).

Due to the singular use of the term "certificate" in the security community, there is still considerable confusion on how to build a PKI. For example, the Internet Engineering Task Force (IETF) has tasked a Public Key Infrastructure X.509 (PKIX) Working Group (WG) to design and build a PKI for the Internet community based on the ITU-T recommendation X.509 [6], whereas the Simple PKI (SPKI) WG has been tasked with producing a certificate structure and operating procedure to meet the needs of the same community for trust management in as easy, simple, and extensible a way as possible. The fear that motivated the IETF to task two WGs is actually due to the possibility that the task of building an X.509-based PKI for the Internet community is too big. Note that the Privacy Enhanced Mail (PEM) WG failed to build and establish an X.509-based PKI for secure electronic mail for the Internet community a couple of years ago [7]. Having a closer look at the two approaches being followed by the WGs, one actually recognizes that the main difference between them is the fact that the IETF PKIX WG assumes the existence of a global namespace, whereas the IETF SPKI WG does not make this assumption and starts from linked local namespaces, such as the ones proposed by Ron Rivest and Butler Lampson in their Simple Distributed Security Infrastructure (SDSI). Furthermore, the SDSI/SPKI effort addresses authorization in addition to authentication (since a PKI that only addresses authentication isn't very useful for e-commerce applications). The results of the IETF PKIX and SPKI WGs and are overviewed and discussed in Chapter 8 of [8]. They are not further addressed in this paper.

One may reasonably dispute whether an X.509-based PKI is actually the infrastructure required for the Internet community and the e-commerce applications that are supposed to take place within the Internet. Anyway, from a

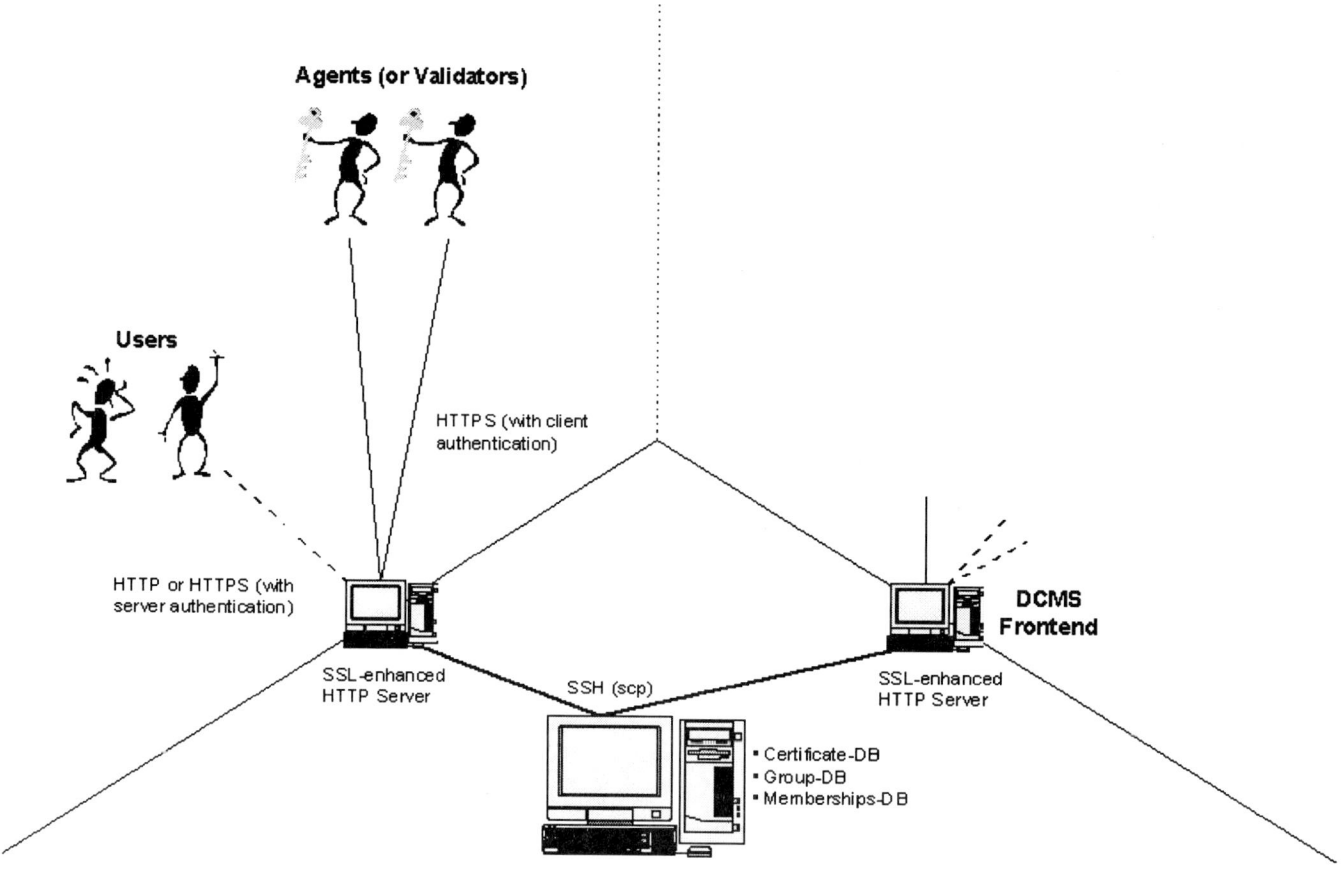

Figure 1: The architecture of the distributed certificate management system (DCMS)

practical (and corporate) point of view, the situation is fundamentally different and simpler. Within a corporate environment, there typically exists a namespace in which each employee is not only identified with a unique name, but is also assigned a unique employee number. Consequently, there exists a namespace (within the corporate environment) that can be used to have certificates bind public keys to unique names. Consequently, ITU-T X.509 provides a useful ground for building a PKI for a corporate environment. In fact, many organizations follow this approach and establish X.509-based PKIs to secure their intranet and extranet connections.

Assuming the existence of an internal (locally unique) namespace within a corporate environment (which can either be a company or an organization), this paper proposes an architecture for a distributed certificate management system (DCMS). In addition to manage X.509-based public key certificates, the DCMS can also be used to provide support for group-based access controls. As such, the DCMS addresses authentication and authorization from an architectural point of view. In short, the aims of the DCMS are two-fold:

- On the one hand, the DCMS architecture is to provide a high degree of delegation and decentralization with regard to the provision of its certification services. The underlying assumption is that a delegated and decentralized certification service can be provided more effectively and efficiently than it centralized counterpart (since existing organizational units, such as the human resources department, can be used).
- On the other hand, the DCMS architecture is to introduce the notion of a group membership to provide support for group-based access controls. This is similar to the use of attribute certificates to facilitate access controls [4,5].

The DCMS architecture has originally been described in [9]. This paper goes some steps further in refining the architecture, elaborating on an existing prototype implementation called PECAN (an acronym derived from "PErl Certification Authority Network"), and pointing out some areas for further study.

The rest of this paper is organized as follows: The DCMS architecture is introduced and overviewed in Section 2. The corresponding prototype implementation is described in Section 3, and areas of further study are addressed in Section 4. Finally, conclusions are drawn in Section 5. The paper refers to ongoing work within the Swiss Federal Strategy Unit for Information Technology (FSUIT). Consequently, future papers will address the experiences that are made with the use and deployment of PECAN within the intranet of the Swiss governmental bodies.

2 DCMS Architecture

The DCMS architecture is illustrated in Figure 1. It basically consists of three components:

- A DCMS core;
- One or several decentralized DCMS frontends;
- A DCMS database that is maintained by the DCMS core. Data that are collected at the DCMS frontends are periodically synchronized, processed by the DCMS core, and replicated and redistributed to the frontends.

The DCMS core is a standalone application that is operated by DCMS administrators with corresponding privileges and access rights. In fact, DCMS administration requires some sort of shell access to the underlying operating system (e.g., UNIX or Windows NT). Contrary to the DCMS core, the DCMS frontends are provided by "normal" HTTP or Web servers that are operated by the corresponding system administrators. The DCMS frontends can run either as normal Web servers or SSL-enabled server-only authenticated Web servers (which is actually the preferred configuration). The same DCMS frontend can also run on a fully operable SSL-enabled Web server (including, for example, client authentication), which then allows certain users, called DCMS agents, to perform specific actions within the database. In essence, a DCMS agent is a user who has been granted special privileges with regard to the verification of user identities or the confirmation of corresponding group memberships. It is up to the DCMS administrators to nominate users as DCMS agents. In either case, communications between the DCMS core and the corresponding frontends must be secured with a cryptographic security protocol, such as the Internet Security Protocol (IPSP), the Secure Sockets Layer (SSL) or Transport Layer Security (TLS) protocol, or the Secure Shell (SSH) [1]. Note that the DCMS topology is a star, simplifying the tasks of key management (for the cryptographically secured communication between the DCMS core and its frontends) and database synchronization considerably.

The DCMS architecture is centered around the notion of a group (to support group-based access controls). In essence, a group is an attribute granted to a certificate to provide its owner with some specific privileges. Unlike other proposals, such as attribute certificates, the privileges that are granted to the certificate owners are not directly encoded into the corresponding certificate data structures, but are stored off-line within a database. The database entries are then used to link certificates to corresponding group membership information. This has the advantage of having certificates in a permanent form, whereas all transient group membership information are stored and maintained dynamically in the database (where it can be managed more easily).

The list of available groups is determined by the DCMS administrators and can be changed at will.

With regard to a given group A, a certificate may be in one of the following states:

- The certificate can be in the "member of A" state. In this state, the certificate has access privileges related to group A. Synonymously, one can say that "membership of A is granted" or "issued" to the certificate, or that the certificate has the "issued" state for A.
- The certificate can be in the "revoked out of A" state. In this state, membership to group A (and its related privileges) has been revoked.
- The certificate can be in the "applied for A" state. In this state, the certificate has been applied for but is not (yet) a member of group A. Eventually, membership will be granted or revoked at some later point in time. Syononymously, one can say that the certificate is in the "pending" state for A.
- Finally, if a certificate does not belong to any of the states mentioned above, it is in the "unknown" state for this particular group A. In this case, no explicit state has been given yet. Consequently, the certificate has no access privileges related to group A (the same is true for the pending and revoked states). A certificate in unknown state is also said to be "external" (external from group A's perspective). All other states mentioned above indicate that a certificate is "internal", meaning that it has a well-defined state. An external certificate can become internal with regard to A either by application from a user, or by an explicit import operation performed by a legitimate agent of the group.

As mentioned above, each group is managed by one or several users who have special privileges (the so-called DCMS agents). In short, a DCMS agent is a strongly authenticated (e.g., through the use of SSL client authentication) user who has the privilege on the DCMS frontends to modify the states of the certificates for "his groups." These are all the groups he's a legitimate agent for. Obviously, a user can be an agent for several groups (all of them are called "his groups"), and a group can be run by one or more agents. Consequently, there exists an (n:m)-relationship between groups and agents (n,m >= 1).

Per definition, DCMS administrators are agents for all groups. Also, there is a special group called ".". Granting a certificate access to the "." group actually means that the identity of the certificate requester has been verified according to a specific policy or certification practice statement (CPS). Similar to any other group, the legitimate agents of the "." group are nominated by the DCMS administrators. In the case of the "." group, DCMS agents are also called validators, meaning that the agents of this group are authorized to verify the identity of the corresponding certificate requesters, and to validate the certificates accordingly. Validation of a certificate implies some policy-driven procedure, such as placing a phone call to the applicant or appearing in person and showing a photo ID. The important point to note is that there may be several validators around. Each validator is authorized to validate any certificate, no matter if it belongs to one of his groups. Actually, a validator does not even need to be an agent of any other group. Also note that each certificate can be subject to several validations. As soon as a validator V1 validates an anonymous certificate, it gets the "V1T1" state (T1 referring to a timestamp for the validation process). But any validated certificate can be revalidated at any time, possibly several times. So, if another validator V2 revalidates the certificate at some later point in time, the validation state gets the "{V1T1,V2T2}" state (T2 referring to the timestamp for the new validation). Consequently, a list of all validators that validated a certificate can be requested and, for example, used by an agent in order to determine whether or not to grant membership to one of his groups. Note, however, that the monotony property of the validation process (meaning that a validation can't be revoked at some later point in time) is important for the scheme to work. In spite of the fact that certificates must be able to be revoked, there is no need to revoke validations (validation revocation doesn't make sense from a logical point of view).

3 Prototype Implementation

The DCMS architecture described so far has been prototyped and is being used at the Swiss Federal Strategy Unit for Information Technology (FSUIT) in a software called PECAN (an acronym derived from "PErl Certification Authority Network"). The name of the software has been chosen due to the fact that it's main parts are implemented with the Perl scripting language.

In the subsections that follow, we address the content of the databases that are used by PECAN, the database synchronization process, access control lists (ACLs) extraction, and the corresponding Perl scripts.

3.1 Databases

PECAN uses a Perl-based database management system (DBMS) called Sprite, but any other SQL-based DBMS could be used instead. The PECAN software currently comprises three main databases (a fourth database that includes the rules that specify how to use the certificates to control access to intranet resources is not addressed in this paper):

- The `Certificate-DB` stores all certificate information, including the original request (e.g., in Netscape's SPKAC format), fields filled in by the user, state of the internal certificate (pending, issued, or revoked), timestamps, and the certificate itself as soon as it is issued. Also, each new certificate gets a unique identifier (ID), called the CERTID, which is a letter followed by a 6-digit number (the letter is unique for each DCMS or PECAN frontend). Consequently, the format of a `Certificate-DB` entry is as follows:

CERTID	Unique certificate ID
TEL	Telephone number of the requester
CN	Common name (CN) of format "surname, firstname :SEQ=\d:" (SEQ referring to a sequence number)
CC	Country code
ST	State/province information
OO	Organization
OU	Organization unit (suborganization)
EMAIL	Electronic mail address
TIMECREAT	Timestamp of certificate request
TIMEMOD	Timestamp of last modification
STATUS	Certificate status ($PENDING, $ISSUED, or $REVOKED)
REQ	Original certificate request
REQFORMAT	Format of REQ (e.g., SPKAC or PKCS7)
CERT	Certificate (as soon as it is issued)
CERTFORMAT	Format (e.g., X509)
EXPIRES	Expiration date

    Note that the certificate's common name (CN) is usually sent by the browser and constructed by a JavaScript code segment. It contains the name entered by the user, and a sequence number given by the user (usually set to 1). Sequence numbers allow reissuing certificates, for example, for certificate renewal or second browsers. Users with the same CN except its sequence number are considered to be the same, whereas certificates with different sequence numbers are considered to be different. The part of the CN field up to the first ":" is called the "owner of the certificate" or "name of the owner of the certificate", whereas the full CN is called the "name of the certificate". Consequently, certificates with CN "Greulich, Andreas :SEQ=1:" and "Greulich, Andreas :SEQ=2:" have the same owner, but are still considered different certificates (the first and second certificate). In either case, the name of the owner is "Greulich, Andreas."

- The `Group-DB` stores group-related information. More precisely, each entry in the `Group-DB` contains a unique group ID for the group, the name of an agent, and eventually a group description (only one entry may contain a group description). As such, the `Group-DB` also stores validators and DCMS administrators; validators being agents of the group ".", and DCMS administrators being agents of the group "CA". The entries of the Group-DB can only be modified by DCMS administrators by direct writing to the core `Group-DB`. The format of a `Group-DB` entry is as follows:

GROUPID	Unique group ID
OWNER	Name of an agent for the group
DESC	Description of the group

Note that several entries with the same GROUPID may exist, but only one should have a non-empty DESC field. The OWNER field contains the name of the owner of authorized certificates, so entering "Greulich, Andreas" as owner labels all certificates of the form "Greulich, Andreas :.....:" as being agents for this particular group (validators for the "." group and administrators for the "CA" group). In this case, the colon is just a separator that is discarded (simply to avoid having to modify the database when certificates are renewed). Finally, note that each GROUPID/OWNER pair is unique and must appear only once in the entire database.

- The `Memberships-DB` links the other two databases (the `Certificate-DB` and `Group-DB`). As such, each entry is keyed with a CERTID and a GROUPID, and provides state information for the certificate (identified with CERTID) with regard to the corresponding group (identified with GROUPID). A certificate can either be internal or external, in the former case being either in the pending, issued or revoked state. There might be only one entry for a given CERTID and GROUPID, except when the GROUPID is ".", as there may be several validators for a certificate. The `Memberships-DB` is readable by anybody, and anybody may also append to it because each new certificate request automatically generates pending memberships for all groups a user selected, plus one "pending" membership for group "." indicating the certificate is not yet validated. Only SSL-authenticated agents, validators and DCMS administrators may modify entries belonging to "their" (and only their) groups. The format of an entry in the `Memberships-DB` is as follows

    CERTID   Link to the `Certificates-DB`
    GROUPID Link to the `Group-DB`
    STATUS   Certificate status
    BY   Name of the person who created
              or modified the database entry
    TIMEMOD Time of the creation or modification

When a user requests a certificate from a DCMS or PECAN frontend, the following steps are usually performed:

1. A `Certificate-DB` entry is created with a unique CERTID, containing all fields, except CERT and EXPIRED. The value of the STATUS field is set to $PENDING (meaning that the certificate is in pending state).
2. A `Memberships-DB` entry is created with a GROUPID value set to "." and a STATUS value set to $PENDING (meaning that the certificate requester is waiting to be validated).
3. For each group the certificate requester selected, a corresponding entry with status value set to $PENDING is created in the `Memberships-DB` (meaning that the certificate requester is waiting to be granted membership to specific groups). Note that steps 2 and 3 are not fundamentally different, since "." can also be seen as a special group.

A special case occurs if the connection of the certificate request was mutually authenticated between the user and a PECAN frontend (through the use of SSL with client authentication). In this case, the user has already been issued a certificate at some earlier point in time. All validations and granted group memberships that have been granted to the non-revoked certificates of the requester are automatically inherited. For example, if the owner "Greulich, Andreas" of the certificate "Greulich, Andreas :SEQ=2:" with CERTID "A111111" requests a new certificate "Greulich, Andreas :SEQ=3:" (with CERTID "A222222") using an SSL-authenticated access, demanding membership to groups A and B, while "Greulich, Andreas :SEQ=2:" is already a member of A (but external to B), the generated certificate automatically inherits its $ISSUED state for group A. The fields of the corresponding entry in the `Memberships-DB` are initialized to the following values:

    CERTID   A222222
    GROUPID A
    STATUS $ISSUED
    BY   INHERIT-A111111
    TIMEMOD ...

If more than one non-revoked certificate with a matching owner name exist (such as "Greulich, Andreas :SEQ=1:" with CERTID "A100000"), multiple inheritance may happen ($ISSUED memberships are inherited, whereas $REVOKED memberships are ignored). So, if "Greulich, Andreas :SEQ=1" is issued, but "Greulich, Andreas :SEQ=2" revoked, the issued state is inherited. For obvious reasons, revoked certificates must not be considered for inheritance. In the example given above, "BY" would be set to "INHERIT-A111111-A100000."

The inheritance mechanism should make certificate renewal easier, as group memberships need not be regranted by the corresponding agents. Note, however, that this subject is still under investigation, and that security inconsistencies can't be excluded at this point in time.

3.2 Database Synchronization

From time to time, the `Certificate-DB` and `Memberships-DB` must be synchronized among the various frontends and the core (note that the `Group-DB` is stable and must not be synchronized). The synchronization process can happen on a regular basis (for example, twice a day) or on an administrator's request. In the PECAN implementation, database synchronization is performed using the SSH `scp` tool to securely copy the frontend `Certificate-` and `Memberships-DBs` to the core, where they are synchronized as follows:

1. The new entries in the frontend `Certificate-DBs` are added to the corresponding core `Certificate-DB`.
2. The entries in the frontend `Memberships-DBs` for a particular CERTID/GROUPID pair that appear in more than one DB (core plus all frontend DBs) are sorted chronologically, and the most recent one is chosen. For each entry it is then checked if the BY field matches an agent in the appropriate `Group-DB`. BY fields starting with INHERIT and AUTO are just taken for granted ("AUTO" is only added to allow importing or therwise issued certificates).
3. The log files from all frontend DBs are collected into a central logfile. Any intrusion detection algorithm would be applied to this central logfile (intrusion detection algorithms have not been implemented so far).

After the synchronization process, the new core DBs are replicated and redistributed to the frontends. In addition, a certificate-signing procedure can be started at this point in time. The corresponding script operates on the core DB only and performs the following actions: All certificates in issued state (meaning that their STATUS field is set to $ISSUED) that are validated (i.e., they have at least one "." membership granted) and have all their memberships in issued state are considered as candidates. Their requests plus a list of all candidates is extracted and shown for acknowledgment to an administrator. If the administrator gives his acknowledgment, all certificate candidates are signed in one step. Obviously, this interactive step must be skipped if the certificate-signing procedure is run in batch mode. In either case, the resulting certificates are put into the appropriate fields in the `Certificate-DB`.

3.3 Access Control Lists Extraction

To support group-based access controls, PECAN can also be used to extract access control lists (ACLs) from its databases (using a Perl script called `acls.pl`). More specifically, for each group A, a file `A.acl` can be extracted that contains the CN fields of all issued certificates with granted membership to this group (multiple certificates that belong to the same user will appear several times). For example, a file `A.acl` may look as follows (specifying two users):

```
Greulich, Andreas :SEQ=1:
Oppliger, Rolf    :SEQ=3:
Oppliger, Rolf    :SEQ=4:
```

Such a file is suitable for Stronghold's `SSL_Require` directive. Something like the following script may work in Stronghold's (and other Web server's) HTTPD configuration file (`httpd.conf`):

```
<VirtualHost *:1943>
SSLFlag on
SSLVerifyClient 2
<Location>
SSL_Group A
"cn INFILE /opt/WWW/ACLs/A.acl"
SSL_Require 'A'
ErrorDocument 403 "Your certificate is
    not member of the A group. To
    join it, please contact Mr. X."
</Location>
ProxyPass / http://A.bfi.admin.ch/
...
</VirtualHost>
```

Furthermore, a certificate revocation list (CRL) can be extracted and used in a similar directive.

3.4 PERL Scripts

As mentioned above, PECAN is currently implemented as a set of several Perl scripts:

- The script `CA.cgi` implements the PECAN frontend (the user interface);
- The script `sync.pl` implements the synchronization procedure mentioned above;
- The script `sign.pl` implements the signing procedure mentioned above;
- The script `acls.pl` implements the ACL extraction process mentioned above;
- The script `index.pl` is used for backward compatibility. It reads in SSLeay-style `index.txt` for "old" certificates, automatically validates them, and adapts memberships specified as attributes in the CN field (meaning that "Greulich, Andreas :SEQ=1:A:B:" automatically gets memberships to A and B). BY-fields are put to "AUTO";
- The script `importOldCerts.pl` scans trough directories containing ".pem" files and adding their certificates into the core DB, if latter contains issued certificates without certificate data whose CN fields match. This script is usually used together with `index.pl` to include old certificates to the core DB.

4 Areas of Further Study

Obviously, the most important component of the DCMS architecture is the signing key that is required to issue digitally signed public key certificates. In one way or another, the DCMS administrator must have access to this key, and this access must be controlled accordingly. The key is either stored in the DCMS core and protected accordingly (e.g., encrypted with a key derived from a password or pass phrase that is known only to DCMS administrators), or it is provided by a DCMS administrator for temporary use (e.g., using smartcard technologies). In practice, the first option is preferred if the process of issuing digital certificate must be automated and included into a batch processing file. In general, however, it is less secure than the second option. In this case, it is up to the DCMS administrator to secure the key, and to provide it to the DCMS core whenever needed.

With regard to protecting the private signing key, one could think of using secret sharing or group signature schemes:

- In a secret sharing scheme, a secret (such as a private signing key) can be shared among many users (or DCMS administrators) in such a way that any qualified group of users can reconstruct the secret, but any unqualified group of users have absolutely no information about the secret (in the case of a perfect secret sharing scheme). This concept was first proposed in [10,11], and has been subject to a lot of cryptographic research and development meanwhile.
- In a group signature scheme, a digital signature can only be computed if a qualified group of users and holders of corresponding secrets) cooperate. More precisely, each user (or DCMS administrator) holds a signing key that allows him to compute a partial signature for a certificate. All partial signatures together constitute the signature for the certificate [12].

Note that using secret sharing or group signature schemes is equally useful in centralized and decentralized (and distributed) certificate management systems. It is assumed that the problem of protecting private signing keys for generating certificates will become more important in the future.

As of this writing, the database synchronization scheme used in the prototype implementation is fairly simple. In fact, database synchronization must be initiated by a DCMS administrator (e.g., twice a day). In large domains, it may be required that databases are resynchronized periodically. Ideally, database resychrnonization is made a permanent task that is performed in the background. Any database replication and synchronization technique can be used. Note, however, that the star topology of the DCMS should be taken into account when optimizing the corresponding database replication and synchronization schemes. Due to the star topology, the DCMS frontends need not be synchronized among each other.

In this paper, the DCMS architecture has been described for a corporate environment (for example, an intranet setting). In practice, the situation is much more complicate with groups including members of several companies and organizations. Consequently, issues related to cross-organization and inter-domain DCMS will be important in the future. For example, how can DCMS administrators cooperate across organizational borders, and how can agents do the same? These questions are left for further study. Similarly, the question of how to efficiently revoke public key certificates is addressed in [8] and not further elaborated in this paper.

Finally, a field that is left for further study is related to the granularity of group membership. Note that in this paper, group membership has always implied that a user (who has been granted group membership) has obtained privileges with regard to this group. Consequently, group membership is a boolean value (either group membership is granted or not). This granularity may not be sufficient for real-world access controls, where a user can be a member of group and have several roles within this group (e.g., leader, moderator, secretary, ...). Against this background, one can reasonably assume that applying role-based access control models to the DCMS architecture will lead to new insights that can be used to further refine the DCMS architecture and its application for access controls. This approach may actually lead to a group- and role based access control model [13].

5 Conclusions

To overcome the problems related to build and operate a scalable public key infrastructure (PKI), this paper proposed an architecture for a distributed certificate management system (DCMS) that can also be used for group-based access controls. In short, the DCMS consists of three components: a DCMS core, one or several DCMS frontends, and several databases that are periodically synchronized with a core database. The DCMS core is operated by administrators with corresponding privileges, whereas the DCMS frontends are operated by agents that have the privileges to either verify the identity of requesting users, or to confirm their memberships to specific groups. Consequently, the operational task of running a CA or PKI is distributed among severalpeople, each of them responsible only for specific tasks.

Meanwhile, the DCMS architecture has also been prototyped and is being used by the IT Security Group of the Swiss Federal Strategy Unit for Information Technology (FSUIT). The corresponding prototype implementation is called PECAN (PErl Certification Authority Network). It consists of a database system and several Perl scripts. Experience has shown that a distributed approach to managing certificates in a corporate environments offers many advantages with regard to the scalability of the resulting solution.

References

[1] R. Oppliger, *Internet and Intranet Security*. Artech House Publishers, Norwood, MA, 1998

[2] R. Oppliger, *Authentication Systems for Secure Networks*. Artech House Publishers, Norwood, MA, 1996

[3] L.M. Kohnfelder, *Towards a Practical Public-key Cryptosystem*, MIT S.B. Thesis, May 1978

[4] R. Oppliger, G. Pernul, and C. Strauss. Using Attribute Certificates to Implement Role-based Authorization, submitted for publication

[5] R. Oppliger, Authorization Methods for E-Commerce Applications. Proceedings of the International Workshop on Electronic Commerce held in conjunction with the 18th IEEE International Symposium on Reliable Distributed Systems (SRDS '99), Lausanne (Switzerland), October 19 - 22, 1999

[6] ITU-T Recommendation X.509: *The Directory - Authentication Framework*, 1988

[7] S.T. Kent, Internet Privacy Enhanced Mail, *Communications of the ACM*, Vol. 36, No. 8, August 1993, pp. 48-60

[8] R. Oppliger, *Security Technologies for the World Wide Web*. Artech House Publishers, Norwood, MA, 1999

[9] R. Oppliger, A. Greulich, and P. Trachsel. Der Einsatz eines verteilten Zertifikat-Managementsystems in der Schweizerischen Bundesverwaltung. Proceedings of the German Informatics Society (GI) Working Conference "Verlaessliche IT-Systeme" (VIS '99), Essen (Germany), September 22 - 24, 1999

[10] A. Shamir, How to share a secret, *Communications of the ACM*, Vol. 22, No. 11, November 1979, pp. 612 - 613

[11] G.R. Blakley, Safeguarding cryptographic keys, Proceedings of AFIPS 1979 National Computer Conference, pp. 313 - 317

[12] C. Boyd, Some Applications of Multiple Key Ciphers, Proceedings of Eurocrypt '88, pp. 455 - 467

[13] R.S. Sandhu and E.J. Coyne, Role-Based Access Control Models, *IEEE Computer Magazine*, February 1996, pp. 38 - 47

Fast Checking of Individual Certificate Revocation on Small Systems

Selwyn Russell
Information Security Research Centre
School of Data Communications (Information Technology)
Queensland University of Technology
2 George Street, Brisbane 4000, Australia
S.Russell@qut.edu.au *

Abstract

High security network transactions require the checking of the revocation status of public key certificates. On mobile systems this may lead to excessive delays and unacceptable performance. This paper examines small system requirements and options with a view to improving performance. It is shown that the use of keyed hash functions (message authentication codes) with a pre-registration option reduces network latency and allows stateless servers.

1. Introduction

The Internet and its large public audience have stimulated interest in commercial transactions across Wide Area Networks. The World Wide Web and its stateless HyperText Transfer Protocol were devised for access from heterogeneous platforms to public documents and are unsuitable for commercial transactions where confidentiality, access control, authorization, financial transactions, etc are concerned. Security enhancements generally involve the use of digital certificates as discussed in the next section. Mostly a certificate contains information regarding the start and finish of its intended valid life. After a certificate has been created and circulated, it is possible for it to be revoked before its internally specified expiry date. In the absence of a revocation status, a revoked certificate may be mistakenly accepted as valid for a transaction. Verification of the authenticity of a certificate in very important transactions will probably require checking of the revocation status. Revocation notification practices and proposals are considered in section 3. While the processing associated with these status checking techniques is a minor burden on desktop and larger systems, their use of digital signatures can lead to unacceptable delays on small systems such as pocket-sized mobile units because of their limited processing power, limited storage, and relatively low speed network connections.

This paper investigates the use of message authentication codes as alternatives to digital signatures for authenticating revocation status replies from a server by the enquiring client. Section 4 discusses requirements for small systems, and proposes four options for authenticable responses not requiring digital signatures. Two of these options which do not require a prearranged relationship between the two parties are investigated in Section 5. The other two options make use of a prearranged relationship are discussed in Section 6.

2. Background

Recent interest in making transactions across public WANs commercially secure, with assured confidentiality, integrity and authentication, has lead to various proposals for a public key infrastructure (PKI). These proposals commonly involve the concept of a certificate to provide some reliable information about the other party. A "certificate" [10] [5] is usually thought of as a block of data which provides information on the public key of one party and which has been attested to by another party which creates the certificate and is known as the Certification Authority (CA) for that certificate, but the Simple Public Key Infrastructure (SPKI) project of the Internet Engineering Task Force has generalized [7] it to include any required information about the first party, which may not include the public key in some applications. A CA may be a "well known" entity or may be an entity within an organization which provides certificates for others within the organization. A certificate may be self-certified by an individual and accepted by friends and other individuals but would not be accepted in electronic commerce for example.

---

*This research is part of the co-operative project "Security Technologies in Wireless Communications" between Queensland University of Technology and Korea Telecom.

The life cycle of a certificate begins when an individual approaches a CA and provides certain identification information. In some cases, the individual may provide details of a pre-selected public key; in others, the CA generates a private and public key pair for the applicant. An individual would probably use a CA which provides services to the public. For a member of a small organization, the approach to the public CA is more likely to be made by authorized officers of the organization on behalf of the individual. For a large enterprise the use of a public CA is not cost effective, and the enterprise would more likely have its own internal CA for issuing certificates to its employees or clients.

The top level internal CA would have acquired a certificate from a publicly accepted CA. There may be several levels of internal CAs, particularly in a geographically dispersed enterprise so that verification of the initial identification of the applicant is more certain.

An issued certificate contains an expiry time after which it is to be regarded as unacceptable for further usage. After that expiry time, the certificate should not be accepted by a recipient for performing transactions or other operations, but it may be required after its expiry date for audit, taxation, or other legal purposes. The maximum lifetime might be specified by the applicant but public CAs commonly impose limits such as one year.

If it is decided by the certificate holder or the issuing CA or some other authorized person that the certificate is not to be used anymore before the expiry date, e.g. the person has left the organization or the customer has closed the account, the CA who issued the certificate is approached and notified of the desire for termination. The CA maintains a publicly accessible database of revoked certificates, and newly revoked identities are added in accordance with the CA's policies.

3. Revocation Notification, Practice and Proposals

There are numerous well known methods of notifying the public of identities of certificates which have been revoked before their expiry date. This section covers the better known ones and compares their benefits.

3.1. Certificate Revocation List

Under the X.509 framework[5], a CA will periodically publish a Certificate Revocation List (CRL) containing the identities of all revoked but unexpired certificates issued by that CA. The size of the list is unlimited.

For validation of an incoming certificate by using CRLs, the computer will obtain, either immediately or at some regular or irregular intervals, the most recently published CRL from each of the issuing CAs, of which there are probably at least two, one master CA for the enterprise and the well known public CA who issued a certificate to the enterprise master CA. If there are other internal CAs involved in a certificate chain, they may have to be contacted for their latest CRLs.

For a large computer, a CRL may be stored locally once fetched from the source. Depending on the transaction, a CRL known to be a week old may be considered satisfactory but for a mission-critical financial transactions, anything older than one hour may be rejected. Fetching the latest CRL is not a great burden for a large computer attached to a high speed network but can lead to unacceptable elapsed times for mobile units.

To determine if the certificate in question is in a CRL, the computer needs to

1. determine the class of CRL
2. determine the version
3. extract the individual items of data (issuer name, signature, certificate list, etc)
4. identify the validity period
5. if expired, reject the CRL and take security actions
6. identify the signature
7. identify the signature algorithm used
8. reconstruct the original unsigned CRL
9. calculate the corresponding hash
10. identify the signer
11. obtain the signer's public key
12. from the signer's key and the signature algorithm, calculate the hash signed by the signer
13. if that hash is different from that of the local calculation, reject the CRL and take security actions
14. search through the list of identifiers of revoked certificates, looking for a match with the identifier of the certificate under analysis.

The elapsed time for this process is greatly influenced by the format of the individual elements, the structure of the certificate, and any encoding of the structure.

A CRL is a poor way for a client to obtain information on a single certificate because of the size of the download and the storage and processing required, but is very efficient if many certificates can be checked from the extracted certificate identifiers before the next version of that CRL is available, as is possible if a mainframe in a large enterprise is involved. A benefit to the CA server is that the number of CRL fetches will be lower than if only information on single certificates were available. The CA will only build the CRL at scheduled intervals and will have a relatively low processing load. However there is still a problem for the irregular enquirer of a single certificate and this is being investigated by various groups.

Although the CRL is current at the time of publication, the CRL will grow stale as further certificates are revoked by the holders before the next publication date. In some scenarios, this is of no consequence, but will be a serious security flaw for others.

Consequently, other means of determining currency of certificate have been investigated including Certificate Revocation Trees (CRTs) [9] and special purpose protocols to access special purpose online databases such as those discussed below.

3.2. Certificate Revocation Tree (CRT)

A Certificate Revocation Tree (CRT)[9] is a patented method which allows a receiver of a certificate to obtain information on its status in the form of fragments of a Merkle tree built and signed by a CA. To reduce the enquiry load on the CA, the tree may be replicated at convenient distributed locations.

The fragments may accompany the certificate or may be obtained from one of the distributed licensed servers ("Confirmation Issuer") which has the replicated complete tree. The fragments relating to the one certificate (actually the fragments define a range of certificate serial numbers) are smaller in size than a typical X.509 CRL with information on all revoked certificates, and can be processed by a sequence of calculations of hash values plus the validation of the signature of the revoking CA.

For the server replying to enquiries on the status of a single certificate, the benefit to the server is that it does not have to sign each reply. It selects the appropriate fragments of the complete CRT which it has obtained from the CA, and forwards them with the signature of the CA on the complete tree. There is no encryption required of the server and its working efficiency is therefore quite high and it can support high hit rates. To check the certificate status, the client must calculate hashes, the number of which is approximately the binary logarithm of the number of leaves in the tree. For a tree of 100,000 leaves containing information on the status of possibly millions of certificates, about 17 hash calculations would be involved. A benefit of the client is that the reply from the server is much smaller than the corresponding CRL. The principle benefit appears to be to the server, which does not have to sign any reply. Network traffic can be reduced by locating mirror servers where convenient.

3.3. Realtime Enquiry of the CA Database

In some cases, it is necessary to verify that the certificate is still active prior to conducting or completing a transaction. CRLs and CRTs cannot provide this realtime assurance and direct enquiry of the certificate database is necessary. The X.500 Directory provides for realtime enquiries using the Directory Access Protocol on OSI networks, as does the derived LDAP system using the Lightweight Directory Access Protocol on TCP/IP networks. There are a number of proposed protocols for authenticated realtime enquiries which are underway as part of the IETF's Public Key Infrastructure using X.509 (PKIX) project.

- Online Certificate Status Protocol (OCSP)

  This proposal [4] is designed around ASN.1 and its related Distinguished Encoding Rules (DER) encoding and uses signed responses.

- Web-based Integrated CA services Protocol – ICAP

  This proposal [13] is designed around the HyperText Transfer Protocol and does not use DER encoding and allows for signed or unsigned responses. OCSP is not designed to be transport protocol dependent but ICAP is designed to use HTTP to ensure it can traverse security firewalls. On the other hand, OCSP points out that HTTP caching can lead to unexpected results if configurations are not carefully set.

- Real Time Certificate Status Protocol – RCSP

  The draft proposal [1] has expired and this proposal seems to have been superceded by OCSP.

- WEB based Certificate Access Protocol – WebCAP/1.0

  This proposal [12] is similar to ICAP in that it uses HTTP but uses XML to encode the contents of the HTTP replies.

3.4. Suitability for use with small systems

Small systems, such as hand held mobile units and palmtop computers, by their nature have limitations on processing power, memory, local storage, speed of network link, which do not apply to enterprise servers or high powered desktop work stations. For these small systems, their performance in processing security functions is critical. If the processing is perceived as unacceptably long by the user, they will be turned off.

In this paper we are concerned with the issue of performing revocation checks from small systems. The issue of processing certificates is beyond the scope of this paper. Certificate structure and processing are being considered by groups such as the IETF's PKIX and SPKI groups. The former is proceeding with X.509 certificates with extended attributes, ASN.1 specifications, DER encoding and decoding; the latter avoids ASN.1 and DER and favours multiple application-specific certificates rather than one multi-purpose certificate. For small systems, the SPKI proposals offer the superior processing speed.

PKI proposals are generally not explicitly platform dependent, but they assume that the client has all the necessary computing power and storage to perform the required operations. Typically, authenticated responses require the client to verify at least one digital signature on the response from a CA or agent, which is relatively time consuming, especially if DER decoding is also involved, as with X.509 certificates and associated systems.

If a certificate chain is involved, then each certificate in the chain will need to be tested for revocation, adding noticeably to the elapsed time for a small system with a low speed network connection. An X.509 CRL is the worst in that it may require the small system with limited local storage to download a 50K CRL, perform DER decoding and analysis and a digital signature verification, for each certificate in the chain, before a transaction can proceed.

4. General Requirements and Options

In this section we will look closer at some of the requirements of clients and servers involved with information on status of certificates.

If a revoked certificate is used by mistake, the fact will be discovered during routine checking and no harm will be done. The certificate holder will probably be notified and will submit a current certificate. The security problem arises when a revoked certificate is used deliberately, implying that the attacker has a compromised key and is impersonating the certificate owner. In this situation, the attacker will try to prevent certificate status checks from revealing that the certificate has been revoked, i.e. will either modify the entries in the database or will actively modify network messages so that the client will receive a good reply rather than the notice of invalid status.

For slow network links, short requests and short responses are desirable. To reduce the elapsed time at the client, short processing time at client and server are desirable. The structure of a request should minimize the work to process it, i.e. not involve processing which could be avoided with a more efficient design. The client requires correct reply, authentication of source, and integrity.

In most cases, the certificate will be valid and the response from the CA will indicate so. This leads to the possibility of a precalculation on the client of a valid response to reduce elapsed time, easy with threaded operating systems. The received response can be compared with the pre-calculated value of a valid reply. If they match, the transaction can continue. An example where this can be used effectively is the case of a pre-arranged relationship treated below in section 6.1.

If the time for a hash calculation is t, and the most likely response occurs with probability p, two or more hashes will be needed at most only with a probability of $1 - p$. Even on small systems, t is very likely less than the transmission latency.

Because of uncontrollable network latency, the design should minimize the number of message exchanges across the network, preferably using only one request message and one reply message.

4.1. Options

Options for authentication of responses include

- unauthenticated response from CA
- conventionally signed response
- authenticatable but non-signed response
    1. no pre-arranged relationship between client and server, anyone can authenticate the response
    2. no pre-arranged relationship between client and server, only the client can authenticate the response
    3. pre-arranged relationship between client and server based upon a persistent shared value
    4. pre-arranged relationship between client and server using a transient or one-time shared value

We will not discuss insecure responses which cannot be authenticated or responses which have a conventional digital signature, but will seek methods where the elapsed time is much shorter. The remainder of the paper discusses the four classes of authenticatable but non-signed responses.

5. No Relationship Between the Parties

In this section we consider the case where the parties have not made prior arrangements before beginning transactions, e.g. an Internet shopper chances across a shop and begins impulsive purchasing. We will use CA to represent the authority providing replies regarding the current status of a certificate, even though this may not necessarily be the issuing Certification Authority.

5.1. Anyone Can Authenticate the Response

The most desirable situation is where anyone can authenticate the status checking response without having made prior arrangements with the CA but no one other than the CA can construct one. The client can easily share the response as received with others and they can verify the origin independently. In legal investigations, the client does not have to reveal any secret information.

One implementation of this asymmetric situation would be the use of an asymmetric cryptosystem, which is undesirable on a small system. Some proposals, e.g. OCSP, use public key signatures. An advantages is that a stateless protocol can be utilized.

The Guy Fawkes protocol [2] has been proposed for signing bidirectional digital streams. It uses hash functions rather than conventional digital signatures. This protocol requires a signed delivery of initial values but subsequent stages do not need digital signatures, only hash calculations. It could be used for a single enquiry only, and restarted from the beginning on the next enquiry, requiring another digital signature creation and one verification. For multiple enquiries over a period of time, the subsequent digital signatures could be avoided but the state would need to be stored. A disadvantage in either case is that a stateful server is required for the steps in the protocol. Another disadvantage is the number of steps involved, leading to increased elapsed time.

5.2. Only the Client Can Authenticate the Response

This group satisfies the client's request but the response cannot be independently verified by other parties.

One possible implementation is the use of a Diffie-Hellman shared key [6] [11], which requires knowledge of the enquiring client's public key and the published value of the key of the CA (or agent) server. If the client has public value $g^c \bmod p$ and the server uses $g^s \bmod p$, the shared value, which either can calculate, is $shVal = g^{cs} \bmod p$. An efficiency consideration is that the client could calculate the shared key once and store it for reuse. Alternatively, other one pass mutual key values, such as an El Gamal key agreement value [11], could be used. With more network traffic, stateful application programs, and more time, a two pass key agreement [11] could be used.

Assuming we have a $shVal$, we will briefly outline two general ways of using it for authentication.

5.2.1 Symmetric Key Based Authentication

Using a key agreement value from the above calculation, either the value $shVal$ or a derivative, e.g. its hash, could be used as a symmetric key to encrypt a response, or to encrypt a data encrypting key which is then used to encrypt the response. Conventional symmetric methods for message authentication can then be used.

5.2.2 Hash Based Authentication

The value $shVal$ calculated above could be used in the calculation of a hash value, effectively performing a keyed message authentication code. In the following, $TrNum$ is a transaction number used here to thwart replay of reply attacks, and CID is the identifier of the certificate in question. Party A represents the enquiring client and party B represents the CA server.

$$A \rightarrow B: \quad TrNum, CID$$
$$A \leftarrow B: \quad TrNum, response,$$
$$H(shVal, response, TrNum, CID)$$

Here there is one hash calculation $H(\ldots)$ each and one calculation each of the shared value $shVal$. Some small systems would be able to calculate the shared value for a most-likely-to-be-accessed-CA once and store it or may have it built into a SIM type device provided with the unit, as with mobile phones.

This principle appears to be suitable for small systems in some environments, mainly when $shVal$ is precalculated and stored securely as in a smart card.

6. Prearranged Relationship Between Client and Server

Many Internet servers require a client to register and establish a user identity and password with it before providing information, even if there is no charge for the subsequent accesses. One reason is to obtain statistics on the usage of the server. A revocation-enquiring client could register with a CA server and obtain a user-specific password (shared value) which would be used in subsequent enquiries. This value could be permanent, i.e. persist unchanged from one access to the next, as is usual with human enquirers, or it could form the basis of a calculated one-time value. These two cases are investigated in the remainder of this section.

6.1. Permanent Shared Value for Each Transaction

If there is a large persistent random value $shRVal$ known to both parties, it can be used in the hash preimage to implement a keyed message authentication code:

$$A \rightarrow B: \quad TrNum, CID$$

$$A \leftarrow B: \quad TrNum, response,$$
$$H(shRVal, response, TrNum, CID)$$

A nice feature of this is that the client can calculate the response corresponding to the most likely status, viz. $VALID$, while waiting for the server to reply. If the received value corresponds to the precalculated value, then the elapsed time at the client is reduced link, to the comparison time plus the maximum of the network latency and the (pre)calculation time rather than the sum of all three as would be the case if digitally signed responses were used. Calculating a keyed message authentication code will be significantly quicker than verifying a digital signature supplied with a response followed by extracting the status content. Having to wait for a reply from the CA before digital signature processing can begin makes the total elapsed time for the digital signature method even worse. If there is a certificate chain to be worked through, the hash based method is even more desirable.

As mentioned above, an attacker will attempt to send a valid response to hide the fact that a certificate has been revoked. In such a case, if the attacker intercepts the reply and alters the plaintext *response*, the reply will be

$$Attacker \leftarrow B: \quad TrNum, INVALID,$$
$$H(shRVal, INVALID,$$
$$TrNum, CID)$$
$$A \leftarrow Attacker: \quad TrNum, VALID,$$
$$H(shRVal, INVALID,$$
$$TrNum, CID)$$

The client will note that the plaintext response contains $VALID$ and that the hash does not correspond to the precalculated hash corresponding to $VALID$. The next step is to calculate the hash corresponding to $INVALID$. If this matches the received hash, the fraud attempt is exposed. If it fails to match, the client will either repeat the request assuming transmission errors or server errors, or abandon the transaction.

If the most likely response, $VALID$, occurs with probability p, two hashes will be needed at most only with a probability of $1-p$. The average number of hashes per enquiry is $2-p$, which is close to unity.

One hash calculation is required of the client and the server. The server can be stateless so HTTP can be used. The server needs to know the identity of the enquirer to use the appropriate $shRVal$ and such identities are commonly provided via a cookie in the header of the HTTP request. Alternatively party A, the client, can provide its identity explicitly in the request. If a brute force attack is considered a threat, the actions could be extended to provide a one-time nonce from the client:

$$A \rightarrow B: \quad TrNum, CID, nonce_c$$
$$A \leftarrow B: \quad TrNum, response,$$
$$H(shRVal, response, TrNum,$$
$$CID, nonce_c)$$

If a chosen plaintext attack is considered a threat, the actions could be extended to provide a one-time nonce from the server but the client will not be able to perform a precalculation while waiting for a reply:

$$A \rightarrow B: \quad TrNum, CID$$
$$A \leftarrow B: \quad TrNum, response, nonce_s,$$
$$H(shRVal, response, TrNum,$$
$$CID, nonce_s)$$

An alternative is to use a modification of the well known KryptoKnight [3] family of protocols developed at IBM which provide for hash-based authentication and form the basis of some IBM products. Modifying the three steps of the KryptoKnight "secure two-way authentication protocol" by adding a transaction number $TrNum$ and a certificate identification CID in the enquiry, and adding a status reply *response* from the server, we obtain the following, where $H(shRVal,...)$ represents the Message Authentication Codes in the original:

$$A \rightarrow B: \quad TrNum, CID, A, B, Nonce_A$$
$$A \leftarrow B: \quad TrNum, response, B, A, Nonce_B,$$
$$H(shRVal, Nonce_A, Nonce_B, B)$$
$$A \rightarrow B: \quad A, B, H(shRVal, Nonce_A, Nonce_B)$$

$shRVal$ is either a shared value or some derived value available to both parties, e.g. $shRVal = H(TrNum, PSV)$ where PSV is the permanent shared value arranged in a prior transaction. In this latter example, each party must calculate three hashes. If $shRVal$ requires no hash calculation, e.g. it is a stored value, there are two hash calculations required for each enquiry. Because of the three steps involved, a server using this KryptoKnight protocol would not be able to function using the simple stateless HTTP but would require a state-aware application running on the server machine.

6.2. Different Value for Each Transaction

The principle is to initially arrange a shared value, then, for each transaction, derive a working value from it which is used as the message authentication key.

Synchronous modification of an initial prearranged value is workable on a small system. An example is a simple extension of the above shared constant value method of section 6.1 is to increment the stored value by a prearranged amount after each enquiry. Because of the avalanche property of the hash function, this will dramatically alter the observed value even if other preimage components were unchanged.

A more complicated option is to use a variation of S-key, almost a reverse S-key. In the S-key system [8] of authenticating a client to a server, there is a value stored at the server for which an authentic client is able to provide the preimage. At successful login, the supplied preimage becomes the stored value to be used for the next login attempt. For our purposes, the client wants to authenticate a communication (the revocation status reply) from the server. An authentic server will know the preimage of the value used on the previous reply, and will be able to use it for the current reply.

Set N as the intial value, each can calculate $F_i(N)$ for any value i, where F is a one way function, and $F_n = F(F_{n-1}(N))$.

$$A :\rightarrow B : TrNum, CID, accessNum$$
$$A :\leftarrow B : TrNum, response,$$
$$H(TrNum, response, CID, accessNum,$$
$$F_{N-accessNum}(N))$$

The value $accessNum$ is incremented by the client at each enquiry.

This system places more computation load on the client, which has to calculate $N - accessNum$ hash values at the time of the enquiry, or requires sufficient local storage for a table of precalculated hash values (as is done in some S-key systems).

Another option is a modified Guy Fawkes system, where the server at each stage provides a hash value whose preimage is revealed at a later stage. However this protocol involves numerous stages of networked communications and stateful behaviour of both parties and hence fails to meet our requirements for small systems.

7. Summary

Realtime status verification of certificates is necessary in some situations. If an attempt is made to submit a revoked certificate, it may be a mistake or fraud may be involved. If fraud is involved, authentication is essential. Authentication involving digital signatures can be a performance problem on small systems connected to low speed network links, such as hand held mobile digital units. As an alternative more suitable for small systems, this paper has proposed some uses of hash functions in keyed message authentication codes to provide shorter elapsed times and faster processing with satisfactory security assurance. The use of pre-registration with a constant value used in a hash function allows precalculation during network latency and allows stateless servers.

References

[1] C. Adams, A. Malpani, R. Ankney, and S. Galperin. Internet Public Key Infrastructure Real Time Certificate Status Protocol – RCSP. Technical report, IETF, Mar. 1998. Internet Draft draft-malpani-rcsp-00.txt.

[2] R. Anderson, F. Bergadano, B. Crispo, J.-H. Lee, C. Manifavas, and R. Needham. *A New Family of Authentication Protocols*. Available at http://www.cl.cam.ac.uk/ftp/users/rja14/fawkes.ps.gz.

[3] R. Bird, I. Gopal, A. Herzberg, P. Janson, S. Kutten, R. Molva, and M. Yung. The KryptoKnight Family of Light-Weight Protocols for Authentication and Key Distribution. Technical report, Dec. 1993.

[4] M. Branchard. X.509 Internet Public Key Infrastructure Online Certificate Status Protocol – OCSP. Technical report, IETF, Mar. 1998. Draft RFC draft-ietf-pkix-ocsp-08.txt.

[5] CCITT. *The Directory - Authentication Framework*. Number CCITT X.509. International Telegraph and Telephone Consultative Committee, Switzerland, Nov. 1988.

[6] W. Diffie and M. Hellman. New directions in cryptography. *IEEE Trans. Inform. Theory*, IT-22(6):644–654, Nov. 1976.

[7] C. Ellison. SPKI requirements. Technical report, IETF, Oct. 1998. IETF draft RFC draft-ietf-spki-cert-req-02.txt.

[8] N. M. Haller. The s/key one-time password system. In *Proceedings of the ISOC Symposium on Network and Distributed System Security*, pages 151–157, San Diego, California, Feb. 1994. The Internet Society. (Available from National Technical Information Service, U.S. Department of Commerce, Springfield, VA 22161, USA.

[9] P. C. Kocher. *On Certificate Revocation and Validation*. Springer-Verlag, Anguilla, British West Indies, Feb. 1998. Proc. of the Second International Conference Financial Cryptography, ISBN 3-540-64951-4.

[10] L. M. Kohnfelder. *Towards a Practical Public-key Cryptosystem*. May 1978. MIT B.S. Thesis.

[11] A. J. Menezes, P. C. van Oorschot, and S. A. Vanstone. *Handbook of Applied Cryptography*. CRC Press, 1997. ISBN 0-8493-8523-7.

[12] S. Reddy. WEB based Certificate Access Protocol – WebCAP/1.0. Technical report, IETF, Apr. 1998. IETF draft RFC draft-ietf-pkix-webcap-00.txt.

[13] Y. Sameshima, H. Kikuchi, M. Sakurai, H. Hattori, and H. Kumagai. Web-based Integrated CA services Protocol – ICAP. Technical report, IETF, Jan. 1999. IETF draft RFC draft-sakurai-pkix-icap-01.txt.

A Model of Certificate Revocation

David A. Cooper
Computer Security Division
National Institute of Standards and Technology
Gaithersburg, MD 20899-8930
david.cooper@nist.gov

Abstract

This paper presents a model for the distribution of revocation information using certificate revocation lists (CRLs). This model is used to highlight inefficiencies in the "traditional" method of distributing certificate status information using CRLs. Two alternative CRL-based revocation distribution mechanisms, over-issued CRLs and segmented CRLs, are then presented. The original model is then expanded to encompass each of the alternative mechanisms and these expanded models are used to demonstrate the advantages of the alternative mechanisms to the "traditional" method. Finally, the paper offers some suggestions for choosing the best CRL-based revocation distribution mechanism for any particular environment.

1. Introduction

Public key infrastructures (PKIs) are being fielded in increasing size and numbers, but operational experience to date has been limited to a relatively small number of environments. As a result, there are still many unanswered questions about the ways in which PKIs will be organized and operated in large scale systems. Some of these questions involve the ways in which individual certification authorities (CAs) will be interconnected. Others involve the ways in which certificate status information will be distributed. In a 1994 report, the MITRE Corporation suggested that the distribution of revocation information has the potential to be the most costly aspect of running a large scale PKI [1].

The MITRE report assumed that each CA would periodically issue a certificate revocation list (CRL) that listed all of the unexpired certificates that it had revoked. Since the MITRE report was published, several alternative certificate status distribution mechanisms have been proposed. Each of these mechanisms has its own relative advantages and disadvantages in comparison to the other schemes. NIST is working to create mathematical models of some of the proposed certificate status distribution mechanisms. These models could be used to determine the circumstances under which each of the mechanisms is most efficient.

Most of the proposals have involved variations of the original CRL scheme. Examples include the use of segmented CRLs and delta-CRLs [2]. However, some schemes do not involve the use of any type of CRL (e.g., on-line certificate status protocols [4] and hash chains [3]).

This paper presents models for various methods of distributing certificate status information using CRLs. In modeling the various methods, it is assumed that relying parties request CRLs only when needed to perform a validation (i.e., no pre-caching of CRLs) and that they have perfect caches (i.e., no CRLs are deleted from the cache until they have expired). For each option, the request rate is computed for CRLs as a function of time. As this paper shows, request rates vary over time. However, in building a repository for a PKI, it is necessary to build one that is capable of handling incoming requests, even when the request rate is at its peak, without unreasonable response times. As such, this paper focuses on distribution methods that minimize peak loads on repositories as opposed to methods that minimize average loads.

The paper begins by presenting a model for the "traditional" method of distributing certificate status information using CRLs. This model is then used to point out some of the deficiencies inherent in the "traditional" method. Finally, models for two alternative CRL-based certificate status distribution methods are presented and the manner in which these methods overcome some of the deficiencies in the "traditional" method is described.

2. A model for the traditional method

The traditional method of distributing certificate status information involves a CA periodically issuing a CRL, which it posts to a repository. The CRL includes all unexpired certificates issued by the CA that have been revoked. Each CRL includes a **nextUpdate** field that spec-

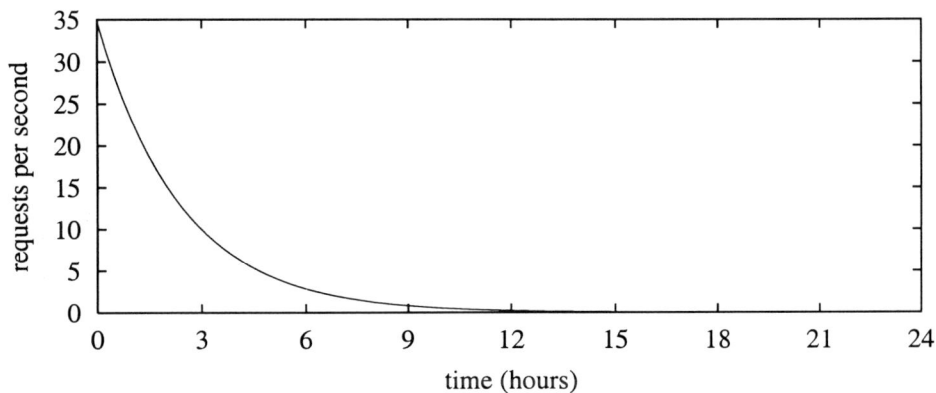

Figure 1. Unsegmented CRL

ifies the time at which the next CRL will be issued. Any relying party requiring certificate status information, that does not already have the current CRL, retrieves the current CRL from the repository. In order to enhance performance, copies of the CRL may be distributed to several sites. The model in this paper, however, assumes that all relying parties obtain CRLs from the same repository[1].

In order to examine the load on the repository from CRL requests, the rate at which requests for CRLs are made over time must be determined. With the traditional method, every relying party needs the most current CRL in order to perform a validation. Once a relying party has retrieved the most current CRL, it will not need to request any more information from the repository until a new CRL has been issued. This is the case with the traditional method since each CRL specifies the status of all unexpired certificates issued by the CA and each CRL includes a **nextUpdate** field stating when the next CRL will be issued. As a result, over the period of time in which a CRL is valid (i.e., the most current), each relying party will make at most one request to the repository for a CRL. This request will be made the first time after the current CRL is issued that the relying party performs a validation.

In order to compute the overall CRL request rate, the probability density function for validation attempts for a single relying party must be known. In particular, if a CA issues a new CRL at time 0, it must be determined, for any time t, the probability that a relying party will perform its first validation after time 0 at time t. If the number of relying parties is reasonably large, then it can be assumed that the times at which validation attempts are made are independent of each other (i.e., they occur at randomly distributed times). Based on this assumption, an exponential interarrival probability density [5] can be used to model the timing of validation attempts. In this model, the probability that a relying party's first validation attempt will occur in the interval $[t \ldots t + dt]$, in the limit $dt \to 0$, is

$$ve^{-vt}dt \qquad (1)$$

where v is the validation rate (i.e., average number of certificates per unit time that a relying party attempts to validate). Since each relying party downloads a CRL at the time of its first validation attempt after time 0, this equation also represents the probability that any given relying party will send a request to the repository for a CRL in the interval $[t \ldots t + dt]$. If this equation is multiplied by the number of relying parties, N, and divided by dt, the result is the request rate for CRLs from the repository at time t:

$$R(t) = Nve^{-vt} \qquad (2)$$

Figure 1 shows the request rate for a CRL, issued using the traditional method, over the course of 24 hours. The graph in figure 1 was drawn assuming that a CRL was issued at time 0 and that no other CRLs were issued during the period of time shown in the graph. It was also assumed that there are 300,000 relying parties each validating an average of 10 certificates per day.

3. Over-issued CRLs

The graph in figure 1 makes the problem with the traditional method of issuing CRLs apparent. The problem is that the CRLs cached by every relying party expire at the same time. Immediately after the CRLs expire, and a new CRL is issued, every relying party will need to obtain a CRL from the repository in order to perform a validation. As a result, there is a relatively high request rate when a new CRL is issued followed by an exponential decline in the request

---

[1] If more than one repository is used, then the load on each repository could be approximated by dividing the number of relying parties by the number of repositories.

cRLNumber = 1 **thisUpdate** = Mon. 12:00am **nextUpdate** = Tues. 12:00am	**cRLNumber** = 2 **thisUpdate** = Mon. 6:00am **nextUpdate** = Tues. 6:00am	**cRLNumber** = 3 **thisUpdate** = Mon. 12:00pm **nextUpdate** = Tues. 12:00pm
cRLNumber = 4 **thisUpdate** = Mon. 6:00pm **nextUpdate** = Tues. 6:00pm	**cRLNumber** = 5 **thisUpdate** = Tues. 12:00am **nextUpdate** = Wed. 12:00am	**cRLNumber** = 6 **thisUpdate** = Tues. 6:00am **nextUpdate** = Wed. 6:00am

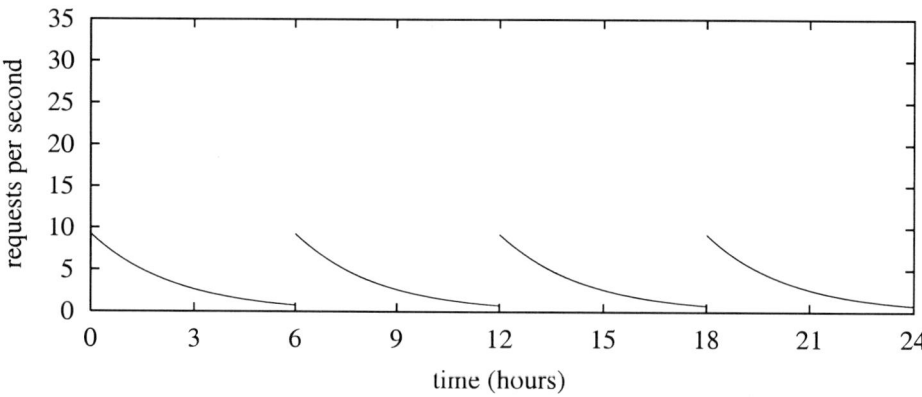

Figure 2. Over-issued CRLs

Figure 3. Request rate for over-issued CRLs

rate. If CRLs are valid for a reasonably long period of time, then there will be periods of time in which the repository is practically unused. In the example depicted in figure 1, the request rate begins at 34.72 requests/second and then drops to 0.24 requests/second after 12 hours. After 24 hours, the request rate is only 1.6×10^{-3} requests/second.

One way to reduce the peak load on the repository is to spread out requests for CRLs. This can be accomplished by issuing CRLs in such a way that the CRLs in relying parties' caches do not all expire at the same time.

With the traditional method, a new CRL is not issued until the time specified in the **nextUpdate** field of the previously issued CRL has been reached. As a result, a relying party with a CRL in its cache will not request a new CRL from the repository until the time specified in the **nextUpdate** field of the cached CRL has been reached. If a new CRL is issued before the previous one expires (i.e., before the **nextUpdate** time of the previous CRL has been reached), then some relying parties will retrieve this new CRL while other relying parties continue to use the previously issued CRL. If each issued CRL is valid for the same length of time, then the relying parties that retrieved the new CRL will still have valid CRLs in their caches when the original CRL expires.

The idea of issuing a new CRL before the previously issued CRL has expired is not entirely new. Many people have considered the idea of issuing an "emergency" CRL whenever a certificate has been revoked as a result of a key compromise. If the validity period of this CRL is the same as that of the "regularly scheduled" CRLs, then the issuance of the "emergency" CRL may lead to a temporary reduction in the peak request rate when the next "regularly scheduled" CRL is issued. However, in order to maintain a consistently low peak request rate, CRLs must consistently be issued at a rate greater than that required by the validity periods of the CRLs.

Figure 2 shows an example of over-issued CRLs. In this figure, each CRL is valid for 24 hours, but a new CRL is issued every 6 hours. Figure 3 shows the request rate for CRLs over the course of 24 hours assuming CRLs are issued as in figure 2 and that there are 300,000 relying parties each validating an average of 10 certificates per day. By comparing figure 3 to figure 1, it can be seen that the result of over-issuing is to spread out the requests for CRLs, thus significantly reducing the peak request rate (from 34.72 requests/second to 9.25 requests/second). Of course, even in figure 3 the request rate varies over time. If CRLs were issued more frequently, requests would be spread out even more evenly and the peak request rate would be further reduced. In the limit, if CRLs were issued continuously, the request rate in this example would be 3.16 requests/second. Figure 4 shows the peak request rate as a function of the

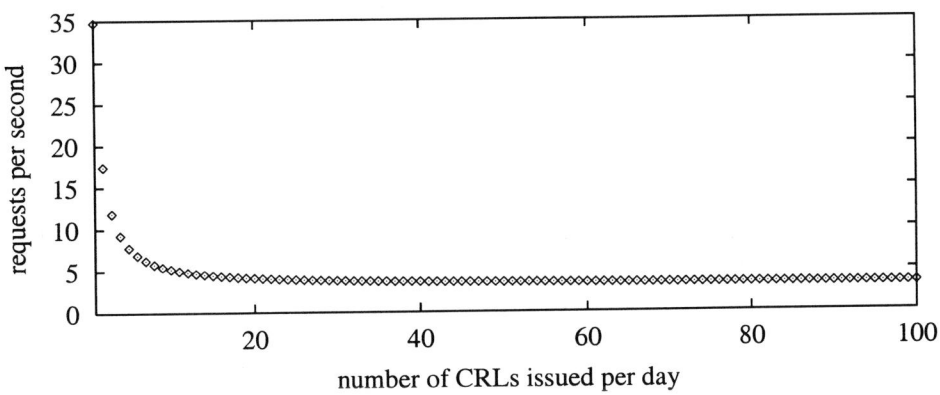

Figure 4. Peak request rate as a function of number of CRLs issued per day

number of CRLs that are issued per day. As can be seen, most of the advantages of over-issuing in this example scenario can be obtained by issuing CRLs once an hour.

3.1. A model of over-issued CRLs

The graphs in figures 3 and 4 are only illustrative of the benefits of over-issued CRLs. The degree to which over-issuing can reduce the peak request rate for CRLs depends on the validation rate of relying parties and the length of time that CRLs are valid. In general, higher validation rates and longer CRL validity periods lend themselves to greater relative improvements in the peak request rate as a result of over-issuing. In this section, a model for over-issued CRLs, which can be used to determine the benefits of over-issuing in any particular scenario, is presented.

Suppose that the period of time between the issuance of two CRLs is called an interval. In order to compute the request rate for CRLs over the course of an interval, the probability that a relying party will request a CRL during that interval needs to be determined.

As was described above, a relying party will only request a CRL from the repository in a given interval if it performs a validation in that interval and it does not have an unexpired CRL in its cache. If O represents the number of CRLs that are valid at any given time ($O = 4$ in figure 2) and P_{val} is the probability that a relying party will perform a validation in any given interval, then the probability that a relying party will request a CRL in interval n is P_{val} times the probability that the relying party did not request a CRL in any of the previous $O - 1$ intervals:

$$P_{I,n} = P_{val} \left[1 - \sum_{j=n-O+1}^{n-1} P_{I,j} \right] \quad (3)$$

Once the system has reached a steady state, the probability that a relying party will request a CRL in an interval will be the same in each successive interval (i.e., $P_I = P_{I,n} = P_{I,n-1} = P_{I,n-2} = \ldots$). So, in the steady state

$$P_I = P_{val}[1 - (O-1)P_I] \quad (4)$$

Equation (4) can be solved for P_I:

$$P_I = \frac{P_{val}}{(O-1)P_{val} + 1} \quad (5)$$

If an interval begins at time 0, then the probability that a relying party will request a CRL from the repository between times t and $t + dt$, in the limit $dt \to 0$, is the probability that the relying party performs its first validation attempt of the interval between times t and $t + dt$ multiplied by the probability that the relying party does not have a valid CRL in its cache that it retrieved in a previous interval. The probability that the relying party performs its first validation attempt of the interval between times t and $t + dt$ is $ve^{-vt}dt$ (see equation (1)). The probability that the relying party does not have a valid CRL in its cache can be computed as the probability that the relying party will request a CRL during the interval divided by the probability that the relying party will perform a validation in the interval (i.e., equation (5) divided by P_{val}). Thus, the probability that the relying party will request a CRL between times t and $t + dt$ is

$$\frac{ve^{-vt}dt}{(O-1)P_{val} + 1} \quad (6)$$

If equation (6) is multiplied by the number of relying parties, N, and divided by dt, the result is the request rate for CRLs from the repository at time t:

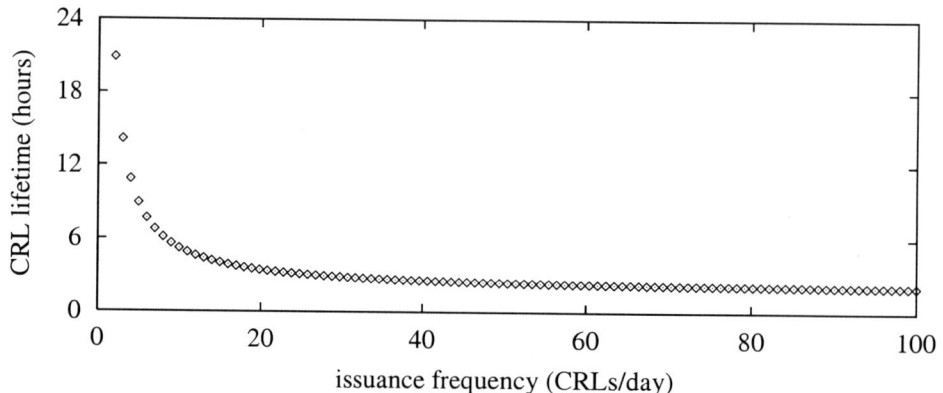

Figure 5. Minimum CRL lifetime as a function of CRL issuance frequency

$$R_I(t) = \frac{Nve^{-vt}}{(O-1)P_{val}+1} \quad (7)$$

Since validations follow an exponential interarrival probability distribution, the probability that a relying party will perform no validations during any given interval is $e^{-vl/O}$ where l is the length of time that a CRL is valid (i.e., an interval is of length l/O). Thus, $P_{val} = 1 - e^{-vl/O}$. So, the request rate for CRLs over the course of an interval is

$$R_I(t) = \frac{Nve^{-vt}}{(O-1)\left(1-e^{-vl/O}\right)+1} \quad (8)$$

and the peak request rate is

$$R_I(0) = \frac{Nv}{(O-1)\left(1-e^{-vl/O}\right)+1} \quad (9)$$

When O equals 1, equation (9) simplifies to the request rate for CRLs issued in the traditional manner, $R_I(0) = Nv$. At the other extreme, if CRLs are issued continuously, the request rate will be

$$\lim_{O \to \infty} \left[\frac{Nv}{(O-1)\left(1-e^{-vl/O}\right)+1} \right] = \frac{Nv}{vl+1} \quad (10)$$

Equation (10) represents the theoretical minimum peak request rate that can be achieved by over-issuing CRLs. While it is impossible to achieve this minimum rate, as illustrated in figure 4, one can get a peak rate close to the theoretical minimum with a moderate amount of over-issuing.

Equation (9) was derived under the assumption that the goal in choosing a revocation distribution mechanism is to minimize the peak request rate for CRLs from the repository while maintaining a given CRL lifetime, l. An alternative approach, however, is to assume that the repository can handle a given peak request rate and then use the equation to determine how short the CRL lifetime can be made. If, in equation (9), lf is substituted for O (where f represents the number of CRLs that are issued per unit time), then the equation can be solved for l, the minimum CRL lifetime that can be achieved if the peak request rate must be at most R:

$$l = \frac{Nv - Re^{-v/f}}{(1-e^{-v/f})Rf} \quad (11)$$

The graph in figure 5 shows an example of how CRL lifetime can be reduced as over-issuing is increased. In this figure, it is assumed that there are 300,000 relying parties each validating an average of 10 certificates per day and that the repository can handle at most 20 requests per second. As the graph shows, the more frequently CRLs are issued (i.e., the more they are over-issued) the more up-to-date relying parties can keep their caches while still not overloading the repository. In this particular example, if CRLs are only issued twice a day, the CRL lifetime must be set to at least 21 hours in order to prevent the repository from being overloaded. On the other hand, if CRLs are issued continuously, the CRL lifetime can be reduced to 1 hour and 46 minutes, thus ensuring that status changes are propagated more quickly.

4. Segmented CRLs

Another way to improve performance over the traditional method of distributing certificate status information is to segment CRLs. While segmenting CRLs may not reduce the peak request rate for CRLs, it will usually reduce the size of each CRL. This may allow a repository to service requests for CRLs at a faster rate.

In this section, a model for segmented CRLs is presented which is used to determine the effects of segmentation on request rates. In some cases, certificates may be allocated to CRL segments in a way that attempts to minimize the number of CRL segments that a relying party will need to download. The model in this paper, however, assumes that certificates are allocated to CRL segments at random. It is then assumed that each validation attempt is equally likely to require access to any of the CRL segments.

As in section 2, the probability density function for a single relying party with respect to a single CRL segment (e.g., segment 1) must be determined. If CRLs are not over-issued, and a new CRL for segment 1 was issued at time 0, then a relying party will request segment 1 from the repository in the interval $[t \ldots t + dt]$ if and only if it attempts to validate a certificate in the interval $[t \ldots t + dt]$ that requires the use of segment 1 and it has not validated any certificates in the interval $[0 \ldots t]$ that required the use of segment 1.

First, the probability that a relying party will not have requested segment 1 in the interval $[0 \ldots t]$ will be determined. Since an exponential interarrival probability for validation attempts is assumed, it is known from the Poisson law [5] that the probability that n validation attempts will be made during an interval of length t is

$$\left[\frac{(vt)^n}{n!}\right] e^{-vt} \qquad (12)$$

If there are s CRL segments, then there is a probability of $1/s$ that segment 1 will be needed to perform any given validation attempt. Thus, the probability that segment 1 will not be needed for any of n validation attempts is

$$\left(1 - \frac{1}{s}\right)^n \qquad (13)$$

Equations (12) and (13) can be combined to determine the probability that any given relying party will not request segment 1 during the interval $[0 \ldots t]$:

$$\sum_{n=0}^{\infty} \left(1 - \frac{1}{s}\right)^n \left[\frac{(vt)^n}{n!}\right] e^{-vt} = e^{-vt/s} \qquad (14)$$

Next, the probability that a relying party will need segment 1 during the interval $[t \ldots t + dt]$ (in the limit $dt \to 0$) must be determined. The probability that one validation attempt will be made in the interval $[t \ldots t + dt]$ is[2]

[2]Since the interval $[t \ldots t + dt]$ is infinitesimally small, it can be assumed that the probability of more than one validation attempt occurring is 0.

$ve^{-v\,dt}dt = v\,dt$. Since the probability that any given validation attempt will require the use of segment 1 is $1/s$, the probability that segment 1 will be needed in the interval $[t \ldots t + dt]$ is

$$\frac{v\,dt}{s} \qquad (15)$$

Combining equations (14) and (15) and multiplying the result by the number of relying parties results in the total expected number of requests for segment 1 in the interval $[t \ldots t + dt]$:

$$N'_s(t) = \frac{Nve^{-vt/s}dt}{s} \qquad (16)$$

Dividing both sides of equation (16) by dt and multiplying by the number of segments results in the total request rate:

$$R_s(t) = \frac{s\,N'_s(t)}{dt} = Nve^{-vt/s} \qquad (17)$$

Equation (17) shows how CRL request rates change with the amount of segmentation. Since $R_s(0) = Nv$, it is clear that the peak request rate is not affected by the amount of segmentation. Increasing the amount of segmentation only affects the rate at which the request rate drops off after a group of CRL segments have been issued. This can be seen by comparing figure 1 to figure 6.

5. Over-issued segmented CRLs

The reason that the peak request rate for segmented CRLs (equation (17)) is the same as the peak request rate for unsegmented CRLs (equation (2)) is that they both suffer from the same problem. In both models, all CRLs expire at the same time. As a result, there is a moment in time in which every relying party's cache is empty. At this moment, every validation attempt will result in a request for revocation information from the repository. Since the validation rate is Nv, this is the peak request rate.

Sections 3 and 4 have presented two techniques for improving the performance of repositories, with section 3 demonstrating how peak request rates can be reduced and section 4 demonstrating how the sizes of CRLs can be reduced without increasing the peak request rate. To a certain degree, the advantages of these two techniques can be combined. However, as the amount of segmentation increases, the degree to which over-issuing can reduce the peak request rate decreases.

There are two basic ways that over-issuing can be combined with segmentation. The first is to issue all CRL segments at the same time, but issue the CRL segments more

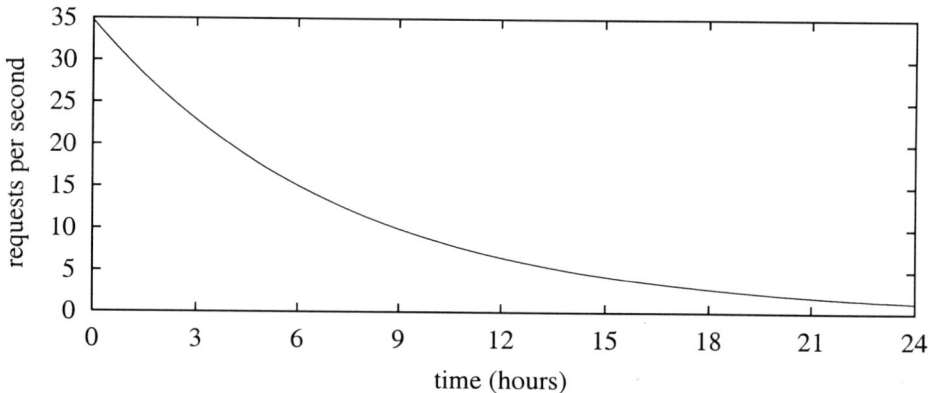

Figure 6. Request rate for three CRL segments

often than is required by the CRLs' validity periods. The other way is to issue each segment only as often as necessary, but to stagger the issuance of each segment so that the peak request rates for the different segments occur at different times.

In order to demonstrate the advantage of staggering the issuance of CRL segments, the scenario from figure 6 will be used as an example. The request rate for each segment at the time of issuance is 11.57 requests/second. However, after 8 hours the request rate has dropped to 3.81 requests/second and after 16 hours the request has dropped to 1.25 requests/second. So, if the issuance of the three CRL segments were staggered by 8 hours then the peak request rate would be only 16.64 requests/second as opposed to a peak rate of 34.72 requests/second if all three segments were issued at the same time (see figure 7). Unfortunately, the peak request rate does not continue to decline with increasing numbers of segments. With 4 CRL segments issued at 6 hour intervals, the peak request rate increases slightly to 17.15 requests/second. As the number of CRL segments approaches infinity, the peak request rate approaches the peak rate for an unsegmented CRL.

In general, the request rate for segmented CRLs issued at evenly separated intervals is

$$\frac{Nve^{-vt'/s}}{s} \sum_{i=0}^{s-1} e^{-ivl/s^2} = \frac{Nve^{-vt'/s}\left(1-e^{-vl/s}\right)}{s\left(1-e^{-vl/s^2}\right)} \quad (18)$$

where $t' = t \mod \left(\frac{l}{s}\right)$.

If a CA is willing to over-issue each CRL segment, then the peak request rate can be reduced even further. Using the example from above, if three CRL segments are used and each segment is issued once every 8 hours, then the peak request rate will be only 14.83 requests/second. Furthermore, the more frequently the segments are issued, the more the peak request rate can be reduced. If the three CRL segments from the example above were issued continuously, then the peak request rate would be only 8.01 requests/second. As was described above, however, as the number of segments increases, the degree to which the peak request rate can be reduced also decreases. So, if revocation information is divided among a large number of segments in order to reduce the size of each CRL segment, then there may be no advantage, in terms of peak request rate, to over-issuing the CRL segments or to staggering the issuance of the segments.

In general, the request rate for over-issued segmented CRLs is

$$R_I(t) = \frac{Nve^{-vt/s}}{(O-1)\left(1-e^{-vl/sO}\right)+1} \quad (19)$$

where t is the amount of time since the latest CRL segments were issued. As in section 3, the lowest possible peak request rate can be determined by computing equation (19) in the limit as O approaches infinity. The resulting request rate is

$$R_I = \frac{Nvs}{vl+s} \quad (20)$$

6. Choosing a method for issuing CRLs

A number of factors must be taken into account when choosing the best method for distributing certificate status information using CRLs. In addition to the validation rates of relying parties and the validity periods of the CRLs, one must consider the expected number of revoked certificates and the environments in which relying parties will be operating.

All of the techniques described above rely on the re-use of cached information in order to reduce peak request rates.

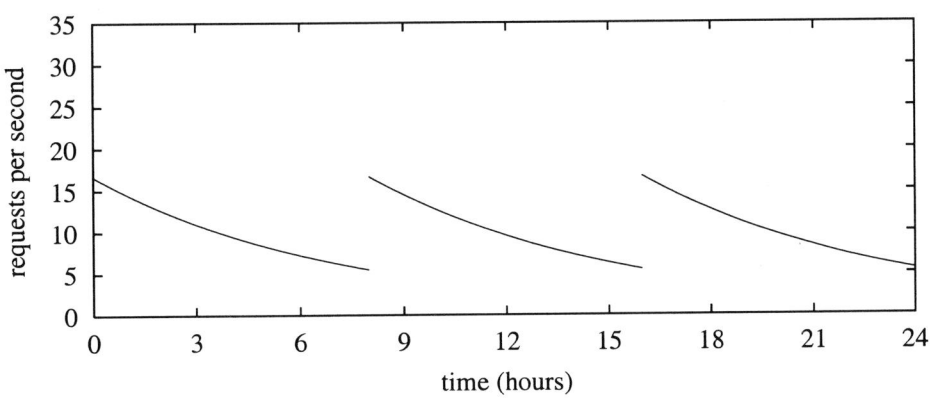

Figure 7. Request rate for three CRL segments with staggered issuance

If relying parties must obtain fresh revocation information from the repository each time a validation is performed, either because CRLs are valid for a very short period of time or the validation rates of the relying parties are relatively low, then none of the techniques described in this paper will be effective at reducing the peak request rate. As an example, if CRLs were valid for only 10 minutes instead of 1 day, then the lowest peak request rate that could be obtained by over-issuing for the example in section 3 would be 32.47 requests/second. This represents a mere 6.5% improvement over the traditional method as opposed to the 90.9% improvement that was possible when CRLs were valid for a day. The best solution in this case is to break up CRLs into as many segments as possible in order to minimize the time required to service a request.

If CRLs are valid for a sufficient length of time to make caching effective, then the best choice of certificate status distribution method will depend on the expected number of revoked certificates. If it is expected that very few certificates will be revoked, then segmentation will not be very effective in reducing the size of CRLs. This may be the case with an authority revocation list (ARL) since it is expected that certificates issued to certification authorities will rarely need to be revoked. For these environments, the best option is to issue unsegmented CRLs, but to over-issue them in order to reduce the peak request rate.

If there will be a large number of revoked certificates, then it may be more important to reduce the sizes of CRLs than to reduce the peak request rate. If this is the case, then segmentation should be used. If certificate status information is divided among a sufficiently large number of segments, however, then there is no need to over-issue the segments as over-issuing will not substantially reduce the peak request rate.

One final variable to consider when choosing a method for distributing certificate status information is the environment in which relying parties will be operating. If relying parties will be operating off-line, then segmentation will not be effective. Relying parties that operate off-line will not know which certificates they will be validating at the time that they obtain CRLs from the repository. As a result, if CRLs were segmented, these relying parties would need to obtain all of the segments. Over-issuing, on the other hand, will be very useful for these relying parties. If CRLs are over-issued, then relying parties will be guaranteed to always obtain relatively fresh information from the repository each time they request a CRL. Without over-issuing, some relying parties requesting certificate status information would receive CRLs that are about to expire. These CRLs would be of little or no use to the relying parties.

7. Conclusions and future work

This paper has presented a model for the traditional method of distributing certificate status information using CRLs along with models for two improved methods for using CRLs. As was shown, these improved methods can reduce peak loads on repositories, and thus improve response times, in almost all environments.

One method of certificate status distribution that this paper did not cover is the use of delta-CRLs. With delta-CRLs, one can have base CRLs whose lifetimes are relatively long, allowing for re-use, while at the same time using delta-CRLs with relatively short lifetimes in order to ensure that relying parties have up-to-date certificate status information. We are working to develop models for the use of delta-CRLs that will demonstrate how they can be used most effectively. This work will be described in a future paper.

References

[1] S. Berkovits, S. Chokhani, J. A. Furlong, J. A. Geiter, and J. C. Guild. *Public Key Infrastructure Study: Final Report.*

Produced by the MITRE Corporation for NIST, Apr. 1994.

[2] R. Housley, W. Ford, W. Polk, and D. Solo. *Internet X.509 Public Key Infrastructure Certificate and CRL Profile*. RFC 2459, Jan. 1999.

[3] S. Micali. Efficient certificate revocation. Technical Memo MIT/LCS/TM-542b, Massachusetts Institute of Technology, Laboratory for Computer Science, Mar. 1996.

[4] M. Myers, R. Ankney, A. Malpani, S. Galperin, and C. Adams. *X.509 Internet Public Key Infrastructure Online Certificate Status Protocol - OCSP*. RFC 2560, June 1999.

[5] A. S. Tanenbaum. *Computer Networks*. Prentice-Hall, Inc., second edition, 1989.

Track B: Forum

Information Security Education for the Next Millennium: Building the Next Generation of Practitioners

Chair

Ron Ross, NIST

As we move into the 21st century, our personal and professional lives continue to be dominated by information technology. Our nation's growing dependence on the Internet has increased our concern about the security and privacy of information being stored, processed, and transmitted on supporting computer systems and networks. Each day, new vulnerabilities are discovered in those systems and networks giving rise to difficult and challenging information security problems. How will this nation meet these information security challenges and develop cost-effective solutions to an ever-increasing array of security-related problems?

This forum will present the ideas of several leading university educators—educators who are also experts in the field of computer and information security. The panelists will discuss the specialty area of information security education and address the following specific questions:

- How can we ensure that our nation's colleges and universities develop needed information security curricula and what are some of the obstacles that might prevent success in this area?
- What types of information security courses are most appropriate for these colleges and universities and what types of supporting classroom materials are needed to effectively engage students?
- How can government and industry be effectively engaged in creative partnerships for information security education?
- How can we balance the requirements for information security education and training?

Track A

Public Key Infrastructures

Chair

Klaus Keus, GISA/BSI

Generic Support for PKIX Certificate Management in CDSA

Shabnam Erfani
WatchGuard Technologies
serfani@watchguard.com

Sekar Chandersekaran
Microsoft Corporation
sekarcha@microsoft.com

Abstract

The Common Data Security Architecture (CDSA) from the Open Group is a flexible standard that defines APIs for security services needed for implementing Public Key Infrastructure (PKI). The emerging IETF Public Key Infrastructure (PKIX) standards provide certificate management protocols geared toward the Internet. The PKIX specifications define the expected behavior of the PKI, but do not provide abstractions that can be used by exploiting applications. In this paper we show the feasibility and design methodology of extending CDSA abstractions to support PKIX certificate management. To achieve this, we model a general, end-to-end system architecture based on CDSA that 0 PKIX certificate management model, and discuss the merits of this system from the application and system architecture perspectives. We conclude the paper with a discussion of the resulted generic CDSA version 2.0 API that support PKIX certificate management model.

1. Introduction

As the applications exploiting public key infrastructure (PKI) grow more complex, the market demands integrated security services that are platform independent, scalable and standards compliant. Integration of PKI into distributed applications such as health care and E-commerce requires availability of basic security services such as cryptography, certificate management and secure storage services in various components of the system in a ubiquitous and transparent manner. Furthermore, as the application security models become more mature and distributed, provision of the basic security services needs to become configurable according to a given policy. For example, different countries (jurisdictions) exercise import/export policies for providing strong cryptography to applications. Or, an enterprise may need to impose a policy for key storage and backup that needs to be enforced transparently in the infrastructure. Last but not least, software maintainability mandates that applications not embed policies or the details of a particular PKI protocol. Otherwise, if policies or protocols change the application has to be modified or rewritten. Clearly, appropriate services should be provided as an encapsulation and based on the configured policy enforced by a mediating layer. A good approach to address these issues is to provide a functionally rich set of security services in a controlled manner through a framework-based architecture such as the Common Data Security Architecture (CDSA). This is the goal and motivation behind our approach to integrate PKIX management services into CDSA.

CDSA defines a framework-based approach to providing basic security services as depicted in Figure 1. The framework layer defines Application Programming Interfaces (APIs) for each category of service that can be called by the application, and a matching Service Provider Interface (SPI). Pluggable service provider modules that implement the actual services support the SPI. The framework mediates and dispatches an API call to the appropriate SPI implemented by a selected service provider. This architecture not only provides a well-defined set of APIs and SPIs, but also transparent policy enforcement and integrity checking within the framework. This method separates the application from a particular service implementation since the application calls the same API, but different implementations (in the form of different service providers) can be selected at run-time. The services can be used to implement another layer that provides system security services as depicted in Figure 1. Framework architecture is also used in Microsoft Cryptographic API and Java Cryptography Architecture, and has proven merits.

CDSA provides 5 service categories to applications: Key recovery (KR), Cryptography (CSP), Certificate library (CL), Trust Policy (TP), and Data Library (DL). CDSA also provides APIs for module management and run-time discovery of service provider capabilities. Service provider modules benefit from the module management services in the framework. A service provider can invoke the services of another SP by calling that provider through the CDSA API. For example, a CL performing certificate verification can invoke a CSP to check the cryptographic signature on

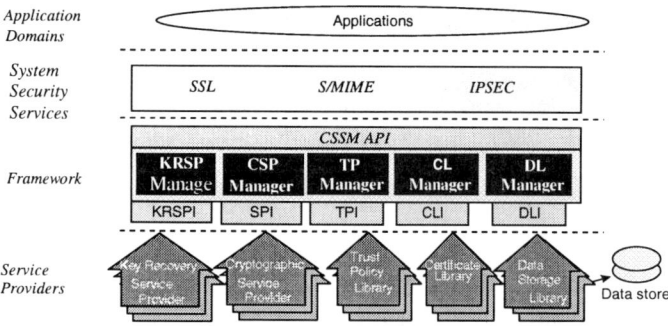

Figure 1. CDSA Architecture

the certificate. In this respect, the CL acts as an application to CSP.

In this paper, the CL and TP APIs are areas that we consider for further development. The CDSA version 1.2 defined a number of APIs in CL and TP that were appropriate for smaller, localized applications that needed certificate services such as issuance, trust policy validation and revocation. They did not permit distributed or asynchronous certificate lifecycle operations. The CL provided APIs for syntactic manipulation of the certificates and certificate revocation lists (CRLs), and the TP allowed certificate and CRL validation. This model however was not adequate for implementing the PKI standards that are becoming dominant. Specifically, we felt a need for expanding the CL and TP abstractions to accommodate a PKIX-based certificate management model. This work has been a joint effort with Intel Architecture Labs and has been included in the CDSA version 2.0.

The Public Key Infrastructure Drafts (PKIX) from the I-ETF establish a model for certificate lifecycle management. They also define a common profile for X.509v3 certificates and certificate revocation lists (CRLs) geared toward the Internet, providing a common ground for interoperability. The discussion of PKIX requirements and architecture in this section is a distillation of [3]. The goal is to provide a background and set of requirements for the extending CDSA certificate and trust policy services described later in the paper. The existing APIs for data storage and cryptographic services are functionally rich enough to support implementation of a complex PKI.

The PKIX architecture is composed of three entities: the end entity (EE) or the client, the registration authority (RA) and the certificate authority (CA). Note that the RA presence as a separate entity is optional and can be combined with CA into one entity (certificate server) if needed. Without loss of generality, in this paper we assume that the RA is a separate entity. The RA acts as a broker between the CA and the EE, however, the EE can contact the CA directly as well in the PKIX model. Typically, the RA performs tasks such as EE authentication, policy verification, key generation, and archival, etc. The CA in fact relies on the RA to perform almost all the necessary checks on incoming requests. The CA acts only as the signer of certificates and CRLs. This division of labor has several benefits:

- The CA can work 1 in a protected manner
- The CA can be generic and applicable to many installations of the RA
- The RA can be customized for various policies and business workflow and CRL distribution
- Multiple RAs can be present in the system, permitting scalability and distribution of the workload

The PKIX certificate management model, however, does not clearly divide the labor between RA and CA. It is up to the system administrators and designers to determine which functions are performed by which entity in the PKI. In the current state of PKIX, the EE configuration is performed out of band. The RA initialization and certification process (enrollment) by CA is also performed statically out of band. In future, PKIX may provide protocol primitives to perform RA enrollment programmatically. The PKIX certificate management is composed of a number of stages as summarized below:

1. CA establishment where the CA is installed and configured independently or as part of a hierarchy with CA Keys. The CA certificate is published in the directory and CA policies are established. PKIX does not specify how this operation is accomplished.

2. EE initialization involves the following steps:
   - Request and import a root CA public key certificate (out of band)
   - CA/RA issues a secret values (initial authentication key) and reference value that is transported to EE via an out of band channel
   - EE Key pair may be generated elsewhere but has to be transported to EE by some means

3. Certification results in creation of a certificate for an entity and is composed of the following steps:
   - Initial registration/certification
   - Key pair update
   - Certificate update
   - CA key pair update
   - Cross certificate request
   - Cross certificate update
   - Certificate confirmation

4. Certificate/CRL discovery is the step taken to publish or distribute the issued certificate or CRL. PKIX provides messages for publication, or the PKI can use the directory to publish the certificates and CRLs.

5. Recovery operations are part of PKI management and are needed when an end entity loses its Personal Security Environment (PSE). The PSE is the collection of EE keys, certificates and trusted roots that are essential for performing secure operations. The recovery operation typically is performed to recover the client key archived or backed up at RA or CA.

6. Revocation is done when an authorized party requests the CA to revoke a certificate. This request results in a change to the CRL and possible publication of the CRL

7. PSE operations include actions such as changing the pin and key backup that are not in the scope of PKIX.

PKIX defines a certificate management protocol (CMP) that enables some the stages described above. The CMP defines protocol messages for initial registration and certification, certificate publication, and revocation. Other stages are either considered out of the scope of PKIX, or are under development. Furthermore, PKIX also mandates EE authentication and proof of possession (POP) of the private key by the RA/CA. The details of how these operations are performed can be found in [3].

The PKIX certificate management model is an enabling technology that is moving to become standard and widely accepted. Therefore, it is desirable to provide support for P-KIX in security infrastructure architectures such as CDSA. There are more advantages to building support for PKIX in CDSA. PKIX is still evolving, therefore hiding the implementation inside a service provider as done is CDSA is highly desirable. Furthermore, CDSA allows separation of PKIX certificate management model and the actual implementation of the protocol. The system can be designed such that the application is aware of the certificate lifecycle, but the service provider encapsulates the underlying management protocol. Additionally, other management protocols also can be implemented within the service provider without affecting the application drastically.

In the rest of this paper, we describe the methodology we used to design the CDSA abstractions needed for PKIX certificate management support. We present a model for a generic system that uses PKIX entities to enable certificate management. Then, we further show how the model can be built using CDSA as an 0 and the properties that CDSA should satisfy to enable the construction of the model. Based on the developed model we infer the requirements and the design pattern that we need to build the relevant API in CDSA. We also present an analysis of the system properties and then describe the generic CDSA APIs that neatly enables support for the PKIX certificate management model.

2. System Architecture Model

The three entities in the PKIX model exploit cryptography, secure storage for keys, certificate management and trust policy services to accomplish their tasks. Therefore, CDSA is an ideal candidate for providing infrastructure services for these entities since it provides a rich set of APIs for each category. PKIX requires these entities to support a wide set of cryptographic algorithms for encryption, MAC and digital signatures. The current set will grow as new algorithms are introduced. CDSA Cryptographic Service Providers can easily satisfy this requirement. Furthermore, by encapsulating trust policy and certificate generation capabilities into CDSA TP and CL, CA and RA can be easily combined into one entity. The most important task of RA is to perform policy checks and user authentication on various incoming requests. CDSA service providers can be designed to encapsulate such functions. If the RA for some reason becomes optional, the service providers can be moved to CA and exploited there. Furthermore, the CDSA services can be exploited for key management. For example, PKIX defines primitives for user key recovery and update. The key recovery APIs and service providers in CDSA can be exploited to implement these required services in P-KIX.

Figure 2 below depicts how the system composed of EE, RA and CA can be modeled using CDSA API and service providers. Note that we only discuss the part of the architecture that is relevant to the PKIX flow and its interaction with CDSA APIs. Other internal details of EE/RA and CA implementation (policy configuration and contents, permanent storage for audit records, etc.) and system issues are not considered in this paper.

As illustrated in the figure, each entity can be implemented as a layer on top of CDSA taking advantage of the underlying service providers. The components of the architecture are:

1. **End Entity:** The End Entity (EE) is the client side of the system where most of the requests are generated. The EE application places a call to TP API to make a request (authenticated or unauthenticated) from the PKI. The service provider in turn uses the PKIX protocol to submit a request to the PKI. The box labeled as the PKIX protocol manager on the EE side is composed of a set of libraries that encapsulate mechanisms for creation and parsing of PKIX protocol messages. We have 0 separated the EE components from the P-

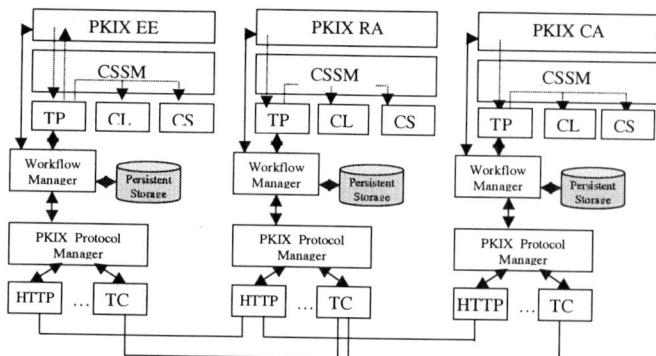

Figure 2. System model based on CDSA for implementing PKIX entities

KIX protocol handler to decrease architecture dependency on PKIX and increase reusability of the system components.

2. **Registration Authority:** The RA entity acts as the intermediate node between the EE and the CA. If the RA is present in the system, it must be certified by the CA and be configured with appropriate certificates, private keys and policies that it enforces for that CA. We assume that this information is established during RA initialization. Similar to EE, the RA relies on a separate component to interface with other PKIX entities (CA and EE), the PKIX Protocol Manager. The PKIX RA can be a separate process initiated by a master RA that dispatches various requests to the appropriate subordinate RA. The RA design is composed of an application layer that sits on top of the CDSA framework, and takes advantage of TP, CL, and CSP modules that provide lower level PKIX services. The TP module encapsulates all the trust primitives needed for validation and verification of incoming requests. The CL module provides the syntactic manipulation capabilities for certificates, and finally CSP can be used for cryptographic functions. A DL module can be used to access LDAP, or to store records needed for auditing, etc. at RA.

Since the presence of an RA is optional, one can move all of the RA functionality to the CA system by incorporating the RA application properties within the CA application and making the RA-preferred providers (TP, CL, CSP and possibly DL) available on the CA system. Using this mechanism, combining an RA and CA would involve attaching and using the RA-preferred service providers and the CA-preferred SPs on a single CA system. The CDSA-based architecture easily supports migration of system configuration. Another aspect of RA architecture is interoperability with different CAs. It is desirable to have an RA that not only works with a PKIX CA but can also interoperate with non-PKIX CAs. We believe using CDSA in the architecture will significantly reduce the complexity of achieving this goal. The fact that the PKIX protocol handling (the message format and message forwarding operations) are encapsulated inside the TP module allows the RA application to interface with non-PKIX CAs by attaching a TP module that can handle a different protocol while preserving the semantics of the certificate management model.

3. **Certificate Authority:** The CA entity in terms of architecture is quite similar to the RA. The main functionality of CA is to provide a signing facility where the approved requests are processed and returned to the source of the request, EE or RA. Similar to RA, the CA relies on a PKIX protocol manager to manipulate PKIX messages and a master CA to dispatch the requests to other peer CAs. The PKIX CA application is a layer on top of CDSA that takes advantage of service provider services. Similar to RA, most of the trust and 0 certificate operations are encapsulated inside CL and TP service provider. By specializing the SPs, and allowing the PKIX CA application to select different service providers, a PKIX CA can interoperate with non-PKIX CAs.

4. **PKIX Protocol Manager (PPM):** The PKIX protocol manager is a logical entity that provides PKIX protocol management and queuing services (through the depicted persistent storage) for the three PKIX entities EE, RA and CA. Note that physically at least between the RA and CA the PPM can be shared if needed. Moreover, the PPM 0 can use any generic storage facility to queue messages and store other transport layer information where the application and Service Provider can access them. The PPM, however, does not provide PKIX session management and state services. All state information pertaining to PKIX request sessions is managed by the workflow manager. The PPM provides PKIX specific services such as message encoding and verification. To provide a transport, it relies on another underlying layer that provides transport protocol services. As a result, the PKIX messages can be encapsulated in various transport protocols such as HTTP, TCP, SMTP, etc.

5. **Workflow Manager (WM):** The PKIX model relies on exchange of requests and responses to determine the state of every session and object in the system. The state information can be can be managed by a separate entity that we call the Workflow Manager. This component is either a generic or customized component. The WM is responsible for keeping track of the

state of work objects in the system. Object structures are defined based on the events they must record, the creating entity, the current state and the entity where they are located. The work objects can be persistent or not. The workflow manager relies on a persistent storage that contains information that could be used for system recovery and auditing as well. 0, the unit can be used to implement a customized 0 process. For example, if a CA only operate offline, the WM on the CA can be designed to batch the incoming requests, and send them to CA when it is online and send the responses back when available.

The workflow manager and the protocol manager cooperate to provide session 0 and message forwarding on behalf of the application. These two are reusable components on all three entities. The basic flow in this architecture starts when the application calls a TP API to place a PKI request such as certificate request, renewal or revocation. The TP performs policy checks on the request and forwards it to the workflow manager. At this point, the request becomes a workflow object that can be transported to another platform and contains a state. The object state and other relevant information are updated as the protocol messages are exchanged between entities. This architecture allows clean encapsulation of functions within the service providers. It also provides a model for development of APIs with the 0 transactional properties required by PKIX. Also, the architecture insulates applications from the details of the PKIX protocol. The application knows about the states in the lifecycle of requests and objects, but not the underlying protocol. Therefore, the PKIX service providers could be updated or replaced with minimal impact on the application.

3. CDSA Trust Policy APIs for PKIX

The PKIX certificate management model assumes certain properties in the system that need to be addressed by the designed APIs. There are other properties that are nice to be designed into the system that enhance interoperability and scalability. Furthermore, since PKIX is an evolving standard, there has to be backward and forward compatibility in the APIs to minimize the impact on applications.

The PKIX transaction model is designed to cater to both centralized and distributed systems. It also allows for either synchronous or asynchronous operations. The Certificate Management Protocol (CMP) includes authenticated and unauthenticated flows, depending on how the system decides to do certain operations. For example, depending on how the system is designed to perform POP (directly or indirectly) the CMP flow may or may not be authenticated. Also, the CMP allows batch messages and responses.

These requirements introduce other issues that need to be taken into consideration when designing a suitable API. Should the API support polling, callbacks or event notification? How do we incorporate the appropriate transactional properties into the API to enhance performance and scalability while supporting PKIX requirements?

Given the CDSA design patterns, we addressed these requirements by defining various primitives that helped create an elegant and generic set of APIs that not only accommodate PKIX, but also can be used to support non-PKIX protocols. These primitives are:

- **Caller authentication context:** This data structure encapsulates the input parameters, method and timing of the caller authentication process. This context is supplied to the API from the application to be used for the requested operation. The context allows applications to control the granularity of the credentials usage. The same context can be used across many API calls, or can be change between calls. The information in the context can be used locally to authenticate the caller or can be passed on to the protocol manager to perform signing of PKIX messages, or be transported to another entity.

- **Groups and Sets:** We introduced groups of objects that can be used for batch processing. Defining structures that support groups of objects such as CRLs, fields and requests supports the PKIX requirement and also allows scalability and interoperability in the container objects.

- **Operation Contexts:** This data structure is defined for certificate operations such as certificate verification similar to cryptographic contexts. The verification context encapsulates all the necessary parameters for certificate validation such as the trust roots, CRLs, parsed certificates, etc. Introduction of the context collects all the relevant information into a manageable container object that can be used across APIs. It can also act as storage for caching information.

- **Transaction Model:** : We designed a granular polling mechanism for supporting distributed operations. This model allows use of the same API for both local and distributed operations and is suitable for PKIX model. When a request API is called, a transaction reference identifier and an estimated time is returned to the application. The application can use these parameters to call the corresponding receive APIs to get the results back.

- **Protocol Sequence:** We observed that almost all PKIX CMP messages follow the same pattern:

- The application submits a request on a client entity such as EE or RA
- The client application retrieves the response from server
- The client application confirms the response if needed
- The server application awaits the confirmation from client before closing the session

Many data structures also turned out to be common for multiple service types. These patterns were used to design generic APIs that support multiple service types.

The generic APIs fall into three categories: Submit, Retrieve and Confirm. The Submit interface accepts service-specific inputs and a service type to perform. The Retrieve interface outputs service-specific results. Each of these interfaces can be authenticated (get a caller authentication context as input) or not. The Confirm interface allows confirmation of the results from the client to the server. This function also can be authenticated or non-authenticated. Each category interface also receives an input that specifies the requested service type. Based on this parameter, the service provider can identify the data structure types passed in. For the sake of interoperability and following the PKIX certificate management model, the following certificate service types and the corresponding data structures have been defined:

- **Issuance:** for requesting certificates. Certificate renewal can also be accomplished using this service type.
- **Revocation:** for handling certificate revocation operations requested by authorized parties
- **Verification:** enables remote certificate validation operations
- **Notarization:** specifies data notarization services
- **Key Reclaim:** enables recovery of a private key associated with an issued certificate
- **Hold and Release:** allow changing the state of a certificate. For example, using this service type an authorized party can suspend or resume a certificate

The API also provides a CRL issuance service type. Full details of the API and supporting data structures can be found in [1], however, we give an overview of the API functions:

- **TP_SubmitCredRequest(**
CSSM_TP_HANDLE TPHandle,
const CSSM_AUTHORITY_ID *PreferredAuthority,
CSSM_AUTHORITY_REQUEST_TYPE RequestType,
const CSSM_TP_REQUEST_SET *RequestInput,
const CSSM_TP_CALLERAUTH_CONTEXT *CallerAuthContext,
sint32 *EstimatedTime,
const CSSM_DATA_PTR ReferenceIdentifier)

- **TP_RetrieveCredResult(**
CSSM_TP_HANDLE TPHandle,
const CSSM_DATA *ReferenceIdentifier,
const CSSM_CALLERAUTH_CONTEXT *CallerAuthCredentials,
sint32 *EstimatedTime,
CSSM_BOOL_PTR ConfirmationRequired,
const CSSM_TP_RESULT_SET_PTR RetrieveOutput)

- **TP_ConfirmCredResult (**
CSSM_TP_HANDLE TPHandle,
const CSSM_DATA *ReferenceIdentifier,
const CSSM_CALLERAUTH_CONTEXT *CallerAuthCredentials,
CSSM_TP_CONFIRM_RESPONSE *Responses,
const CSSM_AUTHORITY_ID *PreferredAuthority)

- **TP_ReceiveConfirmation (**
CSSM_TP_HANDLE TPHandle,
const CSSM_DATA_PTR ReferenceIdentifier,
CSSM_TP_CONFIRM_RESPONSE_PTR *Responses,
sint32 *ElapsedTime)

4. Conclusion

In this paper, we presented an overview of CDSA and PKIX, two standards that provide infrastructure services to PKI enabled applications in different forms. We described the rationale and a model for implementing the PKIX certificate lifecycle management in systems that take advantage of CDSA for providing infrastructure security services. Observing the patterns in the PKIX model we described how the APIs that support PKIX have been designed as part of CDSA version 2.0. This architecture unification allows a more coherent design for the PKI infrastructure of secure applications. Future work entails implementation and evaluation of the CDSA based system and introduction of new APIs as more PKIX services become available

5. Acknowledgements

This work is the result of cooperation of two teams at IBM and Intel Architecture Labs and funding from IBM Internet Division. We would like to thank and acknowledge the following people for their contributions to the API development, and their thoughtful review and feedback on this paper: Denise Ecklund and Marion Shimoda from Intel Corporation who did considerable amount of work on collecting requirements and revisions of the API, as well as Ian Morrison and Sohail Malik from IBM Corporation. We would like to also thank the members of the IBM Vault Registry team – Hatem Ghafir, Tom Gindin, Khalid Asad, Mark Fisk, and Dave Rusnak – for their excellent review and suggestions on development of the system architecture model.

References

[1] Common Data Security Architecture Specifications, version 2.0, HTTP://www.opengroup.org

[2] PKIX RFC 2459. http://www.ietf.org/html.charters/pkix-charter.html

[3] PKIX RFC 2510. http://www.ietf.org/html.charters/pkix-charter.html

Efficient Certificate Status Handling within PKIs: an Application to Public Administration Services

Marco Prandini

DEIS – Department of Electronics, Computer and System Science
University of Bologna – Viale Risorgimento 2, 40136 Bologna, Italy
E-mail: mprandini@deis.unibo.it

Abstract

Public administrations show a strong interest in digital signature technology as a mean for secure and authenticated document exchange, hoping it will help reducing paper-based transactions with citizens. The main problem posed by this technology is with the necessary public-key infrastructure, and in particular with certificate status handling. This paper describes the definition and deployment of a web-based environment suitable for offering administrative services to citizens and for accepting authenticated documents from citizens. The best features of two different certificate status handling schemes, namely CRL and OCSP, have been exploited within this environment to obtain a good balance between security, timeliness and efficiency.

1. Introduction

As the free exchange of people and goods within Europe becomes effective, the efficiency required to public administrations must increase in order to meet the expectations of the new and enlarged market.

The adoption of electronic data processing (EDP) has already speeded up most of the internal procedures of public administrations, but the potential improvement of EDP can't be fully exploited until document hardcopies are needed at different moments during the process. Of course, this isn't a technological constraint, but a legal issue, mainly related to signature and archival operations.

During the last few years, powerful tools like digital signatures have become widely available. Their usage is currently being put under legal regulation, with the aim of giving digital signatures the same value of autographed ones, and of substituting digital archives for hardcopy.

Various Italian public administrations the author has worked with (Regione Emilia-Romagna, Comune di Modena, Comune di Cesena) are deploying experimental infrastructures to support the exchange of digitally signed documents. This paper discusses some technological issues arisen during these experiences.

2. Technology overview

A general definition of a digital signature can be stated as follows: a digital signature is a bit string computed by the signer over a digitally formatted document, which can both prove the integrity of the document and authenticate the signer.

While these properties can be achieved in different ways, the most viable option these days seems to be *asymmetric cryptography* [1,2]. Within an asymmetric cryptosystem, each signer owns a pair of numbers, called *private key* and *public key*, used for, respectively, signing and verifying signatures. The first key must be kept strictly secret by its owner, while the second one should be made widely available.

Since legal and economic transactions occur between individuals or organizations, and not between "keys", the fundamental task of binding each public key to its owner is performed by Public-Key Infrastructures (PKIs). The entities of a PKI and their mutual relationships, described in detail in [3], are shown in Fig. 1.

When a user presents a request to a Registration Authority (RA) to become a PKI member, a certificate is issued containing the user identity (ascertained in a secure way) and the associated public key, together with some other relevant information such as the certificate issue and expiration dates. The certificate is signed by the Certification Authority (CA), so that its integrity is guaranteed, and published to the directory where it is made available to all PKI users. The CA's public key, which is required to verify any CA's signed document, is transferred to the new user via a secure channel.

It may be necessary to revoke a certificate before expiration of its validity period, commonly one year, due to events like private key compromise or changes in user identification data (e.g., affiliation). As a consequence, proper use of a certificate implies not only expiration date verification, but also revocation checking.

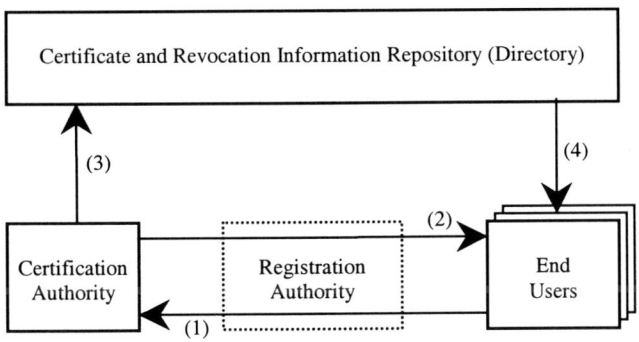

(1) Users registration, certificates revocation and update requests
(2) Certification Authority's public key distribution
(3) Certificates and associated status information publication
(4) Certificates and associated status information distribution

Fig. 1 – Architectural model of a PKI.

The implementation of a certificate status handling scheme must be devised according to security, timeliness and efficiency requirements. A more precise description of these requirements within this context can be helpful:

Security: certificate status information, as known to the CA, should be made available to users without the possibility of alteration.
Timeliness: there should be the minimum possible delay between any certificate status change (e. g., certificate revocation) and its reflection on the replies to user queries.
Efficiency: the algorithms and protocols involved in status updating shouldn't be limiting factors for the secure and timely behavior of the infrastructure.

In many applications, the security requirement is considered of primary concern. To this end, the only secure method currently recognized in the Internet Society standard track, namely the *Certificate Revocation List* (CRL) scheme [3], is exploited. Under this scheme a CA periodically timestamps, signs and sends to the directory a list of (the serial numbers of) all revoked certificates, together with the corresponding date and time of revocation. This very simple solution, which prevents any hostile intervention by the directory (except, of course, denial of service), has the advantage of requiring a single cryptographic operation both by the CA at each update and by the user at each check. It exhibits, however, a serious drawback, since the status of a certificate is verifiable by a user only by obtaining the complete, comprehensive list of all revoked certificates. Moreover, since the list authentication is performed off-line by the CA, timeliness is somewhat limited.

In other applications, the timeliness requirement is considered of primary concern. To this end, the *On-line Certificate Status Protocol* (OCSP) [4], derived from the original proposal of the *Real-Time Certificate Status Protocol* [5], is exploited. Within an OCSP-based system certificate status authentication is delegated to a *responder*, usually integrated in the directory, i.e. it isn't directly guaranteed by the CA signature, but by a signature produced with a key that the CA and/or users trust. The drawback of this solution is that the responder, can be attacked through the network or perform malicious alteration of information sent to users, without CA and users can promptly realize it. Proper behavior of an OCSP-based system is therefore possible if and only if the directory is trusted.

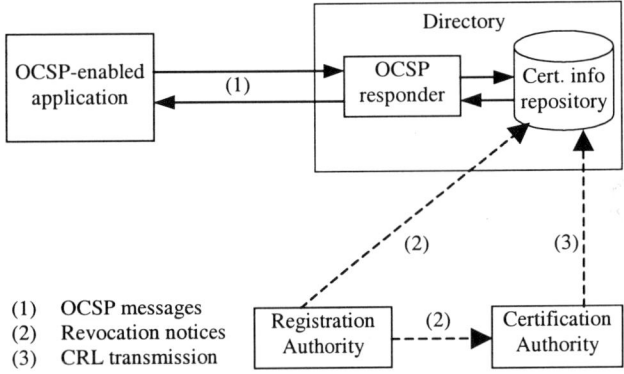

(1) OCSP messages
(2) Revocation notices
(3) CRL transmission

Fig. 2 – Architectural model of a CRL/OCSP-based system

The idea behind the work reported in this paper is that the combined use of OCSP and CRL (Fig. 2) may provide a better overall performance. OCSP, in fact, makes available explicit, concise and timely updated information regarding each single certificate. CRL may conveniently add periodic guarantee of authentication and unforgeability.

3. Efficiency of the CRL/OCSP architectural model

The efficiency of a PKI relying on both CRL and OCSP for certificate status handling can be conveniently estimated before effective deployment, in order to evaluate the impact of PKI operations over the existing information system. In this section, both communications traffic between PKI entities and computational load over each entity are analytically expressed as functions of the relevant PKI parameters. Particular emphasis is placed on the computational load deriving from application of each scheme, a matter which only recently has received the attention it deserves [6]. The parameters usually considered of primary concern in similar contexts are related to:

i) certificate status generation and publication:
- number of cryptographic operations performed by the CA or by the directory to update the status of all certificates;
- amount of data transferred from the CA to the directory at each update;

ii) certificate status checking:
- amount of data transferred from the directory to a user;
- number of cryptographic operations performed by a user.

These parameters have been computed under the usual assumption that a PKI works in stationary conditions as regards the number of revoked certificates, that is, within any certificate status updating period, the average number R of new revocations is balanced by as many revocation removals. R is simply given by:

$$R = \frac{N \cdot P}{365T}$$

where, according to NIST notation [7], N indicates the total number of certificates handled within a PKI, P the revoked certificates fraction, and T the daily number of certificate status updates.

3.1. Computational load and traffic deriving from the CRL protocol

(a) CA computational load evaluation

CRL is essentially (ignoring the header specifying the CA identity, the timestamp, and the adopted signing algorithm) a signed list of $N \cdot P$ (revoked certificate serial number, revocation date and time) pairs. Each pair, according to NIST estimates, can be represented with 68 bits: 20 for the serial number and 48 for the revocation date and time. A list therefore consists of $l_{info} = 68 N \cdot P$ bit. At each update, the list must be signed with the usual process: a message digest function is first applied, then the resulting hash is signed with the CA's private key. The daily computational load of the CA is therefore given by:

$$L_{CA} = T(l_{info} \cdot L_{hash} + L_{signature})$$

With the aim of expressing the overall load of an operation which involves very different cryptographic algorithms, two symbols have been introduced: $L_{signature}$, which represents the computation time needed to perform a signature operation, and L_{hash}, which represents the equivalent marginal load of a 1-bit message digest, computed as the inverse of the function's bit rate [8].

(b) Directory incoming traffic evaluation

At each update the list is published on the directory. The deriving directory incoming traffic, in bit/day, is then given by:

$$T_{CA-DIR} = T(l_{info} + l_{signature})$$

where $l_{signature}$ indicates the number of bits involved in the representation of the signature.

(c) Directory computational load evaluation

In a CRL-based system, no cryptographic operations are requested to the directory in order to reply to a user query.

(d) Directory outgoing traffic evaluation

Each time a user needs to check a certificate status, the whole list has to be sent. The overall directory outgoing traffic, in bit/day, is then given by:

$$T_{DIR-U} = Q(l_{info} + l_{signature})$$

where Q is the daily number of user queries.

(e) User computational load

To perform a certificate status check, a user needs to search the CRL for the corresponding serial number and verify the signature on the list. It is reasonable to assume the latter contribution as the most relevant, so that the computational load can be estimated as:

$$L_U = l_{info} \cdot L_{hash} + L_{verification}$$

where $L_{verification}$ represents the computational load of a signature check operation.

3.2. Computational load and traffic deriving from the OCSP protocol

(a) CA computational load evaluation

OCSP does not rely on synchronous certificate status updates by the CA, that is, it doesn't involve any CA cryptographic operation or any communication between CA and directory.

(b) Directory incoming traffic evaluation

Each time a certificate status change is reported to the RA, immediate action is taken to directly inform the directory. This originates a negligible daily directory incoming traffic, given by:

$$T_{CA-DIR} = \frac{20N \cdot P}{365}$$

(c) Directory computational load evaluation

When a user issues a query about the status of one or more certificates, the OCSP responder performs a repository search to extract the selected up-to-date information. The signed reply contains a data section reporting, for each queried certificate, the target certificate identifier, the certificate status value, the response validity interval and, possibly, optional extensions. The reply contains also a header specifying the responder identity and version, and the adopted signing algorithm. The header size can no more be ignored with respect to the data section size as in the CRL case, since the status representation of a certificate calls for very few bits (possibly two bits only, discriminating whether the certificate is valid, revoked or unknown), and a reply most frequently deals with a single certificate. The overall size of the reply is therefore a fixed quantity, which can be indicated with $l_{OCSP\ reply}$. The resulting daily computational load can be estimated as:

$$L_{DIR} = Q(l_{OCSP\ reply} \cdot L_{hash} + L_{signature})$$

(d) Directory outgoing traffic evaluation

With the OCSP protocol, a user receives data about the certificate he wants to check. The deriving outgoing traffic for the directory, in bit/day, is:

$$T_{DIR-U} = Q(l_{OCSP\ reply} + l_{signature})$$

(e) User computational load evaluation

To perform a certificate status check, a user needs to verify the signature on the reply. The corresponding computational load is:

$$L_U = l_{OCSP\ reply} \cdot L_{hash} + L_{verification}$$

4. Applications and experimental results

The architectural model illustrated in this paper has been applied for the design of the PKI which will handle in the near future the public administrative services for the town of Modena (Italy). Following open standards, ensuring a high degree of interoperability, gathering as much awareness as possible during the development process, all have been primary design concerns dictated by the public administration. The implemented system is therefore based on well-established underlying architectures and protocols, on open-source software libraries, and on PKI components developed by the Italian participants to the ICE-TEL project [9]. Both the CRL and OCSP schemes have entered the testing phase to experimentally validate the foreseen performances.

It is important to notice that the main objective of this first deployment phase is not to build an all-purpose PKI for the citizens, but to evaluate the real benefits of substituting the traditional paper exchange with authenticated digital documents exchange between the citizens and the city administration offices. To this end, a test-bed has been created for submission of signed forms and certificate-based access control to services.

Working within this specific application field, it is possible to introduce a variant of the illustrated CRL/OCSP architecture. Since the public administration is at the same time both the entity in charge for certificate status updating and the only user which really needs high timeliness in status handling, the OCSP responder access could be restricted to the administration intranet, so gaining two important advantages:
- the responder can be placed in a secure network, where malicious attacks are much less probable;
- being the responder highly trusted, once a reply has been computed it can be cached for a longer time than it would normally be allowed to, easing the computational load associated with reply signing.

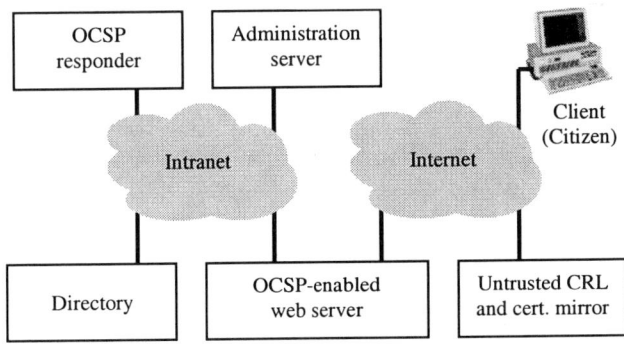

Fig. 3 – Architectural model of the implemented CRL/OCSP-based system

A possible architectural solution is represented in Fig. 3. The CA-authenticated information, such as certificates and CRLs, is both placed on the Intranet directory and mirrored on an Internet-accessible, untrusted directory, thus allowing public, secure usage of certificates for transactions which don't need the timeliness provided by OCSP. The revocation notices, as soon as they are received by some PKI front-end (like RAs), are sent to both the CA for insertion in the CRL and the Intranet directory for updating the OCSP database.

The public administration offers its services by way of a secure web gateway, which performs client authentication and validates the client certificate status using both the CRL and an integrated OCSP client. A good timeliness/security tradeoff is obtained by tuning the frequency of CRL issuing. The gateway, in fact, caches a copy of the CRL each time it is updated, in order to get a secure, long-term reference list of revoked certificates. Each certificate that doesn't appear in the CRL is verified by means of the OCSP protocol, allowing real-time information to be retrieved.

A key step in the implementation of this gateway has been an ad-hoc extension to the well-known *mod_ssl* module [10] for the *Apache* web server [11]. It is worthwhile pointing out that this extension is candidate for definitive inclusion within *mod_ssl* in the near future. Of course, the resultant OCSP-enabled web server can be used in conjunction with every OCSP responder, being its application absolutely not restricted to the proposed secure-network-based architecture.

The prototypal system has undergone a testing phase under various realistic usage conditions, in order to evaluate the system behavior before full deployment. The same parameters analytically expressed in section 3 have been measured for different simulated values of the number of certificates handled in the PKI, of the update frequency, etc.. The results, as expected, were in good accordance with the analytically estimated figures.

Fig. 4 reports in graphical form two of the most interesting parameters, directory incoming and outgoing traffic, showing their dependence on the number of certificates handled in the PKI. It is evident how a big saving in the directory outgoing traffic can be achieved by exploiting OCSP instead of CRL for the greater part of the status checks. The directory incoming traffic is the sum of the CRL- and OCSP-induced traffic, which is only negligibly higher than the CRL-induced traffic alone. Again, there is a performance tradeoff as the traffic reduction is balanced by a computational load increase, due to the OCSP reply signing.

5. Conclusions

This work summarizes the experience gathered during a complex work, which involved deep study, application and extension of the concepts related to public-key certificate handling. The resulting architecture exploits the best features of two different certificate status handling schemes, namely CRL and OCSP, to obtain, within a peculiar citizens-to-administration communication model, a good balance between security, timeliness and efficiency.

Research studies currently being undertaken aim to devise schemes based on untrusted directories that make both the communication traffic, particularly the directory incoming traffic, and the overall computational load less dependent from the number of PKI users and certificates status update frequency. Interesting results seem to emerge from approaches exploiting OWA cryptographic primitives [12], and incremental cryptography techniques [13-16].

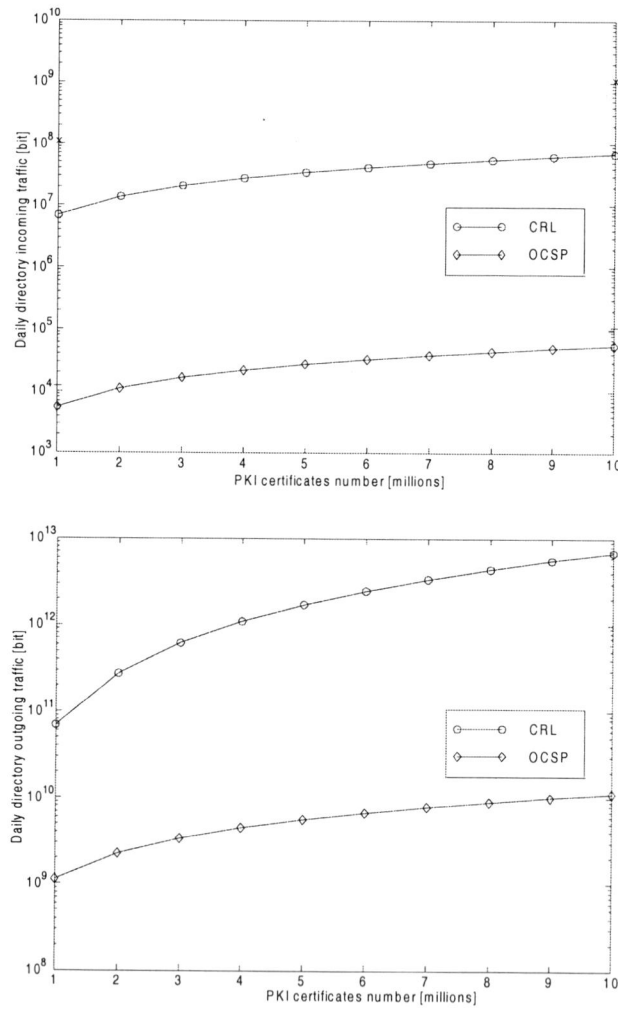

Fig. 4 – Directory traffic dependence on the number of certificates handled in the PKI

Acknowledgements

The author gratefully acknowledges the contribution of Modena city administration in developing the prototype system. The author would also thank Prof. Eugenio Faldella, University of Bologna (Italy), and Mr. Giovanni Faglioni, IS consultant, for their support with several useful discussions, and Dr. Andrea Giacobazzi for the actual development of OCSP code within *mod_ssl* as part of his CS Engineering Master's thesis.

References

[1] W. Diffie, M. E. Hellman: *New directions in cryptography*, IEEE Transactions on Information Theory, v. IT-22, n. 6, Nov 1976, pp. 644-654.

[2] R. Rivest, A. Shamir, L. Adleman: *A method for Obtaining Digital Signatures and Public-key Cryptosystems*. Communications of the ACM, v. 21, n. 2, Feb. 1978, pp. 120-126.

[3] R. Housley, W. Ford, W. Polk, D. Solo: *RFC 2459 – Internet X.509 Public Key Infrastructure Certificate and CRL Profile*. The Internet Society, Jan. 1999 – http://www.rfc-editor.org/rfc/rfc2459.txt

[4] M. Myers, R. Ankney, A. Malpani, S. Galperin, C. Adams: *X.509 Internet Public Key Infrastructure Online Certificate Status Protocol – OCSP*. IETF, Sep. 1998 – ftp://ftp.ietf.org/internet-drafts/draft-ietf-pkix-ocsp-08.txt

[5] A. Malpani, C. Adams, R. Ankney, S. Galperin: *Internet Public Key Infrastructure Real Time Certificate Status Protocol – RCSP*. IETF, Mar. 1998 – ftp://ftp.ietf.org/internet-drafts/draft-malpani-rcsp-00.txt

[6] E. Faldella, M. Prandini: *Efficient Handling of Certificates within Public-Key Infrastructures*. Proceedings of the 3rd IMACS/IEEE International Multiconference on Circuits, Systems, Communications and Computers (CSCC'99), post-conference book, v. 2.

[7] NIST: *Public-key Infrastructure Study*. Gaithersburg, MD, April 1994.

[8] W. Dai: *Speed Comparison of Popular Crypto Algorithms* – http://www.eskimo.com/~weidai/benchmarks.html

[9] *Internetworking Public Key Certification Infrastructure for Europe (project programme)* http://www.darmstadt.gmd.de/ice-tel/programme/programme.html

[10] The *mod_ssl* web site: http://www.modssl.org

[11] The *Apache* web site: http://www.apache.org

[12] J. Benaloh, M. de Mare: *One-Way Accumulators: A Decentralized Alternative to Digital Signatures (Extended Abstract)*. Eurocrypt '93 Proceedings, pp. 274-285.

[13] M. Bellare, O. Goldreich, S. Goldwasser: *Incremental Cryptography: the Case of Hashing and Signing*. Crypto '94 Proceedings, Lecture Notes in Computer Science, v. 839, pp. 216-233, Springer-Verlag, 1994.

[14] M. Bellare, O. Goldreich, S. Goldwasser: *Incremental Cryptography and Application to Virus Protection*. Proceedings of the 27th Annual ACM Symposium on the Theory of Computing, pp. 45-56, 1995.

[15] M. Bellare, R. Guerin, P. Rogaway: *XOR MACs: New Methods for Message Authentication Using Finite Pseudorandom Functions*. Crypto '95 Proceedings, Lecture Notes in Computer Science, v. 963, pp. 15-29, Springer-Verlag, 1995.

[16] M. Fischlin: *Incremental Cryptography and Memory Checkers*. Eurocrypt '97 Proceedings, Lecture Notes in Computer Science, Vol.1233, pp.393-408, Springer-Verlag, 1997.

Track B

Mobile Code

Chair

Dan Thomson, Secure Computing Corporation

User Authentication and Authorization in the Java™ Platform

Charlie Lai   Li Gong

Sun Microsystems, Inc.
charlie.lai,li.gong@sun.com

Larry Koved   Anthony Nadalin

International Business Machines, Inc.
koved,drsecure@us.ibm.com

Roland Schemers

onebox.com
schemers@onebox.com

Abstract

Java™ security technology originally focused on creating a safe environment in which to run potentially untrusted code downloaded from the public network. With the latest release of the Java™ Platform (the Java™ 2 Software Development Kit, v 1.2), fine-grained access controls can be placed upon critical resources with regard to the identity of the running applets and applications, which are distinguished by where the code came from and who signed it. However, the Java platform still lacks the means to enforce access controls based on the identity of the user who runs the code. In this paper, we describe the design and implementation of the Java™ Authentication and Authorization Service (JAAS), a framework and programming interface that augments the Java™ platform with both user-based authentication and access control capabilities.

1 Introduction

The Java™ technology [8, 12] emerged in 1995 with a prominently stated goal of providing a safe programming environment. This means that Java security must provide a secure, readily-built platform on which to run Java enabled applications. It also means that Java security must provide adequate and extensive security tools and services implemented in Java technology that enable independent software vendors (ISVs) to build a wider range of security-sensitive applications, for example, in the enterprise world.

The latest release of the Java platform (Java 2) introduces a new security architecture [7] that uses a security policy to decide the granting of individual access permissions to running code (according to the code's characteristics, e.g., where the code is coming from and whether it is digitally signed and if so by whom). Future attempts to access protected resources will invoke security checks that compare the granted permissions with the permissions needed for the attempted access. If the former includes the latter, access is permitted; otherwise, access is denied.

Such a code-centric style of access control is unusual in that traditional security measures, most commonly found in sophisticated operating systems, are user-centric in that they apply control on the basis of who is running an application and not on the basis of which application is running. One major rationale behind code-centric access control is that when a user uses a web browser to surf the net and runs executable content (e.g., mobile code written in Java) as needed, the user variable remains essentially constant. On the other hand, the user may trust one piece of mobile code more than others and would like to run this code with more privileges. Thus it is in fact natural to control the security of mobile code in a code-centric style.

Nevertheless, it is obvious that Java is becoming widely used in a multi-user environment. For example, an enterprise application or a public Internet terminal must deal with different users, either concurrently or sequentially, and must grant these users different privileges based on their identities. The Java Authentication and Authorization Service (JAAS) is designed to provide a framework and standard programming interface for authenticating users and for assigning privileges. Together with Java 2, an application can provide code-centric access control, user-centric access control, or a combination of both.

The rest of the paper is organized as follows. Sections 2 and 3 introduce the basic concepts used by JAAS. Section 4 describes the authentication model implemented by JAAS. Section 5 describes the authorization framework for JAAS, and is broken up into several subsections. Section 5.1 defines the JAAS user-based security policy, Section 5.2 covers the JAAS access control implementation, and Section 5.3 discusses scalability issues regarding the security policy. Section 6 discusses the issue of logging into the Java virtual machine. Section 7 follows with a summary.

2 Subjects and Principals

Users often depend on computing services to assist them in performing work. Furthermore services themselves might subsequently interact with other services. JAAS uses the term, *subject*, to refer to any user of a computing service [9, 17]. Both users and computing services, therefore, represent subjects. To identify the subjects with which it interacts, a computing service typically relies on names. However, subjects might not have the same name for each service and, in fact, may even have a different name for each individual service. The term, *principal*, represents a name associated with a subject [11, 17]. Since subjects may have multiple names (potentially one for each service with which it interacts), a subject comprises a set of principals. See Figure 1.

```
public interface Principal {
    public String getName();
}

public final class Subject {
    public Set getPrincipals() {}
}
```

Figure 1. Subject Class and Principals

Principals can become associated with a subject upon successful authentication to a service. Authentication represents the process by which one subject verifies the identity of another, and must be performed in a secure fashion; otherwise a perpetrator may impersonate others to gain access to a system. Authentication typically involves the subject demonstrating some form of evidence to prove its identity. Such evidence may be information only the subject would likely know or have (a password or fingerprint), or it may be information only the subject could produce (signed data using a private key).

A service's reliance on named principals usually derives from the fact that it implements a conventional access control model of security [10]. This model allows a service to define a set of protected resources as well as the conditions under which named principals may access those resources. Recent studies (PolicyMaker [4] and SPKI [5]) have focused on the limitations of using conventional names in large distributed systems for access control, and note that public keys, instead, provide a more practical and scalable name representation. JAAS, and SPKI as well, do not impose any restrictions on principal names. Localized environments that have limited namespaces, or that do not rely on public key cryptography, may define principals that have conventional names. Large-scale distributed systems may use principals that allow the principal name to be a public key (encoded as a hex string, as in PolicyMaker).

3 Credentials

Some services may want to associate other security-related attributes and data with a subject in addition to principals. JAAS refers to such generic security-related attributes as *credentials*. A credential may contain information used to authenticate the subject to new services. Such credentials include passwords, Kerberos tickets [16], and public key certificates (X.509 [9], PGP [21], etc.), and are used in environments that support single sign-on. Credentials might also contain data that simply enables the subject to perform certain activities. Cryptographic keys, for example, represent credentials that enable the subject to sign or encrypt data. JAAS credentials may be any type of object. Therefore, existing credential implementations (java.security.cert.Certificate, for example) can be easily incorporated into JAAS. Third-party credential implementations may also be plugged into the JAAS framework.

JAAS credential implementations do not necessarily have to contain the actual security-related data; they might simply reference the data. This occurs when the data must physically reside on a separate server, or even possibly in hardware (private keys on a smart card, for instance). Also, JAAS does not impose any restrictions regarding credential delegation to third parties. Rather it allows each credential implementation to specify its own delegation protocol (as Kerberos does), or leaves delegation decisions up to the applications.

JAAS divides each subject's credentials into two sets. One set contains the subject's public credentials (public key certificates, Kerberos tickets, etc). The second set stores the subject's private credentials (private keys, encryption keys, passwords, etc). To access a subject's public credentials, no permissions are required. However, access to a subject's private credential set is security checked. See Figure 2.

```
public final class Subject {
    ...
    // not security checked
    public Set getPublicCredentials() {}

    // security checked
    public Set getPrivateCredentials() {}
}
```

Figure 2. Subject Class and Credentials

4 Pluggable and Stackable Authentication

Depending on the security parameters of a particular service, different kinds of proof may be required for authentication. The JAAS authentication framework is based on PAM [18, 20], and therefore supports an architecture that allows system administrators to plug in the appropriate authentication services to meet their security requirements. The architecture also enables applications to remain independent from the underlying authentication services. Hence as new authentication services become available or as current services are updated, system administrators can easily plug them in without having to modify or recompile existing applications.

The JAAS *LoginContext* class represents a Java implementation of the PAM framework. The LoginContext consults a configuration that determines the authentication service, or *LoginModule*, that gets plugged in under that application (See Figure 3). The syntax and details of the configuration are defined by PAM.

```
public final class LoginContext {
    public LoginContext(String name) {}
    public void login() {} // two phase process
    public void logout() {}

    // get the authenticated subject
    public Subject getSubject() {}
}

public interface LoginModule {
    boolean login();   // first phase
    boolean commit();  // second phase
    boolean abort();
    boolean logout();
}
```

Figure 3. LoginContext Class and LoginModule Interface

JAAS, like PAM, supports the notion of stacked LoginModules. To guarantee that either all LoginModules succeed or none succeed, the LoginContext performs the authentication steps in two phases. In the first phase, or the *login* phase, the LoginContext invokes the configured LoginModules and instructs each to attempt the authentication only. If all the necessary LoginModules successfully pass this phase, the LoginContext then enters the second phase and invokes the configured LoginModules again, instructing each to formally *commit* the authentication process. During this phase each LoginModule associates the relevant authenticated principals and credentials with the subject. If either the first phase or the second phase fails, the LoginContext invokes the configured LoginModules and instructs each to *abort* the entire authentication attempt. Each LoginModule then cleans up any relevant state they had associated with the authentication attempt.

In addition to JAAS, the Generic Security Services Application Programmer's Interface (GSS-API) and Simple Authentication and Security Layer Application Programmer's Interface (SASL) [13, 14] define frameworks that provide support for pluggable authentication. However, the GSS and SASL authentication frameworks are designed specifically for network communication protocols and, as such, provide additional support for securing network communications after authentication has completed. While JAAS does accommodate general network-based authentication protocols (including Needham-Schroeder and EKE [15, 2]), it also focuses on addressing the need to support pluggable authentication in stand-alone non-connection oriented environments.

5 Authorization

Once authentication has successfully completed, JAAS provides the ability to enforce access controls upon the principals associated with the authenticated subject. The JAAS principal-based access controls (access controls based on who runs code) supplement the existing Java 2 codesource-based access controls (access controls based on where code came from and who signed it).

5.1 Principal-Based Access Control

As stated earlier, services typically implement the access control model of security, which defines a set of protected resources, as well as the conditions under which named principals may access those resources. JAAS also follows this model, and defines a security policy to specify what resources are accessible to authorized principals. The JAAS policy extends the existing default Java 2 security policy, and in fact, the two policies, together, form a single logical access control policy for the entire Java runtime.

Figure 4 depicts an example codesource-based policy entry currently supported by the default policy provided with Java 2. This entry grants code loaded from *foo.com*, and signed by *foo*, permission to read all files in the *cdrom* directory and its subdirectories. Since no principal information is included with this policy entry, the code will always be able to read files from the *cdrom* directory, regardless of who executes it.

```
// Java 2 codesource-based policy
grant Codebase "http://foo.com",
      Signedby "foo" {
    permission java.io.FilePermission
        "/cdrom/-", "read";
}
```

Figure 4. Codesource-Based Policy Entry

Figure 5 depicts an example principal-based policy entry supported by JAAS. This example entry grants code loaded from *bar.com*, signed by *bar*, and executed by *duke*, permission to read only those files located in the */cdrom/duke* directory. To be executed by *duke*, the subject affiliated with the current access control context (see Section 5.2) must have an associated principal of class, *bar.Principal*, whose *getName* method returns, *duke*. Note that if the code from *bar.com*, signed by *bar*, ran stand-alone (it was not executed by *duke*), or if the code was executed by any principal other than *duke*, then it would not be granted the FilePermission. Also note that if the JAAS policy entry did not specify the Codebase or Signedby information, then the entry's FilePermission would be granted to any code running as *duke*.

```
// JAAS principal-based policy
grant Codebase "http://bar.com",
      Signedby "bar",
      Principal bar.Principal "duke" {
    permission java.io.FilePermission
              "/cdrom/duke", "read";
}
```

Figure 5. Principal-Based Policy Entry

JAAS treats roles and groups simply as named principals [10]. Therefore access control can be imposed upon roles and groups just as they are with any other type of principal. See Figure 6.

```
// an administrator role can access user passwords
grant Principal foo.Role "administrator" {
    permission java.io.FilePermission
              "/passwords/-", "read, write";
}

// a basketball team (group) can read its directory
grant Principal foo.Team "SlamDunk" {
    permission java.io.FilePermission
              "/teams/SlamDunk/-", "read";
}
```

Figure 6. Role-Based and Group-Based Policy Entries

For flexibility, the JAAS policy also permits the Principal class specified in a grant entry to be a *PrincipalComparator* (the class implements the PrincipalComparator interface). The permissions for such entries are granted to any subject that the PrincipalComparator *implies*. See Figure 7.

Figure 7 demonstrates how PrincipalComparators can be used to support role hierarchies [19]. In this example assume that an administrator role is senior to a user role and, as such, administrators inherit all the permissions granted to regular users. To accommodate this hierarchy, *bar.Role* must simply implement the PrincipalComparator interface, and its *implies* method must return, *true*, if the provided subject has an associated "administrator" role principal.

```
public interface PrincipalComparator {
    boolean implies(Subject subject);
}

// regular users can access a temporary
// working directory
grant Principal bar.Role "user" {
    permission java.io.FilePermission
              "/tmp/-", "read, write";
}
```

Figure 7. PrincipalComparator Interface and Example Policy Entry

Note that although the JAAS policy supports role hierarchies via the PrincipalComparator interface, administrators are not limited by it. JAAS can accommodate alternative role-based access control mechanisms (such as that defined in [6]), as long as the alternative access controls can be expressed either through the existing Java 2 policy or the new JAAS policy.

5.2 Access Control Implementation

The Java 2 runtime enforces access controls via the *java.lang.SecurityManager*, and is consulted any time untrusted code attempts to perform a sensitive operation (accesses to the local file system, for example). To determine whether the code has sufficient permissions, the SecurityManager implementation delegates responsibility to the *java.security.AccessController*, which first obtains an image of the current *AccessControlContext*, and then ensures that the retrieved AccessControlContext contains sufficient permissions for the operation to be permitted.

JAAS supplements this architecture by providing the method, *Subject.doAs*, to dynamically associate an authenticated subject with the current AccessControlContext. Hence, as subsequent access control checks are made, the AccessController can base its decisions upon both the executing code itself, and upon the principals associated with the subject. See Figure 8.

```
public final class Subject {
    ...
    // associate the subject with the current
    // AccessControlContext and execute the action
    public static Object doAs
        (Subject s,
         java.security.PrivilegedAction action) {}
}
```

Figure 8. Subject doAs Method

To illustrate a usage scenario for the doAs method, consider when a service authenticates a remote subject, and then performs some work on behalf of that subject. For security reasons, the server should run in an AccessControlContext bound by the subject's permissions. Using JAAS, the server can ensure this by preparing the work to be performed as a *java.security.PrivilegedAction*, and then by invoking the doAs method, providing both the authenticated subject, as well as the prepared PrivilegedAction. The doAs implementation associates the subject with the current AccessControlContext and then executes the action. When security checks occur during execution, the Java 2 SecurityManager queries the JAAS policy, updates the current AccessControlContext with the permissions granted to the subject and the executing codesource, and then performs its regular permission checks. When the action finally completes, the doAs method simply removes the subject from the current AccessControlContext, and returns the result back to the caller.

To associate a subject with the current AccessControlContext, the doAs method uses an internal JAAS implementation of the *java.security.DomainCombiner* interface, newly introduced in version 1.3 of the Java 2 SDK. It is through the JAAS DomainCombiner that the existing Java 2 SecurityManager can be instructed to query the JAAS policy without requiring modifications to the SecurityManager itself. Details of the interaction between the Java 2 SecurityManager and DomainCombiners are documented in the javadocs for the java.security.DomainCombiner interface.

5.3 Scalability of the Access Control Policy

The JAAS principal-based access control policy was intentionally designed to be consistent with the existing codesource-based policy in the Java 2 platform. The default policy implementations provided with both Java 2 and JAAS reside in a local file, and assume that all policy decisions can be defined and made locally. Obviously, this design does not scale beyond small localized environments. KeyNote [3] and SPKI both address the limitations of such access control designs, and discuss alternative solutions that enable the delegation of policy responsibilities to certified 3rd parties. By delegating policy-making responsibilities, access control policies can easily scale to serve larger systems.

To improve scalability, both the Java 2 and JAAS file-based policy implementations can be replaced with alternative implementations that support delegation. This is achieved by specifying the alternative implementations in the *java.security* properties file located in the lib/security subdirectory from where the Java runtime environment was installed. The designs of potential alternative implementations are beyond the scope of this paper.

6 Logging in to the Java Virtual Machine

With support from the JAAS framework, the Java virtual machine (VM) can be augmented to provide a general login facility for users. This would enable the VM itself to impose access controls based on who logged in. In fact, [1] investigates and describes the constructs necessary to support a multi-user environment within a VM. In such an environment, individual users log into the VM and are each given an execution shell in which to launch commands and applications (similar to Unix). The VM imposes access controls based on the identity of the user, and special UserPermissions may be granted to code running as a particular user to permit access to particular resources.

JAAS can serve as the underlying authentication architecture for such a system. Also, the environment described in [1] focuses on user-based authentication and access control from the point of view of the Java virtual machine. The JAAS framework supplements this environment by providing the support necessary for developers to build the same user-based authentication and access control capabilities into their own applications.

7 Summary and Future Directions

In this paper, we have outlined the design and implementation of the *Java*™ *Authentication and Authorization Service (JAAS)*, a framework and programming interface that augments the Java™ platform with both pluggable authentication and principal-based access control capabilities, without requiring modifications to the Java 2 core. Although individual pluggable LoginModules can be written in native code, the basic JAAS framework can be written entirely in Java. A prototype implementation of the framework has been developed, and is currently packaged as a Java 2 standard extension consisting of approximately 25 classes partitioned into four packages.

As Java technology is used to construct not just a single desktop but a full-fledged distributed system, a whole new range of distributed systems security issues (such as those we touched upon in the Introduction chapter) must be tackled. For example, additional mechanisms are needed to make RMI secure in the presence of hostile network attacks. For Jini, service registration and location must be securely managed if the environment contains coexisting but potentially mutually hostile parties. There is a full set of higher-level concepts and services that must be secured, such as transactions for electronic commerce. There are also many lower-level security protocols that we can leverage on, such as the network security protocols Kerberos and IPv6. JAAS is a critical building block for all these issues.

8 Acknowledgements

We are grateful to Bob Scheifler for his comments and feedback on the JAAS architecture. We also thank Bruce Rich, Kent Soper, Anat Sarig, Maryann Hondo, and David Edelsohn for their work in helping to define JAAS' functional requirements, and for their assistance in testing and documenting JAAS' features. Whitfield Diffie, Gary Ellison, Rosanna Lee, Jan Luehe, Peter Neumann, Jeff Nisewanger, Jerome Saltzer, Fred Schneider, Michael Schroeder, Scott Seligman, and Rob Weltman all contributed to early JAAS designs. Maxine Erlund provided management support for the JAAS project. Sriramulu Lakkaraju and Narendra Patil wrote product tests for JAAS. Scott Hommel helped edit this paper.

References

[1] D. Balfanz and L. Gong. Experience with Secure Multi-Processing in Java. In *Proceedings of ICDCS*, May 1998.

[2] S. Bellovin and M. Merritt. Encrypted Key Exchange: Password-Based Protocols Secure Against Dictionary Attacks. In *Proceedings of the IEEE Symposium on Research in Security and Privacy*, May 1992.

[3] M. Blaze, J. Feigenbaum, and A. Keromytis. Keynote: Trust Management for Public-Key Infrastructures. In *Proceedings of the Security Protocols International Workshop*, 1998.

[4] M. Blaze, J. Feigenbaum, and J. Lacy. Decentralized Trust Management. In *Proceedings of the IEEE Conference on Security and Privacy*, May 1996.

[5] C. M. Ellison, B. Frantz, B. Lampson, R. Rivest, B. M. Thomas, and T. Ylonen. SPKI Certificate Theory. Internet Engineering Task Force, November 1998. Internet Draft.

[6] L. Giuri and F. U. Bordoni. Role-Based Access Control in Java. In *Proceedings of the 3rd ACM Workshop on Role-Based Access Control*, 1998.

[7] L. Gong, M. Mueller, H. Prafullchandra, and R. Schemers. Going Beyond the Sandbox: An Overview of the New Security Architecture in the Java™ Development Kit 1.2. In *Proceedings of the USENIX Symposium on Internet Technologies and Systems*, December 1997.

[8] J. Gosling, B. Joy, and G. Steele. *The Java Language Specification*. Addison-Wesley, Menlo Park, California, August 1996.

[9] R. Housley, W. Ford, T. Polk, and D. Solo. Internet X.509 Public Key Infrastructure Certificate and CRL Profile. Internet Engineering Task Force, January 1999. Request for Comments 2459.

[10] B. Lampson. Protection. *ACM Operating Systems Review*, 8(1):18–24.

[11] B. Lampson, M. Abadi, M. Burrows, and E. Wobber. Authentication in Distributed Systems: Theory and Practice. *ACM Transactions on Computer Systems*, 10(4):265–310.

[12] T. Lindholm and F. Yellin. *The Java Virtual Machine Specification*. Addison-Wesley, Menlo Park, California, 1997.

[13] J. Linn. Generic Security Service Application Program Interface, Version 2. Internet Engineering Task Force, January 1997. Request for Comments 2078.

[14] J. Myers. Simple Authentication and Security Layer (SASL). Internet Engineering Task Force, October 1997. Request for Comments 2222.

[15] R. M. Needham and M. D. Schroeder. Using Encryption for Authentication in Large Networks of Computers. *Communications of the ACM*, 21(12):993–999.

[16] B. C. Neuman and T. Ts'o. Kerberos: An Authentication Service for Computer Networks. In *IEEE Communications*, volume 39, pages 33–38.

[17] T. Ryutov and B. C. Neuman. Access Control Framework for Distributed Applications. Internet Engineering Task Force, November 1998. Internet Draft.

[18] V. Samar and C. Lai. Making Login Services Independent from Authentication Technologies. In *Proceedings of the SunSoft Developer's Conference*, March 1996.

[19] R. S. Sandhu, E. J. Coyne, H. L. Feinstein, and C. E. Youman. Role-Based Access Control Models. *IEEE Computer*, 29(2):38–47.

[20] www.opengroup.org. X/Open Single Sign-On Service (XSSO) - Pluggable Authentication. In *Preliminary Specification P702*, June 1997.

[21] P. Zimmerman. *PGP User's Guide*. MIT Press, Cambridge, 1994.

Transactions in Java Card

Marcus Oestreicher
IBM Zurich Research Laboratory
8053 Rueschlikon, Switzerland
oes@zurich.ibm.com

Abstract

A smart card runtime environment must provide the proper transaction support for the reliable update of data, especially on multiapplication cards like the Java Card. The transaction mechanism must meet the demands by the applications and the system itself within the minimal resources offered by current smart card hardware. This paper presents the current transaction model implied by the Java Card 2.1 specification, highlights its shortcomings and presents a detailed discussion of possible implementation schemes and their optimizations. It especially addresses the problem of object instantiations within a transaction in the Java Card 2.1 specification and presents an effective solution.

1 Introduction

Smart cards provide the secured access to stored data. Data on the smart card is usually not accessible for an external application until it has authenticated itself to the card sufficiently. If the communication only consists of read accesses, the card can deliver the requested data without compromising the security and integrity of the stored data. If the external application creates or updates data on the card, care must be taken that the integrity of the data is preserved throughout the communication. Either all updates take place during the communication or the data on the card is reverted to its initial state in case of an interrupted execution.

The terminal applications set up and control the communication with the smart card and mostly also control the consistency of their data on the card completely. Current applications typically flag their data on the card to be inconsistent with the first write access during a series of updates. After all updates, the terminal application finally records its data on the card to be consistent again. If a terminal application is confronted with a card in an inconsistent state, its state may be reset by the terminal application itself, but more often must be fulfilled under special authority within a trusted environment. The dependency of the smart card consistency on external applications can be accepted as long as the smart card is only used for a few critical applications where any irregularity must be recorded and checked at a central site. Otherwise, a smart card should not only be able to verify the access rights of an external application, but should also provide a tighter control over the consistency of the internally stored data. Especially, on multiapplication cards where each application on the card has access to its own data, applications must also be able to control the integrity of their data. Thus the underlying system must provide a proper transaction mechanism which ensures the correct transition between consistent states of applications and offers its functionality to all applications residing on the card. The task of the system is then twofold [1]. First, the system is required to ensure that all updates of an application are performed atomically; second, it must perform crash recovery to provide stability: the system must recover its state and the state of the applications to a consistent state if a transactional computation fails.

A simple transaction model on the card may only support userlevel transactions in the traditional sense [2]. Transactions can be assumed to begin and end within the communication with a terminal application, are thus short lived and need not be split in multiple subtransactions even if multiple applications cooperate together. However, the implementation of a transaction mechanism is hindered by the extremely limited resources on a smart card. With RAM capacities around 1 KByte and writable EEPROM capacities around 16 KByte the transaction implementation must be carefully chosen. In case of the Java Card, the underlying standard Java environment must first be extended to offer integrated transactional computations. The familiar programming convenience of Java should be retained while the necessary resource demands must be kept as minimal as possible.

Section 2 gives an overview over the possible integrations of transactions into the different types of smart card systems, especially into interpreter based systems. Among them is the Java Card whose execution and memory management model is introduced in Section 3. Section 4 discusses transactions on the Java Card in depth. Section 4.1 presents its transaction API and details its pros and cons. Section 4.2 presents the minimum functionality which is expressed in the Java Card 2.1 specification. However, the Java Card specifications inhibits some problems described in Section 4.3. Section 4.4 explains the transaction implementation options on the card, especially the possible log strategies. Section 4.5 deals with the problem of object instantiations within transactional boundaries and presents a solution. Section 5 finally draws our conclusions and presents future ideas.

2 Approaches in Smart Card Operating Systems

As soon as a smart card is inserted into a smart card reader, an external application can start a communication and send commands to the smart card. The card acts as a server, fulfills the requested operation and returns a reply. A set of basic commands is described in the ISO 7816-4 specification which defines an interoperability standard at the level of the command exchange [3]. A smart card conforming to this specification presents the stored data as a secured file system to an external application. An external application can select files in directories and read and update their data after a successful authentication. The ISO specification does not prescribe a transactional concept for the update of stored files. While individual commands updating data should be executed atomically, a sequence of updating commands needs not to be atomic, especially as extremely memory limited smart cards may not provide the necessary resources for such additional guarantees. Thus the external application is supposed to keep track of and manage consistent states. An ISO file system based card could be extended to provide the atomicity of all requested updates. However, an external application might need a more fine granular control over which records belong to the transaction or not. In this case, new commands for transaction control must be introduced limiting the interoperability of the card.

Some smart cards offer a convenient transaction model in form of a database application or even a database operating system [5]. External applications can access and update the information stored in relational tables by providing sufficient indexing information and authentication. In contrast to filesystem based access, updates are transactional by definition. The database model remains sufficient as long as the necessary data can be easily modeled within a relational table and the application does not rely on specific authentication and encryption schemes.

Multiapplication and post issuance smart cards allow the deployment of many applications on a smart card and the extension of the card functionality by installing new applications at a later time on the smart card. Each application is independently selectable by an external application and is responsible for servicing its requests. In multiapplication cards where machine code serves as the executable content, the applications are fully responsible for providing transactional semantics as applications are allowed to directly access the contents in memory. However, direct write accesses to memory which must be logged during a transaction can in general only be caught by explicit support in the language and compiler.

Control over memory access is a basic benefit of an interpreter as the basic execution engine. Interpreters can easily ensure that different applications only access the parts of the memory which have been assigned to them so far. Other than that, an interpreter can make sure that no memory cell is overwritten during a transaction where its previous content has not been saved for potential restore at a later time. Any computation within an application on the smart card can be part of a transaction and transactional computations can be integrated easily in the programming language.

Smart Card interpreters achieve memory protection in two different ways. Systems like MULTOS realize a software memory management unit where the instructions may refer to memory by address but each access gets guarded and checked towards granted areas [6]. Smart card environments like the Java Card offer the possibility to rely on the protection mechanisms of a type safe language which prevents arbitrary accesses to memory. The referential integrity of the language is preserved. An application is only allowed to access the elements or fields in an object or class. One might use this information to record the changes during a transaction at a higher level and record the operations applied to the individual objects. This provides additional information about transaction failures during future investigations, but increases heavily the information needed for the transaction recording.

3 Java Card Introduction

3.1 Applet Execution

The Java Card environment shares the basic architecture with the standard Java environment. However, due to the limited resources on current smart cards the Java Card sacrifices a number of Java features. For instance, the Java Card does not support all primitive types and does not allow the dynamic download of classes [7]. Instead, a converter is used to package all classes of a Java Card application into one executable file and to reduce its size by prelinking it for the execution on the card as far as possible. The converted package can then be downloaded on the card where a Java

Card application, an applet, can be installed in a separate step.

The runtime environment initiates the applet installation by calling the *install()* method of its class instantiating an applet object and registering it at the runtime environment. From now on, an external application can initiate a *session* with the installed applet by selecting it first at the runtime environment. The select command will be forwarded by the runtime to the applet's *select()* method, each following command will be forwarded to its *process()* method. The applet processes each command and returns from its invocation with a response for the terminal application. Thus the invocation of the applet is event driven until the remote application finishes the card session or selects a different applet where the current applet is notified by the invocation of its *deselect()* method.

3.2 Memory Management

The applet instance and associated persistent objects of an application must survive a session. Therefore they are placed in the non volatile storage on a card, usually EEPROM. EEPROM provides similar read and write access as RAM does, but with the important difference that the number of physical writes is limited and writes to EEPROM cells are typically more than thirty times slower than writes to RAM. Performance of writes can be increased on many current chips by initiating block writes instead of multiple single EEPROM writes where individual bytes are written in parallel to EEPROM. Neither single byte nor block writes are guaranteed to succeed in case of sudden power loss, the write operation can suddenly fail after an arbitrary number of bits have already been written. Thus the runtime environment can only rely on the outcome of a single flag write as the basic building block for transactions. Both RAM and EEPROM size is extremely limited on current smart card hardware, ranging typically up to 1 KByte for RAM and up to 16 KByte EEPROM for current Java Cards.

In contrast to EEPROM, RAM looses its value in case of a power loss. For repeated, performance- and security-sensitive computations, RAM must be usable by Java Card applications. For instance execution state, operand stack and local variables must be placed in RAM by the virtual machine. Other than that, the Java Card 2.1 specification allows applets to allocate array instances explicitly in RAM. Our model extends the Java Card specification by allowing any type of object to be placed both in EEPROM as well as in RAM. The system is described in detail in [9] and especially allows the easy deployment of a RAM garbage collector.

Data located in RAM, i.e. execution state and transient objects, is not considered to be part of the persistent state and its manipulations are not recorded during the transaction due to a number of reasons, among which are performance penalty and security implications. Thus, only changes to the applet objects in EEPROM must be covered by the transactional mechanism.

4 Transactions in Java Card

4.1 Language Integration

The described memory model shares its main properties with the Java Card transaction model. The persistence or transience property is orthogonal to the type of an object. Any update of an object can be transactional independent of its concrete type. Other than that, the transaction scheme provides the following features:

1. Persistent updates are independent of transactional updates. Changes to objects residing in EEPROM persist even when occurring outside of transaction boundaries. While a single EEPROM field access has to be atomic regarding to the Java Card specification, multiple writes to EEPROM inside or outside a transaction may differ in their behavior.

2. Transactional independence: Source code executed inside or outside a transaction can look exactly the same.

3. Execution within transactions do not compromise Java security:
   No changes have been applied to the language or to the instruction set. Thus the converter remains independent of the transaction mechanism. The recording of state changes is invisible and unaccessible to the executing applet.

Figure 1 shows the current API in the Java Card specification for initiating, committing and aborting transactions. The control of transactions by static methods has a number of disadvantages. The begin and end of a transaction is not connected to each other, neither in the program text nor at runtime. As a result, the execution state can not be reset to a consistent state when a transaction is aborted by request of an applet using *abortTransaction()*. Instead, execution continues right after the *abortTransaction()* call. Transactional

Figure 1. Transaction API

```
JCSystem.beginTransaction();
JCSystem.commitTransaction();
JCSystem.abortTransaction();
```

systems like Transactional-C extend the language by constructs allowing the linguistic connection between begin, commit and abort blocks [10]. In case of abort or commit execution continues at well defined locations. PJama achieves a similar effect by expecting the transaction to be coded within one single instance method [11]. The runtime environment will then execute the given method within a transaction and return in any case, commit or abort, from its invocation.

Such a mechanism adds the overhead of one temporary instance per transaction which might still be acceptable even within the resource constrained Java Card environment. However, the encapsulation within one method interferes with the event triggered execution model of an applet in the Java Card 2.1 specification. It is not possible to extend the lifetime of a transaction across multiple commands during a session as soon as the transaction is encapsulated within a method invocation. As a method invocation can only last as long as the invocation of the *process()* method, the transaction boundaries can not be connected with each other as soon as transaction lasts longer than one single command. The current API therefore favors flexibility and resource friendliness although the missing linguistic connection is partly responsible for some of the problems described in Section 4.6.

4.2 Basic Java Card Transaction Model

As soon as a transaction is started, the system must keep track of the changes to the persistent environment. The system must at least record the state before the transaction and the most current value for any given element during the transaction. The updates must be logged at the granularity of a single access. Large transactional systems group objects in pages, manipulate them in RAM during the transaction and log changes lazily at the granularity of the page into stable storage. However, the necessary RAM resources are by no means available on current smart card hardware.

The transaction system must provide two guarantees. If the system commits a transaction on request by an applet, it must guarantee that the changes to the persistent set are applied in any case. Any necessary commit information must be stored persistently at commit time to allow for the restart of the commit process in case of sudden power loss. If the commit process succeeds without a crash, execution continues after the return from the commit method.

Whenever a transactional computation aborts, the system must be able to restore the state at the beginning of the transaction. The reason for an abort firstly includes system crashes, e.g. sudden power losses, or system initiated aborts of applet computations. The system throws an exception in case of any irregularity during the transaction processing, for instance due to a transaction buffer overflow, and may abort the applet computation for instance in case of an exception not being handled by the applet. The system then recovers the previous applet state where the recovery information had to be stored persistently to be able to restart the recovery process in case of a sudden power loss. The system is then free either to deselect the current applet or to let it continue in its current session.

An applet can always explicitly request the transaction abort by an *abort()* method invocation, for instance after it caught an exception thrown by the system. The applet remains selected to be able to react to the abort and to further communicate with the external application.

4.3 Java Card 2.1 Limitations

The Java Card specification expects the recovery process to take place immediately at the invocation of the *abort()* method. The persistent state is brought back to its initial state while the execution state and temporary instances are not affected and applet execution continues after the return from the *abort()* invocation. As the state has been recovered, the applet can for instance immediately try to restart the aborted transaction. As it will turn out, the point in time defined for the recovery process has severe implications on the flexibility of the transaction mechanism. In general, the action and the point in time of the recovery can be varied and still allow the future execution of the same applet during the same session.

Although the Java Card 2.1 specification limits the maximum lifetime of a transaction to the duration of one APDU communication, there are scenarios where computation must be transactional over multiple APDU's. For instance, a download of a new application should be encapsulated within a transaction. Other than required for system relevant processes, applications in general benefit from the extension of the maximum transaction duration. For example, downloads of new keys of arbitrary length can span multiple APDU's, should be possible with the regular transaction mechanism, and should not require additional transaction logic by the application.

Allocations by the system or applications must also be covered by the transaction mechanism. The Java Card specification indeed specifies the installation of applets as a transactional process. All objects which are created during a failing applet initialization must be freed. Other than that, the current 2.1 Java Card specification does not require the release of allocated memory within transaction boundaries in case of an abort. In contrast to standard Java, the Java Card specification assumes all object instantiations to take place at installation time and not at any later time. However, some applications may not know or do not have any real worst case requirement which they could allocate at installation time. A general database or data storage application on a card might want to allocate dynamically as many records as an external application may need [13]. In these cases the system should limit the application resources, but not the application itself. Especially with a garbage collection scheme on the card and increasing memory capacities, memory releases and new instantiations are easily affordable for applications. The system must then guarantee that no memory is lost when new objects are created during a transaction aborted at a later time. Indeed, reclaiming this memory is already required by the definition of a transaction, but hard to enforce in the resource limited Java Card environment.

Our Java Card implementation tries to avoid native code as often as possible. System services like the secure download of new applications and the update of keys, part of the implementation of the Visa Open Platform specification, are almost completely written in Java [12]. Thus the transaction mechanism can be tailored completely towards the requirements of Java applications and need not be designed to support explicitly processes written in native code. As we rely on the general transaction mechanism for performance sensitive applications like the application download, the transaction implementation must be runtime efficient. Other than that, the transaction implementation must take the scarce resources on the card into account and be space efficient.

4.4 Old versus New Value Logging

Updates or writes to the persistent set occur within the interpreter loop only on the access of persistent instance fields, static fields and arrays. A second source are native methods which must use special access operations to not bypass the transaction mechanism. Especially the native *Util.arrayCopy()* methods allow the transactional update of a number of array elements at once [8].

Two schemes are well known for the logging of write accesses during a transaction, e.g. either new value or old value logging [2]. In case of old value logging, the update of a location during the transaction occurs in place, e.g. directly at the referenced location. The general properties of old value logging are:

- fast read accesses as the up-to-date values are always stored at the referenced location.

- the original value for a given location must be saved in a transaction buffer, typically once at the time of the first write access to the location.

- committing a transaction is cheap as the new value are already in place.

- aborting a transaction is expensive as the saved values have to be written back to the original locations.

In case of new value logging, each value for a store operation to a given location is saved in the transaction buffer during the transaction while the original value remains at the affected location. The general properties are here:

- a slow read access as the up-to-date value for a location must be searched in the buffer.

- write operations always have to update the buffer as any new store operation has to be recorded there.

- committing a transaction is expensive as the new values have to be written to their target locations.

- aborting a transaction is cheap as the original values are still in place.

Although the advantages and disadvantages still apply in general in case of the Java Card, their degree depend on the exploitation of the memory characteristics found on a smart card. For instance, the performance aspect depends here mostly on the number of necessary single or block EEPROM writes whereas accesses to RAM are negligible to a large extent. One might also include the typical access pattern of Java Card applications into account where writes to the same location during a transaction are usually rare. So what are reasonable implementations and the achievable performance for both schemes on a Java Card ?

Old Value Logging

Read performance always remains excellent in case of old value logging. In case of a write, the referenced location has to be checked for having already been saved. A reasonable implementation for current smart cards scans the transaction buffer linearly for the given location and if found, the write succeeds directly to the target location. As multiple updates of the same location are rare, the best case for the write performance -one single EEPROM write - does not occur too often. If the former value of the given location has not been saved so far, a new entry consisting of location and original value must be added **persistently** to the transaction buffer to support a recovery process in case of sudden power loss.

Two schemes are conceivable, a mark or counter based transaction buffer scheme. The latter one adds first the new entry to the buffer and then increments the entry counter of the buffer. The counter must be incremented atomically, for instance with the help of a shadow counter and a flag indicating which counter is currently valid. Thus three EEPROM writes are necessary. One block write for the new entry, one write for the incremented shadow counter and one write for flipping the counter flag. Performance can be increased with the mark scheme where a flag after the last entry in the buffer indicates its end. Entries are added to the buffer by first appending the new entry with the new end marker in a single block writte and then clearing the previous end marker in a second single EEPROM write access. The number of EEPROM accesses is reduced to two while the entry size is increased by an additional byte.

Table 1 summarizes the properties of a old value logging scheme with a marked buffer implementation. Appending a new entry needs two EEPROM writes. In case of commit, the expected total number of EEPROM writes per location is then expected to consist typically of three assuming multiple updates of the same location are rare; two for adding an entry, one for updating the target location.

In case of commit, the transaction buffer must just be marked invalid and the transaction is completed. In case of abort, the saved values in the buffer are written back to their former locations. After a sudden power loss the write process may just be restarted from the beginning of the buffer as locations and values in the buffer remain constant and thus can be rewritten as often as possible (although the number is actually limited by the physically possible number of EEPROM writes).

Table 1. Logging Scheme Comparison

Logging Strategy	New Value	Old Value
Commit Costs	High	Minimal
Abort Costs	Minimal	High
Minimum E2 Accesses for Logging	1	2/Log Entry
Maximum E2 Accesses for Logging	1/Store	2/Log Entry
Expected E2 Accesses per Committed Store	1 + 1/Store	3/Store
Expected E2 Accesses per Aborted Store	1	3/Store
Writes per Log Entry on Abort	0	1

New Value Logging

Similar overall performance can be achieved in the new value logging scheme dependent on the implementation and the available resources. Read performance lags always behind as the transaction buffer must be scanned - typically linearly - for a formerly written value. The situation can be better in case of the much more expensive write operations. A straightforward solution will scan the transaction buffer for a formerly written entry for the given location and replace its value with the new value in a single EEPROM write operation. If the location is accessed the first time - the most common case for typical Java Card applications - a new entry must be added to the buffer **non atomically**, e.g. with one single EEPROM block write. Thus the performance can be increased significantly if the transaction buffer is cached in RAM and written out lazily to EEPROM on overflow. If the RAM resources are not too limited and the transaction does not involve too many write operations, all memory accesses can be logged within the cache in RAM and are only written to EEPROM in one single EEPROM block write at commit time. The buffer must then be saved persistently as any started commit operation has to be completed after a sudden power loss at the time of the next card reset. The runtime environment will then scan through the transaction buffer and apply the stored values to the given locations. Aborts are again free in the sense that the contents of the transaction buffer can just be discarded.

Table 1 summarizes the properties of a new value logging scheme with RAM caching. Best commit performance can be achieved if all log entries can be cached in RAM and all entries are saved at commit time in EEPROM with *one* single block write. The value in *each* entry must then be flushed to its target location with another EEPROM write. In the worst case however, EEPROM has to be accessed on each log operation for instance if log entries are reused and an entry for a given location is already existent in EEPROM.

Other than pure performance, the necessary memory resources are another key aspect for choosing the right logging scheme which are for instance high in case of a cache based new value logging scheme. However, there is still another general advantage of the new value logging scheme which arises from the fact that an abort or a sudden power loss is more likely to occur during the application processing than during the commit or abort process by the system. Thus someone might choose the new value logging scheme in general as it reduces the amount of work for the recovery process in case of an application abort drastically.

4.5 Object Instantiations within Transactions

The Java Card specification does not enforce possible object instantiations outside of the installation method. Other than that, it also explicitly states that object allocations within transactions may fail and any allocated space is allowed to get lost forever in case of an abort [8]. Clearly, this does not conform to proper transactional semantics where the state of the applications and the system is expected to be exactly the same as before the transaction in case of an abort and thus any allocated space in between is released. This is especially very harmful as there is a practical need for object instantiations outside of the applet installation method and under a proper transaction control.

For instance, our Visa Open Platform implementation relies completely on a real transaction mechanism for the download of new applications [12]. During the transaction, a new array is created and the executable content is downloaded and stored in the newly allocated object. If the transaction fails, the transaction mechanism ensures that the newly allocated object will go away during the abort process. Indeed, if any change to the persistent memory is included in the transactional mechanism, including the changes by the system to the heap management structures etc., the persistent state is recovered completely in case of an abort and any newly allocated object is automatically released.

However, there are a few remaining problems. The newly allocated array for the code to be downloaded in the given example can be huge and as any write to the array incurs an additional entry in the transaction buffer, the buffer is likely to overflow during the transaction. However, each access to a newly created object can be easily detected within the interpreter and directly forwarded to the contents of the newly created array. In the object aware Java bytecode, objects are always addressed by an object reference and offset. When the object header and its heap management information is logged at instantiation time, the transaction mechanism can decide on each access whether a given object already existed before or has been allocated during the transaction. The referenced object is just searched in the buffer and if it is not found, the object already existed before and the store operation is regularly logged. If it is found, it has been newly allocated and the value can commence directly within the newly allocated region at the given offset. In case of commit, the object header and its heap management information is written permanently, the object thus becomes allocated persistently. In case of an abort, it is automatically released. This optimization can therefore reduce extremely the necessary transaction buffer size during a transaction.

The most hindering problem is the fact that the transaction mechanism logs only writes to persistent fields. Thus, temporary references stored in RAM may still reference the newly instantiated objects after an abort. As long as these references exist, the virtual machine can not release the referenced objects. If the runtime releases the objects, it must reset the relevant references to a defined state. The most simple approach for avoiding this problem is to deselect an applet immediately in case of an abort and to recover the persistent set. However, if an applet gets automatically deselected, it depends completely on the external application to reselect and reactivate it again.

There are two potential sources for references within RAM to the areas of aborted object instantiations. First, an application might have stored such references in transient objects. These can be found and reset by a RAM garbage collector [9]. It has just to be adapted to search for specific persistent objects and reset the referencing location in RAM. Other than that, local variables in the current execution frame may contain such references in case of an abort due to the missing linguistic connection between the transaction boundaries. Figure 2 shows a code example where f is a local variable which is still accessible after the application initiated an abort and still refers to the newly instantiated object. If the semantics for *abortTransaction()* are

Figure 2. Problematic JCSystem.abort()

```
Foo f;
JCSystem.beginTransaction();
...
f = new Object();
...
JCSystem.abortTransaction();
f.doIt();
```

defined to recover the state and release the allocated objects immediately, the references on the stack must be reset, too. Which elements on the stack are references can be gathered practically in two ways. Firstly, the interpreter may implement a type tagged stack where each stack slot is marked with its type. This allows the reset of problematic references immediately in case of abort, but reduces the interpreter performance in general and increases the size of the runtime stack. Secondly, instructions can be checked lazily at execution time not to operate on invalid references and throw an exception in case. However, this still introduces a performance penalty and especially makes it very hard to reuse and reallocate the space for an aborted object instantiation as the system must ensure that no other reference to this area still exists. This seems to be the main reason why the Java Card specification allows memory to get lost in case of allocations within transactions.

The restrictions on the interpreter implementation can be reduced when the point in time for the recovery process is delayed until the applet returns from its *process()* invocation by the system. The stack is then unwound and only the temporary objects have to be scanned for problematic references. The applet is then limited in so far that it can not immediately try to restart the transaction, but must wait for another command by the external communication. However, we expect an applet to return an error code in case of a failure anyway and wait for new commands for further processing. Instead of restricting the system with an expensive and fixed interpreter architecture, we propose instead a small limitation on the possible communication behavior of Java Card applications. We therefore suggest that *abortTransaction()* throws an exception by default to remember a programmer that his applet is going to operate on still unrecovered data and will be recovered on return from the current applet invocation.

5 Conclusion And Future Work

This paper presents the effective integration of transaction support in the Java Card. It reports the basic transaction semantics required by the Java Card 2.1 specification which only requires the minimum functionality needed for simple transactional computations. For instance, the Java Card specification and especially its transaction model suffers from its static allocation model where any space allocated within transactions may not be released in case of an abort. In contrast, we have shown that object instantiations can easily be integrated in the transaction mechanism even in case of the tight memory resources on a smart card. The various possible implementation choices are discussed in detail, including various log schemes, their impact on performance and memory usage and possible optimizations.

An extended transaction mechanism can be used by a wide range of applications, for instance by system services like the download of applications, or by applications to download and update arbitrary data like keys. It is also used by applets to reliable audit the progress of computations. Java Cards do not provide enough memory resources and symbolic information to allow a general audit of application processes by the system. Thus, current applications need to record any audit information by themselves. In the future, we want to extend our transaction mechanism to provide a standard audit mechanism which can be used by a broad range of applications. However, as specifications like Visa Cash or Geldkarte can not rely so far on a standard audit service, they specify their own and different audit mechanisms which then have to be implemented by the applications themselves [4].

The described application scenarios are already fully supported with the transaction mechanism proposed in this paper and the Java Card platform therefore provides a flexible and reliable platform for smart card applications.

References

[1] Jim Gray, The Transaction Concept: Virtues and Limitations, Very Large Data Bases, 7th International Conference, September 9-11, 1981, Cannes, France, Proceedings

[2] Jim Gray, Andreas Reuter, Transaction Processing: Concepts and Techniques, Morgan Kaufmann 1993, ISBN 1-55860-190-2

[3] ISO/IEC 7816-4, Identification Cards - Integrated circuit(s) cards with contacts - Part 4: Interindustry commands for interchange, 1995, ISO/IEC 7816-4:1995(E)

[4] Leo van Hove, A selected bibliography on electronic purses, http://cfec.vub.ac.be/cfec/purses.htm

[5] E. Dufresnes, P. Paradinas, J.-J. Vandewalle. CQL, a Data Base in Smart Card for healthcare Applications, Height World Congress on Medical Informatics, Edmonton Canada, July 1995

[6] Scott Guthery, alt.technology.smartcards FAQ, 1998, http://www.scdk.com/atsfaq.htm

[7] Sun Microsystems Inc., Java Card 2.1 Virtual Machine Specification, Final Revision 1.0, March 1998, http://java.sun.com/products/javacard/JCVMSpec.pdf

[8] Sun Microsystems Inc., Java Card 2.1 API Specification, Final Revision 1.0, March 1998, http://java.sun.com/products/javacard/htmldoc/index.html

[9] Marcus Oestreicher, Krishna Ksheeradbhi, Object Lifetimes in Java Card, USENIX Workshop on Smart Card Technology, May 1999

[10] Paul Taylor, Transactions for Amadeus, Thesis, Department of Computer Science, Trinity College Dublin, August 1993

[11] Atkinson M.P., Jordan M.J., Daynes L., Spence S., Design Issues For Persistent Java: a type-safe, object-oriented, orthogonally persistent system, Seventh International Workshop on Persistent Object Systems, February 1996

[12] Visa International, Open Platform Main Page, http://www.visa.com/nt/suppliers/open/main.html

[13] RSA Laboratories, "PKCS #11: Cryptographic Token Interface Standard", December 1997, RSA Data Security, Inc., http://www.rsa.com/rsalabs/pubs/PKCS/html/pkcs-11.html

Track A: Panel Session

Legal and Technical Responses to Protecting the U. S. Critical Infrastructures

Chair

Art Friedman, NSA

Last year President Clinton ordered the strengthening of the nation's defenses against emerging unconventional threats to the United States and the protection of our critical infrastructures. The Critical Infrastructure Protection directive (Presidential Decision Directive – 63) calls for a national effort to assure the security of the increasingly vulnerable and interconnected infrastructures of the United States. Such infrastructures include telecommunications, banking and finance, energy, transportation, and essential government services. The directive requires immediate federal government action including risk assessment and planning to reduce exposure to attack. It stresses the critical importance of cooperation between the government and the private sector by linking designated agencies with private sector representatives.

Both the federal government and private industry have become more proactive to protect our national infrastructure, such as telecommunications, energy, defense, transportation. There have been many legal, technical, and possibly ethical issues in developing capabilities to respond to attacks. What should be the United States position to protect our telecommunications networks, banking and finance, and our livelihoods? How proactive should industry become? What partnerships should be developed between government and industry? These are some of the questions that the panel will consider.

The panel consists of experts that represent the National Incident Response Team, law enforcement, industry response to protecting our networks, and legal advice to both government and industry.

Track B

Middleware

Chair

Vince Reed, MITRE Corporation

A Middleware Approach to Asynchronous and Backward Compatible Detection and Prevention of ARP Cache Poisoning

Mahesh V. Tripunitara
CERIAS
Purdue University
West Lafayette, IN, USA
tripunit@cerias.purdue.edu

Partha Dutta
Internet Platforms Organization
AT&T Labs
San Jose, CA
ppd@ipo.att.com

Abstract

This paper discusses the Address Resolution Protocol (ARP) and the problem of ARP cache poisoning. ARP cache poisoning is the malicious act, by a host in a LAN, of introducing a spurious IP address to MAC (Ethernet) address mapping in another host's ARP cache. We discuss design constraints for a solution: the solution needs to be implemented in middleware, without access or change to any operating system source code, be backward-compatible to the existing protocol, and be asynchronous.

We present our solution and implementation aspects of it in a Streams based networking subsystem. Our solution comprises two parts: a "bump in the stack" Streams module, and a separate Stream with a driver and user-level application. We also present the algorithm that is executed in the module and application to prevent ARP cache poisoning where possible, and detect and raise alarms otherwise.

We then discuss some limitations with our approach and present some preliminary performance numbers for our implementation.

1. Introduction

The Address Resolution Protocol (ARP) [5, 9] is used by hosts on a Local Area Network (LAN) to find a link layer address given a network layer address. In the context of this paper, a network layer address is an IP [6] address, and a link layer address is an Ethernet address. This assumption is not necessary for the issues in this paper to be valid.

Hosts on a LAN maintain the IP address to Ethernet address mappings in a local table called an ARP cache. A mapping may be dynamic: the entry corresponding to the mapping is removed after a certain time-period unless refreshed.

ARP cache poisoning is the act, by a malicious host in the LAN, of introducing a spurious IP to Ethernet address mapping into another host's ARP cache. Some specific examples of ARP cache poisoning are discussed in [12].

This paper discusses ARP cache poisoning and specifies the context and design constraints for a solution. It then presents a solution that satisfies those design constraints and discusses the security and performance properties of the solution.

The remainder of this paper is organized as follows. The next section discusses ARP and the problem of ARP cache poisoning. Section 3 discusses the design constraints and context for a solution. The context for the solution is an operating system that uses the Streams paradigm for its networking subsystem. Section 4 presents the solution. Section 5 discusses some disadvantages and shortcomings with our approach. Section 6 presents some perfunctory performance studies. We conclude in section 7.

2. ARP and ARP Cache Poisoning

In this section, we briefly discuss the Address Resolution Protocol (ARP) [5, 9] and what it means for a host's ARP cache to be poisoned. We also discuss various attack scenarios and special cases in the use of ARP.

2.1. ARP

We adopt the scenario of hosts in a LAN communicating using the TCP/IP suite [6, 7] over a shared Ethernet. IP packets need to be encapsulated in Ethernet frames before they can be transmitted. Hosts are identified at the IP layer with an IP address, and at the Ethernet layer with an Ethernet address. We assume that there is a one-to-one mapping between the set of IP addresses and the set of Ethernet

---

*Portions of this work were supported by sponsors of the Center for Education and Research in Information Assurance and Security.

addresses for the LAN. This is necessary for hosts to be uniquely identified, both at the IP layer and at the Ethernet layer.

Before an IP packet can be encapsulated in an Ethernet frame, the sender needs the recipient's Ethernet address so the Ethernet frame can be constructed. Given the destination IP address, ARP is used to find the Ethernet address corresponding to that IP address. ARP is employed when static configuration of the IP to Ethernet address mappings in each host in the LAN is not feasible or preferable.

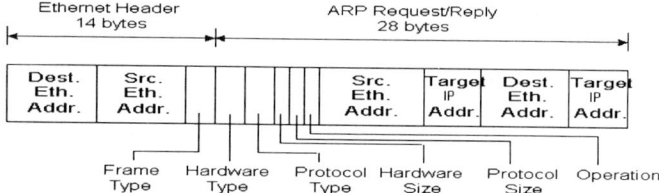

Figure 1. The format of an ARP frame when used on an Ethernet. This figure is adapted from [9].

Figure 1 shows the format of an ARP frame. ARP is a request–response protocol. An ARP request is broadcast on the LAN. The request contains the source IP and Ethernet addresses and the target IP address.

Each host on the LAN checks the target IP address in a request against its own IP address. If a host is configured with the target IP address, it sends an ARP response with its Ethernet address. The response is unicast: it is addressed only to the sender of the request.

Proxy ARP may be employed in situations in which it is desirable to have an ARP (proxy) server respond to all or some resolution requests. The server responds on behalf of the target host. Proxy ARP is discussed in [2].

2.2. ARP Cache Poisoning

ARP cache poisoning is the act of a malicious host in the LAN, of introducing a spurious IP to Ethernet address mapping in another host's ARP cache. The effect of ARP cache poisoning is that IP traffic intended for one host is diverted to a different host, or to no host.

Following are ways in which a host's ARP cache can be poisoned. We have tested that these attacks do work against the ARP implementations of Solaris 2.6 and 2.5.1, Windows 95, Windows 98, Window NT 4.0 server and workstation and Linux (various versions of the kernel).

- Unsolicited Response: A response that is not associated with a request will be honored by an ARP implementation. A malicious host only has to send a response ARP packet on the LAN with a spurious mapping to poison the ARP cache of the victim. This response can be broadcast to poison the ARP cache of every host on the LAN.

- Request: ARP implementations cache entries based on requests they receive. That is, if host A sends out a broadcast ARP request for host B, host C might cache the mapping information about host A based on the request host A sends out. An attacker only has to pretend to be sending out a legitimate request to poison the ARP cache of a victim.

- Response to a request: Rather than send an unsolicited response, or a spurious request, a malicious host may wait till a victim issues a request and send a spurious response to that request. If another host (legitimately) responds to the request, there is a race condition that the malicious host may win. The response that is received later will supersede the entry in the victim's cache corresponding to the response that is received earlier.

- Request and response: A malicious host could send out both a spurious request, and a spurious response corresponding to that request. This may be used to poison a victim's ARP cache in the case that the victim has a partial solution to the problem and "remembers" a request: either its own, or from another host and only caches a response to a request.

3. The Design Considerations and Context for a Solution

We first discuss design considerations for a solution in section 3.1. Then, in section 3.2 we discuss the Streams [8, 10] paradigm and the portion of the protocol stack of interest to us implemented using that paradigm.

3.1. Design Considerations

The design considerations for a solution to the problem of ARP cache poisoning discussed in the previous section are:

- Backward Compatible: we only want to protect the ARP caches of some of the hosts in a LAN. These could be "special" machines such as routers. All other hosts in the LAN continue to use ARP unaware that some of the hosts are protecting their respective caches.

- Asynchronous: we want a solution that does not involve checking ARP cache consistency every few units of time. A solution that involves such a technique would leave us with the problem of deciding what is an appropriate time interval between checks for consistency.

- Middleware: we do not want to have access to source code for ARP or other components of the networking subsystem to be able to develop or deploy the solution. A middleware solution is preferred, by which some components are introduced into the networking subsystem without any change to existing components. The Streams paradigm, discussed in section 3.2, facilitates such a solution.

The design constraint for backwards compatibility means that a "conventional" cryptographic solution of establishing a public key infrastructure for the LAN, and attaching a message authentication code with every ARP packet, cannot be used. We do not seek cryptographically strong security, but we still want confidence in the validity of entries in a host's ARP cache.

Where possible, we want to prevent the host's ARP cache from being poisoned. For situations in which we are unable to perform prevention, we would like to detect and respond to attempts to poison the ARP cache. In discussing our solution in section 4, we discuss our choice of situations for prevention versus detection and response.

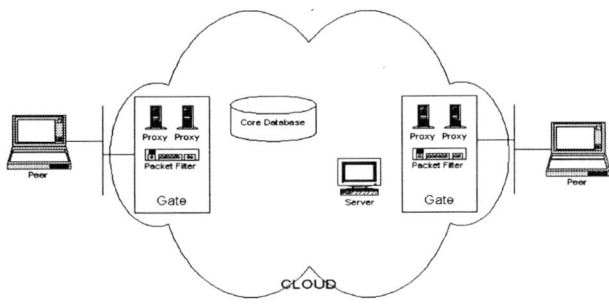

Figure 2. The Common Open IP Platform (COIPP) and some of its components. The COIPP is an integrated data communications infrastruture.

These design constraints arise in the context of the Common Open IP Platform (COIPP) [1, 4] (see figure 2). In the COIPP architecture, a network cloud is used for communication between peers. A peer is either a client or a server, or both. At the edges of a cloud are gates. The gate is a bastion to the cloud. Its ARP cache needs to be protected. But peers only run "standard" software (such as web browsers) and therefore nothing can be changed in them.

The COIPP is a network operating system. A peer is a "user" that "logs into" the cloud and uses services exported by the cloud and by other peers. The cloud provides functionality that does not have to be available at the peer, such as authentication, access control and usage recording.

These design constraints are not unique to the COIPP. In any situation in which the ARP caches of only select machines on a LAN need to be protected, these design constraints are appropriate. No changes are necessary in any of the other hosts.

3.2. Streams and Solaris

We assume that a host that we need to deploy the solution in has a Streams [8, 10] based networking subsystem. Streams is a paradigm that prescribes modularity. Modules can be created that implement some functionality, and can be selected and interconnected without any kernel reprogramming or linking. Drivers act as interfaces between a (possibly virtual) device and the kernel.

Streams modules and drivers are organized as a stack, with a stream head on top, any number of modules beneath the head, and a driver at the bottom. Data is transferred using units called message blocks, and a messaging queue is associated with each of the upward and downward directions.

Solaris 2.6 is an example of an operating system that uses a Streams based networking subsystem. Part of the functionality associated with each of ARP and IP is implemented using Streams modules. We refer the reader to [8, 10] for more details on Streams and Streams modules and drivers.

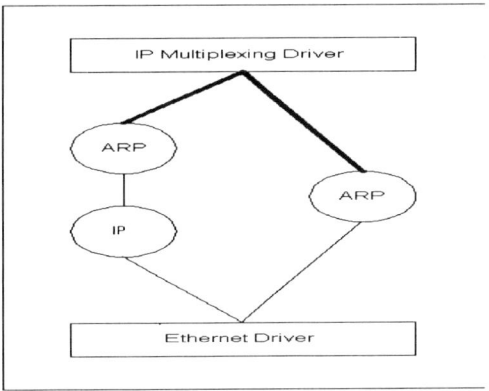

Figure 3. The portion of the protocol stack that pertains to ARP. The ovals are Streams modules, and the rectangles are Streams drivers. The bold lines represent links to the multiplexing driver, and the thin lines represent the links in a Stream.

Again, using Solaris 2.6 as an example, the portion of the protocol stack that pertains to ARP is shown in figure 3. The ARP module is pushed above the IP module for the IP module to be able to make resolutions based on the local ARP cache. All ARP traffic from and to the network flows

305

on the "branch" on which there is only the ARP module below the IP multiplexing driver.

4. The Solution

In this section, we present our solution to the problem of ARP cache poisoning that satisfies the design constraints specified in section 3.1. Our solution is for a Streams-based network subsystem. We first describe a Streams module, driver and user-level application as components of our architecture in section 4.1. In 4.2, we discuss heuristics that we adopt in the Streams module to address the attacks mentioned in section 2.2.

Our implementation is for the Solaris 2.6 operating system, and we discuss details from the implementation where appropriate.

Note that our solution can also be implemented in other platforms, including ones that do not use the Streams paradigm for their networking subsystem. For instance, we could write a kernel device driver to realize the functionality in the Streams module in a non–Streams environment.

4.1. Streams Module, Driver and a User-Level Application

Our prevention and detection architecture for solving the problem of ARP cache poisoning is shown in figure 4.

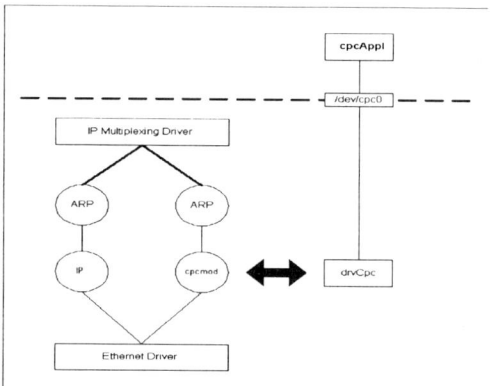

Figure 4. Figure 3 modified to show our solution in place. cpcmod is the Streams module, drvCpc is the Streams driver, and cpcAppl is the user–level application. /dev/cpc0 is the device used for communication between cpcAppl and drvCpc.

"CPC" stands for "Cache Poisoning Checker." The CPC module intercepts ARP traffic in both the downward and upward directions. Traffic in the upward direction can be checked for whether it will poison the cache. If a decision is made that the traffic should not be allowed through, that is enforced. Traffic in the upward direction could be either ARP requests or responses.

Traffic in the downward direction is ARP requests and responses from the host. This traffic is used to record what requests have gone out of the host, so responses may be matched to the requests. As there are separate queues for downward– and upward–flowing traffic, requests sent from the local host can be differentiated from requests sent by a malicious host pretending to be the local host.

The CPC driver is used to provide an interface to the user-level application. The device /dev/cpc0 provides an interface to the driver. The application performs an open( ) [11] on the device and then communicates with the driver using ioctl( ) [11] to send messages to the driver, and getmsg( ) [11] to receive messages from the driver. The module and driver communicate with each other using function calls.

The application is used for two reasons: to have access to the local ARP cache, and to raise alarms if an attack is detected. COIPP has its own management and monitoring system in a cloud to raise such alarms. Alarms can also be raised using the Syslog facility [11]. Note that the driver and the application are on a Stream of their own. That Stream does not have modules between the Stream head and the driver.

Note that the CPC module cannot do what the IP module (see figure 3 or figure 4) does to make Ethernet address resolutions. As we mentioned in section 3.2, the IP module uses the ARP module to make such resolutions. But the "protocol" used between the IP module and the ARP module is not publicly documented. Therefore, we use the separate Stream that has the driver and application.

No kernel reboot is required to "plumb" the solution into the Stream in the kernel. If the host in the which the solution is deployed has multiple interfaces, each interface has a Streams module plumbed in, but the host has only a single driver and application.

4.2. Heuristics for Detection and Prevention

In this section, we discuss the heuristics we employ in the module and application to prevent and detect ARP cache poisoning. As we mentioned earlier , we prevent poisoning where possible, and detect an attack otherwise. If an attack is detected, an alarm is raised.

There are four events of potential interest to us: receiving a request, receiving a response, sending a request and sending a response. The event associated with sending a response can be ignored: it does not affect the ARP cache of the host in which our solution is installed.

The CPC module maintains two queues of IP addresses called requestedQ and respondedQ. When the host sends out an ARP request, this fact is remembered by recording the target IP address in the requestedQ. When a response is received by the host, the requestedQ is checked for whether a request for that IP address is outstanding. If a request is outstanding, the response frame is allowed to flow up the Stream so it can be cached in the host's ARP cache. The entry corresponding to the request is moved from the requestedQ to the respondedQ.

If there is no entry in the requestedQ corresponding to the response, the respondedQ is checked for a corresponding entry. If an entry exists, the response is characterized as a duplicate and the application is consulted via the driver for whether the response is consistent with the entry already in the cache. If it is, the entry in the cache is refreshed. If it is not, an alarm is raised and the entry for that IP address is flushed.

Thus, our characterization of whether a response is unsolicited or a duplicate is based on whether a request corresponding to that response is in the respondedQ or not.

When a request is received, the request is checked for whether it is a request for this host's Ethernet address. If it is not, the request is dropped. If it is, the Streams module responds to the request and does not allow the request to flow up the stream. Thus, we enforce a policy that information from requests is not cached. Only information from responses to requests from this host is cached.

The size of the requestedQ plus the respondedQ is fixed. When an entry needs to be added to the requestedQ, the oldest entry in the respondedQ is overwritten with the new request information and moved to the requestedQ. If the respondedQ is empty, the oldest entry in the requestedQ is overwritten with the new information and becomes the newest entry in the queue.

The algorithm executed in the Streams module and the application is as follows.

If a frame is received:
    If this is a response:
        If there is a corresponding entry in
        the requestedQ:
            Move the entry to the respondedQ
            and let the frame flow up the Stream
            to be processed by the host's ARP
            implementation.
        Else, there is no corresponding entry in
        the requestedQ, and:
            If there is a corresponding entry in the
            respondedQ, then we have received a
            duplicate response, so:
                Check the local ARP cache (via the
                application) for whether there is an
                entry for this IP address. If there is:
                    Check whether the entry in
                    the ARP cache corresponding
                    to the IP address is the
                    same as that in the response.
                  If yes:
                      Refresh the entry in the
                      ARP cache.
                Else, the ARP cache entry is
                not consistent with the frame:
                    Raise an alarm and log
                    the fact. Drop the
                    frame. Flush the cache
                    of the entry with
                    that IP address.
            Else, there is no entry in the ARP
            cache for this IP address, and:
                The entry has expired in the
                ARP cache. To avoid the risk
                of poisoning the ARP cache,
                drop the frame.
            Else, this is an unsolicited response.
            Drop it and log the fact.
    Else, this is a request, and:
        If this is a request for a resolution of this
        host's IP address:
            Send a response and drop the frame.
        Else, this is a request for resolving another
        host's IP address:
            Drop the frame.
Else, a frame is being sent, and:
    If this is a response:
        Let the frame flow down.
    Else, this is a request, and:
        Add a corresponding entry in the requestedQ.
        Let the frame flow down.

4.3. Special Cases with ARP

Two special cases not mentioned in the above algorithm are gratuitous ARP and the use of an ARP (proxy) server.

Gratuitous ARP is used by a host to find out if another host on the LAN has also been assigned its IP address [9]. A situation in which this is useful is when DHCP [3] is used for dynamic IP address assignment. When a host gets an IP address from the DHCP server, it sends out a gratuitous ARP frame. A gratuitous ARP frame is an ARP request, and has that IP address as both the source and target IP addresses in the frame (see figure 1), and the host's Ethernet address as the source Ethernet address. The frame is broadcast, just like any other ARP request.

The expectation is that a host that has the same IP address will respond to the request, and thus, the two hosts know that they are using the same IP address. How they resolve the conflict is not relevant to this discussion, and the reader is referred to [9] for a discussion on the issue.

When our Streams module receives a gratuitous ARP

frame, it checks for whether the IP address corresponds to the IP address of the host. If it does, the frame is allowed to flow up the Stream. If it does not, the frame is dropped. This is done so that a spurious gratuitous ARP frame is not allowed to poison the host's ARP cache.

Some LANs use a proxy ARP server to respond to ARP requests for the Ethernet addresses of some hosts. The host that our solution is deployed in can act as proxy server with some modifications to our solution. If some of the other hosts in the LAN use such a proxy server to give out their Ethernet address information, that does not adversely affect our solution. The responses from such a server have the source address in the Ethernet frame that the ARP frame is encapsulated in, as the server's address. But the source address in the ARP frame (see figure 1) is the address of the host for which the proxying is being performed.

5. Disadvantages with the Approach

We discussed the design constraints for the solution in section 3.1. The design constraints also express the advantages with the approach. In this section we discuss some of the disadvantages with our approach and implementation.

Our solution does not offer cryptographically strong protection for entries in the host's ARP cache. Cryptographically strong security would be ideal, but because of our necessity for backward-compatibility with ARP, we are unable to incorporate cryptography into our solution.

We have only implemented our solution in a Streams environment, and we have tested that it works successfully with Solaris 2.5.1 and 2.6. We have not directly investigated the portability issues to other operating systems. But we conjecture that implementing the solution in a non–Streams environment is possible.

Our heuristics do not work in all situations. For instance, in our solution we expect the legitimate host to respond to requests so we are able to detect duplicates. If an attacker can "choke" the legitimate host so it is unable to respond, he will succeed in poisoning the ARP cache of the host we are protecting.

The combined size of the two queues is very critical to the proper functioning of the solution. If the total size is too small, our solution will effect a denial of service even in situations where there is no attack. This would happen if the host has more ARP requests outstanding that the requestedQ can accommodate. When a response is received for a request that is not in the queue, that is characterized as an unsolicited response.

One of the solutions to the problem with the combined size of the two queues is to make them dependent on the expected traffic characteristics. Alternately, it is possible to design an algorithm to make the queue size determination dynamically, based on observed traffic characteristics.

6. Performance Impact

ARP is not intended to be a high performance protocol. ARP traffic is expected to be "few and far between" in comparison to "real" network traffic, such as IP datagrams. Nevertheless, it is useful to study the impact our solution introduces. We conducted a preliminary study of the impact as discussed in this section.

We deployed the solution in a SparcStation 20 with 32 MB of RAM on a 10 Mbps Ethernet. We then ran a "ping test" as discussed below against a 133 MHz Pentium on the same LAN running Linux.

We measured the latency introduced by the solution as follows: we sent 50,000 ICMP Echo Requests (ping packets) from host A, the host the solution was deployed in, to host B. The ARP caches at both A and B were cleaned before each (echo-request, echo-response) pair was generated. Each ICMP echo request from A causes A to make an ARP request for B's Ethernet address. The requestedQ and respondedQ at A are set up so that with each request, an entry has to be moved from the respondedQ to the requestedQ. B also has to make an ARP request for A's Ethernet address before it can respond.

We performed the above "ping test" in two situations: with the solution deployed at A, and without the solution. We observed a performance degradation of 4% when the solution is in place when compared to when the solution is not in place. The mean of the total times when the solution was in place was 2.56 ms, with a standard deviation of less than 0.1, and the mean when the solution was not in place was 2.47 ms, with a standard deviation of 0.08.

7. Conclusions

In this paper, we discussed the Address Resolution Protocol (ARP) and the problem of ARP cache poisoning. ARP is an example of a protocol designed for a benign environment, but sometimes used in insecure environments. We presented the design constraints for a solution: backward compatible, middleware and asynchronous. We then discussed our context for a solution: a Streams based protocol stack implementation.

Using the Solaris 2.6 operating system as an example platform, we discussed our solution. We also discussed some implementation aspects of our solution. Based on initial performance studies, the solution does not seem to severely impact network performance.

8. Acknowledgements

The first author would like to thank Karen Kelley at AT&T Labs for all her hard work behind the scenes on this and other publications.

References

[1] AT&T Labs, Internet Platforms Organization. *Twenty First Century Advanced Network Services Platform Technology Overview*. White Paper, April 1998.

[2] S. Carl-Mitchell and J. S. Quarterman. Using ARP to implement transparent subnet gateways. *RFC 1027*, October 1987.

[3] R. Droms. Dynamic host configuration protocol. *RFC 2131*, March 1997.

[4] N. Mihai. Geoplex – an open service platform. *IEEE Open Signaling Workshop (keynote address)*, October 1998.

[5] D. C. Plummer. An ethernet address resolution protocol or converting network protocol addresses to 48.bit ethernet address for transmission on ethernet hardware. *RFC 826*, November 1982.

[6] J. Postel. Internet protocol. *RFC 791*, September 1981.

[7] J. Postel. Transmission datagram protocol. *RFC 793*, September 1981.

[8] S. A. Rago. *UNIX System V Programming Guide*. Addison–Wesley Professional Computing Series, July 1993.

[9] R. W. Stevens. *TCP/IP Illustrated, Volume 1: The Protocols*. Addison–Wesley Professional Computing Series, January 1994.

[10] Sun Microsystems. *STREAMS Programming Guide*. Solaris 2.6 AnswerBook Library.

[11] Sun Microsystems. *Manual Pages for Solaris 2.6*. 1994.

[12] Y. Volobuev. Playing redir games with ARP and ICMP. *The BUGTRAQ mailing list, http://www.goth.net/iceburg/tcp/arp.games.html*, September 1997.

A Resource Access Decision Service for CORBA-based Distributed Systems

Konstantin Beznosov
Baptist Health Systems
of South Florida
6855 Red Road,
Miami, FL 33176
konstanb@bhssf.org

Yi Deng
Florida International University
University Park
Miami, FL 33199
deng@cs.fiu.edu

Bob Blakley
DASCOM
3004 Mission Street
Santa Cruz, CA 95060
blakley@dascom.com

Carol Burt
2AB
3178-C Highway 31 South, Pelham, AL 35124
cburt@2ab.com

John Barkley
National Institute of Standards and Technology
Gaithersburg, MD 20899-0001
jbarkley@nist.gov

Abstract

Decoupling authorization logic from application logic allows applications with fine-grain access control requirements to be independent from a particular access control policy and from factors that are used in authorization decisions as well as access control models, no matter how dynamic those polices and factors are. It also enables elaborate and consistent access control policies across heterogeneous systems. We present design of a service for resource access authorization in distributed systems. The service enables to decouple authorization logic from application functionality. Although the described service is based on CORBA technology, the design approach can be successfully used in any distributed computing environment.

1. Introduction

Traditional access control mechanisms [1] provide limited capabilities for authorization decisions to be based on factors that are specific to the application domain. The complexity of access control policies in such application domains as healthcare requires exercising access control policies that are more sophisticated and of finer granularity than the general ones used in security services of such distributed environments as CORBA.[1] This complexity leads application designers to embed domain-specific authorization logic inside their applications. Some even document patterns of designing "application security" [2].

CORBA environment, including the CORBA Security Service, provides a general-purpose infrastructure for developing distributed object systems in a broad range of specialized vertical domains. The CORBA Security service defines the interfaces to a collection of objects that provide a versatile set of services for enforcing a range of security policies using diverse security mechanisms. Some of these mechanisms require application systems to be aware of security. Such security models currently require application system designers to implement complex access control decisions based on content and context of interactions between client and target objects.

Security requirements in such a domain as healthcare mandate domain-specific factors (e.g. relationship between the user and the patient, emergency context) to be used in access control policies. At the same time, commonality of business domain tasks and security requirements across an enterprise computing infrastructure requires exercising fine-grained access control policies in a uniform and standard way.

This paper describes a CORBA-based authorization service, utilization of which allows fine-grain application-level access control in such a way that the functional design of application systems is separated from complexity and idiosyncrasies of particular enterprise access control policies. We show how decoupling of the authorization logic from application logic can be done if the described authorization service is used. In addition, our approach allows having a multi-policy authorization model, and it permits security administrators and application developers to maintain a clear separation of responsibilities.

The authorization service is by no means a replacement or substitution of standard CORBA Security service [3]. In

---
[1]Common Object Request Broker Architecture

fact, the concrete design proposed in this paper assumes existence and takes advantage of CORBA-compliant security infrastructure. More over, our solution is of general value and it is applicable to any distributed computing environment such as Sun RPC, DCOM, DCE or Java.

The design of the authorization service provides a way to have any level of access control granularity, allows integration with existing authorization models and systems, and supports such dynamic attributes as patient–caregiver relationships using existing authorization models. To achieve these benefits, our design requires application-level enforcement of authorization decisions and assumes agreement on semantics of resource names between the application developer and the owner.

This paper shows that decoupling of authorization logic from application can be done without complicated interactions between an application and the authorization service and without significant communication overhead. Factors specific to the application domain can be supported by authorization systems using the traditional access matrix as an underlying implementation. The body of the work described in this paper has been served as a foundation of the recently voted specification [4] of Resource Access Decision Facility from the Object Management Group. The initial design was prototyped and the current design has been implemented.

The rest of the paper is organized as follows: the next section provides an overview of CORBA security model and describes its access control model; Section 3 discusses the problems that we address in this paper; the service design is presented in Section 4; pros and cons of the design are discussed in Section 5; our approach is compared to related work in Section 6; the implementation status is reported in Section 7; we draw conclusions and discuss future work in Section 8.

2. Overview of CORBA access control model

CORBA environment, including the CORBA Security Service, provides a general-purpose infrastructure for developing and deploying distributed object-based systems in a broad range of specialized vertical domains. All entities in CORBA computing model are identified with interfaces defined in the OMG Interface Definition Language (IDL). A CORBA interface is a collection of three things: operations, attributes, and exceptions. An implementation of a CORBA interface is called a CORBA object. Hence, we use "CORBA object" or just "object" to mean "implementation of a CORBA interface", where it does not cause confusion. Object functionality is exposed to other CORBA-based applications only through the corresponding interfaces. Objects have object references by which they can be referenced. An object reference is a handle through which one requests operations on the object.

CORBA Security service (CS) defines interfaces to a collection of objects for enforcing a range of security policies using diverse security mechanisms. It provides abstraction from an underlying security technology so that CORBA-based applications could be independent from the particular security infrastructure provided by user enterprise computing environment. Due to its general nature, CS is not tailored to any particular access control model. Instead, it defines a general mechanism which is supposed to be adequate for the majority of cases and could be configured to support various access control models. CS model comprises the following functionalities visible to application developers and security administrators: identification and authentication, authorization and access control, auditing, integrity and confidentiality protection, authentication of clients and target objects, optional non-repudiation, administration of security policies and related information.

One of the objectives of CS is to be totally unobtrusive to application developers. Security-unaware objects should be able to run securely on a secure ORB without any active involvement on the site of application objects. In the meantime, it must be possible for security-aware objects to exercise stricter security policies than the ones enforced by CS. In CS model, all object invocations are mediated by the appropriate security functions in order to enforce various security policies such as access control. Those functions are part of CS and are tightly integrated with the ORB because all messages between CORBA objects and clients are passed through the ORB.

CS uses the notion of principal. "A *principal* is a human user or system entity that is registered in and authentic to the system" [3]. In translation to the traditional security terminology, a principal is a subject. CS manages access control policies based on the security attributes of principals and attributes of objects as well as operations implemented by those objects. Objects that have common security requirements are grouped in security policy domains. Access control policies control what principals can invoke what operations on what objects in the domain the policies are defined on. Policies can be enforced either by the ORB or by the application. In the latter case, such an application is called a *security-aware application*. Domains allow application of access control policies to security-unaware objects without requiring changes to their implementations or interfaces.

As it can be seen in Figure 2, the client-side and target-side invocation access policy governs whether the client can invoke the requested operation on the target object on behalf of the current principal. This policy is enforced by the ORB in cooperation with the security service it uses for all (security-aware and unaware) applications. A client may invoke an operation on the target object as specified in the request only if this is allowed by the object invocation ac-

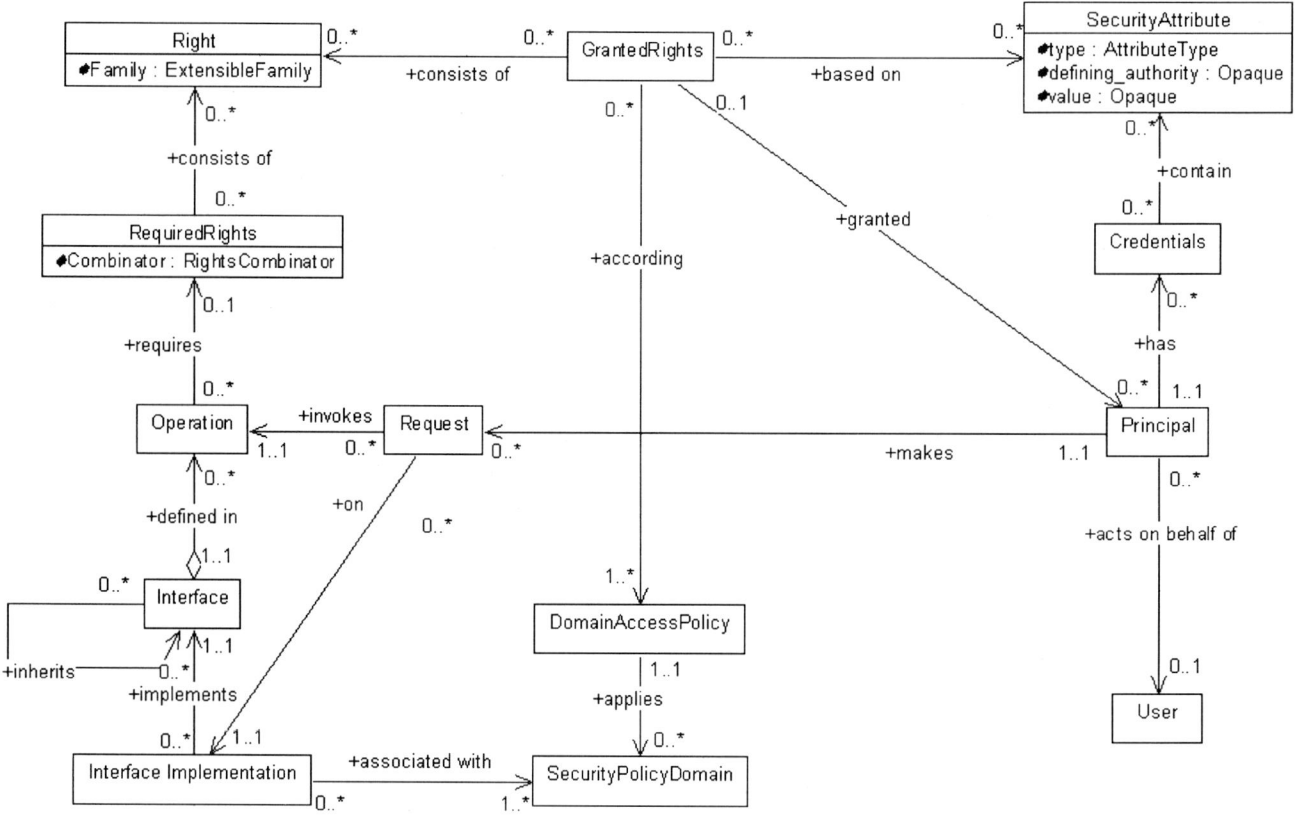

Figure 1. CORBA access control model

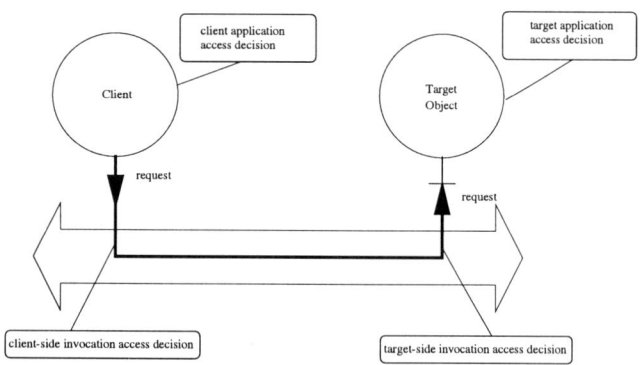

Figure 2. CORBA Security service access control model (from [3])

cess policy.

A user uses a *UserSponsor* to authenticate to the CS environment. A *UserSponsor* is an implementation artifact which handles user authentication process. After the user is successfully authenticated, a new principal with locality constrained *Credentials* object is created. The information in *Credentials* constitute the identity of the new principal which initiates requests on CORBA objects on behalf of the user. Principal authenticated security attributes are part of the information stored in *Credentials* object.

We provide an illustration of the following CS access control (AC) description in Figure 1. The concept of a user is absent from CS AC model. Instead a principal represents the user completely. The notion of a session is indistinguishable from the notion of a principal. Thus multiple principals can act on behalf of a single user. They all potentially have different sets of credentials and therefore exist in CS as completely independent entities. Among other data, principal credentials contain security attributes. Hereafter, we understand attribute to mean security attribute. From CS AC model point of view, a principal is nothing but an unordered collection of authenticated attributes. All attributes are typed. Attribute types are partitioned into two families: privilege attributes and identity attributes. The family of privilege attributes enumerates attribute types that identify principal privileges: access identifier, primary and secondary groups the principal is a member of, clearance, capabilities, etc. Identity attributes, if present, provide additional information about the principal: audit id, accounting id, and non-repudiation id, reflecting the fact that a principal might have various identities used for different purposes. Principal credentials may contain zero or more attributes of the same family or type.[2] Due to the extensibility of the schema for defining security attributes, an implementation of CS can support attribute types that are not defined by CORBA Security standard. Although the normative part of CS does not mandate the way attributes are managed, assignment of such attributes to users is meant to be done by user administrators.

All a principal does in the CORBA computational model is invoke operations on corresponding interface implementations. Such implementations are also called objects. Every object implements an interface. In order to make a request one needs to know two things: object reference, which uniquely identifies an object, and operation name. CORBA interfaces can inherit from other CORBA interfaces via interface inheritance. An operation name is unique for an interface[3] the object is implementing. Thus, any operation is uniquely identified by its name and by the name of the interface it is defined in. In this paper, we use notation $i_k m_n$ to refer to n-th operation on k-th interface.

There is a global, i.e. not dependent on a policy domain in which the object is located, set of rights (*RequiredRights*) for each operation. This set, together with a combinator (*all* or *any* rights), defines what rights a principal has to have in order to invoke the operation. It is assumed that required rights are defined and their semantics are precisely documented by application developers who know the best what each operation does. Depending on the access policy (*DomainAccessPolicy*) enforced in a particular AC policy domain,[4] a principal is granted different rights (*GrantedRights*) according to what *SecurityAttributes* it has. For the sake of brevity, we omit delegation state qualifier for granted rights. This does not change the correctness of the discussion, as we show below. Each *DomainAccessPolicy* defines what rights are granted for what security attributes. Security administrators are responsible for defining what rights are granted to what security attributes in what delegation state on domain per domain basis. Whenever a principal attempts an operation invocation, principal's effective rights are computed via operation *AccessPolicy::get_effective_rights*.[5] CS specification purposefully does not define how the operation combines rights granted through different privilege attribute entries. The specifiers let CS implementers to define the operation internal behavior ([3, p. 122]). A simplest implementation of *get_effective_rights* could be when the set of rights granted to a principal is a union of rights granted to every security attribute the principal has.

3. Problem description

This section shows why there is a need in security-aware implementations of CORBA objects to enforce their own access control policies, as well as problems with embedding such control into application systems.

3.1. Why application-level access control

There are two main reasons for application-level access control, namely the necessity in fine-grain access control and the need for authorization decisions based on factors that can be "known" only to the application.

Fine-grain access control is necessary because sometimes the sensitivity of the information accessed via the same *operations*[6] of a CORBA service interface differs. In healthcare for instance, different parts of the patient medical record have different levels of sensitivity. Obvious examples are patient name and HIV-related test data.

Another crucial reason for application-level access control is the need in using application domain-specific factors in authorization decisions. Analyses made by one of the authors and discussed elsewhere [6], [7] reveals the necessity of sophisticated access control policies in healthcare systems. They are due to the various legal and liability requirements imposed by state and federal legislation [8]. Ideally, authorization decisions in the healthcare domain should be based on the following factors [9]: subject affiliation, subject role, subject location, access time, and relationship between the subject and the patient whose records are to be accessed.

Relationship is a good example of an authorization decision factor, which is specific to the healthcare vertical domain. Its value ideally should be derived from the information scattered across various clinical, billing, and patient registration systems. Some types of relationships that need to be managed in the healthcare context are: patient's primary care provider; admitting, attending, referring, or consulting physician of a particular patient; part of the patient care team; healthcare staff explicitly assigned to take care of the patient; patient's immediate family; patient's legal counsel or guard; personal pastoral care provider. The relationship factor is very dynamic and ideally it should be computed dynamically every time a decision is made. We expect that other vertical domains have similar requirements

---

[2]This rule applies to all attribute types including access id, although it is hard to foresee a useful implementation of CS where a principal would have multiple or no access identities.

[3]Interface inheritance in CORBA does not allow to inherit from interfaces with operations of the same type. This rule resolves the problem of operation name overloading.

[4]In CORBA security model, a security policy domain is just a collection of objects.

[5]Regular caching techniques can be used by an implementation to avoid repetitive computations.

[6]Operation is a synonym to method in OO terminology. We use it according to the object management model [5] from the OMG.

in access control policies regulated by domain-specific factors that cannot be modeled using groups, roles, or identities.

3.2. Problems with authorization logic embedded in application systems

Since the application programmer understands the application functionality most intimately, building authorization logic into the application allows the application to control access at an arbitrary granularity level and to use authorization rules of an almost unlimited complexity. However, authorization logic coupled with application logic produces serious consequences. Embedding authorization logic into application systems causes problems that can be qualified as software engineering and information enterprise security administration. This paper discusses problems related to operation and administration of enterprise security.

With authorization logic embedded into application systems, enterprise security administrators end up having to configure such access logic on an application-by-application basis, which brings tremendous administrative overhead and highly increases chances of human error. Because each application system has its own access control model, which is administrated via proprietary interfaces, multiple inconsistent security authorization models co-exist in the same information enterprise. It is difficult to ensure consistency of authorization policies across the enterprise. Most of the time, security administrators end up having no guarantee, whatsoever, that access rules and, especially, changes to them are consistent across all application systems as well as with required company policies. In addition, an environment with mixed authorization and application logic merges an administrator's responsibilities with an application developer's responsibilities and vice versa.

The approach presented in the next section permits security administrators and application developers to maintain a clear separation of responsibilities, as well as to avoid most of the software engineering shortcomings of embedding authorization logic in the application.

4. Resource access decision service

In this section, first we describe the scope of the authorization service and the interactions between the service and application systems. Then, we describe the design of the authorization service.

As it was shown in Section 2, the granularity of CORBA access control mechanisms is at the level of operations on CORBA objects. The authorization service is to make authorization decisions for access to those information and computational resources by CORBA services that are not first class CORBA objects and their operations, as shown

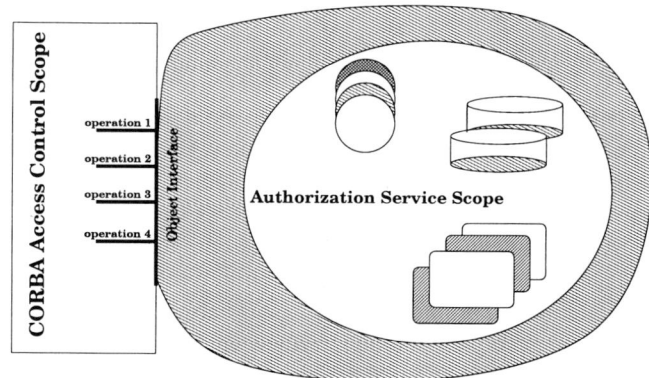

Figure 3. Scope of the authorization service

in Figure 3. Thus, the service complements CORBA security access model. It relies on and uses CORBA security environment.

4.1. Interaction Between Application Service and Authorization Service

The main objective of RAD is to decouple application-level authorization logic from application logic. Authorization logic is encapsulated into an authorization service external to the application, which is traditionally part of an application program. A simplified schema of interactions among application client, application service and an instance of authorization service is depicted in Figure 4. To perform an application-level access control, an application requires an authorization decision from such a service and enforces that decision. Simple interfaces between the application and the authorization service are used, where an application programmer only needs to make a single invocation on the authorization service in order to obtain a decision.

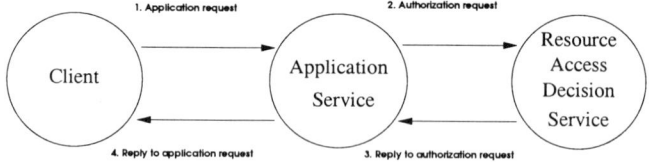

Figure 4. Interactions between client, application system, and authorization service.

The sequence of the interaction, illustrated by Figure 4, is as follows:

1. An application client invokes an operation on the application service (application, for short).

2. While processing the invocation, the application requires an authorization decision from the RAD.

3. The RAD makes an authorization decision, which is returned to the application.

4. The application, after receiving an authorization decision, enforces it. If access was granted by the RAD, the application returns expected results of the invocation. Otherwise, it either returns partial results or raises an exception.

An application obtains an authorization decision only from one instance of RAD. It is the contract between the application and its enterprise environment to request an authorization decision and to enforce it. Before we proceed with greater details on the design of an authorization service, we will describe syntaxes and semantics of a request for authorization decision.

From RAD perspective, any application requesting an authorization decision is an RAD client. From now on, we will use the term "RAD client" to refer to any entity of the distributed system that requested an authorization decision from an RAD.

A nominal amount of data is passed between the application and the authorization service in order to make authorization decisions. When making a request for an authorization decision, an RAD client passes the following three parameters: a sequence of name-value pairs representing a name of the resource to be accessed on behalf of the client; name of access operation (e.g. "create", "read", "write", "use", "delete"); authenticated security attributes of the subject on behalf of which the client is requesting access to the named resource.

Security attributes here are regular attributes of the current user session. The interesting parameters passed by RAD client are the first two: resource name and access type. They are described below.

We introduce an abstraction called "protected resource name" or just "resource name." Resource name is used to abstract application-dependent semantics and syntaxes of entities under application-level access control. A resource name can be associated with any valuable asset of an application owner, which is accessed by a client on behalf of a subject using it, and access to which is to be controlled according to the owner's interests. For example, electronic patient medical and billing records in a hospital are usually its valuable assets. The hospital administration is interested in controlling access to the records due to various legal, financial and other reasons. Therefore, the hospital administration considers such records as protected resources. Moreover, different information in those records count as different resources. Examples of different resources can be records from different visits or episodes for one patient. At the same time, a resource name can be associated with less tangible assets, such as computer system resources, including CPU time, file descriptors, sockets, etc. The RAD does not attempt to interpret semantics of the resource name. We will show in the discussion of the RAD design that it uses the resource name only to obtain additional security attributes and to look up a set of policies that govern access to the resource associated by an application system with the resource name.

Access operation abstracts semantics of access to resources associated with resource names. An application may manipulate with patient records on behalf of different care-givers, or may provide different hierarchies of menus to different technicians of the hospital lab. In either case, it is up to the application system developers and the enterprise security administrators to agree on semantics of the operation name used for each access. The RAD does not interpret semantics of access operation as it is shown in the description of the RAD design.

Before an application requests an instance of RAD for authorization decision, it is supposed to identify what the resource name and the access operation name are associated with servicing the client request. There is not any particular algorithm defined for performing such an association. For every application, or at least for every application domain, the way of associating protected entities with abstract resource names can be different.

4.2. Design of the service

RAD service is composed of the following objects[7]: *AccessDecisionObject* (ADO) receives requests on authorization decisions from RAD clients. Zero or more *PolicyEvaluators* provide evaluation decisions for those policies that govern access to the given resource. If a policy evaluator does not have any policy associated with the given resource name, the evaluator returns a result meaning "don't know," therefore delegating the decision combinator to apply its combination policy while combining results from potentially several evaluators, depending on the combinator configuration. *PolicyEvaluatorLocator* keeps track of and provides references to potentially several policy evaluators. *DynamicAttributeService* provides dynamic attributes of the principal in the context of the intended access operation on the given resource associated with the provided resource name. *DecisionCombinator* combines results of the evaluations made by policy evaluators into a final decision by resolving evaluation conflicts and applying combination policies.

Figure 5 shows the interaction among the parts of the authorization service. Once the authorization service received

---

[7]Since in OMA a service entity can implement multiple interfaces, and objects are nothing else but implementations of interfaces, we refer here to an object to signify a particular interface implementation. An implementation of the authorization service described here can implement any number of the specific interfaces in one entity of the CORBA environment.

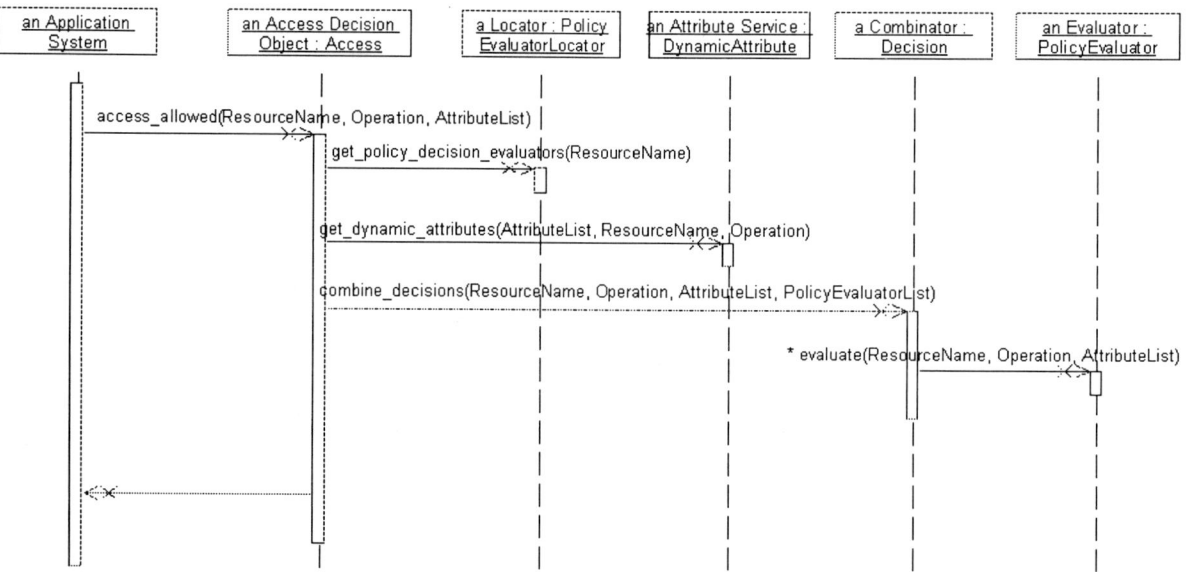

Figure 5. Interaction diagram of the authorization service components

a request via the ADO interface: *ADO* obtains object references to those *PolicyEvaluator*s that are associated with the resource name in question and an object reference for the *DecisionCombinator* which will combine the decisions. *ADO* obtains dynamic attributes of the principal in the context of the resource name and the intended access operation on it. *ADO* delegates an instance of *DecisionCombinator* for polling *PolicyEvaluator*s (selected in step 1). A *DecisionCombinator* obtains decisions from *PolicyEvaluator*s and combines them according to the combination policy. The decision is returned to *ADO*. The *ADO* returns the decision to the application.

4.3. Dynamic security attributes

One of the significant points of the design is handling the factors specific to the application domain in the manner neutral to their semantics. All such factors are handled as dynamic attributes. We introduce qualifier "dynamic" to distinguish them from regular privilege attributes of the subject, which we call "static attributes" here. They are obtained from the enterprise environment via specialized dynamic attribute services. An authorization service does not interact with such services directly. It delegates the generic dynamic attribute service to collect all dynamic attributes from specialized services. The semantic of a particular application domain (patient – care-giver relationship) can be expressed in the form of dynamic attributes. This allows utilization of already existing authorization mechanisms such as the traditional access matrix [10].

Dynamic attributes are those attributes that express properties of a principal but are not administrated by security administrators. A user usually has dynamic attributes due to the various activities the user performs in the enterprise work-flow. Dynamic attributes are so called because their values usually change more frequently than traditional user privilege attributes. Traditional "static" security attributes are used for describing relatively fixed properties of users and/or resources. The values of static attributes are typically set by security administrators and are obtained by an application in an environment specific manner, e.g., from a principal's credentials in case of CORBA environment. While the use of a dynamic attribute in an access decision is determined by a security administrator, the values of dynamic attributes are usually set as part of normal processing, i.e., dynamic attribute values are usually part of information content not separately maintained security meta-data. Consequently, dynamic attribute values must be obtained at the time an access decision is required. This is in contrast to traditional "static" privilege attributes whose values are usually obtained when a session is established. The values of dynamic attributes may change during a session as a result of normal work-flow processing.

Consider the following example of a dynamic security attribute. Physician John Smith attends patient B. The physician has an attribute specifying such a relationship when principal with access_id=*johnsmith* (speaking for John Smith) is accessing resources associated with medical records of patient B. This relationship attribute is an example of a dynamic attribute in our model. It has the value "attending physician" returned by a generic DAS only when John Smith accesses B's records. The generic DAS obtains the value of this relationship attribute by consulting a specialized DAS, which has capabilities to compute the value of relationship attribute. For instance, by looking at the corresponding fields of B's patient record which contains a list of B's attending physicians. When John Smith is accessing resources not associated with any patient, this dynamic attribute of type *relationship* is not returned by the corresponding specialized DAS and consequently it is not returned by generic DAS.

4.4. Policy Evaluators

Another significant design element is encapsulation of authorization policies and their evaluators into separate entities in the computational environment. Policy evaluators can be considered either as distinct authorities each representing a different set of authorization policies, or they can be considered as policy evaluation machines each supporting a particular policy language. Such design insulates representation and interpretation of policies from the authorization service. It also allows adding and removing policy evaluators dynamically. By encapsulating the evaluation of those policies in *PolicyEvaluator* objects, the design supports implementation of arbitrary authorization policies.

4.5. Separation of concerns

Separation of concerns among various stake-holders involved in the authorization process enables control of different factors in the authorization process by appropriate parties. Application developers decide what functions of their application map into what access operations. User administrators control what users (or roles) are assigned what static security attributes. Implementors of the authorization services and other third party vendors control quality, performance and other properties of the authorization service implementation. Work-flow administrators indirectly control what dynamic attributes are assigned to what users in the context of what resources. Security administrators administrate what access control policies govern what access to what named resources.

5. Discussion

Our solution has the following advantages:

Simplicity. Simple interfaces between the application and the authorization service are used. An application programmer is required to make a single invocation on the authorization service in order to obtain a decision. All required information is represented by such simple structures as resource names, operation names, and principal security attributes. A nominal amount of data is passed between the application and the Authorization Service in order to make authorization decisions.

The programming complexity of making authorization decisions for an individual policy is encapsulated in *PolicyEvaluatorLocator, DynamicAttributeService,* and *PolicyEvaluator* objects. Thus, simple policies allow overall simplicity of the model. The complexity increases only by introducing complex types of authorization policies and sophisticated *specialized DynamicAttributeServices*. *PolicyEvaluatorLocator* can be as simple as an implementation of relational table indexed by resource name.

Generality. Due to the design, the authorization service can be utilized in various application domains. It introduces the notion of resource name, which in its turn allows arbitrary granularity of protected resources. The application system decides, depending on the application domain, how small the unit of access control is. The resource name, principal security attributes as well as request dynamic attributes, and the intended operation name should communicate any semantic information that can be used for applying reasonable[8] authorization policies. The design supports arbitrary authorization policies by encapsulating the evaluation of those policies in *PolicyEvaluator* objects.

Flexibility. Due to the use of CORBA infrastructure with object implementation location transparency and its services such as Naming and Trader, the proposed design enables implementations adaptable to changes in authorization policies and their types as well as in the workflow of the user organization via replacement of *PolicyEvaluators* and *specialized DynamicAttributeServices*. New *PolicyEvaluators* can be registered with the *PolicyEvaluatorLocator* and new *specialized DynamicAttributeServices* can be registered with the *DynamicAttributeService* object or obtained via CORBA Naming or Trader services. The semantic of a particular application domain (patient–caregiver relationship) can be expressed in the form of dynamic attributes. This allows utilization of already existing authorization mechanisms such as the traditional access matrix. Separation of concerns among various stake-holders involved in the authorization process enables control of different factors in the authorization process by appropriate parties.

There are three main issues with the proposed approach. It is not clear whether it is possible to abstract all protected resources into resource names. The proposed solution requires such abstraction. Matching in dynamic attribute semantics between policy evaluators and specialized dynamic attribute services has to be maintained. One of the ways to reduce performance penalties of obtaining a decision from an authorization service is to co-locate an application system and an authorization service. Simple co-location increases the number of authorization service instances to ad-

---

[8]We do not define here what policies fall in the scope of reasonable ones. We think it is the subject of separate research, which we describe in Section 8.

ministrate. On the other hand, an optimum administration solution would be such that it requires to administrate only one instance of administration interfaces. Current design of the authorization service does not provide ways to have a single set of administration objects and multiple instances of authorization services.

There are also implementation issues that have to be addressed in order to develop an efficient and scalable implementation. One of them is proper parallelization in order to avoid bottlenecks. The back-end data needed by PolicyEvaluators and DASs could become a bottleneck in accessing authorization service, when multiple ADO clients consult instances of ADOs. This could decrease scalability of the system. Regular caching and replication techniques should be sufficient for maintaining system scalability.

6. Related work

The ideas of discretionary access control (DAC) model proposed by Lampson in [10] has led to the concept of a reference monitor outlined by Anderson in [11]. When an application enforces its own access control policies, a reference monitor is embedded in the application. Our authorization framework allows externalization of a reference monitor from an application without losing the capability for an application to define its own space of protected resources and its semantics.

Abadi et al. [12] and Lampson et al [13] developed a unified theory of authentication and access control in distributed systems. Practical implementations reflecting some results of the theory have been implemented in security architectures of such distributed environments as DCE [14], DCOM, and CORBA [3]. Our work suggests an authorization framework for implementing multiple fine-grain and workflow-dependent access control policies in application systems developed for such environments. Even though we present a concrete solution that uses CORBA security infrastructure, the underlying schema should be implementable for DCE and DCOM, because the only requirement for the underlying security infrastructure is the capability of an application to query the infrastructure for the principal security attributes of the client.

Multi-policy authorization paradigms and frameworks have been proposed by a number of research projects ([15], [16], [17], [18]). They use an object method in Argos [17] or a database table record in [18] as the finest level of access control decisions. In our approach, the authorization decision is obtained after the method on the object is invoked. Hence, an application can exercise access control of any granularity level by associating a resource name with protected elements of any size and semantics. One reference monitor (supporting a particular policy) per request is used in Argos to evaluate requested access. Due to introduction of multiple evaluators and a combinator, we provide ways for more than one policy (of different types), as in Bertino et al. [18], to govern authorization decisions for the same request. Bertino and Jajodia in [18] define an explicit authorization model with conflict resolution and overriding rules. Such rules have to be implemented by a particular instance of decision combinator in our framework. This is left as future work for our framework.

The proposed concept of dynamic attribute service gives enough flexibility in using enterprise-specific factors to support all implicit access rights that Argos does as well as PICASSO's [19] patient-specific roles of the principal and other types of access rights. Our approach allows Argos and PICASSO policy engines to be used as one of the policy evaluators in the authorization service described here. This would be similar, although not exactly the same, to what Johnscher and Ditrich suggest in [17] when they write that "Argos can be used as an access control service for any application that is connected to the corresponding object request broker."

7. Implementation status

A prototype of the first version of the authorization service design has been implemented by 2AB, Inc. and is available at http://www.omg.org/docs/corbamed/99-01-19.zip. It includes the implementation of the authorization service with interfaces as defined in [20], a policy administration system necessary to allow resources and policies to be defined, and a client program to test sample policies. A functioning prototype of the design outlined in this paper and specified in details in [4] has been implemented at the Center for Advanced Distributed Systems Engineering (CADSE)[9] of Florida International University.

8. Conclusions

In this paper we presented an approach in decoupling authorization logic from application logic for those CORBA-based application systems, which resort to application-level access control in order to achieve fine granularity of protection or to use factors specific to the application domain in authorization decisions, or both. We described the design of an authorization service that allows any level of access control granularity, applying authorization policies of different types and from different authorities, as well as providing application domain-specific factors for evaluating such policies.

The following two results are the main contributions of the paper: (1) decoupling access control from applications can be done without complicated interfaces and without

---

[9]http://cadse.cs.fiu.edu

sending much information between an application and the authorization service; and (2) dynamic attributes, such as the patient–caregiver relationship, can be supported using a traditional access matrix as an underlying implementation.

The body of the work described in this paper has been served as a foundation of the recently voted specification [4] of Resource Access Decision Facility from the Object Management Group.

We plan to show what types of policies can be supported by the proposed design effectively, to develop a more precise specification of the authorization service, and to obtain experimental data on performance and scalability of the described solution.

References

[1] Ravi Sandhu and Pierangela Samarati. Access control: Principles and practice. *IEEE Communications*, 32(9), September 1994.

[2] Joseph Yoder and Jeff Barcalow. Application security. In *Proceedings of The 4th Pattern Languages of Programming Conference*, 1997.

[3] Object Managment Group. *CORBAservices: Common Object Services*, July 1998. OMG document number: formal/98-07-05.

[4] Object Management Group. *Resource Access Decision Facility*, May 1999. OMG document number: corbamed/99-05-04.

[5] Richard Mark Soley and Christopher M. Stone. *Object Management Architecture Guide*. John Wiley & Sons, 3 edition, June 1995.

[6] Wayne Wilson and Konstantin Beznosov. *CORBAmed Security White Paper*. Object Management Group, November 1997. OMG document number: corbamed/97-11-03.

[7] Konstantin Beznosov. Issues in the security architecture of the computerized patient record enterprirse. In *Proceedings of Second Workshop on Distributed Object Computing Security*, Baltimore, Maryland, USA, May 1998. The Object Management Group and the United States National Security Agency.

[8] Konstantin Beznosov. Taxonomy of CPR enterprise security concerns at Baptist Health Systems of South Florida. http://www.bhssf.org/IT/Projects/cpr/security/progress-reports/categorize-requirements.html, December 1997.

[9] Konstanantin Beznosov. Requirements for access control: US healthcare domain. In *Proceedings of the Third ACM Workshop on Role-Based Access Control*, page 43. Fairfax, Virginia, USA, October 1998.

[10] Butler Lampson. Protection. In *In 5th Princeton Symposium on Information Science and Systems*, pages 437–443, 1971.

[11] James Anderson. Computer security technology planning study. Technical Report ESD-TR-73-51, Vols. I and II, Air Force Electronic Systems Division, 1972. NTIS document number AD758206.

[12] M. Abadi, M. Burrows, B. Lampson, and G. Plotkin. A calculus for access control in distributed systems. Technical Report 70, DEC, March 1991.

[13] Butler Lampson, Martin Abadi, Michael Burrows, and Edward Wobber. Authentication in distributed systems: Theory and practics. Technical Report 83, DEC, February 1992.

[14] Open Software Foundation, 11 Cambridge Center Cambridge, MA 02142. *OSF DCE Application Development Guide: Core Components*, 1.2.1 edition, 1996.

[15] Dobson J. and McDermid J. A framework for expressing models of security policy. In *Proceedings of IEEE Symposium on Security and Privacy*, pages 229–239, May 1989.

[16] Hosmer H. Multipolicy paradigm. In *Proceedings of the New Security Paradigm Workshop*, Little Compton, RI, 1992.

[17] Dirk Jonscher and Klause R. Dittrich. Argos – a configurable access control system for interoperable environments. In *Proceedings of the IFIP WG11.3 Ninth Annual Working Conference on Database Security*, pages 39–66, Rensselaerville, NY, 1995.

[18] Bertino E., Jajodia S., and Samarati P. Supporting multiple access control policies in database systems. In *Proceedings of the IEEE Symposium on Research in Security and Privacy*, Oakland, California, May 1996. IEEE Computer Society Press.

[19] Dixie B. Baker, Robert M. Barnhart, and Teresa T. Buss. PCASSO: Applying and extending state-of-the-art security in the healthcare domain. In *Annual Computer Security Applicatications Conference*, 1997.

[20] Object Management Group. *Healthcare Resource Access Control (Initial Submission)*, October 1998. OMG document number: corbamed/98-10-02.

Non-repudiation Evidence Generation for CORBA using XML

Michael Wichert
GMD - German National Research Center for
Information Technology
SIT - Institute for Secure Telecooperation
64295 Darmstadt, Germany
wichert@gmd.de

David Ingham and Steve Caughey
Department of Computing Science
Newcastle University
Newcastle upon Tyne
NE1 7RU, UK
[dave.ingham, s.j.caughey]@ncl.ac.uk

Abstract

This paper focuses on the provision of a non-repudiation service for CORBA. The current OMG specification of a CORBA non-repudiation service forces the programmer to augment the application with calls to functions for generating or validating evidence. Furthermore, the application itself has to manage the exchange of this evidence between parties and its storage. The paper describes our design for a generic CORBA non-repudiation service implementation. Our approach provides a separation between the application business logic and the generation of evidence allowing non-repudiation support to be incorporated into applications with the minimum of programmer effort. Our design is described in this paper using the example of ordering goods over the Internet. The non-repudiation service provides the parties with evidence proving that the transaction has taken place. This proof is a XML document based on the proposed IETF Internet standard Digital Signatures for XML.

1. Introduction

It is predicted that U.S. business trade on the Internet will explode from $43 billion in 1998 to $1.3 trillion in 2003, meaning that more than 9% of total U.S. business sales will be done on the Internet in four years time [3]. The first e-commerce systems were based on point to point communication, where the buyer communicated directly to the seller and submitted orders using e-mail or Web forms. The complexity is now increasing with tighter integration with back-office systems to allow order data to be electronically transferred between businesses. The order phase is only one aspect of a typical transaction, for example, an interaction could include product selection from a categorised catalogue, electronic payment, and in the case of soft goods, electronic delivery.

One of the popular e-commerce models is the electronic marketplace which enables purchasers to select products from multiple vendors. This idea is being extended in the EU-funded MultiPLECX project (Multi-party Processes for Large-scale Electronic Commerce Transactions) which is looking at the issues involved in linking together federated marketplaces [8]. Figure 1 shows an example in which a single categorised product catalogue is available at all linked marketplaces. Each marketplace has a set of 'local' buyers and sellers but the marketplaces are inter-connected to allow buyers to see products from sellers hosted at remote marketplaces. For the buyer, this has the advantage that a broad selection of products are available through his home marketplace which provides a well-understood policy concerning payment, and terms and conditions of delivery.

These more complex models place additional requirements on the underlying technology; simple e-mail and Web communication is not sufficient. Distributed object technology is a good candidate for building such systems as it provides a strong separation between a service interface and its implementation thereby facilitating the construction of inter-organisation applications. The currently available technologies include Microsoft's DCOM (Distributed Component Object Model) [1] and the Object Management Group's CORBA (Common Object Request Broker Architecture) [10]. Trading systems with interfaces specified in CORBA can easily be integrated in existing enterprise resource planning systems (ERP) to avoid multiple manual data input. This enables a continuous data flow from the vendor's back end system to the client's system possibly via several marketplaces using a Web browser with its familiar user interface.

In an Internet based trading system, communication between the parties is notoriously insecure; transferred data could be eavesdropped or worse still, tampered with by an attacker. Because business data is often sensitive, it should be protected by security mechanisms like

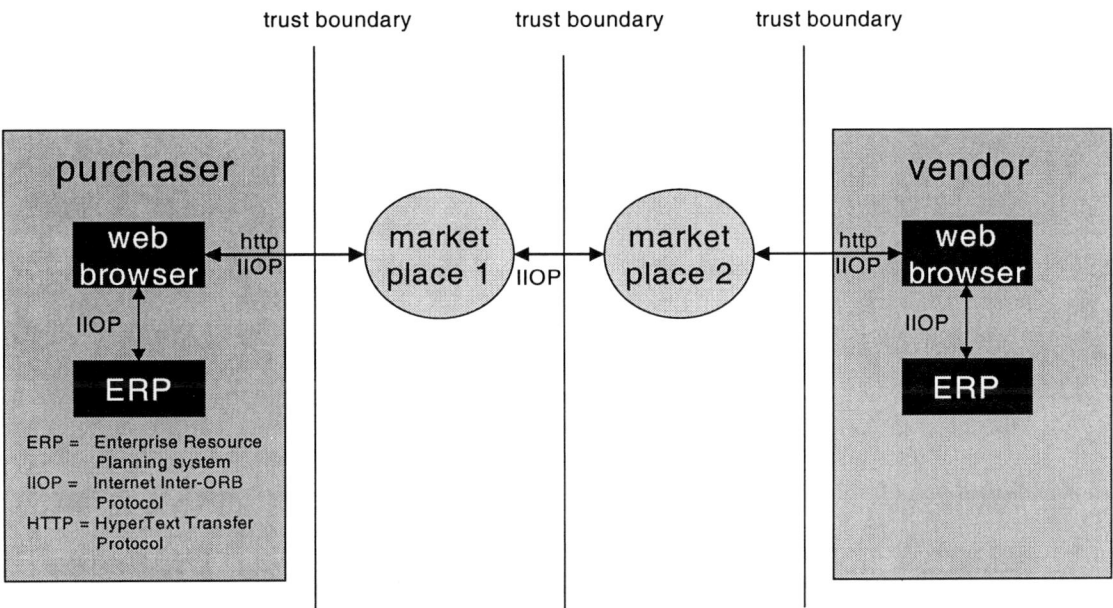

Figure 1. Data Flow in a Trading System

encryption and digital signatures to provide privacy, integrity and authenticity of the data. In trading, several partners are involved with different interests and there is often only limited trust between them. This leads to a need for a system that provides non-repudiation to compensate for the lack of trust between different companies across trust boundaries. Non-repudiation is necessary for commercial transactions like placing an order by a client or updating an internet catalogue that is located at a market place by a vendor.

Non-repudiation is provided by generating an unforgeable evidence that is held by each party that can be used after the fact to resolve disputes. If the non-repudiation system includes both proof of origin and proof of delivery then both business partners have equal rights and none of them is preferred in contrast to traditional e-commerce systems where vendors of goods are in a preferred position.

To provide security for CORBA applications the Object Management Group (OMG) has specified the CORBA security services [9]. This specification describes interfaces to services that provide access control, integrity, confidentiality, non-repudiation and others. These services are designed to be as transparent as possible so as to minimise the impact on the business logic of the application. However, in the case of the non-repudiation service, the programmer has to augment the application with calls to functions for generating or validating evidence. Furthermore, the application itself has to manage the exchange of this evidence between parties and its storage. This paper describes the design of a non-repudiation service that relieves this programmer burden by separating the evidence generation and management from the business logic of the application. The application programmer has to identify for which method invocations non-repudiation is required and the non-repudiation service automatically generates the appropriate evidence, transparently transfers it between parties, verifies its authenticity and stores it. Orthogonal to the management of the evidence is the issue as to what form the evidence should take.

The remainder of the paper is structured as follows: Section 2 gives an overview of the background technologies of non-repudiation and CORBA. Section 3 describes our design in two parts, first the mechanics of evidence management and secondly the form of the evidence itself. Finally, we draw conclusions.

2. Background

This section gives a short introduction into non-repudiation and CORBA. It also explains the specification of the CORBA non-repudiation security service.

2.1 Non-repudiation

Non-repudiation is one of five security services defined by the International Organization for Standardization (ISO), the others being authentication, access control, data confidentiality, and data integrity [4]. According to ISO, non-repudiation is defined as follows:

> "The Non-repudiation service involves the generation, verification and recording of evidence, and the subsequent retrieval and re-verification of this evidence in order to resolve disputes. Disputes cannot be resolved unless the evidence has been previously recorded." [5]

Non-repudiation itself can be split in different types [6], the main types being:

- non-repudiation with proof of origin;
- and non-repudiation with proof of delivery.

The *non-repudiation with proof of origin* service provides the recipient of the data with evidence proving that the sender has sent the referenced data at a certain time. The n*on-repudiation with proof of delivery* service is also often called non-repudiation of receipt. It provides the sender of the data with evidence that proves that the recipient has received the referenced data at a certain time but it does not prove that the recipient has also processed the data.

Usually the evidence is generated using asymmetric cryptography where the data is digitally signed with the private key. The proof is sent to the communication partner where the digital signature is verified with a public key digital certificate issued by a trusted third party. It is important for the recipient to store the evidence to resolve later disputes. It is also possible to use symmetric cryptographic algorithms for creating a proof. But then an online trusted third party is needed to digitally sign the data with its secret key (notary service).

For a trading system both non-repudiation with proof of origin and proof of receipt are necessary. The non-repudiation service is required to provide the following functions:

- evidence generation;
- evidence delivery;
- evidence verification;
- evidence storage;
- evidence retrieval;
- and evidence re-verification.

2.2 CORBA

CORBA [10] was introduced by the Object Management Group (OMG) in 1991. The OMG was founded in 1989 as a non-profit organisation which now includes more than 800 members. Its main task is to standardise CORBA in a specification that allows interoperability between products of different software vendors. CORBA provides a mechanism for objects with interfaces defined in an Interface Definition Language (IDL) to communicate with each other no matter in what language they are implemented nor on what platform they are located. The objects invoke methods on a server object through the Object Request Broker (ORB) using the Inter-ORB Protocol (IOP). The IOP was specialised for objects to communicate over the Internet in the specification of the Internet Inter ORB Protocol (IIOP). Using CORBA, method invocations can be performed in a distributed environment where the client does not have to know where the server object is located whether locally or across a network. The ORB finds the object if only a reference to it is known, transfers a method call with its parameters to the server, invokes the method and returns the result to the client.

2.3 CORBA non-repudiation service

The CORBA security service specification describes the following services [9]:

- identification and authentication;
- authorisation and access control;
- security auditing;
- security of communication;
- and non-repudiation.

Implementations of the first four services are available from a number of vendors but, at the time of writing, no non-repudiation service is known to exist. There are a number of reasons for this. Firstly, the importance of non-repudiation is not currently widely acknowledged by software manufactures and Internet traders alike. This is reinforced by the fact that support for non-repudiation is an optional part of the specification and therefore vendors are able to sell compliant products without it. The specification is also somewhat incomplete in that mechanisms for evidence delivery, evidence storage and interoperability of non-repudiation evidence is missing.

The specification of a non-repudiation service by OMG is based on an ISO standard [6] that specifies the non-repudiation service functionality in terms of:

- evidence generation and verification;
- evidence storage and retrieval;
- and delivery authority.

Evidence generation and verification are specified in detail and several functions are defined to generate or verify non-repudiation evidence (e.g., generate_token, verify_token). The evidence is generated in the form of a non-repudiation token that cannot be repudiated later. Any holder of such a token can use the non-repudiation service to verify the evidence and may store it in case of

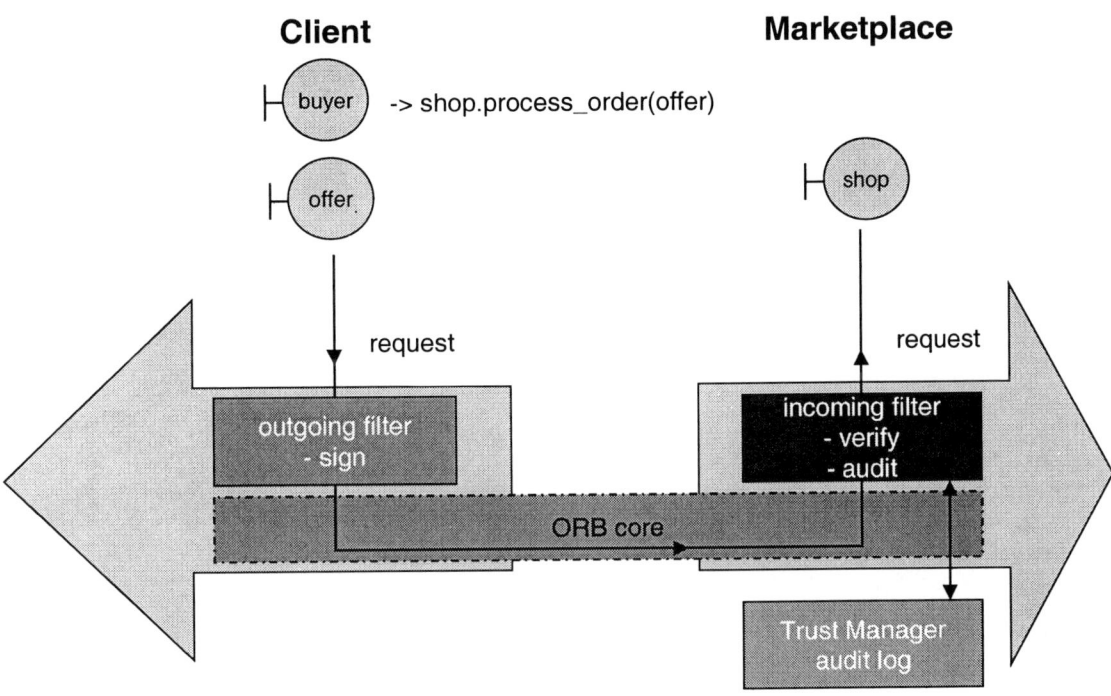

Figure 2. Non-repudiation of an order

later disputes. Because the specified CORBA non-repudiation services are under the control of the applications rather than used automatically on object method invocations the possessor of a token is normally the application that generated it. The specification lacks of a description of storage and retrieval of tokens that means that the application is responsible for administering the tokens. It is also not specified how the token is sent to the recipient but it is proposed to pass it on an invocation as a parameter to a request. According to the specification, a non-repudiation token should be composed of the following components:

- non-repudiation policy (or policies) applicable to the evidence;
- type of action or event;
- parameters related to the type of action or event;
- date and time of action or event;
- digital signature or secure envelope.

Though the token components are defined the format of it is not. This will lead to interoperability problems between products from different vendors. Depending on the chosen cryptographic technology non-repudiation tokens are generated as secure envelopes in the case of symmetric cryptography (requiring a trusted third party) or in the case of asymmetric cryptography the content is digitally signed with the initiator's private key and the corresponding public key is certified by a trusted certification authority. It is not specified what digital signature algorithms and formats to use, nor is it clear how a secure envelope should be composed. The conclusion is that the non-repudiation service for CORBA specified by OMG describes a general approach how a non-repudiation service could be implemented but it doesn't specify an interface to a non-repudiation service that satisfies interoperability criteria.

3. A Transparent non-repudiation service

One of the main design goals for our CORBA non-repudiation service was the minimisation of the burden of evidence management on the application programmer. To this end, we separate the format and specification of evidence from its creation, transport and storage. Application objects, such as an order, are responsible for defining the format of their non-repudiation evidence and application programmers tag object interfaces to indicate the requirement for evidence generation. The non-repudiation service then automatically requests an object to provide evidence where appropriate, transports it between the parties, verifies its authenticity and finally stores it securely. We shall first describe these evidence management mechanisms before discussing the format of the evidence itself.

In the CORBA environment, object interfaces are defined using language-independent IDL, as previously mentioned. The IDL is pre-processed to create language-specific *stubs*. A client application invokes a method on a stub object and the underlying ORB-core transparently passes the request to the target object which may reside in a remote process. Our non-repudiation service uses the concept of *filters* (or *interceptors*) to transparently manage evidence generation, transport, verification and storage. Filters operate by trapping method invocations as they flow through the ORB. Using filters it is possible to manipulate method invocations at four points:

- as the request leaves the client (*pre-request*);
- when the request arrives at the server but before it is passed to the target object (*pre-dispatch*);
- after the target object has serviced the request but before the response leaves the server (*post-dispatch*);
- and before the response is returned to the client (*post-request*).

The filter interface provides access to the name of the invoked method, to the target object to which the method belongs and to the parameters of the invocation. The C++ signature of the preRequest filter is shown below[1]:

```
virtual bool preRequest (
          CORBA_Object_ptr p,
          CORBA_ULong reqId,
          const char* op,
          OBBuffer& buf);
```

Our service operates by using a pre-request filter (the *outgoing filter*) to create appropriate evidence, sign it and append it to the request. A pre-dispatch filter (the *incoming filter*) removes the evidence, verifies it and store it for later use. The invocation is then passed up to the application for process as normal.

Consider the example of a Marketplace with a categorised catalogue offering goods for sale on the Internet. A Client selects some goods he intends to buy. The Marketplace then sends an offer to the Client and the Client has to decide whether to accept or reject the offer. If it is accepted, e.g., with a button press in a Web browser user interface, then the offer is sent to the Marketplace. This is done with the invocation of the method `process_order` on the object `shop` with the object `offer` passed as parameter as shown in Figure 2.

---

[1] This C++ code is taken from the filter mechanism that we have added to the ORBacus 3.1 ORB from OOC. See <URL:http://www.ooc.com/>.

The method invocation is intercepted by our *outgoing filter* which then generates a non-repudiation token that contains:

- date and time;
- type of non-repudiation (*non-repudiation with proof of origin*);
- method name (`process_order`);
- and a representation of the parameters (the `offer`).

Note: the representation of the parameters and the format of the evidence will be discussed further in later sections, we will first describe the basic operation of the mechanism.

To provide non-repudiable evidence, the token is digitally signed. The public key certificate and the digital signature are also appended to the token. For interactions which involve human participants, the information to be signed can be presented to the Client before the digital signature is applied. Typically, the Client will be requested to type in a PIN to unlock a smart card, where the private key is located. In other situations where the interaction does not involve human participants the signature can be applied automatically. Finally the filter appends the digitally signed token to the existing buffer of the request parameters.

The request is sent via IIOP to the *Marketplace* where the *incoming filter* verifies the signature on the token and sends the token to the *Trust Manager* which is responsible for storing and retrieving non-repudiation tokens. The *Trust Manager* thus has the task of evidence storage and retrieval defined by the CORBA non-repudiation service specification. The token is then removed from the parameter list before the message is passed up to the application level `shop` object. The token can be retrieved from the *Trust Manager* in case of disputes to prove that a specific action has taken place as claimed.

3.1 Representing user class objects

Passing instances of user classes as parameters in a non-repudiable method call requires special attention. Until very recently, CORBA has only supported the passing of user objects by reference whereas instances of basic types, such as integers are passed by value. In our example, this means that under normal circumstances it will be a reference to the `offer` rather than its state that is passed in the `process_order` invocation. Any invocations that the implementation of the `process_order` method makes on the `offer` object will result in remote communication back to the `offer` object in the client address space. Clearly, this is inappropriate for the purposes of non-repudiation as including the object reference in the non-repudiation token will not provide evidence as to the state of the offer when the request to process it was made.

CORBA 2.3 maintains this default parameter passing model but also introduces the concept of *valuetypes*, which are user objects that are passed by value. Since, at the time of writing, CORBA 2.3 compliant ORBs are not widely available, we will first present a design assuming no support for valuetypes and then show how they can be used to simplify our design for CORBA 2.3 compliant ORBs.

Without ORB support for value types

Without ORB support for valuetypes, it is necessary to implement our own pass-by-value mechanism for the purposes of non-repudiation. The requirement is that the state of the parameters that are manipulated by the implementation of the method be the same as the states that are preserved in the non-repudiation token.

Our approach operates by tagging user classes that are required to be passed by value by inheriting them from a service-provided IDL interface, `ByValue`. The `ByValue` interface defines methods for packing the state of the object into a buffer and for unpacking the state from a buffer into the object. Illustrative IDL is shown below:

```
interface ByValue {
    void pack (in Buffer buffer);
    void unpack (in Buffer buffer);
};
```

User objects that inherit from `ByValue` implement their own class-specific pack and unpack routines. The pack and unpack operations must encode sufficient information so that packed objects can be recreated at the server side. The format of the packed data is configurable, further details are provided in the next section. The *outgoing filter* invokes the pack operation on each `ByValue`-derived parameter. The packed states are used in the non-repudiation token.

It is not sufficient to simply use the packed state for evidence but allow the implementation of the target method to use a reference to the original object within its processing. Instead a copy of the object is created in the server address space based on the packed state held in the token. This is done automatically by the *incoming filter*: for each user class parameter, a new object is created and the unpack operation is used to recreate its state from the packed data. Before passing the invocation up to the application, the filter modifies the object references in the parameter list to point to these newly created objects causing the implementation of the method to use the local copies rather than references to the originals.

Unfortunately, this results in an altering of the semantics of the parameter passing model as there now exist two copies of the objects with no mechanism to ensure that their states are consistent. Application developers have to be aware of this feature when using the non-repudiation mechanism.

With ORB support for value types

The value type mechanism specified in CORBA 2.3 can be used instead of the aforementioned bespoke approach to provide non-repudiation evidence for user classes. Value types are defined at the IDL level and the ORB automatically serialises their state when they are passed as parameters to method invocations. The semantics of value types are very similar to our implementation in that a copy of the object is created in the server address space and there is no consistency mechanism between the copy and the original. The advantage of using the value type facility is that the semantics are well defined. The ORB provides default support for packing (marshaling) and unpacking (unmarshaling) value types. However, it is possible to provide custom marshaling code to control the representation of the packed objects.

3.2 Evidence format

Deciding on the format that the evidence should take is non-trivial; it is essential that there is no possibility of any misinterpretation of the token. The critical part of a token in this sense is the invocation parameter list. There are three requirements regarding the form of a serialised object state. Firstly, it must be complete, in that all of the salient information about the state of the object has to be included so that an identical clone of the object can be created at the server side. Secondly, the state has to be machine-understandable to allow the creation of the clone. Thirdly, the state of the object should be human-understandable otherwise validating and interpreting the evidence in case of dispute would require the availability of the software to 'decode' the binary information.

Consider an example where the parameter part of a non-repudiation token consists of three 16-bit integers like "0000 0000 0000 0001 0000 0000 0000 0010 0000 0000 0000 0011". It could be interpreted the following way: the client has ordered one item of an article with order number 2 for 3 dollars. Or it could be read as, the client has ordered three pieces of article with order number 1 for 2 pounds each, depending on the sequence. To overcome these possible misinterpretations, the implementations of the serialise and unserialise operations would have to be agreed upon (i.e., signed) by each party and stored safely. This would greatly complicate the evidence management system. Without care, software versioning could also lead to possible misinterpretations. Conversely, an ASCII text representation of the object state could be interpreted correctly by humans but would be difficult for machine interpretation. Another possibility is to have two structures, one for the machine and one for the user. But it is impossible to be sure that both have the same meaning without interpreting both structures by the same entity. Our design goal is therefore to have a single representation that is both machine and human readable. To simplify inspection of stored evidence, tool support is necessary that can interpret the state in a way that it could not be misinterpreted. Additionally a conversion algorithm must exist that transforms the text structure into an Java or C++ object to allow processing of the non-repudiable data by the *incoming filter*. This is also important for transferring the data to an enterprise resource planning systems (ERP) for further processing.

Several languages comply with this requirement, for example XML (eXtensible Markup Language) and ASN.1. For our implementation, we have chosen XML due to the widespread availability of interpreters in different implementation languages. Furthermore, current trends suggest that XML is to be the de-facto standard structure description language of the future. XML [13] is specified by the World Wide Web Consortium (W3C) and is a subset of SGML (Standard Generalized Markup Language) [7]. It is a language that describes the structure of documents and data. The most important syntax element of XML is the markup which encodes a description of the document's layout and logical structure. Example markups are tags like <form> or </form> in HTML. XML could be used to describe the content of an object which is done by its pack method. The produced document can be displayed if required to the user after parsing it with an XML parser. It is also possible to reconstruct the original object when it is described in XML. Such a document is shown in the following example, which shows how the content of an offer object could be described.

```
<?xml version='1.0'?>
<offer>
 <purchaser>
  <name>Tom Buyer</name>
  <address>
   15 Vendor St.,Shopcity
  </address>
 </purchaser>
 <article>
  <quantity>1</quantity>
  <order_number>1345</order_number>
  <name>KTM Sorento</name>
  <catogory>bicyle</catogory>
  <price>795</price>
  <currency>EUR</currency>
 </article>
</offer>
```

Not only can the object be described in XML but also all parameters of a method invocation or even the whole non-repudiation token. If this evidence token is a document described in XML then the applied digital signature could be integrated in XML as well. There are several initiatives specifying standards for digital signatures incorporated in documents. One important initiative is the proposed Internet standard *Digital Signatures for XML* [2]. It specifies the syntax of a digital signature within an XML document. A digitally signed non-repudiation token complying with this standard could look like:

```
<NR-token>
 <Token-data id="to-be-signed">
  <nr-type>origin</nr-type>
  <method>process_order</method>
 <parameters><offer>...</offer><parameters>
 </Token-data>
 <Signature>
  <Manifest>
   <Resource>
    <Locator href="#to-be-signed"/>
    <ContentType type="text/data"/>
    <Digest>
     <DigestAlgorithms>
      ...
     </DigestAlgorithms>
     <Value encoding="base64">
      pkKE6o2pK7EldfdiIK8Sfb5FjT3V=
     </Value>
    </Digest>
   </Resource>
   <OriginatorInfo>
    (identification information block)
    (keying material information block)
   </OriginatorInfo>
   <RecipientInfo>
    (identification information block)
    (keying material information block)
   </RecipientInfo>
   <Attributes>
    <Attribute type='signing-time'
               critical='true'>
     <Date value='1999-12-12T03:11+0100'>
    </Attribute>
   </Attributes>
   <SignatureAlgorithm>
    (algorithm information block)
   </SignatureAlgorithm>
  </Manifest>
  <Value encoding="base64">
   uSDdfa2sSD82fAS4FD52dfaDsdf3=
  </Value>
 </Signature>
</NR-token>
```

The non-repudiation token (*NR-token block*) consists of the non-repudiation token data (*Token-data* block) and the digital signature referring to the token-data (*Signature* block). The *Token-data* block describes the type (non-repudiation with proof of origin, non-repudiation with proof of delivery), method name and parameters of a method invocation. The signature block refers to the *token-data* block with the *Locator* markup and contains the digital signature, information on the used algorithms, the originator, the recipient, date and time. This or the like could be an evidence for non-repudiation for CORBA using XML and a standard digital signature format.

4. Conclusions

The specification of the CORBA non-repudiation service describes the functionality of such a security service but lacks interface details and interoperability. This paper describes an implementation of a non-repudiation service for CORBA that has minimum impact on application programmers. Evidence management is performed automatically, relieving programmer burden in creating, transporting, validating and storing evidence. Non-repudiation tokens are digitally signed and contain date, time, non-repudiation type, method name and method parameter information. Our approach uses the same data for both non-repudiation evidence and application processing improving system integrity. It is proposed to encode the non-repudiation tokens using digitally signed XML documents specified by the proposed Internet standard *Digital Signatures for XML*. It is believed that this approach could form the basis for a proposal for interoperable non-repudiation tokens.

In the EU funded project MultiPLECX we are implementing the generic non-repudiation service described in this paper. The service will be used to provide security for the created infrastructure required to support multi-party Electronic Commerce. The project will run pilots of commercial applications which will demonstrably enable multi-party business-to-business e-commerce transactions over the Internet in a fashion which is secure, robust and scaleable.

5. References

[1] Microsoft Corp., Distributed Component Object Model, http://www.microsoft.com/com/tech/dcom.asp.

[2] Richard D. Brown: *Digital Signatures for XML*. Proposed Internet Standard, January 1999, http://www.ietf.org/internet-drafts/draft-brown-xml-dsig-00.txt, 42 pages.

[3] Forrester Research, Inc., http://www.forrester.com .

[4] ISO 7498-2: *Information processing systems -- Part2: Security Architecture*. International Organization for Standardization, 1989.

[5] ISO 10181-4: *Information technology – Security frameworks for open systems: Non-repudiation framework*. International Organization for Standardization, 1997.

[6] ISO 13888-1: *Information technology – Security techniques – non-repudiation – Part 1: General*. International Organization for Standardization, 1997.

[7] ISO 8879: *Information processing – Text and Office Systems – Standard Generalized Markup Language (SGML)*. International Organization for Standardization, 1986.

[8] MultiPLECX: *Multi-party Processes for Large-scale Electronic Commerce Transactions*. EU funded ESPRIT project. http://www.multiplecx.org, 1999.

[9] OMG (Object Management Group): *CORBA security specification*. Http://www.omg.org, 1998.

[10] OMG (Object Management Group): *Common Object Request Broker Architecture (CORBA)*. http://www.omg.org, 1999.

[11] Robert Orfali, Dan Harkey: *Client/Server Programming with Java and CORBA*. John Wiley & Sons Inc., New York, 1997

[12] Alan Pope: *The CORBA Reference Guide*. Addison Wesley, Reading, Massachusetts, 1998.

[13] Tim Bray et al.: *Extensible Markup Language (XML)* 1.0. W3C Recommendation., http://www.w3.org/TR/1998/REC-xml-19980210.html, February 1998.

Track A

Security Architectures

Chair

Daniel P. Faigin, The Aerospace Corporation

Security Relevancy Analysis on the Registry of Windows NT 4.0

Wenliang Du
CERIAS*
Computer Sciences Department
Purdue University
West Lafayette, IN 47907
duw@cs.purdue.edu

Praerit Garg
Microsoft Corporation
Redmond, WA 98052
praeritg@microsoft.com

Aditya P. Mathur
Computer Sciences Department
Purdue University,
West Lafayette, IN 47907
apm@cs.purdue.edu

Abstract

Many security breaches are caused by inappropriate inputs crafted by people with malicious intents. To enhance the system security, we need either to ensure that inappropriate inputs are filtered out by the program, or to ensure that only trusted people can access those inputs. In the second approach, we sure do not want to put such constraint on every input, instead, we only want to restrict the access to the security relevant inputs. The goal of this paper is to investigate how to identify which inputs are relevant to system security. We formulate the problem as an security relevancy problem, and deploy static analysis technique to identify security relevant inputs. Our approach is based on dependency analysis technique; it identifies if the behavior of any security critical action depends on certain input. If such a dependency relationship exists, we say that the input is security relevant, otherwise, we say the input is security non-relevant. This technique is applied to a security analysis project initiated by Microsoft Windows NT security group. The project is intended to identify security relevant registry keys in the Windows NT operating system. The results from this approach is proved useful to enhancing Windows NT security. Our experiences and results from this project are presented in the paper.

1 Introduction

To build a secure system, it is important to understand system behaviors, especially those behaviors that respond to inputs; to understand those behaviors, knowing whether an input is *security relevant* is important. The *security relevancy* of an input is defined based on the definition of a security critical action. A security critical action is an action, which, if conducted in a uncontrolled manner, can compromise system security. For example, in UNIX, `system()` is a security critical action since it invokes a command, which could be any command if the argument passed onto `system()` is not appropriately controlled. Generally speaking, an input is *security relevant* if the data from this input will affect the behavior of at least one security critical action. A formal definition is given in section 2.

There are many different kinds of inputs to a program. The most obvious ones are the input from users. Less obvious ones are inputs from files, from network, from environment variables, from other processes, or from the Windows NT Registry. Some of these are critical to system security, some are not. By saying "critical to system security", we mean that if the input data is validated incorrectly or the validation is missing, the system security could be compromised by the manipulation of the input in certain way.

Let us take Windows NT Registry as an example. Windows NT Registry is essentially an organized storage for operating system and application data. This data is globally shared by different applications and different components of the operating system. Please see section 3.1 for the definition of *Registry* and *registry key* terminology. When a program gets data from the Registry, the data now becomes an input, and some of this input are benign while some are not. For example, in one scenario the program gets an input from a registry key and treats this input as a file name, then displays to the user this input in a message window. Even if somebody can arbitrarily manipulate the data, no harm will be done to system security itself (though the message can be changed in such a way that the user is tricked to do something harmful). In another scenario, the data retrieved from the registry key is still treated as a file name, but the program proceeds to execute the file represented by this name, This input now becomes a dangerous input, which means leaving the source of the input (the registry

---
*Center for Education and Research in Information Assurance and Security (CERIAS)

key in this case) unprotected or using the input without an appropriate validation might now lead to a security breach.

Consequently, knowing which inputs are critical to system security is essential to enhancing system security. In the previous Windows NT Registry example, knowing that a registry key is critical to system security will enable us to put a protection on that key to prevent unauthorized modification. However, there is no easy way to know that. Furthermore, one protection configuration might become invalid in the new version of the operating system because changes to the code could make a security non-critical registry key become security critical, and vice versa. It is not always obvious to identify which part of the configuration is not valid any more since people who made the decision that certain keys are security critical might have left the company without leaving the corresponding documentation on why that protection decision was made. From discussions with NT developers, we have learned that they are constantly looking for the reasons why they have put some registry keys into protection mode. Their customers, after all, want to know whether they themselves should really put certain keys under protection or not. Sometimes, they may decide to put less restriction on certain keys, but they want to know how much risk that would bring to the system. Moreover, every time developers made a major revision on the operation system program, people want to know whether those reasons still stand.

Knowing whether an input is critical to system security is also important to security testing. It can help testers allocate their resources wisely. The key difference between secure software and other high quality software is that secure systems have to be able to withstand active attacks by potential penetrators. When developing a secure system the developers must assure that intentional abnormal actions can not compromise the system. In another words, secure systems must be able to avoid problems caused by malicious users with unlimited resources [9]. Knowing that an input is not critical to system security, testers do not need to spend time in designing attacks against that specific input; instead, they can focus on those inputs that are critical to system security. Furthermore, knowing that an security critical action depends on the value of an input provides testers with more information for security testing cases. If they know, for instance, that the value of an input is treated as a file name and is subject to execution, their test cases would thus involve using files with different properties, permissions, owners etc. We have developed an environment perturbation technique based on this knowledge in [4].

Knowing whether an input is critical to system security is not trivial. It is not sufficient to just look at the content of an input. In the example used before, the input data in both case are exactly the same (file names), but they are used for different purposes, thus implicating different consequences. How can we identify their purposes?

This problem can be formulated as a dependency problem [7]. An example can help illustrate this point. As is known, in UNIX, `system` action is a security critical action, the consequence of which depends on the value of the actual argument passed to this action. If the action takes the form of `system("rm /etc/passwd")`, it will erase `/etc/passwd` file, which will cause a severe security problem. But, if the action takes the form of `system("ls")`, it will not do as much harm as the former action. From this perspective, the value of the actual argument passed into the `system` action actually decides the security consequence. The value in the actual argument can be affected by various sources. If an input is one of these sources, we say that this `system` action depends on the input and thus the input is considered security relevant. Dependency relationship exactly models the correlations among various variables. If variable a affects variable b's value, we say b depends on a. Therefore, to find out if an input is security relevant to system security is equivalent to finding out the dependency relationship among the program's variables, especially dependency relationships between arguments sent to a security critical action and variables that represent inputs.

Dependency analysis technique has already been used in detecting a variety of anomalies in program, in testing, and in program slicing [7]. The work presented here appears to be the first attempt to detect security relevancy of inputs using dependency analysis. Also presented is our experience with the application of this technique to Windows NT 4.0 source code.

In addition to static analysis, another possible way of identifying this kind of dependency relationship is to derive it from design specification. By analyzing specification, one can understand how the program will use the input data. This, to some extent, can generate more precise information about the dependency. However, this is not always feasible. In reality, many inputs are hidden from the design specification because it belongs to implementation details. For example, inputs from files or from the Registry are frequently hidden from design specification, and thus learning the security relevancy of these hidden inputs is impossible from specification analysis. Another drawback via this approach is the difficulty of automation unless the specification is written in a strictly formal language.

The remainder of this paper is organized as follows. Section 2 describes the dependency and security-relevancy analysis. Section 3 presents the application of the security-relevancy analysis on windows NT 4.0 source code. Section 4 briefly reviews related works in this research area.

Finally, section 5 draws conclusions and points out future work.

2 Analysis

This section describes dependency analysis technique and based upon which, we will discuss security relevancy analysis.

2.1 Dependency analysis

Dependency analysis has been discussed in several works [18], [8], [7], [13], [16]. However, most of those works focus on finding data and control dependency relationships among statements. We, however, discuss a similar technique to identify dependency relationships among variables.

A program P has a dependence relation D among its variables
$$D(P) : Var \leftrightarrow Var$$
where a pair $(x, y) \in D(P)$ means that the value of the variable x, after execution of P, depends on the value of y before execution of P. Each of such pair represents a dependency relationship in the program P.

To specify the dependency relationship formally, we borrow the notation from [7]: Representing the behavior of program P as a function p over some set of program variables like a, b, c, etc.
$$p : (a, b, c, ...) \rightarrow (a, b, c, ...)$$
we say that variable x depends on variable y when there are two prestates s and s' that are distinguishable only in their y components and lead, under P, to corresponding post-states having different x components:
$$(x, y) \in D(P) \text{ iff } \exists s, s'. \forall v \neq y.$$
$$s|v = s'|v \cap p(s)|x \neq p(s')|x.$$

(Here $s|v$ means the value of variable v in state s.) In other words, x depends on y if the computation of x uses y.

A direct dependency relationship is a dependency relationship derived from a primitive statement, which could be assignment or procedure call. A Data Dependency Graph (DDG) could be built based on the direct dependency relationships among variables.

A DDG is actually a directed graph, the node of which represents a variable, and the edge of which represents a direct dependency relationship. If there exists a direct dependency between variables A and B, say B directly depends on A, then in the DDG the relationship is shown as a directed edge from A's node to B's node. Since the dependency relationship is transitive, with DDG the dependency relationship between two variables can be rephrased as the following: a variable x depends on another variable y if and only if there exists a path from y's node to x's node in the Data Dependency Graph. Therefore, for the purpose of capturing dependency relationships among variables, all one needs to do is to build a DDG. We will use $DD(P)$ to represent direct dependency relationships derived from program P.

During the analysis, we will assume that each variable, whether a local variable, global variable or formal parameter, has a different identifier. This can easily be achieved by renaming.

Simple dependence analysis

If two or more variables denote the same memory address, we say that the variables are *aliases* of one another. The presence of pointers makes data-flow analysis more complex because they cause uncertainty regarding what is defined and used [18]. In this part of the analysis, we temporarily suppose that no alias exists in the program; thus, each variable represent a distinguished memory location.

The primitive statement that generates direct dependency relationships is an assignment statement:
$$DD(x = y) = (x, y)$$

A composite statement generates direct dependency relationships in the following way:

$$DD(\text{if } W \text{ then } S \text{ else } T) = DD(W) \cup DD(S) \cup DD(T)$$
$$DD(\text{while } W \text{ do } S) = DD(W) \cup DD(S)$$
$$DD(S; T) = DD(S) \cup DD(T)$$

Now let us analyze dependency relationships among variables across different procedures. As we know, this kind of relationship is caused by inter-procedure call. So, let us use a general form of procedure invocation S: $w = f(x_1, x_2, ...x_m)$. To simplify the discussion, suppose the identifier for the return value of f is r, and the formal arguments of f is $v_1, v_2, ...v_m$.

Since we have supposed that there is no alias type, the data of actual arguments are passed onto formal arguments via pass-by-value, i.e. during the invocation, it actually has a set of assignment statements: $v_i = x_i$, where $i = 1...m$. Therefore, the resultant dependency relationship is:

$$DD(S) = \{(v_i, x_i), \text{where } i = 1...m\} \cup \{(w, r)\}$$

With alias

If two variables denote the same memory address, namely, they are aliases of one another, the analysis becomes more complicated because the presence of pointers causes uncertainty regarding what is defined and used. An assignment of *x = *y could cause the dependency of u and v if x and y are the aliases of u and v respectively.

The safest assumption is that a pointer p can point to any variable in the program. Thus, a single assignment like *p = *q causes a dependency relationship between any two variables. Although a knowledge of variable scope can cut down the number of dependency pairs, the assumption is still too strong for dependency analysis to derive an accurate relationship.

Several methods of alias analysis and point-to analysis have been proposed [12, 6, 19, 2, 20]. By using these methods, one can compute a *points-to* set for each variable. The *points-to* analysis is beyond the scope of this paper, and we assume that a *points-to* set for each variables could be obtained via this analysis. The main concern of this paper is how to use the *points-to* sets to build a Data Dependency Graph, and based on which, how to conduct security-relevancy analysis. In the following analysis, we use $\phi(a)$ to represents the *points-to* set of variable a.

With a *points-to* set for each variables available, one can compute dependency relationships from the following assignments:

$$DD(*p = *q) = \{(x,y)|x \in \phi(p), y \in \phi(q)\}$$
$$DD(*p = v) = \{(x,v)|x \in \phi(p)\}$$
$$DD(u = *q) = \{(u,y)|y \in \phi(q)\}$$

2.2 Incomplete program

An assumption underneath the above analysis is that the source code for a program is complete. However, in practice this assumption is not always true. Library routines, for instance, usually come with no source codes. To solve this problem, a dependency digest for each of those library subroutines is manually computed. A dependency digest of a subroutine represents the dependency relationship among its formal parameters and return value.

For example, char * strcpy(char *s1, char *s2) subroutine will copy the contents pointed by $s2$ to the location pointed by $s1$, and return the value of $s1$. Thus the dependency digest is:

$$\{(*s1, *s2), (*r, *s1), (r, s1)\}, \text{ where } r \text{ is the return value.}$$

Therefore, for the statement S: x = strcpy(a, b), we have

$$\{DD(S) = \{(x,a)\} \cup \{(\phi(x), \phi(a))\} \cup \{(\phi(a), \phi(b))\}$$

2.3 Security Relevancy Analysis

Security critical action

Some of actions conducted by a program could be benign while some might be *security critical*, which means that if the target of the action is not verified correctly, the action could lead to breach, such as impairing system integrity, confidentiality, accountability, or availability. Examples of such actions are system calls like write(), unlink(). Take write() as an example: if the target of the write action is not appropriately validated, this operation could be applied to an unwanted target, thus overwriting the target.

In operating systems such as Windows NT, UNIX, a security critical action usually is represented by a system call or by a procedure from library that invokes system calls. A security critical attribute is associated with each of of this kind of procedure indicating whether its invocation has any potential consequence on system security. We define a variable's security relevancy based on these security critical actions.

Definition 2.1 *(Security Relevancy of Variable)* A variable x is security relevant in program P (denoted as $x \in SR(P)$), if one of the following situations is true:

1. x is passed as a parameter passed onto function f, where f is security critical.

2. $(v, x) \in D(P)$ and v is security relevant.

After obtaining the direct dependency relationships among all variables of the program, one can build a Data Dependency Graph (DDG). A DDG is actually a directed graph, the node of which represents a variable, and the edge of which represents a direct dependency relationship. If there exists a direct dependency between variables A and B (say B depends on A), then in the DDG the relationship is shown as a directed edge from A's node to B's node.

We will distinguish those variables which represent inputs from other variables by marking each of their nodes with an I. We will also distinguish the variables which are fed directly to security critical actions from other variables by marking each of their nodes with an S. The rest of variables are marked with an O. Now the problem of determining whether an input is security relevant is transformed into the following problem statement:

Definition 2.2 *(Security Relevancy Problem)* Given the directed graph $G = (V, E)$, where $V = I \cup S \cup O$, and I, S, O are three sets of nodes with different properties, finding all security relevant inputs is equivalent to finding all nodes $i \in I$, such that $\exists s \in S$, and there exists at least a path from i to s,

Proof: Since set S contains all security relevant nodes, and set I contains all input nodes, if there exists a path from an I node to an S node, from the dependency definition, we know that the S node depends on the I node. From the definition of security relevancy of a variable, the I node is a security relevant variable. The input it represents is thus a security relevant input.

An intuitive solution to this graph problem is to first reverse the direction of each edge, then to find the complete reachable set for each S node, then check whether the set contains any I node. If so, one can decide that the I node is security relevant. A straightforward implementation would have the running time of $O(|S| \times n)$, where n is the number of security relevant variables. In the worse case, where $|S|$ is in the order of n, the algorithm would take $O(n^2)$ time.

An improved algorithm would (1) reverse the direction of each edge like the above solution; (2) choose a node s from S set, find the reachable set for node s; (3) delete all nodes that are in this reachable set from the graph, as well as all the edges connected to these nodes; (4) choose another unchosen node from S set, and repeat step (2) until there are no more nodes to choose. Finally, if any node from I appears in the union of all reachable sets, we say that the node is security relevant. Since the improved algorithm only traverses each security relevant node once, the total running time would be $O(n)$, where n is the number of security relevant variables.

To further increase the performance of the algorithm, one could compress the Data Dependency Graph to some extent. For example, once a set of dependency relationships for each procedure is obtained, all relationships among local variables could be removed if they are not related to any input. Thereby, only the dependency relationships among parameters, global variables, and input-related local variables are kept. Of course, one can not simply get rid of those local variables, since, for example, some formal parameter might depend on a local variable, which itself depends on another formal parameter, This circumstance makes the first formal parameter depend on the second one. The indirect dependency relationships among formal parameters and global variables should be preserved while the dependency relationship set is reduced.

3 Registry Security Analysis Project

3.1 Background of the Project

The Registry in Windows NT 4.0 is laid out in a hierarchical structure of *keys* and *name-value pairs*. This structure is used as a central configuration database for the user, application, operating system, and computer information. A **key** is a node of the hierarchical Registry structure. It consists of sub-keys and name-value pairs. A **sub-key** is the child of a parent key. A **name-value pair** is the holder of the data within a registry key. Each key may have any number of sub-keys and/or name-value pairs [3]. We will use registry key/value in this paper to refer to both key and name-value pairs.

Definition 3.1 *Security relevant registry key:* a registry name-value is security relevant if a change in its value in some way could lead to violation of system security, which includes confidentiality, integrity, accountability, and availability. A registry key is security relevant if any of its containing name-value pairs are security relevant.

A project is initiated for the purpose of identifying all security relevant registry keys in Windows NT Registry. There are several motivations behind this project. First of all, some registry keys should be configured as protected resources which non-privileged user can not make arbitrary modification on. Usually, the decision about which registry keys should be protected comes either from specification, or developers' formal or informal documentations. As time goes on, however, the specification might become obsolete; it is hard to keep up with the evolution of software. Furthermore, people who made the decision regarding which registry keys should be protected might have left. So, from time to time, people might ask: "why is this registry key protected? what is the consequence if I do not protect it"? To answer these questions, software vendors have to turn to the developers, provided that the developers who made the decision are still there; otherwise they have to go through the specification and find out the result themselves. Specification could be obsolete and incomplete as well. yet nevertheless, compared with specification, program source code would provide more accurate, more complete and more up-to-date information. Therefore, if we can derive the security relevancy information from the program itself, especially if automatically, we can keep up with the evolution of the software regarding to the security relevant registry keys.

Secondly, various enterprise customers or developers from other groups want to know why a registry key is protected. These customers might want to build their own software on NT or port their software to NT. Sometimes, the software requires that a non-privileged user have the right to modify a certain registry key which is in the protection mode. They should either modify the software or remove the protection from the registry key. To make the right decision they would need to do risk analysis on whether it is appropriate to just remove the protection from the registry key. If the risk is not high enough, they might trade a little bit of security for the cost of modifying software. Usually customers are not satisfied with the specifications that only specify that a registry key should be protected without providing further details. The more details they have, the more accurate the risk analysis is.

Thirdly, the project hopes to identify security flaws related to the Registry. There still are several world-writable registry keys after the Windows NT 4.0's fresh installation. Several NT security books [17, 10] have pointed out that some of the registries should be protected. We hope to identify the known one, as well as uncover the unknown ones if any.

3.2 Design and Implementation

Through the project we want to be able to answer the following questions:

1. Which registry keys/values are used in the program?
2. Where are they used?
3. Are they security relevant?
4. Why are they security relevant?

For the ease of implementation, we divide our task into two different steps. In the first step, we try to answer the first two questions by gleaning registry keys/values information from the program. The data itself is quite valuable, since it gives a global overview of the usage of the Registry by various components. For example, from the data we collected from Windows NT4.0 SP3 source codes, we found that Winlogon registry key is used 256 times throughout 33 different modules, and Lsa registry key is used 190 times throughout 24 different modules. This information suggests that we should be very cautious about changing the value, configuration, or the meaning of such registry keys. Fortunately, these two registry keys are protected in the default configuration and only Administrators and system can modify them. A data collection tool has been implemented for collecting the Registry usage information. Although it is impossible to resolve all the names of registry keys/values that are used in a program since some names of the keys/values are dynamically generated, we have indeed resolve 80% of them.

In the second step, the dependency and security relevancy analysis techniques discussed in section 2 are used for analyzing the security relevancy of each input from the Registry. Without the result from the first step, one can tell only whether an input from a registry key is security relevant or not without knowing in particular which registry key is security relevant. But when the first step and the second step results are combined, the security relevancy of a specific registry key/value is now ascertainable.

Data organization

The final results from the above two steps are stored in a database that contains the following fields:

- Registry key: this field records the name of a registry key used in a program, or whose value is used.

- Registry value name: if a registry value is retrieved, the field records the value name.

- Access permission for "Everyone" on this registry key: Since we are concerned with whether the key is world-readable or world-writable, only the permission for "Everyone" group (this group includes every user in the system) is recorded.

- Link to source file: this field provides a link to the source file that uses the registry key/value.

- Line number: this field records where in the source file the registry key/value is used.

- Security relevancy: the decision made as to whether the registry key/value is security relevant. The decision is based on the security relevancy analysis.

- Criterion: the reason of why the registry key/value is categorized as security relevant. Such reasons could be: the input is passed as a file name into a deletion function; or the input is passed as a file name into an execution function; or the input is used as condition to decide if a network connection function should be invoked, and so on.

Security relevancy analysis

Before security relevancy analysis is conducted, one question has to be answered: what consists of security critical action in the Windows NT operating system? The security action in the Windows NT is defined at system calls and library calls level, namely, system calls and library calls are categorized into two categories (security critical actions and security non-critical actions) based on the targets to which the actions are applied. Security critical actions in Windows NT are described in the following, and they are categorized by the targets to which the actions are applied:

- *Executable* : this kind of action usually involves executing a program, loading a DLL and executing its procedure, invoking a service and etc.

- *Permission or Privilege*: this kind of action usually involves setting or modifying a permission or a privilege on a target.

- *File or Directory*: this action involves accessing a file or a directory including reading, writing, and deleting.

- *Registry*: similar to accessing files, this kind of action only involves actions of accessing registry keys or values.

- *Network*: this kind of action involves accessing network, such as connecting, sending or receiving on network.

- *Environment Variable*: since a lot of other unexpected actions, whether security relevant or not, depend on environment variables, so a change to a security variable is considered security relevant.

- *Process and Service*: changing a process or a service is security critical, since an action might cause a denial-of-service problem if the target is inappropriate.

- *Security Policy*: Security policy, such as whether to allow somebody to login, is critical to system security, so any change to the security policy is considered security critical. However, in the Windows NT operating system, there is no standard API (Application Programming Interface) for this functionality. Sometimes, a policy is specified in a registry key, sometimes, it is specified in a file. It is very difficult to distinguish a normal file or a registry key accessing operation from the operations of accessing security policy. Our approach depends on manual annotation (either by programmers themselves or by code inspectors) to identify such an action.

Example

An example is used here to illustrate how the analysis technique presented in section 2 is applied to analyze security relevancy of registry keys/values. The program used in this example is the following:

```
f(){
  RegQueryKey(hkey, ... input)
  g(input);
}

g(char *str){
  char name[30];
  strcpy (name, "\\Winnt\\");
  strcat(name, str);
  h(name);
}

h(char *n){
  CreateProcess(n)
}
```

Figure 1 shows the dependency relationships among variables. Because CreateProcess is a security critical action, node $*n$ in the figure is marked as an S node, and because RegQueryKey is an input procedure, node $*input$

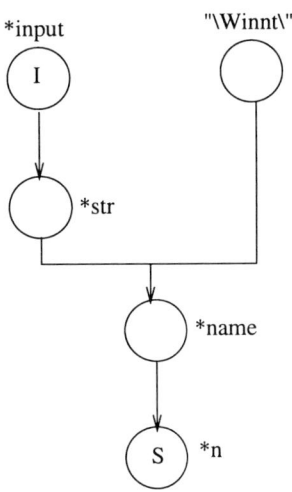

Figure 1: Data Dependency Graph

is marked as an I node. From the figure, a path from $*input$ node to $*n$ node exists, therefore, according to security relevancy analysis, input from RegQueryKey() is considered security relevant.

3.3 Results

We have applied the data collection tool on the whole Windows NT4.0 (SP3) source tree. There are 16,009 places where the Registry is accessed. The names of registry key/values used in 80% of those places have been resolved. The reason that the names of registry keys/values used in the other 20% have not been resolved is mainly because some registry key/value names are dynamically generated during the program execution; therefore, static analysis is impossible to resolve them.

Among all those 16,009 entries, 48% are just an "open" or "close" operation, which does not involve the real data exchange between the program and the Registry. 14% are "set" operations, which are considered as output as opposed to input. 25% are "query" operations which actually input data from the Registry to the program. The rest 13% consist of other registry operations which are of no interest to this project. Although "open", "close" and "set" operations sometimes have security impact on the system, they are beyond the scope of this work because we are only concerned about the security relevancy of the "input". For the "set" operation, if the output from this operation is never used as an input, the involved registry key is not security relevant; if the registry is used as an input somewhere, it will be under the category of "input", and will be analyzed in our approach. Therefore, in this project, only the registry keys involved in a "query" operation will be the target of our security relevancy analysis.

Based on the Registry usage information we have collected, experimental analysis using the technique discussed in section 2 was conducted on about 50 registry keys, 21 of which were found security relevant for various reasons. Among those security relevant registry keys, 11 are world-writable, which means if the program does not perform appropriate checks on the those inputs, an unprivileged user could be able to cause security breaches by modifying those registry keys. The rest of this section presents part of the results obtained from the analyses.

One of the interesting keys is ``HKLM\Software\Microsoft\Windows NT\CV\Type 1 Installer\Type 1 Fonts'' [1]. From the name of the registry key, it seems that this key contains information about fonts, which are unlikely to cause a serious security breach even if somebody can tamper with it. This is probably why the key is not protected. However, the analysis reveals that a `delete` action on files specified by this value. Therefore, if somebody makes the registry key point to an important file, this action will seriously affect the system.

HKLM\Software\Microsoft\Windows NT\CV\ProfileList\(sid) (sid is not a registry key name; it is a user's security ID and is user dependent) registry key contains a `ProfileImagePath` value, which is considered a directory name and will be appended with a string to form a file name. In a module executed in privileged context, this generated file name is passed onto a `delete` action, i.e. the file represented by this name will be deleted. If somebody can modify this value, such as making it point to other people's profile directory, the execution of this module will actually delete a undesired file, thus breaking system integrity.

The same registry key and same value are used to set the user's several environment variables. Considering that many applications may depend on those environment variables, a corruption of their values will lead to an undesired or, even worse, unsecured consequence.

HKLM\Software\Microsoft\Windows NT\CV\Winlogon registry key contains a `PolicyHandler` value. This value is treated as the name of a dynamic link library (`dll`) and a procedure name as well. The `dll` name is used to load the corresponding dynamic link library into the memory, and the procedure name is used to find the corresponding procedure from the loaded library to be invoked by the program. Thus, this value actually points to a piece of code, and compromising of this value will lead to the execution of an arbitrary code by the Winlogon module, which runs as a privileged process. Fortunately, this registry key is protected in the default configuration.

HKLM\Software\Microsoft\NetDDE\Parameters\General registry key contains a `DebugPath` registry value. This value contains the name of a log file. Our analysis result discloses that, in one of modules, the program conducts a `write` operation to the file specified by this registry value. A closer look at the program reveals that the programmer has not checked whether the registry value is trusted or not before going ahead to write to the specified file. Consequently, an implicit assumption is made by the programmer on the registry value. If the registry value is not protected, a malicious user can cause any file to be overwritten if that module is executed by a privileged user.

Knowing what registry keys/values are security relevant along with the permissions set on each of the registry key, it takes just a simple query on the database to find out all registry keys/values that are both security relevant and writable to "Everyone" group. Based on the result we have collected, we have identified 11 such registry keys/values, 4 of which are not documented in any literature that we are aware of. These results have been acknowledged by Microsoft Corporation.

As of the writing of this paper, only 50 registry keys have been analyzed at the initial stage of the analysis. We believe that with an analysis of all of the registry keys the number of unprotected security-relevant registry keys will be far more than 11. The results of this project are considered very useful by Windows NT security group, and thus are incorporated into the secure configuration of the Windows NT.

4 Related work

Several books [17, 10] have been published about NT security, most of which mention that some registry keys that should be protected are not protected in the default configuration Most of the suggestions come from analyses on windows NT operating system, from specification and documentation, or purely from experience. Ours analysis provides another perspective, which takes into consideration the final version of the source code. We therefore avoid the potential problems caused by inaccurate or obsolete documentation.

Static analysis technique has long been used as a technique to enhance program security. Although these studies are very similar in the way to deploy the technique, they deploy the technique to achieve different goals.

Bishop and Dilger studied one class of the time-of-check-to-time-of-use (TOCTTOU) flaws [1]. A TOCTTOU flaw occurs when an application checks for a particular characteristic of an object and then takes some action that assumes the characteristic still holds when in fact it does not. This approach focuses on a source-code based technique for identifying patterns of code which could have this programming condition flaw.

---

[1] For the sake of convenience, the following description uses HKLM to represent HKEY_LOCAL_MACHINE, and CV to represent CurrentVersion.

Fink and Levitt employ application-slicing technique to test privileged applications [5]. This static analysis technique is used for the program slicing according to the criteria derived from the specification. Orbek and Palsberg [14] have introduced trust analysis for high-order languages. Trust analysis encourages the programmer to make explicit the trustworthiness of data, and in return it can guarantee that no mistakes with respect to trust will be made at runtime. The similar static analysis technique is used in this paper to analyze the trustworthiness of data.

The difference between our work and those other works that uses static analysis technique in enhancing system security are the following: First of all, most of those techniques focus on detecting security violation, whereas our work focuses on pointing out the dependency relationship between inputs and the program's critical actions. While this dependency does not necessarily indicate a security vulnerability in the program, it reveals that as long as the input is not protected, or the input is not correctly checked, a security vulnerability is possible. This information may not lead to the discovery of a security vulnerability, but it indeed helps the testers look in the right place for the purpose of security testing; it also helps the developers make the right decision about whether or not to put extra efforts into validating an input. Secondly, some techniques require the modification of source code, such as annotating a source code. With the annotation of the code, analysis technique could collect more information from the code, thus leading to a more powerful analysis. However, given such a large system as the Windows NT, it is infeasible to modify the source codes before analysis.

Penetration testing [11, 15] is another way of discovering whether an input is security relevant or not by demonstrating that certain inputs could cause security breaches. In the case where the source code is not available this is an effective approach because all that needs to be done is to come up with a different input and feed it to the system to see whether the system security will be compromised? The disadvantage of this approach is that one has to see a security breaches to believe that an input is security relevant. If an execution path is never covered, it is difficult to determine whether the input related to that path is security relevant. In addition, devising a test case itself could be difficult.

5 Summary

We have argued and demonstrated that knowing the security relevancy of inputs is important to enhancing program security. In addition, we have presented a technique that reveals the security relevancy of an input. This technique is based on the insight that finding whether an input is security relevant is equivalent to finding the dependency relationship between the input and any security critical action.

We have also conducted experimental analyses on the Windows NT 4.0 source code. The results not only reveal the security relevancy information of registry keys/values, but also point out several vulnerabilities in the configuration of the Registry. These results demonstrate that security relevancy analysis is a useful technique in enhancing program security by pointing out the existing and potential vulnerability in the programs.

6 Acknowledgement

The authors are indebted to Peter Brundrett, Margaret Johnson, Kirk Soluk and other people in the Windows NT Security group for their insightful advice throughout the whole project. We are also grateful to Microsoft Corporation for providing us with the chance to conduct experimental analyses on the Windows NT 4.0 source code. We also thank the anonymous reviewers for their useful comments.

References

[1] M. Bishop and M. Dilger. Checking for race conditions in file acesses. *The USENIX Association Computing Systems*, 9(2):131–151, Spring 1996.

[2] J. Choi, M. Burke, P. Carini. Efficient flow-sensitive interprocedural computation of pointer-induced aliases and side effects. In *ACM-20th PoPL*, 1993.

[3] W. Chen and W. Berry. *Windows NT Registry Guide*. Addison-Wesley Developers Press, 1997.

[4] W. Du and A. Mathur. Vulnerability testing of software system using fault injection. Technical report, Purdue University, 1998.

[5] G. Fink and K. Levitt. Property-based testing of privileged programs. In *Proceedings of the 10th Annual Computer Security Applications Conference; Orlando, FL, USA; 1994 Dec 5-9*, 1994.

[6] R. Ghiya and L. J. Hendren. Putting pointer analysis to work. In *POPL*, San Diego, CA USA, 1998.

[7] D. Jackson. Aspect: Detecting bugs with abstract dependences. *ACM Transactions on Software Engineering and Methodology*, 4(2):109–145, April 1995.

[8] D. Jackson and E. J. Rollins. A new model of program dependences for reverse engineering. In *SIGSOFT*, New Orleans, LA, USA, 1994.

[9] R. Kemmerer. Security, computer. In *Encyclopedia of Software Engineering*. 1994.

[10] N. Lambert and M. Patel. *PCWEEK Windows NT Security: System Administrator's Guide*. Ziff-Davis Press, 1997.

[11] R. R. Linde. Operating system penetration. In *AFIPS National Computer Conference*, pages pp. 361–368, 1975.

[12] A. Diwan, K. S. McKinley and J. B. Moss. Type-based alias analysis. In *SIGPLAN*, Montreal, Canada, 1998.

[13] J. Ferrante, K. J. Ottenstein and J. D. Warren. The program dependence graph and its use in optimization. *ACM Transactions on Programming Languages and Systems*, 9(3), July 1987.

[14] J. Palsberg, and P. Orbek. Trust in the λ-calculus. In *Proc. 2nd International Symposium on Static Analysis*, pages 314–329, September 1995.

[15] C. Pfleeger, S. Pfleeger and M. Theofanos. A methodology for penetration testing. *Computers and Security*, 8(7):613–620, 1989.

[16] S. Horwitz, T. Reps and D. Binkley. Interprocedural slicing using dependence graphs. *ACM Transactions on Programming Languages and Systems*, 12(1):26–60, January 1990.

[17] C. Rutstein. *Guide to Windows NT Security: A Practical Guide to Securing Windows NT Servers & Workstations.* McGraw-Hill, 1997.

[18] A. Aho, R. Sethi and J. D. Ulman. *Compilers Principles, Techniques, and Tools.* Addison-Wesley Publishing Company, 1986.

[19] M. Shapiro and S. Horwitz. Fast and accurate flow-insensitive points-to analysis. In *POPL*, Paris, France, 1997.

[20] B. Steensgaard. Points-to analysis in almost linear time. In *POPL*, St. Petersburg FLA, 1996.

Security Architecture Development and Results for a Distributed Modeling and Simulation System

Dr. Richard B. Neely, CISSP
Science Applications International Corporation

Abstract

This paper reports on an ongoing effort to define the security architecture for the Joint Simulation System (JSIMS), a joint military modeling and simulation system. It also describes the use of the security architecture to support the accreditation of the system.

The JSIMS security architecture must coordinate not only enclaves at different classifications, but also the independent configurations of the multiple stakeholders. These include the various military branches and their separate designated approving authorities.

It has therefore been necessary to develop the security architecture with sufficient breadth and flexibility to describe a variety of JSIMS instantiations, allowing an integrated accreditation by the multiple authorities without necessitating entirely independent accreditations. We have addressed the objective of flexibility by establishing a base, logical architecture along with customized versions of the architecture to meet the joint security objectives.

1. Introduction and background

This paper describes the security architecture of the Joint Simulation System (JSIMS), including the development approach of the security architecture as well as use within the system. JSIMS is a joint military modeling and simulation system being developed to provide a distributed training environment that integrates a number of government and military simulation models. Major security objectives are automated communication between enclaves processing data at different levels of sensitivity; supporting need-to-know based access controls throughout the distributed system; and providing accreditability in an environment of multiple independent Designated Approving Authorities (DAAs). Two major releases will be provided: Initial Operating Capability (IOC) and Full Operating Capability (FOC).

The purpose of the JSIMS security architecture is to provide a common understanding of security and a security engineering direction for JSIMS among all stakeholders: JSIMS Alliance military and government development agents (DAs), the user community, security engineers, infrastructure and model software developers, and accreditors.

The JSIMS security architecture is based on a combination of source information and constraints, including the system architecture, a variety of security requirements and needs, and development limitations. It was developed and described by a collaboration of the development agents, the Security Team, and the user community, with important input from infrastructure developers, system engineers, and accreditors. This paper reports the results of that collaboration, and the method by which the collaboration was used to produce the results.

Section 2 of this paper characterizes the problem to be solved by the security architecture, describing JSIMS security needs, limitations of available security assurance mechanisms, and other JSIMS-related challenges. Section 3 describes the objectives of the security architecture development, description, and application in solving those problems. Section 4 explains the approach used to develop the security architecture as driven by the objectives. Section 5 summarizes the result of that effort: the security architecture description. Finally, conclusions deriving from the effort are presented in Section 6.

2. JSIMS security characteristics and needs

This section presents an explanation of the need within JSIMS for a security architecture. The explanation includes the ambitious security goals of JSIMS, and in contrast the intrinsic limitations of the available security assurance mechanisms. Furthermore, constraints on the JSIMS security solution include JSIMS characteristics that are not directly related to security.

2.1. JSIMS security objectives

The security needs of JSIMS have been described in several forms, and those descriptions have required some restatement and integration to achieve a simple, coherent description of security objectives. Described briefly, the security objectives of JSIMS are to provide security support for:

- enclaves processing data at different levels of sensitivity, with a requirement for simulation-oriented communication between the enclaves;
- need-to-know separation requirements among multiple developers and data owners; and
- multiple user/developer groups with independent accreditors: all their concerns must be accounted for.

The security architecture analysis has been valuable in integrating the security needs, in formulating the security objectives, and in assuring that the JSIMS design complies with the security needs.

The JSIMS security needs derived from several sources: formal security requirements, informal security concerns of the developers and data owners, and accreditor guidance and mandates. The formal security requirements were provided by multiple sources in the combined customer/developer community and are thus based on multiple security standards. Various data owner participants have expressed additional concerns regarding protection of data, particularly in the intelligence community. Multiple DAAs associated with the various development agents must grant approval to operate JSIMS. Further, separate DAAs are associated with the TS/SCI enclave and the Secret enclave.

2.2. Assurance mechanism limitations

Design decisions driven by simulation engine performance have created the need for a monolithic process architecture on each simulation model platform, which results in a serious security assurance limitation. This tends to limit the value of incorporating a high-assurance ("trusted") operating system. Nevertheless, the use of an operating system with sensitivity label functionality and high assurance at Common Criteria (CC) [1] EAL4, with sensitivity label functionality, has other value, as explained below. The CC's EAL4 is essentially equivalent to the DAA-directed protection level.

Available automated security guards for information flow have notable limitations in functionality and assurance. Nevertheless, it is anticipated that reductions in those limitations will occur in the time frame when JSIMS needs the additional functionality and assurance, i.e., for the FOC release.

Because of the JSIMS cost profile and schedule (as well as limited availability of appropriate products), it was not possible to use a multilevel secure (MLS)-like solution, which would have eliminated the need for an enclave-based architecture and the resulting inter-enclave communication issues.

The consequence of these limitations is that multiple sources of assurance have been necessary to provide acceptable security safeguards to drive risk down to an acceptable level for accreditation. The combination of security risk management and the structure provided by the security architecture for assurance mechanisms has provided the best use of the sources of assurance.

2.3. Additional constraints

JSIMS presents several challenges in meeting the security objectives beyond those directly related to security. They include:
- the need for a "building-block" approach in order to meet early, IOC requirements while addressing FOC cost effectively;
- the lack of early accreditor availability; and
- a mandate for simulation High-Level Architecture (HLA) compliance for interfacing with external simulation exercises. (HLA is an emerging standard for modeling and simulation systems.)

The technical structuring effect of the security architecture has been beneficial in each of these areas. In particular, the security architecture description has proved to be flexible, admitting of revision and of "multi-faceted" descriptions (e.g., descriptions of earlier and of later system releases).

By a "building-block approach," we mean that while measures are taken to comply with the security requirements levied on JSIMS at IOC, such measures must be directly on the path for satisfying the greater extent of FOC security requirements. In that way, little of the pre-IOC effort must be discarded after that release, and no post-IOC cost spike will occur in preparing for FOC.

Multiple DAAs associated with multiple participating organizations and with different parts of the system architecture present an extraordinary challenge to supporting accreditation. This challenge has been increased by the limited and late involvement of DAAs, typically because of scheduling conflicts. The result has been a lack of direct guidance by the accreditors at times when security decisions have had to be made. Our approach to specifying and validating a security assurance approach has mitigated the potential risk associated with that lack of direction. In particular, the security architecture approach has organized the specifics of the security requirements and the security controls in a way that is somewhat independent of specific direction, by incorporating general, broadly accepted standards, such as the Common Criteria [1] class and family structure.

3. Objectives of the security architecture

The purpose of the JSIMS security architecture is to provide the technical structure needed to coordinate a wide variety of JSIMS development artifacts that affect information security protection. The artifacts include the system architecture, the security objectives, the security risk management process, and security requirements to be allocated to various components. We have found, in the process of developing and communicating the security architecture, that a derived (but no less important) purpose of the security architecture is to provide feedback (sometimes not of a security nature) to many aspects of JSIMS development.

To accomplish the purpose described, the security architecture must:

- be flexible so that anticipated and even unanticipated changes to JSIMS can be addressed without debilitating impact;
- be produced, including occasional updates, in a timely way; and
- assure its content is communicated where it is needed within the system development process.

Flexibility of the security architecture has been in part a result of the security architecture development approach. Timely production of the security architecture is partly a result of flexibility, because development flexibility leads to reuse of previous work, and so a rapid turnaround.

A security architecture (and any other development artifact) would be worthless were it not communicated to appropriate audiences within the Alliance. Such communication must address both understandability and ease of interpretation. That means the security architecture must be a working document, analogous to the blueprints on a construction site that (if they are any good) end up covered in sawdust and smudged fingerprints. The JSIMS security architecture document itself forms part of the accreditation package, but it also must be a workable reference document for developers. Further, certain aspects of its content have ended up as "training" or orientation briefings for both members of the Extended Security Team and for other JSIMS developers.

It is useful to note that—though arrived at independently—these purposes and objectives for the JSIMS security architecture closely resemble the security architecture objectives and principles developed by DARPA's Information Assurance (IA) program for the Advanced Information Technology Services Reference Architecture [3]. This is particularly notable in the areas of (1) providing a structural basis for security risk management and application of security requirements (particularly to system enclaves); (2) allowing flexibility of security documentation; and (3) enabling effective integration of multiple sources of assurance.

4. Approach

This section describes the approach used in developing and communicating the JSIMS security architecture to assure that it meets the security architecture objectives given above, in turn supporting the JSIMS security objectives.

This approach consists of several facets:

- the architecture development method;
- multiple views of the security architecture as a framework;
- security risk management as a driver;
- informal effectiveness metrics; and
- documentation of the security architecture and its use.

4.1. The architecture development method

Our method for developing the security architecture has included several important characteristics:

- It has been substantially driven by the primary stakeholders, particularly the model builders ("users" of JSIMS).
- It has involved groups with a variety of needs and backgrounds.
- Multiple interaction mechanisms have been used to refine the architecture.

The multiple-view structure of the JSIMS security architecture came from several sources. Regarding the Logical view (cf. Section 5), the government DAs, who were responsible for the development of most of the simulation models, had the most direct interest in this view. They produced the original version of the Logical view, and continued to be involved in its continuing development. The Logical view has been especially important in understanding the relationships among the system architecture, the implementation, and the security objectives, and in communicating that information to a variety of development groups within JSIMS.

At the same time, the development of the entire security architecture was the result of a combination of contributors, including both the Security Team and the DAs, and to a degree the System Engineering Team and other sources. The breadth of background and expertise thus represented was key to assuring that the developed security architecture addresses the full set of security objectives, as well as maintaining consistency with all JSIMS development artifacts.

Another important aspect of the security architecture development that helped assure it met its objectives was the variety of interaction mechanisms. These included small group interaction, discussion in larger groups (e.g., the Extended Security Team, including DAs), and individuals going off to "do homework" and bring the results back for further group discussion. The larger groups were of course necessary to assure that sufficient breadth of knowledge was brought to bear on each issue. Yet smaller groups usually meant more rapid turnaround, more creativity, and more flexibility. Paraphrasing a quote attributed to Albert Einstein: Work groups should be as small as possible, but no smaller. (The original quote: "Everything should be as simple as possible, but no simpler.")

4.2. Structuring the development

The security architecture is a complex development artifact, and must relate to the system and its development in many ways. Complexity has been controlled by defining multiple views and describing their relationships, both to one another and to other development artifacts. Specifics of the views and their relationships are given in Section 5.

A security architecture is a method of allocating security controls within a system to best counter security threats. Security controls must be allocated in a way that limits risk to an acceptable level while minimizing the cost of the controls. This means that the security risk management process defined for the target system must be used to drive the security architecture itself.

4.3. Informal effectiveness metrics

As the security architecture development proceeds, it is important to make sure that progress is being made toward the goals of the security architecture: flexibility, timeliness, and communication (cf. Section 3). To make that determination, we defined and used two informal effectiveness metrics:
- frequent comparison for consistency of the developing security architecture product with system artifacts that relate to the security architecture goals; and
- frequent integration of solicited feedback from the stakeholder security representatives, including the development, customer, and user communities.

Such related development artifacts are: the system architecture; the security needs (in the form of formal security requirements and accreditor guidance); and derived security requirements that are, in part, an outcome of the security architecture. Feedback was obtained by review of interim security architecture results by personnel within the DA organizations and discussions with them. On a less frequent but regular basis, review and working meetings were held that combined the Security Team and DA representatives.

4.4. Security architecture documentation

The goal of the security architecture documentation has been to be as useful as possible by:
- allowing customers and users to understand the security architecture as well as possible, in order to provide an effective basis for determining whether their needs are being met;
- providing security guidance to developers;
- recording decisions in a development environment that requires both strong direction and flexibility; and
- supporting accreditation by documenting security decisions and providing an overview of system security.

Based on feedback from the security architecture target community, it is apparent that this goal has been met in large part.

5. Results

This section presents the JSIMS security architecture as of September of this year. Because JSIMS is a joint program, and because a series of JSIMS releases must each be accredited for multiple security modes, the security architecture remains a living development artifact.

The security architecture is described here in terms of the *Base Logical Architecture* along with a set of *views* and a set of *extensions*. The Base Logical Architecture serves as the starting point for the architecture description. By presenting first this single, logical (i.e., abstracted) description of the security architecture, its important aspects can be simply explained and can lay the foundation for a kind of type accreditation. In that way, more concrete but varying aspects of the architecture, such as system releases and hardware layouts, can be compared with the characteristics of the logical architecture and so avoid a series of start-from-scratch accreditations.

Such comparison is necessary, since it is the implemented, deployed system that must ultimately be accredited. The comparison is given by a mapping between the logical architecture and other architecture representations, including any physical system to be deployed. Such mapping analysis is far from trivial, but is much simpler than would be a full architectural analysis for each JSIMS variation. Complexities of the mapping include its many-to-many nature and the need to demonstrate generic mappings, so that a class of deployments can at once be shown to conform to the logical view.

These aspects of the security architecture are explained in the following subsections, along with the explanation of their use in the joint, multiple accreditation environment. This section also documents feedback provided by the JSIMS stakeholders regarding the security architecture as developed.

5.1. The Base Logical Architecture

Figure 1 depicts the Base Logical Architecture, which includes top-level components, flows, and data

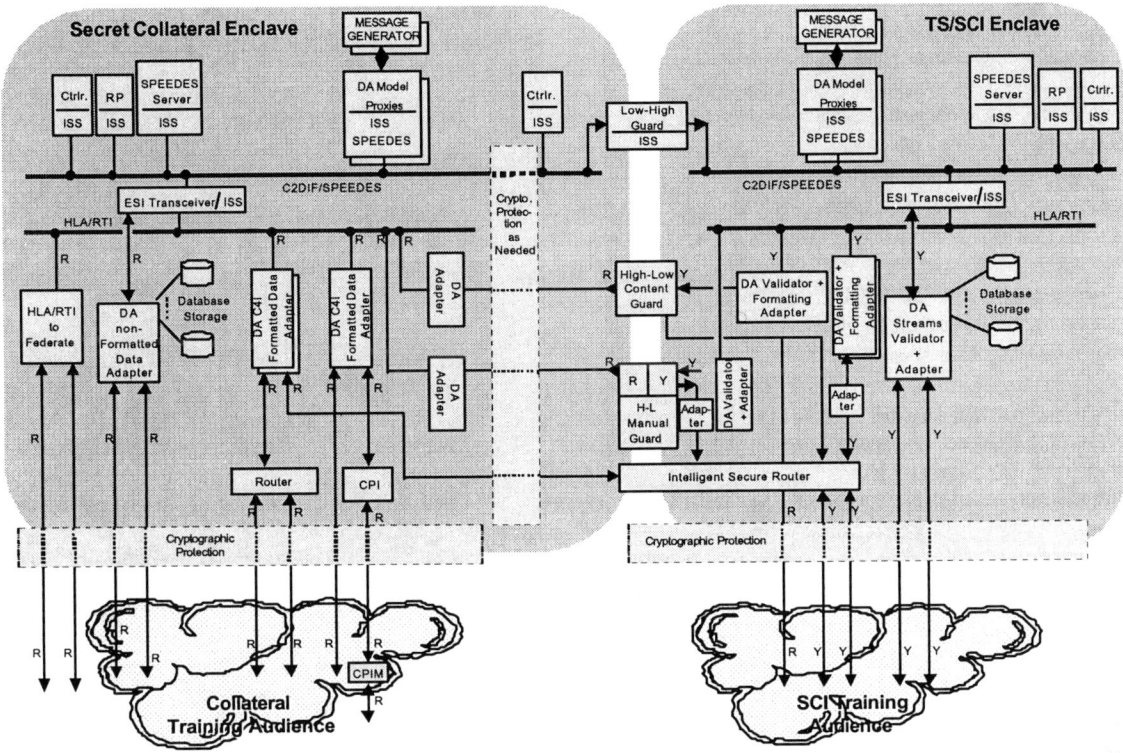

Figure 1. Base Logical Architecture

descriptions (content and format). As allocated security characteristics are applied to the architecture description, it becomes the logical *security* architecture. By "logical" it is meant that *classes* of components and data flows are shown. In that way, security requirements and relationships can be allocated and analyzed for accuracy and risk management purposes. At the same time, the volatility of particular deployments, compositions, and implementation decisions can be addressed by relating them to the logical architecture. In that way, the basic architectural analysis can be stable and accredited on a generic basis.

The two large gray areas in Figure 1 depict the two JSIMS enclaves, which in the Base Logical Architecture process Secret Collateral and TS/SCI information. The top parts of the enclaves, down to the C2DIF/SPEEDES backbone, represent the simulation (models, infrastructure, and simulation engine) part of JSIMS. The lower parts of the enclaves represent support for interfaces to external systems. The guards, which bridge between the enclaves, make up the inter-enclave controlled interface. For geographically remote data communications (enclave-to-enclave and JSIMS-to-external-systems), cryptographic protection is provided.

5.2. The views

The architecture *views* provide multiple ways to perceive the JSIMS security architecture. This base-architecture-plus-views approach is an important part of the support for a generic accreditation. Mappings are provided between the logical architecture and the other views, resulting in constraints on the views. Implementations that satisfy the view constraints maintain the legitimacy of the mappings.

The views of the JSIMS security architecture are depicted in Figure 2. Four of these views are shown as hierarchical layers. The fifth view, Organizational, underlies all the hierarchical views.

Details of the views. In the Abstract view, the distributed, multi-enclave nature of the JSIMS implementation is invisible, and the software infrastructure is seen by simulation models only in terms of the JSIMS API (JAPI). The purpose of the JAPI is to present to the simulation model applications a specification of the simulation mechanisms. The mechanism implementations appear within the Software view. The primary security characteristic of this view is a particular mechanism that supports, in the high

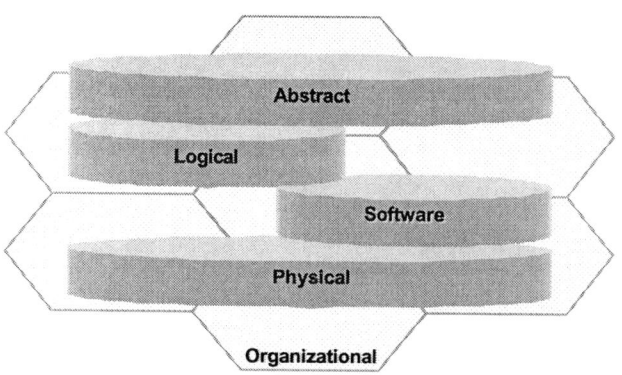

Figure 2. The Views of the JSIMS Security Architecture

enclave, the nomination of simulation objects to be sent to the low enclave via a high-assurance guard.

The Logical view, as indicated previously, describes data flows, including formats and content. One security characteristic of the Logical view consists of the controlled interfaces: guards supporting data flow between the enclaves and between JSIMS and external systems. The other security characteristic is support for integrity of data during transit through lower assurance components.

The Software view contains the operating system, middleware (e.g., database systems), simulation infrastructure mechanisms, and the simulation models. Security in this view deals with assurance needed for off-the-shelf components and developed software; and integrating sources of assurance, for example providing isolation of functions using multiple means.

In the Physical view, a "wiring diagram" of networks and platforms is provided. Security assurance is supplied within this view by hardware mechanisms exploited by software and by constraints on physical connectivity.

The final security architecture view is the Organizational view. This view is not part of the hierarchy, but relates to each of the other views. This view describes the organizational characteristics for both JSIMS development and operation. It provides a place to address management and procedural security controls. In order to manage security risk, such controls must be present and effective in order to complement the product-oriented technical controls. The accreditation process includes evaluation of these controls, so they must be visible in the architecture itself.

View mappings. The Abstract view—the JAPI specification—is implemented by the Software view. Each of the interface objects of the JAPI has been analyzed to determine whether applicable security requirements necessitated a high-assurance implementation. The relationship between the Abstract view and the Logical view has required analysis to determine the effect of security requirements associated with the Abstract view on the distributed nature of the implementation and on its two-enclave nature.

The Physical view is also directly related to both the Logical and Software views. The security characteristics of these related views depend on the characteristics of the hardware platforms and the connectivity established by the Physical view. One example is that the process isolation provided by operating systems is dependent on the correct operation of the hardware memory management scheme. Another example is that the capability for the security guards bridging the enclaves to provide partial isolation between the enclaves is dependent on the physical connectivity (particularly the lack of it) among the various platforms.

The Logical view is dependent on the Software view in that the software implementation controls the logical connectivity. Largely, the model applications specify the data flows, and the underlying software (operating system, simulation engine, and developed infrastructure) executes those specified flows. The control of connectivity takes on a specific security flavor at the low-to-high and high-to-low guards between the enclaves, where developed software takes on a support function for some of the guards.

The relationship between the Organizational view and the other views is one of organizational interdependence and communication in the form of Memoranda of Agreement (MOAs) and Memoranda of Understanding (MOUs). Such communication prevents expectations from "falling through the cracks."

5.3. The extensions

The Base Logical Architecture and related views describe one "point" in a multidimensional space of JSIMS variations. We term other points in the space *extensions* to the base architecture. As depicted in Figure 3, the dimensions are termed *Release, Composition Type*, and *Operational Phase*.

The architecture extensions provide specific support for the accreditation of multiple JSIMS versions and deployments by "reusing" parts of accreditations.

Table 1 describes several aspects of the JSIMS variation space. Each dimension of the space is given by a row in the table, with related extensions in the cells of that row. The extensions are positioned in the table so that one of the columns (shaded) shows where the Base Logical Architecture fits in the variation space. The points on each variation axis are emphasized with a dark border.

JSIMS variations represented by all combinations of extensions (i.e., all points in the space) will be realized and must be accreditable. Consequently, at least 12 ($2 \times 2 \times 3$) variations must be analyzed relative to security constraints

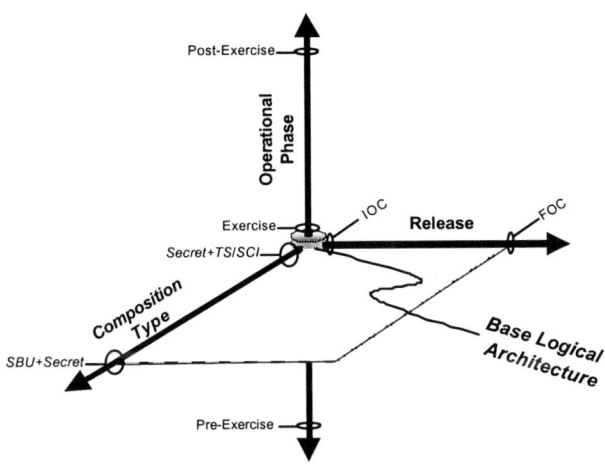

Figure 3. The JSIMS Security Architecture Variation Dimensions

and reuse of accreditation results. The phrase "at least" is appropriate because:

- JSIMS releases requiring accreditation, in addition to IOC and FOC, are possible; and
- a granularity of compositions finer than that of the two types given will be necessary.

Those finer-grained compositions are the result of the needs of the multiple DAs, which also constitute JSIMS user groups.

Table 1. Architecture Extension Descriptions

Dimensions	Extensions with Axes Emphasized		
	In Base Logical Architecture		
Release		At IOC	At FOC
Composition Type	Secret Collateral + TS/SCI	SBU + Secret Collateral	
Operational Phase	Pre-Exercise	Exercise	Post-Exercise

5.4. Effectiveness and use of the security architecture

The JSIMS security architecture is documented in part in the JSIMS Systems Security Authorization Agreement (SSAA) [6]. The DoD Information Technology Security Certification and Accreditation Process (DITSCAP) [2] (the accreditation process used within JSIMS) specifies the SSAA as the primary repository for accreditation support information. Releases of the SSAA are published on a limited-access JSIMS intranet site, making the security architecture is available to all JSIMS stakeholders.

Recall that the two informal metrics of the security architecture are (1) comparison and consistency with related system artifacts and (2) incorporation of feedback from the JSIMS stakeholders. In applying these metrics, it is important to recall that the development of the security architecture has not been unilateral: contributions were made by all the DAs and by the Security Team. Consequently, individuals involved in the security architecture development were often also those involved in providing feedback.

The two metrics are not entirely distinct. Comparison with artifacts has typically been accomplished by obtaining input from "owners" of the artifacts, who are generally JSIMS stakeholders. In particular, we facilitated accurate comparison with system artifacts (e.g., other system architecture representations, security requirements, and software design) by direct analysis of the artifacts with the assistance of the personnel responsible for them. Such personnel include the system architect, the Security Team member responsible for security requirements analysis, the software infrastructure design team, and DA security design teams. In that way we have been able to achieve a consensus of consistency between those artifacts and the security architecture.

Such inputs are obtained frequently via electronic communication and small group meetings, and less frequently in larger meetings, the latter to assure consistency of the inputs themselves. The outcome, as remarked over time, has been that the resulting security architecture continues to address the full complement of system and security concerns.

6. Conclusions

An accurate security architecture is closely related to the underlying system architecture. Ideally, it would be expected that the development of a security architecture would be based on an existing system architecture. What may happen instead (as in the case of JSIMS) is that well into a development effort important aspects of the system architecture are incomplete. The result is then that the system architecture as documented cannot serve as a basis for a security architecture. As a JSIMS example, until early this year, only the Abstract architecture and, to some degree, the Software architecture were documented.

As a result, the security architecture development, description, and dissemination often provide value to a system development far beyond its immediate target of addressing the structure of security constraints. That has been the case with JSIMS. By May 1999, the Security Team had developed the view-and-extension description of the security architecture and. In collaboration with all the DAs, the Security Team had also filled in much of the previously missing detail for particular views. That detail included not only security attributes, but system architecture information as well.

The security architecture development method, with its small-team-plus-larger-group approach, proved to be as effective as hoped, judging from the results. The security architecture itself was effective as judged by the given informal metrics. In particular, as changes came up (such as new expectations provided by DAAs), it was possible to make necessary changes to architecture descriptions quickly and without great upheaval to the overall security architecture.

The Security Team has successfully used the varied-team approach for other security tasks within JSIMS, such as security requirements analysis. Based on the author's experience with other large projects in which security was a major component, the security architecture approach itself is applicable to a broad class of targets. The concept of the multiple views of the architecture has proved valuable, though the identity of the specific views could change for different systems.

Improvements to the process and the results could be made in two areas, one that was beyond our control, and one where we believe, with hindsight, that we could have improved the approach. The first area is in the "wish list" department—it is that more could have been done with less effort had it been possible to make a solid start with security in JSIMS at the beginning of the program, rather than many months into the program. Subsequent to significant system and software design and implementation, bringing the program under control with respect to security was difficult. This is a lesson that security engineers have learned many times over, but it is worth adding yet another data point.

Regarding the second area, we could surely have improved the approach by an early change in priorities. Once the security effort within JSIMS had begun, several tasks were quickly started, one of which was *not* security architecture development. As a result, the effort initially was not well coordinated, and the resulting lack of efficiency limited the initial impact of security on the overall program. Once the security architecture definition was begun, we were able to orient much of the security effort around that definition. After that point our progress notably accelerated.

7. Acknowledgements

Acknowledgements are due three JSIMS groups: the Extended Security Team (DA representatives plus core Security Team), the System Engineering Team, and the software developers. Discussions with those groups provided valuable input into, and in some cases were substantial to, the development of the JSIMS security architecture. Thanks are also due Phil Taylor for his careful reading of the paper.

8. References

1. *Common Criteria for Information Technology Security Evaluation*, version 2.0, May 1998.
2. *DoD Information Technology Security Certification and Accreditation Process (DITSCAP)*, November 1997.
3. Information Assurance Security Focus Group, *Security Architecture for the AITS Reference Architecture*, Revision 1.0, December 1997.
4. *JSIMS System Segment Description Document (SSDD)*, Overview and Discussion volume, version 2.5, January 1999.
5. *JSIMS System Segment Description Document (SSDD)*, version 3.0, Appendix A: JSIMS Application Program Interface Definition Document, April 1999.
6. *JSIMS Systems Security Authorization Agreement (SSAA)*, October 1999.

SecurSight: An Architecture for Secure Information Access

John G. Brainard
RSA Laboratories

Abstract

This paper describes SecurSight, an architecture that combines authentication, authorization, and secure communications. The primary goal of this architecture is to secure access to network resources, while providing a smooth migration path from legacy authentication and authorization methods to a public-key infrastructure. Authentication may utilize either shared secrets or public/private key pairs. Authorization is public-key based and provides both direct support for PKI-aware applications and indirect support for legacy applications. Authorization credentials are portable, and may be used in location-independent fashion, without the need for cumbersome export and import procedures.

1. Overview

The use of public-key technology for authentication and authorization in enterprise environments has been slow in deployment due to a number of factors. The use of "soft" public-key credentials in desktop applications such as Web browsers is convenient, but the portability of such credentials is limited. Truly portable public-key devices, such as smartcards, require infrastructure, in the form of smart card readers, which is not yet widely available.

Access control in applications faces something of a "chicken and egg" problem. Users do not want to go to the trouble of obtaining key pairs and certificates until their applications require it. Major application developers, on the other hand will not use public-key technology in their products until a critical mass of users has keys and certificates. This makes the conversion to public-key an all-or-nothing proposition, where all users and applications must be upgraded at once.

In this paper we will discuss an architecture, called SecurSight, that helps solve these problems by using existing authentication technology as a front end to public-key based services. It provides authorization services directly to public-key based applications. Older applications that know nothing of PKI are supported using public-key aware wrappers. This wrapping, combined with the storage of legacy credentials, such as passwords, inside public key based containers, allows the public-key infrastructure to exist without explicit awareness of it on the part of either end users or applications.

SecurSight's novelty is less in the specifics of its implementation than in the way it uses public-key infrastructure to enhance, rather than replace, existing security methods. This allows users to begin experimenting with public-key authentication and smartcards, without throwing away old passwords and one-time password generators. It allows new PKI-aware services to be integrated seamlessly, without abandoning existing applications.

1.1 SecurSight Design Principles

A primary goal of SecurSight is to provide centrally administered authentication and authorization for all users of a network, regardless of the resource to be accessed. The users log in to a trusted server and then obtain credentials for the resources they are authorized to use. The credentials have a short validity period, to allow administrators to grant and revoke privileges in a timely fashion.

SecurSight authentication is not restricted to a single method. Public-key based authentication, using both smartcards and keys stored in software, is supported. In addition, both traditional static passwords and various forms of one-time password (OTP) are allowed. The mechanism support is flexible enough that new mechanisms, such as biometrics, may be added without change to the basic design.

The authorization mechanism in SecurSight is the same for all users, regardless of the method used to authenticate. This gives all users potential access to the same set of resources. Administrators may require a particular type of authentication for a particular resource, but the choice is not dictated by the architecture.

With SecurSight, a user may log in and obtain authorization credentials from any enabled client system. Any additional credentials, beyond those used for initial authentication, are maintained by the authentication server and downloaded to the user after successful authentication.

The SecurSight system maintains a list of trusted authorities that is used to verify chains of public-key certificates at authentication time. This, in conjunction with the use of an external certificate validation service, moves much of the trust management problem away from the user's desktop where it may lead to both confusion and security errors. All trust paths are processed as part of a user's initial authentication; subsequent authorizations use only a trusted issuer, with no certificate chaining required.

1.2 Components

A SecurSight installation consists of six main components, desktops, managers, Privilege-Attribute Certificate (PAC) issuers, agents, certificate authorities, and a directory service. Each component is described briefly below.

The desktop is an application that runs on a user's desktop or portable computer. It provides the interface through which a user logs in and is authorized. It also provides a repository for the obtained authorization credentials. The desktop software also provides local security services, such as selective encryption of local files. The desktop communicates with the manager using the Cryptographic Security Services Protocol [CSSP]. TCP connections from the desktop to protected applications are redirected through an SSL connection to an agent.

The manager acts as both the authentication service and as the long-term repository for users' access rights. Users authenticate, from the desktop to the manager, then receive a privilege attribute certificate containing their authorization information

The manager must reside in a secure facility. It maintains an internal database containing authentication and authorization data for its users. The manager may be replicated to improve reliability and increase performance.

The manager is also referred to as the CSSP server, after the protocol it uses in communication with the desktop. CSSP provides for user authentication, using a variety of methods, and the subsequent delivery of authorization credentials. CSSP requests and responses are formatted as Lisp-style S-expressions. CSSP requires an underlying secure communications layer. This layer must authenticate the server to the client and provide confidentiality and integrity for the exchanged information. In SecurSight, this layer is provided by the Secure Sockets Layer [SSL] protocol, with server-side authentication only.

The PAC issuer is responsible for creating the short-term authorization credentials (PACs) for users after the manager authenticates them. The credentials are constructed using information from the manager's database and the directory service. In most implementations, the PAC issuer will be the manager, but it may be set up as a distinct service.

Agents come in two varieties: remote access agents and application connect agents. Remote access agents act as proxies for users not directly connected to the local network. These can be considered simplified versions of the desktop, with varying protocol requirements.

Application connect agents protect application-based services on the network. The applications may invoke SecurSight services directly, using an API. Existing applications, not modified to use SecurSight, may be protected with wrappers. These wrappers add both public-key based authorization and secure communications to database servers and other applications that normally provide no such security.

The SecurSight certificate authority issues the identity certificates used by the desktop and for other applications. This is an optional service; either an alternate CA or certificates from an external certification service may be used.

The directory service is an optional component in SecurSight that allows a subset of the authentication and authorization data to be maintained outside of the manager's internal database. Any service that supports version 2 of the Lightweight Directory Access Protocol [LDAP] may be used. Long-term secrets, such as passwords, symmetric keys, and private asymmetric keys may not be exported to the directory service.

2. Authentication: PSDs

The central concept of SecurSight authentication is the Personal Security Device, or PSD. A PSD is a unifying construct defined to enclose a user's authentication credentials, independent of whether the user performs authentication with a password, an OTP, or using a smart card. The PSD may be instantiated either in "hard" form, in a public-key based smart card, or in "soft" form, as data temporarily resident on the desktop. To allow for user mobility, the "soft" PSD data is maintained by the manager and downloaded to the user's desktop after a successful authentication.

PSD Field	Description
Version	An alphanumeric string representing the version number of the PSD format
PackageID	An alphanumeric string containing an identifier for the PSD. The identifier should be unique within the domain of the manager issuing the PSD.
Owner	The Distinguished Name of the PSD's owner.
PublicKey Info	An X.509 *SubjectPublicKeyInfo* structure containing the public key.
PrivateKey Info	An *EncryptedPrivateKeyInfo* structure, as described in PKCS #8 [PK8], containing the encrypted value of the private key corresponding to the above public key.
Attributes	A set of certificates and encrypted private keys belonging to the PSD's owner. This includes a certificate containing the key from the PublicKeyInfo above.
Usage	An integer value indicating whether the PSD may be used for encryption, signatures, or both.
Trusted Keys	A list of trusted public keys and certificates.

Table 1: PSD Fields

2.1 PSD Definition

The PSD consists of a user's private key, a corresponding public-key certificate, and a set of additional attributes. These attributes may be passwords, asymmetric key pairs, symmetric keys, or other user-specific information.

The individual fields of the PSD are described in Table1.

2.2 PSD Generation and Distribution

The manager generates a Soft PSD when a user is enrolled. PSDs may also be generated externally and uploaded to the manager, after authentication. The PSD may be downloaded to the user's desktop after a successful authentication. The manager may also be configured to download PSDs without authentication, with authentication required only to obtain the unlocking keys.

The desktop makes an authentication request to the manager, by sending a CSSP request message. The type of authentication may be negotiated with the server, or a default method may be used. A simplified exchange is represented below, with D representing the desktop and M representing the manager.

```
D->M: <UserID><Methods>
M->D: <Method><Challenge>
D->M: <Response>
M->D: <Result><Cookie>
D->M: <Acknowledge>
```

Figure 1: Authentication

The cookie value returned by the manager contains information specific to the authentication session, encrypted under a symmetric key known only to the manager. The cookie may be retained on the desktop and presented to the manager, as proof of authentication, in subsequent requests. Session encryption, as provided by the secure communications layer (SSL), protects the cookie from interception and replay.

Once the authentication is successful, the desktop may request the user's PSD from the manager. This is done using another CSSP exchange.

```
D->M:   <PSDRequest><Cookie>
M->D:   <PSD>
D->M:   <Acknowledge>
```

Figure 2: PSD Download

The private key in the soft PSD is protected under a key-encrypting key (KEK). This key is stored in the PSD, encrypted using any of several methods, depending on the level of protection desired. If the PSD is protected by a static password, the KEK may be stored in the PSD encrypted under a key derived from the password. This option allows the PSD, once retrieved, to be used off-line, without interacting with the manager. The PSD may also be protected by a one-time password, either software generated or from a hardware token. In this case, the KEK is stored in the PSD encrypted under a symmetric key that is stored on the manager. This key may be downloaded, over the secure channel, from the manager after a successful authentication.

```
D->M:   <PSDKeyRequest><Cookie>
M->D:   <PSD Key>
D->M:   <Acknowledge>
```

Figure 3: PSD Key Request

As an optimization, the desktop may cache the user's PSD, with private fields encrypted. If the PSD is cached, only the "unlocking" key needs to be obtained from the manager. Since the manager may modify the contents of the PSD, the desktop must check if the cached PSD is up to date.

If emergency access, in the case where a user's password is forgotten or token lost, is desired, the KEK may also be stored in the PSD encrypted under a PSD unlocking key or PUK. The PUK is kept in a secure facility, under control of the SecurSight administrator.

2.3 Soft PSD Usage

Once downloaded and decrypted, the private key in the soft PSD may be used to create secure connections to SecurSight protected resources. The desktop initiates an SSL session with the application connect agent at the protected resource. The PSD key is used to provide client-side authentication for the SSL session.

In addition to its role in SecurSight authorization, the soft PSD may be used in other applications. It may be used to sign or decrypt electronic mail. It may be used to gain access to SSL-protected web sites. Any application that is PSD aware, or is built from PSD aware libraries, may use the soft PSD as though it were a physical smartcard. In particular, the SecurSight soft PSD is designed to be used with standard APIs such as PKCS #11 [PK11] and Microsoft's CryptoAPI [CAPI].

The Soft PSD may contain more than one private key. If this is the case, the additional keys are kept in the attributes field of the PSD. The X.509 keyUsage extension is used to distinguish between keys used for authentication, encryption, or non-repudiation. The primary private key, in the PrivateKeyInfo field, is used for SSL client authentication with connect agents.

2.4 Comparison with Other Authenticators

Soft PSDs offer significant advantages over other forms of authentication. Static passwords are portable and may be cached to provide a form of single sign-on. They are subject to a number of attacks, and must be synchronized with every application that requires them. SecurSight soft PSDs provide secure authentication and require no synchronization with applications.

One-time passwords, from software or hardware tokens, provide stronger authentication than static passwords. To use one-time passwords with multiple applications, however, requires that each protected application either stores token secrets or communicates with a server that stores them. In addition, for hardware tokens, the user must perform a new authentication for each resource accessed, which quickly becomes burdensome.

SecurSight soft PSDs are most similar to the soft credentials used by web browsers. The browser-based credentials, however, have limited portability. Some browsers offer the ability to export and import credentials in the PKCS #12 interchange format [PK12]. This requires explicit action on the part of the user, and is not practical for a truly mobile user. The Soft PSD user, on the other hand, may authenticate from anywhere within the enterprise, without any special procedures.

Smartcards using RSA and other asymmetric algorithms, offer greater portability than SoftPSDs, as well as better physical protection of the private key. The smartcards require an infrastructure, in the form of card readers, which is not always present or easy to add.

3. Authorization: PACs

All the authorization information in SecurSight is encapsulated in a form of public-key certificate called a Privilege-Attribute Certificate, or PAC.

3.1 PAC Definition

Privilege Attribute Certificates (PACs) are used in SecurSight to convey information about what privileges or authorizations exists for a subject. PACs are short lived (with a lifetime on the order of hours) and are generated on demand by the PAC Issuer (PI) for access to user applications. A PAC is an internal structure used only by SecurSight components.

PACs are used to simplify the trust path management between desktop users and the application agents they are accessing. A user's identity certificate contained within the PSD may be generated by a range of different CAs interconnected in complex trust chains. These trust chains are validated when the certificate in the PSD is presented during desktop authentication. The user's identity and privileges are then stored as part of the PAC. This allows optimized trust processing when secure links are established within SecurSight. The application agent is required only to validate the PI and need not be concerned with all possible CAs that may have issued identity certificates.

PACs are exchanged and processed by several SecurSight components:

Desktop — The local access agent can request one or more PACs when an application that might need a PAC is to be started. When the local access agent sends a request for a PAC to the PAC Issuer, it may specify which applications it wishes to access.

PAC Issuer—The PAC Issuer receives requests for PACs from desktops. The issuer extracts the appropriate information from the user's Identity Certificate (DN, public key, etc.), adds the privilege extensions, sets the Issuer field to its own DN, and then signs the PAC.

Application — An application can be a client/server system (such as a database) or local to the desktop (for example, a local login). The connect agent verifies the signature and validity time of the PAC, extracts the access control information, and initiates the access control sequence for the application.

3.2 PAC Generation and Distribution

PACs are generated at the manager, in response to a PAC request from the desktop. PACs are provided only after a successful authentication. After authentication, the desktop may request a PAC for the user. The request may be generic, in effect requesting all of the user's authorizations, or contain "hints" as to the particular authorizations desired.

```
D->M:   <PACRequest><Hints>
        <Cookie>
M->D:   <PAC>
D->M:   <Acknowledge>
```

Figure 4: PAC Request

3.3 Use of PACs by Connect Agents

Figure 5 illustrates the sequence of events when a user logs in at the desktop, then uses an application that requests access to a server. The user's PSD contains a certificate that has been issued by a CA outside of the organization, but one that is trusted.

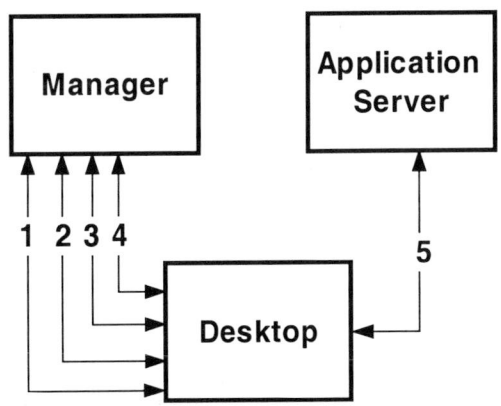

Figure 5: PAC Usage

The numbered items below correspond to the numbered transactions in Figure 5.

1. The user is authenticated at the desktop using a password, a one-time password, or hardware PSD.

2. For software PSDs only, if a current PSD is not cached on the desktop, it may be downloaded from the manager. This transaction requires a cookie from a recent successful authentication.

3. For OTP-protected soft PSDs, the key to decrypt the key-encrypting key in the PSD is then downloaded from the manager. This transaction also requires a prior authentication.

4. After authentication, when access to a network resource is needed, the desktop requests a PAC from the PAC Issuer, in this case the manager.

    The PAC request may be generic or it may contain information regarding the specific resource to be accessed. The PAC request also contains the user's identity certificate, from the PSD, and a cookie, to demonstrate prior authentication.

    The PAC issuer creates a PAC, using the public key and distinguished name from the supplied identity certificate and the user's authorization rights, or the requested subset. This PAC is signed by the issuer and returned to the desktop.

5. The desktop establishes a secure, authenticated channel to the Application Access Agent at the Application Server using the SSL protocol [SSL], with both server and client authentication. The PAC replaces the user's identity certificate in the client authentication portion of the SSL handshake.

    The Application Access Agent extracts the users login credentials from the PAC and communicates the users credentials to the application server. This process is dependent on the application server. The results of the login attempt are communicated back to the desktop.

Once the session is established, the SSL channel is used to securely exchange data between the desktop and the application server.

3.4 PAC format

A PAC is a short-lived X.509 version 3 certificate [X509], with a defined extension handling access rights. PACs may be thought of as the public-key equivalent of the tickets used in systems like Kerberos [KERB]. The PAC may be used in place of an identity certificate in many applications. Some special constraints on the basic certificate fields are described below.

Serial Number – Unlike X.509 identity certificates, SecurSight PACs are short-lived, do not appear on revocation lists, and are not searched for by serial number, so the serial number is not required to be unique.

Validity – As specified in the Internet Public Key Infrastructure [PKIX], UTCTime is used for dates before 2050, and GeneralizedTime for dates after 2050. The validity period for PACs may be configured, at the issuer, but is typically on the order of 24 hours.

Subject – The subject distinguished name must match the subject name in the user's identity certificate.

Subject Public Key – Like the subject name, the public key is copied from the user's identity certificate.

Note that the optional Subject Unique Identifier and Issuer Unique Identifier attributes, as defined by X.509, are not used in SecurSight PACs.

3.5 PAC Extensions – EARs

The only extension vital to the PACs is the entity access right or EAR. The PAC will contain an EAR for each service for which the PAC authorizes access. The EAR contains any service-specific information for the user. Sensitive attributes, such as passwords, are kept in encrypted form.

EAR Field	Description
Service	The name of the service for which the user is authorized.
Method	The access method. This string is specific to the application connect agent on the target system.
Host	The host name on which the service resides. This should match the host name field of the distinguished name in the host PSD for the application connect agent.
Application Data	Application specific data, including access rights and passwords. The data is UTF-8 encoded as set of attribute value pairs, in the form VAR=Value. The values may be a mixture of cleartext and encrypted fields. The encrypted fields are protected with a session key that is, in turn, encrypted under the connect agent's public key.

Table 2: Entity Access Right (EAR) Fields

3.6 Comparison with Other Authorization Methods

SecurSight PACs play a similar role to the tickets used in Kerberos. Both are obtained by the user after an initial authentication, both are short-lived, and both contain information specific to a target service or resource. Unlike Kerberos tickets, however, SecurSight PACs are public-key based, so no shared secret needs to be maintained between the protected resource and the manager.

Both the privilege attribute certificate defined in Sesame [SESM], and the attribute certificate specified by X.509 provide a mechanism for binding authorization information to a user's public key. In both cases, unlike SecurSight, the authorization is in another certificate, linked to the user's identity certificate, and signed by a trusted authority.

Keeping authorization distinct from the identity certificate is useful in distributing management of authorization decisions, but it requires the end application to process and validate two certificates or chains instead of one. In addition, by maintaining the authorization information in a standard identity certificate, this information can be communicated to the target application as part of an SSL handshake, with no additional protocol requirements.

The use of PACs helps make SecurSight a scalable architecture, by requiring transactions with the central server only at authentication time, rather than every time a resource is accessed.

4. Trust Management

The desktop must be configured with the public keys of the managers from which it will obtain services. This trust relationship can be leveraged by allowing the manager to maintain a list of trusted certificate issuers. This list may then be downloaded to the desktop on request. The list is called the Issuing authority table or IAtable.

4.1 Certificate Authority

The Certificate Authority is an optional component of SecurSight that provides certification services. This CA may be used to issue certificates for use with a PSD on the desktop or it may be used independently of desktop and manager to register keys used in desktop browser or other applications

4.2 Certificate Validation Service

The Certificate Validation Service (CVS) is a verification entity within SecurSight. Two types of verification are supported, a simple CRL check, and a full certificate chain validation. The service is used by the desktop, primarily to verify the host certificates for application servers.

The CVS uses the CSSP protocol to communicate validation requests from the desktop to the validation service and to return the responses. SSL is used to protect the integrity of the communication and to authenticate the CVS server to the desktop The desktop supplies only the certificate to be validated. Any additional certificates needed for a full chain validation are retrieved from a directory, using LDAP.

A CVS transaction is quite simple. The desktop or other client application sends a request including the type of service and the certificate to be checked, if any. The CVS server responds with a status code indicating the result of the validation. The transaction can be represented as follows, where D represents the desktop and S represents the CVS server.

```
D->S: <Request><Type>[<Cert>]
S->D: <Status>
```

Figure 6: CVS Request

The types of validation service provided by CVS are described in the table below.

CVS Service	Description
Complete	Complete verification with both revocation check, and certificate signature verification.
no_crl	Verification of certificate signature, but no revocation check.
crl_only	Revocation check only, no signature verification.

Table 3: **CVS Services**

The status returned by CVS indicates if the validation succeeded, partly succeeded, or failed, and the reasons for failure, if any. The possible statuses are listed below.

CVS Status	Definition
0	Verified, in accordance with request
1	Verified, but unable to check revocation status
2	Expired
3	Revoked
4	Verification failed (bad signature, format, etc.)

Table 4: **CVS Status Codes**

The CVS server may cache the result of a request, to make subsequent validations of the same certificate more efficient.

CVS makes the desktop requirements for certificate validation much smaller. In traditional X.509 implementations, the client requests, or receives periodically, a certificate revocation list (CRL) signed by a trusted issuer. The client then checks whether the certificate in question is present on the CRL. CVS avoids the need to download and parse such CRLs, by delegating this responsibility to the CVS server.

The PKIX Online Certificate Status Protocol, or OCSP [OCSP], also centralizes processing of revocation lists, but it does not provide the additional services that CVS does. In particular, CVS verifies the signature on certificates, in addition to checking revocation status. Unlike OCSP, CVS may perform a full chain validation including the retrieval of issuer certificates. CVS also maintains the list of trusted roots, available for download to the desktop.

In contrast, the proposed Data Certification Service [DCS] provides a more extensive set of services than CVS. Specifically, DCS can validate arbitrary signed data, with timestamps, in addition to certificate chain validation. These are valuable services, but they are beyond the scope of the current SecurSight architecture.

The CVS architecture also allows for the addition of new validation methods, without any change required at the desktop.

5. Future Work

SecurSight may be enhanced in a number of ways. New authentication methods, such as biometric devices, may be supported. SecurSight's proprietary PACs may be enhanced or replaced with X.509-style attribute certificates. The Certificate Validation Service may be extended to provide a more generic set of PKI services, like those in DCS.

6. Conclusions

SecurSight provides authentication and authorization services that are similar to those provided by Kerberos, Sesame, or the Distributed Computing Environment [DCE]. The mechanisms used by SecurSight, while differing in specific details, are similar to the mechanisms in those architectures.

SecurSight places emphasis on support for legacy applications and hiding, to the extent possible, the infrastructure from the end user. These features may make it more acceptable in an enterprise environment. This may allow organizations to make a faster and easier transition from their current security methods to a public-key infrastructure.

Finally, SecurSight uses public-key credentials to establish secure connections from user desktops to existing applications. This allows critical data to be protected now, rather than waiting for new applications that employ public-key technology.

Acknowledgments

Special thanks to Alan Abrahams, Bill Duane, Peter Röstin, and the other architects at Security Dynamics for developing the architecture described here. Thanks to Vipin Samar of Sun Microsystems for his work on key formats, upon which much of the PSD design is based. Also thanks to Burt Kaliski, John Linn, and Magnus Nyström of RSA Labs as well as the anonymous referees for their suggestions on improving the content.

References

[CAPI] Microsoft Corporation, *Microsoft® CryptoAPI,* Version 2.0, September 1996

[CSSP] J. Brainard, "The CSSP Protocol: An Architectural Overview." In *Proceedings of the 1998 RSA Data Security Conference,* January 1998

[DCE] The Open Group, *DCE 1.1: Authentication and Security Service,* Open Group Technical Standard C311, August 1997

[DCS] C. Adams and R. Zuccherato, *Internet X.509 Public Key Infrastructure Data Certification Server Protocols* , Internet Draft, draft-ietf-pkix-dcs-00.txt. work in progress, Internet Engineering Task Force, September 1998

[KERB] J. Kohl and C. Neuman, *The Kerberos Network Authentication Service (V5),*
 RFC 1510, Internet Engineering Task Force, September 1993

[LDAP] M. Wahl, T. Howes, and S. Kille, *Lightweight Directory Access Protocol (v3),* RFC 2251, Internet Engineering Task Force, December 1997

[OCSP] M. Myers, R. Ankney, A. Malpani, S. Galperin, and C. Adams, *X.509 Internet Public Key Infrastructure Online Certificate Status Protocol – OCSP,* Internet Draft, draft-ietf-pkix-ocsp-07.txt, work in progress, Internet Engineering Task Force, September 1998

[PK8] RSA Laboratories, *PKCS #8: Private Key Information Syntax Standard,* version 1.2, November 1993.

[PK11] RSA Laboratories, *PKCS #11: Cryptographic Token Interface Standard,* Version 2.0, April 1997.

[PK12] RSA Laboratories, *PKCS #12: Personal Information Exchange Syntax Standard,* version 1.0, April 1997.

[PKIX] R. Housley, W. Ford, W. Polk, and D. Solo, *Internet Public Key Infrastructure: Part I: X.509 Certificate and CRL Profile,* RFC 2459, Internet Engineering Task Force, January 1999

[SESM] T. Parker, *A Secure European System for Applications in a Multi-Vendor Environment,*
March 1992

[SSL] A. Frier, P. Karlton, and P. Kocher, *The SSL 3.0 Protocol,* Netscape Communications Corp., Nov 18, 1996

[X509] CCITT. *Recommendation X.509: The Directory - Authentication Framework.* 1988.

Track B

Intrusion Detection

Chair

Jeremy Epstein, NAI Labs

SAM: Security Adaptation Manager

Heather Hinton[†]   Crispin Cowan   Lois Delcambre   Shawn Bowers

[†] Ryerson Polytechnic University, Canada   Oregon Graduate Institute

E-mail: heather@eecg.utoronto.ca   {crispin, lmd, shawn}@cse.ogi.edu

Abstract

In the trade-offs between security and performance, it seems that security is always the loser. If we allow for adaptive security, we can at least ensure that security and performance are treated somewhat equally. Using adaptive security, we can allow a system to exist in a less secure, more performant state until it comes under attack. We the adapt the system to a more secure, less performant implementation. In this paper, we introduce the Security Adaptation Manager, or SAM. We describe SAM and how we have implemented SAM to take advantage of the different protection strengths offered by the StackGuard compiler. Using SAM to provide StackGuard-based adaptive security provides a form of misuse-based intrusion detection, capable of detecting known and novel attacks.

1. Introduction

It seems that the criteria on which software is evaluated is given in order of "importance" as functionality, performance, and finally security. Given that we are not likely to fundamentally change this ordering we turn to to the practice of adaptive security. Adaptive security allows us to implement a system in a high performance, highly functional state for normal use, and then adapt the system to a less performant/less functional/more secure state in the presence of attacks. That is, we adapt the amount of security offered based on the severity of the attack environment in which a system exists.

In this paper, we describe the Security Adaptation Manager (SAM) tool and the adaptive security it provides. We describe the implementation of SAM and its use with the StackGuard compiler [CPM+98, CBD+99] to adaptively protect against buffer-overflow based stack-smashing attacks. The Security Adaptation Manager (SAM) is a front-end adaptation coordinator that monitors unsuccessful stack-smashing attacks. Together with a General Adaptation Space Navigator, SAM implements adaptive security: more or less protection, providing less or more performance in the presence of a more or less hostile environment. The SAM tool allows us to adapt the level of StackGuard protection in a system to correspond to the (perceived) attack environment.

It is not our position that we implement systems with minimal or no protection. However, recognizing that many such systems are already in place, we offer this approach as a means of mitigating the risk of using such a system.

This paper is structured as follows: the remainder of this Section provides a brief introduction and overview of Adaptation Spaces. Section 2 describes buffer-overflow attacks and defenses. In Section 3 we describe the buffer-overflow adaptation space. The implementation of the Security Adaptation Manager (SAM) is described in Section 4. We briefly discuss the (expected) performance results of SAM in Section 5. Section 6 contains a brief discussion of other software-centered pproaches to intrusion detection.

1.1. Adaptation Spaces

An adaptation space consists of a condition space and a transition graph: these define when and how we implement adaptations. The condition space is a complete lattice of all possible conditions of interest and their settings. Conditions are "of interest" if they are used to define when to adapt an application. As a simple example, a condition might indicate that a resource has experienced a non-maskable failure. If the system is to continue to offer some (reduced level of) service then it must adapt to this non-maskable failure. In a security context, the conditions of interest correspond to different "attack environments" experienced by the system. Each attack environment represents a class of attacks against the environment and the system.

Given a condition space, there is a corresponding transition graph. The transition graph has one node for each system configuration (as defined by the condition space) and defines how we can transition between configurations. For the application defined in this paper, it is possible to transition from any one configuration to any other configuration (all possible transitions are allowable). The transition graph therefore represents an implementation space. This defines the system configurations that can survive and thrive under a given set of conditions. Each individual configuration is referred to as an implementation alternative. It is up to the adaptive application designer to define the available implementation alternatives for an adaptation space.

An implementation alternative is specified by a set of conditions. An implementation alternative is considered a feasible choice when its conditions are true. Conditions are defined over event variables that monitor some aspect of the external environment. Note that for any given condition, there may be more than one implementation alternative that is feasible. For example, it is an artifact of the implementation space that when the system is in its optimal state, we may legitimately implement any of the defined alternatives, including that defined for the worst possible state.

In general, if the most desirable implementation alternative is feasible then all lesser implementation alternatives are also feasible. We specify a default preference order, indicating the "desirability" of the implementation alternatives. This is used to indicate the preferred implementation from the set of feasible implementation alternatives.

An adaptation space formalism is used to navigate among combinations of adaptations [CDM+99]. The adaptation space is represented as a partially-ordered graph (a lattice) with a upper and a lower bound. The upper bound corresponds to the ideal situation, where all required resources are available. In a security context, this is the case where no attacks are experienced. The lower bound corresponds to the worst possible situation, where no resources are available. In a security context, this implies that the system is experiencing indefensible attacks. The lower bound represents the least desirable state; conditions that are higher in the lattice are more desirable.

The adaptation and implementation spaces are rich, in that they specify a complete set of resources and their possible configurations. The adaptation space approach allows us to prune the implementation space so that we define an "optimal" set of implementation alternatives for the system. Similar implementations can be coalesced into a single implementation, triggered by multiple conditions.

2. Buffer Overflow Defenses

Buffer overflows are one of, if not the, most commonly exploited vulnerability in security-sensitive code. These vulnerabilities are commonly exploited in stack-smashing attacks to gain privileged access to a system. There are two "types" of protection against these attacks. We can protect a system against these attacks, using techniques such as non-executable stacks and stack integrity checks. Alternatively, we can attempt to eliminate or reduce the vulnerabilities that lead to these attacks using techniques such as array bounds checking, memory access checking, type-safe languages and debugging tools.

2.1. Protecting the Stack

Non-executable stacks have been implemented with patches to Solaris and Linux [Dik, Des]. These patches make the stack portion of a user process's virtual address space non-executable. Injected attack code cannot therefore be executed. This approach offers a zero performance penalty but requires a specially-patched kernel. These patches are not trivial to implement.

Integrity checks against the stack are also used to protect against buffer-overflow attacks. StackGuard is an example of an integrity check approach. StackGuard is a compiler enhancement to protect programs against stack-smashing attacks [CPM+98, CBD+99] using integrity checks against the stack prior to returning from a function call. StackGuard detects that the return address has been altered before returning from a function (and executing the attacker's injected code). Stack protection is independent of the software executed on a system; protection is provided, regardless of the quality of the code.

2.2. Reducing Vulnerabilities

Reducing a system's vulnerability to buffer-overflow attack occurs at the code level. Richard Jones and Paul Kelly have developed a gcc patch [JK95] that does full array bounds checking for C programs. This method prevents all buffer overflow attacks, not just those attempting to alter function activation records. Unfortunately, this method also imposes a substantial performance overhead: a pointer intensive function (ijk matrix multiply) experienced a 30× slowdown. This compiler is also not mature: complex programs such as elm fail to execute when compiled with this compiler.

Purify [HJ92] is a memory debugging tool for C programs. Purify does integrity checking of memory on every memory access. The performance penalty imposed by Purify is 2 to 5 times the execution time of optimized code. Purify is more suitable for debugging code than for use with production code. More advanced debugging tools have also been developed, such as fault injection tools [GOM98].

Debugging techniques can only minimize the number of buffer overflow vulnerabilities. They provide no assurance that all buffer overflow vulnerabilities have been eliminated. Thus for high assurance, protective measures such as StackGuard and non-executable stacks should be employed.

2.3. StackGuard Protection

The StackGuard compiler provides protection through integrity checks against the function activation record on the stack. StackGuard places a "canary" word next to the return address on the stack (between the return address and the function's local variables). Every function, including main, gets a canary word. When a function returns, it first checks the canary word. If the canary word is still intact (i.e., unchanged), the function will jump to the address pointed to by the return address word.

If the canary word is not intact then the function will invoke the canary_death_handler. This will send a canary-death message to the syslog files and cause the program to (gracefully) terminate. The format of this message is

Immunix type ? Canary[?] = ? died with
  cadaver ???????? procedure ???

This message reports the number of the canary (the ith canary corresponds to the ith function protected), the value of the canary (reported in hexadecimal format) and the procedure name that contains the corrupted canary [1]

StackGuard protection is not infallible. An attack that proceeds without altering the canary value, either by carefully stepping over the canary word or by including the canary word in the attack string, would fail to be detected.

The initial release of StackGuard protected the canary value by choosing a 32-bit random number as a canary value at program exec() time (a random canary). This makes it intractable for the attacker to guess the canary value [CPM+98]. The StackGuard protection has subsequently been extended to use a "terminator" canary [CBD+99]. It is reasoned that an attacker cannot simultaneously deposit a terminator value (for example, a null character) in the canary's location and move on to alter the return address above the canary. The terminator canary is a 32-bit word comprised of a null byte, a carriage return (0x0D), a line feed (0x0A), and an "EOF" (0xFF in the libc representation). Most string copying functions will halt when they encounter one of these bytes.

The random canary is impervious to all string operations, not just those that terminate on the "usual" termination symbols. The random canary is therefore more secure than the terminator canary. Conversely, the terminator canary is faster than the random canary check because it does not have to look up the current canary value.

A final flavor of StackGuard protection is the "terminator with diversity" canary word(s). With this approach, we add a random number of words after the canary word (and before the function's local variables) on the stack, so that the length of the canary word is not predictable. This StackGuard flavor protects against an attack against the terminator canary implemented using do-while gets to overwrite and rebuild the terminator canary word. While not as secure as the random canary, the terminator with diversity is more secure than the terminator canary implementation.

3. StackGuard Adaptation Space

The StackGuard Adaptation Space is defined by the attack environment, that is, the types of buffer-overflow stack-smashing attacks that can be implemented against a system. In the ideal situation, there are no attacks implemented and no special protection is required. In the worst possible situation, it is not possible to defend against the attacks that can be implemented and the only recourse is to take the vulnerable code off-line. The ideal and worst situations bound the adaptation space, which is defined by the (total) ordering shown in Figure 1(a).

Figure 1(b) gives the corresponding implementation space. Note that in Figure 1(b) we do not have an implementation that corresponds to the bounds checking compiler. This is because we have not been able to find a good, working bounds checking compiler for a Linux-based system [2].

The least upper bound of the lattice refers to Unprotected code. We do not recommend, as a rule, that a system contain Unprotected code. However, there may be situations where we can tolerate Unprotected

---

[1] When placed into the syslog files, Date, Time, Host and Program Name information is prepended to the canary death message. For example, one possible prepended message is:
Apr 22 19:52:06 localhost badnull1:

[2] Purify is Solaris-based and the Jones-Kelly bcc is not mature enough for use.

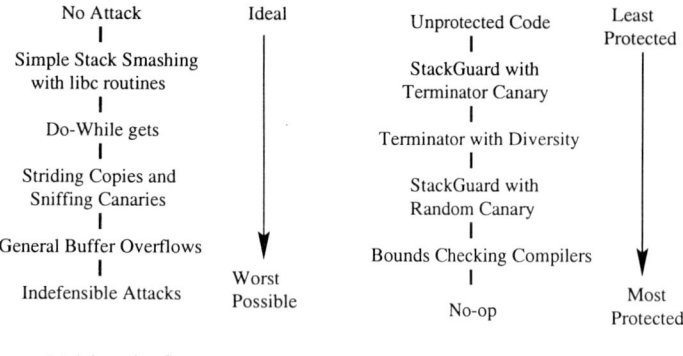

Figure 1. Buffer-Overflow-Based Stack-Smashing Attack Adaptation Space

code, including: we cannot protect the code because we do not have access to the source code and cannot recompile it with the StackGuard compiler; we have a sufficiently good guarantee that the code cannot be accessed (and therefore attacked); the code has been formally verified and proven to be immune to any and all attacks.

The Terminator, Terminator with Diversity, and Random implementations are all flavors of StackGuard-protected code and refer to the type of canary that is used to protect the function pointer. Each flavor protects against the types of attack defined in the corresponding adaptation configuration (Figure 1(a)).

The greatest lower bound of the lattice refers to No-op code. In this situation we are in the presence of an omnipotent and omnipresent attacker and we cannot, by definition, protect the code from attack. This means that our only recourse is to take the affected code off-line and "No-op" it. Because No-op'ing code is a serious action, we do not recommend that entire classes of programs be No-op'ed. Once a vulnerable program is discovered, that program and only that program should be taken off-line [3].

As with a properly defined implementation space, protecting our system at any of the implementation levels defined in Figure 1(b) will provide protection against attacks at that level and all attacks that are higher in the lattice. This means that, for example, the protection provided against general buffer-overflow attacks also implies protection against stack-smashing attacks using libc.

---

[3]This is consistent with real-world practice. For example, CERT will often issue a warning with the advice that a certain piece of code be taken off-line until a work-around can be discovered and put in place.

3.1. StackGuard Monitoring

The SAM tool can be configured to monitor any type of event that is deemed relevant to the system. We provide two types of (StackGuard-relevant) events. The first type of event is the set of death messages reported to the syslog by StackGuard-protected code. We refer to these as monitored events. The second type of event is the set of manual triggers, toggled by the user.

Monitored events are used by SAM to automatically adapt the level of protection within the system. Manual events allow a security administrator to force the adaptation to a more secure implementation than is indicated by the monitored events. This would allow the SA to move to a more secure state as a precautionary measure, for example, after reading a CERT advisory. Note that we cannot use manual events to force an implementation that is less secure than the one specified, and required, by the monitored events.

3.2. StackGuard Monitored Event Variables

SAM monitors the canary death messages reported in the syslog files. Each syslog message contains syslog-generated information (describing the date, time, and "originator" of the message) and StackGuard-generated information (the canary death message). The data contained in this message is parsed and separated into Month, Date, Time, HostName, ProgramName, CanaryType, CanaryValue, and AttackedProcedure fields.

The Month, Date, and Time information is used to determine the frequency of unsuccessful attacks. The CanaryType and CanaryValue fields are used to verify which StackGuard implementation is currently in place. Although not currently used by SAM, the AttackedProcedure field can be used as part of an off-line analysis of the vulnerabilities that are being exploited by the unsuccessful attacks.

The HostName and ProgramName are used to identify the sensitivity of the host and program under attack. We consider three classes of host sensitivity: security server, other server and workstation. A security server is one that is critical to the security function of the network. An example of a security server is a Kerberos authentication or a RADIUS server. An example of a non-security, other, server is a file server or a compute server. We respond to attacks against these classes of servers differently: we take a much more conservative view when considering attacks against a security server.

We classify programs as having nobody, user, or root sensitivity. Attacks against root-level programs are the most serious (have greatest associated risks). Attacks against nobody-level programs are judged to be the least serious. We tolerate fewer unsuccessful attacks against root-level programs than against user-level or nobody-level programs.

3.3. SAM Conditions

The SAM adaptation conditions are given by the following tuple:

(pgm_host_attack_grid, manual_selector)

The manual_selector event variable represents the user-specified implementation alternative.

The pgm_host_attack grid defines the (monitored) conditions for moving to a more or less secure implementation based on the class of program and host that is being (unsuccessfully) attacked. A typical grid is shown below in Table 1. The value in each corresponds to the number of (unsuccessful) attacks that are observed before we move to a more secure implementation. Once the conditions specified by any cell in this grid are satisfied, we must adapt the system. In Table 1, for example, if there is more than one unsuccessful attack on (any) root-level program on a security server, then we will upgrade the system to a more secure implementation.

Originally, we had defined adaptability based on the percentage of possible programs and hosts within a class being under attack. This approach offered flexibility because we cannot know the numbers of different types of servers within an unknown system. For a given system, defining a trigger based on 1% of these servers has the same effect as specifying one server. Defining a trigger based on 50% of the workstations in a system, however, is easier to understand (and justify) than requiring 13 workstations be under attack.

	Security	Other	Workstation
Root	1	5	10
User	5	10	15
Nobody	10	20	25

Table 1: Pgm_Host_Attack Grid

We have found that it is just as easy to base our decisions on a "raw" number of perceived attacks against a given class. While this might result in a more sensitive set of adaptability conditions, this is not seen as a detriment. Indeed, this approach is more flexible in that it does not allow an attacker to hide their actions by moving from host to host.

3.4. Protection Postures

The possible implementation space that SAM needs to consider is quite large. This follows given that we monitor three classes of programs (root, user, nobody), on three classes of hosts (security server, other server, workstation), with five possible security levels (Unprotected, Terminator, Terminator with Diversity, Random, No-op). This leaves us with 9^5 possible implementation alternatives to consider.

We can immediately prune this space by noting that two of the five possible security states are not recommended for entire classes of programs or hosts (Unprotected and No-op). Taking an entire class of programs or an entire class of hosts off-line, or leaving them unprotected, is a drastic action. We postulate that the number of Unprotected and No-op'ed programs will be small and can be represented by N. Based on these assumptions, we can prune our implementation space to $9^3 + N$. Even this space, however, is too large to be practical.

We therefore consider pre-configured states, or Protection Postures. A protection posture is a predefined system implementation, where each program-host class may have different implementation alternatives. Protection postures allow us to prune the implementation space by pre-configuring a small number of postures that are the most effective system implementations. We define three postures, called Calm, Nervous, Panic in order of preference.

When a system has adopted a Calm protection posture, we trade-off protection for performance as shown in Table 2. The most critical code (root-level permission on a security server) is always implemented at the highest (most-protected) protection level, even in the Calm state. The remainder of the code is protected at the least StackGuard-protected level (note that this differs from the least protected level, which is Unprotected).

	Security	Other	Workstation
Root	Random	Terminator	Terminator
User	Terminator	Terminator	Terminator
Nobody	Terminator	Terminator	Terminator

Table 2: Calm Protection Posture

Once we believe that a system is under attack, we move up to the Nervous protection posture. This posture offers protection against a broader range of attacks than the Calm posture. We protect at the highest StackGuard level (with the Random canary) the root-permission code on the security and other servers and the user-permission code on the security server. The remainder of the code is upgraded to the Terminator with Diversity level of StackGuard protection.

	Security	Other	Workstation
Root	Random	Random	TermDiv
User	Random	TermDiv	TermDiv
Nobody	TermDiv	TermDiv	TermDiv

Table 3: Nervous Protection Posture

If a system is heavily attacked, we move into the Panic state. In this state we implement the strongest security we have by taking all code to the Random canary level of StackGuard protection. We also take any root-level programs that are under attack into the No-op state.

	Security	Other	Workstation
Root	Rand/NoOp	Rand/NoOp	Rand/NoOp
User	Rand	Rand	Rand
Nobody	Rand	Rand	Rand

Table 4: Panicked Protection Posture

A protection posture is implemented when a corresponding set of conditions, defined by a pgm_host_attack grid, is true. Table 5, below, defines the pgm_host_attack grids corresponding to the protection postures defined above [4]. If any of the conditions in a grid are true, then we must adapt the system to a more secure implementation, where all conditions are true. If all of the conditions of the grid are false, then we may restore the system to the less secure implementation (for which the conditions are all true).

	Security	Other	Workstation
Root	1	5	15
User	5	10	20
Nobody	5	15	25

Table 5(a): Monitored Event Conditions for Calm Posture

	Security	Other	Workstation
Root	2	10	20
User	10	15	30
Nobody	10	20	40

Table 5(b): Monitored Event Conditions for Nervous Posture

According to Table 5(a), once we have seen one attack against a root-level program on a security server, we can no longer remain calm: we must move into the nervous posture.

---

[4] The values reported in this table correspond to the test values used with SAM.

	Security	Other	Workstation
Root	3	15	25
User	15	20	40
Nobody	15	25	50

Table 5(c): Monitored Event Conditions for Panicked Posture

The protection postures and pgm_host_attack grids are used together to determine the implementation alternatives for a given system given its (attack) environment. For example, let the monitored events indicate that there have been 13 attack attempts against user programs on other servers. This indicates that there is at least one condition required by the Calm posture that is false: we cannot continue with the Calm implementation. From Table 5(b) and (c), we see that this monitored event does not violate the conditions of the Nervous or Panicked postures. Either posture is allowable. However, we prefer to be in the Nervous posture over the Panicked posture for performance reasons, and so the preference ordering will indicate that the Nervous posture is the preferred implementation.

4. Implementation

The Security Adaptation Monitoring tool is implemented in Java and Perl (using JDK 1.1 on a StackGuard-protected Linux distribution). SAM has been tested on a stand-alone system using simulated test data (based on real attack patterns observed at both Ryerson Polytechnic University and the Oregon Graduate Institute). SAM successfully adapted the system: simple attacks that were possible (but difficult to implement and therefore gave rise to auditable failure notices) became impossible as the system adapted to a more secure state. SAM also successfully transitioned the system to a more performant state in the absence of any failed attack attempts.

SAM takes as an input a file generated by the Swatch tool [Atk]. Swatch is a Perl utility used to filter all non-SAM relevant messages from syslog. Currently, only canary death messages are considered SAM-relevant. SAM also receives user inputs from a user interface. SAM parses the relevant event variables from these inputs and passes the information to the Generic Adaptation Space Navigator.

The Generic Adaptation Space Navigator is a (Java-based) tool that enables software applications to adapt to changing environments [Bow99]. The Navigator takes as an input an XML [XML] file specifying an adaptation space. The Navigator also takes as input the values of the monitored event variables, and produces as an output the path to the preferred implementation for the given environment.

Using the preferred implementation returned by the Navigator, SAM must "replace" the existing implementation with the preferred implementation. This is accomplished using a Perl script that is triggered by the Java component of SAM. We maintain three complete "systems", one for each protection posture. That is, we prepend to all directory paths the protection posture that is currently implemented. This means that below the root directory, we have three sub-directories, /calm, /nerv, /panic, as shown in Figure 2.

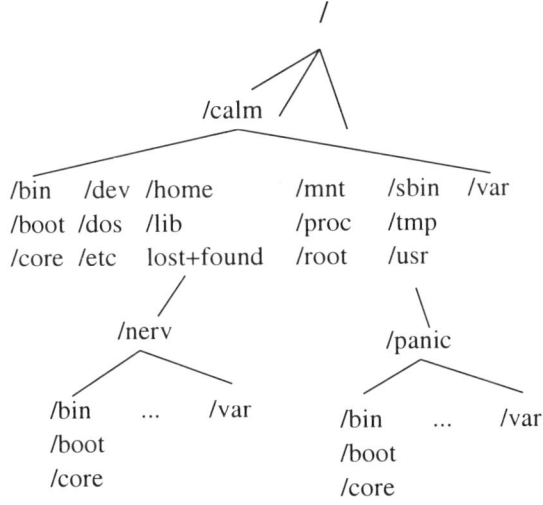

Figure 2. Implementing the Protection Postures

For example, we will have three versions of /etc: /calm/etc, /nerv/etc, /panic/etc. In the /calm directory, all root-level code on a security server will protected with a Random canary, while the remaining code on the remaining servers is protected at the Terminator canary level.

This implementation implies that the details of the protection postures are locally configurable. While we cannot change the fact that there are three postures, we are free to implement these postures as most effective and efficient for a given system.

4.1. When to Adapt

When to adapt is based on the number of programs at a host that are under attack. We have stated, for example, that if there has been an unsuccessful attack against a root-level program at a non-security (other) server, then we cannot stay in the calm posture and must adapt to a more secure implementation alternative. Do we consider attacks over all time or over the last x seconds?

If we were to consider attacks over all time, it is trivial to argue that once the system adapts into the most secure implementation, it can never return to a less secure/more performant implementation. If we consider attacks over some period of time, how do we define this period? This is not a trivial problem.

If we pick a period that is too short, we may not "detect" attacks that should cause us to adapt to a more secure state (a technique known in the hacker literature as a "slow scan"). If we pick a period that is too long, it will be very difficult to "recover" from past attacks. Simply by picking a value, we open ourselves up to a denial-of-service attack: all the attacker must do is ensure that the minimum number of attacks are recognized within this time period.

Associated with this problem is the problem of recovering to a more performant state after the number of detected attacks drops off. Do we use the same waiting period? Do we place stricter requirements on this "direction" of adaptation and use a longer waiting period? If we pick a waiting period that is too short, we can easily set ourselves up for a concerted attack against the system in its weaker state. We also run the risk of thrashing the system, that is, wasting cycles adapting between two alternatives, to the point that there are no cycles available for compute jobs. If we pick a period that is too long, then we are not taking full advantage of the adaptive approach to maximize performance.

We recommend that the downgrade window be set at least 10 times as long as the downgrade window. This value is based solely on our observations of the timing of attacks; it will more than likely need to be fine tuned for each individual system.

Because of the difficulty in picking these adapt and wait times, we do not hard-wire this into SAM. Instead, we allow security administrators to pick these values when configuring SAM for their local systems. We have tested SAM (and set up as default values, easily changed within SAM) using an upgrade window of 60 seconds (measured in milliseconds), and a downgrade window of 3600 seconds. This means that an attacker can attempt at most one attack an hour against the least-protected system.

4.2. Security of SAM

One, very good, means of attacking a system is to attack the system's defense mechanisms. We must consider the security of StackGuard and the Security Adaptation Manager. In order to subvert the StackGuard mechanism, we must recompile code with a non-StackGuard compiler. This implies that even if SAM is subverted, the protection offered by StackGuard will continue to be in place.

SAM relies on the outputs of the syslog files, filtered by the PERL utility swatch. If we can subvert either swatch, the swatch configuration files, or the output produced by swatch, we can fool SAM into thinking that the system is not under attack. SAM will therefore not adapt the system to a more secure or more performant implementation. This implies that we must protect all aspects of swatch.

An easier way to subvert SAM is to replace the various StackGuard-compiled programs with non-StackGuard compiled programs. When SAM adapts the system, it will then (unknowingly) adapt less secure code instead of more secure code. This means that we must tightly control write access to the locations where StackGuard compiled code resides.

Another way to attack SAM is to inject false canary death records to the syslog files. This will give the appearance of a system heavily under attack and will cause SAM to upgrade the system to a low performance/high security implementation. This is a form of denial-of-service attack against the system.

5. Performance Results

We have run a preliminary performance analysis on a 133 MHz Pentium with 16M of RAM, 16K cache memory and a 256K level 2 cache. The SAM components are implemented in Java and Perl scripts. Because SAM is a continuous process (always running) it will affect the performance (elapsed time, or throughput) for all processes. Using a better Java compiler would help this aspect of performance. Nevertheless, we do not believe that this is a serious drawback as SAM should not be running on a "general user" machine. SAM is a priviliged, security-relevant program. As such, it should be run on a bastion host.

We do not yet have performance results for the tool as used in a production-type environment (i.e., with a more powerful processor) or a "true" attack environment, when we must implement attack-based transitions. All testing of SAM has been done using simulated attack data. A preliminary performance justification follows.

Performance analyses of the StackGuard flavors tell us that the Terminator canary is the most performant, followed by the Terminator with Diversity, and the Random canaries. We also know that the performance overhead imposed by StackGuard'ed code is not significant [CBD+99]. This leads us to postulate that the major contributor to performance slowdown with SAM will be the adaptation time. The adaptation time is the time it takes to re-configure the system to reflect the new SAM-specified protection posture.

As the majority of the performance penalty is that incurred by the creating of symbolic links, the performance hit incurred is negligible. Implementing SAM-specified re-configurations on a heavily loaded laptop had no noticeable effect on other jobs.

One ramification of using symbolic links for implementation transitions is that any processes that are currently running will not be re-configured, mid-execution, to a {more, less} secure state. Instead, they will finished executing in their current state. The next time the process is invoked, it will be invoked in the "new" configuration, corresponding to the current implementation.

We have implemented the transition mechanism with the assumption that processes are short-lived and start-on-demand. There are however, several persistent daemons, including nfsd, sendmail, and inetd (which handles the start on demand for all other daemons). Future versions of SAM must develop a solution that allows these persistent daemons to be killed and re-started automatically. Until then, these daemons will need to be re-started manually when the system is transitioned to a more secure state.

6. Discussion

Ghosh et al proposed a software level approach to intrusion detection [GWC98]. They concentrate on the software level because "attacks against computer systems are in fact attacks against specific software programs". Although their approach works best with software that has been modified to provide internal state information, they do allow for intrusion detection based solely on the observable external states of the program. Thus they are not limited to applying this approach to programs for which the source code is available.

Forrest et al. have also proposed a system process level approach [HFS98] to misuse detection. Misuses are those sequences that deviate from those occurring empirically in traces of known normal behavior. This approach requires a modified kernel to trap system calls.

The StackGuard based approach does not require the modification of programs or the kernel. It does, however, require that we have access to the source code, so that we can re-compile it with the StackGuard compiler. We hope that the benefits of a tool such as the Security Adaptation Manager as used with StackGuard will convince more people to release open source.

Together, StackGuard and SAM provide a form of misuse detection, where the misuse pattern is the canary death message reported by a failed StackGuard-compiled program. StackGuard (and therefore SAM) are different from misuse detection approaches in that it is able to "recognize" novel attacks. For example, StackGuard was developed before the recent attack against a particular edition of lsof was known/published [Zbo99]. Where other misuse detection systems may not be able to detect this type of misuse, StackGuard had no trouble in preventing lsof-based stack-smashing attacks. This implies that StackGuard and SAM will be able to detect new, previously unknown buffer-overflow based stack-smashing attacks, and adapt the system correspondingly.

7. Conclusions and Future Work

Although not a "classic" intrusion detection mechanism, the Security Adaptation Manager (SAM) does provide detection of and response to possible attacks. SAM monitors audit logs to detect unsuccessful attacks and to provide an adaptive response. Based on the attack characteristics, SAM will adapt the system to more or less secure states, optimizing the performance of the system in the presence of attacks. SAM also allows the user to force the adaptation to a more secure state than is required by the attack characteristics. This allows security administrators to take pre-emptive steps in the face of (e.g.) CERT advisories.

In future work, SAM can be generalized to arbitrary intrusion detection sources and arbitrary intrusion response adaptations. Because of the generality of the use conditions in an adaptation space, any form of intrusion detection is suitable for driving SAM. Similarly, any portion of the system's security posture that is dynamically configurable can be driven by an intrusion detection-response policy encoded in SAM. For example, SAM can be easily configured to provide adaptability to firewalls and firewall rules. The sample policies presented here only scratch the surface of possibilities.

References

[Atk] Todd Atkins. The simple watcher and filer. available from ftp://ftp.stanford.edu/general/security-tools/swatch or from ftp://ftp.redhat.com/pub/contrib/SRPMS/swatch-2.2-2.src.rpm.

[Bow99] Shawn Bowers. The general adaptation space navigator, April 1999. Heterodyne Project.

[CBD+99] Crispin Cowan, S. Beattie, R. Day, C. Pu, P. Wagle, and E. Walthinsen. Protecting systems from stack smashing attacks with stackguard, 1999. to appear at Linux Expo 1999, http://www.bitmover.com/ linux-expo/ papers.html.

[CDM+99] Crispin Cowan, L. Delcambre, A. Le Meur, L. Liu, D. Maier, D. McNamee, M. Miller, C. Pu, P. Wagle, and J. Walpole. Adaptation space: Surviving non-maskable failures, 1999. Heterodyne Project.

[CPM+98] Crispin Cowan, C. Pu, D. Maier, H. Hinton, P. Bakke, S. Beattie, A. Grier, P. Wangle, and Q. Zhang. Stackguard: Automatics adaptive detection and prevention of buffer-overflow attacks. In Proceedings 1998 Usenix Security Conference, January 1998. San Antonio, Texas.

[Des] Solar Designer. Non-executable user stack. http://www.false.com/security/linux-stack/.

[Dik] Casper Dik. Non-executable stack for solaris. Posting to comp.security.unix January 2 1997.

[GOM98] Anup K Ghosh, Tom O'Conner, and Gary McGraw. An automated approach for identifying potential vulnerabilities in software. In Proceedings of the IEEE Symposium on Security and Privacy, pages 104–114, May 1998.

[GWC98] Anup K. Ghosh, James Wanken, and Frank Charron. Detecting anomalous and unkown intrusions against programs. In Proceedings of Fourteenth ACSAC, 1998.

[HFS98] S.A. Hofmeyr, S. Forrest, and A. Somayajii. Intrusion detection using sequences of system calls. Journal of Computer Security, 6:151–180, 1998.

[HJ92] Reed Hastings and Bob Joyce. Purify: Fast Detection of Memory Leaks and Access Errors. In Proceedings of the Winter USENIX Conference, 1992. Also available at http://www.rational.com/support/techpapers/fast_detection/.

[JK95] Richard Jones and Paul Kelly. Bounds Checking for C. http://www-ala.doc.ic.ac.uk/ phjk/BoundsChecking.html, July 1995.

[XML]   XML. World wide web consortium extensible markup language (xml). http://www.w3.org/XML/.

[Zbo99]   Anthony C. Zboralski. [HERT] Advisory #002 Buffer overflow in lsof. Bugtraq mailing list, http://geek-girl.com/bugtraq/, February 18 1999.

An Application of Machine Learning to Network Intrusion Detection

Chris Sinclair
Applied Research Laboratories
The University of Texas at Austin
sinclair@arlut.utexas.edu

Lyn Pierce
epierce@arlut.utexas.edu

Sara Matzner
matzner@arlut.utexas.edu

Abstract

Differentiating anomalous network activity from normal network traffic is difficult and tedious. A human analyst must search through vast amounts of data to find anomalous sequences of network connections. To support the analyst's job, we built an application which enhances domain knowledge with machine learning techniques to create rules for an intrusion detection expert system. We employ genetic algorithms and decision trees to automatically generate rules for classifying network connections. This paper describes the machine learning methodology and the applications employing this methodology.

1. Introduction

Existing intrusion detection systems rely heavily on human analysts to differentiate intrusive from non-intrusive network traffic. The large and growing amount of data confronts the analysts with an overwhelming task, making the automation of aspects of this task necessary. Whether complete automation is possible or even desirable is debatable. We describe the use of machine learning techniques which provide decision aids for the analysts and which automatically generate rules to be used for computer network intrusion detection.

The Applied Research Laboratories of the University of Texas at Austin (ARL:UT) has developed significant expertise in the area of machine learning through internal research and development. This research has been applied to a number of applications in which machine learning techniques, such as generation of finite state machines and pattern matching, have been used[5][6]. The Network Exploitation Detection Analyst Assistant (NEDAA) is one such application, combining artificial intelligence rule generation with a classic expert system as an enhancement for intrusion detection systems (IDS).[1] In this paper we give an overview of machine learning techniques used and we describe some of the successes and problems encountered in applying these techniques to computer network intrusion detection.

Our application layers machine learning techniques onto an existing network-based IDS deployed to protect military subnetworks. On each military subnetwork there is a probe that filters and logs network traffic to a central database[8]. A rule set is used to analyze archived data for intrusive patterns. The pattern matching has traditionally been simple, looking for exploitive activity such as connections from certain IP addresses with histories of intrusive behavior. However, an intrusion into a computer network can be more complex, with the complexity being both spatial and temporal. An example of this type of intrusion is a 'low and slow' attack consisting of intrusive behavior over hours, days or weeks that may originate from multiple network sources. Machine learning can be applied to this problem to extend human pattern recognition. Automated techniques are ideal for this application because they can monitor and correlate vast numbers of intrusive signatures.

[1] Contracts N00039-0051, Task Order No. 0293 and Task Order No. 0273 and ARL:UT IR&D Programs No. 0000859 and 0000875.

2. Machine Learning Techniques

Our current implementation of NEDAA contains rule generation modules that interface with two ARL:UT artificial intelligence (AI) software packages: a genetic algorithm tool set and a decision tree generator. These modules can be customized for specific applications and data sources. The choice of AI techniques employed stemmed from our previous experience with genetic algorithms, and literature research into other applicable methods. The genetic algorithm software package was a logical platform from which to tackle the difficult problem of intrusion detection. The use of decision trees for rule generation was made to provide a deterministic alternative to genetic algorithms.

VulcanRG, the machine learning component of the NEDAA system, generates rules for compilation into intrusion detection systems. These rules are generated by the genetic algorithm and by decision tree packages developed at ARL:UT. We currently use VulcanRG to generate rules for one deployed IDS and one experimental system. Many of the examples presented in this paper are derived from actual runs of the machine learning components of NEDAA.

2.1. Genetic Algorithms

Genetic algorithms are a family of problem-solving techniques based on evolution and natural selection. They are essentially a type of search algorithm, and as such, can be used to solve a wide variety of problems. This section gives a brief overview of genetic algorithms.

The goal of genetic algorithms is to create optimal solutions to problems. Potential solutions to the problem to be solved are encoded as sequences of bits, characters or numbers. The unit of encoding (usually a single bit in traditional genetic algorithms) is called a gene, and the encoded sequence is called a chromosome. The genetic algorithm begins with a set (population) of these chromosomes and an evaluation function that measures the fitness of each chromosome, i.e. the 'goodness' of the problem solution represented by the chromosome. It uses reproduction (one of several operators collectively called crossover operators) and mutation (the spontaneous alteration of a single gene) to create new solutions, which are then evaluated. The selection of chromosomes for survival and recombination is biased toward the fittest individuals. The recombination/evaluation sequence is iterated many times, and if the problem is well-constructed, strong solutions gradually emerge.

The genetic algorithm package we have developed is a generalization of the classic genetic algorithm. Our genetic algorithm does not mandate the encoding of solutions into low-level chromosomes. If crossover and mutation operators can be imposed on the solutions themselves, domain specific information can be used to expedite the search. If a low-level encoding was required in such cases, this domain specific knowledge would be unusable. In cases where a crossover or mutation operator cannot be imposed on the space of solutions, a classic genetic algorithm (with encoding to chromosomes) is used.

2.2. Decision Trees

Decision trees are structures used to classify data with common attributes. Each decision tree represents a rule which categorizes data according to these attributes. A decision tree consists of *nodes*, *leaves*, and *edges*. A node of a decision tree specifies an attribute by which the data is to be partitioned. Each node has a number of edges which are labeled according to a possible value of the attribute in the parent node. An edge connects either two nodes or a node and a leaf. Leaves are labeled with a decision value for categorization of the data.

Example 1 *A decision tree to detect intrusive behavior based on the data in Table 1*

In this example IP Port, *and* System Name *label the nodes,* intrusion *and* normal *label the leaves, and the labeled arrows are the edges. The generated decision tree is shown in Figure 1.*

Table 1. Example Intrusion Data

IP Port	System Name	category
004020	Artemis	normal
004020	Apollo	intrusion
002210	Artemis	normal
002210	Apollo	intrusion
000010	Artemis	normal
000010	Apollo	normal

Figure 1. Example Intrusion Decision Tree

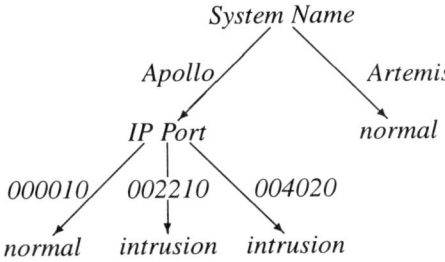

This decision tree could be turned into the following rule (in C++ form):

```
if(System Name == Artemis){
  intrusion = false;
}
else if(System Name == Apollo){
  if(IP Port == 002210){
    intrusion = true;
  }
  else if(IP Port == 004020){
    intrusion = true;
  }
  else if(IP Port == 000010){
    intrusion = false;
  }
}
```

We use Quinlan's[7] ID3 algorithm to construct decision trees from structured data (such as the data in Table 1). The ID3 algorithm uses information theoretic precepts to create efficient decision trees. Given a structured data set, a list of attributes describing each data element, and a set of categories to partition the data into, the ID3 algorithm determines which attribute most accurately categorizes the data. A node is established and labeled by this attribute. The edges coming from this node are labeled with the possible values of the partitioning attribute. The data set is then divided into subsets by the values of this attribute. If a subset is completely categorized, then the edge terminates in a leaf labeled by the categorization. Otherwise the subset is subdivided further by creating a new node and repeating this process recursively.

Figure 2. Pruned Decision Tree

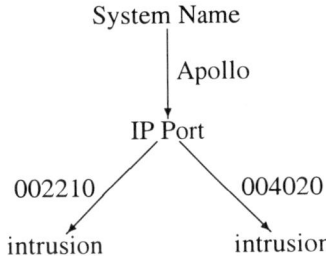

Decision trees constructed by the ID3 algorithm are based on the *training set* used to construct them. In order for a decision tree to generalize the information learned, the decision tree must be *pruned*. Pruning replaces certain nodes with leaves. A simple example of pruning involves removing all nodes and leaves which terminate in a default category. In Figure 2 we show the tree of Figure 1 after it has been pruned. All connections are assumed to be normal if they are not classified as intrusions. The pruned decision tree can be turned into the following code:

```
intrusion = false;

if(System Name == Apollo){
  if((IP Port==002210)||(IP Port==004020)){
    intrusion = true;
  }
}
```

3. Machine Learning applied to Intrusion Detection

The NEDAA machine learning approach uses analyst-created training sets for rule development and analyst decision support. In the current implementation the training information is comprised of database views queried from the archived network events (Table 3). From this training data, the machine learning modules generate rules of the form:

$$\text{if} < condition > \text{then} < action >$$

These rules can be compiled into the expert system for intrusive event detection, or used to simplify the analyst's task by summarizing large sets of training data into simple rule sets. It is important to note that the quality of the synthesized rules depends on the quality of the training set. Any classification errors in the training set will propagate into the resulting rule set.

Table 2. Example Training Data

Source IP	Dest IP	Source Port	Dest Port	Protocol	Intrusion
123.202.72.109	225.142.187.12	001360	000080	IP	true
123.202.72.109	225.142.187.12	001425	000080	IP	true
123.202.72.109	225.142.187.12	001488	000080	IP	true
123.202.72.109	225.142.187.12	001559	000080	IP	true
123.202.72.109	225.142.187.12	001624	000080	IP	true
123.202.72.109	225.142.187.12	002156	000080	IP	true
123.202.72.109	225.142.187.12	002158	000080	IP	true
225.142.147.75	150.216.191.119	001624	000080	IP	true
225.142.187.19	125.250.187.19	004207	000025	IP	true
233.167.15.65	225.142.187.12	004607	000025	IP	false
233.167.15.65	225.142.187.12	004690	000025	IP	false
139.61.51.70	225.142.187.12	001052	000021	IP	false
142.142.5.113	225.142.187.12	001572	000080	IP	false
:	:	:	:	:	:
					false

3.1. Applying Genetic Algorithms

In the current version of NEDAA, we use genetic algorithms to evolve simple rules for monitoring network traffic. These rules are simple single-connection patterns for differentiating normal from abnormal network connections. The rules are evolved by creating patterns which match a set of anomalous connections and a set of normal connections (as reported by an analyst). These patterns are used as the firing conditions of rules of the form if $< pattern\_matched >$ then $< generate\_alert >$.[2] The goal is to develop rules which match only the anomalous connections. Such rules can then be used to filter historical records and new connections so that the analyst can concentrate on those which are suspicious.

The patterns created by the genetic algorithm corresponds to the format of incoming connections and are combinations of specific connection attribute values and 'wild cards'. Examples of attributes used in the current version of NEDAA include: source IP address, destination IP address, source IP port, destination IP port, and network protocol.

The initial population (see section 2.1) is comprised of random rules; an example is shown in Table 3. The chromosome for a rule is comprised of 29 genes: 8 for source IP (2 hexadecimal digits per address field), 8 for destination IP, 6 for source port, 6 for destination port, and 1 for protocol. Each gene can be either a specific numeric value in the appropriate range for the field or a wild card. The chromosome for the rule in Table 3 is shown in Figure 3.[3] When a rule is used to filter connections, each connection is converted to a 29-field format corresponding to the gene structure of a rule as described above. A rule matches a connection if and only if every non-wildcard gene in the rule matches the corresponding field in the connection.

Table 3. Sample rule

Attribute	Value
Source IP	42.22.e5.bc (66.34.229.188)
Dest IP	15.b*.6e.76 (21.176+?.110.118)
Source port	047051
Dest port	912320
Protocol	TCP

Figure 3. Chromosome for rule in Table 3

$$(4, 2, 2, 2, 14, 5, 11, 12, 1, 5, 11, -1, 6, 14,$$
$$7, 6, 0, 4, 7, 0, 5, 1, 9, 1, 2, 3, 2, 0, 17)$$

The evolutionary process of the genetic algorithm requires some form of fitness measure on individual population members. In NEDAA, this fitness measure is based on the actual performance of each rule on a pre-classified data set. Each rule is used to filter a data set comprised of connections marked as either anomalous or normal by an analyst, and the fitness function rewards partial matches of training connections that have been designated as anomalous. If a rule completely matches an anomalous connection

---

[2] As there is a clear 1-1 correspondence between rules and patterns, we will use the terms interchangeably for the remainder of this section.

[3] The value of -1 in the 12th field represents a wild card.

it is awarded a bonus; if it matches a normal connection it is penalized. As a result, succeeding populations are biased toward rules that match intrusive connections only. After a certain number of generations, the genetic algorithm is stopped, and the best unique rules are selected.

The classic genetic algorithm described earlier tends to converge on a single 'best' solution to any given problem. In the case of a rule set, however, it is generally not sufficient to find a single rule. Multiple rules are generally needed to identify unrelated types of anomalies; several 'good' rules are more effective than a single 'best' one. In mathematical terms, this requirement translates to the concept of finding *local maxima* as opposed to the *global maximum* of the fitness function. Genetic algorithms evolve solutions which maximize (or minimize) the fitness function. A traditional genetic algorithm will attempt to find a global maximum of the fitness function, and will continue until all solutions in the population have converged to this maximum. In contrast, the problem of discovering multiple rules to filter incoming connections based on different criteria is essentially that of discovering multiple local maxima of the fitness function.

In order to find local maxima of the fitness function, and hence multiple rules, we employed *niching* techniques. Conceptually, niching in genetic algorithms is similar to that in nature; different species that share an environment generally inhabit different niches in order to exploit resources and minimize competition. In genetic algorithms, niching strategies attempt to create subpopulations which converge on local maxima. The two standard ways of niching are *sharing* and *crowding*[4]. Sharing degrades the fitness of solutions based on the number of other solutions which are nearby (similar). When the fitness is degraded in this manner, overcrowded niches become less hospitable, forcing solutions to other local maxima which may be less populated. In crowding, solutions which are generated by the crossover of two 'parent' solutions replace the nearest (most similar) solutions in the population.

Both sharing and crowding use the concept of *nearness*, or similarity, in order to maintain population diversity. A distance metric must be imposed either on the space of solutions or on the space of chromosomes in order to use either of these niching methods. Unless a domain specific distance metric is determined for the problem, the *Hamming distance* is used[4]. The Hamming distance between two chromosomes is the number of genes which differ between the two chromosomes. We use the Hamming distance and a variation of crowding in order to generate a diverse rule set.

3.2. Applying Decision Trees

We use the ID3 algorithm to create decision trees which classify connections based on the attributes listed in Table 3. The generated decision tree can be pruned to determine connections which have similar attributes to those in Table 3. In this way decision trees generalize information learned during their construction. A pruned decision tree generated by the ID3 algorithm based on data in Table 3 is shown in Figure 4.

Figure 4. Intrusion Detection Decision Tree

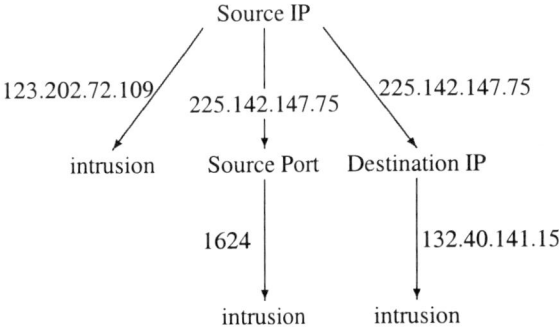

The rules produced by the decision trees are of a slightly different nature than those produced by genetic algorithms. The genetic algorithms use niching to create a population of unique rules; ideally each rule at its own local maxima. Decision trees on the other hand create a single rule with a number of different clauses. Each clause is equivalent to a single rule in the genetic algorithm population. Each element of training data falls into one of the clauses in the decision tree and hence is represented in the final rule. The 'completeness' of the final rule, with respect to the training data, is an advantage that decision trees have over genetic algorithms, and dispenses with the need for niching in the decision tree component.

The rules developed by the decision tree component, like the genetic algorithm rules, are sensor level rules. These rules are used to filter single connections. Currently, the generated decision trees provide an elaboration of the 'Hot IP' list; a list which enumerates IP addresses with previous anomalous activity. This extension of the 'Hot IP' list allows an intrusion detection system to differentiate between normal and anomalous activity from a Hot IP address.

4. Future Plans

The goal of machine learning as applied to network intrusion detection is to generate a minimal rule set which can detect intrusion signatures generalized from previous activity. We want a minimal number of rules for rapid response and efficiency in the expert system. Rule complexity must mirror complexity of attacks; as hackers become more skilled our AI techniques need to create correspondingly complex rules. Our primary near-term goal is to extend the machine learning components to correlate and filter sets of connections as opposed to single connections. We will combine connection filtering with other information the IDS records (events, strings matched etc.) to create complex rules based on data annotated by analysts. More complex rules will look for connection patterns which are extensive in both space and time. Ideally these rules will be able to detect the 'low and slow' attack.

There are many ways to build rules that are based on a number of connections, events, etc. One way is to create rules which can cause other rules to be activated. This method, known as *rule chaining*, allows complex sequences of events to be detected[3]. Given a number of rules of the form $\{\text{if} < predicate > \text{then} < action > \}$, the execution of one rule's action during a cycle may trigger the successful evaluation of another rule's predicate on subsequent cycles. In this way rules may communicate with each other to detect complex behavior. Incoming connections may activate certain rules, which in turn may activate other rules. This process may continue indefinitely until a message triggers an alarm to the intrusion detection system, or until no new messages are created. We are investigating the alteration of the genetic algorithm component to create rules which chain in this manner.

Enhancements to the current decision tree module would be useful for extending their current utility. Decision trees work best for attributes with a small number of values. Planned enhancements would allow for the use of many-valued attributes[1]. The ID3 algorithm builds decision trees from an annotated data set. If the data set is augmented, a new decision tree must be built to encompass the changes. Building a decision tree is computationally intensive. In order to avoid this computation new algorithms have been developed to update existing decision trees based on new information[2]. This allows us to build scalable decision trees, and thus continually refine the rule set as new information becomes known to the analyst. We will investigate scalable decision tree construction as an enhancement to our current system.

We are also looking to employ the decision tree module to identify anomalous sequences of network events. Decision trees can be used to cluster network events into similar categories based on common attributes. Intrusive sequences of network events would be associated with sequences of corresponding clusters. By labeling these sequences as intrusive, we can generalize the specific intrusion sequences to encompass similar sequences.

The decision tree module currently generates decision trees by maximizing the information gain ratio at each level of the tree. This produces a decision tree which attempts to accurately differentiate network events based on their common attributes. By replacing the information gain ratio with a distance function on the set of training data, the resulting decision tree would partition the training set into subsets defined by similarity. By using a distance function with a scalable decision tree builder, one could create a decision tree which clusters the set of archived network events. This decision tree would contain almost all of the information of the archived data, but in a more manageable and compact format.

This decision tree snapshot of the archived network traffic could be used to create rules which chain to detect complex intrusions. Each network event would fall into a unique partition determined by the decision tree. Sequences of network events would be mapped to sequences of corresponding partitions. Since all elements in a given partition are similar, a sequence of partitions could represent a number of related (but distinct) sequences of network events. By building rules based on sequences of partitions generated by known intrusion signatures, rules could be built which detect those intrusions, and other similar sequences of network events.

The decision trees built to cluster data have additional value beyond rule generation for intrusion detection. These decision trees represent snapshots of the archived data, which can be used when lightweight approximations of the archived data are necessary.

In addition to enhancing our current suite of machine learning techniques, we also intend to research other artificial intelligence methods applicable to intrusion detection. Methods such as neural nets, and statistical methods may have utility in expanding our capabilities. The complexity of attacks that we can detect will improve as our machine learning techniques improve.

5. Conclusion

We have adapted existing machine learning applications to develop rules for a deployed IDS. The rule generation component of NEDAA is layered onto an expert system that enhances the ability of the IDS to filter anomalous connections. The current machine learning approach uses genetic algorithms and decision trees. The rules we have developed and deployed differentiate anomalous connections from normal network connections. Planned near-term improvements will allow for more complex rule development.

Created rule sets are to be evaluated against known data sets such as training data from the DARPA Intrusion Detection Evaluation. Preliminary analysis of the DARPA Intrusion Detection Evaluation Data using our machine learning components has yielded patterns in the data set attributed to the contrived nature of the training data.

The main result of the presented material is the production of rules for compilation into the expert system. We are pursuing the creation of rules to detect complex network intrusions to maximize the utility of the expert system, and to produce a dynamic rule base capable of detecting new attack signatures.

References

[1] Roger Gallion, Daniel C. St. Clair, Chaman L. Sabharwal, W.E. Bond (1993). "Dynamic ID3: A Symbolic Learning Algorithm for Many-Valued Attribute Domains," *SAC*: 14-20.

[2] Johannes Gehrke, Venkatesh Ganti, Raghu Ramakrishnan, Wei-Yin Loh (1999). "BOAT - Optimistic Decision Tree Construction," To appear in *Proceedings of 1999 SIGMOD Conference*.

[3] David E. Goldberg (1989). *Genetic Algorithms in Search, Optimization and Machine Learning*. Addison-Wesley, Reading, MA.

[4] Brad L. Miller, Michael J. Shaw (1996). "Genetic Algorithms with Dynamic Niche Sharing for Multimodal Function Optimization," *IEEE International Conference on Evolutionary Computation*: 786-791.

[5] Lyn Pierce, Stan Young (1998). "YAGATS: A Toolset for Genetic Manipulation of Finite-State Machines," Applied Research Laboratories Technical Report No. 99-1 (ARL-TD-99-1), Applied Research Laboratories, The University of Texas at Austin.

[6] Lyn Pierce, Chris Sinclair (1999). "YAGATS IR&D Report," Applied Research Laboratories Technical Report No. 98-1 (ARL-TD-98-1), Applied Research Laboratories, The University of Texas at Austin.

[7] J. Ross Quinlan (1993). *C4.5 Programs for Machine Learning*. Morgan Kaufmann Publishers, San Mateo, CA.

[8] Lane B. Warshaw, Lance Obermeyer, Daniel P. Miranker, Sara P. Matzner (1999). "VenusIDS: An Active Database Component for Intrusion Detection," Submitted to 1999 Annual Computer Security Applications Conference.

A Process State-Transition Analysis and its Application to Intrusion Detection.

Nittida Nuansri,[1]   Samar Singh,[2]   Tharam S. Dillon

Dept. Computer Science and Computer Engineering,
and Applied Computing Research Institute (ACRI)
La Trobe University, Bundoora VIC 3083
Melbourne, Australia.

Abstract

This paper describes a new technique for detecting security breaches in a computer system. For each Unix process, the user credentials, which are user identifiers, determine the process privilege, including whether a process has gained a high privilege, such as that of the superuser. The state transition technique is applied to a suitably defined process state, identified by certain classes of user credential values. A transition takes place when these values change from one class to another. These states are clearly defined, and prohibited state transitions as well as some supporting rules are identified. When many break-ins succeed, either the rules are violated or these prohibited transitions occur, and this implies a violation of system security policy. A specially modified system call, ktrace(), is used by the superuser to monitor the process-state and state transition analysis is applied to the traced information, by the Intrusion Detection System. Tests show that most known security violations belonging to the targeted classes (such as buffer overflow exploits) can be detected (and possibly pre-empted) while the constituent activities are still being processed in the kernel.

1. Introduction.

Intrusion detection has been a long-standing problem in the field of computer security. Despite many intrusion detection systems and methods to detect intrusion activities which have been proposed and implemented, computer systems are still vulnerable to intrusions. We will restrict ourselves here to "intrusions" on a single computer system, and we focus further on that stage of the intrusions where they illicitly obtain high-level access privileges. At this point, the intrusion is synonymous with "misuse" and we shall use these terms interchangeably. In this paper we present a new approach for detecting such (misuse) attempts, using a system call tracing technique which provides the ability to trace all processes while they are being executed in the target system. A novel state-machine technique is applied to model the state of each process according to its current privilege(s), and violations of the system's security policy are identified as "forbidden" transitions or other activities which violate specific rules. The intrusion detection system detects intruder attempts in real-time as their processes are traced in execution. These break-in attempts can then be pre-empted before fully achieving their aims. Our preliminary test results demonstrate that the approach is capable of detecting many intrusion activities, especially those attacks based on buffer overflow and insufficient validation problems.

In the next section we first discuss some Intrusion Detection Systems that have been described in the literature, to put our system in context. Following that, we describe the system call tracing approach that we first tried. We connect the results of our first tracing experiments with an analysis of known break-in attempts. In order to better explain the next step, we

---

[1] Current Address: Head, Computer and Network Division,
    Computer Center, Prince of Songkla University,
    Hat Yai, Songkla, Thailand.

[2] corresponding author.

summarise briefly the various identifiers of a process and their uses, in the Unix environment in Section 3, even though this may be well-known to some readers. A further analysis of break-ins, based on our understanding of section 3, is provided in Section 4, where we also explain the motivation for modifying the system call tracing to include additional information. Section 5 describes our state transition analysis approach and indicates how it can be combined with a few simple *supporting rules* to help in intrusion detection. Section 6, briefly describes the implemented intrusion detection system, and gives examples of preliminary test results of using the system with many well-known break-in methods. It also discusses the shortcomings and possible difficulties with the approach. Section 7 presents our conclusions and indicates the extensions to this work that we are pursuing.

2. Operating System Call Tracing

The literature shows that although there are several different techniques that have been applied for intrusion detection, [7- 10, 12, 15 – 20] most of them share common features. Many of these intrusion detection systems are based on known system or software vulnerabilities, and known break-in methods [2-5, 13, 14]. Although the underlying techniques for recognising such activities might be different, they rely on specific system commands or application program names, or *patterns* of these issued by suspicious users or potential attackers (attack scenarios). However, no matter how well an intrusion detection system has been designed to detect various existing (known) intrusion scenarios, or how easily it can be modified to match the latest situation, it will still lag behind attackers' methods. Furthermore, no single intrusion detection methodology can hope to cover all possible attacks.

In order to provide yet another (partial) solution to the problem, a technique to detect ill-intentioned programs or tools, with a different, and hopefully more robust, approach is presented here. The approach is based on the fact that every program always makes system calls, either directly or indirectly, to accomplish most meaningful tasks. System calls are issued from all programs, which can be user programs, or from "commands" which are programs available in the system for any user. This approach does not rely on any commands, programs, or tools available at the top or shell level. Rather, it focuses attention on the lower level, the kernel level, of the operating system running on each computer system. Thus, the changes of the real world, or the availability of new tools should not effect this approach significantly. In addition, the total number of system calls available is fixed, until new system calls are added to the kernel, which does not happen frequently. Therefore, the system call usage does not change frequently over time. Its usage pattern is also always the same in each command. That is, to make each system call, the calling function has to provide the exact parameters required by the system call.

Based on this knowledge, we decided to study and trace the pattern of system calls of a process, so that later, the tracing technique could be used for an intrusion detection method. We will see later that the final version of this approach depends even less on existing attacks, and has the potential to detect new attacks.

The idea of tracing a user's pattern of system calls has also been explicitly considered in [Hofmeyr, 1998]. In this approach, the sequences of system calls issued are matched against "standard" templates held in a database, and deviations are flagged as suspicious. This system is different from ours, but reinforces the idea that, the use of system calls is critical to the usage of system resources and therefore an important characteristic of a user's profile.

2.1 System Call Tracing Analysis

In order to get information on how each command behaves once it is executed as a process residing in the system memory, it was decided to make use of the *ktrace()* system call to trace processes activities. A *ktrace()* function call first appeared in 4.4BSD [1]. **Only the superuser can use it to trace processes belonging to other users.** This system call is used to enable or disable tracing of one or more processes and provide the information of the specified traced process. The kernel operations that can be traced by this system call include system calls, name translations, signal processing, and all I/O. All system calls are executed in kernel mode. Thus the information provided by the system call *ktrace()*, is that obtained from the kernel area, or the memory area of each traced process. This information is stored in the kernel data structure for each process and is referred to as a process entity. Some of this information is not accessible by general system programs. Further, all this process information is present only at execution time and will disappear from the memory when the process dies.

The tracing function reports all system calls used in a traced process as well as their arguments and return values, an error number and an error message, if any. The information is presented in order of occurrence in the traced process, so that all activities of the traced process are presented in real time. Thus, output obtained from tracing a process contains significant information required for investigating the behaviour of a process. At the beginning of the tracing investigation, several types of user applications and system commands or programs were traced.

2.2 Common Nature of Intrusions

The study of advisories from CERT and other similar security response teams, as well as traces of example (misuse) intrusions led to the conclusion that many a successful (detected) break-in or system compromise was carried out by using the so-called *setuid root* programs, or utilities. Very few, if any, general Unix programs had been directly used to break into a system. Some were used as part of a serial task performed for breaking into a target system. But the turning point was often reached through one of the *setuid* or *setgid* programs. This is because of the nature of the *setuid* and *setgid* programs. They provide higher privileges while in execution in order to perform certain restricted activities or to gain access to some restricted resources, which would not be permitted with the normal user privilege. Although these *setuid* or *setgid* programs should always have been written with greater care than others, experience has shown that it is almost impossible to have programs which do not contain some exploitable shortcoming. Once a single mistake or vulnerability has been found, there are likely to be more, either in the same command or in others with the same structure. Thus, these programs are likely to be the starting point for study by attackers looking for system vulnerabilities. In order to understand more closely what these programs are and what they do, we give a brief summary of the attributes of a process that constitute its credentials in a Unix system.

3. Identifiers and Credentials in Unix

Each user in a Unix system is identified by a set of user and group identifiers and for each process in execution, there is a data structure containing this process information. This data structure is kept in the kernel process table. Part of this information is the user's credentials, the User-Id and the Group-Id, (UID, GID). Along with these two identifiers, there also are *effective* User-Id and *effective* Group-Id, (EUID, EGID)**,** which identify the "effective" ownership of the process at any time. The "effective" id is a means of granting temporary privilege to a process, that is now explained more fully.

Initially, these effective identifiers are set according to the type of a command or a program which is given as an argument to the system call *execve()*. The effective user ID and the effective group ID will be the same as "real" user ID and "real" group ID when a command or program is executed, except for the special class of **setuid** and **setgid** programs. Thus, in the common situation for general non-privileged commands and normal user programs, the value of a real UID and an "effective" EUID are always the same. This is also true for the pair of a real and an effective group ID. In the Unix system architecture, EUID and EGID determine the process privilege. Therefore altering the "effective" user ID or group ID attributes will alter the current privilege of the process. The security control mechanism of the Unix system is based on the idea that any particular resource (object) is accessible by any subject (users or programs) if the subject has the authority to do so. The identifiers of the process are compared with those of the object to determine whether access should be permitted. However, to enable temporary changes in privilege, these identifier values are changeable during the process execution using appropriate system calls such as *setuid()*, *seteuid()*, *setgid()*, *setegid() setreuid(), and setregid()* [4.4BSD User's Reference Manual , 1994]. Of course, these changes cannot be made by any user, or user process. It is only a process with effective UID of the *superuser*, such as the special class of **setuid** (and **setgid**) programs which can do this, and these programs are provided by the system. By the very design of **setuid** programs, they will be executed with an effective user identifier (UID) of the owner of the programs, which is the *root* or *superuser*.

Sometimes, the values of real user (group) and effective user (group) IDs are interchanged, especially in setuid processes. This is performed when a *setuid* program needs to temporarily discard the current privilege of the process and set the effective user ID back to that of the process owner. When that particular operation, which should not be given privilege, has been completed, the effective user ID is set back to the previous privileged value. This can also be applied to the group and effective group user IDs. This transposition procedure is necessary for many privileged programs in order to prevent system resources from being tampered with while using the temporary privilege provided by the programs. The interchanging of these IDs is performed on a regular basis and thus can be represented by certain patterns of attributes and transitions from one to the other. We will see later that this changing pattern of attributes can be characterised by a suitable finite-state-machine diagram in which the change from one class of pattern to another is a transition from one state to another.

From the foregoing, it is easy to see that *setuid* or *setgid* programs or utilities are likely to be a starting point for most attackers to gain unauthorised access or *root* privileges to a system. If an attack is successfully launched while the vulnerable **setuid** command is being executed, the attacker will also gain the effective UID of the target command. For this reason, we decided to pay more attention to these programs.

4. Modifications of the System Call to Enhance the Tracing Method

When it was found that most *setuid* or *setgid* programs are often used to gain higher privileges on a system, we investigated in greater detail as to how an attacker can (illegally) gain privileges. There are several approaches to getting this knowledge, such as studying the source code (which is easily obtained) of each target command. Although it is possible to detect command flaws by such a method, it is time consuming and it is not guaranteed that all possible flaws will be detected. On the other hand, the system call interface is the only mechanism provided by the Unix operating system for a user to access the system kernel portion. Moreover, all system calls are executed in the kernel mode with *superuser* privileges and in order to utilize system privileges, a user or a program has to make some system calls. Therefore, if we are able to follow the trace of these system calls as they are executed we might then be able to detect a suspicious process.

All setuid and setgid programs are executed with effective UID (EUID) or effective GID (EGID) of the owner of the programs (which is the supersuser), or with both, EUID and EGID values, if the command is both *setuid* and *setgid*. These effective IDs are used by the kernel to determine whether a process will be granted a requested permission or not. Furthermore, under Unix, a child process always inherits the parent's environment, and this includes all identifier values. Thus when a process running with a EUID or EGID of the superuser *forks* a child process, the child process would normally be executed in a state just like its parent. Although these values are inherited, in the case of child processes, they are also changeable within the process by using appropriate system calls such as *setuid()*, *setgid()*, etc. Thus, a normal user process can alter its user credential attributes if the right method is employed (as in some cases of successful break-in).

To become the system superuser, which is almost every attacker's goal, these values must be set to satisfy the system authentication and authorisation mechanisms. Every process that belongs to the superuser always has a value of UID and EUID zero. Therefore, these user credentials are important attributes to be monitored for detecting break-in attempts. If it is possible to monitor processes and to extract the UID and EUID values at any time, it should be possible to detect suspicious processes, especially if they suddenly become superuser processes. As already mentioned, Unix operating systems, especially the BSD-derived Unix systems, provide the system call for kernel process tracing, *ktrace()*. The important information that we have now identified, namely the attribute values of real and effective user IDs, is however *not* obtained from *ktrace()* in the version that has been provided. Therefore, we modified the *ktrace()* system call to output these as well and recompiled the kernel. The modified code constitutes a modified version of FreeBSD. With this modification, an approach of tracing all system calls, especially with respect to the process credentials, has become possible. Informally, this approach may be called "uid monitoring".

5. State Transition Analysis and Supporting Rules

After studying traces of break-in attempts, we have classified the credentials into representative "states". Note that these states are different from the usual states of a process, and depend only on these credentials. Changes in these credential values are significant when they cause a transition from one defined state to another, and it is possible to identify certain transitions, "forbidden" by the system's security policies. It is just these "forbidden" transitions that occur in many cases of successful break-in. We have also identified some supporting rules, which if applied, would restrict many break-ins to just these transitions, which could then be detected by tracing the changes in state. Alternatively, the break-ins must violate the rules, so that they can again be detected.

5.1 State Definitions.

We first define the "state" of a Unix process, in terms of its identifiers. Any state is described by a 4-tuple (real user ID, effective user ID, real group ID, and effective group ID) or (UID, EUID, GID, EGID). Each of these components of the 4-tuple is described below.

Real user ID and an effective user ID.

These attributes represent a real and an effective user identifier (UID and EUID) respectively. The real user ID represents the actual user who initiated the command, and the effective user ID the current privileges available to the command. At a particular time, when a process is running, the value of UID and EUID can be denoted by one of the following values:

uid – (user's id) the user identifier number assigned by the system administrator during the user creation process to the user whose process is being traced.

sid – (special id) a user identifier number of high privileged users which are defined here as ***root, daemon, operator, bin, news.*** Any appropriate set could be chosen. For the purposes of the examples presented it can be assumed that all of these users have numeric UID values less than 10.

oid – (other's id) a user identifier number that does not fall into the above two categories. This is the identifier of another non-privileged user.

Real group ID and an effective group ID.

These attributes represent a real and an effective group identifier (GID and EGID) of the process respectively. Similar to the real and effective user ID, the value of GID and EGID can be one of the following values:

gid - a normal group identifier number to which the user who ran the process belongs.

sgid - a group identifier for special system or high privileged groups, such as *wheel* (the highest privileged group in some Unix systems), *daemon, kmem, sys, tty, operator, bin, and news*. All of these groups are assumed, for the purposes of the examples, to have numeric GID values less than 10.

ogid - a group identifier number that does not fall into the above two categories.

States
At a particular time, a process will be in one and only one state depending on the values of the 4-tuple at that time. We differentiate four types of states:

> *Normal, special privileged, superuser, system group, another user.*

Within each type, there are a few different states.

Definition 1: Normal State

A process is said to be in a **normal** state if and only if the process ownership attributes (process 4-tuple) are the same as the ownership values of the user who initiated the process. Thus, the process 4-tuple values are (**uid, uid, ugid, ugid**) for the correspondent attributes of (UID, EUID, GID, EGID).

Definition 2: Special Privileged State.

A process is said to be in a *special privileged state* if and only if some values of the process 4-tuple belong to a privileged group but, at the same time, either the real user ID or effective user ID value remains that of the original process owner, who is not privileged. That is, these two attributes do not share the same privileged identifier. This also applies to the group identifiers. This special privileged state can be the result of several system calls, which cause the transition. We can refer to these special cases with the same name as the system call that caused them. Thus :

setuid :   a state induced by the ***setuid()*** system call
setreuid : a state induced by the ***setreuid()*** system call
setgid :   a state induced by the ***setgid()*** system call
setregid : a state induced by the ***setregid()*** system call

Definition 3: Superuser and System Group States.

A process is said to be in a *superuser state* when a process user ID or group ID attributes have their values changed in one or a combination of the following ways. The states described below can "normally" only be achieved by the system *superuser* or programs run by the *superuser*.

Superuser State
A real user ID and an effective user ID are **both** privileged user IDs (**sid**).

System Group State
A group ID and an effective group ID are **both** privileged group IDs (**sgid**).

Definition 4: Another User State
A process is said to be in *another user state* when a process' user ID or group ID attributes have their values changed in one or a combination of the following ways:

(a) A real user ID and an effective user ID are both changed to other user IDs (**oid**).

(b) A group ID and an effective group ID are both changed to other user group IDs (**ogid**).

Fig.1 below shows some of the important states and their transitions according to the definitions given above. The "forbidden transitions" are clearly marked, while the "another user" state is not shown.

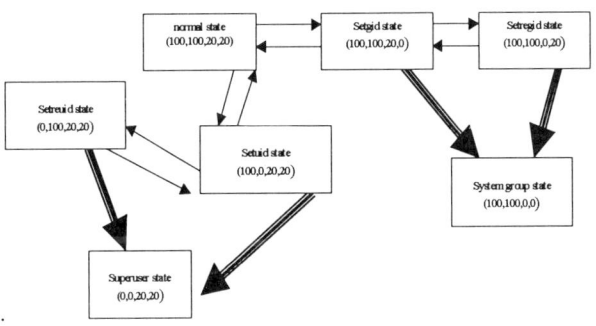

Fig. 1. State transition diagram for some system states. The heavy arrows represent "forbidden" or intrusion activities.

The actions indicated by the state transition arcs are system calls, which, if successfully executed, result in the changes of state tuple attributes (UID, EUID, GID, EGID). The state 4-tuple attributes (UID, EUID, GID, EGID) are illustrated by numeric values representing user identifiers at a particular time for each state. In this example, a user who initiated a process, is identified by user ID 100, and belongs to group ID 20. The user ID 0 (zero) represents the *superuser* identifier (in all Unix systems). At the beginning of a user process execution, the process is always started in a normal state where (uid, euid, gid, egid) tuple attributes are always presented by the user and group IDs, e.g., (100,100,20,20). When the process is in a state where one of the state tuple attributes is of the privileged value, the state is then labelled with state name as, *setuid, setgid, setreuid, or setregid* state. The actions, which cause a state transition, each arc, are process activities. These can be a system call, program, or other activities that create state transitions. The forbidden transitions, as illustrated in Figure 1, are examples of successful intrusion activity.

5.2 Supporting Rules for Intrusion Detection.

Since some break-in methods are able to change the computer system in such a way, that they can return, in a later session with superuser privileges, five rules were identified and used in the intrusion detection system to support the state transition analysis described above. These rules are given below, with brief explanations wherever the reasons for the rules are not entirely self-explanatory. It should be noted that these rules serve actually to enforce the system security policy.

Rule 0: Only the special system calls *setreuid()* and the *setregid()* are permitted to change the (real) UID or GID respectively.

If any system call or program other than these changes the real UID or GID of the process, it is flagged as an intrusion.

Rule 1: No *execve()* call is allowed in a *special privileged* state.

While a process is in the special *setuid/ setgid/ setreuid /setregid* state, it should not be allowed to *execve()* another program or command, because that new process will inherit the special privileges. If it is essential for the process to *exec()*, it must temporarily give up its current privilege. If the new program also requires a system or root privilege to perform its particular task, it can be implemented as a *setuid* program rather than inheriting its privileges from the parent process. Implementation of this rule will prevent a number of buffer overflow and insufficient boundary check attacks, where an exploited command is forced to run an arbitrary command so that an attacker can gain root access. For intrusion detection, any *execve()* call from a process in a *special privileged state* is flagged as suspicious. Notice, that while this may lead to false alarms, it will highlight dangerous or vulnerable implementations.

Rule 2: A process in a *special privileged* state is not allowed to create a *setuid/setgid* program.

Only the *superuser (root)* should be allowed to do this.

Rule 3: A process is not allowed to modify system programs.

Thus, a special rule can be set for these files so that no other programs or processes, especially a *setuid* state process, are able to access to or modify them. These files are identified, by being in a special directory or belonging to "root" which is checked when the *open()* system call is executed. A similar rule is used in [Porras92]

Rule 4: For intrusion detection, we consider any process creating new user accounts as suspicious unless it has *superuser* credentials.

Again, only the *superuser* should be allowed to create new accounts.

Rule 5: Some system call functions are strictly limited to *superuser (root)*.

Like general commands which might provide several options, some system calls accept several options, in terms of parameter values. These options are available to all users except in a few system calls where one option is limited to *root* only. These system calls are *mount()*, *umount()*, *nfssvc()*, *quotactl()*, *reboot()*, *settimeofday()*, *swapon()*. For detection purposes, an alarm is raised if the restricted option is not called by real user *root*.

6. Intrusion Detection System.

To demonstrate the effectiveness of the state-transition analysis, and rule-checking applied to system call tracing, a C program for an intrusion detection system was implemented based on these techniques. It takes trace output from (the modified version of) *ktrace()*, which is used to trace a process of interest, and extracts all important information, related to the rules, and applies the state-transition analysis to determine break-in attempts. The program maintains process information of all processes including child processes in a tree data structure. The first process to be traced is at the top of the tree, and is an ancestor process to every process forked after the tracing starts. The program also stores the real user ID of the user initiating the traced process. This user ID is used as an origin user ID to determine if a process violates the security rules. The program monitors results from several especially important system calls, such as *execve()*, *open()*, *chmod()*, etc. and uses the rules described above.

6.1 Example Trace of a Break-in Program

Many break-in programs, available from the Internet, were used to test the capability of this program. An example trace of a break-in attempt is given here as illustration and shows how the "forbidden" transition finally takes place. In the trace below, the first four integers in each line represent the state-quadruple (UID, EUID, GID, EGID), as described in Fig.1, and the rest of the line represents the process-id, the process name, the system call and the parameters etc. Some lines have been folded.

```
100 100 20 20    2980 bash      CALL
execve(0xa290c,0xb58cc,0xa0b0c)
100 100 20 20    2980 bash      NAMI
"/var/home/noi/Trace/src/kdump/bsd_procfs
_1"
```

```
100 100 20 20    2980 bsd_procfs_1 CALL
write(0x1,0x4000,0x24)
```

   "Demonstration of 4.4BSD procfs hole"
   after you see "setuid changed", enter
the pw for the user
   Be warned, searching for the setuid()
function takes a long time!

```
100 100 20 20    2980 bsd_procfs_1 CALL
fork
100 100 20 20    2980 bsd_procfs_1 RET
fork 2981/0xba5
100 100 20 20    2980 bsd_procfs_1 CALL
open(0xefbfd6d8,0x2,0xefbfd72c)
100 100 20 20    2980 bsd_procfs_1 NAMI
"/proc/2981/mem"
100 100 20 20    2980 bsd_procfs_1 RET
open 3

100 100 20 20    2981 bsd_procfs_1 CALL
execve(0x165c,0x14000,0xefbfd73c)
100 100 20 20    2981 bsd_procfs_1 NAMI
"/usr/bin/su"
100 0 20 20      2981 su        RET    execve 0

100 0 20 20      2981 su        CALL
write(0x3,0x1b000,0x9)"Password:"
```

**** *some password entered here*

```
100 0 20 20      2981 su        RET    write 9
100 0 20 20      2981 su        CALL
lseek(0x3,0,0,0,0)
100 0 20 20      2981 su        RET    lseek 0
100 0 20 20      2981 su        CALL
read(0x3,0x1b000,0x10000)
100 100 20 20    2980 bsd_procfs_1 PSIG
SIGALRM caught handler=0x804cec0
mask=0x2000 code=0x0
100 100 20 20    2980 bsd_procfs_1 RET
sigsuspend -1 errno 4 Interrupted system
call

100 100 20 20    2980 bsd_procfs_1 CALL
write(0x1,0x4000,0x21)
```

   "searching - please be patient."

```
100 100 20 20    2980 bsd_procfs_1 CALL
lseek(0x3,0,0x8003000,0,0)
100 100 20 20    2980 bsd_procfs_1 RET
lseek 134230016/0x8003000
100 100 20 20    2980 bsd_procfs_1 CALL
read(0x3,0xefbfd6d8,0xd)
100 100 20 20    2980 bsd_procfs_1 GIO
fd 3 read 13 bytes
100 100 20 20    2980 bsd_procfs_1 CALL
write(0x1,0x4000,0x1b)
```

```
        "setuid changed (0x8042b94)"

100 100 20 20   2980 bsd_procfs_1 RET
write 27/0x1b
100 100 20 20   2980 bsd_procfs_1 CALL
kill(0xba5,0x13)
100 0 20 20     2981 su    PSIG  SIGCONT
caught handler=0x803d3bc mask=0x0
code=0x0
100 0 20 20     2981 su    RET   read
RESTART

100 0 20 20     2981 su    CALL
read(0x3,0x1b000,0x10000)
100 100 20 20   2980 bsd_procfs_1 RET
kill 0
100 100 20 20   2980 bsd_procfs_1 CALL
wait4(0xffffffff,0,0,0)
100 0 20 20     2981 su    GIO   fd 3 read 8
bytes

    NOTE: A (correct) USER PASSWORD WAS
ENTERED HERE

100 0 20 20     2981 su    CALL
connect(0x3,0x808a8d0,0x10)
100 0 20 20     2981 su    NAMI
"/var/run/log"
100 0 20 20     2981 su    RET   connect 0
100 0 20 20     2981 su    CALL
sendto(0x3,0xefbfca70,0x30,0,0,0)
100 0 20 20     2981 su    GIO   fd 3 wrote
48 bytes
    "<37>Feb 24 14:46:45 su: noi to noi on
/dev/ttyp6"

***below is a violation of rule 1

100 0 20 20     2981 su    CALL
execve(0x686f,0x4050,0xefbfd764)
100 0 20 20     2981 su    NAMI
"/usr/local/bin/bash"
100 0 20 20     2981 bash  RET   execve 0

**** notice this bash is running with
EUID = 0 - already a disaster ******

100 0 20 20     2981 bash  CALL
open(0x109c,0,0)
100 0 20 20     2981 bash  NAMI
"/usr/libexec/ld.so"

    jasmine 503 # ../break_1

100 0 20 20     2981 bash  CALL  fork
100 0 20 20     2981 bash  RET   fork
2994/0xbb2

**** another violation of rule 1

100 0 20 20     2994 bash  CALL
execve(0xb500c,0xb1f8c,0xa220c)
```
```
100 0 20 20     2994 bash  NAMI
"../break_1"
100 0 20 20     2994 break_1 RET  execve
0
```

****** this is a violation of rule 0 and
causes the forbidden transition below

```
100 0 20 20     2994 break_1 CALL
setuid(0)

0 0 20 20       2994 break_1 RET  setuid 0
```

****** this user program, 2994 break_1,
is now running with superuser status

Other (similar) detected break-in attempts are too numerous to list, so some representative ones of the types that would be detected are listed in an appendix. Some of these attacks no longer work on the current versions of Unix because the vulnerabilities described have been "patched". However, all these attacks worked by making the forbidden transitions of our state model, or violating one of the rules, and thus they would have been detected by our system.

It needs to be stressed that the "uid monitoring" approach has the potential to detect new (hitherto unseen) attacks if they make use of the forbidden transitions, or violate the rules. Indeed, the method actually attempts to detect violations of a "policy", and it has been brought to our notice that (an enforcement version of) it fits in with the formal approach described in [21]. The concept there is of an "enforcement automaton" that monitors the behaviour of a process for violations of some aspect of a security policy.

6.2 Difficulties and Deficiencies

We hope to implement this detection system in a real "production environment" after efficiency and operational issues have been properly addressed. The deployed intrusion detection system must not overly degrade the performance of the system, by utilising too many system resources. Currently, the problem is that the *ktrace()* call writes into a file, which is then read by the intrusion detection system. Efficiency requires that the output of *ktrace()* be sent via a "pipe" to the detection program, but so far such an implementation has not been possible because of an intrinsic difficulty with the way the *ktrace()* call operates.

It also needs to be stressed that our method makes no claim to detecting all possible intrusions. Rather it concentrates on a certain class of intrusion (misuse) techniques. Indeed, it has been pointed out that if the kind of "uid monitoring" proposed by us becomes widespread, attackers will change their tactics. However, we believe this argument applies to almost any intrusion detection technique. Further, by restricting the possible attacks, we hope to make the system more secure.

An additional difficulty, is that the necessary modifications to the *ktrace()* routine can only be made if the source code of the operating system is available, as in the case of FreeBSD. For example, no such system call is available in other Posix compliant versions of Unix or even Linux.. Nevertheless, we believe that the principle behind our method would apply in these cases also. Indeed, one can hope that our results would encourage the implementers of these operating systems to provide such a system call in future releases.

Finally, only a full implementation on a running system will give us realistic data about any "false positives". It has been suggested by some reviewers that our rules may "break" some existing applications. However, as the system is designed in such a way as to enforce a certain "policy" (see also our proposed extensions below), even the false positives that do occur, will point out deficiencies in existing software, or highlight practices that present possible vulnerabilities.

7. Conclusions.

We have provided a discussion of the observations that can be made for intrusion detection and their common features. This has led to a suitably defined process state-transition model and its application to system call tracing techniques. The outcome of this analysis has led to a new approach for intrusion detection. A few rules for supporting the state-transition analysis have also been presented. A system for intrusion detection based on this approach has been implemented in a system running FreeBSD and has been tested with several real break-in programs obtained from the Internet. The system can detect many attacks, especially buffer overflow attack scenarios.

The natural extension of our approach, particularly its proposed rules, and the concept of forbidden transitions, lead naturally to the idea that these can be programmed into the operating system itself. This approach would be in line with the formalism proposed and analysed in [21]. We are examining this possibility for the next level of system security, the goal of which is a more secure operating system kernel. This would involve modifications of the current kernel, particularly of some important system calls. Thus the intrusion detection module would become embedded in the modified kernel which will provide the ability of detecting intrusion attempts and pre-empting them while they are in progress. However, that extension is a major task.

Acknowledgement

The suggestions and comments of the anonymous referees have contributed enormously to the final shape of this paper.

8. Bibliography.

1. 4.4BSD Berkeley Software Distribution, User's Reference Manual (URM), The USENIX Association and O'Reilly & Associates, Inc. (1994)

2. R. P. Abbott, " Security Analysis and Enhancements of Computer Operating Systems", Technical Report NBSIR 76-1041, Institute of Computer Science and Technology, National Bureau of Standards (1976)

3. T. Aslam, "A Taxonomy of Security Faults in Unix Operating System", Master Thesis, Department of Computer Science, Purdue University (August 1995), http://www.cs.purdue.edu/coast/coast-library.html

4. T. Aslam, I. Krsul, E. H. Spafford, "Use of a Taxonomy of Security Faults", Technical Report TR-96-051, Department of Computer Science, Purdue University (September 1996), http://www.cs.purdue.edu/coast/coast-library.html

5. M. Bishop, D. Bailey, "A Critical Analysis of Vulnerability Taxonomies", Technical Report CSE-96-11, Department of Computer Science, University of California at Davis (September 1996), http://seclab.cs.ucdavis.edu/papers.html

6. J. Carlstead, R. Bibsey II, F. Popek, "Pattern-directed Protection Evaluation", Technical Report, Information Sciences Institute, University of Southern California (June 1975)

7. D. E. Denning, "An Intrusion Detection Model", IEEE Transactions on Software Engineering, Vol. SE-13 No. 2, pg. 222-232, (February 1987)

8. S. A. Hofmeyr, S. Forrest, A. Somayaji, "Intrusion Detection using Sequences of System Calls", Department of Computer Science, University of New Mexico, (1998), http://www.cs.unm.edu/~steveah/publications/ids.ps

9. R. A. Kemmerer, "NSTAT: A Model-based Real-time Network Intrusion Detection System", Technical Report

TRCS97-18, Department of Computer Science, University of California, Santa Barbara (1997), http://www.cs.ucsb.edu/

10. C. C. W. Ko, "Execution Monitoring of Security-Critical Programs in a Distributed System: A Specification-Based Approach", Ph.D. Thesis, Department of Computer Science, University of California, Davis California, (1996), http://seclab.cs.ucdavis.edu/ papers.html

11. V. Krsul, "Software Vulnerability Analysis", PhD Thesis, Department of Computer Science, Purdue University (May 1998), http://www.cs.purdue.edu/coast/coast-library.html

12. S. Kumar, E. H. Spafford, "A Pattern Matching Model for Misuse Intrusion Detection", Proceedings of the 17th National Computer Security Conference, (1994)

13. C. E. Landwehr, A. R. Bull, J. P. McDermott, W. Choi, "A Taxonomy of Computer Program Security Flaws", ACM Computing Surveys, Vol. 26 No. 3, pg. 211-254, September 1994

14. B. Marick, "A Survey of Software Fault Surveys", Technical Report, UIUCDCS-R-90-1651, University of Illinois at Urbana-Champaign, December 1990

15. B. Mukherjee, L. T. Heberlein, K. N. Levitt, "Network Intrusion Detection", IEEE Network, Vol. 8(3), pg. 26-41, May/June 1994

16. P. Porras, "STAT – A State Transition Analysis Tool for Intrusion Detection." Master's thesis, Computer Science Department, University of California, Santa Barbara, June 1992.

17. P.A. Porras, P.G. Neumann, "Conceptual Design and Planning for EMERALD: Event Monitoring Enabling Responses to Anomalous Live Disturbances", Technical report, Computer Science Laboratory, SRI International, Menlo Park, CA, (October 1997), http://www.csl.sri.com/intrusion.html

18. J. R. Raymond, "Quantitative Aspects of Software Validation", SIGPLAN Notices, Vol. SE-5(3), pg. 276-286 (May 1975)

19. S. E. Smaha, "Haystack: An Intrusion Detection System", Proceedings of The 4th Aerospace Computer Security Applications Conference, Florida, pg. 37-44, (December 12-16, 1988)

20. M. Sobirey, B. Richter, H. Konig, "The Intrusion Detection System AID - Architecture, and Experiences in Automated Audit Analysis", IFIP-TC6 Workshop on Communications and Multimedia Security, (September 1996).

21. F.B. Schneider, "Enforceable Security Policies", TR98-1688, Cornell University (Revised July 24, 1999)

Appendix. Sample Vulnerable Commands

Some past system programs with problem of buffer overflow and insufficient boundary check. are given below.

rcp	CERT Advisory CA-89:07, "Sun RCP vulnerability", Computer Emergency Response Team Advisory, October 26, 1989
rexecd	CERT Advisories CA-92:04, "AT&T /usr/etc/rexecd Vulnerability", Computer Emergency Response Team Advisory, February 25, 1992
syslog()	CERT Advisories CA-95:13, "Syslog Vulnerability", Computer Emergency Response Team Advisory, October 19, 1995
rdist	CERT Advisories CA-96.14, "Vulnerability in rdist", Computer Emergency Response Team Advisory, July 24, 1996
sendmail	CERT Advisories CA-96.20, " Sendmail Vulnerabilities", Computer Emergency Response Team Advisory, September 18, 1996
in.telnetd	CERT Advisories CA-91:02a, " SunOS in.telnetd Vulnerability", Computer Emergency Response Team Advisory, March 27, 1991
chroot	CERT Advisories CA-91:05, "DEC Ultrix Vulnerability", Computer Emergency Response Team Advisory, May 1, 1991
login	CERT Advisories CA-91:08, "AT&T System V Release 4 /bin/login Vulnerability", Computer Emergency Response Team Advisory, May 23, 1991
xterm	CERT Advisories CA-93:17, "xterm Logging Vulnerability", Computer Emergency Response Team Advisory, November 11, 1993
NFS vulnerabilities	CERT Advisory CA-94:15, "NFS Vulnerabilities", Computer Emergency Response Team Advisory, December 19, 1994
mail	CERT Advisory CA-95:02, "Vulnerabilities in /bin/mail", Computer Emergency Response Team Advisory, January 26, 1995
ps	CERT Advisory CA-95:09, "Solaris ps Vulnerability", Computer Emergency Response Team Advisory, August 29, 1995
suidperl	CERT Advisory CA-96.12, "Vulnerability in suidperl", Computer Emergency Response Team Advisory, June 26, 1996

Author Index

Anderson, R. xix
Archer, M. 109
Areizaga, E. 84
Arona, A. 199
Baker, J. 129
Barkley, J. 310
Benecke, C. 67
Beznosov, K. 310
Blakley, B. 310
Bogle, J. 134
Bouabdallah, A. 84
Bowers, S. 361
Brackin, S. H. 99
Brainard, J. G. 349
Broccard, P. 170
Bruschi, D. 199
Burt, C. 310
Caughey, S. 320
Chandersekaran, S. 269
Cooper, D. A. 256
Cowan, C. 361
Delahaye, C. 84
Delcambre, L. 361
Deng, Y. 310
Dillon, T. S. 378
dos Santos, A. L. M. 35
Du, W. 331
Dutta, P. 303
Eppinger, B. J. 143
Epstein, J. 45
Erfani, S. 269
Fayad, A. 119
Fox, C. 55
Friedman, A. 299
Froscher, J. N. 143
Fung, F. 129
Galiasso, P. 219
Garg, P. 331
Gärtner, F. C. 3
Gombault, S. 75
Gong, L. 285
Greulich, A. 241
Hale, J. 219
Hearn, D. 12

Heitmeyer, C. 109
Herrmann, G. 22
Hinrichs, S. 209
Hinton, H. 361
Hoyt, M. V. 170
Iglio, P. 189
Ingham, D. 320
Irvine, C. 183
Jajodia, S. 119
Kang, M. H. 143
Karro, J. 161
Kemmerer, R. A. 35
Kirby, Jr., J. 109
Koved, L. 285
Lai, C. 285
Laurent, M. 75, 84
Leitold, H. 84
Levin, T. 183
Long, D. L. 129
Mateos, J. M. 84
Mathur, A. P. 331
Matyas, Jr., S. M. 155
Matzner, S. 371
McCollum, C. D. 119
McDermott, J. 55
Munawer, Q. 229
Nadalin, A. 285
Neely, R. B. 341
Newman, R. E. 170
Nuansri, N. 378
O'Brien, R. 134
Oestreicher, M. 291
Oppliger, R. 241
Pagnia, H. 3
Papa, M. 219
Paul, O. 75
Payne, C. 134
Pernul, G. 22
Pierce, L. 371
Posch, R. 84
Prandini, M. 276
Roginsky, A. 155
Röhm, A. W. 22
Ross, R. 265

Rosti, E.	199
Russell, S.	249
Sanders, M.	170
Sandhu, R.	229
Schemers, R.	285
Shenoi, S.	219
Sinclair, C.	371
Singh, S.	378
Swanson, T.	170
Thomsen, D.	134
Trachsel, P.	241
Tripunitara, M. V.	303
Vogt, H.	3
Wang, J.	161
Wichert, M.	320
Wilkinson, T.	12
Winner, J.	170
Wiseman, S.	12

Notes

Press Activities Board

Vice President and Chair:
Carl K. Chang
Dept. of EECS (M/C 154)
The University of Illinois at Chicago
851 South Morgan Street
Chicago, IL 60607
ckchang@eecs.uic.edu

Editor-in-Chief
Advances and Practices in Computer Science and Engineering Board
Pradip Srimani
Colorado State University, Dept. of Computer Science
601 South Hows Lane
Fort Collins, CO 80525
Phone: 970-491-7097 FAX: 970-491-2466
srimani@cs.colostate.edu

Board Members:
Mark J. Christensen
Deborah M. Cooper – Deborah M. Cooper Company
William W. Everett – SPRE Software Process and Reliability Engineering
Haruhisa Ichikawa – NTT Software Laboratories
Annie Kuntzmann-Combelles – Objectif Technologie
Chengwen Liu – DePaul University
Joseph E. Urban – Arizona State University

IEEE Computer Society Executive Staff
T. Michael Elliott, Executive Director and Chief Executive Officer

IEEE Computer Society Publications

The world-renowned IEEE Computer Society publishes, promotes, and distributes a wide variety of authoritative computer science and engineering texts. These books are available from most retail outlets. Visit the Online Catalog, *http://computer.org*, for a list of products.

IEEE Computer Society Proceedings

The IEEE Computer Society also produces and actively promotes the proceedings of more than 141 acclaimed international conferences each year in multimedia formats that include hard and softcover books, CD-ROMs, videos, and on-line publications.

For information on the IEEE Computer Society proceedings, send e-mail to *cs.books@computer.org* or write to Proceedings, IEEE Computer Society, P.O. Box 3014, 10662 Los Vaqueros Circle, Los Alamitos, CA 90720-1314. Telephone +1 714-821-8380. FAX +1 714-761-1784.

Additional information regarding the Computer Society, conferences and proceedings, CD-ROMs, videos, and books can also be accessed from our web site at *http://computer.org/cspress*